Volume III of *The Papers of Adlai E. Stevenson* illuminates Stevenson's determination to inform, to educate, to interest the people of his state in their government. In his own words — in letters, speeches, memoranda and articles — *Governor of Illinois, 1949–1953* shows Stevenson speaking out on the local and national issues of his day and wrestling with such problems as revising the state's constitution, improving its public welfare and aid to education programs, drafting antidiscriminatory employment laws, revamping road and highway programs, fighting against organized crime and juvenile delinquency, reorganizing branches of the state government, and battling corruption within his own administration.

Written in his familiar style — witty, pungent, sharp, free of pomposity — illustrated with twenty photographs, these papers brilliantly illustrate Stevenson's maturing political philosophy and the continuing growth in knowledge and prominence that eventually led him to the presidential nomination. The papers dealing with that nomination and

Walter Johnson, the editor of *The Papers of Adlai E. Stevenson*, is a professor of history who has taught at the University of Chicago, where he received his M.A. and Ph.D., and at Oxford, where he was Harmsworth Professor of American History. He presently teaches at the University of Hawaii. He is the author and editor of nine previous books, including *1600 Pennsylvania Avenue: Presidents and the People 1929–1959*, *William Allen White's America*, *How We Drafted Adlai Stevenson*, and *Selected Letters of William Allen White*.

Carol Evans, the assistant editor, originally worked in the law firm where Stevenson was a junior partner. In 1948 he asked her to join him in his campaign for governor of Illinois. She accompanied him to Springfield as his personal secretary and remained with him until July 1961.

Books by Walter Johnson

THE BATTLE AGAINST ISOLATION

WILLIAM ALLEN WHITE'S AMERICA

THE UNITED STATES: EXPERIMENT IN DEMOCRACY
(with Avery Craven)

HOW WE DRAFTED ADLAI STEVENSON

1600 PENNSYLVANIA AVENUE: PRESIDENTS AND THE PEOPLE, 1929–1959

THE FULBRIGHT PROGRAM: A HISTORY
(with Francis J. Colligan)

Edited by Walter Johnson

SELECTED LETTERS OF WILLIAM ALLEN WHITE

ROOSEVELT AND THE RUSSIANS: THE YALTA CONFERENCE
By Edward R. Stettinius, Jr.

TURBULENT ERA: A DIPLOMATIC RECORD OF FORTY YEARS, 1904–1945
By Joseph C. Grew

THE PAPERS OF ADLAI E. STEVENSON
Volume I: Beginnings of Education, 1900–1941
Volume II: Washington to Springfield, 1941–1948
Volume III: Governor of Illinois, 1949–1953

The Papers of Adlai E. Stevenson

WALTER JOHNSON, *Editor*

CAROL EVANS, *Assistant Editor*

The Papers of

Advisory Committee

Adlai E. Stevenson

VOLUME III

Governor of Illinois
1949–1953

LITTLE, BROWN *and* COMPANY • *Boston* • *Toronto*

308.0973

St 48 p

v. 3

FIRST EDITION

T 11/73

The editors gratefully acknowledge the permission of the following authors, publishers, individuals and institutions to reprint selected materials as noted:

Herbert Agar, *American Bar Association Journal*, Ayer Direct, George W. Ball, Morris A. Bealle, Edgar Bernhard, Melvin Brorby, Ralph J. Bunche, James C. Colvin, Paul S. Cousley, Kenneth S. Davis, Edison Warner Dick, Jane Warner Dick, Sherwood Dixon, Doubleday & Company, Inc., Thomas H. Eliot, William I. Flanagan, Don Forsyth, Dorothy Fosdick, Watson Gailey, Richard Paul Graebel, Mrs. Parker Hardin, Harper & Row, Publishers, Robert M. Hutchins, Lawrence E. Irvin, Mrs. Ernest L. Ives, Mrs. Edward L. Joyce, Arthur Krock, L. Duncan Lloyd, Archibald MacLeish, Carl McGowan, Porter McKeever, Nicholas A. Masters, T. S. Matthews, George W. Mitchell, Stephen A. Mitchell, Thomas Mulroy, Charles S. Murphy, *The Nation,* Reinhold Niebuhr, John J. Parish, Noble J. Puffer, Random House, Inc., Whitelaw Reid, Robert H. Salisbury, Walter V. Schaefer, Eric Sevareid, Vincent Sheean, Paul Simon, Mr. and Mrs. Hermon D. Smith, Mrs. Harry E. T. Thayer, Ronald Tree, Rexford G. Tugwell, Basil L. Walters, Mrs. John Paul Welling, Fred Young and George Young for all items from their publications and writings as detailed in the footnotes.

Harper & Row, Publishers, for excerpts from *As We Knew Adlai: The Stevenson Story by Twenty-two Friends.* Edited and with Preface by Edward P. Doyle. Copyright © 1966 by Harper & Row, Publishers, Inc.

Library of Congress Cataloging in Publication Data

Stevenson, Adlai Ewing, 1900–1965.
    The papers of Adlai E. Stevenson.

    Includes bibliographical references.
    CONTENTS: v. 1. Beginnings of education, 1900–1941.--
                        v. 3. Governor of Illinois,
1949–1953.
        1. Stevenson, Adlai Ewing, 1900–1965. I. Title.
E748.S84A25 1972   973.9'092'4 [B]   73-175478
ISBN 0-316-46752-9

*Published simultaneously in Canada
by Little, Brown & Company (Canada) Limited*

PRINTED IN THE UNITED STATES OF AMERICA

Foreword

On January 10, 1949, Adlai E. Stevenson was inaugurated as the thirty-first governor of Illinois. Four years later he wrote of his experience:

> I was elected by the largest majority in the State's history. There followed four years of toil in Springfield, more rewarding and satisfying than I dreamed possible. The governorship of a great state is an intensive education in politics, people and public administration that has few counterparts in American public life. There I discovered that in a political job there are usually two ways to do things: the politically expedient way or the right way. Sometimes they do not coincide but in the long run the right way is the best politics.[1]

On January 28, 1952, *Time* magazine said of Governor Stevenson: "His manner is lawyerlike, earnest and — sometimes patiently, sometimes anxiously — engaging. He has a rueful laugh, nervous and sudden, a tongue in his head and a head on his shoulders." Adlai E. Stevenson's own words — in letters, postcards, speeches, and his abortive attempts at keeping a diary — are presented in the volumes of *The Papers of Adlai E. Stevenson*. These volumes are a documentary biography of Governor Stevenson and, at the same time, a documentary history in his own words of the extraordinary, and often bewildering, changes that remolded the United States and the world during his lifetime from 1900 to 1965.

In selecting the materials from Governor Stevenson's papers to be published in these volumes the editors decided to emphasize the material that helped answer such questions as: How did he educate himself? How did he become the man he became? What were the key influences in his life? How did he understand his times? How did he articulate the problems of his times?

[1] *Major Campaign Speeches of Adlai E. Stevenson, 1952* (New York: Random House, 1953), p. xxi.

[*vii*]

Stevenson's four years as governor are chronicled in Volume III. The papers pertaining to his nomination for President in 1952 and his campaign for that office are omitted from this volume. They are included in Volume IV of *The Papers of Adlai E. Stevenson.*

It is impossible for the governor of any state to acknowledge and properly respond to all the mail he receives without the help of his staff. Governor Stevenson was no exception.

Stevenson authorized his assistants to draft letters over his name, to be signed, usually by Mrs. Anne Risse at the State House or Miss Carol Evans and Mrs. Margaret Munn at the mansion, without going over the Governor's desk. Although he dictated and signed an impressive number of letters himself, he once told his secretary Carol Evans that he did not think his signature was important or added anything to a letter. Letters from personal friends were put on his desk, as were those of special interest, and he either dictated replies or sent his own handwritten response. Usually letters of great importance went first either to Walter V. Schaefer, Carl McGowan or James W. Mulroy, depending on the nature of the matter, and were brought to the Governor's attention by them.

When letters were written over the Governor's name by an aide, the author's initials with those of his secretary were typed in the left-hand margin of the carbon copy to identify the writer and the person who typed the letter.

For example, if on a carbon copy of a letter drafted for the Governor the initials "CMcG/FR" are found in the left-hand margin, this indicates that it was dictated by Carl McGowan and typed by his secretary, Frances Ruys. If Mr. McGowan deemed it unnecessary to clear the letter with Governor Stevenson before it went out, the letter was signed by one of the three secretaries authorized to do so. If the letter was considered important enough to be read by the Governor before mailing, it was usually presented to him first in draft form, then typed in final form and signed by one of the authorized persons, or by the Governor himself.

When the Governor dictated letters, his initials with those of the secretary were placed in the left-hand margin of the carbon. Some of these letters were returned to his desk for one reason or another (he sometimes added a postscript by hand, or he might redraft the letter) and were signed by him. The others were signed by one of the authorized secretaries.

Because the collection of Stevenson's papers consists mainly of carbon copies, it is impossible to know whether the Governor or one of his authorized subordinates signed them. It is, of course, possible to determine whether he was actually their author. But whether he composed and signed them personally or not, the letters and memoranda are considered to be his because he authorized them to be done on his behalf. In view of the huge volume of papers during the four years as governor, the editors have been more highly selective than in Volumes I and II. All letters published in this volume were written from Springfield, Illinois, unless the editors indicate otherwise.

Governor Stevenson wrote many letters to Mrs. Edison Dick and her family during the years he was in Springfield. Some were dictated and transcribed on the typewriter, and some were handwritten. Mrs. Dick has submitted extracts to the editors from handwritten letters she received from Governor Stevenson. She has indicated with ellipses material that was deleted by her. The originals of all the handwritten letters are in her possession.

The editors of these volumes searched widely for handwritten documents. Stevenson enjoyed writing by hand — he must have, since he wrote so many letters and postcards. Some people, particularly before Stevenson became governor of Illinois, failed to save them. Many people were most cooperative, placing all their Stevenson items at our disposal. Some preferred to send us only selections from their collection. A few refused to send us any material at all.[2]

Some letters, which would cause unnecessary anguish in people still living, the editors have not included in these volumes or have made appropriate deletions within such letters. These deletions are indicated by ellipses. The location of handwritten letters, postcards or originals of typewritten letters is given in the footnote references.

We indicate for the speeches we publish whether the draft we used was a press release, a carbon copy, or the original — that is, the final copy from which the speech was actually delivered. There are several speeches taken from "ribbon" copies, where some doubt exists as to whether they are in fact the originals. These are designated as ribbon copies.

Stevenson customarily rewrote a speech practically up to the minute of delivery. It would, therefore, be best if we could always have used the original copy. Many of these, however, have disappeared. Stevenson frequently gave the original to a friendly reporter and it was never returned.

When we have made deletions from letters, speeches, or other papers, we indicate this by ellipses. We have provided editorial comment on any item where it was necessary for clarity or continuity.

Stevenson provided in his will that material about his governorship of Illinois be deposited in the Illinois State Historical Library and the re-

---

[2] Katie Louchheim wrote: "These were [some of] the women who owned a share in Adlai's destiny." *By the Political Sea* (Garden City, New York: Doubleday, 1970), p. 108.

mainder of his papers be deposited in the Princeton University Library. Stevenson's most important correspondence, drafts of speeches, and fragments of diary were at his home in Libertyville when he died. The editors selected some of the material for this volume from the material at Libertyville before the collection was divided between the two depositories. Some items are still in the possession of Adlai E. Stevenson III.

Since the majority of the papers for his gubernatorial term are at the Illinois State Historical Library (some in the distribution, probably inadvertently, went to the Princeton University Library), the editors identify the location of only those papers that are *not* in the Springfield collection. Those papers that are in the Elizabeth Stevenson Ives collection at the Illinois State Historical Library are identified by the abbreviation E.S.I., I.S.H.L. The papers that are in the Adlai E. Stevenson collection, Princeton University Library, are identified as A.E.S., P.U.L.

Handwritten letters or postcards and original typewritten letters that are in the possession of individuals will be so designated.

All Stevenson's letters on official business were signed with his full name over the title "Governor." Both name and title on all such items are omitted in this volume. Because we have had to work, in most cases, with carbon copies it is impossible to know how these letters and memoranda were signed. Hence, signatures have been omitted from such items. Whenever we have located the original letter, and he signed it "Ad" or "Adlai," we have included the signature.

When he wrote by hand, Stevenson had several idiosyncrasies. He spelled "it's" without the apostrophe; he used "thru" for "though," etc. We have left them as he wrote them and have not added a *sic*.

Under the legal agreement between Walter Johnson and Adlai Stevenson III, Borden Stevenson, and John Fell Stevenson, Adlai III agreed to read each volume before publication. If he objected to the inclusion of any particular item of his father's papers, and Walter Johnson refused to accept the objection, the matter in dispute went to Judge Carl McGowan for final — and irrevocable — decision. Adlai III found nothing in this volume to which he objected.

Contents

Illustrations

Part One

1949

O n January 9, 1949, Stevenson and his family, friends, and personal staff traveled to Springfield for his inauguration as governor the following day. The ceremonies took place in the Armory building at a joint meeting of the legislature, which was also attended by an overflow audience of interested citizens and political workers. Later in the evening there was an inaugural ball led off by the new Governor and his attractive wife, Ellen.

Because of her background as a belle of Chicago society, the legislators and Springfield residents had anticipated a glamorous social life, but they were to be disappointed. Mrs. Stevenson returned to their home near Libertyville, Illinois, the day after the inauguration, because, as she stated, she did not wish to take their youngest son John Fell away from his classes at Lake Forest Country Day School. She came to Springfield only a few times, and only for formal legislative dinners. There was much talk about her absence, and finally, in September, 1949, the Governor, sadly and by formal statement, announced their separation.[1]

The Governor's sons were away at school: Adlai III at Harvard University, Borden at the Choate School in Connecticut, and John Fell in Lake Forest (and later that year at Milton Academy in Massachusetts). Shortly after the inauguration the Governor persuaded his chief administrative aide, Walter V. Schaefer, who was living in a hotel, to move into one of the many rooms of the Governor's mansion. Schaefer's room was destined to be occupied in turn by Carl McGowan and later by William

[1] Jane Warner Dick writes of the divorce: "Adlai regarded marriage, home and family with old-fashioned reverence. The break-up of his marriage after twenty years and just after his election as Governor was a staggering shock. Only his close friends ever knew the scars it left. His dignity throughout this ordeal, his reticence about discussing personal problems, and his solicitous endeavors to preserve the affection and loyalty of his sons to both parents revealed as much as anything the quality of this man." "Forty Years of Friendship," in *As We Knew Adlai: The Stevenson Story by Twenty-two Friends*, edited and with preface by Edward P. Doyle, foreword by Adlai E. Stevenson III (New York: Harper & Row, 1966), pp. 271–272.

McCormick Blair, Jr., both acting as assistants to the Governor with offices in the mansion.

After the divorce his sister and brother-in-law, Mr. and Mrs. Ernest L. Ives, visited him frequently and were extremely helpful to him, although they maintained two homes elsewhere: one at Bloomington, Illinois, and one at Southern Pines, North Carolina. Mrs. Ives acted as her brother's official hostess when she was in Springfield. When she was absent or otherwise engaged, the Governor would ask the wife of a cabinet member, department head or prominent Springfield citizen to act as his hostess at mansion social affairs.

The Governor made sure there were many guests at the mansion, both American and foreign, and it was said that the mansion had never had such a wide range of visitors.[2] During 1949 the following, among others, were mansion guests: Vice President Alben Barkley, Mr. and Mrs. Gregg Sinclair (he was then president of the University of Hawaii), Vincent Sheean; Charles Taft, Mary Garden, columnist Doris Fleeson and other members of the press, including two from the British Broadcasting Corporation, a representative from the Department of Agriculture of Uruguay, as well as personal friends and members of his family.[3]

Stevenson had looked forward to many visits from one of his most treasured friends: Lloyd Lewis, writer, historian and newspaper editor, and Stevenson's neighbor in Libertyville. Lewis died suddenly on April 21, 1949. The loss of his friend had a depressing effect on Stevenson, and deepened for him the gloom of the mansion and the complexities of his new job.

Another occupant of the mansion, and one to which the Governor was devoted, was his Dalmatian dog, King Arthur, dubbed "Artie." Artie was a running dog and in his restlessness took to roaming the Springfield streets, resulting in phone calls to the mansion from neighbors to report on his activities. But frequently enough he could be found late at night at the Governor's feet in his basement office.

Although the mansion was not entirely unoccupied, Stevenson was a lonely man. Former State Senator John J. Parish, of Centralia, Illinois, said: "A Governor is a lonesome man, and Governor Stevenson had much to contend with and he was lonesome. . . . I was in his office when a friend called him from Chicago . . . and he started to complain how he was cooped up and felt like a mole, and life was nothing but work. When he hung up I gave him a lecture telling him that he was honored to have

[2] From an interview by Walter Johnson with Mrs. Thomas Masters, wife of a prominent Springfield physician, April 20, 1966.

[3] Taken from the 1949 desk calendar of Carol Evans.

been elected Governor . . . and that no one liked a cry baby. I never heard him complain after that, but he really had a right to." [4]

The result of his loneliness was a devotion to his work, spending long hours learning the intricacies of his job, that of governing the state of Illinois. As one biographer, Kenneth S. Davis, wrote: "In the immediate aftermath of the divorce he was convinced of his own failure. He worked incredibly hard for incredibly long hours all during the divorce period. . . . One midnight [his sister] Buffie went down to his basement office in the mansion to plead with him to go to bed. . . . He shook his head stubbornly and made, unwittingly, one of his rare revelations of his hurt and of his excessively conscientious response to it. 'I've failed as a husband,' he said. 'I've failed as a father. I will succeed as governor!' " [5]

He did not fail as a father, although he did not then realize it. His sons came to Springfield at every opportunity and later to their home near Libertyville, or they would join their father, after the governorship, on his numerous trips abroad if they could possibly arrange it. Later he was to acquire daughters-in-law and grandchildren who delighted in and adored him.

His interest in and appeal to young people extended far beyond his sons. During his term as governor he received many letters from young people, and whenever possible he answered them himself rather than passing them along for his staff to acknowledge. He took special pleasure in talking with young people about public affairs, was always interested in what they were thinking or doing, and urging them to participate in their government. He inspired Paul Simon, a young newspaper editor in the small Illinois city of Troy, to write of him after his death: "As I look back on it now, Stevenson appealed to youth and had an interest in them because he was always young himself, always growing, always eager to explore and probe untried paths." [6]

Governor Stevenson maintained two offices in Springfield: one in the capitol building and one on the first floor (sometimes called the basement) of the ninety-three-year-old executive mansion. He also had an office in Chicago.

His capitol office was small and could be reached only by passing through an enormous reception room. It was necessary to exit by the

[4] Letter to Carol Evans, undated, but written in December, 1967.

[5] Kenneth S. Davis, *A Prophet in His Own Country: The Triumphs and Defeats of Adlai E. Stevenson* (New York: Doubleday, 1957), pp. 316–317. "The multitude of letters of commendation that came to him during his administration as Governor attested to the fact that he was, indeed, successful as being considered Illinois' greatest Governor." Mrs. Robert Risse, letter to Carol Evans, April 21, 1968.

[6] Paul Simon, "Young People Loved Him," in *As We Knew Adlai*, p. 130.

same route as there was no private passageway, making him easily acces-sible to anyone who wanted to see him, with or without an appointment. He used this office during legislative sessions when it was important for him to be quickly available to legislators, although it was necessary at times to schedule appointments and meetings at his mansion office. When the legislature was not in session he used the more spacious and con-venient offices in the mansion, going to the capitol infrequently. Cabinet and legislative meetings were held at the mansion offices, and most ap-pointments were scheduled there except during legislative sessions.

When Stevenson took office he brought with him, from his campaign headquarters in Chicago, James W. Mulroy to act as his executive secre-tary and Louis A. Kohn, on leave through the legislative session from his lucrative law practice, to act as appointments secretary. William I. Flan-agan became head of the Division of Department Reports. (This agency released information about all state agencies to the communications media, but the usual practice was for an incoming governor to appoint someone to head it who would also act as his press secretary.) These three men had offices in the capitol building.

In the Governor's capitol office also were T. Don Hyndman, administra-tive aide to the former governor, and Mrs. Anne Risse, who had served five previous governors. Hyndman had been a newspaperman. He drafted statements, proclamations and speeches, and acted as an adviser. Mrs. Risse continued to act as supervisor of the Governor's staff. They both served Stevenson effectively and loyally throughout his term of office.

All the clerical and stenographic help in the Governor's capitol office had their jobs by virtue of patronage appointment from the outgoing Re-publican governor and were not covered by civil service. Stevenson asked them to continue with him if they wished, and they all stayed.

During 1949 Stevenson also added to his capitol staff Lawrence Irvin, of Bloomington, Illinois, over whose desk all patronage requests passed. He had been a Red Cross field director and business manager of Illinois State Normal University and was well known in Illinois. Later, Richard J. Nelson joined the capitol staff as administrative aide to the Governor. He was a young lawyer who became president of the Young Democratic Clubs of America. He accompanied the Governor on numerous speech-making and political journeys. He was later to become a vice president of Inland Steel Corporation. On August 1, 1971, he became president of Northern Illinois University.

At the mansion offices Walter V. Schaefer acted as the Governor's chief counselor and assistant. He took a leave of absence from his teaching duties at Northwestern University Law School to continue with Stevenson through the 1949 legislative session. He had previous government experi-

ence at both state and national levels, and had assisted Stevenson during the campaign and post-election period in formulating his program for Illinois. He was later to be appointed by the Governor to fill a vacancy on the Illinois Supreme Court and at the end of that term to win the office by election.

When Schaefer returned to Chicago in the fall of 1949, his place as chief adviser and assistant to the Governor was taken by Carl McGowan, also from the faculty of Northwestern Law School. McGowan grew up in Paris, Illinois, but he had practiced law in the East and during World War II had worked closely with Stevenson in the Navy Department. He remained as adviser to the Governor throughout his administration and during the 1952 campaign. He then returned to the practice of law in Chicago, and later became a judge of the United States Court of Appeals, District of Columbia Circuit.

J. Edward Day, a native of Springfield, was a young attorney who had been associated with the law firm in Chicago of which the Governor had been a partner. During the war he was in the Naval Reserve which he left as a lieutenant commander. He joined the mansion staff in March, 1949, and worked closely with Schaefer and McGowan on the legislative program, also advising the Governor on personnel and general matters. He was later to become Postmaster General during the administration of President John F. Kennedy. He had a gift for light and witty verse, was a clever punster and an accomplished storyteller.

Day was to remain as assistant to Stevenson for approximately a year. In 1950, on the resignation of the director of the Department of Insurance, the Governor appointed Day to fill the vacancy, a position he held throughout the remainder of the administration. He brought many effective changes into that department and continued to serve the Governor as adviser and friend.

William McC. Blair, Jr., was to succeed Day as adviser to the Governor. Blair first met Stevenson in 1940, at twenty-three, when he worked as a volunteer for the Committee to Defend America by Aiding the Allies. He was a second cousin of Colonel Robert R. McCormick, publisher of the Chicago Tribune, and scion of one of Chicago's wealthiest and most distinguished families. He served in the Army during World War II in the China-Burma-India theater as an intelligence officer, and was mustered out a captain. He was associated with the law firm of Wilson & McIlvaine in Chicago, but resigned when Stevenson asked him to come to Springfield. He screened appointments for Stevenson and became, generally, a "diplomatic troubleshooter," a role for which he was well qualified with his calm, intelligent and friendly manner. He lived at the mansion and had an office on the first floor. He was to remain with

Stevenson until 1961, when President Kennedy appointed him ambassador to Denmark.

Carol Evans, who had served during the campaign, became Stevenson's personal secretary at the mansion. She had earlier worked part-time in his law office while attending the University of Chicago, and was to remain with him until 1961 when he became U.S. ambassador to the United Nations.

Others of the mansion secretarial staff were Phyllis Gustafson, a young woman from Chicago who had worked in the campaign headquarters. She returned to Chicago late in 1949 to join the Department of Finance and to help the Governor in his Chicago office. (After the governorship she became, successively, secretary to William McC. Blair, Jr., and Adlai E. Stevenson III.) Margaret Munn transferred from the capitol staff and worked closely with Mr. Blair, Miss Evans and the Governor. She was a native of Springfield and her knowledge of local politics was extremely helpful. Frances Howe Ruys, Stevenson's secretary in his Chicago law office, having married, acquired a family, and moved to Springfield, became secretary to Carl McGowan. Both Mrs. Munn and Mrs. Ruys remained in Springfield after the governorship.

Although there was some rivalry between the staff at the capitol and the mansion, on the whole it was muted, and morale throughout the entire four years of the administration was excellent. Mrs. Risse, of the capitol staff, said: "The first contact I had with Governor Stevenson was when he visited his office in the Capitol Building following his election in 1948. He turned to me and said, 'Mrs. Risse, I've heard so many, many, fine things about you!' How he knew who I was I never found out, but he was like that. He made it a point to know everybody." And Frances Ruys, at the mansion, said: "His sense of humor eased many a difficult situation. As I look back on those years, he seemed more like a close personal friend or your next door neighbor than employer." [7]

The household staff consisted of the housekeeper and her husband, Everett Van Diver, a captain in the state police, who acted as the Governor's chauffeur, driving the ancient Cadillac the Governor insisted on keeping throughout his administration. Van Diver had served four previous governors. In addition, two police officers were on duty outside the mansion at all times to admit callers, drive mansion visitors, and provide security. There were several servants in addition to the housekeeper, all of whom lived away from the mansion and went to their homes at night.

[7] "A Statesman's Epitaph," *State Journal-Register*, Springfield, Illinois, July 18, 1965. The headline of this full-page story was taken from a line in the article: "It is said epitaphs are written by one's own actions. Adlai Stevenson has left an enviable one."

Captain and Mrs. Van Diver lived on the premises in an apartment over the garage.[8]

The Governor also kept an office in downtown Chicago in a large building occupied entirely by state offices. His suite was located on the top floor and consisted of a spacious office and reception room, with adequate but not large living quarters attached. It was necessary for him to go into Chicago about once a month to consult with agency and commission heads and to keep other appointments. He kept no full-time employees in this office.

The Governor and his staff were all relatively young. The Governor was approaching his forty-ninth birthday when he took office, and most of his staff were in their thirties and forties. Paul Simon wrote: "Part of the impact he had on Illinois and on me was the wave of able people he brought to Springfield: Carl McGowan, Newt Minow, Bill Blair, Dick Nelson, Bill Flanagan, Larry Irvin, Leonard Schwartz, to mention just a few." [9]

Although it is extremely difficult to recruit first-rate people to serve in state government, Stevenson was able to persuade a surprising number of well-qualified people to serve with him in his administration. His wide acquaintance in government circles and in the business world were helpful to him, but the loyalty and effectiveness of his appointees were tributes to his personal and leadership qualities. Stevenson once told his son Adlai III that the test of any administrator was whether he could draw good people to help him; that after all, a governor could not do it all by himself; that during the governorship he drew a top group of people into his administration; and from that time on he knew how to draw on talent to secure ideas and assistance.[10]

In recruiting personnel, Stevenson could not offer much in the way of material rewards. His own salary was only $12,000 a year; that of his cabinet and department heads $8,000.

Stephen A. Mitchell, one of the original members of the Stevenson for Governor Committee, recalled in 1966: "Governors as well as candidates nearly always have trouble about money, whether it be campaign funds, expense accounts or state budgets. . . . After the 1948 campaign our first hasty audit indicated we had a deficit, and we welcomed a number of

[8] Both Kenneth S. Davis in *A Prophet in His Own Country* and Elizabeth Stevenson Ives and Hildegarde Dolson in *My Brother Adlai* (New York: William Morrow, 1956) give excellent and detailed accounts of life at the executive mansion during the governorship.

[9] "Young People Loved Him," in *As We Knew Adlai*, pp. 136–137. Newton N. Minow did not join the Governor's staff until the summer of 1952. Leonard Schwartz was appointed by Stevenson as director of Conservation, a post he held throughout the four-year administration.

[10] Adlai E. Stevenson III, conversation with Walter Johnson, February 3, 1966.

'late contributions' which poured in in the wake of victory — and declined quite a few, too. With these we were able to repay certain loans and out-of-pocket expenses. . . . I proposed that this fund be held and disbursed at the Governor's discretion. Adlai was beginning to realize the problem of getting quality talent at the low state salary level, and this situation was in our minds." [11]

Mitchell then developed the idea of forming a charitable corporation as a depository for funds to be used for additional compensation to certain high-level employees, and set about exploring the possibilities. The problems were so overwhelming that it was abandoned.

However, Stevenson did use campaign funds to supplement salaries of some of his appointees who took their positions at considerable sacrifice, and to pay certain other ongoing expenses. The fund was added to by gifts from old friends and supporters whose sources and motives were considered to be above suspicion. It was not a "secret" fund. Stevenson talked about it openly, as he did about his problems of recruiting first-rate people who believed in decent government. But it was to cause him embarrassment in the 1952 presidential campaign. [12]

Early in 1949, Edward D. McDougal, Jr., treasurer of the Volunteers for Stevenson, wound up his services and instructed the First National Bank of Chicago to honor only checks signed by James W. Mulroy, Stevenson's executive secretary. [13]

Both Stevenson and Mulroy were concerned about the method of raising funds and their source. Mulroy wrote Stevenson on May 30, 1950:

> As a result of talks we have had in recent days I have the following tentative program to offer you on the subject of raising money. . . . All monies in the form of contributions by those who are personal friends of yours or who specify that they wish to help out the Stevenson for Governor Committee fund should come to me and be deposited in the Stevenson for Governor Committee bank account. . . . All money received from solicitations made by friends of yours who approach those who have done business with the State of Illinois should be deposited in the Stevenson for Governor bank account. Under no circumstances should friends of yours be allowed to solicit money on a percentage basis and such people should be warned that any money going to the Committee bank account should come in on a voluntary basis. [14]

[11] "Adlai's Amateurs," in *As We Knew Adlai*, p. 79.

[12] Richard M. Nixon has an inaccurate statement about the fund in his *Six Crises* (Garden City, N.Y.: Doubleday, 1962), p. 106.

[13] From a copy of a typewritten letter, undated, in the possession of Mr. Mulroy's widow, Mrs. Helen Kaste.

[14] This handwritten memorandum is in the possession of Mrs. Helen Kaste.

Prior to the inauguration, patronage requests as well as applications for top-level positions were routed through regular party organizations. Many names came to the attention of the Governor and were screened through a "patronage committee" appointed by him and operating from his campaign headquarters after the election. No positions could be filled until after the inauguration.

With respect to all appointments, the Governor adopted the policy from the outset that "deserving" Democrats were to be granted preference if they were qualified for the job; otherwise, positions were to be filled by anyone who did qualify regardless of party affiliation. This policy did not endear him to some Democratic politicians who were starved for patronage, since the Republicans had held the governorship for eight years.

Although a few appointments to departments and agencies were made soon after he became governor, Stevenson and his advisers decided to take their time on some top-level appointments. Their hands were full with the legislature and it was considered wise to allow some Republican directors and commission chairmen to remain until specially qualified personnel could be found to replace them.

Stevenson had been elected by the largest plurality in the history of Illinois: 572,067 votes. He won not only Cook County but 48 counties out of the other 101. Cook County, with Chicago as its capital, usually voted Democratic; the rest of the state was normally heavily Republican. (Although a few counties lie to the west and a little north of Cook County, in Illinois all the counties except Cook are referred to as "downstate.") The General Assembly was divided: 72 Republicans to 81 Democrats in the House; 32 Republicans to 18 Democrats in the Senate. Thus the Senate Republican majority was 14, the House Democratic majority, 9. But when the legislature met in joint session the Republicans had a majority of 5.

The legislature at the time the Governor assumed office had been in session for five days. Between election day, November 4, 1948, and the date of his formal installation as governor, he struggled with patronage problems, top-level appointments, a heavy load of correspondence, made public appearances when necessary, and, most important, formulated a legislative program and prepared his inaugural address.

In Illinois as in other state legislatures bills can originate in either house. The governor can exert his leadership by recommending to the legislature what he believes to be not only urgent but desirable.[15]

[15] There were some issues Stevenson thought extremely important but did not include in his inaugural address. For example, he wrote on January 13, 1949, to Guy E. Reed, president of Harris Trust & Savings Bank, Chicago: "The Crime Commission

Stevenson needed all the political skill he could muster to get his program enacted. He was an amateur in the sense of never having held elective office, but because of his family's political background and his own experience in the national government, neither was he a complete stranger to practical politics, and he rapidly became more expert. Of Stevenson's role as a politician, Carl McGowan, who served as the Governor's chief aide in Springfield, said:

It is, I think, one of the emptiest myths of our time that Adlai Stevenson was a political sport — an unhappy and uncomfortable accident in the unlikely milieu of professional politics, ill at ease with others who followed that trade, ineffective in his relationship with them because of his instinctive distaste for them and their way of life. . . . During his first year in office, it was common to hear about the halls of the capitol and in the hotel bars the bland assumption that he was an accident, a one-termer who would be retired to the lusher pastures of the North Shore without being reslated. By the end of the first year or so, this talk had disappeared completely and, if referred to at all, it was in the homely locution that he could not be beaten for a second term with a baseball bat.[16]

Stevenson believed that the most vital measures to be considered by the legislature were the calling of a constitutional convention to revise the state's outdated constitution, improvement in personnel practices, improvement in aid to dependent children and the aged by incorporating these assistance programs into the Department of Public Welfare, extending and increasing benefits of unemployment compensation, passage of a fair employment practices law to prevent discrimination in employment, extension of grand jury terms in Cook County to help curb organized crime; improvement and maintenance of highways, extension of civil service to the Department of Mines and Minerals, reorganization of the state police under a merit system, reorganization of the Illinois Commerce Commission, and massive state aid to education.

He did not get all the legislation he asked for, but approximately two-thirds of it was passed. Some of the legislation he so earnestly desired was doomed to defeat when some Chicago Democrats joined Republicans to vote against it. For example, the so-called Chicago West Side Bloc Democrats were anxious that the Crime Commission bills not be passed because of gambling interests in their districts; and many legislators of both parties were distressed because a constitutional convention would

Bills were eliminated along with several other things in order to shorten that long and tedious speech."

[16] Washington *Post*, July 18, 1965.

*have meant redistricting the state, with new political lines drawn, and
would also have paved the way for a state income tax.*

On January 10, 1949, Stevenson delivered his Inaugural Address.[17]

Mr. President, Mr. Speaker, Members of the Sixty-sixth General Assembly, Governor and Mrs. Green and Fellow Citizens:

Every Governor of Illinois has tried, I suppose, to make his inaugural address brief. Few have succeeded. I, too, have tried, and failed, even though I have reserved for future comment many subjects deserving discussion.

I cannot fail, however, to note the significance and perhaps the historical opportunity for you and me in this hour when Illinois is passing from one epoch to another exactly as it did 100 years ago.

Historians say that 1848 was a transition year in the history of Illinois. A steel plow to cut the tough sod had, at last, been invented. The reaper had come to our prairies. Plank roads had begun to lift Illinois out of the mud. The Germans and the Irish were coming. With 25,000 souls, Chicago was struggling out of the swamps. A railroad was creeping westward. Illinois was emerging from the log cabin frontier era and was taking its place in the new industrial day that was breaking upon the Union.

Illinois was to meet the test of a century ago. It was to become a pillar of strength and a progressive leader in the sisterhood of States. Behind vast barriers of sea and land, Illinois grew to maturity relatively remote and aloof from world affairs.

Today, Illinois stands at the threshold of another era — an era in which almost any event in any part of the world can have immediate and profound impact upon us. Barriers of time and space no longer isolate or protect us. And to a degree hitherto undreamed, events in America have prompt repercussions around the globe. Many watch us intently. Our mistakes, our failures, all are quickly exploited by those who watch with malice. But more watch with prayers.

Two convulsive conflicts have made our revolutionary generation the bloodiest in the history of man. And now with the post war period of gay optimism ending, the world settles down to a long trial of strength between individualism and collectivism — a trial of strength not limited to military and economic potentials but to moral and spiritual actualities.

Will Illinois in this new era take the leadership that it took in the

[17] The text is based on a copy printed by the State of Illinois, entitled "Inaugural Address of Governor Adlai E. Stevenson of Illinois Delivered Before a Joint Session of the General Assembly of Illinois at Springfield, January 10, 1949."

materialistic era of the past hundred years? We can if we will it. We who meet here in Springfield today can take a long step toward making our government a model, a precept in the best tradition of self government. The forces of progress are at hand. In the century that stretches back to the log cabin door, nature, agriculture, industry, learning, and an energetic, diverse population have combined to bless us, enrich us, enlighten us. Nothing can stop us unless it be our own moral inadequacy, greed, selfishness, prejudice, excessive partisanship.

We are here, chosen by the people, not as party agents but as the peoples' agents. A common concern for the future unites us. A common desire to serve the state unites us. Political parties and party principles are essential to our system of government, but economic and social principles upon which a healthy electorate divides, diminish in importance as government descends from the national to the local level. Basic divisions between Democrats and Republicans on national issues have little bearing upon state or municipal problems. Mere partisan struggle for advantage will serve neither party nor state, because where you, as legislators of Illinois, and I as Governor of Illinois, now stand, it is only performance that will count.

I would not be misunderstood as to the role that Illinois can take in this titanic struggle for the future that plagues the world. What Illinois can and must do is to make itself the strongest link in that mighty chain which we call the United States.

We can set our own house in order. We can hearten our countrymen; we can demonstrate for all to see that representative government is healthy, vigorous, enterprising; that representative government *is* the best government. We can show the world what a government consecrated to plain talk, hard work and prairie horse-sense can do.

In accordance with the Constitution and tradition I shall today make a few suggestions calculated, I think, to put our house in order.

State and Local Finances

Let's assess first our basic problem. With the many new services which modern civilization demands of government revenue is the basic problem, because the amount of money available to do a given job determines how the job is done.

We must bear in mind that the period of manpower and material shortage of the war years when many services and expenditures of government were necessarily curtailed is now over. Instead of an opportunity to accumulate excess revenues we now have an accumulation of imperative demands for capital improvements and services at greatly increased cost.[18]

The state's taxing system is today producing revenue at the unprecedented rate of approximately 450 million dollars a year. But some of the major taxes are earmarked for special expenditure programs. Federal grants add about 75 million dollars a year, but these grants are also earmarked. As my predecessor, Governor [Dwight H.] Green, said to you last week, we have an unencumbered balance of about 100 million dollars in the State Treasury after allowing for anticipated deficiency appropriations and all legal or moral commitments.

On the other side of the ledger our bonded debt is 466 million dollars, the second largest of any state in the union. Moreover, to operate those state functions which are not financed from earmarked sources, we are now spending at a rate in excess of our income. Recent estimates show that expenditures of non-reserved funds in this fiscal year will exceed revenues by some 40 million dollars.

This is the background against which we must assess the obligations of our state to its citizens. Many school units are hard pressed despite increased property taxes. Many face increasing enrollments with inadequate buildings. Low salaries make it difficult to recruit and retain the best teachers. Likewise municipalities quite generally face grave difficulties in maintaining their essential services.

The people are impatient with bickering between the state and local governments over the division of duties and revenues. They look only for efficient and responsible government by whatever agency is best fitted. As taxpayers, they are entitled to a governmental structure both state and local which will insure the most economical administration of all government services. There is no justification for preserving the frills and extravagances of one government when the functions of other governments within the boundaries of the same state have been reduced beyond the minimums of common welfare. The citizens of the towns and school districts of this state are also the citizens of the state. We want no feast within our borders when there is also famine.

The problems of all governments in Illinois are the concern, indeed

[18] During the war years, when almost all construction materials were used for the war effort and none for housing, public buildings or roads, most state treasuries accumulated generous surpluses. In 1949 the surplus in Illinois was approximately $150 million. On taking office, Stevenson learned that about $80 million would be needed to cover deficiency appropriations and commitments already made by the prior (Green) administration. This did not deter the Republicans from claiming full credit for the entire surplus and charging Stevenson with being a reckless spender when he began using these funds. Mimeograph memorandum by J. Edward Day, "The Stevenson Administration — The First Three Years," May 7, 1952, pp. 43–44.

the major concern, of the state. Consistent with maintaining the state's credit and discharging its own prior responsibilities for the general welfare, our greatest single challenge lies in finding the means for better financing of schools, roads and local services. To shoulder this heavier responsibility certainly it is our obligation to squeeze the water and the waste out of governments at every level. Before imposing additional state taxes, certainly it is our obligation to enforce completely and effectively those we already have.

A greater participation in the financing of local government requires that the state demand economical and efficient local government. I do not think that state funds should be used to perpetuate structures that cannot do an economical and effective job of good administration. But for well-organized local units the state should relax restrictions for its aid so as to insure the maximum of local initiative and responsibility in the management of local affairs.

The able Revenue Commission appointed by the 65th General Assembly, of which Senator Merrit J. Little [19] is chairman, will shortly make detailed recommendations to you concerning these basic problems of revenue and state aid. I anticipate that its conclusions will reflect its concern for our best interests and will be made with a vision which transcends fleeting political considerations.

Constitutional Convention

Directly related to the problem of revenue, and to other road blocks to better government is, of course, the Constitution of 1870.

I cannot now describe in detail all of its impediments. But everyone knows that uniformity of taxation of property, commanded in 1870 when land was the principal form of wealth, is impossible today. We avoid compliance by individual and official evasion and subterfuge. The price we pay is an inequitable taxing system with real estate carrying a disproportionate share of the burden, and a serious breakdown in respect for law. Irreverence for constitutions threatens the foundations of constitutional government itself.

The flat constitutional command of legislative reapportionment every ten years has not been complied with since 1901. Realistically, I apprehend that it is not going to be complied with so long as reapportionment would give control of both houses of the General Assembly to Cook County, as it would under the present Constitution. And in the meantime there is practical disenfranchisement of a very large number of citizens.

The present constitutional limitation on municipal indebtedness has resulted in a proliferation of local governments which increases costs,

[19] Republican, 14th District.

diffuses responsibility and hampers effective control of government by the people.

The rigid constitutional pattern for the administration of the state's justice has resulted in a complex, unbusinesslike judicial establishment.

The hands of the legislature are tied in many respects by detailed unnecessary constitutional legislation. To use Governor Lowden's [20] words of 32 years ago: "To withhold necessary power from a public official because he may abuse it, is to confess the failure of our form of government."

Experience has demonstrated [the] virtual impossibility of revising the Constitution by the process of piecemeal amendment. The need, therefore, is to assemble a constitutional convention to deal with the problems, promptly and comprehensively.

Accordingly, I request the General Assembly to adopt a joint resolution submitting to a referendum the question whether a constitutional convention shall be called. I am confident that the General Assembly will afford our people the opportunity to express themselves on this important question.

But legislative action alone is not enough. We must overcome those obstacles which have combined to defeat so many past efforts to revise our Constitution.

The fear so frequently expressed that a new constitution will permit a graduated income tax or turn over to Cook County domination of the legislature is probably the best assurance that the convention will refrain from doing so.

I know of no large number of our people who favor a state income tax. I know a great many who oppose it. Rather than risk the rejection of a new constitution because of this apprehension I would urge the convention to leave the income tax problem precisely where it stands at present.

I do not believe that Cook County wants legislative dominance in both houses. Even if Cook County wanted that dominance it could not get it in a constitutional convention, for there the distribution of voting strength as between Cook County and downstate would be precisely the same as in the General Assembly. The problem of achieving a balance of legislative power is neither novel nor complex. It was solved in our federal system and it has been solved in the constitutions of other states.

Other objections will be raised to a constitutional convention. Some will oppose it because of the ensuing uncertainties of interpretation, or because of the fear that hard won gains and advantages will be lost. At

[20] Frank O. Lowden, Republican governor of Illinois, 1917–1921.

best this is going far afield to borrow trouble; at worst it is according the convenience of the few precedence over the welfare of the many.

In the past political parties in Illinois have laid aside partisan differences in the consideration of basic constitutional issues. A vigorous nonpartisan effort is again imperative. The support of interested groups must be enlisted. And I hope you will change our election laws and restore to political parties the responsibility for constitutional issues which the men who wrote the Constitution of 1870 contemplated they should have.

I firmly believe that if we approach the task of revising our Constitution in the manner I have outlined, our people will not fear or mistrust a constitutional convention and that such a convention, when assembled, will approach its responsibilities in the solemn spirit of retaining all that is of proven value while adapting our fundamental law to the needs of the present day.

Personnel

Government, however good the laws, will not rise above the quality of the men that comprise it. Administration will be no better than the administrators. Revitalizing public service can't be achieved with good intentions and elocution about good government. The conditions of good morale are a sense of mission, self respect and dignity.

The problem of personnel administration in a business spending half a billion dollars a year merits the closest attention of you, the board of directors, and of us, your executive officers. It will have mine, I assure you.

Meanwhile let me comment on three aspects of the personnel problem. In the first place, responsibilities of this magnitude demand highly competent and scrupulous men at the top. It is obvious to all that many of the senior positions in the state's service do not pay enough to support, let alone attract the quality of management and leadership these positions demand and the people deserve, except upon a basis of unselfish sacrifice. And too often, as many have noted, the reward for sacrifice in public service is not gratitude in lieu of dollars, but abuse, criticism and ingratitude. Government cannot, will not, and should not attempt to match the salary scales of private business. But government can and must, if it is to be good government, pay salaries which are not an invitation to carelessness, indolence or even worse — corruption. And in good government, good men will find their supplementary reward in personal satisfaction, public esteem and respect.

I will propose, therefore, while you are considering general salary levels, substantial increases in the salaries of key positions.

In the second place, competent and incorruptible men at the top are not enough. It is the men and women in the ranks who translate legislation and executive policy into action, who give government its meaning and character. In a real sense they *are* the government. And its quality depends not on the majestic buildings symbolic of the power and dignity of government but upon the spirit and competence of these people who *are* the government.

These employees of the state are not employees of a political party. They must not be so considered.

Today the major emphasis in civil service administration is on recruiting, training and promoting the best possible body of men and women to administer the public business. I have carefully considered whether, in view of our lack of progress in this most important field, I should urge you to consider the adoption of a more modern system of personnel administration to secure the necessary emphasis upon recruitment and training aspects of a genuine merit system.

I have concluded, however, that a sincere effort must first be made to achieve progress under our present machinery. One significant legislative change is essential, however. The function of position classification is an integral part of personnel administration, and I urge the General Assembly to restore that function to the Civil Service Commission where it belongs.

In the third place, the modern goal of government is career service. Too large a segment of our employees are political transients rather than career servants. Ideally a change of administration should mean a change in policy-making personnel only. Hard, practical considerations point to the same goal. Current appropriations for personnel service are some one hundred million dollars a year. The prudent expenditure of such a sum for the best possible public service imposes a grave responsibility upon the General Assembly and the Governor.

I have no illusions that progress in this field will be easy. But I know that the patronage system of the past is inefficient because effective administration is impossible when employees owe their allegiance and responsibility not to their supervisors but to their political sponsors. And I know that the system is even of diminishing political value as the electorate finds it more and more distasteful. Witness the last election in Illinois.

I believe sincerely that we are sufficiently mature to encourage the policy of career service and an expanding merit system in Illinois.

Incidentally the phrase "the government of Illinois belongs to the people of Illinois" has too often been abused by empty lip service. A healthy antidote to payroll padding and familiar political practices would be to invite constant public scrutiny of payroll facts and figures. The policy of my administration will be to require as complete and current payroll information as is feasible and looking to the future I urge the adoption of legislation expressing that policy.[21]

Public Welfare and Assistance

Public welfare is perhaps our most moving and urgent problem. During the early stages when we were setting up assistance programs for dependent children, the aged and the handicapped, we developed a two-headed organization to provide welfare services and assistance, frequently at the same time to the same people. It duplicates procedures and costs, and provides a double standard which affects salaries and methods of operation.

We have now had a broad experience in this field. I believe that by integrating the related services of the Illinois Public Aid Commission and the Department of Public Welfare into a single unit, we shall achieve not only economies and increased efficiency but better service to the citizen who does not want two, three, or four agencies visiting his home. I urge that legislation effecting this integration be adopted.

I also recommend for the director of this much enlarged department a strong advisory and policy approving board.

Our dependent children, our old people, our handicapped and mentally ill whose welfare would be entrusted to this single department will in the future as in the past merit our first attention on humane grounds and also because such a large segment of the state's dollar will be allocated to their care.

I assume the General Assembly will wish to proceed promptly by emergency legislation to increase aid to those for whom the last Congress made additional provision. The old age pensioners, and the blind are in need of this additional aid which will increase maximum payments under old age assistance to at least fifty-five dollars a month.

In this connection I believe the legislature should also give consideration to providing pension payments for the aged and blind solely on basis of need and without arbitrary maximum. Ceilings other than the need of the recipients have been eliminated for old age pensions in one-fourth of the states and made subject to administrative change in an equal number of jurisdictions.

The population of our mental institutions is growing at an alarming rate. The deficiencies in their accommodations, care and treatment are well known. So is the appalling cost of new building on a scale to meet

[21] During the prior administration payroll information was not open to the public, a fact which Stevenson made an issue in his campaign. See, e.g., *The Papers of Adlai E. Stevenson,* Vol. II, pp. 561–562.

the demand. So also is the dearth of competent trained personnel to properly staff existing facilities, let alone large additional facilities.

Humanity, prudence and good sense compel us to attack this problem all along the line. Fire hazards, structural and sanitary deficiencies endanger the well-being and even the lives of too many of our wards and must be eliminated. The building program to enlarge our capacity and reduce pitiful overcrowding in some of our hospitals and to replace obsolete units cannot be deferred. Moreover the population of our mental institutions which now exceeds 40,000 can and should, I think, be reduced. Many of these patients are merely aged and infirm or senile. They do not need elaborate psychiatric and nursing care. Segregation with proper custodial facilities and care should both cost less and provide more humane care. Others could be discharged and maintained in their own or foster homes with the aid of old age pensions. Still other patients could be discharged and maintained at home, treated and cared for through local agencies under the supervision of the State.

And to arrest the rapid increase in the mental hospital population we must also find ways and means of providing that treatment before hospitalization is necessary. With proper early treatment in their own communities many tragic souls could have remained in their homes and lived useful lives.

Too often the easiest way has been to commit people to institutions. Added to the human tragedy of hurrying merely distressing cases off to institutions is the ever-mounting long-term cost of institutional care, whereas these same people would get along better in their own communities and with proper treatment many would recover.

So I am suggesting a shift of emphasis from state hospitalization to home care. This will require time and the assistance of the ablest authorities in the fields of health and welfare. It will require the mobilization of all our public and private resources. It will involve a change in our philosophy and attitude toward these victims of troubled minds in a troubled world, with less emphasis on institutional care and more on prevention and clinical treatment.

This is but the pattern of a beginning, but a beginning must be made to conserve useful human life and control the cost of institutional care.

In the service of helpless people we have a special responsibility for the careful selection of personnel. To attract doctors, nurses, social workers and skilled attendants we will have to give unmistakable proof of our determination to establish an attractive career service in public welfare in Illinois for those who have a sincere urge to help the less fortunate.

Labor

Our position as one of the leading industrial regions of the world underscores our responsibility for enlightened leadership in protecting the welfare of labor. That the role of a state in labor legislation is less dramatic than the role of the national government, makes it no less important. In fact the foundation of the safety and welfare of the worker rests on state legislation. The gains already made must not be impaired, and the foundation requires constant re-examination to insure its adequacy.

Accordingly, it is necessary that you review again the adequacy of workmen's compensation awards in the light of the increased living costs of the injured workman. And it is imperative that I insure scrupulous and disinterested administration of a law which is of such critical importance to the workman and his employer.

The maximum benefits payable under our unemployment compensation act were last adjusted in 1944. The purpose of this legislation is to enable the unemployed worker to continue to purchase the necessities of life. Increases in wage scales and living costs since 1944 have obliterated the correlation between earnings and unemployment benefits which are now insufficient to cover non-postponable necessities.

Our statute extends the benefits of unemployment compensation only to workers in establishments which employ more than six employees. Twenty-seven states, employing more than 60% of all the workers covered by unemployment compensation have extended their coverage to establishments employing less than six, without, apparently, encountering serious administrative difficulties. I urge you to consider this matter with other legislative adjustments in the field of unemployment compensation.

Here too, there are problems for the executive as well as for the legislature. The importance of security to workers, the heavy cost to employers, the volume of claims presented — all combine to demand the utmost administrative care to protect our unemployment compensation system against abuse by officials as well as undeserving claimants.

When the employment service was restored to the state at the end of the war, Illinois separated the related functions of unemployment compensation and the free employment service. Experience has shown that this separation impedes efficient service and I recommend corrective legislation to permit close coordination of these functions.

While I think weekly benefits payable to unemployed workers should be raised, consideration should also be given to a reduction of employer contribution rates taking into account the present size of the fund and the potential need for funds in the foreseeable future.

I trust that when the legislature is considering unemployment compensation it will also explore the related question of temporary disability insurance.

I also ask you to consider the advisability of enacting legislation to enable the State to take an affirmative role in the settlement of labor disputes. The Federal government has, of course, its Mediation and Conciliation Service which participates in most labor disputes. Many states have such agencies, some successful and some unsuccessful. While I do not expect spectacular achievements from a state agency operating in this field, there may be a useful place for a state agency, operating on a modest budget with the cooperation of industry and labor, to render useful public service. I believe the possibility should be explored.

I should like to urge your consideration of a subject which, while it is connected with labor, has even broader implications. I refer to Fair Employment Practices legislation. The ideals we so proudly proclaim cannot be reconciled with economic discrimination upon racial or religious grounds. To fall short of our professed ideals today, and in this field, has implications of hypocrisy and insincerity we dare not disregard. The eyes of the world are riveted upon our democracy. Prejudices can no longer find safe refuge in rationalizations. How we deal with this subject is intimately related to the world wide conflict of ideologies which is the battle for tomorrow.

Moreover it is obvious that only as new opportunities for employment are opened will those now at a disadvantage be able to help themselves. I earnestly bespeak your thoughtful consideration of legislation to that end and toward the solution of one of our most difficult problems.

Highways

I have mentioned the formidable needs of our schools, of the distressed local governments and of our welfare institutions. Governor Green said to you last week: "One of the principal functions of modern state governments is the maintenance and improvement of highways." And I might add that it is also one of the most expensive. But good highways, country roads and city streets are no longer a luxury or a convenience; they have become essential to our agricultural and industrial economy.

We already have an enormous investment in our highway system. We face an even larger investment to conserve what we have already invested and to improve and reconstruct our highways. Consistent with other urgent demands for capital improvements and with an eye to the timing of public construction work in prosperity and depression, we must have the courage to adopt and initiate a long-range program suitable to our needs.

The 65th General Assembly created a commission to study the whole problem of highway traffic, construction and financing with a view to recommending a long-range highway program. Its report will be submitted to you by March 1.

If it is based, as I think it will be, on truth rather than conjecture, on demonstrable need rather than expediency; if it meets conflicts between political practice and public interest with courage and realism, I confidently believe that we will unite on its adoption. And I assure you that this administration will strive to execute it with honesty, non-partisanship and relentless determination to accomplish the maximum improvement of our highway system within the desire and ability of the people to finance.

Agriculture

It must be the vigilant duty of the General Assembly and the Executive, working hand in hand, to foster the agricultural eminence of our prairie state, to cooperate with the Federal Government in control of floods and erosion, and in kindred problems. We must support the University of Illinois in its extension to the farmer of improved agricultural methods, but over and beyond all else we must think of the farm in terms of a living — a way of living and a place to live. Life on the farm in this age can and should be as attractive as urban life. I think we can well afford to give more thought to the amenities of life on the farm if we are to maintain the proud position of our basic industry, agriculture.

Housing and Rent Control

The outstanding paradox of our advanced age is the persistence of an acute shortage of one of the most elemental requirements of mankind — shelter — in the nation which beyond all others is the wealthiest, most productive and most resourceful.

It is not necessary to present statistics depicting the scope of the problem. It affects almost every community in the state, large or small. We know now that rural areas have their slums as well as do our larger urban centers. And we know the major part of the price we pay for our acute housing shortage is measured in the intangible but cruelly real terms of broken homes, moral deterioration, juvenile delinquency, cynicism and despair.

I have no magic formula to offer. I wish I did. It is clear that the problem is inherently one for private enterprise. And it is also clear that it cannot do the job at rentals or costs within the reach of those most in need. The combined resources of national, state and local governments are necessary for the solution of this problem. Presumably this Congress will enact legislation along the lines of the Wagner-Ellender-Taft bill [22] which will provide the basis for an enlarged attack upon the problem. We must be receptive to new ideas and prepared to support the federal program with such legislation as is necessary.

However, there is one specific legislative change I would suggest. It is not a panacea, but legislation permitting more rapid acquisition of land for slum clearance and housing purposes should accelerate solution of the problem. Other states have had such legislation for many years. Ample provision can be made for the protection of property owners, and I urge you to consider legislation to this end.

One phase of the problem — the acute shortage of rental housing — requires a further word. Not only in Chicago, but throughout the state abnormal conditions prevail in the rental housing markets. The continued existence of federal rent control has substantially alleviated the potential hardships. One important deficiency in federal rent control is its failure to provide for control of accommodations for non-transient occupants of hotels. The result has been that thousands of permanent residents of hotels have suffered rapid and often unwarranted rent increases.

The legislation enacted by the 65th General Assembly did not meet this problem. By its language no local controls can become effective until all federal control ceases. Hence local action to control this situation is impossible. But as the existing federal control terminates March 31, 1949, and an extension is probable, I presume you will wish to defer any action to remedy this situation pending determination of the federal course.

Mines and Minerals

The time has come, I believe, for you to give attention to the state's agency for discharging its responsibilities to those engaged in the mining and petroleum industries. The elements of good government are power

[22] With the end of World War II the nation was faced with a critical housing shortage. This bill, introduced in the Senate in November, 1945, by Robert A. Wagner (Democrat, N.Y.), Allen J. Ellender (Democrat, La.) and Robert A. Taft (Republican, Ohio), proposed liberalization of the terms on Federal Housing Authority mortgages "yield insurance" for investors in large-scale rental housing; 500,000 units of public housing over a period of four years; loans and grants for farm housing research aimed particularly at bringing down the cost of housing; federal grants for urban redevelopment; and a permanent national housing agency. It enjoyed the support of the administration and many civic and social organizations but was opposed by powerful real estate and financial interests. It was passed by the Senate in 1946 but died in the House Banking and Currency Committee. It was put forward again in 1947 as the Taft-Ellender-Wagner bill, in a greatly watered-down version, and was finally passed and signed into law by President Truman in June, 1949.

and strict accountability for its exercise. I believe that in this light the organization of the Department of Mines and Minerals requires re-examination. In due course I will submit to you concrete proposals for its reorganization.

As there seems to be some ambiguity at present, I will also urge you to extend the civil service to include most of the employees of this de-partment. Moreover, our mining laws contain much that is obsolete, and I strongly urge that they be rewritten in their entirety. Agencies are at hand to assist in this work and I shall have more to say to you in this connection at a later date.

Conservation

Our natural resources of forest and wild life are presently admin-istered by an executive department headed by a Director appointed by the Governor. Some twenty-seven states have adopted the non-political commission form of administration of their comparable services. None of them has reverted to the method which we retain. I think Illinois in its quest for more efficient and economical public administration could well take the same progressive step.

State Police

Another highly specialized field of the state service which should be removed from political control is the Highway Maintenance Police. A public service charged not only with fearless and equal enforcement of the law but with the protection of human life itself demands charac-ter, discipline and undiluted loyalty. The men who undertake this re-sponsible and exacting work are entitled to a merit system which in-sures them protection and recognition for their service without fear or favor. It has been done in other states and it can and should be done in Illinois if our first interest is the quality of our government.

Public Utility Regulation

I invite your attention to the Illinois Commerce Commission. It is regulating public utilities whose rates and charges now exceed two billion dollars a year. The five men who comprise the Commission have vast power, authority and responsibility. Because of the enormous volume of its work, the technical character of its proceedings, and the tremendous importance of its decisions, the qualifications of the men who serve as Commissioners are not alone the concern of a Governor but of the public and the utility companies alike.

Under existing legislation the men who are charged with these re-sponsibilities are appointed by the Governor to serve for a two-year term. Their annual compensation is $7,500. In earlier years under the administrations of Governors Dunne [23] and Lowden the approach toward this important agency was somewhat different. In those days members of what was then more aptly called the Public Utility Commission received $10,000 a year and served for a term of six years. The terms of the Commissioners were staggered to insure continuity and independence.

The importance of the work of the Commission has not declined in the intervening years; rather it has increased. Yet the system in Illinois is hardly conducive to indifference to the caprices of political fortune, nor is the compensation compatible with the responsibilities of the office.

I believe that the public will be better served by a Commission whose independence and continuity is increased by lengthened and staggered terms of office. And I further believe that to attract to this vital public service the character of men it deserves the compensation must more adequately reflect its responsibility.

Conclusion

In an effort to limit my remarks severely I have omitted any reference to many other matters of grave concern — the veteran, higher education, public health. I will have something more to say to you later about these and other subjects, and doubtless you will have still more to say to me!

In conclusion, I hope I have made it clear that the State of Illinois appears to me to be well off financially at present, but that with just demands increasing rapidly, and with matching revenue at best doubtful, in the next biennium if not this one, we may well face acute difficulties.

I hope I have made it clear that we should anticipate the future now, that I will have no reluctance to break boldly with the complacent, quiet past; that to match the relentless demands of these searching times for thrifty, efficient, honest government is the only desire of my colleagues and myself who have been so signally honored by our fellow citizens.

I hope I have made it clear that with sincere purpose, if limited talents, I want to execute your will, and serve my only ambition — to help to make of Illinois an example of the best in our democratic tradition, a leader in a noble future as it was in a noble past.

We Americans are proud that we were born of revolutionaries with a passionate faith in freedom and human worth.

[23] Edward F. Dunne, Democratic governor of Illinois, 1913–1917.

We Illinoisans are proud that our state was born of simple folk who believe in an ever better future.

This is our inheritance. To preserve it, to enrich it in the great age that lies ahead we ask that God, in His infinite power for good, help us make of Illinois a land where justice, honesty and progress abound.

Mr. and Mrs. Edison Dick and their son, Edison Warner Dick (called "Eddie"), were among those who came to Springfield for the inaugural festivities. They stayed at the executive mansion overnight. So did Carl Sandburg, the Illinois poet and biographer of Abraham Lincoln, who came to speak at the ceremonies. The next morning the Governor's youngest son, John Fell, and Eddie Dick, thinking it would be fun to peek in on the poet in his slumbers, were trapped in the elevator they used to get up to his third-floor bedroom. Sandburg did not awaken, but the boys were imprisoned for over an hour until help arrived. After Eddie returned to school he wrote thanking the Governor for "the most Historical event I have ever witnessed . . . this morning . . . John Fell and me gave talks on the inauguration."

To Edison Warner Dick

January 14, 1949

My dear Edison:

You were very good to write me and I can assure you that I enjoyed having you here just as much as you enjoyed being here. Moreover, I hope you will come back. Indeed you would be welcome almost any time. Perhaps when you and your parents have little to do you will come down and spend a week end with me.

The elevator is running very well and we could have some good rides together. There are many things to see around Springfield which are even more historical than my inauguration.

I am so glad that you entertained the assembly with an account of the inauguration, and I hope you and John Fell managed to tell the same story.

Affectionately,

Mr. and Mrs. Ralph Hines (Mrs. Hines was Mrs. Stevenson's sister Betty) and their two children came from New York for the inaugural ceremonies. Mr. Hines wrote to the Governor on their return to New York thanking him for having invited them, and added: "Much rests upon you and I have the greatest confidence in your ability to assume your responsibilities. We, now, hear a great deal of you here in the East especially in regards to your future."

To Ralph Hines

January 25, 1949

Dear Ralph:

I have your encouraging and thoughtful letter. I need not tell you what a comfort it was to have you and Betty and the children here. I only wish it could be more frequent. The family means a great deal to me, and I am very much alone in this new enterprise. I wish you were all coming back tomorrow.

Love to Betty.

Yours,

P.S. I hardly need add you were most helpful and that if you ever want a job as the Governor's Aide, consider yourself hired!

AES

Mr. and Mrs. A. B. Perry, of Bloomington, Illinois, had worked hard for Stevenson during his campaign. Mrs. Perry expressed her bitter disappointment in a letter to Stevenson on January 28, 1949, that her husband was not to be appointed State Fair manager. It was a post for which he had no specific background or experience, and Mr. Perry wrote the Governor on January 28 that the decision was "agreeable" to him.

To Mrs. A. B. Perry

January 29, 1949

Dear Esther:

I have your letter and I am sure you realize how deeply disappointed I am that I could not see my way clear to ask Abe to accept this job. That I did not in no way minimizes my deep gratitude for what you did for me or my long personal affection for you. One has to do the best he can in these positions and every appointment results in far more disappointments than satisfactions, as I am sure you realize.

But I did hope that Abe might be useful to me here, not just in discharge of any feeling of political responsibility but because I need and the public needs honest, competent and reliable servants.

I hope you can find it in your heart to forgive me for this seeming ingratitude.

Yours,

To A. B. Perry

January 29, 1949

Dear Abe:

I had a disappointed letter from Spotty [24] and enclose a copy of my reply. I am sure you know some of the things I am confronted with in my desperate efforts to solve this appalling Chinese puzzle, as your letter so well implies.

Please come in to see me some time when you are here — and my enduring thanks for all of your loyalty and help.

Yours,

Melvin Brorby, a Chicago advertising executive, wrote on January 29, 1949, suggesting that when he approached the end of his term, Stevenson should write an account of his years of office "which would answer both for the student of American history and Democracy, and for the average citizen some important questions. How does our system really work? What can honest men do when they are elected? What are the compromises that must be made; what are the frustrations?"

To Melvin Brorby

January 29, 1949

Dear Mel:

Your letter interests me a great deal, although I cannot accept the assumptions of the future importance of my present horrors!

At all events, I am giving it some thought and maybe I can work out some arrangement to keep the sort of a journal I have always wanted to keep in my many prior dramatic and even more important experiences. Unhappily, my besetting problem is adequate and competent staff. As you well know, to write a proper interpretive history of even a small segment in American public affairs needs a competent and constant chronicler. I have none nor do I see any prospect of finding one nor of hiring one if I found him, in view of my budgetary limitation.

However, I am going to see what I can do — thanks to your admoni-

[24] Mrs. Perry.

tion to keep some rudimentary records. Some day I should like to talk with you about this interesting idea.

Yours,

P.S. After Frank Knox died after four years as Secretary of the Navy in its most critical historical interval, I was approached by publishers to write his biography, or at least the war portion. I was shocked to realize that with almost daily contact there were great spaces of ignorance about critical conferences where I was not present or, worse still, about the volumes I had already forgotten with not a scratch to refresh my recollection. I declined.

AES

Frank E. Beatty, a friend from Stevenson's days in the Navy Department (1941–1944) was in 1949 a rear admiral stationed at the U.S. Naval Ordnance Laboratory at Silver Spring, Maryland. He and his wife attended the inauguration of President Truman, where they saw the Governor and Mrs. Stevenson.

To Rear Admiral Frank E. Beatty

January 31, 1949

Dear Frank:

It was good to catch even a confused glimpse of you and Pat in that chaos in Washington, and the next time I get there I hope I can take you up on that invitation to White Oak for a leisurely visit. There is much ground to cover!

Yours,

Throughout his administration Stevenson discussed all key appointments with his department heads and watched appointments to the various departments carefully.

To the Directors of All Code Departments [25]

February 3, 1949

I request that you be guided by the following procedure with respect to securing personnel for your Department. This will apply to all posi-

[25] This term in Illinois designates the departments established as parts of the executive branch of the state government under the Civil Administrative Code, as passed by the legislature in 1917 and subsequently amended. There were thirteen such departments in 1949.

tions excepting those for which the Civil Service Commission has existing eligible lists.

1. Requisitions for employment shall be directed to my office in duplicate. For this purpose use the "Personnel Requisition" form, sample of which is attached and marked Appendix A. You will also attach in duplicate a statement of the position qualifications and duties of the job. Appendix A–1.

2. When an applicant has been recommended for the position, the Director will receive a "Recommendation for Employment" form in triplicate from the Governor's Advisory Committee on Employment, sample of which is attached, and marked Appendix "B."

3. The Director of the Department or his subordinate will then notify the applicant for the position when and where to report for interview. If the applicant is accepted by the Director of the Department, the Department will complete the "Recommendation for Employment" form and return two copies to my office. The employee will fill out the employment record card in triplicate, one copy for your files and two copies for my office.

4. If the applicant is not accepted, the Director of the Department will so indicate at the bottom of the "Recommendation for Employment" form and return all three copies to my office.

5. Upon receipt of notice that the applicant has been rejected by the code department, another applicant will be recommended and the procedure will continue as outlined above.

Please understand that I wish to discuss with you any appointments to policy-making or key positions.

Very truly yours,

Lincoln's Birthday in Springfield was observed by day-long ceremonies. Among others, the American Legion, of which Stevenson was a member, sponsored a pilgrimage to the Lincoln tomb at Oak Ridge Cemetery, about three miles outside the city. Governor Stevenson's brief message at the tomb was broadcast by radio.[26]

We come to the Tomb today to pay homage to the saviour of the Union, our fellow townsman of Springfield, Abraham Lincoln.

He was a good man and a brave man; he was gentle, friendly and loved the people. He took with him to the grave human slavery. He left behind him a nation indestructably united for the first time, and a

[26] The text is based on a ribbon copy. There are no insertions or other marks in the text, and the editors therefore assume it is not the copy from which Stevenson read his remarks.

world which had, because of him, a wider concept of freedom and of human rights.

Today everyone honors him, everyone everywhere. But it was not always so. In the Presidential election of 1860 he barely carried this his home town; all but three of the Springfield clergymen opposed him; he lost this county. In his time of severest trial during the Civil War, the leading Chicago editor wrote that complete success in the war "has become a moral impossibility" and that "Lincoln is only half awake and will never do much better than he has done." Bitterness, defeatism and the vengeful partisanship of little men were his lot. In 1864 he was defeated for reelection in this his home county by 400 votes.

No President, and probably few figures in history have been so mistrusted, reviled and hated.

But the abuse and ridicule is long since stilled. Today there is only applause. Today we stand by his side, our heads bowed in reverent homage to this man who loved the people — the fickle people, quick to condemn, who did not always make his path easier.

He never lost faith in the people and when the great decisions came he decided the great way, the hard way, because the disadvantages were patent and present, the advantages obscure and remote. It was his faith in us that sustained him — his faith that the people, once they understood him and his purposes, would support him, for his purposes were good, his purposes were their betterment and salvation, his purposes were to save the republic and expand human freedom, not only here but everywhere. In both he succeeded because he had faith in ultimate understanding and justice.

In death he has become an immortal leader of the people because in life he believed in the people. In the first inaugural address, while attempting to preserve the union by splicing the few common bonds that remained between North and South, he turned to the people, asking, "Why should there not be a patient confidence in the ultimate justice of the people. Is there any better or equal hope in the world?"

We legionnaires, we Americans, who have lived through two world wars against autocrats and dictators can well ask the same question when our hearts are faint — Is there any better hope in the world than the people? As long as our answer is Lincoln's answer we have nothing to fear — there will be no dictators in America.

Vice President Alben Barkley spoke at a meeting of the Illinois State Historical Society, in Springfield, on February 12. President Truman sent Stevenson a message to be read at the meeting.

To Harry S. Truman [27]

February 13, 1949

Dear Mr. President:

Last night we read your beautiful message at the Abraham Lincoln day celebration here in Springfield just before Vice President Barkley's speech. It added immeasurably to what will be a memorable Lincoln's Birthday in Springfield and I am deeply grateful for your thoughtfulness.

Command me if I can ever be of any service.

Faithfully yours,

Elmer Davis, veteran newscaster and political analyst of the American Broadcasting Company, wrote Stevenson on February 10 that after reading his inaugural address "I take it that, if I may borrow the language of another statesman, Illinois needs the biggest untangling, unsnarling, unraveling housecleaning in its history. . . . May the Lord strengthen your arm."

To Elmer Davis

February 15, 1949

Dear Elmer:

You were good to write me and I am most grateful for your thoughtful and very understanding note. I only hope the Lord strengthens both my arms.

Let me know if you pass this way.

Sincerely yours,

To Mrs. Edison Dick [28]

February 15, 1949

Dear Mrs. Mumps: [29]

Your letter has arrived and . . . I am much relieved to hear that the ravages of the disease have impaired neither your wit nor, shall I say, interest in public affairs.

As for your appearance [I regret?] that I shall not have a chance to see a perfect circle. My temptation is to enlist the services of your men

[27] The original is in the President's Personal File, the Harry S. Truman Library, Independence, Missouri.
[28] This handwritten letter is in the possession of Mrs. Dick.
[29] Mrs. Dick was suffering from the mumps.

folk to provide me a photograph which I am quite sure would be of great interest to the innocent inhabitants of this house — including for myself, especially because of my horrid taste for abnormal physiology. Side shows fascinate me!

[P.S.] Your visit was a blessing and the office staff are already begging for a return. I am much relieved to hear about Miss Hazard's [30] patience — you certainly must have captivated that lady and I hope you can stop for an inspection on the next trip. You could get off the train there and I could send a car to bring you down. . . .

I am planning to come up Friday — if I can make it. [James] Mulroy — my master — has ordered me to go to a dreadful dinner Sat night but I'll be home Friday & a bit of Sunday & I'll try to call you — You're so good to keep interested and to do all these things for me and I'm deeply grateful — Mrs. Mumps!

Please give my warm and affectionate regards to Mr. Mumps and Master Mumps.

Yours
THE GOV.

Tues. A M—(8 o'clock — and the breakfast conference starts at 8:30, so enough of this dawn drivel!)

Mrs. Walter V. Schaefer was ill in Passavant Hospital in Chicago, while her husband was assisting Stevenson with his legislative program in Springfield.

To Mrs. Walter V. Schaefer [31]

February 21, 1949

Dear Margo:

I have this afternoon's report from Wally on your progress, and I am much relieved to hear that all is well. I have a profound feeling that you are going to harbor forever a bitter resentment for the Governor who keeps your husband on the job when he should be at the hospital. Forgive me!

Sincerely yours,
ADLAI

[30] Miss Helen Hazard, superintendent of the State Reformatory for Women at Dwight, Illinois. The institution was within the jurisdiction of the Department of Public Welfare. Stevenson appointed Mrs. Dick as a member of the Board of Public Welfare Commissioners and she expected to visit the reformatory.

[31] The original is in the possession of Mrs. Schaefer.

Porter McKeever, director of public information of the U.S. mission to the United Nations, wrote Stevenson congratulating him on his inaugural address. He said he and others at the UN had been interviewed by Joe Alex Morris in connection with an article on Stevenson for the Saturday Evening Post, *and added, "I'm sure that we told him nothing that would give you cause for libel suits." He and his wife, Susan, were expecting their first child, hoping it would arrive on St. Patrick's Day.*

To Porter McKeever

February 21, 1949

Dear Porter:

I was delighted to have your letter. You were good to think of me and your generous reading of the inauguration speech is far more than that tedious document deserves.

I am a little alarmed that my fortunes in the Saturday Evening Post were exposed to your tender mercies, but I know Mr. Morris got nothing but the truth — and how it hurts!

The news of another McKeever is spectacular, and I am sure St. Patrick's prayers are going to be even more effective than mine to have it born on his birthday. Give Susan my love — and all good wishes to you both. I wish you were coming out here to see me in my unfamiliar role of big-time politician!

Sincerely yours,

William Benton, publisher of the Encyclopaedia Britannica, *sent the Governor an article from the* Economist *describing the difficulties facing his administration.*

To William Benton [32]

February 21, 1949

Dear Bill:

Many thanks for your note and the copy of the article from the Economist. I am not a little flattered that my troubles are even preoccupying the English!

Yours,
ADLAI

[32] The original was in the possession of the late Mr. Benton.

To Merritt A. Hewett [33]

February 25, 1949

Dear Mr. Hewett:

My youngest son, John Fell Stevenson, was 13 in February. He has been at the Lake Forest [Country] Day School and had done reasonably well, but I am confident that the time has come when he should go away. He has matured more slowly than the other boys, but is now growing up rapidly and I suspect with him, as with Adlai and Borden, that this school has about served its usefulness.

I would appreciate it if you would let me know whether or not he could be admitted to Milton this autumn should Mrs. Stevenson agree to send him off. Also, please review my recollection about how many boys there are in the lower school, both boarders and day scholars. John Fell is a highly responsible lad and will, I have little doubt, get to work promptly once the environment is right.

With warm regards, I am

Sincerely yours,
ADLAI

Mrs. Joseph T. Bowen, grandmother of William McC. Blair, Jr., was one of Chicago's outstanding citizens. On the occasion of her ninetieth birthday, Stevenson sent her this message.

To Mrs. Joseph T. Bowen [34]

February 26, 1949

My dear Mrs. Bowen —

St. Francis prayed not so much to be consoled, as to console; to be understood as to understand; to be loved as to love. I think of you. And because it is in giving that we receive, you will have the blessings of thousands who don't know you and of all who do on your ninetieth birthday, including this devoted admirer —

ADLAI E. STEVENSON

Alicia Patterson and Adlai Stevenson had been friends since about 1925 or 1926. In July, 1926, Stevenson went on a trip to Russia and Miss Pat-

[33] Registrar of Milton Academy, Milton, Massachusetts. The original is in the possession of Milton Academy.
[34] This handwritten letter is in the possession of William McC. Blair, Jr.

terson married and moved to London and later to New York. He did not see her again until he went to New York in 1946 as a delegate to the General Assembly of the United Nations, when they renewed their friendship. In 1948 (and until her death in 1963) Miss Patterson was publisher of Newsday *on Long Island, and, in private life, Mrs. Harry Guggenheim. Shortly before the following letter was written, she apparently wrote him that* Newsday *had reached 100,000 circulation.[35]*

To Alicia Patterson[36]

March 8, 1949

. . . 100,000 circulation!

So you've made it. . . . I know what it means to win, when people smiled and had no faith — just damnable courtesy. But why this Napoleonic — "I'll found an empire?" Must Caesar forever gather laurels to be happy. . . . The stuff of greatness is goodness, serenity, wisdom — not conquest. . . .

I'm back tonight from my hasty trip to Wash — for the White House Corrs [pondents]. dinner for the Pres[ident]. 3 hours down from Libertyville with a tail wind, 5½ hours back to Springfield. I suppose it was worthwhile — all the dignitaries turned out and the entertainment was superb. I was the only gov. at the head table — the Pres was very cordial indeed — and many others. What was it Polonius said: "Crook the bended pregnant knee, that thrift may follow fawning" — or something. Anyway I find this courtesy & voluble flattery from those who sniff the wind too sharply highly distasteful. Perhaps newspaper-women have spoiled my taste for newspaper-men.

Now to my damnable income tax; then to a speech for the radio on Constitutional Convention — then to bed. . . .

A

Sunday night . . .

Adlai Stevenson realized that his wife did not want to go to Springfield with him, but he hoped she could be persuaded to change her mind. She appeared at the mansion only two or three times, on the most formal occasions, returning immediately to their home near Libertyville. Stevenson, in a letter to Mrs. Edison Dick reporting on the trip he had just made to Washington, expressed his feelings about the separation and impending divorce.

[35] Miss Patterson's letters were not available to the editors.
[36] This handwritten letter is in the possession of Adlai E. Stevenson III.

To Mrs. Edison Dick [37]

March 8, 1949

. . . Back from my journey to Washington — 3 hours down from Libertyville with a tail wind and 5½ hours back to Spring[field]. with a head wind. It hardly seemed worth the effort but at least [James] Mulroy had his way with me for once!, and perhaps the brief diversion was a good thing. The dinner — White House Correspondents Assoc — was very fine, the notables out in full force and the Governor of Illinois the only Gov. at the Speakers table. The entertainment was superb and the Pres. [Truman] *very* cordial to the Guv.

What was it Shakespeare said — Crook the bended pregnant knee, that thrift may follow fawning — or something. At all events I find the adulation of those who sniff the wind too sharply distasteful. And little do the fools knows how they waste their flattering words. Serve them right — it will.

On the spur of the moment — because we had Athletic Commission business to talk — Saturday night I asked Lloyd Lewis if he wanted to fly down with me for a talk on the plane. He seized the invitation and will spend a couple of day in the Library there re Grant. . . .[38]

I'm alone, utterly alone, for about the first time in the Mansion and brooding over this appalling pile of papers without a word written in my speech for Wednesday — gloating in self-pity, oppressed with forebodings of disaster and dishonor. Surrounded with everything for happiness and usefulness I'm desolate and destitute — and think of nothing except the creeping morrows. . . .

During his administration, Stevenson received many letters from friends urging that he not work so hard. Edgar Bernhard, a Chicago lawyer, wrote: "I have asked very little of you since you became Governor, but I do have one urgent request which I hope you will grant: Take a little time off! Slow down! There is no danger that you will do a slovenly job or go back on the people who have confidence in you."

[37] This handwritten letter is in the possession of Mrs. Dick.
[38] Lloyd Lewis was working on a multivolume study of U. S. Grant, of which only *Captain Sam Grant* (Boston: Little, Brown and Company, 1950) was published, posthumously.

To Edgar Bernhard

March 10, 1949

Dear Edgar:

For once someone has asked me to do just what I want to! I think I will follow your suggestion — and heartfelt thanks for reminding me.

Yours,

Stevenson's friend Laird Bell, a Chicago lawyer, also admonished him about trying to do too much and hoped he would use more discretion in the way he drove himself; he argued that it was important for Stevenson to serve the full four years, if not longer.

To Laird Bell

March 15, 1949

Dear Laird:

I don't know what prompted you to write that letter of March 11, but I am awfully tempted to take your advice — as usual! The dreadful thing about it is that I don't see any escape. There is so much pressing for attention and so little time. Some of the wretched things just don't seem to be able to wait until tomorrow.

But you are right, and I shall long remember the personal concern that prompted such a letter.

Yours,

To Mrs. Edison Dick [39]

March 15, 1949

. . . Last night it snowed. Today its spring. Its 7:30 & I'm in my bedroom sniffing the good air by the window. Now I'm going to take some violent exercises. You've shamed me — maybe I care after all. Or is it this gigantic mirror that doesn't let me escape my obesity!

Have a good time. . . .[40]

I'm happy, gayier [gayer], less frightened, more carefree this morning than for months. What is it? Spring? . . . Surely it can't be these damn exercises that hurt my tummy! . . .

[39] This handwritten letter is in the possession of Mrs. Dick.
[40] Mrs. Dick and her family were about to leave for a vacation in Florida.

The Governor received some complaints that department heads had retained many Republicans in non–civil service jobs. He questioned his executive secretary, James Mulroy, about the matter.

To James Mulroy [41]

March 16, 1949

Any views on this? What is the trouble with the Departments or is there any? Why not ask [Lawrence] Irvin to study an illustrative payroll from some department so that we can more accurately determine if there is a problem and what it is.

Several members of the Governor's staff were Irish, including Margaret Munn and Anne Risse. On St. Patrick's Day Mrs. Risse saw to it that Stevenson had a pot of shamrocks on his desk.

To Anne Risse [42]

March 17, 1949

Dear Mrs. Risse:

You were sweet to think of me, and my littered desk has at least one bright spot on this St. Patrick's Day — thanks to you!

Sincerely yours,

Mrs. Chalmer Taylor, an old friend living in Bloomington, Illinois, wrote to congratulate the Governor on his presentation of the need for a constitutional convention, and warned him against working too hard.

To Mrs. Chalmer C. Taylor

March 18, 1949

Dear Aenid:

No one has written me a better letter than that. You have a realistic philosophy about public administration which I envy. But I am getting there — the hard way! I wish I could find some way out of the overwork. I know it will pay no dividends in the long run, but meanwhile it seems to be easier than letting too many things drift. I wish you and the

[41] The original of this memorandum is in the possession of Lawrence Irvin.
[42] The original is in the possession of Mrs. Risse.

Bohrers,[43] et al, would come down and spend an evening with me some-time. As for Joe I am appointing him to the Normal Board,[44] as you know, and I am sure he will be a great help.

Yours,

In March, 1949, the Dick family was vacationing on the west coast of Florida. The Governor was in Springfield struggling with the legislative program.

To Mrs. Edison Dick [45]

about March 20, 1949

. . . The report from the Survey Commission on Florida resort life among the family type of migrant (?) fascinates me. I only wish there were pictures and more details. It sounds like a strange never-never land and the inhabitants beautiful and healthy. I assume they read and write and also talk, but probably very little. And why should they. Do they chew betel nut or just gin? I hope to go to see them sometime and I gather they are not actively hostile toward sight seers. I have heard more of the Herd or Cafe variety which flourishes on the East Coast and they have not excited my curiosity quite as much. At all events I begin to understand why so many of my subjects are emigrating to those regions. It is quite disturbing to my kingdom but never being a jealous ruler I always say "what's Illinois' loss is the cormorants' gain."

My only concern then, aside from lively curiosity, is that the survey commission doesn't vanish forever. The idea was to reconnoiter the region and make friends with the inhabitants — not to colonize — at least not until I can abdicate decently and gather up squaw and young and come too.

Speaking of the squaw, she sends her love to you all — but I warn you hastily, reject it. She's in bed with the mumps as big as a full grown pumpkin!

She came to Springfield and presided at two riotous dinners for the Senate — accompanied by thousands of toasts and . . . a proposal from her to kiss any Senator who voted *against* the Broyles bills.[46] Now, fol-

---

[43] Mr. and Mrs. Joseph F. Bohrer. See Mr. Bohrer's "Boys in Bloomington," in *As We Knew Adlai,* pp. 1–14.

[44] The board of trustees of Illinois State Normal University.

[45] This handwritten letter is in the possession of Mrs. Dick.

[46] A series of bills to investigate and curb "subversive activities," sponsored by Republican Senator Paul Broyles. The only one passed by the 1949 legislature was for an appropriation to inquire into such activities at the University of Chicago and

lowing public disclosures of her condition, which overtook her Thurs. morning following the last dinner, she has notified the Senators by wire that she will *now* kiss any who voted *for* them!

Regards — jealous, envious, nasty regards — to the Clan Dick and all and sundry of my faithless subjects. Tell them I'm a kind, good man — that they can come home — all is forgiven! And the sooner you get back on the job the better. As someone said as soon as Mrs. Dick went to Florida the Republicans took after me!

Yours

ADLAI REX

Sat. on the train — in haste!

P.S. I get no comfort out of the Governor of Florida's troubles! [47]

To Harry S. Truman [48]

March 23, 1949

Dear Mr. President:

The community of Cahokia in southwestern Illinois, near St. Louis, has the distinction of being the oldest settlement in the Mississippi Valley.

The 250th Anniversary of its settlement is to be observed in a week of public ceremonies starting May 15.

A committee of prominent citizens representing the sponsoring organizations has asked me to extend to you their most cordial invitation to come to Illinois on May 15 to participate in the opening of this public observance. I am advised that Representative Melvin Price of Illinois has spoken to you personally about this event. While I realize how extremely busy you are, I share the committee's fervent hope that you may find it possible to accept this engagement and thus insure the success of the anniversary celebration. I am sure you will recognize its unusual historical significance.

Both the Illinois and Missouri State Historical Societies, and a dozen or more other prominent organizations, are cooperating in the arrangements for the event. The Governors of all the states within the area of the old Northwest Territory are being invited.

An interesting account of Cahokia's history has been written by Mr. Irving Dilliard, past president of the Illinois State Historical Society and

---

Roosevelt College, and Stevenson allowed it to become law without his signature. In 1951 the legislature passed the other Broyles bills, which Stevenson vetoed. See E. Houston Harsha, "The Broyles Commission," in *The States and Subversion*, edited by Walter Gellhorn (Ithaca: Cornell University Press, 1952).

[47] Not known what Stevenson alludes to.

[48] The original is in the President's Personal File, Harry S. Truman Library.

a member of the editorial staff of the St. Louis Post-Dispatch. I am attaching a printed copy of this for your further information.

If you find it possible to undertake this appearance, I shall, of course, be happy to send along all details of the program as they are developed by those in charge. I do very much hope that you will find it possible to come.[49]

With cordial personal regards and all good wishes, I am

Sincerely,

On March 28, 1949, Governor Stevenson made a revealing off-the-record speech to the Commercial Club of Chicago about the difficulties and successes of his first three months in office. A court reporter recorded the speech. A copy of the speech is in the Stevenson Papers at the Princeton University Library.

In introducing the Governor, Vice President Graham McCorkle said: "General comment on what he has been doing since he took office shows his actions are keyed to his words. The Governor's administrative problems in this short period must have been very trying. Most of you operate large institutions. Suppose you were suddenly confronted with a need to replace all your vice presidents, general managers, superintendents, supervisors and even assistant supervisors in your organization, with men well qualified for these positions! You'd find it quite a task, especially so if the salaries you could offer were less than other businesses were offering. Well, looking at it this way, will give you some idea of the magnitude of one part of the job facing the Governor when he took office. There is clear evidence that he's winning out."

Mr. Chairman and fellow Democrats, if any: I should say, at the outset, that I am very much alarmed to see a court reporter here. The last time I spoke before The Commercial Club, at one of these closed meetings some few years ago, as I recall, there fell from me, to use the graceful expression, so many indiscretions that it took me almost three weeks to edit my remarks, and by the time I had finished them for publication in the Annual Year Book, they bore absolutely no resemblance to anything I said at the meeting. I suspect I will be obliged to do the same thing again today. At least I am thankful for one thing, and that is I have not been exposed to a photographer. Sitting between a great utility on my left, and a great bank on my right, that would cer-

[49] The President replied on March 31, 1949, saying that although he recognized that the significance of the occasion extended beyond the boundaries of Illinois he felt he could not accept the invitation as the result of the press of official business. The editors were not permitted to quote directly from any of Truman's letters to Stevenson.

tainly terminate my career in politics. (Laughter) I trust that I can pledge you all to everlasting secrecy that I found myself so exposed.

And speaking of exposure, my wife has just exposed all 50 members of the Senate of the State of Illinois to the mumps. (Laughter) I want you to know that she exposed them indiscriminately. There was no selection whatever. (Laughter)

I was asked by somebody a moment ago upstairs if anything funny had happened to me since I have been in office, and as he said that I reflected on something that did happen to me within forty-eight hours after I was inaugurated. A flood, a very serious flood in Southern Illinois came along, as you know, from the Little Wabash and the Big Wabash and the Muddy River, and a number of other rivers in Southern Illinois, and we had to send out the National Guard and do a lot of things.

Well, I said to myself, "I am going to be different from all Governors. I am going to take a personal interest in the affairs of these poor, wretched, homeless people in the affected areas." So I promptly seized the phone one morning and started to call the Mayors of all the cities affected by the flood. I disposed of the Mayor of Carmi pleasantly and agreeably, pledging him all of the support of all of the State agencies. And then I asked the girl to get me the Mayor of Murphysboro. She said, after a few minutes, "The Mayor is on the phone." I picked it up and said, "How do you do, Mayor. This is Adlai Stevenson, Governor Stevenson in Springfield." "Oh, how do you do, Governor? Well, I never had a Governor call me before." I said, "I have been so alarmed about your condition down there. How are you?" "Oh, fine. I never was better. How are you, Governor?" Finally I said, in desperation, "Well, we want to do everything we possibly can for you," having been previously informed that the flood was almost up to the foundations of the waterworks. And I said, "Mayor, how is your water?" He said, "My water! What the hell are you talking about? My water is fine. How's yours?" (Laughter)

This exchange of epithets went on, each of us getting more and more indignant, and finally I said, "Say, who the hell am I talking to? Is this the Mayor of Murphysboro?" He said, "No, this the Mayor of Murraysville, and my water is fine." Bang! (Laughter)

Well, I had one other brief moment of levity out of one of these dinners to the Senators at the Mansion. As they left, after a series of toasts, one of them got up and said, "Governor, I want to thank you particularly for the dessert. Nothing has been finer. Three Senators in my immediate vicinity have eaten their doilies and never even noticed it." (Laughter)

My wife, at that point, rose to her feet and said that she would be glad to kiss any Senator who voted against the investigation of the University of Chicago. The next day she came down with mumps. (Laughter) She sent a telegram to the majority leader of the Senate and said that in her present condition she would have to alter her proposal and she would now kiss any Senator who voted for the investigation. (Laughter)

I have no speech for you, I regret to say, nor have I been an elected officer long enough to have developed sufficient reminiscences to entertain you, or to permit me to engage in any philosophical comments or speculations about the future of Democratic government in the State of Illinois. I would like to talk to you a little while and then perhaps after I have subsided, if time permits, you will be good enough to ask me any questions and I will answer them as best I can. I will talk to you about what I found there and what I am attempting to do about it.

As I think all of you know, in Illinois, in contrast to some other States, in addition to the Governor the people also elect a Lieutenant Governor, the Attorney General, the State Treasurer, the Secretary of State, the Auditor of Public Accounts and the Superintendent of Public Instruction. All of these, except the Superintendent of Public Instruction, were elected with me in the election in November. They are all of them Democrats.[50] I can't say that, with the exception of one or two, they were all intimate or long-time friends.

It is terribly important, as long as we have this system which is, in my judgment, partially right and partially wrong, of electing so many officers who are essential to the successful functioning of the executive branch, to enjoy a harmonious personal relationship. As some of you know, perhaps one of the greatest misfortunes or inconveniences or difficulties that my predecessor, Governor Green, confronted was the open and notorious dis-union, disharmony between himself and his Attorney General, which created many awkward difficulties on both sides.

My situation in that respect is very, very satisfactory indeed. I hope it will continue to be so, and I have no reason to think that it will not. In all events, what I am saying is that I have no control whatever over those five important elective officials, with large budgets, with the exception of the Lieutenant Governor, and large staffs of their own, other than the influence of cooperation, persuasion and happy harmony. Sometimes that is not always enough as personal ambitions or other motives intervene.

It is a difficulty that I think might to some extent be corrected if we were to have a new constitution, and is one of what seems to me a more minor reason for modernizing our basic law.

[50] The exception, Republican Superintendent of Public Instruction Vernon L. Nickell, had served continuously since 1943. He was reelected to a four-year term in 1950.

Now, as to our department offices, as Governor I have 13 code departments, each having come down since the Administrative Code was first inaugurated in Illinois under Governor Lowden. There were originally created 11 code departments. Subsequently one has been eliminated, and three new ones have been added. I have 13 code departments under my immediate jurisdiction, and some 105 Boards and Commissions. The code departments range in magnitude and importance and administrative complexity from the Department of Aeronautics with 65 or 70 employees, and a budget of a few hundred thousand dollars, to the Department of Public Welfare, for example, with 10,000 employees, and a budget neighboring $100,000,000.

With respect to the Commissions, they vary in size and importance from one that I encountered the other day called the Bee Keepers Commission that has two employees, to those like the Illinois Commerce Commission, with which you are entirely familiar, and the Illinois Public Aid Commission, with two or three thousand employees, and a budget of $150,000,000.

So that, in the aggregate, I have under the jurisdiction of my office some 30,000 employees, and a budget neighboring perhaps a billion dollars or more for the biennial period.

Now, of this enormous personnel, this enormous staff of, say, 30,000 — I can't tell you exactly, I wish I could but it is still in the future statistics, how many are under civil service, and therefore secure in their tenure. I would imagine that the figure was probably in the neighborhood of 15,000 and somewhat more. In all events, that leaves some 10,000 to 15,000 employees who are my so-called personal appointees — ten to fifteen thousand. That is the area known as: Patronage, which is the curse of all public officials, so far as my experience extends, and which has been my principal obstacle and difficulty to date and will be as long as I endure in this office.

The job that confronted me was to first organize the business of this magnitude with some 30,000 employees, an annual expenditure of $500,000,000, prepare a program in the interests of the State, as I see it, and prepare a budget, and put all of this through a legislature which was sitting and waiting for me the day before I got there.

Of course, I think anybody who has been through this experience realizes that that is a very bad way to attempt to do public business. You can't possibly organize anything in this order of magnitude, you can't possibly prepare and articulate a program, and prepare a budget of this size, and handle a legislature simultaneously. And I would suggest that if the time ever came when we could elect the legislature in the odd numbered year, the way they do in New York, or provide a Governor some time within which he can get his bearings and get his staff together, and equip at least his major positions, by postponing, as one alternative, the convening of the legislature in the year of the inauguration by two or three months, it would be a great blessing and make for economy and efficiency.

I have at the present time in the 13 code departments, so-called, that I mentioned to you, three carry-overs; three directors that I have not replaced since I took office. Of the remaining 10, the first job, of course, was to select the best people I could find. There are three ways, as best I have been able to make out, how you select major administrative officials.

One is to invite the party, your political party, to make recommendations and select whomever they recommend. That is the orthodox way. Unhappily that has been the too common way, I am afraid. A second way to do it is to select the best people of the candidates, those people who aspire to the position, and there are always a great many, I can assure you. I have had some classical illustrations of it. I had 107 applications for membership on the Court of Claims, for example. A third way to do it is to disregard both, and to go out and try to find your own men. If you can better what the political party has to suggest, if you can better what you have in the way of applications, you are that much better off.

Out of these 10 that I have appointed so far, of the so-called Cabinet, 4 represent my best judgment among the candidates. None of them represent the nominees of my political party, not one. The other six represent my own selections, people that I have gone out and enlisted. They include, incidentally, 3 Republicans. It has not been easy. I can assure you it has been very difficult. You start with this obstacle that the maximum amount that you can pay an officer to run a department like, we will say, Public Works and Buildings, with 8,000 employees and a tremendous budget, is $8,000.

In the case of some of these appointees, I suspect I spent far too much time. I am beginning to feel now that maybe I did. My theory at the outset was that if I worked very diligently over the selection of these top personnel it would save me a great deal of trouble and anxiety. I have no doubt the latter is true, but the expenditure of the time in the selection of these people has perhaps been at the cost of the program, and at the cost of my relations with the Legislature. I am hoping that the quality of the administration will make up anything I have lost in those respects in the interim.

I can illustrate the quality by telling you that in the case of the selection of the director of one department, I first tried nine men before I was able to induce one to take it at a very large financial sacrifice. In the case of another department, the Department of Mines and Minerals, which is an interesting sort of illustrative case, although that is a department which is perhaps not so familiar to most of you unless you are in the coal or the oil business, but is perhaps one of the most difficult in the State — it has to do with the policing and the administration of the mining industry, not only coal mining, but all of the other aspects of the mining industry in Illinois, and the oil industry — I, at great length, commencing in November, late, after the election, selected a man for this position [51] and finally induced him to come by, in turn, inducing his company to protect him, through a very devious device that I would not care to have known publicly, on the differential between his salary and the salary that they were paying. He had been in office three weeks when he died. He died in the end of January, and I have been ever since trying to find a successor, off and on, almost continuously with, to date, no luck whatever. If I get hold of a good man, as I did find today, one entirely new name of the some 17 names that arc before me I find that his wife refuses to permit him to move to Springfield. If I get the most qualified man that I now have before me on the record, I find that his brother is in the slot machine business in Macoupin County and his brother-in-law runs a handbook in East St. Louis. If I get the next best qualified man who is a superintendent of one of the largest mines in the world, in Southern Illinois, I find that I am going to be criticized by some segments of the press because of the fact that, entirely innocently, he was superintendent of a mine some years ago where there was a disaster.

It is that sort of thing that you run into all the time. Meanwhile, John Lewis [52] watches every move you make. If I take one of these fellows he has threatened to call a strike on all Illinois mines. If you go with the United Mine Workers, the Progressives [53] take after you. If you go with either one of them the operators take after you.

So that I finally enlisted, some weeks ago, the Professor of Mining and Metallurgy from the University of Illinois to take over the job temporarily until I could find a new man, and I had within 24 hours over 600 telegrams, expressing their resistance and their opposition and their extreme distaste for this Professor because he had never been a miner underground, although he is one of the most distinguished people in this field in the country.

[51] James W. Starks, superintendent of underground operations of the Peabody Coal Company of Taylorville, Illinois, was appointed director of Mines and Minerals on January 17, 1949. He died on February 3, 1949.
[52] John L. Lewis, president of the United Mine Workers of America.
[53] The animosity between the United Mine Workers and the Progressive Mine Workers of America was considerably more bitter than the normal rivalry between competing labor unions.

Well, it is that sort of thing that drives you nuts. (Laughter)

I finally selected, at long last, a gentleman who heads a certain institution downstate, and after I selected him some several days passed when a Republican member of the Senate brought me a transcript of a criminal proceeding in a downstate county showing that he had been indicted for rape some twenty-four years before; and convicted for carrying concealed weapons.

I stopped, at the last moment, the appointment to a major position of a fellow just because I was not quite satisfied with his record and I got the Bureau of Criminal Identification to go into his record and see if there was any, and I found that he had never been indicted, but there was a record on him back in 1934 in connection with graft in the awarding of some contracts.

It is that kind of thing that makes me feel that you can't ever screen too meticulously and that it is perhaps worth the effort.

Meanwhile the patronage pressure is incessant and dreadful. It is not like organizing a business. It is not like going out and getting the best men you can for the money — the way you would do with any position in your businesses — because you are dealing in an area that is quite dissimilar. You are dealing with a political party. You are dealing with a Legislature. You have to have the Legislature or all the best intentions in the world will come to naught, and the pressure from them to put inadequate people and unsatisfactory people into positions is incessant.

I do not know whether you are familiar with the process that we have. It works, roughly, this way: I select, without any interference from the party — and I must say that both on behalf of Colonel Arvey[54] in Chicago, and the leaders downstate, they have given me no suggestions and no interference whatever with respect to any of these major appointments — but when it comes to the secondary and the tertiary, and then with minor appointments running into thousands of people in every little, every ordinary job, every day — they have the most ingenious devices for misrepresenting to the Governor, for carrying messages from one to another.

I finally worked out a most elaborate system[55] whereby requests for

[54] Jacob M. Arvey, chairman of the Democratic Cook County Central Committee.

[55] Carl McGowan wrote the editors: "Somehow Part I [of Volume III] gives the impression that Adlai was against the patronage system and that, accordingly, he was not very faithful to it. His antipathy to the patronage system was mainly where it placed an incompetent or a time-server on the public payroll. With respect to those jobs where this was not likely to happen, he was a loyal party man and believed that, all other things being equal, a Democrat should have the job rather than a Republican. So long as so many jobs in Illinois remained subject to the patronage system, and were not taken out of it by legislative action, he thought the existing

the appointment move from the director by form of document describing the qualifications required for the job, and from thence they go to the screening committees that are established in a hotel in Springfield, and in a hotel in Chicago, known as the Morrison,[56] and then the Democratic party solicits applicants for these jobs from all of the county chairmen and then they make their own screening, and send along what they deem to be the best qualified man, and then, in turn, he has to be selected or rejected by the chief of the division to which he has been assigned. It makes a lot of machinery and a lot of tiresome, tedious detail.

In the past it has been the practice to put all the people engaged in those screening processes on the state payroll. I can say in this case not one of them is on the state payroll. Not one of them has an employee who is on the payroll. Not even an automobile. And they do not use state space. How in the world they are going to be paid, I don't know.

Whatever you do, you are wrong. You can't ever satisfy anybody as far as I can see.

I have here something that came to me the other day that was distributed through the Legislature on everybody's desk. It is printed on a little slip of paper which says at the top:

"what do you mean,
i gotta be screened

"gov. stevenson: Did you attend Princeton?
precinct capt.: No, I went to the Morrison.
stevie: Do you know the duties of a U.N. delegate?
pre. capt.: You got me, I always bet on Notre Dame.
stevie: Name three foreign diplomats.

---

system should be made to work in favor of party workers. You will recall how he deviled John Weigle [John C. Weigel, president of the Illinois Civil Service Commission] to provide him with monthly reports, comparing the rate of employment of Democrats in the first years of his administration with that of Henry Horner. That statistic always indicated, to his relief and satisfaction, the balance to be in Adlai's favor. He had two concerns in this regard: One was to have ammunition to meet the complaints from the party professionals that he was not replacing the Republicans as fast as he should, and the other was that he did not want to let unskillful handling of patronage get him into a position where, like Horner, he would have to face a primary fight in 1952. As you know, he always thought that it was Illinois's tragedy that Governor Horner's chances of continuing good state government in his second term were completely ruined by the alliances he had to make to win the primary in 1936. . . ." Letter to Carol Evans, April 2, 1970.

[56] The St. Nicholas Hotel in Springfield housed the Democratic State Central Committee headquarters; the Morrison Hotel in Chicago was the headquarters of the Cook County Central Committee.

PRE. CAPT.: Charlie Weber, Senator Connors and Pete Fosco.[57]
STEVIE: Are you a C.P.A.?
PRE. CAPT.: No, I am a Democrat.
STEVIE: What is a Lame Duck?
PRE. CAPT.: Me canvassing my precinct in the rain.
STEVIE: Who is the No. 1 man in the State?
PRE. CAPT.: Paddy Bauler.[58]
STEVIE: Were you in Service?
PRE. CAPT.: Sure, twenty years a Precinct Captain.
STEVIE: You understand this process of screening?
PRE. CAPT.: Naw, I don't want to be a Movie Star, I wanna JOB."

(Laughter)

The other day there was distributed all over Springfield and placed on all of the legislators' desks a little pamphlet very beautifully printed, and on the outside of it, it said:

"Americans of Polish descent. List of the offices enjoyed by the largest voting block [bloc] in Illinois, under the administration of Governor Adlai Stevenson." Then it says:

"1 * denotes director of code department.

"2 ** denotes assistant director of code department.

"3 *** denotes other important positions."

Then you open the thing up and there are six pages of blank paper. (Laughter)

Well, you have to put up with this business. It has not worried me too much, but it is terribly time-consuming.

When we took over my first instruction to the new department heads, and to the existing ones that we carried over, was to first eliminate all of what are called the deadheads; that is, people on the payroll who perform no services, or make no pretense of performing any service.

Secondly, to eliminate all those who were not working in the sense of working a full day on their job. We were going to eliminate the part-time employee, which is something new and unheard of in Illinois.

I found that between the election and the first of January thousands of people had been dropped from the payroll already. Since the middle of January, up to the 1st of March, we have eliminated 1,563 more people with a net saving to the state of salaries in personal services alone of $35,000 a month. Now, that seems to you all to the good, and obviously manifestly desirable, but every time one of these men is discharged or let go, or permitted to resign, you get a repercussion from somewhere.

[57] Powerful Chicago Democrats.
[58] Chicago Democratic Ward Committeeman Mathias Bauler, who achieved fame among other things for saying: "Chicago ain't ready for reform."

Usually it is from his Republican sponsor, who usually is a member of the State Legislature, and generally he comes in to you and says, "You are making a great mistake. You are going to need my vote for this or for that."

I do not see any way to trifle with the thing. You simply go ahead and do it, and that is what we have attempted to do.

We have kept on a good many Republican employees. Actually up to date, I guess, more than 50 percent are carry-overs in the second level jobs and down, and we will keep on a whole lot which we probably could dispense with. That is always hard to explain to people of your own party. Living in their country communities it irks them to see Republicans still on the payroll getting the salaries that they feel they should have. One reason you keep them, of course, is until you can find as good or better men to replace them. A second reason, in many cases, is that you keep them in order to have, if you please, the cooperation of their sponsor. I am shameless about it. I will keep on a lot of Republicans in some of these positions that I would be perfectly glad to replace with equally qualified Democrats, just to try to propitiate their sponsors in the Legislature, because I am confronted, as you know, with a divided Legislature, a very meager Democratic majority in the house, and an overwhelming Republican Senate.

What we do is keep a black book, and it is nothing new. It is commonplace, I am told, in state and federal politics, and has been for a long time. Then we watch how this Senator or Representative who sponsors this particular Republican job-holder votes. If he votes badly you always have the threat of reprisal that his patronage will be fired; if he goes along with you, you will keep him. Perhaps it is not a very worthy way to do it, but somebody has got to show me a better one.

Now, as to my program. I do not know that I need to spend any of your precious time on that. You know about my passionate anxiety to reform our organic law, the constitution, and I think you are conscious of the reasons for it and why it has become virtually unamendable,[59] especially if we are going to have efficient, thrifty, and orderly government in this State. You know how desirable it would be to redistrict the State and accord proper representation to the metropolitan center of Chicago, and at the same time subordinate downstate. And it can be done; it can be easily done. I could talk to you at length, but I won't, about a matter with which you are all familiar: The difficulty of dis-

[59] The Illinois constitution could only be amended by a majority vote of all persons voting in an election. Since many voters ignored the separate ballot containing the proposed amendment, such a majority was seldom achieved. Stevenson had made constitutional reform a major issue of his campaign. See, e.g., *The Papers of Adlai E. Stevenson,* Vol. II, pp. 491–492, 563–567.

tributing the burden of property taxes equitably between real estate and personal property, particularly intangible personal property.

You know how archaic our court system is, how cumbersome, and how entirely unsatisfactory it is. Our Supreme Court's time is preoccupied with fee cases which constitutionally it has to hear at the expense of a large volume of litigation which is much more important in the times in which we now live, in the modern economy in which we live.

You know about the 5 percent debt limitation which has resulted in the duplication of municipal taxing bodies until not long ago when we started this consolidation program in school districts we had in Illinois something over 15,000 municipal taxing bodies, in contrast to the national average of under 6,000; undoubtedly the most cumbersome and expensive State in the Union.

I also feel that we could do much in the way of consolidation of governmental units from the township on up, which would eliminate duplication of administration expense, which would simplify ballots, and which would make on the whole for a much more intelligent and inexpensive representative government — not to mention the moral problem of respect for constitutional government, which I do not think any of us can afford to wholly overlook. You can't expect people, the younger people who have a disrespect for the Constitution, even the State Constitution, to have respect and admiration for a system which they are taught to die for if they can't even respect its basic documents.

I think I would have no trouble whatever with a resolution calling for a constitutional convention if it was not for the companion piece I introduced: The so-called party responsibility bill,[60] which was calculated to bring about a constitutional convention rather than merely a meaningless resolution which would be voted down by the people at the next general election in 1950, not because they were against it, but because, as has been the case for the last fifty-five years, they just failed to vote on the proposition at all. That is what causes the trouble. All of the members of the Legislature on both sides of the aisle, Republicans and Democrats alike, are perfectly willing to vote for a constitutional convention resolution, and are perfectly willing to go back to their people and say, "Well,

[60] This is the same as the "Party Circle" bills referred to by Stevenson in his speech to the League of Women Voters in Chicago, October 8, 1948 (see *The Papers of Adlai E. Stevenson*, Vol. II, p. 569).

Kenneth S. Davis explained: "This called for a revision of the ballot law so that political parties, at their conventions, could endorse the calling of a constitutional convention, the endorsement then to appear at the top of the election ballot under the party's circle. A straight ticket vote in the circle, for all party nominees, would also be a vote for the calling of the convention. Split-ticket voters would be able to vote 'yes' or 'no' specifically on the constitutional question." *A Prophet in His Own Country*, p. 342.

this is nothing more than to give the people an opportunity to vote whether or not we should have a constitution" — They are quite willing to do that, because they are confident that it will fail. As soon as you introduce legislation which is calculated to make it succeed, then they run away from you, and their opinions are, for the most part based on self-interest. For the most part many of them have told me in so many words, "We are afraid to redistrict because we know we will lose our job. We are very much afraid of your proposal because we know that the Democratic party in its party convention, or its primary, will undoubtedly adopt it and it will go on the ballot, and that will force all the independents to vote in the Democratic column, and we will probably be voted out of office."

I think that is foolish, but many of them assert it. I even have a lot of trouble with my Democrats in the Legislature on it because they come from downstate districts where they have gone so far as to say to me, "Well, I can't tell you why we are against it, but we are just fearful if there should be a constitutional convention that the big cities, Chicago, and the big towns in the State will be represented by the smarter delegates than we will be able to delegate from our districts." They are afraid somehow through inarticulate, inchoate fears that they will be at a disadvantage.

Now, I have also proposed that the ceiling shall be removed on old-age pensions. Some people said that that was a frivolous thing to do. My motives were quite clear, and I think any people who have had any experience with the administration of relief will understand what I had in mind. If you make it clear that the responsibility of every agent in the field, that it is based on need and need alone, and deprive him of the protection of a statutory ceiling, you create a greater inducement to thrift, and to successful administration than you do if he always knows he can go up to the ceiling and still be protected. In all events that will fail and I am quite content to let it go to the ceiling. It will be above $65.

Senator Thompson [61] on the Republican side has proposed a fluctuating ceiling depending on the cost of living index, which is also entirely all right with me. Actually I think this won't cost more money in the long run than the other system will.

I promise to take the Department of Mines and Minerals out of politics, and I am in the process of succeeding in that regard. We have conducted over bitter, bitter protests of the Democratic party, mine examinations without asking any applicant for his political credentials, and by admitting Republicans and Democrats alike to participate in the examination, and I am retaining all of the State mine inspectors who had qualified

[61] Wallace Thompson (43rd District), president pro tempore of the state Senate.

under these examinations after the Centralia Disaster two years ago.[62] I have some important legislation I mean to offer in order to make clear the responsibility of the Director of the Department of Mines and Minerals. As it is now, I defy any lawyer in this room to read the statutes and determine whether the Director of the Department, or the Mine Board, as it is called, is ultimately responsible for the administration of the Department's affairs. Nobody knows. The result is you can't assess responsibility, and it is a situation that seems to me must be corrected.

I hope to merge the Illinois Public Aid Commission with the Department of Public Welfare. I feel that although it is questionable as to whether or not it has not been better administered, and I think it has under the Commission than it would be under the Department, administratively it makes for great difficulty, and that probably it would be far better if it were incorporated in the Department which is directly responsible for the cognate activities.

I have asked the President of the University of Illinois, Dr. [George] Stoddard, who has been most cooperative, to relinquish the Galesburg Branch of the University, and shut it up, and to let me take over that enormous erstwhile Federal hospital in order to concentrate seniles in the Department of Public Welfare, so as to create more room and relieve the overcrowding in the other State institutions which, as you know, is now one of the worst in the country. That will save the State about $6,000,000 in construction in the next biennium in additional hospital facilities, and will reduce the problem and will enable concentrating a lot of these people who should not be in mental institutions and who are merely taking up space, requiring not only custodial care, but remedial care.

I am trying to reorganize the State police.

Heretofore the State police in Illinois — some of you in the city seldom come in contact with them, but it is of first importance to the people living in the small towns — the State police has been wholly political.

When Governor Green [63] was inaugurated, 97 per cent of the existing State police that had served under Governor Horner [64] were fired and replaced by Republicans, on the recommendation of County chairmen.

[62] On March 25, 1947, a coal mine explosion in Centralia killed 111 miners. Governor Green's mine inspectors had collected campaign funds from mine operators and ignored violations of safety regulations. For a full account of this, see John Bartlow Martin, "Blast in Centralia," *Harper's*, March, 1948. Stevenson had made mine safety and the depoliticization of the Department of Mines and Minerals an issue in his campaign. See, e.g., *The Papers of Adlai E. Stevenson*, Vol. II, pp. 487–489, 525–526.

[63] Dwight Green served two terms as governor prior to Stevenson's inauguration. He was a Republican.

[64] Henry Horner, Democratic governor of Illinois, 1933–1940.

The same thing happened in Governor Horner's term when he took over from Governor Emerson.[65]

I think the time has come when we can no longer afford to permit that sort of improvident situation and entirely inefficient situation to continue. So we are proposing now that we fill all the vacancies with deserving Democrats. I have hired Mr. Kremmel [66] from Chicago and his staff to establish new standards and qualifications for the State police, which, I am sorry to say, they perhaps are putting a little too high. Then we will screen out sufficient of the weakest Republicans, so that we will bring the force of 500 men into, roughly, equivalent balance — 250 surviving of the best Republicans and 250 of the best Democrats we can recruit around the State. Then I will go to the Legislature and introduce legislation similar to that in Michigan and Pennsylvania to put the State police under a permanent merit system, and thereafter it will be impossible to even ask a candidate's political affiliation.

With respect to the Commerce Commission, I have been very hopeful that that could be put on a proper level, a level equivalent to what it is in some states like New York, by increasing salaries, by staggering terms, and by taking it out of politics entirely. For that reason I have retained, as you know, some three Republicans out of five on the Commission, and I am hopeful that the Legislature will go along with me on that. They actually went into office back under Governor Dunne's administration, and in Governor Lowden's administration — and it was not until Governor Small [67] amended the Commerce Commission Act that it became a purely political body.

Now, with respect to the schools. I should like to do far more for the schools than has been done in recent years, and I should like to do it by not merely increasing the amount of money appropriated to the School Distribution Fund, but in increased inducement for consolidation of school districts throughout the State, and in raising the tax level so that more of this money will go where it is needed, and less of it where it is not needed.

Probably the most organized lobby in the State is the school lobby, and it is the most difficult to deal with. It is hard for me because I am sympathetic with it, although the impression seems to have been circulated that I am against liberal aid to schools.

I hope I can do something about our road program. You are not so familiar with it here, but if you travel downstate you will find, next to

[65] Louis B. Emmerson, Republican governor of Illinois, 1929–1933.
[66] Franklin M. Kreml, director of Northwestern University's Traffic Institute.
[67] Len Small, Republican governor of Illinois, 1925–1929.

schools, it is of the greatest concern to our citizens. It is an appalling situation. The report of the Griffenhagen Associates [68] indicates, and nobody has successfully challenged it although it has been examined by engineers now very generally, that we should be spending in the neighborhood of $450,000,000 a year on our roads if we are ever going to get them back into anything like proper shape. It is pressing, because the roads are deteriorating so rapidly that the cost of maintenance is eating up the entire road dollar that is in the State.

A projection of the curve of the last few years would indicate that four years from now we won't have a dollar to spend on construction — every dollar that we get in Illinois from Federal or State sources will be spent on maintenance alone.

You know, when one of these hard roads gets past a certain point then you can no longer resurface it, blacktop it. So they have to be blacktopped while they are still worth saving.

I am hopeful, although I have not said this publicly and I will ask you to protect me because it is a difficult matter with respect to the legislature to get somebody else to assume some leadership on the Republican side — that the report of the Joint Committee which Governor Green appointed, headed by Hugh Cross, which has done a very extraordinary piece of work, will be adopted insofar as an increase in the gas tax is concerned from 3 cents to 5 cents.[69]

We are among the last of the great states to still cling to the 3-cent gas tax. There are only two others, Iowa and Ohio. In every other State in the Union, New York, Pennsylvania, California, Indiana, Kentucky, Wisconsin, all the surrounding States, the tax runs anywhere from 5 to as much as 9 cents. It is bitterly opposed by the oil people — why, I can't understand, except it be from a very short-range point of view, but if they understood the deterioration that is taking effect, it would be more and more apparent if it is not raised in this biennium it would have to be next time, and it will be just that much longer before we can do a proper job in restoring our roads.

Purchasing is a good illustration of the importance of minor vices in the State. The State spends for commodities of one kind and another perhaps 75 to 100 million dollars a biennium, and the manner in which pur-

[68] A private consulting firm in the field of public administration and finance, employed by the state to conduct a scientific study of traffic needs. The report, "A Highway Improvement Program for Illinois," is dated November 1, 1948.

[69] The 1947 General Assembly created the Illinois Highway and Traffic Problems Commission, consisting of five members each of the Illinois state Senate and House of Representatives, as well as five "citizen" members appointed by Governor Dwight Green, who also appointed Lieutenant Governor Hugh W. Cross as chairman. The commission made its report to Governor Stevenson in February, 1949.

chases are requisitioned, and the appliance of standards to bids, is entirely unsatisfactory. There is very little, if any, policing. Pilfering, loss, waste, stupid disregard of specifications is commonplace. The people are corrupt, I am afraid, from top to bottom. It is something that is going to take a long time to correct.

I think I have got a Director of Purchases who is dedicated to the correction of this evil, but it will need the installation of new auditing systems and a spot-checking staff to go around and check on the receiving end of State purchases.

Now, as to the budget, and I will take only a minute longer.

Roughly I will have 531 million dollars for the general revenue fund this year from the sales tax, the racing tax, the liquor tax, the cigarette tax, and all of the other taxes — and I mean estimated at the full probable return — not at 80 per cent of it as has been the estimate in the recent past. The sales tax, incidentally, declined in February, 8 percent for the first time in ten years. I have already had to use up 50 million dollars of the so-called surplus I inherited for deficiency appropriations to carry the government through the balance of this biennium. If I use 50 of the 100 that remains, that will give me 581 million dollars to work with for the general fund. 195 of that, roughly, after three weeks of night-and-day work on this budget, will go for the Legislature, for the courts, for all of the executive branches of the government for normal operations. About 71 million for higher education, the University of Illinois and the five State normal colleges.[70]

For the schools the total estimates at the moment are $147 million — it is 123 for the School Distribution Fund and 23 for State Aid Handicapped Children, transfer, school buses and all that sort of thing.

The best we have been able to do with the Illinois Public Aid Commission budget is $158 million.

Adding $20 million for miscellaneous, including $12 million which, under the law, has to be taken out of the general fund for the retirement of Soldier Bonus Bonds,[71] gives me $591 million, or $10 million more than the total revenue that we can possibly estimate. In other words, we are under water about $10 million without setting aside 5 cents for any building whatever, any construction; without 5 cents of aid to the City of Chicago, or to any of the other municipalities.

[70] Eastern State Teachers College at Charleston, Western State Teachers College at Macomb, Northern State Teachers College at De Kalb, Southern Illinois University at Carbondale, and Illinois State Normal University at Normal. All of these institutions are now part of the Illinois State University system.

[71] In 1947, the General Assembly enacted a law granting a bonus, to be financed by a bond issue, to all Illinois veterans who were residents of the state at the time of their entrance into service during World War II.

Now, what are we going to do? I think we can squeeze about $50 million more out of it by improved administration of sales tax collections, and by extending the sales tax to cover presently exempted industries.

I also think we can squeeze about 10 percent on the average out of every one of the personnel bodies, across the board, by eliminating jobs, and so on. That, I am afraid, is going to be entirely absorbed by granting a 10 per cent salary raise to State employees. I do not know whether we can do that. I do not know whether we should do it. In all events, there is an incessant demand for it, and perhaps on the basis of statistics, and comparison with private industry, they are entitled to it.

You can see that the position is exceedingly acute. We have spent a great deal of time trying to squeeze everything out everywhere we can. For example, I discovered only a few days ago in going over the budget for the Military Department, that it is costing the State $77,000 a year just to maintain a headquarters for the Commanding General of troops here in the City of Chicago. I think that is the sort of thing we can deal sharply with. It will be very distasteful, and it will be very unpopular with the National Guard, but it is entirely unnecessary to have a stratification of Headquarters, it seems to me, in the National Guard, as unfortunately we have so often in the military service in the Federal Government.

Now, as to the Legislature. My huge majority by which I was elected last fall has been a great asset, as you can imagine. I am reaching now the point of diminishing returns; the point of increasing complaints; the point of increasing dissatisfaction, and diminishing satisfaction. The honeymoon is, undoubtedly, over.

I was amused last week when the Republicans who only increased the budget for the schools last year by $9,000,000, made a fuss in the House demanding that the committee be discharged and the Bill reported increasing the budget for the schools this year 100 percent.

Now, not an hour had elapsed before that was tried, and I was charged with bottling up and stalling the school budget, when the leader of the minority in the House came to see me at the Mansion, and said, "Of course, Governor, you will forgive me; I know perfectly your position. I am not in favor of any substantial aid to the schools myself, not as much as you are, but the time has come when we had to call you names."

I suppose I will get used to that.

In connection with the discontinuance of the University Branch at Galesburg, I went and called in the majority leader, the Republican majority leader in the Senate, who comes from there.[72] He is a very fine man, one of the finest, I think, if not the finest I have encountered, and I

72 Wallace Thompson.

told him I was going to do that. He said, "Well, of course, you are dead right. You can't possibly afford to go on giving free education at the expense that it is costing you down there, but I will have to oppose it in my community."

Well, that is the sort of thing you are up against. I am not surprised. I expected about as much.

Now, as to a typical day. Somebody asked me here at luncheon — I guess it was Dave McDougal,[73] "What do you do?" Well, here was Friday of last week. I wrote it down. It is fairly typical.

I started in the morning with a conference with sixteen ministers of the gospel from Pulaski and Alexander Counties who complained about gambling conditions in their counties and demanded immediate intervention by the State to force the State's Attorneys to do what they will not do.

Then follows a meeting with a delegation from the Illinois Oil and Gas Association to discuss a conservation bill for Illinois, which is sharply disputed apparently within the industry. I spent a lot of time in owlish silence listening to them, and did not know any more about it when I got through than when I started.

Then I am visited by a delegation from Rock Island County demanding some patronage for their men which they say has been cruelly neglected, and demanding that I fire three notorious Republicans who are presently on the State payroll while a Mayoralty campaign is going on there. They pressed me intensively, and I listened patiently, and gave them an arbitrator for the Industrial Commission.

Then I am waited on by one of these honest downstate politicians I have made Postmaster at one of the largest cities outside of Chicago, who makes an impassionate plea, literally weeps for the appointment of a thief and scoundrel to the Illinois Liquor Commission.

Then I am waited on by the Budgetary Commission to report to me some of the bad news that I have already suggested to you, after some of their preliminary talks about the building program for the next biennium.

Then, by a delegation from Joliet to demand 3-½ million dollars at once in order to divert the course of the Hickory Creek so Joliet is not flooded every two years.

And then finally a delegation of politicians who complain that in the selection of the new State policemen the standards are so high that all the boys from their respective counties have been rejected. Upon investigating that I find that in one case the boy had an IQ of 6 percent in his test, and in another case the boy has congenital syphilis.

Well, I am afraid I have talked much too long, and in a much too

[73] David McDougal, vice president of the Northern Trust Company of Chicago.

desultory way, and I appreciate your patience and apologize for this very uninformative talk.

I should like to feel that in the course of these few years in which I seem to be destined to sit in this high seat that I might do something in the way of increasing public respect for the career service. That seems to me one of the most difficult problems I have to confront; enlarging not only the area of the civil service and the merit system, but primarily a regard by the public of some of the public servants as career servants irrespective of politics.

I should hope very much that I could do something more for the schools whose plight, particularly downstate, is really acute.

I would like to do something for roads and that should be of interest to everyone in this room, because it is going to be more expensive later if it is not done now.

I should like to do something in the way of making the administration of all State welfare institutions, particularly the mental hospitals, show an improvement, and to decentralize, if possible, part of that burden before it eats us up alive. As it is now, that population is increasing at a net rate of about a thousand a year, and it is costing fifteen thousand to twenty thousand dollars per bed to build, and we can't even keep up with it any more.

There are many things, such as removing Mines and Minerals from politics; the State Police from politics; extending the civil service to cover areas like the Factory Inspection service, and some of these other things that are badly abused — and most of all I should like to at least establish a record for the decrease of payroll padding, if nothing else. Perhaps the worst abuse to which we all as taxpayers have been exposed from time immemorial, is just that abuse. It can be done, and I have had very little trouble with my party or with the Republicans about doing it now. They were educated in this campaign by seeing a great proud and noble party brutally defeated in Illinois for perhaps no greater reason than that alone.

It is no longer party machines built on jobs that win elections. It is public respect for public office and public office holders.

Thank you. (Applause)

Governor Stevenson and his aides and department heads spent long hours in preparation of the budget.

To James Mulroy [74]

[undated]

Mr. Mulroy:

At the time I talked yesterday about the timing on the budget I should have made a strong precise little statement that I was personally cutting in each dept. and screening every request, to insure the utmost economy and caution etc. I wish someone could be thinking about this sort of thing.

AES

To George D. Stoddard [75]

April 22, 1949

Dear George:

The other day it came to my notice that John K. Morris,[76] a member of the Legislature, was anxious to be appointed Associate Director of Extension Services in Agriculture and Home Economics at the University.

I am taking this opportunity to say to you personally, and not officially, that I could not disregard this information without doing both him and the University an injustice. I came to know this young man a few years ago before I got into politics, and I have developed a most genuine and sincere admiration for him and for his marked intelligence and talents. I am sure Dean Rusk [77] knows all about him, and I should be sorry to see him leave the Legislature were he appointed, but also, with my limited understanding of the qualifications for the position, I should be disappointed to see the University miss an opportunity to pick up a really first-rate man with a high moral purpose, considerable worldly experience, a fine intelligence, and a cracking good farmer.

Let me say again that I am writing you as an old friend and not as Governor.

Sincerely yours,

---

[74] The original of this memorandum is in the possession of Robert Notti.

[75] President of the University of Illinois.

[76] A Democratic member of the legislature, a graduate of the University of Illinois College of Agriculture and a professional farmer specializing in purebred Guernsey and Aberdeen cattle and white Leghorn chickens. He was helpful to the Governor during the legislative sessions.

[77] Henry Perly Rusk, dean of the College of Agriculture and director of the Agricultural Experiment Station and Extension Service.

To Mrs. Edison Dick [78]

April 3, 1949

. . . Of course if you should decide that the effects of Florida had sufficiently subsided and that you were yearning for a trip to Springfield to crawl under the heavy yoke of public service — I would with little notice — provide you with suitable accommodations.

But I warn you — you will find a weary, distracted, rh[e]umatic, unattractive Governor awaiting you!

Respectfully
AES

L. Duncan Lloyd, a Chicago lawyer, wrote the Governor on March 30, 1949. He addressed his letter to the attention of "Messrs. Mulroy, Kohn or Schaefer," referring to them as the "Gold Dust Triplets," saying if they would allow his letter to get to the Governor he would "know there is one Republican who thinks you have made a number of very outstanding appointments for key positions. . . . Have you had to buy your second pair of striped trousers?" This referred to a charge in the 1948 campaign that Stevenson was conducting a "striped pants" campaign, the implication being that he was more at ease with diplomatic relations at the national level than with state issues.[79]

To L. Duncan Lloyd

April 3, 1949

Dear Dunc:

The Gold Dust Triplets let your letter get by, and I am flattered in the extreme. No, I haven't bought a second pair of striped trousers — indeed, I haven't bought the first pair!

Yours,

To Merritt A. Hewett [80]

April 4, 1949

Dear Mr. Hewett:

John Fell has been very immature for his age, but I think he is beginning to grow up now and is making better progress all the time.

[78] This handwritten letter is in the possession of Mrs. Dick.
[79] See *The Papers of Adlai E. Stevenson*, Vol. II, pp. 472–474; Davis, *A Prophet in His Own Country*, p. 297.
[80] The original is in the possession of Milton Academy.

Although I cannot say that our conclusions are final, I suspect he should go away in the autumn, and I wish you would therefore consider him as an active candidate and send along the tests in May. I hope Mrs. Stevenson will be able to bring him down but she has been so preoccupied with affairs here that it may be difficult. Moreover, she has been in bed with the mumps all during his spring vacation.

With warm regards, I am

Sincerely yours,

In 1949 Governor Stevenson's oldest son was a student at Harvard University.

To Adlai E. Stevenson III

April 4, 1949

Dear Bear:

Mother has sent me your letter, and I hope the vacation will work out without too much exhausting travel. It sounds to me as though you were attempting to cover a lot of territory.

I was more than delighted to hear about the improvement in your marks and I wish I could say the same for Borden.* [81] His difficulties don't seem to yield to increasing application and I am really troubled about him.

The selection of Eliot House seems to me good and if there is anything I can do, let me know. I was a close friend of Robert Finley who went to Harvard, and who now practices law in New York and lives in Princeton, New Jersey. Possibly the Eliot House Master, Finley,[82] whom you mentioned, is a relative of Bob's.

I hope you got to hear [Winston] Churchill speak at MIT [Massachusetts Institute of Technology]. I wish I had.

Mother is still in bed with the mumps but she has not been at all uncomfortable and I suspect the swelling will disappear soon. I only hope Borden does not get it after being exposed to her. John Fell was down here for a couple of days last week with Mr. and Mrs. Hermon Smith [83] and their little girl Adele. We have not yet decided on a school for him, and I think Mother is planning to go East late in April to look at Asheville and some others. I suspect he will end up at Milton.

[81] Borden was at the Choate School, Wallingford, Connecticut.
[82] John H. Finley, Jr., professor of Greek literature at Harvard University.
[83] The Smiths were old friends and neighbors of the Stevensons. Mr. Smith was a member of the original Stevenson for Governor Committee in 1948. See his chapter entitled "Politics and R & R," in *As We Knew Adlai,* pp. 28–41.

The work here is appalling just now due to the budget and a myriad of other things. It has not been much fun so far, but once the Legislature is over I think we can relax a little and begin to think at last. I like Springfield more and more, and yesterday — Sunday — went out horse-back riding with Uncle Ernest [Ives] and Mr. [Walter] Schaefer along the shores of Lake Springfield. It was very fine and I hope to get more of it as time goes on, and also some tennis at the Country Club early in the morning.

Love,
DAD

P.S. Your Aunt Buffy [Ives] has given you three boys 5000 in bonds which I will put in your envelopes in my safety deposit box soon. You must thank her — its a magnificent gift and touches me deeply.

It looks as tho Con Con [84] would pass the House next week by a very narrow margin which is more than I expected a couple of weeks ago.

Early this morning I flew down to Effingham to inspect the ghastly hospital fire there.[85] They're still taking the bodies out of the ruins. Looked like Germany in the war.

How about this summer? Any ideas?

* A letter from him today says he's going to the infirmary for 10 days with the mumps!

Emmet L. Richardson, Stevenson's cousin, and his wife Harriet were in Florida in the early spring of 1949. Mrs. Richardson wrote to congratu-late Stevenson on the article that appeared about him in the April 2, 1949, issue of the Saturday Evening Post, *entitled "Rebel in Illinois," by Joe Alex Morris.*

To Mrs. E. L. Richardson

April 4, 1949

Dear Cousin Harriet:

You were sweet to write me, and it was good to hear from you again. I thought the article a little superficial and silly, to tell the truth — nor

[84] The bill sponsored by the administration for a constitutional convention referendum. It failed to pass.

[85] A fire broke out at midnight, April 3, 1949, at St. Anthony's Hospital in Effingham, Illinois, in which fifty-eight persons died, including all the babies in the maternity ward and a nurse who refused to leave them. Only the walls of the building remained when the fire was extinguished. Stevenson mobilized all the state's relief and resources, including the National Guard, the state health and fire departments, and the state police, to aid the victims.

did I know anything about my golfing prowess or store of limericks! All the same, I am glad you liked it.

Give my best to Cousin Emmet, and maybe I could induce you both to stop off for a night with me here in Springfield to get reacquainted.

Best love,

Joseph Sam Perry, of Wheaton, Illinois (later to become a judge of the U.S. District Court), wrote the Governor commending him for his good work and careful screening of job-seekers. But he reminded him that in order to keep up his good work there must be a supporting organization; and urged the Governor to appoint people from northern Illinois in order to strengthen the Democratic party in that Republican area.

To Joseph Sam Perry

April 6, 1949

Dear Mr. Perry:

I was delighted with your letter and have taken careful note of your advice. It is very difficult, as you well know, and I get some comfort from the fact that on the few occasions I have wobbled I have made some mistake.

I wish I could take advantage of your suggestion about a better representation in the northern counties. Most of the subordinate patronage has been delegated so much that I have little knowledge of what has been going on, and I should welcome any help you can give me in that direction, either as to names of people to replace promptly or as to candidates who may not have passed the screening committee whom I could well consider.

You were good to write to me, and I hope you do it often.

Sincerely yours,

Mrs. Carlos Salamanca was with the U.S. Delegation to the United Nations Preparatory Commission in London in 1945 when Stevenson was head of that delegation. On April 5, 1949, she wrote him with news of herself and other personalities at the UN at Lake Success, New York, and told him that a group of students from Rockford College had come into her office. When they learned she knew the Governor they became excited and told her she must write and tell him to veto the Broyles Bill.[86]

---

[86] For the state antisubversive legislation, see note 46, above.

To Mrs. Carlos Salamanca

April 6, 1949

Dear Janet:

You were an angel to write me, and it was good to hear from you again. As usual you have that happy faculty of packing more news in a short space than anyone I know.

We had a good evening with the Stonemans,[87] but unhappily it was all too brief and too much preoccupied with Illinois due to the presence of other people — who plague my life continually. I think you are right and that Bill will be happier back in the newspaper business. I have a feeling he felt that he had served his usefulness with Mr. Lie.[88]

Reading between the lines, I can only assume that you are flourishing and still happy with your job. I hope so, for God knows as things get worse the UN gets more and more important, it seems to me.

Ellen and John Fell are in Libertyville and the other two boys are away at school, the oldest one at Harvard and the second one at the Choate School in Connecticut — the latter now enjoying the mumps!

I wish I could be in New York for at least a glimpse of the General Assembly, but that world of yours gets more distant for me every week as the horrors of my own job multiply.

Remember me to Carlos, and Bill Agar,[89] and don't forget me yourself!

Yours,

To Alicia Patterson [90]

April 11, 1949

. . . And now its Monday morning at 8 o'clock and I'm in my plane winging thru the bright spring sky back to Springfield and my miseries.[91] I take off from a war born auxiliary field just south of your old house and only a few minutes from the farm which makes it all very convenient. I had all day Sunday at home — two sets of tennis in the morning with Ellen Smith and work on my budget in the afternoon plus a canoe ride with my precious John Fell. I love him so much it hurts. And I think he really loves me. . . .

[87] William H. Stoneman, a member of the Chicago *Daily News* foreign service before joining the staff of the Secretary-General of the United Nations. He later returned to the *Daily News*.

[88] Trygve Lie, Secretary-General of the United Nations.

[89] William Agar, then with the Department of Public Information, United Nations.

[90] This handwritten letter is in the possession of Adlai E. Stevenson III.

[91] Stevenson had just been in Chicago.

Stuyvesant Peabody [92] has given me 4 tickets to the Ky Derby with his party May 7 — I think. Luncheon first & afterward to French Lick for the night. Would you & Harry [93] like to come — or you? . . .

There is much to tell you — my constitutional convention resolution comes up for a vote on Wed. in the House. It takes ⅔ & if it carries it will be a great triumph. I've worked like the devil for it. Keep your fingers crossed for me. I'm crushed with the awful job of putting together a balanced budget of 1-¼ billions & writing a message all against a deadline & a million thoughtless people who seem to think I've nothing to do but talk to them. . . .

A

Under the Illinois constitution, the governor may either sign a bill passed by the legislature or use his veto power to prevent its becoming law. He has a third option: If he fails to sign a bill within ten days of its submission to him, the measure automatically becomes law.

On March 29, 1949, House Bill No. 418 was passed by the General Assembly, appropriating $2500 to the State Seditions Activities Investigation Commission. On April 12, Governor Stevenson sent the bill to the Secretary of State for filing without his signature, with this message.[94]

I am letting House Bill 418 become law without my approval. This bill implements a Joint Resolution of the House and Senate to investigate "subversive activities" at The University of Chicago and Roosevelt College [in Chicago].

I doubt the legality of this investigation. "Subversive" means "tending to overthrow." We already have laws in Illinois making it a crime to advocate overthrow of the government by violence or other unlawful means. If the purpose of this investigation is to determine whether these institutions or certain students or professors have violated these laws then the investigations should, it seems to me, be conducted by the courts with full opportunity for defense against specific charges.

I doubt the necessity for this investigation. The Resolution says that a large group of students from these universities appeared in opposition to pending legislation to control subversive activities. It goes on to

[92] A Chicago coal company president who had important mining and racing interests in Illinois. Stevenson appointed him chairman of the Illinois Racing Commission.

[93] Miss Patterson's husband, Harry Guggenheim.

[94] The text is based on a typewritten draft bearing corrections and interlineations in Stevenson's handwriting.

say that "it appears that these students are being indoctrinated with Communistic and other subversive theories." Because some 100 students from institutions numbering 15,000 exercise their rights as citizens to oppose anti-subversive legislation, it hardly follows that they are being indoctrinated with Communism as this Resolution seems to imply.

Nevertheless I am reluctant to interfere with the Legislature's power of investigation. Also, in view of the serious charges, I think The University of Chicago, one of the great centers of learning in the world, and Roosevelt College, a new institution dedicated to education for those of limited means, should now be given an opportunity to be heard. I donot want to stand in the way of a fair and responsible investigation.

I am, accordingly, permitting this appropriation to become law without my signature. I trust that the Commission will conduct the investigation with a scrupulous respect for the rights and reputations of individual citizens, the University of Chicago and Roosevelt College.

Suppression and intimidation are not among the weapons we ought to use in the current warfare of ideas, lest we abandon the very things we seek to preserve. Academic freedom, freedom to think and freedom to speak, are the best antidote to Communism and tyranny.

To Alicia Patterson [95]

April 15, 1949

. . . I thought you would enjoy your distinguished cousin's comments [96] on my heartbreaking effort to give the people at least a chance to vote on whether they would like a constitutional convention — not a new const. just a convention to draft a new const. which would then have to be submitted to the people.

I guess my honeymoon with that medieval SOB is over & its OK by me!

I'm now crushed under the damnable budget. Its the worst headache yet & I have to deliver it to a joint session with radio next Tuesday — . . .

A

Friday — in dreadful haste.

---

[95] This handwritten letter is in the possession of Adlai E. Stevenson III.

[96] Robert R. McCormick's Chicago *Tribune*, April 20, 1949, denounced Governor Stevenson as a spendthrift and asserted: "A vote for 'con-con' is a vote for a state income tax. The Stevenson budget makes that certain."

To Mrs. Edison Dick [97]

April 21, 1949

. . . Its late. I'm in bed after a legislative dinner and a concert by a really remarkable High School band from Elmhurst at the Armory. I had to do the usual autographing, make a little speech & now I'm alone at last. . . .

I'm glad you thought well of the budget message [98] — it was the worst ordeal yet, and then I had to fly up to Chicago last night & speak at a bond drive dinner and then fly back afterward, arriving at 11:45 A.M. Ellen [Stevenson] & her mother arrived this afternoon — and return tomorrow morning. No talk.

I'll be coming up Sat. I think for over Sunday. Hope you'll come back with me — bring your men folk if they want to come. . . .

Ho Hum — I think my head will split what with the myriad of things here that are accumulating each day. . . .

Would you and Eddie [99] like to fly down to the Derby with me on May 7 — Stuyvesant Peabodys party?

Governor Stevenson and Lloyd Lewis were the closest of friends and neighbors for many years. Lewis was a reporter-editor for the Chicago Daily News, *a columnist for the Chicago* Sun, *and biographer of General U. S. Grant and of General William T. Sherman. He enjoyed drafting a message he thought the Governor might use in vetoing a bill passed by the legislature (the so-called "Cat Bill") and sent it along with a note on April 21. About midnight that same day Lloyd Lewis died suddenly and unexpectedly. The news came as a shattering blow to Stevenson.*

The funeral was held two days later on April 23, 1949, in the Lewises' garden on the banks of the Des Plaines River, with services of Quaker simplicity. Author-playwright Marc Connelly and Stevenson were asked to speak. The Governor declined, saying that he was emotionally not prepared, but after Connelly finished he made the following impromptu remarks.[100]

[97] This handwritten letter is in the possession of Mrs. Dick.

[98] On April 19, 1949, Stevenson delivered in person his message accompanying the budget he presented to the General Assembly. The message is not reprinted here since the Governor presented many of the same general points in his radio reports to the citizens of Illinois on May 23, 1949, and July 7, 1949, below.

[99] Mr. Dick.

[100] Mrs. Quincy Wright arranged to have the services recorded for Mrs. Lewis's sister, who could not be there. The text is based on a carbon copy of the stenographer's transcript.

I have been asked to share in these farewells to a friend.

I think it is a good day for this meeting. It is April now and all life is being renewed on the bank of this river that he loved so well. I think we will all be happy that it happened on this day, here by the river with the spring sky so clear, and the west wind so warm and fresh. I think we will all be the better for this day and this meeting together.

He was my neighbor. He was the neighbor of many of you. He was a very good neighbor; quick in time of misfortune, always present in times of mirth and happiness — and need.

I think Mr. Connelly was right when he said he was the most successful man he ever knew. I don't know much about the riches of life, and I suspect few of you have found the last definition. But I do know that friendship is the greatest enrichment that I have found.

Everyone loved this man. He enriched others and was enriched. Everyone was his friend — everyone who knew him or read him. Why was that? Why is he the most successful man that many of us will ever know? Our answers will differ. For me it was his humility, gentleness, wisdom and wit, all in one. And most of all a great compassionate friendliness.

I think it will always be April in our memory of him. It will always be a bright, fresh day full of the infinite variety and the promise of new life. Perhaps nothing has gone at all — perhaps only the *embodiment* of the thing — tender, precious to all of us — a friendship that is immortal and doesn't pass along. It will be renewed for me, much as I know it will for all of you, each spring.

On April 23, 1949, Governor Stevenson signed one of his first veto messages. A small but devoted group of bird-lovers were able to have a bill introduced in the legislature designed to protect birds by restraining cats. In previous years it was passed by one house, only to be turned down by the other. In 1949 it passed both houses and the decision was finally shifted to the Governor. Stevenson's message returning the measure became known as the "Cat Bill Veto" and received widespread publicity because of its wit and good humor.[101] On April 27, 1949, the Chicago Daily News *stated "Many Adlaiphiles immediately proclaimed it one of the noble pronouncements of our time, comparable to the boldest state documents from the pen of F.D.R. or Winston Churchill. . . . Mr. Stevenson did no pussyfooting on pussy's perambulations. He did not seek to make a cat's paw out of the Supreme Court by citing de-*

[101] In the final version of the message, Stevenson used very little of the material sent to him by Lloyd Lewis.

cisions of dubious relevancy. He categorically assumed full responsibility for his momentous decision. He did not assert that the bill's effort to restrict felines to lives of sedentary domesticity was a violation of the Constitution. He invoked a higher law — the law of Nature."

To the Honorable, the Members of the Senate of the Sixty-sixth General Assembly [102]

April 23, 1949

I herewith return, without my approval, Senate Bill No. 93 entitled, "An Act to Provide Protection to Insectivorous Birds by Restraining Cats." This is the so-called "Cat Bill." I veto and withhold my approval from this Bill for the following reasons:

It would impose fines on owners or keepers who permitted their cats to run at large off their premises. It would permit any person to capture, or call upon the police to pick up and imprison, cats at large. It would permit the use of traps. The bill would have statewide application — on farms, in villages, and in metropolitan centers.

This legislation has been introduced in the past several sessions of the Legislature, and it has, over the years, been the source of much comment — not all of which has been in a serious vein. It may be that the General Assembly has now seen fit to refer it to one who can view it with a fresh outlook. Whatever the reasons for passage at this session, I cannot believe there is a widespread public demand for this law or that it could, as a practical matter be enforced.

Furthermore, I cannot agree that it should be the declared public policy of Illinois that a cat visiting a neighbor's yard or crossing the highways is a public nuisance. It is in the nature of cats to do a certain amount of unescorted roaming. Many live with their owners in apartments or other restricted premises, and I doubt if we want to make their every brief foray an opportunity for a small game hunt by zealous citizens — with traps or otherwise. I am afraid this Bill could only create discord, recrimination and enmity. Also consider the owner's dilemma: To escort a cat abroad on a leash is against the nature of the cat, and to permit it to venture forth for exercise unattended into a night of new dangers is against the nature of the owner. Moreover, cats perform useful service, particularly in rural areas, in combatting rodents — work they necessarily perform alone and without regard for property lines.

We are all interested in protecting certain varieties of birds. That cats

[102] *Veto Messages of Adlai E. Stevenson, Governor of Illinois, on Senate and House Bills Passed by the 66th General Assembly of Illinois* (published by the State of Illinois, 1949), pp. 8–9.

destroy some birds, I well know, but I believe this legislation would further but little the worthy cause to which its proponents give such unselfish effort. The problem of cat versus bird is as old as time. If we attempt to resolve it by legislation who knows but what we may be called upon to take sides as well in the age old problems of dog versus cat, bird versus bird, or even bird versus worm. In my opinion, the State of Illinois and its local governing bodies already have enough to do without trying to control feline delinquency.

For these reasons, and not because I love birds the less or cats the more, I veto and withhold my approval from Senate Bill No. 93.

Respectfully,

Although Stevenson never advocated a state income tax, it was widely rumored that he favored such a tax. His mail on the subject was sometimes misguided. On April 8, 1949, Wylie G. Okenson, of Chicago, wrote protesting the Governor's advocacy of a constitutional convention that would permit a state income tax, and also objecting to any tampering with the bill of rights of the Illinois constitution.

To Wylie G. Okenson

April 25, 1949

Dear Mr. Okenson:

Thank you for your letter. I have never proposed a state income tax nor have I ever proposed tampering with the Bill of Rights. I am afraid you read the [Chicago] Tribune and not what I say. Indeed, I wonder if you know why you are for the Old Constitution, which makes government so inefficient and costly in Illinois.

At all events, I am delighted that you are interested in the subject. The more people who become interested, the more certain a convention becomes, and I hope you will join us too.

With kind regards, I am.

Sincerely yours,

Nils K. G. Tholand, of New York City, accompanied Stevenson in 1943 as a member of a Foreign Economic Administration team to make a survey of economic conditions in Italy. He wrote the Governor that he had read the Saturday Evening Post *article entitled "Rebel in Illinois," and that it had aroused "nostalgic memories." He said he was just leaving New York for Geneva, Switzerland, to rebel against the U.S. Tariff*

Act of 1930; and added that he might pay a visit to Stevenson's "castle" in Springfield.

To Nils K. G. Tholand

April 25, 1949

Dear Nils:

I didn't recognize anything about myself in that article in the Saturday Evening Post — and neither did you. Anyway, we are both rebels and I only wish I could pick up the cudgels for tariff reform again alongside such a doughty warrior as yourself.

You will be welcome in my "castle" — indeed, you will have a hell of a time getting out of it.

Yours,

R. Keith Kane, a friend of Stevenson's since their Harvard Law School days sent him an article entitled "Illinois Tests the Liberals," from the Economist *of London,[103] and inquired when the Governor might visit New York.*

To R. Keith Kane

April 25, 1949

Dear Keith:

You were good to send me the clipping from the Economist. I wish it had a larger circulation in Illinois!

I see no prospect of visiting New York. Indeed, I have all the sensations of the man in the iron mask and the only daylight I see is through a window. Why did you ever talk me into this!

My love to Amanda.[104]

Yours,

P.S. If any of the Kane tribe are traveling west this summer, you will avoid serious trouble by stopping here for a visit in my gloomy mansion.

AES

Stevenson read in the April 20, 1949, issue of the Chicago Tribune *that retired Admiral Alan G. Kirk had been appointed U.S. ambassador to the Soviet Union.*

[103] January 29, 1949, p. 193.
[104] Mrs. Kane.

To Alan G. Kirk

April 25, 1949

Dear Alan:

I seldom get any information of value or importance from the Chicago Tribune. But you are the exception!

Nothing has pleased me more in a very long while than the announcement of your assignment to Moscow, although no doubt Lydia [105] has the usual misgivings. Everything I have heard hereabouts would warm your heart and I have a strong feeling that you can bring something of what we all pray for to that post and our relationships with the Russians.

I cannot say I envy you, and even my present seat feels more comfortable when I think of yours.

With love to Lydia, and breathless hopes for this appalling mission —

Yours,

Fred D. Fagg, Jr., president of the University of Southern California, wrote Stevenson on April 18, 1949, sending belated congratulations on his election, and mentioned that he had read the April 2 Saturday Evening Post *story about the Governor. He expressed pride in Stevenson's splendid record, predicting an even larger opportunity for him in the future.*

To Fred D. Fagg, Jr.

April 25, 1949

Dear Fred:

You were good to write me and I am most grateful for your thoughtful letter.

I have heard about you from time to time — and always with envy! You wouldn't like to trade jobs, would you?

Sincerely yours,

Miss Helen Kirkpatrick, special correspondent for the Chicago Daily News, *had expected to visit the Governor in Springfield but was called to Washington instead. She wrote to express her disappointment, saying she was off to London and Paris, and that she expected to join the State Department when she returned. She reported having heard in Chicago*

[105] Mrs. Kirk.

widespread and enthusiastic approval of Stevenson's performance as governor.

To Helen Kirkpatrick

April 25, 1949

Dear Helen:

Your letter has mollified me, but only a little! And now you are off to London and Paris, and then the State Department. I have enough to think about without trying to dope all this out, and whenever a more lengthy report of your eccentric behavior is out it will be by His Imperial Highness, the Groaning Governor of Illinois!

Yours,

Ronald Tree, former Conservative Member of Parliament, first met Stevenson in London in 1942. In subsequent years Mr. Tree and his second wife, Marietta, became extremely close friends of the Governor. Mr. Tree wrote Stevenson from Chicago on April 21, 1949, that "I hear on all sides what a good job you are doing despite tremendous difficulties. Stick to it & we shall all proudly see you in Washington one of these days."

To Ronald Tree

April 25, 1949

Dear Ronnie:

I have just now run across your note of April 21 and I am more than a little disappointed that we did not see you and Marietta on this visit. I flew up to Chicago early Saturday morning for Lloyd [Lewis]'s funeral and we might at least have had a word by telephone.

This has been a frightful ordeal and I only wish you had both been down here for a night to get a taste of it. Bear it in mind for the next trip — and give my love to Marietta.

Yours,

One citizen wrote Stevenson protesting what he termed the Governor's program to tax the state heavily in order to make grants to municipalities. He felt that the municipalities should raise their own funds.

To E. F. Lawrence

April 26, 1949

Dear Mr. Lawrence:

Thank you for your letter. Of course, I am sure you realize that the practice of state aid to municipalities started many, many years ago and most large states support the common schools far better than Illinois. I have no program to "tax this state heavily in order to make grants to municipalities" beyond extending the coverage of the sales tax to include service businesses. I agree with you heartily that towns and cities should provide their own revenue. I hope they will find ways of doing so before we have any general revolt of real estate owners.

Sincerely yours,

Walter V. Schaefer, who accompanied the Governor to Springfield, expected to return to his teaching position at Northwestern Law School in the autumn of 1949, and Stevenson hoped to persuade his friend Carl McGowan to take Schaefer's place as his chief aide and counselor.

To Carl McGowan

April 30, 1949

Dear Carl:

Many thanks for your note. I am still hopeful that we can work out some sort of arrangement which will find you carrying my weary head about in your pocket, and I hope we can talk about it one of these days.

Yours,

To Irving Dilliard [106]

April 30, 1949

Dear Irving:

It was as sad a day as I can remember, but it was all very simple and in Quaker style. Marc Connelly made a beautiful talk, and I followed with a few choked and incoherent remarks. Ellen [Stevenson] reports Kathryn [107] well and in good heart. I hope she will come down and stay here with me for a while when she gets pulled together.

You didn't miss much at the press dinner, but I hope you will find it

[106] Editor of the St. Louis *Post-Dispatch*.
[107] Mrs. Lloyd Lewis.

[78]

convenient to come over for an evening some time when we can have a respectable talk about all that ails the State of Illinois — as long as you don't seem loath to take on two states!

I was delighted with your editorial about Lloyd. It put things and his stature in a fitting measurement. Also, your quote from the Courier-Journal was a help, and I had not seen it before. I am afraid Barry Bingham [108] is neglecting me.

Ellen sends her best.

Yours,

To Harry S. Truman [109]

April 30, 1949

Dear Mr. President:

I am tentatively planning to fly to Washington on Saturday morning, May 21, to attend the Gridiron Dinner that night. Because I remember so well your gracious suggestion that I stop in to see you, I am taking the liberty of suggesting the possibility of a moment's visit on that Saturday afternoon, if it is convenient.

I have no business to discuss, and I am loath to even suggest an appointment, so please do not hesitate to postpone it to a more convenient time.[110]

Faithfully yours,

Clay Judson, of Lake Forest, Illinois, wrote the Governor to commend him on his "Cat Bill" veto. "You correctly handled what might have been a touchy question with a light touch and delicious humor." He also expressed his appreciation of the Governor's remarks at Lloyd Lewis's funeral.

To Clay Judson

April 30, 1949

Dear Clay:

You were good to write me, and I am happy that you found the "Cat Bill" veto in proper vein. It was not easy to keep it restrained!

[108] President and editor of the Louisville *Courier-Journal.*

[109] The original is in the President's Personal File, the Harry S. Truman Library, Independence, Missouri.

[110] President Truman replied on May 10, 1949, saying that he was looking forward to seeing Stevenson and asking him to come to Blair House, where the Trumans were living temporarily, on Saturday, May 21. The editors were not permitted to quote directly from any of Truman's letters to Stevenson.

The Lloyd Lewis business took me without advance notice and I was in a childish state of disorder. I am happy that you didn't find it as bad as I fear it was.

I wish you and Sylvia [111] could come down and stay a night with me sometime. If she is at large, tell her to let me know any time.

Yours,

Edwin A. Lahey, a Washington columnist for the Chicago Daily News, *had known Stevenson for many years. He wrote that he had been "on the New York run with the Communists for a couple of months. . . . The death of Lloyd Lewis was a real shock."*

To Edwin A. Lahey

April 30, 1949

Dear Ed:

Thanks for your letter. It was a sad, sad day on the sandy banks of the DesPlaines when we all said goodbye to Lloyd. But the sky was clear and the buds popping, and I think you would have liked the simple Quaker ceremony, with Marc Connelly as the speaker, and Stevenson as a poor second.

I don't know why you have to chase Reds around New York. According to the menagerie around the State House, Illinois is alive with them, and I gather in the opinion of a few citizens of our domain that they also reside in the Executive Mansion.

So you will be more than welcome!

Yours,

R. D. Dexheimer, superintendent of the Temperance League of Illinois, had supported Stevenson during his 1948 campaign but was dismayed when the Governor appeared in Peoria to cut a ribbon opening the Pabst Brewing Company's new plant. In his letter to the Governor he said that two million adults would be asking him questions about it.

To R. D. Dexheimer

April 30, 1949

Dear Mr. Dexheimer:

Thank you for your very candid letter about the hour I spent at the Pabst Brewery Company opening in Peoria. I am sure you realize that

[111] Mrs. Judson.

I have also to consider labor and industrial development in Illinois, as well as friendship. Yesterday I went to Peoria and dedicated in a far more impressive ceremony the new Caterpillar Plant.

This is not to ask you to excuse my visit to Pabst. It was made against my own judgment and strong objection. I shall always appreciate your candid comments, and I hope I can merit your sympathetic interest as well.

Sincerely yours,

During the campaign in 1948, the practice of payroll padding was exposed. In county after county there were those on the state payroll who made no pretense of doing any work for the state. The practice of subsidizing many editors and publishers of newspapers throughout the state was also exposed.

On April 25, 1949, H. R. Tolle, of Mattoon, Illinois, wrote Stevenson, sending him a local newspaper article listing some of the "payrollers" from the prior administration. These included, for example, "Bill Mc-Cauley of the Olney Daily Mail who received $41,281 from Feb. 1, 1941, to Jan. 15 last. He also received the use of a Buick and a generous expense account."

"As a taxpayer, I wish I could be assured by some one," wrote Mr. Tolle, "that the recent record breaking state budget presented to the Legislature does not carry any such apparently phony jobs as these mentioned."

To H. R. Tolle

April 30, 1949

Dear Mr. Tolle:

I have your letter of April 25, and share your concern for the elimination of unnecessary State employees. I think you will be pleased to hear that we have thus far succeeded in eliminating some 1,300 positions. Total reduction in personnel is far more than that, but some of them will have to be replaced for seasonal work on highways and also in the State institutions where there is a dangerous shortage of attendants.

I hope I can succeed in eliminating every unnecessary employee and that people like yourself will let me know if they find any in my administration.

Sincerely yours,

[*81*]

It has been said that Governor Stevenson felt that the failure of his marriage was the greatest defeat of his life. The following excerpt from a letter to Jane Dick refers to his impending divorce.

To Mrs. Edison Dick [112]

May 2, 1949

. . . I wish I could buck myself up — or had someone else to buck up. I really never thought anything could hurt quite as much as this has. But I *am* emancipated — and there is nothing to worry about whatever. . . .

To Alicia Patterson [113]

May 1, 1949

. . . The [Edison] Dicks came down for the week end and brought their little boy and my enchanting John Fell and I took off a whole 24 hours from my ghastly routine. This afternoon we all went to the opening of the baseball season and I had to walk out on the diamond say the inevitable "few words" and then pitch a ball from the box to the Mayor of Springfield at the plate. I was scared to death — but my arm *didn't* fly off and the ball got there!

. . . I wish you hadn't mentioned Lloyd Lewis. He was my dearest friend — my comfort and encouragement and help in need more than I can tell you. I loved him like I've loved no other man. Catherine [114] asked me to speak at his funeral — I choked up like a silly ass and made a fool of myself on top of everything else. I shall never have such another friend. . . .

A

Harold H. Helm, president of Chemical Bank and Trust Company, New York, wrote the Governor that while attending a bankers' convention he had talked with their mutual friend Solomon B. Smith, executive vice president of the Northern Trust Company of Chicago. Helm reported that Smith's admiration for the Governor was so great he was about to turn Democrat, and that Smith had confided there was no office in the country that Stevenson could not acceptably hold.

---

[112] This handwritten letter is in the possession of Mrs. Dick.
[113] This handwritten letter is in the possession of Adlai E. Stevenson III.
[114] Kathryn Lewis.

To Harold H. Helm

May 3, 1949

Dear Harold:

It was good to hear from you again, and I am gratified to hear that the conservative Northern Trust Company has some regard for any Democrat!

Best regards.

Sincerely yours,

During legislative sessions, the Governor spent the greater share of his time at the capitol, but there were times when it was imperative for him to schedule appointments and meetings at his mansion offices. Guy E. Reed, vice president of the Harris Trust and Savings Bank and chairman of the Chicago Crime Commission, wrote to Stevenson on May 4 that there seemed to be some discouragement, and even resentment, that members of the legislature did not have easy access to his office, and that he did not call in the leaders among the independents frequently enough. He also suggested that the Governor talk with Representative Bernice Van der Vries, who, although a Republican, admired the Governor's program as well as his philosophy, and supported him on the constitutional convention issue in spite of great pressure from some of her own party leaders. Reed was particularly eager to get certain bills onto the Senate floor, and expressed the opinion that if the bill lengthening the grand jury term in Cook County were passed it would be extremely helpful in breaking up a gang who were the chief opponents of good government.

To Guy E. Reed

May 5, 1949

Dear Guy:

Many thanks for your letter. I know precisely what you mean. It has been more than I could handle, and I am afraid I have missed many opportunities to cultivate some people usefully. The reason is time and the appalling amount of work I have to get out.

At all events, I had a good talk with Bernice Van der Vries only yesterday, and I have had in all of the Democrats who voted against the Crime Commission Bills, one by one. You will see some different results, I am confident, when they come up next week.[115]

[115] The Crime Commission Bills passed the Senate but were lost by a narrow margin in the House when they came to a vote in June.

You were good to write me, and I hope you will do it more often. It helps.

Sincerely yours,

To Alicia Patterson [116]

Sunday [probably May 8, 1949]

. . . It was a gala day at the Derby. I even won some money. A new experience. Today we've played golf and I've had about the first 24 hours of solid holiday since my troubles commenced. . . .

Now for a bar B-que and then to Springfield by air and back to my everlasting travail.

. . . Get at your tennis. I think we're going to have a lot at Libertyville this summer. I hope to be there much of July. . . .

A

Carl Sandburg wrote Stevenson on May 4, 1949, "It's hard to lose Lloyd Lewis. Your loss is great. His affection for you and his admiration of you ran away deep. He could talk on and on about you, keen and warm. . . . He knew the best heart of both you and me away deep."

To Carl Sandburg

May 9, 1949

Dear Carl:

Your letter is here and I am very grateful for it. It will be my best reminder of him — should I ever need any!

It was a windy, bright spring morning on the river bank and a very sad day. Sometime we will talk about him.

Yours,

Harold C. Havighurst, dean of Northwestern University Law School, wrote Stevenson suggesting that the Governor and Walter Schaefer take a day off to play on the faculty softball team against members of the Law Review. He added that he had enjoyed and approved some of Stevenson's messages to the legislature — cats included.

[116] This handwritten letter is in the possession of Adlai E. Stevenson III. It was written from French Lick, Indiana.

To Harold C. Havighurst

May 6, 1949

Dear Harold:

As always I am on the side of youth — hence, I will do my best to withhold the Faculty Ace. Moreover, Schaefer is in no condition to play baseball or anything else — except politics!

I am glad you approve my recent literary efforts. They seem to be highly non-productive.

Yours,

Columnist Doris Fleeson visited Stevenson in Springfield. On returning to Washington, D.C., she wrote him that Illinois Senator Scott Lucas was in the hospital suffering from an ulcer and fatigue.

To Doris Fleeson

May 10, 1949

Dear Doris:

Many thanks for your note. Paul Douglas [117] was here yesterday and confirmed what you said about Senator Lucas.

It was a more than agreeable interlude and I hope you will come back again. I felt a little mortified about being so preoccupied with my own affairs when I had such a rare opportunity to learn from you something of the "outside" world.

By all means send me your remarks on the welfare state. Meanwhile, I am enclosing mine on the "Cat Bill," lest you have any doubt about the extent of the legislature's welfare program in Illinois!

Yours,

To Mrs. Lloyd Lewis

May 16, 1949

Dear Kathryn:

Wally Schaefer gave me the package on the plane yesterday.[118] The papers, photo and dress buttons I need not tell you will be among my dearest possessions, and you were thoughtful and good to let me have

[117] Democratic U.S. senator from Illinois.
[118] Mrs. Lewis had sent some memorabilia of her husband to Stevenson by Walter Schaefer.

them. If you should run across a *spare* copy of his editorial obituary on FDR in the Daily News I would like to include that too.[119]

I hope you will decide to come down here and enjoy a little languid luxury for a while.

Affectionately,

Mrs. Smith wrote Stevenson in May, 1949, that "Along about this time of year . . . we start thinking of Desbarats [120] and the peace and complete escape from the woes of the world. I don't know what you plan to do this summer but we think that you should also think of Desbarats. . . . You don't have to decide now . . . but you must start thinking about how blue the water is and how clear the air is and the fishing with John Fell."

To Mrs. Hermon D. Smith [121]

May 19, 1949

Dear Ellen:

Why did you ever write me that wretched letter? Start dreaming! I shan't dream of anything else — and me with a Legislature on my hands!

You are an angel — as always — and don't be surprised if I land at the Soo some morning and call up just two hours ahead of time. And with — I hope — some boys in tow.

Affectionately,

ADLAI

William Burry, a Chicago lawyer, wrote the Governor on May 10, 1949, that he had just learned that one house of the legislature had appropriated $5700 for a new automobile for the lieutenant governor. In his opinion nothing could cost that much except a Cadillac limousine. Although he had nothing against Lieutenant Governor Dixon, whom he considered to be a "good guy," he hoped Stevenson would be able to prevent this extravagance.

[119] Chicago *Daily News,* April 13, 1945.

[120] The Smiths' vacation retreat, Thorne Camp, in the Canadian wilds at Desbarats, Ontario. The story of Stevenson's visits there is told by Mr. Smith in "Politics and R & R," in *As We Knew Adlai,* pp. 34–41.

[121] The original is in the possession of Hermon D. Smith.

To William Burry

May 19, 1949

Dear Bill:

I have your letter, and I am sure Dixon was as much embarrassed as anyone. But this seems to be an old practice of the Legislature. Moreover, there also seems to be a story about the car he was supposed to inherit from his predecessor which the latter carried away with him. This in confidence — more to follow.

Yours,

To Mrs. Edison Dick

May 19, 1949

Dear Jane:

Things are stealing up on us from all sides — several that I think you could help with in case you have any spare days. Also, Fred Hoehler [122] was over the other night and baffled me with the multitude of his ideas. I think he would like to get a little "special assisting," and I am sure I would like to get some sorting out of what comes first.

Tell Eddie [123] I am most grateful for his painstaking and comprehensive explanation of the world government legislation in the various states. At least I understand what is going on, and I am disposing of Fyke Farmer's letter along the line he suggested. Some day we should discuss this, although I doubt if there is much that can be done in Illinois at this session.[124]

I enclose a letter and I would be glad to have Eddie's comments before I discuss it with Dr. Cross.[125]

Sincerely yours,

George D. Kells, chairman of the Democratic State Central Committee, wrote Stevenson on May 10, 1949, sending him an article entitled

[122] Director of the Department of Public Welfare.

[123] Mr. Dick.

[124] Mr. Dick sent the Governor information as to action recommended by the United World Federalists and taken by various state legislatures. Mr. Farmer was an attorney in Nashville, Tennessee, active in liberal and civil rights causes, who had urged the Dicks to become members of the United World Federalists. Letter from Mrs. Dick to Walter Johnson, July 10, 1968.

[125] Mr. Dick was a member of the Board of Public Health Advisors, appointed by Stevenson. He does not recall what the letter was about. Dr. Roland Cross, director of the Department of Public Health, was a holdover from the Green administration.

"Founder of Jocism," from the May issue of the Catholic Mind. *Mr. Kells explained that Jocism meant "Young Christian Workers," a movement that had become powerful in Belgium and France. He pointed out that the Church had lost contact with the proletarians — that when a worker entered the seminary he seemed to lose touch with his people; and that in politics there was some similarity. He expressed the opinion that the Democrats were losing contact with workers in the large cities and states.*

To George D. Kells

May 23, 1949

Dear George:

I have read the article on Jocism with much interest. I believe that the Moral Rearmament movement is attempting to do something of the same by working more with labor leaders than with labor itself. Actually I feel that in the political arena we are closer to the working people than the church has been. All the same I agree that we could do much better, and I hope we can discuss it in a more leisurely fashion sometime.

Yours,

P.S. The Des Moines Conference,[126] although partisan in purpose, has something of the same apostolical idea of bringing the farm program direct to the farmer.

A.E.S.

On May 23, 1949, Governor Stevenson made a radio report to the people of Illinois, a practice he followed periodically throughout his administration.[127] On this occasion he reported on the progress of the legislation he had proposed in his inaugural address in January.

The last time I had an opportunity to speak over the radio to a large audience was March 9. I am grateful for this further invitation to talk to you about the legislation being enacted — and not being enacted — here in Springfield by the Illinois Legislature.

On March 9 I told you that we would need some changes in our Constitution in order to meet the needs of today; that we should have more equitable property taxation; more home rule for cities; that our repre-

---

[126] A Midwest Democratic conference, attended by three hundred national committeemen and state chairmen from sixteen states, which had, among other objectives, the formulation of a program to attract the farm vote.

[127] The text is taken from a mimeograph copy of a news release.

sentation in the Legislature was unfair; that there was too much waste and duplication in government throughout Illinois; and that to have good, efficient and economical government, our Constitution of 1870, which it has been so difficult to amend, should be revised by a convention of delegates selected for that purpose who would submit such revisions to the people for acceptance or rejection.

I told you that I was very anxious for the Legislature to at least give the people a chance to vote on calling such a Constitutional Convention. Thereafter, more than three-fifths of the members of the House of Representatives did vote to give the people a chance — the Democrats almost unanimously. But the resolution required a two-thirds vote and we fell a few short. If I had been willing to trade off other desirable legislation it would have passed, but I don't think that is right and I don't believe you think so either.[128] So the resolution to submit the question of calling a convention to the people failed, and the prospect for modernizing government in Illinois in an orderly, comprehensive way to help us solve problems which affect every taxpayer has been postponed.

Almost as disappointing was the vote on this question which affects everyone in the country or the city and is not a political question. I had hoped that the welfare of the people and the common desire for better government would raise the issue above partisanship. Some of the Republicans in the House supported the Constitutional Convention resolution, and I am very grateful to them for voting their convictions on a proposition which has been supported by almost every Republican governor in the past 30 years. But far more of them voted against it; some even voted against it who voted for it two years ago under a Republican governor.

When the convention resolution was defeated I promptly endorsed the Gateway Amendment,[129] introduced by the Republicans, because I be-

---

[128] Two Democrats and four Republicans, all members of Chicago's West Side Bloc, voted against the resolution. Stevenson was approached with the proposal that they would support it if he would withdraw his active support from the Crime Commission bills to extend the length of grand jury sessions in Cook County. This he declined to do. Later he was approached with another deal: In exchange for his promise not to veto legislation permitting dog racing in Illinois he would have the support of the West Side Bloc on "Con-Con." This he also turned down. To his friends the Hermon Smiths, he expressed his view that consent to the offers would have meant giving decisive power to the worst political elements in the state, and correctly predicted that he would lose both the crime bills and Con-Con. See Davis, *A Prophet in His Own Country,* pp. 344–345.

[129] This amendment, which was passed by the 1949 legislature and adopted by the people of Illinois at the 1950 election, permitted up to three proposed amendments to the state constitution to be placed before the voters in a given election, instead of only one as formerly. More importantly, it allowed the enactment of any amendment by a two-thirds vote of those voting on the amendment, rather than requiring, as in the

lieve in constitutional reforms more than party victories. The Gateway proposition has now been adopted by both Houses, with almost unanimous Democratic support, and I sincerely hope the people will approve it at the 1950 election. I will do everything I can to insure its adoption, although it has been defeated five times in the past, and although I seriously doubt if there is much hope of really fundamental constitutional progress through this method of patchwork amendment.

But it is certainly better than nothing, and there is at least a possibility that some much needed changes can be achieved pending the time when we can have a Constitutional Convention and do in Illinois what more progressive states like Missouri and New Jersey have done very recently.

This session of the Legislature, which began in January, ends on June 30. There are only about 30 legislative days remaining to complete its job. To date 126 bills have been passed as against 54 at this time in the last session. There is an enormous amount of work to be done in the remaining days, because so many more bills have been introduced in this session than in the last.

Among the first bills which the Legislature passed was the bill to restrict cats from wandering off an owner's premises. As is often the case, this bill which was fraught with so much human interest, attracted far more attention, both in Illinois and throughout the country, than an important measure like constitutional reform. And people are still writing me all the way from Maine to Texas. I felt obliged to veto this bill because, as I said, it is in the nature of cats to do a certain amount of unescorted roaming. Their useful work in combatting rats and mice they perform alone and without regard to property lines. In my opinion the State of Illinois and the local police already have enough to do without trying to control feline delinquency.

An important bill which has passed the House and is on its way to the Senate is a Fair Employment Practices Act to end discrimination on account of race, religion, color or national origin in obtaining or keeping a job. This bill creates a commission to investigate unfair practices and to resolve them by conference and conciliation. If that fails, the commission may hold a public hearing. If its orders to end unfair practices are not obeyed it can seek remedy in a court.

There is much opposition to this bill on the ground that a man should be entitled to hire and fire whomever he pleases, and that morals and racial prejudice cannot be regulated by law. There is, of course, much

---

past, a majority of those voting in the election. (Cf. note 59, above.) The first Gateway Amendment was introduced in 1892, and four subsequent attempts had also failed. *Illinois Blue Book, 1949–1950* (printed by authority of the State of Illinois), pp. 291–293.

merit to these objections, and I wish no such legislation was necessary. But I cannot concede that the alarm and dire prophecies of the opponents are justified. In other states like New York, New Jersey and Connecticut which have adopted more stringent FEPC laws under Republican governors, these laws have not caused any important difficulties for employers, and I do not anticipate any in Illinois. Moreover, there is economic discrimination and prejudice against Negroes, Jews, Catholics and people of various national origins. The ideals we so proudly proclaim cannot be reconciled with such discrimination upon racial or religious grounds. For one American to discriminate against another because of color or religion is a blow at the very foundation of our democracy, which is faith in equality of opportunity for all. We must not play into the hands of the Communists by giving them propaganda material about democratic hypocrisy and further injure democratic prestige and sincerity with the myriads of brown and yellow peoples of Asia.

The quality of liberty is not divisible. When we deny its privileges to another, we place our own in jeopardy. And finally, we know that every human being is created in the image of the Almighty and by the same token is entitled to an equal opportunity for life, liberty and the pursuit of happiness.

I think this legislation is not only simple justice, but will actually strengthen our economy and our society by reducing prejudice and discrimination and their ugly offspring — racial tension.

Another important bill which I have caused to be introduced will take the State Police force out of politics and establish a police merit system for the first time in Illinois. During the campaign I promised to do this if I could. And after months of work and study with experts in police administration, I think we have proposed legislation which will be a permanent and important contribution to better government in Illinois.

Most of you are acquainted with the political control of our State Police that has prevailed in the past. With every change of administration, the personnel of the force has changed. The policemen have been picked by politicians as part of the spoils of victory. Consequently the loyalty of the man has been divided between the politician who got him the job and his superiors. In many cases unqualified men have been appointed to the force, and for the qualified, conscientious man there has been little hope of making a career in the State Police. The men, the system, the public and our purses suffer accordingly. This is not a good way to run anything, especially a police force.

To evidence our sincerity, and in an effort to gain non-partisan support for this legislation, we have proposed to split the force as evenly as possible between Republicans and Democrats before giving it over to non-political control. So the legislation provides that prior to January 1, 1951, all appointments and promotions shall be made in such a manner as to achieve equality between the two major political parties.

After that, all applicants would be selected by a police Merit Board without regard to politics on the basis of rigid physical, mental and moral tests and the successful completion of police training school courses. Promotions will be made by the Board on a man's record in the service, and no policeman could be removed or demoted without a hearing by the Board. Partisan political activity would be prohibited, and it would be unlawful to solicit campaign contributions from members on the force.

One hundred young men selected on rigid standards from about 300 applicants have already graduated from a police school set up at the State Fair Grounds. I went to their graduation exercises the other day, and I wish all of you could have been there. You have never seen a finer group of men — mostly combat veterans — anywhere. Nothing more heartening in my first difficult and sometimes frustrating months as Governor has happened to me. These men want to be policemen — the best policemen in the country. They want to do their jobs without political fear or favor. And I think that's what you want. So I hope the Legislature will set aside politics and pass this bill. If they do I am sure it will be a great thing for better government in Illinois.[130]

There is another bill of great importance I want to tell you about. Our welfare services constitute the State's biggest business and biggest expense. The welfare department looks after some 48,000 people in our mental and welfare institutions. It also has many other responsibilities in the welfare field. The Public Aid Commission administers old age

[130] Jacob M. Arvey, many years later, wrote that when Stevenson proposed the removal of the state police from patronage, he was at first "stunned and distressed," since the Democratic organization had just won the disposition of the hundreds of jobs involved. "All my cajolery went for nought. He was decisive and he was courageous as well. This was his idea, this was his conviction; and I finally found myself pleading with the legislature to enact Adlai Stevenson's program, the removal of politics from the state police system." "A Gold Nugget in Your Backyard," in *As We Knew Adlai,* pp. 54–55.

Walter V. Schaefer, who was then the Governor's chief assistant, also told about the meeting referred to by Colonel Arvey: "Most of the leading Democratic politicians in Illinois were in the Governor's office. They were opposed to the Bill. . . . The discussion was heated, and it went on for several hours. No one spoke in favor of the bill. The only support that the Governor had was from me . . . and that was silent support — because I did not feel that I was entitled to participate in the discussion. . . . Several of the leading party figures bluntly and bitterly told the Governor that he would definitely not be re-nominated unless he withdrew his support from the Bill. He was offered face-saving amendments, since he had made it an essential part of his platform. He refused any form of compromise. I think I have never admired any man so wholeheartedly as I admired him that night." Letter to Carol Evans, Feb. 2, 1968.

pensions, aid to the blind and aid to dependent children. Together these two agencies will spend in the next two years about 356 million dollars of State and Federal funds, or almost one-third of our total budget. And the cost of these services is constantly rising. It is more and more imperative, therefore, to manage all of these welfare services with the utmost efficiency and economy. But as it is now we have an executive department managing some of them and a commission the balance. There is no common control or direction. So I propose to combine them all under one head, the Department of Public Welfare. Thereby we could streamline these services, consolidate and reduce the number of regional offices, eliminate much of the duplication of effort and double standards of salaries and operations, to achieve not only greater efficiency but better service to the people who need these services. Some homes now are visited not by one but by several state agencies. Just as an example of possible improvements, the Public Aid Commission's carefully developed medical program could serve the Welfare Department's functions in child welfare and family service programs and eliminate duplicate or parallel medical services.

As I say, public welfare services now affects the lives of men, women and children in every community. Unification of these two agencies is in the interest of greater efficiency and economy. We must economize whenever we can.

I am hopeful that the Legislature will reach the same conclusion and not perpetuate a dual administration of our welfare services.

There are many other measures which I wanted to talk to you about which the Legislature must act upon in the remaining few weeks. I can mention only a few, and those briefly.

Sometime ago I arranged a meeting between employer groups and representatives of labor and asked them to work out an agreement, if possible, and as soon as possible, to increase benefits to injured workmen under the Workman's Compensation and Occupational Diseases Acts. They went to work in a fine spirit of conciliation, and on May 6 I had the pleasure of attending a meeting with them in Chicago at which we announced increases averaging 15 per cent, the largest single increase ever agreed upon by both labor and industry.

I am working now with the same groups in an effort to reach agreement on a new scale of unemployment compensation payments which were last adjusted in 1944 and are no longer in step with living costs. Also there have been abuses of unemployment compensation by unscrupulous people which must be corrected. I am confident that once again a mutual spirit of fairness and compromise will reconcile widely conflicting views and yield agreed legislation.

A bill urgently desired by law enforcement officials to extend the term of grand juries in Cook county is pending in the House. It has already passed the Senate. It would give Cook county, where the crime situation is the worst, only the same weapons all the other counties already have. I believe this bill is of such importance that the House of Representatives should at least have a chance to vote on it, but its opponents threaten to hold up the whole legislative program by filibuster and delaying tactics to keep this bill off the floor and prevent a vote. More important than any legislation, it seems to me, is the principle of majority rule in an American legislative body. If the majority want to vote on such important legislation they should have the right, and I deplore the spectacle of filibuster and delay in the House of Representatives of Illinois to frustrate that basic principle.

For a long while I've been working on legislation to improve the administration of the laws protecting the lives of miners. The present situation is unsatisfactory. We have an executive department of Mines and Minerals, but the health and safety laws are administered by a Mining Board whose members serve on a part-time basis. The whole setup is ambiguous and it is difficult to fix responsibility for lax, inefficient or corrupt administration. I want to end that, and legislation is being presented to place responsibility for the administration of that department and enforcement of the laws governing mining operations squarely on the director of the department and no longer scattered between a department and a board.

In my inaugural address I emphasized my desire to strengthen the State civil service and to create conditions more attractive to career service. If we can do that I think it will be a long step toward better public servants and better government. The first step is a strong, competent Civil Service Commission. I have already asked for a substantial increase in the appropriation for that Commission and now I am going to propose to the Legislature that the office of president of the three-man Civil Service Commission be made a full-time job. Heretofore Civil Service in this state has been administered by a part-time commission of three members. None has had full-time responsibility and their work for the commission has been a side-line. The results have not been good. I think we must take it more seriously and have a full-time president in day-to-day contact with the problems of the staff and with the heads of the operating departments. This is the pattern of organization recommended for the Federal government by the Hoover Commission. I believe its adoption for Illinois will be a long step forward because if we are going to make much enduring progress toward better government the place to start is with the men and women who are the government — who do the day-to-day work year in and year out — the civil servants.

But most of all tonight I wanted to say something about the budget — the largest in the State's history. I am a frugal man, which may account for a lot of letters from friends who have seen me pinch pennies who can't understand why after criticizing the past administration for waste and extravagance, I have proposed to spend during the next two years 130 million dollars more than was spent during the last two. They all complain that with local taxes so high and federal taxes so high, I should be economizing and not spending more like everyone else.

Well, I want to say to them that I am economizing. I want to say to them that I have already cut the cost of operating the departments under my control by 14 per cent, and I have just begun. I want to say that the increases in the state budget are going to cut or at least slow down the increases in their local taxes. Most of the complaints, whether from newspapers or individuals, seem to overlook that; they seem to overlook that the increased expenditures are largely for schools, for aid to municipalities and distributions which, if they were not made by the State, would have to be made locally with an increase in their local taxes.

They seem to overlook that with an increase of 130 millions in the total, there has been an increase of over 140 millions in new and increased distributions of State funds for aid to schools, aid to municipalities, and old age pensions, aid to dependent children and aid to the blind, over which I have no control. They also overlook that the cost of servicing our soldier bonus debt is up 27 millions for the next two years alone. They seem to overlook that only one-third of this budget goes to pay the costs of operating the whole state government, and two-thirds is for construction and distributions to local governments and individuals.

In short, they seem to overlook that this budget is a significant step toward local tax relief — and that it has only been possible by some sharp cuts in state expenditures. I have already eliminated more than 1,000 jobs from the state payroll and I hope to eliminate a lot more. We have, for example, been compelled to abandon the program of building lakes all over the state for recreation purposes — not because they are not desirable, but because we can't afford everything. We felt that the schools and local tax relief came first because they involve all the people and not just a portion. The same is true of the ambitious airport construction program which I reluctantly had to stop. And the same is true of many other projects and programs which I had to halt because we couldn't afford them.

But we are setting aside 40 million dollars to aid the cities, of which some six millions is to help local hospitals with tuberculosis control, and 34 millions is to help maintain fire, health and police services; and we are increasing aid to schools by 54 millions, or 70 per cent, because if we have any greater responsibility than giving our boys and girls a good common school education I don't know what it is. And we have also increased our aid for operating the State University and teachers' colleges by some 14 millions.

People also overlook that we have to, in common justice, and to get better employees, increase the pay of state employees, whose wages have not kept pace with those in business and industry. A 10 per cent increase in state salaries alone will cost the state some 20 millions. I guess there are a lot of things people overlook about this budget — for example, the state's population has increased by 300,000 since the last budget was prepared and most of the increase comes in the young people of school age and the old people, which adds to the cost of our services to the young, the poor and the sick.

And then, frankly, I hope I won't have to spend all the money covered in the budget. But you have to figure two years ahead in Illinois — this is a two-year budget — and you can't foresee exactly what you are going to need if prices change, for example — or exactly what you can save or where.

You know, my friends, I'm not proud of this budget. I would much prefer to hear applause than criticism, but I'm not the least ashamed to have eliminated non-essentials, and increased what seemed to me the essentials. And I am not ashamed of letting the people know just what they're up against if we are going to continually demand an increase in state services and then complain about paying for them. It's a funny thing, or rather a pleasing thing, that when people come in to complain and I explain the budget, what we have cut off and cut down, how we have assumed more of the local tax burden, etc., and then ask them what they would have done — well, they usually have no more to say and no more complaints. But I'm sure the budget isn't perfect by any means. We had to prepare it hastily and many of the detailed items had already been presented by the prior administration to the Budgetary Commission and approved before I was even inaugurated.

I don't mind it when someone complains about something specific — I like it; it helps us to restudy what we're doing. What I don't like — what doesn't help anyone to understand government and where we're going in Illinois — is the usual unreasoning, unthinking, broadside denunciation which is all too common. But I am getting some specific complaints — particularly with respect to the appropriation for automobiles — which represents about 1 per cent of the budget. They say we asked far too much. Perhaps we have, but the fact is that only one car, an ambulance for the Kankakee State Hospital, has been purchased in my part of the government since I took office.[131] I'm trying to find out just how many cars we really need and how many will have to be replaced before mileage and repair expense gets too high for economical operation or trade-in during the next two years. It looks thus far as though we had inherited from our predecessors 100 to 200 more cars than we need or should have, including a lot of high-priced Buicks.

There's going to be no joy-riding at state expense if I can prevent it, and I think I can. And I would be only too glad if the Republicans in the Senate would tell us first where and how much the budget for automobiles should be cut for the next two years. But they didn't do that. Instead they cut out the entire appropriation in several departments, like Agriculture and Conservation, with loud declamations about economy. But that's not economy — it's politics, and not very good politics either, because it is manifest extravagance to use large numbers of cars until you can't turn them in for anything and repair expense eats you alive. I think we can make some reductions in this small item we inherited, and we will — but not that way. But really it's not the appropriations that count — it's the performance, it's what we spend, in fact, that I have to account to you the people for two years hence.

After listening to this clamor about automobiles I've about decided that politics is the biggest export commodity in Illinois. I used to think it was corn and hogs. The trouble is that we export the corn and hogs, but not the politics.

Another word about the budget.

To finance part of these increased expenditures for local units of government, largely schools, we have asked the legislature to extend the coverage of the present 2 per cent sales tax to construction contractors and other occupations which are now exempted. Of course there is organized concerted opposition as always. But these aid programs to assist the school districts and distressed municipalities which can no longer make both ends meet, like Chicago, depend on the passage of this revenue measure because the State of Illinois cannot borrow to meet revenue failures, and if the money is not forthcoming from taxes it cannot be spent.

And speaking of revenue, let me say that the operating expense of our highways is scheduled to increase ten millions in the next two years due largely to the increasing cost of maintaining our rapidly deteriorating roads. In other words, our roads are in such bad shape, as all of you who

---

[131] The expenditure of the appropriation for a new automobile mentioned in Stevenson's letter to William Burry of May 19, 1949, above, was the responsibility of Lieutenant Governor Dixon and was not within the Governor's jurisdiction.

travel extensively know, that maintenance expenditures are now half as large as construction expenditures. Each year the situation will get worse and, as I said in my budget message to the Legislature a month ago, "If we are to arrest wasteful deterioration and put our road system in first-class condition we must not only exact full value for every dollar spent, but we must promptly invest far more."

I have reviewed some of the legislation which I want because I think it is in the public interest. It's a large, ambitious program. There's nothing new, nothing I didn't propose long ago. It would have been far easier for me to sit still, administer the state as I find it, avoid trouble, give the schools and distributive aid programs a niggardly increase and keep things rocking along. But I don't think that's what you elected me for. I'm going to trim the ship as best I can and I'm going to fulfill every campaign pledge a politically divided Legislature will allow.

I am going to do the job as economically, as efficiently, as sensibly as strength, time and wisdom permit. I think I have the most honest, competent and conscientious department heads in the history of Illinois. I know I have the most patient, tolerant and understanding electorate in the United States.

Since the legislature does most of its business during the last days of the session, there is an avalanche of bills immediately after its adjournment. They go to the attorney general's office for an opinion on their constitutionality before reaching the governor, and some are held in that office for a short time, thus easing the load on the governor and his staff. During the session the governor and his aides follow all bills through the legislature and usually know which ones he intends to veto.

Vetoes by the governor must be accompanied by a message. Because Stevenson was under great pressure at the end of the legislative session, his principal aides (in 1949, Walter V. Schaefer and J. Edward Day) assisted him in preparing drafts of messages. These were then sent to the Governor, who reworked them into an end product that was his own.

Carl McGowan, who helped prepare the veto messages in 1951, said: "I think I could write a history of the Stevenson administration and an exposition of his philosophy of government from the vetoes alone. Anybody can make a speech. But a veto represents the Governor's final decision. It is not just talk." [132]

Stevenson used his veto on sixty-eight different bills in 1949. He was to use it even more extensively in 1951.

[132] John Bartlow Martin, *Adlai Stevenson* (New York: Harper, 1951), p. 101.

The legislature passed a bill appropriating funds to maintain the Senate Chambers and rooms when not in use, an action that provoked Stevenson's sense of economy. He vetoed the bill.

To the Honorable, the Members of the Senate
of the Sixty-sixth General Assembly,

May 27, 1949 [133]

I herewith return, without my approval, Senate Bill No. 58 entitled "An Act creating the Senate Chambers Maintenance Commission, defining its powers and duties, and making an appropriation therefor." I veto and withhold my approval from this Bill. The Bill appropriates $20,000 to a commission to maintain the Senate chambers and rooms during the period the General Assembly is not in session. A similar bill (House Bill 598) appropriating $20,000 for the maintenance, between the sessions of the chambers and rooms of the House of Representatives, was passed yesterday and will reach my desk next week.

At a time when economy is so necessary I cannot believe that $40,000 is needed for guarding, cleaning and exhibiting the legislative rooms during a period of eighteen months, particularly since the Secretary of State, as custodian of the Capitol, already has funds and personnel available for that purpose.

For this reason I veto and withhold my approval from Senate Bill No. 58 and I intend to disapprove House Bill 598 when it comes to my desk.

Respectfully,

Charles Wheeler, of the Chicago Daily News, *in 1949 was dean of the press corps covering the state government in Springfield.*

To Charles Wheeler

May 27, 1949

Dear Charlie:

You might like to know I have just read a letter from a constituent who thought the Gateway Amendment had something to do with restaurants in railway depots. Yes, I thought you'd enjoy it!

Yours,

[133] *Veto Messages of Stevenson, 66th General Assembly,* p. 7.

Governor Stevenson kept in close touch with what the newspapers reported about the state government. He sent suggestions from time to time to his aides about getting items into various newspapers. The following memoranda to his executive secretary, James W. Mulroy, were handwritten and undated, but probably written by the Governor in 1949 during the legislative session.

To James W. Mulroy [134]

[no date]

Jim Mulroy —

Don't overlook press possibilities in Rep[ublican]. opposition to ICC [Illinois Commerce Commission] bill — naming no names. I'm sure Beardsley [135] would like that morsel —

AES

To James W. Mulroy [136]

[no date]

Mr Mulroy —

If it hasn't been done, copy of this should be sent to M[arshall]. Field, Jr.[137] with comment that he might like to see it.

AES

In May, 1949, Alger Hiss was being tried in the U.S. District Court in New York on a charge of perjury, growing out of accusations of espionage by Whittaker Chambers and subsequent congressional hearings. Hiss's counsel asked Stevenson to testify as to the reputation of Hiss when Stevenson knew him. Stevenson consented to answer the interrogatories in Springfield. He did not give his own opinion concerning Alger Hiss, but merely testified as to the reputation of Hiss based upon the opinions of other persons with whom he had come in contact.

Stevenson's willingness to answer the interrogatories was distorted and used against him many times in the years to come. On March 28, 1952, he wrote his sister, Mrs. Ernest Ives, who confessed that she did not know what to tell people who accused her brother of defending Hiss:

[134] This handwritten memorandum is in the possession of Mrs. Helen Kaste.
[135] Harry Beardsley, legislative reporter for the Chicago *Daily News*.
[136] This handwritten memorandum is in the possession of Mrs. Helen Kaste.
[137] Publisher of the Chicago *Sun-Times*.

You can say about the Hiss case that I knew him slightly during my few weeks in the State Department in 1945 and I saw something of him again when he accompanied the American Delegation to the General Assembly of the United Nations in London in 1946. At that time he occupied a very important position in the State Department. One has to tell the truth in response to interrogatories propounded by the judge and sent to me in Springfield. I said that from what I had heard others say his reputation 'was good.' To have said anything else would have been a lie. To have refused to say anything might have resulted either in a subpoena and would be a clear evasion of what seems to me the simple responsibility of any citizen. I don't think you either tell a falsehood or evade acting as a character witness in a criminal trial for fear the defendant may later be convicted. When that time comes it will be a sorry day for Anglo-Saxon justice.

I could add that other character witnesses were John W. Davis, Justice Frankfurter, Justice Reed, and that John Foster Dulles hired him as President of Carnegie Foundation.[138] Was I, who saw him only a few times in the State Department and in London supposed to know about his connections eight years before?

Direct Interrogatories in Behalf of Defendant Alger Hiss [139]

Q. NO. 1   State your name and address.

A. NO. 1   Adlai E. Stevenson, Executive Mansion, Springfield, Illinois.

Q. NO. 2   What is your official position at the present time?

A. NO. 2   Governor of Illinois.

Q. NO. 3   State the official positions which you have held in the past.

A. NO. 3   I was special counsel to the Agricultural Adjustment Administration, Washington, June, 1933 to January, 1934. I was assistant general counsel of the Federal Alcohol Control Administration, Washington, January, 1934 to September, 1934. I was special assistant to the Secretary of the Navy, Washington, from July, 1941 to June, 1944. I was special assistant to the Secretary of State from February, 1945 to August, 1945. I was United States Minister in London, September, 1945 to March, 1946. I was United States representative to the Preparatory Commission of the United Nations,

[138] John W. Davis was congressman from Virginia, 1911–1915; ambassador to Great Britain, 1918–1921; Democratic candidate for President, 1924. Felix Frankfurter and Stanley F. Reed were Justices of the U.S. Supreme Court. John Foster Dulles was chairman of the Carnegie Endowment for International Peace, and appointed Alger Hiss president of that organization in December, 1946. In 1952 Dulles became Secretary of State.

[139] The case was filed in the United States District Court for the Southern District of New York by the United States of America against Alger Hiss, Defendant, Case No. C–128–402. The editors have omitted the formal legal language preceding and following the interrogatories.

London, September, 1945 to January, 1946. I was senior adviser to the United States Delegation to the General Assembly of the United Nations, first session, London, January-February, 1946. I was alternate United States Delegate to the General Assembly of the United Nations, New York, September, 1946 to November, 1946. I was alternate United States Delegate to the General Assembly of the United Nations, New York, September, 1947 to November, 1947. I think that is all.

Q. NO. 4 How long have you known Mr. Alger Hiss, the defendant?

A. NO. 4 Since June or July, 1933.

Q. NO. 5 Where, when and under what circumstances did you first become acquainted with him?

A. NO. 5 We served together in the Legal Division of the Agricultural Adjustment Administration in Washington in 1933.

Q. NO. 6 State the nature and extent of your association with him from that time until the present.

A. NO. 6 In the Agricultural Adjustment Administration in 1933 we were working on different commodities. Our contact was frequent but not close nor daily. I had no further contact with him until I met him again in the State Department when I went to work there in 1945. Upon my arrival in the State Department at the end of February or early March to the end of April, when Mr. Hiss left for the San Francisco conference, he was, I think, largely preoccupied with the arrangements for that conference, for the United Nations conference on international organization at San Francisco. During that interval, from the first of March to the end of April, I was engaged in other matters and met him mostly in intra-departmental meetings and in connection with some aspects of the plan for the San Francisco conference, largely relating to matters pertaining to the handling of the press at the conference. I was at the conference, myself, as assistant to the Secretary of State from about the 10th of May until the end of June. During that interval Mr. Hiss was Secretary General of the conference and I was attached to the United States Delegation. Our paths did not cross in a business way but we met occasionally at official social functions.

Back in Washington during July, I had some conferences with him in connection with preparations for the presentation of the United Nations charter to the Senate for ratification.

I resigned from the Department early in August, 1945, and so far as I recall I did not meet Mr. Hiss personally again until he came to London in January, 1946, with the United States Delegation to the First General Assembly of the United Nations. During that conference in January and February we had offices nearby each other and met frequently at delegation meetings and staff conferences.

I returned to the United States in March, 1946 and I do not believe I met Mr. Hiss again until the United Nations General Assembly in New York in 1947. At that time he was connected with the Carnegie Endowment for International Peace and I visited with him on one or two occasions at my office in the United States Delegation Headquarters in connection with the budget for the United Nations, which was one of my responsibilities as a member of the American Delegation. I have not seen him since.

Q. NO. 7   Have you known other persons who have known Mr. Alger Hiss?

A. NO. 7   Yes.

Q. NO. 8   From the speech of those persons, can you state what the reputation of Alger Hiss is for integrity, loyalty and veracity?

A. NO. 8   Yes.

Q. NO. 9   (a) Specify whether his reputation for integrity is good or bad?

A. NO. 9   (a) Good.

Q. NO. 9   (b) Specify whether his reputation for loyalty is good or bad?

A. NO. 9   (b) Good.

Q. NO. 9   (c) Specify whether his reputation for veracity is good or bad?

A. NO. 9   (c) Good.

Cross Interrogatories in Behalf of United States of America, Complainant in Said Cause

Q. NO. 1   Were you ever a guest in the home of defendant Alger Hiss at any time in 1935, to and including 1938?

A. NO. 1   No, I have never been a guest in Mr. Hiss' home.

Q. NO. 2   Did you, prior to 1948, hear that the defendant Alger Hiss during the years 1937 and 1938 removed confidential and secret documents from the State Department and made such documents available to persons not authorized to see or receive them?

A. NO. 2   No.

Q. NO. 3   Did you, prior to 1948, hear reports that the defendant Alger Hiss was a Communist?

A. NO. 3   No.

Q. NO. 4   Did you, prior to 1948, hear reports that the defendant Alger Hiss was a Communist sympathizer?

A. NO. 4   No.

Q. NO. 5   State whether or not you ever attended Harvard College or Harvard Law School?

A. NO. 5   Harvard Law School, September, 1922 to June, 1924.

Q. NO. 6   State whether or not you ever attended Princeton University?

A. NO. 6   Yes, September, 1918 to June, 1922.

I, Adlai E. Stevenson, do hereby certify that the foregoing questions were put to me by William B. Chittenden, United States Commissioner for the Southern District of Illinois, and the foregoing answers were made by me; that my testimony, after being fully transcribed, was submitted to me for examination, and has been read by me and such changes therein as I have desired have been entered upon the said deposition by the said William B. Chittenden, with a statement of the reasons given by me for making the same; in witness whereof, I have hereunto subscribed my name this 2nd day of June 1949. . . .

Columnist Doris Fleeson wrote to Stevenson on May 30, 1949, sending him a copy of her remarks about the welfare state. She said she expected to attend the Governors' Conference to be held that year in Colorado Springs, Colorado, and she hoped to have her daughter with her.

To Doris Fleeson

June 3, 1949

Dear Doris:

Many thanks for your note and the enclosure, which I shall carry off with me for a little careful attention.

I am delighted to hear that you are going to be at Colorado Springs. My situation is so hideous that I doubt if I can stay long, and I hope I can produce at least one, and possibly two of the Stevenson sons. I hope they are not too junior for your charming daughter.

Yours,

To Richard Finnegan [140]

June 13, 1949

Dear Dick:

I had hoped you would be down here to stay a night with me and see the Legislature in session long before this. Should you find it convenient to do so I hope you will let me know. There is always room here at the Mansion and I would welcome an opportunity to discuss my many problems with you.[141]

Sincerely yours,

[140] Editor of the Chicago *Sun-Times*.

[141] Mr. Finnegan declined the invitation. In his letter of June 15, 1949, he also said: "My faith in your character and ability is so high that I'm sure you will conquer your many problems. Keep faith in yourself above all things. There are so many specious arguments for getting you off the track. Henry Horner had his first breakdown when he fully understood how many men — some of them, to his horror, his own friends — were in politics solely to make money. My observation has been that if there were fewer such men the problems of every governor would be fewer and less weighty."

Fred K. Hoehler had served on many boards and commissions at state, national and international levels and his qualifications were impressive. As director of the Department of Public Welfare, Stevenson considered him to be one of his outstanding appointments. Some Democratic politicians found the activities of Mr. Hoehler disconcerting. A Democratic member of the Illinois Public Aid Commission complained to the Governor, calling Mr. Hoehler a Republican. Hoehler felt constrained to defend himself and in a long letter to Stevenson recounted his past political activities. "This letter might be called the confession of a mugwump," he concluded. "By choice, I guess I am an Independent."

To Fred K. Hoehler

June 15, 1949

Dear Fred:

Thank you for your "confession." It is a moving document and it is all I can do to restrain my Democratic tears!

I hope you feel better now that you have come clean.

Yours,

Joan Pirie, Stevenson's niece, wrote him: "Mother [142] *said she had been out to Springfield last week to see you, and I wish I could see you too. But as I can't this will have to say for me how very much we love you and are thinking of you." She also expressed her distress that she would not be able to see him during the summer as she expected to be in Europe.*

To Joan Pirie

June 13, 1949

My dear Joan:

You were sweet to write me. I had hoped that when the time came I might be numbered among those who made the pilgrimage to Westover.[143] But, alas, my destiny seems to be in the hands of a disorderly and sometimes hostile Legislature!

You are through school now and have a whole exciting panorama of useful life ahead of you. You have a splendid preparation and I am delighted to hear that you are going abroad this summer and under such intelligent auspices. You will find in time that it will pay rich dividends if you make every moment count to learn more and more about your fellow

[142] Ellen Stevenson's sister, Mrs. Ralph Hines.
[143] She was a student at Westover School, Middlebury, Connecticut.

men, not only home but abroad. Much of what you discover will be distasteful, but much will be good and fine. The important thing is to note which is which and how to make quick discards.

When you come home I shall hope to hear all about it. And I warn you, if you don't come to see me I will come to see you!

With all my love,

One of the measures Stevenson considered to be important to his high-way program was legislation providing for a two-cent rise in the gasoline tax to increase state revenues. A conflict arose between city and rural interests as to distribution of the revenue. The Governor waited in vain for a satisfactory compromise to be worked out, and, toward the end of the legislative session, endorsed a bill that was passed in the Senate but badly defeated in the House on the last day of the session. The following message from the Governor was sent, probably to all Democratic House members, toward the end of the session.[144]

Imperative we know exact position of all Democratic members of House on Gas tax increase and allocation. Will you be present next Monday and vote for the bill as it passed Senate. Please send your answer to me at speakers office today or write me at St. Nicholas Hotel.[145]

To Alicia Patterson [146]

June 19, 1949

. . . I'm sitting in my office at the while the clamor goes on unabated in the House & Senate & messenger boys & pols run in and out to get my orders on every damn thing. In a few minutes the extension of the sales tax will come to a vote in the Senate & I'll know whether the Rep[ubli-can]. program of months to embar[r]ass me if they can has worked. They are trying to pass larger appropriations than revenue and leave me with an unbalanced budget and thus force me to veto a lot of popular things.

Kennelly has run out on me on the gas tax increase [147] and all in all things are in a mess and so am I!

[144] The original of this handwritten message is in the possession of Mrs. Helen Kaste. Although it is not so marked, the editors assume it was sent as a telegram.

[145] The Springfield hotel which housed Democratic state headquarters.

[146] This handwritten letter is in the possession of Adlai E. Stevenson III.

[147] Martin H. Kennelley, Democratic mayor of Chicago, was never noted for his support of Stevenson. The gasoline tax increase was one of the revenue bills submitted by the administration that failed to pass.

I wish you were here for the last 24 hrs of this fantastic show. . . .

A

P.S. . . .

Stevenson attended the Annual Governors' Conference held in Colorado Springs, Colorado, June 19–22, 1949. He was asked to make some comments on federal aid programs.[148]

Mr. Chairman, I confess I am a beginner here, and I find myself a little confused by this discussion. I don't know whether we're trying to save the states or the taxpayers. I'm not sure that their interests are always identical.

We all believe, I know, in the federal system, and there seems to be little point in belaboring that proposition.

There are certainly those of us who feel that the rapid extension of federal grants-in-aid is threatening the integrity of the states and the federal system. There are some, who, while against extending federal influence and the federal dollar, are also very eager for that dollar. Some see less threat to states from federal encroachment than others, and expect less federal domination than others.

All of us, certainly, have profited from the federal aid programs, but all of us know that there must be some limit to the extension of federal programs. I suggest that those limits may well be determined more effectively by the taxpayers' pocket books than by issuing proclamations about states' rights.

To be realistic, we must recognize that we can't lay down any arbitrary principles which will determine the future of our federal-state relations, but we can properly recognize, as I believe this conference has done in the past, that this is a problem that will only be solved by incessant, insistent, temperate study of our intergovernmental relations at all levels.

As Governor Warren [149] and Governor Driscoll [150] have said, with the industrialization of this country, with the growing complexities of modern life and the stresses of our machine age, a host of new problems has been created. Old problems have taken on new meaning and importance with the freedom of movement which our federal system has established for individuals and for their goods as well.

---

[148] The text is based on a carbon copy. There is no indication on the copy as to what date the remarks were made.

[149] Earl Warren, governor of California, 1943–1953.

[150] Alfred E. Driscoll, governor of New Jersey, 1947–1954.

The plain, hard fact of the matter is that the industrial age has created problems of health, housing, education, transportation, and employment which inexorably flow over state boundaries. No amount of talk is ever going to reverse this trend.

We must face the fact that in many instances the states either won't or couldn't begin to cope with these vast industrial problems. We must admit this fact to ourselves, and recognize that the people — not particularly concerned with philosophical problems of states' rights versus national government — have turned to that source which would give them help. We must admit, I think, in all honesty that in some instances the federal government has acted as a lever to get us going. If we agree that all the citizens of this great land are entitled to an equal opportunity, we must also admit that only through assistance by the entire country could some areas provide these essential minimums.

And further, because of the mobility of wealth and industry, the money which must be raised to support these programs, most particularly the individual and corporate income taxes, must be levied on a national basis.

Another question is the extent to which effective democracy demands local decision and administration. Naturally, the source of all political power rests with the voters in the community and on the farms. All officials, at whatever level, stem from that source. Here the record of the states, it seems to me, must be carefully scrutinized, and we must ask ourselves the question: "Have we provided the most efficient and the best organized administration? Have we granted to our subordinate jurisdictions — the counties, towns, and cities — the same right of autonomy which we, ourselves, are demanding? Does the maximum degree of state sovereignty necessarily go hand in hand with efficiency?"

Here we must candidly admit, I think, that our hopes and aspirations have generally outrun the realities. As has been said so often, to demand greater state autonomy and control requires that we place our own house in order, that we must demonstrate effectively that we ourselves are deserving of the trust of our people. And I don't hesitate to say here that public administration at every level of government in my state, if not in all of the states, could be vastly improved.

I think we must ask ourselves: Are we willing and do we have the financial means and the moral desire to carry out the functions which we say we want to perform but don't want the federal government to do?

I believe there is a way for all of the levels of government to pull together in a harmonious manner. That is our major task. I suggest that we recognize the need for cooperation rather than hostility or capitulation between levels of government, that we should root out every unnecessary duplication in federal, state, and local services, assigning those services to each unit most fitted to administer them in the public interest. For example, I don't see why the city of Chicago should be inspecting dairy farms in Minnesota. We can encourage both federal and state studies to reduce the number of governmental units. Specifically, the bill pending in Congress for a commission on intergovernmental relations seems to me to be an intelligent and promising approach.[151]

I think we should expand interstate agreements, as has been suggested here; that we should press constantly for efficient administration of our federal grants with only those controls which the public interest requires, and limited to fields of legitimate national concern; that we should return to the states or localities those few tax sources which could best be handled at their levels; and that we should see that the states are as fair with the localities as they demand that the federal government be in its relationships with them.

In conclusion, Mr. Chairman, I would say that I suggest that we all have a big job to put our own houses in order. Certainly we should press for the relinquishment of some of these areas of taxation, as has been suggested by the Council of State Governments.[152] Certainly we should study constantly and continuously all existing and all future grants-in-aid with a view to rational, considered extensions or reductions. However, I don't see how we can arbitrarily lay down here any specific percentages for cuts in federal-aid programs until we know, far better certainly than I know, exactly what the impact these cuts would be on our states today, in our present uncertain economic situation.

To Alicia Patterson [153]

June 22, 1949

I'm 17000 feet in the air. I think its Nebraska beneath but I *know* its my tall and handsome son Adlai beside me. We're homeward bound from

---

[151] In 1953 Congress created a Second Hoover Commission to investigate invasions of federal power into "the realm which was the primary interest and obligation of the several states and the subdivisions thereof" (Public Law 109, 83rd Congress). One of the permanent results of the work of the commission was the establishment of a continuing Advisory Commission on Intergovernmental Relations.

[152] Actually, this was the product of a joint conference of governors and members of Congress. A committee composed of the governors of fifteen states, ten congressmen and six senators, met for the first time in September, 1947. The overall objectives of the joint committee were to "develop an equitable and adequate tax structure throughout the country; to avoid, to the extent possible, duplication of taxation; and to make available to all levels of government sufficient taxable resources to perform necessary public services." *State Government,* September, 1948, p. 204.

[153] This handwritten letter is in the possession of Adlai E. Stevenson III.

the Governors' conference at Colorado Springs — a very de luxe affair, contributing an hour of fine trout fishing, a short sun bath by the pool, a series of long dinners and divertis[s]ements and very little education for a young governor. Adlai & Borden were with me besides an assorted retinue & I shipped Bordie off by air at 7 this morning to Durango & thence on his archeological expedition in the Mesa Verde park. Adlai goes back with me to work in the Springfield paper if I can contrive it. . . .

To Mrs. Edison Dick [154]

June 24, 1949

. . . I'm back from Colo. Springs, little enlarged in wisdom, but some refreshed in spirit. At least I was until I had spent a few hours hearing the bad news from the legislature!

There is much to report. I hope you'll be coming down for the final holocaust [155] — the bonfire of my hopes — next week.

Do *you* believe these things that Buffy writes me so beautifully? Why does everyone — except the Senate Reps! — feel they have to buck me up all the time? Am I so poor in spirit? . . .

Hale Bondurant, who was leaving radio station WJBC in Bloomington (owned by the Stevensons and Merwins through the Daily Pantagraph Corporation), wrote the Governor just before his departure. He said he never again expected to work for an organization with higher business ethics. He congratulated Stevenson on his performance as governor.

To Hale Bondurant

June 25, 1949

Dear Hale:

I had hoped to see you before your departure. You were good to write me.

I have heard from Loring [156] about the fine opportunity you have in Wichita, and I can understand perfectly your decision to take it. All the same I am much disappointed to see you leave Bloomington, and I sin-

---

[154] This handwritten letter is in the possession of Mrs. Dick.
[155] The adjournment of the legislature.
[156] Loring C. Merwin, publisher of the Bloomington *Daily Pantagraph,* and Stevenson's cousin.

cerely regret that we have not had more time together since your joint enterprise.

I hope you will find opportunities to stop in to see me whenever you come through Illinois.

With warmest good wishes, I am

Sincerely yours,

Mary Gilson wrote Stevenson from Florida that when she taught at the University of Chicago he was one of her heroes because he was always so straight-thinking — and that he always would be. She hoped he would be President someday.

To Mary Gilson

June 25, 1949

Dear Miss Gilson:

Remember you! I only wish you were in Illinois doing battle for good causes. Our ranks are sparse.

Many thanks for your nice note.

Sincerely yours,

Stevenson received many letters requesting an autographed photo. One of his minor problems was choosing a suitable picture for this purpose, and he called on his press secretary for aid.

To William I. Flanagan, James Mulroy and Ernest L. Ives [157]

June 27, 1949

Apparently we do not yet have a photograph and the requests for autographed copies are becoming a little embarrassing. I still wish you could provide us with some cheap glossy prints of the two that I picked out of the group done by Time Magazine sometime ago. I rather preferred the shaggy unkempt one which you all seemed to disapprove. Would there be much expense involved in getting 50 of each for use here at the mansion?

---

[157] The original of this typewritten memorandum is in the possession of Mr. Flanagan.

To William I. Flanagan [158]

[no date]

Mr. Flanagan —

I wish there was some way to end once & for all the use of this photo which was sent out by Chamberlain [159] early in the campaign without my permission.

AES

To William I. Flanagan [160]

October 25, 1949

Bill —

I like this photo *very much* and suggest we use it for awhile, until something else turns up. I hope it will not be retouched to smooth out the hair or anything. Its a very dark background for autographing, but I don't suppose any thing can be done about that and I'll have to autograph at the bottom —

AES

To Mr. and Mrs. Edward K. Welles [161]

June 27, 1949

Dear Ed and Betty:

If by any chance you want to come down to Springfield to witness the concluding holocaust in the State legislature on Wednesday or Thursday, or both, don't hesitate to let me know. There will be plenty of room for you, and it might be at least an unfamiliar spectacle for you.

Sincerely,

In the closing days of the legislature, the Republican Senate had passed bills approving $65 million in expenditures for which no budget provision was made. Stevenson declared his intention to veto them. Since most legislation is passed during the last days of the session, a governor can ordinarily exercise his veto without fear that it will be overridden, but the Republicans were determined in this case to override Governor Stevenson's. This was possible only if the legislature remained in session. Walter Schaefer described what occurred:

[158] This handwritten memorandum is in the possession of Mr. Flanagan.
[159] Don Chamberlain, staff member in the Division of Department Reports.
[160] This handwritten memorandum is in the possession of Mr. Flanagan.
[161] Lake Forest friends of the Stevensons.

On June 21, 1949 Senator Wallace Thompson, the leader of the Republican majority in the Senate, offered a joint resolution providing that when the two houses adjourn on June 30, 1949, they stand adjourned until July 18, 1949, at 4:00 P.M. This resolution was adopted by the Senate and transmitted to the House of Representatives on the same day.

It had been the uniform custom of the General Assembly to adjourn *sine die* on June 30, and the adoption of this resolution alerted the Governor's staff to the fact that the Republican majority in the Senate wanted to keep the General Assembly in session so that it would have an opportunity to attempt to override the Governor's veto. The Governor's assistant, Walter Schaefer, explored the possibility of proroguing the General Assembly under the constitutional power granted to the Governor, and prepared appropriate resolutions and a proclamation proroguing the General Assembly.

No formal action was taken until June 30. When the House of Representatives convened on that day it immediately voted not to concur in the Senate resolution, and adopted its own joint resolution that when the two houses adjourn on June 30 they stand adjourned *sine die*. Thereafter the Senate refused to concur in the House resolution and refused to recede from its own resolution.

So matters stood, with the clocks in both legislative chambers stopped, until well after midnight on June 30. The House then adopted a resolution certifying to the Governor the fact that the two Houses "have disagreed and cannot agree" as to the time of adjournment, and after the remaining essential bills had been passed, the proroguing proclamation was read by [House majority leader] Paul Powell.[162]

To Chester Bowles [163]

July 2, 1949

Dear Chet:

At 5:30 A.M. night before last I prorogued the Illinois Legislature after the Republican Senate had refused to adjourn sine die. But my animals were better trained than yours, and thanks to fast footwork and the Lieutenant Governor (Democratic President of the Senate), they left town with most of the work completed.

I bleed for you!

Yours,

---

[162] Letter to Carol Evans, April 15, 1970.
[163] Governor of Connecticut, 1949–1951; later ambassador to India (1951–1953); congressman from Connecticut (1960–1961); and Under Secretary of State (1961).

On July 7, 1949, after the legislature had adjourned, Stevenson gave his final report on the session to the people of Illinois, delivered over forty-eight radio stations.[164]

My dear friends:

Just six weeks ago I told you about what the Legislature was doing and not doing. Now the legislature has adjourned — at 5:30 last Friday morning — and I am grateful to many radio stations for this opportunity to tell you what the Illinois legislature did and what it didn't do during the past six months here in Springfield.

I'm afraid some people think the Legislature spent most of its time on cats and dogs. It's true there was quite a bit of time given to the Cat Bill and the Dog Bill — and also to bills about badgers and turtle doves — but much of the real time and effort was on highly important legislation affecting people — and that's what I want to talk about.

Humorists used to say, "Congress has adjourned and the Republic is safe for another year." I don't feel altogether that way about the Illinois Legislature. Of course I was glad to see its work finished and all the uncertainties ended. But government is not like business and it is only by legislation that we can make desirable changes in basic policies. In a big state like this with so many complex problems and spending so much money for public services of all kinds, I think it might be better if the Legislature met every year but for a much shorter session.[165] Tax revenues and expenses could be more accurately estimated on a year to year basis; I think there would be less time wasted; foolish legislation would get less attention; the influence of lobbies, the existence of bribes and corruption, the over-emphasis on politics would all be more apparent to the public if the legislative process were more continuous. And the only way those things can be controlled is by public vigilance and public indignation. But an annual session would take a constitutional amendment, which is only one more reason for revision of our Constitution.

Speaking of politics, I was surprised to see to what an extent party politics influenced legislative decisions. I believe in the two party system. In order to function properly that system requires a division of opinion on major problems, but the basic divisions between Democrats and Republicans on national issues have little bearing upon State and municipal problems. Perhaps there are some few cases where division on

[164] The text is based on a copy printed in pamphlet form by the State of Illinois, entitled "Report to the People on the 66th General Assembly by Governor Adlai E. Stevenson."

[165] The Illinois legislature met once every two years. It convened early in January and adjourned the last day of June. The budget was projected on a two-year basis.

party lines on State issues is proper; but they are very rare. I feel that the executive officers and the legislators are chosen by you to come here to Springfield united in a common desire to serve the State — not as the agents of a political party, but as the agents of the people. I don't think mere partisan struggle for advantage serves either party or State.

After I was elected Governor, I felt confident that, while the Republican controlled Senate might not always accept my suggestions, it would always be guided by the public interest rather than partisan interest. I was fortified in this belief by a letter I received a few days after my election last November from one of the leading Republican Senators. He said this: "Dear Mr. Stevenson: During the time the Republicans controlled the State government, members of your party in the State Senate have been entirely cooperative in helping us develop our program. It is my hope that members of the Republican party in the Senate will be as cooperative with you as your party has been with us."

But instead, as the session developed, I saw Republican Senators vote against legislation they themselves had recommended. I saw Republicans vote *against* measures *I* proposed who had voted for identical proposals made by Governor Green. And, finally, I think I saw the summit of legislative irresponsibility and ruinous partisanship when Republican Senators, after protesting loudly about the budget, killed the revenue bills but voted all of my appropriations and a lot more besides, and then refused to cut them back to fit the revenue.

I was reminded of the wolf who posed as Little Red Riding Hood's grandmother. With one hand they cozened me, and with the other sprang the trap. I suppose their motive was to embarrass me.

But fortunately some of the Republican Senators would not follow their leaders. They practiced what they preached and, thanks to their help, we carried the day and brought the budget almost into balance. I can do the rest by vetoes.

Now I don't blame the Republican Senators so much. I blame myself. I thought they really believed in conservative financial management. But I think you people want legislators who do not put some small party advantages, real or fancied, over courage, intellectual integrity and public responsibility. I think people are sick and tired of old fashioned political fencing. I don't think most people even care much about party labels any more. What they want is honest, sincere, courageous performance. And what's more I think the sooner politicians realize that that's the best politics the better it will be for them and for the people.

But in spite of difficulties, in spite of many disappointments, the Assembly enacted about two-thirds of the legislation I particularly recommended. I think I'm fortunate to have got that much of what I told the people I would try to do — especially when I proposed probably the most extensive and ambitious program any Governor has ever tried to enact in a single session. Maybe we tried to do too much all at once. Probably we did, but I think campaign talk should be more than sweet, deceitful words. It's easy to talk big and act small when the responsibility suddenly falls on you like a ton of coal. So I made a conscientious effort to do about everything I proposed in the campaign, and in terms of legislation it was a very large order.

Now about the defeats and failures first. I think we need a new, up-to-date constitution for Illinois to help us correct many of the cumbersome, obsolete, wasteful and unjust practices of our governments — State and local. I said so during the campaign and I said to the Legislature as soon as I was inaugurated that the people should have an opportunity to vote on calling a constitutional convention. More than three-fifths of the members of the House voted for the resolution — the Democrats almost unanimously. But we needed a two-thirds majority and fell five votes short of the necessary 102. Several Republicans who supported the same resolution under the previous administration voted against it this time. This defeat closed again what is probably the only satisfactory door to major reforms in Illinois, to more equitable property taxation, more home rule for cities, fair representation for all sections of the state in the legislature and elimination of duplication and waste in State, county and municipal government.[166]

With the constitutional convention resolution defeated, I endorsed the so-called Gateway amendment in order to salvage even an unsatisfactory substitute. It permits three amendments to the constitution to be placed before the voters at one time, instead of only one. It also permits enactment of these amendments by a vote of two-thirds of those voting *on the question,* instead of the present majority of those voting *in the election.* The Gateway proposal is to be voted on by the people in November 1950, and I sincerely hope that it is approved. I shall give it my full support, although neither my hopes nor my efforts for a constitutional convention will diminish.

Another disappointment was the defeat of legislation to create a Fair Employment Practices Commission, which was intended to give everyone in Illinois, regardless of race, color or creed an equal opportunity to get and keep a job. This bill was passed by the lower house, but defeated in the Senate and the Republicans cast 24 of the 25 votes against it. I think there was much misinformation and alarm spread about this bill.

[166] Illinois voters finally, in 1968, were able to vote to hold a constitutional convention in 1969.

It has not injured or harassed employers in other states where it has been adopted under Republican leadership. Nor was it designed to do a favor for Negroes and Jews. It is not doing a favor to anyone to discharge a duty which all American citizens owe to each other — the duty to live, as well as talk, democracy. The right of every man to equal treatment regardless of his creed, color or the origin of his grandfather is an implicit American right, basic to the whole concept of our democracy. I think FEPC was the most effective and practical anti-Communist bill of the many introduced in this session.

We also failed in our efforts to give distressed cities, including Chicago, financial aid to relieve the burden of local real estate taxation, because the Senate refused to provide the funds. A Commission was appointed two years ago by my predecessor to study our revenue laws and make recommendations to this legislature. It was composed of seven Republican and three Democratic legislators and five business and professional leaders, including the President of the Illinois Manufacturers' Association. It had a fine staff, worked for almost two years and spent $75,000 of the taxpayers' money. Among its many recommendations it proposed that the sales tax be extended to cover transactions which it was originally intended to cover and which are now exempt. I adopted this recommendation. It seemed only fair to treat all alike and it was estimated that it would yield about $25 millions per year in additional revenue. I proposed that the money be used to aid cities, schools and tuberculosis hospitals all of which would have relieved local property taxes. But only two of the seven Republicans on the Commission who recommended this broadening of the sales tax voted for their own recommendation. They said they were against any tax increases. They might have said they were against equal treatment for all under the sales tax and in favor of higher local taxes, because without this additional revenue I had to abandon the aid for cities program and cut $11 million off the school appropriation. And I could only save the tuberculosis aid by cutting out a much needed medical school building for the University of Illinois at the Medical Center in Chicago.

The Senate also refused to help Chicago to help itself. It defeated the licensing bill proposed by Chicago officials to raise revenue to maintain city services without further increasing real estate taxes. I believe in more home rule for all our cities. They shouldn't have to come to Springfield begging help. I agree that direct state aid to cities is not the long term answer, and I was not enthusiastic about the Chicago licensing bill as a way to raise money. But it seems to me very unfair to deny the city any aid and at the same time deny it the means of aiding itself.

The Senate also defeated my proposal to integrate the Illinois Public

Aid Commission which administers old age pensions, aid to dependent children and the blind with the Department of Public Welfare for better, thriftier administration. I choose to think this proper, inevitable step toward better public administration is only delayed.

I wanted also to consolidate the Free Employment and Unemployment Compensation services which deal with the same people for greater efficiency and economy. But the Senate defeated that. They also rejected my proposal to give Civil Service in Illinois increased strength and improved direction by having a full time president at its head, although the Hoover Commission has recently proposed and President Truman has recommended the same thing for the Federal government.

I asked the legislature to authorize me to appoint an expert, non-political commission to study the administration and financing of higher education which is now absorbing about 20 per cent of the State funds expended for operation of the State government. With an elected Board of Trustees for the University of Illinois, an appointed Board for the Teachers' Colleges, a separate Board for Southern Illinois University, with Eastern and Western State colleges both demanding changes in their functions, and all of them competing for funds with little coordination, I felt it was high time to ask the best people in the country to help us decide where we are going in Illinois and why. The House approved the proposal but the Senate rejected it.

With some Democratic help, I am sorry to say, the Senate also defeated a bill to help us cut operating costs at the Soldiers' and Sailors' Children's Home by admitting dependent children of non-veterans.

I also lost under an avalanche of Senate votes a bill to increase truck license fees. The lobbies were very active in Springfield — as usual, and in spite of the notorious damage heavy trucks do our highways Illinois will continue to collect much lower truck license fees than most of the other states.

I am sorry the Senate defeated the bill to tax the capital stock of out-of-state corporations doing business in Illinois the same as Illinois corporations are taxed.

I must say for the Senate, however, that it did pass the bills proposed to improve the administration of criminal justice. One of the misfortunes was their defeat in the House, particularly the bill extending the term of grand juries in Cook County. Cook County with the largest crime problem asked for no more than the downstate counties already have, but the House denied it to them.

So much for the disappointments. On the positive side, I think our major achievement has been in legislation pointing the way to better schools approved by both houses almost unanimously. Not only have we provided more money than ever before, but with the advice of an advisory committee of experienced specialists we worked out reasonable and attainable permanent objectives for the Illinois common school system and the legislature adopted many of them. Our problem is not simply more and more money for schools, but how to make the most of it; how to provide our grade and high school children all over the State with basic education of a breadth and depth which will fit them for the world in which they must live. This large appropriation and the accompanying changes in the law is only a beginning but I am hopeful that it will prove a memorable advance in the direction of larger, better, more economical schools, and a permanent state policy which will enable the legislature in the future to appropriate for schools not what political pressure and expediency dictate but rather what is necessary to attain clear, sound and reasonable educational objectives.

I am sorry that the failure of the Senate to pass the revenue bills in the last hours of the session forced me to cut the $112 millions I originally proposed for schools by 10 per cent in order to balance the budget. But the $100 millions remaining is still an increase of 53 per cent over the last appropriation for schools.

Another important achievement was the Police Bill to remove the State Police force from politics once and for all. The General Assembly adopted the legislation I proposed and at last we can establish in Illinois a police force wholly emancipated from the political domination and control of the past. With newly established standards for selection, rigorous training of recruits, assurance of tenure and promotion on merit alone, without political fear or favor, we can in time have as efficient and fearless a police system as any in the country. The men in the service and the people will be the beneficiaries.

I also proposed legislation to remove the Illinois Commerce Commission from political interference, control or intimidation by providing better salaries to attract better men, six-year staggered terms to provide greater independence and continuity and membership from both political parties. This Commission is charged with the regulation of the rates we all have to pay for light, heat, telephone and other services. It is one of the most important agencies of state government. It should be above and beyond political interference. But the Republican Senate cut the terms back to four years. Happily the House refused to concur in this agreement and they compromised on five-year staggered terms. It's not all I wanted, but it is most all, and I'll risk the prophecy that we've taken another very significant if not spectacular step in the direction of better government in Illinois.

With the disastrous holocaust at the Effingham hospital fresh in our memories, we turned our attention to the mute but imperative cries of the men, women and children who have perished in the flames of Illinois fires. Legislation was offered and passed authorizing the State to promulgate reasonable rules necessary to protect the public from fire hazards.

In another field of safety, the legislature passed our bills to reorganize the Department of Mines and Minerals. By eliminating perplexing ambiguities we have fixed the responsibility squarely in the Director of the Department for the administration of a state service charged with the protection of human life and we have provided additional safeguards and more rigorous inspections to protect the miner.

Early in the year I asked labor and management to meet together and increase the scale of payments under the Workmen's Compensation and Occupational Diseases Acts. They did so and I want to publicly acknowledge my gratitude for the conciliatory attitude of both the unions and the employers which made possible agreed legislation substantially increasing awards to injured workmen.

After prolonged negotiations with labor and management we also agreed upon and the Legislature enacted major changes in the unemployment compensation law to increase benefits from $20 to $25 per week and to sharply tighten the law to prevent abuses which have been too prevalent in the past.

I might add that earlier in the session in recognition of the rapid increase in the cost of living in the past years the Legislature also increased old age pension and blind assistance rates. Also in recognition of increased living costs we proposed and the Legislature approved increased salaries for state employees and officers to enable us to attract and keep more competent and conscientious people, and help us to eliminate the inefficient and expensive system of part time employees.

As I have said, we did not succeed in getting a full time president of the Civil Service Commission, but we did accomplish part of our program to reinvigorate Civil Service administration by removing the position classification of employees from the Governor's office where it could be too susceptible to political control. Henceforth it will be under the Civil Service Commission.

Much additional legislation of importance was passed. I have already referred to the program of State aid to public tuberculosis sanitariums. The day is almost at hand when that dread disease can be virtually eliminated in Illinois, and I felt the State should lend a hand. Besides aid from Springfield will help the local tax burden of maintaining these tuberculosis sanitariums.

An important, far-reaching step toward the elimination of inequities and injustices in local property taxation and also toward the fulfillment of a campaign pledge, was taken with the passage of the bill providing for county supervisors of assessment which was recommended by the Revenue Laws Commission created by the 1947 General Assembly.

The public assistance laws have been codified; a state reformatory for youthful felons has been authorized; a commission to study reorganization of our complex state government has been established and many other desirable bills were passed. Maybe I can summarize the results by saying that of the major measures in which the administration was particularly interested some 21 were passed and 13 defeated. I am well content; we have much of what we wanted; our budget can be balanced. I think it was a good start, and I am grateful to Speaker Paul Powell of the House and the presiding officer of the Senate, Lieutenant Governor Sherwood Dixon, for the dignity, good order and impartiality with which the legislative deliberations were conducted. I am grateful to Representative James Ryan and Senator William Connors, the Democratic floor leaders, for their tireless support of the administration's program. I am grateful to all the members of both parties who supported it, and to the opponents I am grateful for the utmost courtesy and consideration.

As the prizefighters say: It was a great fight, ma — and I'll be right home for supper.

Before I close, let me say that the total increase in the budget for the next two years from State sources is $120 million. Increased support for schools of $44 million, increased cost of the soldiers' bonus debt of $27 million, increased cost of higher education of $17 million, and increased cost of public assistance and health services of $30 million alone make up this total increase. So you will see that the large budget you've heard so much about is not for the current operations of the State but for the soldiers' bonus, education, health and aid to the old, to dependent children, and the blind — expenditures over which we have little control.

There is one more bill that passed the Senate but did not pass the House which I want to mention — the gas tax increase from three cents to five cents per gallon. Like every one of you I don't like tax increases. But like every one of you I also want good roads in Illinois. Our economy, let alone our recreation, depends on roads and streets. Twelve hundred communities in Illinois have no railroad connection. Ninety-eight per cent of all farm produce moves to market over the highways. Two thousand people were killed on the highways in Illinois last year, and so on and so on.

I know it is always bad politics to advocate tax increases that affect everyone. But I also know it's my duty to tell you what I think and why, whatever the consequences. I studied the report of a commission of legislators and private citizens appointed two years ago which recommended this gas tax increase. I studied and discussed for endless hours the engineering reports. I came to the conclusion that in spite of what we could do to cut costs we could never get our highways, roads and streets in good condition again without investing much more money, and that the longer we waited the more it would cost. Paying taxes for good roads is something like the bride who remarked that it is tough to pay 80 cents a pound for steak, and was reminded by her mother that it's tougher if you pay only 40 cents!

I came to the same conclusion that practically every other state has come to — that we would have to raise the gas tax to do the job and the sooner the cheaper. Thirty-nine states have increased their tax since 1929. We haven't. Only three states have as low a tax as ours. Twelve states have increased since the war and the increase has not been paid by the motorist. The oil companies have absorbed most of it. Today I'm told we pay more for gas with a 3 cent tax than some other states with higher taxes.

So I endorsed the recommended increase in the gas tax, fully conscious that it was unpopular and that no one liked the idea — including myself.

But we can't blink the fact that 3,000 miles, ¼ of the state's primary system, is in need of immediate repair or reconstruction. There is a deficiency of $11 million to carry out vitally needed improvements in the Federal aid primary system. There will soon be a deficiency of $22 million in the non-federal aid system. Maintenance costs are rising as the whole system deteriorates. The time will soon come when available state funds will not even cover maintenance costs, let alone new construction.

The need of many cities for more funds for street maintenance and construction is similar. The counties are not in as bad shape, but with the failure of the gas tax bill the townships will have no state funds to supplement their tax resources. I deplore this, particularly because farm roads in many sections must be improved not only for commercial transportation but for school bus transportation.

Then there is the horror of traffic fatalities — five a day in Illinois. With constant deterioration of our roads there is little prospect for arresting the accidents, injuries and deaths.

Before another session of the legislature rolls around I think you will all consider this major problem of our state. Meanwhile I will do my best to reconcile as between the state, the cities, the counties and the townships the conflicts over the distribution of any increase in gas tax revenue which had so much to do with defeating it in this session.

A final word. All in all the Legislature passed 829 bills. Most of them I will sign. Some appropriations I will have to veto in order to bring the budget into balance. Some bills I will have to veto because I do not think they are in the public interest. That's my next job; some 550 still to be acted on, many appointments to make to boards, commissions and offices, and then I hope we can settle down to the cold, hard, day to day job running this enormous business — the State of Illinois — more efficiently and economically than it has ever been run before. That's my ambition and that's what you sent me here to do.

I hope I will have an opportunity to report to you from time to time and I hope you will want to hear how I am getting along and how your business is being conducted. It is your business, because it's your State[;] it doesn't belong to any party or any group of politicians. It belongs to you.

To Richard J. Daley [167]

July 7, 1949

Dear Dick:

I enclose a memorandum from Steve Mitchell [168] reminding me again of Judge John J. Sullivan's [169] interest in the appointment of a Mr. Frank Smith as Chief Oil Inspector. Judge Sullivan was helpful to me in the campaign and I should like to return the favor, assuming of course that this is a position which *must* be filled and that Mr. Smith has suitable qualifications. I know nothing of the other applicants for the position.

Sincerely yours,

After the legislature adjourned, Stevenson received several letters from legislators thanking him for the privilege of working with him and commending him generally on his program. Among these was Senator Robert Young, Democrat, of Hurst, Illinois, who expressed his gratitude for being able to handle some of the Governor's legislative program and offering his services between sessions.

[167] Daley was appointed by Stevenson to be director of the state Department of Revenue. He became county clerk of Cook County, 1950–1955, and mayor of Chicago in 1955.

[168] Stephen A. Mitchell, Chicago lawyer, charter member of the Stevenson for Governor Committee. He later became chairman of the Democratic National Committee in 1952.

[169] Justice of the Illinois Appellate Court, First District (Cook County), Second Division. Appellate court justices were appointed by the Illinois Supreme Court.

To Robert Young

July 7, 1949

Dear Bob:

You were good to write me and I only wish you had handled a lot more of our program in the Senate. You'd better rest up because I will be counting on you heavily next time!

I wish I could think of something for you to do which is consistent with your office. If you have any ideas, please pass them along promptly, and be sure to stop in to see me whenever you are in Springfield. I value your friendship, loyalty and help in this appalling job more than I can tell you.

Sincerely yours,

Harry L. Topping, Republican state representative from Kankakee, Illinois, wrote the Governor on July 5, 1949, thanking him for courtesies during the legislative session. He wrote that he was happy that the Governor had already signed four of his bills, especially the one to increase the governor's pay. Mr. Topping said he had not used the Governor's name or position at any time while on the floor of the House, as he previously stated he would not.

To Harry L. Topping

July 7, 1949

Dear Mr. Topping:

I am most grateful for your kind and thoughtful letter. You have been more than good to me and I am deeply grateful both for your support and your wise counsel.

If there were more like you hereabouts I might feel more like struggling for that salary increase you arranged for somebody! [170]

With warm regards and happy memories of all our encounters, I am

Sincerely yours,

State representative Paul Taylor, of Effingham, Illinois, a Democrat representing the Illinois 42nd District, wrote Stevenson on July 5, 1949,

[170] Under the Illinois constitution the increase in the governor's salary could not take effect during the term of the incumbent governor. The legislature voted to increase the governor's salary from $12,000 to $25,000 per year, effective in 1953.

that several times during the session he had wanted to communicate some ideas about legislation and the legislature but hesitated because of the Governor's limited time, and also because he felt that he was a very minor and unimportant member and his ideas would have little value. He expressed pride in the Governor for maintaining the high ideals he promised during the political campaign.

To Paul Taylor

July 7, 1949

Dear Paul:

I am disappointed that I did not see you before you left Springfield. Be sure to let me know when you are in town again. I am grateful to you for all of your support and encouragement during the session but more than a little disappointed that our paths did not cross more often. It is an appalling undertaking to organize this enormous business, prepare a budget and prepare a legislative program all simultaneously. I was obliged to do it at the expense of many personal contacts which would have been both a pleasure and a help.

With warm regards, I am

Sincerely yours,

Noble J. Puffer, director of the Department of Registration and Education, a Stevenson appointee, wrote to express his pride in the Governor's leadership. He realized Stevenson's disappointment in the failure of some of his key legislation. "There are those who will accuse you of not being practical, and of being too idealistic. For the sake of Illinois, please don't let those who put politics and practical considerations first, convince you that you must give in on your high ideals in order to achieve your goals."

To Noble J. Puffer

July 8, 1949

Dear Noble:

Many thanks for those encouraging words which greeted me on the morning of July 1. But I didn't really feel too disappointed about the session. I think we got as much as we could have reasonably expected. As for the ideals, I hope I didn't lose them with the sleep!

Yours,

On July 11, 1949, Governor Stevenson introduced Dr. Albert Schweitzer to a luncheon group in Chicago.[171]

We pay our respects and homage today here in our great American city of Chicago and our State of Illinois to a visitor to our shores for the first time; to one of the great men of our time. He comes to us not from London, Paris, Rome or Shanghai. He comes to us from Lambarene in French Equatorial Africa — he comes to us from everywhere, because he has a reverence for life — because he is in the service of all mankind — their minds, their bodies and their spirit.

"Thought will not work except in silence; neither will virtue work except in secrecy." At 30 — already a renowned theologian and the greatest organist in Europe — he renounced a spectacular career to lift the burden of disease, in silence and secrecy, from the African natives. At 74 he comes to us from the jungles, one of a small company whose words and work ennoble this 20th Century of the Christian era.

It was Maeterlinck who said, "Experience still shows that we risk less by keeping our eyes before us than by keeping them behind us; less by looking too high than by not looking high enough. All that we have obtained so far has been announced and, so to speak, called forth by those who were accused of looking too high.

"It is wise therefore when in doubt to attach oneself to the extreme that implies the most perfect, the most noble and the most generous form of mankind."

In a world careless of human, ethical, and spiritual values you, Dr. Schweitzer, have attached yourself to that extreme. And we here in Illinois, like the natives in the jungles of Africa and the musicians, theologians and philosophers everywhere, are enriched and enheartened by your well spent years, your well stared [stored] mind and your spirit beautified by renunciation, dedication and boundless loyalty to life, Dr. Schweitzer.

Paul Scott Mowrer, formerly editor of the Chicago Daily News, *wrote Stevenson from Paris that he and his wife were returning to their home in New Hampshire after having lived abroad for several years. His son Richard was anxious to return to the* Daily News, *and Mowrer solicited the Governor's help.*

[171] The text is based on a carbon copy.

To Paul Scott Mowrer

July 11, 1949

Dear Paul:

I was delighted to have your letter and will do what I can regarding Richard and the Daily News Foreign Service at once. I have not seen Jack Knight [172] or Stuffy Walters [173] for months, but I shall contrive a prompt contact and I hope something can be worked out. I think they would be lucky to get him back. Bill Stoneman and his wife and daughter stopped here at the Executive Mansion for a night with me sometime ago on their way to Europe. He seemed to feel quite satisfied that he had a completely sufficient understanding and looked forward to his prospects with confidence. I wonder if he has not been to Paris and you had not best be in touch with him about the situation in the office at Chicago. He might have some suggestions which would be helpful for Richard.

I have been through a hideous six months of travail, with the legislature in session, trying to organize the administration, prepare a budget and an enormous legislative program all at once. The legislature has gone home now — thank God — and in the course of time I hope to at least feel that I have the thing under better control.

Helen Kirkpatrick stopped in to see us in Libertyville a few weeks ago, looked thin but very well and seemed to be enjoying her work in Washington. She brought news of you and Hadley,[174] and I hope it won't be too long before we can all meet again.

My love to Hadley — and I am passing your letter along to Ellen.

Yours,

Carl McGowan, who had planned a trip to Springfield with his wife Jodie, found he had to go to the hospital instead. Walter Schaefer informed the Governor that McGowan had surgery on his thyroid gland.

To Carl McGowan [175]

July 15, 1949

Dear Carl:

I have neglected your letter of June 28 in the late confusion, and now Wally tells me that you have been in to St. Luke's and are now out with

---

172 John S. Knight, publisher of the *Daily News.*
173 Basil L. Walters, editor of the *Daily News.*
174 Mrs. Mowrer.
175 The original of this typewritten letter is in the possession of Mr. McGowan.

half of something removed! I am glad to hear that your progress is good, and I hope our visit will not be much longer delayed. You better come down here with Jodie and enjoy the luxury of the mansion for a few days. She can have breakfast in bed!

Yours,

ADLAI

Governor Stevenson consulted frequently with Jane Dick, whom he had appointed as a member of the Board of Public Welfare Commissioners, about personnel and policy, not only in the Welfare Department but in other areas of the state government. The Dicks were on vacation when Stevenson wrote them this letter.

To Mr. and Mrs. Edison Dick

July 15, 1949

Dear Dicks:

Lest you are biting your nails about developments in the State of Illinois, let me report that the arrival of Mrs. Dick's letter this morning is as important as anything that has happened. The additional names are most helpful, and of course all orators like to hear flattering remarks about their orations. I think John Miller's wife, Katherine, is an excellent suggestion and must be used.[176] Moreover, I think it would be pleasing to John who has been such a long and warm friend of mine.

Miss Hazard [177] has been taken ill and we have hastily sent to Dwight a Mr. Lewis who used to be warden at Pontiac.

After working a day and a night on Ed McDougal, Fred Hoehler and I have our fingers crossed. I am a little apprehensive that when he said he would think it over he was politely saying no.[178] I don't know what to try next.

I have asked Dr. Cross [179] to arrange with the U.S. Public Health Service to make an efficiency analysis of his entire staff. Perhaps I acted impetuously, as I suspect there is a sort of fraternity among public health people and instead of finding a lot of unnecessary jobs they will recommend more!

[176] Mrs. John D. Miller was offered an appointment but preferred not to state what it was. She could not accept it. Letter to Carol Evans from Mrs. Dick, May 30, 1968.

[177] Helen Hazard, superintendent of the State Reformatory for Women at Dwight, Illinois. The prison was administered by the Department of Public Welfare.

[178] Edward D. McDougal, Jr., was asked to serve as chairman of the Illinois Public Aid Commission, but had to decline because of other commitments.

[179] Dr. Roland Cross, director of the Department of Public Health.

At all events, I think there will be some material for Eddie to work on.

I have about 300 bills out of the way and about 350 more to go. In between I received countless delegations of irritable politicians and have been making appointments right and left, day and night, but the important, critical ones are still ahead.

I am afraid there is little prospect of the journey to Vancouver. Ellen [Stevenson] is leaving Monday for the East to visit her mother, with John Fell, and will return around the first of August. I hope then we can get off for a little holiday, perhaps in Desbarats with the [Hermon D.] Smiths, but I must be back here by the 11th to speak at a celebration for my grandfather in Metamora, and then a fortnight of hell with the State Fair going on and everyone in Illinois to entertain and smile upon.

What a life. Ride 'em cowboy! And come back strong, brown and hungry for work.

Yours,

Stevenson not only read many of the state publications that reached his desk, but was observant of their style and quality. He felt that many state publications were unnecessarily expensive.

To William I. Flanagan [180]

July 16, 1949

I have just run across the "30th Annual Report of Division of Highways for 1947." This seems to me an entirely too expensive and elaborate book and I can see no justification for it. In accordance with our earlier discussion I trust you are reviewing all these publications with a view to economies.

To Alicia Patterson [181]

July 16, 1949

. . . Ellen is leaving Monday to be with her mother in Beverly Mass. until July 30. She is taking John Fell with her and will return then when the boys will all be back until they leave for school Sept 20. Borden & J.F. have to do some tutoring. If we can work out a settlement in the meanwhile she will then go to Nevada or somewhere in late Sept. Its all

[180] This memorandum is in the possession of Mr. Flanagan. A copy was also sent to the director of Public Works and Buildings.
[181] This handwritten letter is in the possession of Adlai E. Stevenson III.

very painful and difficult, but I'm long since reconciled to it as the only solution. . . .

A

Good fishing! I'm sure you'll catch Bertie [McCormick] if nothing else! . . .

To Mrs. Franklin D. Roosevelt [182]

July 21, 1949

Dear Mrs. Roosevelt:

. . . We were all delighted with Frank's success [183] out here — and I recall that in London in January 1946 you told me you felt he should have five years of practice before he went into politics. Evidently he anticipated you a little, but I hope you share the confidence of all of his friends that he was "right"!

With warmest regards,

Faithfully yours,

Mrs. Emmons Blaine, of Chicago, was the daughter of Cyrus Mc-Cormick, who invented the reaping machine. She had worked closely with Stevenson in the Committee to Defend America by Aiding the Allies. [184] *On July 18, 1949, she sent him her check for $2,500 as a "belated arrival for some small service of work for you and therefore for Illinois. In the pressure of the campaign it got sidetracked. . . . It may be a slight help to you in your great undertaking. . . ."*

To Mrs. Emmons Blaine

July 21, 1949

Dear Mrs. Blaine:

I think the best letter I have ever received was your note enclosing your magnificent gift. The gift is more of a help than you can understand. I find that for almost ten years I have been earning little and spending much on a large and expensive family. That seems, however, to be the unhappy plight of public servants generally and I suppose it is my own fault!

But more than the gift your good will and affection and encouragement

[182] The original is in the Franklin D. Roosevelt Library, Hyde Park, N.Y.
[183] Franklin D. Roosevelt, Jr., was elected as a U.S. congressman from New York.
[184] See *The Papers of Adlai E. Stevenson*, Vol. I.

mean a lot to me. I only wish we had more time to sit beneath an apple tree and talk about the state of the world and men's hearts and minds.

I am very, very grateful.

Affectionately,

To Charles Wheeler

July 22, 1949

Dear Charlie:

I hear that you are horizontal.[185] I was disturbed until I had a report that it was nothing serious. I hope you will be your usual self again — and soon! When you are, why don't you plan to come down here and stay a few nights with me and enjoy the luxury of the Mansion and share the misery of a distracted Governor? You can even have breakfast in bed, but I can't recommend it because I have never tried it.

With best wishes for a speedy recovery.

Yours,

The legislature passed a bill providing for a limited type of certificate that would lower qualifications for teaching in certain categories. The Governor vetoed this bill.

To the Honorable, the Secretary of State [186]

July 23, 1949

I herewith file in your office, without my approval, House Bill No. 444, entitled "An Act to add Section 21–3.1 to 'The School Code,' approved May 1, 1945, as amended." The adjournment of the General Assembly having prevented the return of this Bill to the House in which it originated within ten days (Sundays excepted) after its presentation to me, the same is filed in your office with my objections. I veto and withhold my approval from this Bill for the following reasons:

This Bill provides for the issuance of an additional type of limited elementary school teacher's certificate. The qualifications for this new certificate are substantially lower than those regularly required for such a certificate.

Well qualified school teachers are critically important to the improvement of our school system. Lowering of the required standards could be justified only by severe teacher shortage. Apart from emergency relaxa-

---

[185] Mr. Wheeler was in Grant Hospital in Chicago.
[186] *Veto Messages of Stevenson, 66th General Assembly*, p. 35.

tions, our progress must be toward higher standards of qualification, not lower.

I believe that this Bill militates against desirable objectives of our common school system and for this reason I veto and withhold my approval from House Bill No. 444.

Respectfully,

Stevenson's cousin Julia Scott Vrooman and her husband, Carl, were traveling abroad during the summer of 1949. On July 5, Mrs. Vrooman wrote the Governor from England that she hoped he would be able to persuade the legislature to allocate some of the funds set aside for public monuments to restore the home, in Springfield, of the famous poet Vachel Lindsay. Mr. Vrooman also wrote, putting in a good word for a friend, Fred Meyer, who wanted a state job as game warden.

To Mr. and Mrs. Carl C. Vrooman

July 24, 1949

Dear Vroomans:

I was delighted to have your letter and I only wish I could jump on a magic carpet and join you for a "spell." I doubt if much can be done about the Lindsay House through the Legislature, at least at present. Buffie is hard at work on it and maybe in the next session something can be worked out.[187]

I will make an inquiry about Fred Meyer. I don't recall him and have had little time for the mine-run patronage, as you will understand. But Lawrence Irvin probably knows something about it.

Affectionately,

---

[187] When Stevenson's father was Illinois secretary of state and the family lived in Springfield, Vachel Lindsay used to recite his poetry at receptions in the Stevenson home, and young Adlai was stirred by such renditions as "Eagle Forgotten," "Bryan, Bryan, Bryan," and "Abraham Lincoln Walks at Midnight." When Stevenson became governor, the Lindsay home, a large frame house to the rear of the governor's mansion, was in a shabby and deteriorating condition. The Vachel Lindsay Association, already in existence, had been unable to attract public interest in restoring the home. Because of Stevenson's interest, his sister, Mrs. Ernest L. Ives, became active in the restoration project and a committee of local citizens, headed by the Reverend Richard Paul Graebel of the First Presbyterian Church, formed a corporation which raised the funds to restore the home. After the restoration the home was leased to the Vachel Lindsay Association. Thousands now visit the house annually, and it is also open for special affairs. "The Lindsay House was saved for ages to be when Adlai took the idea enthusiastically and Buffie carried it to the committee stage." Letter from the Rev. Richard Paul Graebel to Carol Evans, July 17, 1967.

To Mr. and Mrs. Edison Dick [188]

July 25, 1949

Dear Dicks:

. . . There is much to report — to much for this feeble pencil. The Kennelly trouble is ridiculous and irritating. From the start it has been understood that the city aid program depended on the revenue bills. It was so stated — even using the word "contingent" — in two places in my budget message in April & in many speeches & radio talks. Everyone in the legislature so understood — and now he comes out in July and says it wasn't contingent and its my fault it didn't pass. I enclose copy of a letter I wrote him yesterday — *very confidential*.[189] [Jacob M.] Arvey & [George] Kells are much aroused & so are the members of the legis. who worked so long and hard for this "package" program. Evidently Martin K[ennelly] is being "needled" by the Tribune and some ambitious men who think they will profit from a split which will weaken the Democratic party. . . .

My love & thanks to you all —

ADLAI

To Vernon L. Nickell [190]

July 27, 1949

Dear Vernon:

I am always reading in the papers about things "I said," and I see in the [Chicago] Tribune that I promised "to cut up the sales tax" according to you. I don't mind being confronted with what I said but I don't like to be charged [with] what I didn't say. If you can point out to me where I ever recommended cutting up the sales tax I would be glad to have the citation.

Sincerely yours,

Governor Stevenson allowed Senate Bill No. 511, appropriating $225,-500 (commonly referred to as the "Christmas Tree Bill"), to twenty nongovernmental organizations, to become law without his signature. For some years certain organizations had become accustomed to receiving legislative appropriations and Stevenson wished to prepare them for a

188 This handwritten letter is in the possession of Mrs. Dick.
189 A copy of this letter was not available to the editors.
190 Superintendent of Public Instruction. A Republican, he was first elected in 1942.

*veto in case a similar appropriations bill should be passed by the next
legislature.*

To the Honorable, the Secretary of State [191]

July 28, 1949

I herewith file Senate bill No. 511, entitled "An Act to provide for the
ordinary and contingent expenses of certain associations and organizations." I am allowing this bill, which appropriates $225,500 to twenty
non-governmental organizations, to become law without my signature,
and in connection therewith I wish to make the following comments:

I have refrained from vetoing this bill only because appropriations of
this type to private organizations have become customary in recent
sessions of the legislature and a number of the benefited organizations
have presumably relied upon the continuance of this financial assistance.
However, I feel that the donation of public moneys to private organizations is undesirable, discriminatory and not in accord with proper governmental policy. Furthermore, such appropriations are of very doubtful
validity legally.

During the last ten years appropriations of this kind have steadily increased. New organizations have been added and appropriations to some
have been increased. In 1941 a total of $89,100 was appropriated to ten
organizations; in 1943, $107,400 to eleven organizations; in 1945,
$142,640 to fourteen organizations, and in 1947, $171,900 to seventeen
organizations. The total appropriation proposed by Senate Bill No. 511
as originally introduced was $218,000. By virtue of amendments the
total was increased to $225,500 with twenty beneficiary organizations.

These grants of public funds are for the use of non-governmental organizations in any manner they may determine, and there are no provisions for reporting to the General Assembly how the funds were expended. There are hundreds of worth while non-profit organizations
carrying on various meritorious activities in the State of Illinois and I
do not see why appropriations of as much as $25,000 per organization
should be given to groups representing only a fraction of a per cent
of the total organizations in the State.

I am making this statement now to invite the attention of the Legislature and the public to a practice doubtful at best which has grown to
burdensome limits. I think it should be stopped and that the organizations
involved should make other provision for financing such of their activities
as have previously been supported by the taxpayers.

[191] The text is based on a mimeograph copy prepared by the Governor's office for
release to the press. A copy is in A.E.S., P.U.L.

After the legislative session, Walter Schaefer and Louis A. Kohn re-
turned to their jobs in Chicago. Stevenson asked his sister and brother-
in-law, Mr. and Mrs. Ernest Ives, to help him find suitable gifts for his
departing aides.

To Ernest L. Ives

July 29, 1949

Dear Ernest:

The suggestion about Wally is excellent. It would be a godsend if you
and Buffy could get something appropriate and have it inscribed something like this:

> *To Wally and Margo Schaefer, with*
> *grateful memories of the Battle of*
> *Springfield*
> *January–August 1949*

Also, I think something similar should be done for Lou Kohn:

> *To Louis A. Kohn from his grateful friend*
> *Adlai E. Stevenson – 1949*

I recall so well the wooden salad bowl which Ed Stettinius gave me in
San Francisco with a silver plate. Perhaps something like that is useful.

I also think the idea of the party for the staff is excellent. Perhaps
you could do it in August either just before or just after the Fair.

Sincerely yours,

Harley Notter, whom Stevenson knew during his State Department
days, was in San Francisco in April and May and wrote the Governor
that he had found many people thinking of him in the highest political
terms.

To Harley Notter

July 29, 1949

Dear Harley:

I was delighted to have your good letter and I hope that you will let
me know when and where I can get your book after it is published.[192]

[192] Published as *Postwar Foreign Policy Preparation, 1939–1945*, Department of
State Publication 3580, General Foreign Policy Series 15 (Washington, D.C.: Government Printing Office, 1950).

I have been so distracted with the fantastic difficulties of this job that I don't find the vistas you mentioned the least attractive! It has been a rough but enlightening experience and there have been long hours when I wished I were once more there in the department — or even dealing with the Russians. . . .

You were good to write me and I hope our paths will cross before too long.

Sincerely yours,

Lucy P. Williams, of Bloomington, Illinois, wrote Stevenson on July 21, 1949, to say how proud of him she was and to congratulate him on his record as governor. She remarked that he was a true statesman and predicted that not only would all Bloomington and Illinois be proud of him but the entire nation whose President she hoped he would become someday.

To Lucy P. Williams

July 29, 1949

My dear Miss Lucy:

I was delighted and touched by your warm and encouraging letter. One does not get that sort of spontaneous letter very often and it is better coming from oldest friends.

Affectionately,

Governor Stevenson, as commander in chief of the state's military and naval forces, desegregated the Illinois National Guard. The following order was issued on July 30, 1949.

There shall be no racial segregation nor shall there be any discrimination in accepting enlistment in the service of any unit, company, regiment, corps, division, department or any other subdivision of the National Guard or Naval Militia because of race, creed or color.

To Mrs. Edison Dick [193]

August 2, 1949

. . . I had a long session with Kennelly in Chicago Saturday & told him my position in no uncertain terms. He insists no one ever told him

[193] This handwritten letter is in the possession of Mrs. Dick.

that aid to cities depended on the revenue bills being passed in spite of all our conferences, the budget message & countless statements & radio speeches. Its an odd business & there's no doubt he's done the party damage by giving aid & comfort to the enemy & letting those rascally Chi[cago] Rep[ublican]. senators off the hook by attacking me instead of them. I've kept still and will continue to & am suffering no pain! Arvey & Kells are "in my corner" & many of the politicians are very resentful.

I still have about 275 bills to dispose of, but the appointment situation is excellent! Yesterday Henry Tenny finally accepted the chairmanship of the Ill. Pub. Aid Com! [194] You can picture my relief and I'm getting more and more of the major appointments lined up in my own mind — including a successor for Schaefer, Carl McGowan who is here with his wife now looking things over while Ed Day searches madly for a house. . . .

I'm so glad your holiday has been a success — even the fishing! — and I envy you that visit to the Kelloggs beautiful place.[195] Give them all my love. I wish this letter could be longer but the thundering herd is thundering.

Best to Eddie & plan to come down for a look at the State fair and a fine assortment of jobs when you get back!

Yrs

ADLAI

P.S. I'm hoping for a fortnights holiday with Adlai the last of August & early Sept. but where I don't know.

To Mrs. Ernest L. Ives [196]

August 2, 1949

Dear Buffy:

I quote as follows from a letter from an old man which will interest you:

"Years ago I heard tell of a luncheon at which your grandfather and Mark Twain were present. The newspapers quoted the great humorist as delivering himself of this gem:

[194] Stevenson appointed his friend Henry F. Tenney, a Chicago lawyer, to be chairman of the Illinois Public Aid Commission. Mr. Tenney was also a member of the board of trustees of the University of Chicago and the board of governors of the American Red Cross, and other organizations.

[195] The Dicks were vacationing at the summer home of Mr. and Mrs. John P. Kellogg on Salt Spring Island, Victoria, B.C. The Kelloggs were neighbors of the Dicks and the Stevensons in the Lake Forest-Libertyville area.

[196] The original of this typewritten letter is in E.S.I., I.S.H.L.

> *'Philologists sweat and lexicographers*
> *bray,*
> *But the best they can do is to call*
> *him Ad-lay.*
> *But at longshoremen's picnics, —*
> *where accents are high —*
> *Fair Harvard's not present — so*
> *they call him Adlai.'"*

Love,
ADLAI

James Phinney Baxter, president of Williams College, wrote Stevenson that the latter's mother-in-law and a friend of hers at a luncheon meeting had told him the Governor was discouraged in not getting more of his program through the legislature. He added that Stevenson's aide J. Edward Day was a friend of his oldest son.

To James P. Baxter III

August 3, 1949

Dear Jim:

You were good to write me and I enjoyed the simile, but perhaps I'm not quite as discouraged as the good ladies thought. After all, I got a lot more of the program enacted than I had any right to expect in view of the political situation in the Legislature. But all the same I'd like to go to Maine *or* Colorado for a nice long vacation!

Ed Day is with me and I literally don't know what I could do without him. He will be delighted to hear from you and I am passing your letter along to him.

I hope you will not overlook me if you pass through Illinois on your occasional wanderings.

Warm regards,

Sincerely yours,

In vetoing a bill requiring the imprisonment of anyone addicted to the use of narcotic drugs, Stevenson said the bill "seeks to accomplish a commendable purpose by a method which is inappropriate and likely to cause injustice."

To the Honorable, the Secretary of State [197]

August 9, 1949

I herewith file in your office, without my approval, Senate Bill No. 264, entitled "An Act to add Section 62a to Division I of 'An Act to revise the law in relation to criminal jurisprudence,' approved March 27, 1874, as amended." The adjournment of the General Assembly having prevented the return of this Bill to the House in which it originated within ten days (Sundays excepted) after its presentation to me, the same is filed in your office with my objections. I veto and withhold my approval from this Bill for the following reasons:

This Bill provides that any person who is addicted to the use of narcotic drugs, with specified exceptions, shall be guilty of a misdemeanor and "shall be sentenced to imprisonment for a term not less than that required to effect a medical cure of the addiction to be determined by proper medical authority, but not more than one year." The Bill also provides that the court in its discretion may place such person on probation conditioned upon such person entering an institution for the treatment of narcotic addicts and remaining in such institution for one year or until cured. The Bill further states that its purpose is to provide a method by which addicts may be compelled for their own benefit, and the benefit of the general public, to take medical attention to cure them of such addiction.

It appears that the provision in this Bill authorizing imprisonment may have been intended only as a threat to compel the addict to undergo treatment, but whatever may have been the intention in this regard, the Bill does authorize imprisonment for a condition which it is admitted does not constitute a criminal act. The place to which the court is empowered to sentence an addict to "imprisonment" is not fixed by the Bill. Whether it is intended that the confinement should be in the Illinois State Penitentiary, the Illinois State Farm or in a county jail, none of those places are sufficiently equipped for treatment of drug addicts to make them suitable places for such confinement. The administration of this Act might well require the establishment and maintenance of institutional care and treatment for a large number of persons, in order to avoid the entirely undesirable situation of having such addicts treated as criminals. Providing the necessary special facilities would require substantial expenditures which have not been provided for by the General Assembly. In my opinion the Bill seeks to accomplish a commendable

---

[197] *Veto Messages of Stevenson, 66th General Assembly*, p. 15.

purpose by a method which is inappropriate and likely to cause injustice.

For the foregoing reasons, I veto and withhold my approval from Senate Bill No. 264.

Respectfully,

Stevenson vetoed a bill that would have doubled the number of scholarships to the University of Illinois to be awarded each year by members of the legislature.

To the Honorable, the Secretary of State [198]

August 10, 1949

I herewith file in your office, without my approval, Senate Bill No. 288, entitled "An Act to amend Sections 30-9 and 30-10 of 'The School Code,' approved May 1, 1945, as amended" . . . I veto and withhold my approval from this Bill for the following reasons:

This Bill increases from one to two per year the number of scholarships to the University of Illinois which may be awarded by each of the 204 members of the General Assembly. Since these are four year scholarships the Bill would increase the authorized number of legislative scholarships to a total of 1632.

There is no requirement that the scholarships be awarded to needy students nor on any competitive or merit basis. In my opinion the proposed increase bears no relation to improvement of educational standards at the University or to enlarged opportunity for higher education for the ambitious and deserving. There are already a large number of free scholarships to the University provided by various laws and I see no justification for adding to this number, particularly where the scholarships are non-competitive.

For the foregoing reasons I veto and withhold my approval from Senate Bill No. 288.

Respectfully,

To the Honorable, the Secretary of State [199]

August 12, 1949

I herewith file in your office, without my approval, House Bill No. 316, entitled "An Act to amend Section 11 of 'An Act to regulate the civil

[198] Ibid., p. 17.
[199] Ibid., p. 28.

service of cities,' approved March 20, 1895, as amended." . . . I veto and withhold my approval from this Bill for the following reason:

This Bill exempts from civil service the staff and employees of public libraries in cities of less than 500,000 inhabitants. These employees have been included in civil service under the statute since it was originally adopted in 1895 and no reason now appears for removing them from its protection. On the contrary, because of the specialized character of their work, civil service selection and tenure is particularly appropriate for these employees.

For this reason I veto and withhold my approval from House Bill No. 316.

Respectfully,

Archibald MacLeish, poet and public servant, and Boylston Professor of Rhetoric and Oratory at Harvard University, and Stevenson had become close friends and colleagues in Washington during World War II.[200] *MacLeish sent Stevenson an article he had written entitled "The Conquest of America,"* [201] *on which he wrote by hand: "Adlai my boy: I salute you! I revere you! Goddam but I love you. Archie."*

To Archibald MacLeish

August 13, 1949

Dear Archie:

Thanks — for the fifth copy of your much discussed piece. All my friends have sent it to me, but I had not expected one from the author himself — and with what an inscription!

I had planned to take it off with me on the mythical holiday that keeps beckoning beyond the garden gate. But now that you have sent the copy I shall have to read it even if it keeps a couple of bills from being signed and a couple of "pols" from getting jobs.

From all I hear it has attracted more attention than anything you have written for some time, but it still won't suffice unless it tells me precisely what I think about this cockeyed world. I have about come to the conclusion that I had better stop thinking about what I think.

I yearn for you, and should the Boylston Professor at Harvard want to dig his fingers in the roots, I will provide the roots.

My love to you both.

Yours,

[200] See *The Papers of Adlai E. Stevenson*, Vol. II.
[201] *Atlantic*, August, 1949.

p.s. Adlai E. Stevenson III is a sophomore at Harvard this fall. I will insist that he call upon you which he won't do, but if need be I will come down and present him in person!

AES

On August 16, 1949, Stevenson vetoed a bill passed by the legislature to control the price of cigarettes.

To the Honorable, the Secretary of State [202]

August 16, 1949

I herewith file in your office, without my approval, House Bill No. 494, entitled "An Act to prevent unfair competition and unfair trade practices in the sale of cigarettes." . . . I veto and withhold my approval from this Bill for the following reasons:

House Bill No. 494 is, in essence, a mandatory price-fixing Bill. It prescribes mark ups by which wholesale and retail minimum cigarette prices shall be fixed and provides penalties for any sale below such prices.

Price fixing for the benefit of limited business interests without compensating benefit to the consuming public who pay the price is, in my opinion, objectionable. In periods of emergency there may be justifications for the exercise of the police power of the State by controls which have a substantial relationship to the public welfare. I see no such relationship in this Bill.

Ours is basically a free enterprise economy. Free enterprise has historically meant competition. In our market place free competition has not only been encouraged but any interference with it has been abhorred. Price regulation has traditionally been sharply limited to public utilities and price fixing legislation to the protection of trade marks, brands, etc., through voluntary contracts. But this Bill is not concerned with the protection of trade names or brands of cigarettes. It is an out and out mandatory price fixing measure on the wholesale and retail level.

If it is argued that the State under its police power may prevent ruinous competition, why do we single out the distribution of one product — cigarettes — for this special privilege? If we depart from the long established policy of this State against price fixing and prohibit competition when some group deems it ruinous where do we stop?

Also, the administration and enforcement of this Act would be costly, and even if the general welfare was more apparently involved, the

[202] *Veto Messages of Stevenson, 66th General Assembly,* pp. 35–36.

burden of policing the price of a product sold through so many outlets as cigarettes should not be undertaken lightly without some strong economic and social justification.

Moreover, this Bill is, I think, of very doubtful legality. Virtually all legislation which has had price fixing as its primary purpose has been invalidated by the courts. This Bill far transcends the limited exceptions to the Sherman Act provided by the Miller-Tydings amendment [203] permitting producers by "fair trade" agreements to protect brands, trade names and marks by fixing retail prices and it offends the policy of our State and the Federal Anti-Trust Laws.

I therefore veto and withhold my approval from House Bill 494.

Respectfully submitted,

On August 16, 1949, Hermon D. Smith wrote the Governor that his son, Farwell, was in Paris and wanted to go to a few out-of-the-way places, such as Yugoslavia (off limits because of its Communist regime), Iran and Iraq, and was encountering some difficulty in securing the necessary visas. He suggested that a letter from the Governor vouching for Farwell's character and financial responsibility could be very helpful.

To Whom It May Concern

August 19, 1949

The bearer of this letter, Farwell Smith of Chicago, I have known since birth. He is a graduate of Harvard University and served in the Merchant Marine in the Pacific and Mediterranean during the War while I was Assistant to Frank Knox, Secretary of the Navy. Following college he is travelling about "seeing the world" before settling down to business or a profession.

Mr. Smith's parents, Mr. and Mrs. Hermon Dunlap Smith of Chicago and Lake Forest, Illinois, have been my very close friends for many, many years. Mr. Smith Senior is the head of one of the largest, if not the largest, insurance brokerage firms in the world,[204] and is a very prominent citizen of Chicago both in civic and philanthropic and educational affairs. He is a Trustee of the University of Chicago and of many other large and important institutions, both public and commercial.

---

[203] The Miller-Tydings Act of 1937 amended the Sherman Antitrust Act (1890) to provide that contracts or agreements to maintain resale prices, when made under state "fair trade" laws, did not violate the Sherman Act, and that such contracts did not constitute an unfair method of competition under Section 5 of the Federal Trade Commission Act.

[204] Marsh and McLennan.

I would count it a great favor if any American officials into whose hands this letter may fall would extend to my young friend, Farwell Smith, and his problems sympathetic consideration. He is a young man of exceptional enterprise and curiosity and I am hopeful that he will have an opportunity to enrich his already extensive experiences and knowledge of the world. He is discreet; his judgment is good; and I am confident that he will cautiously avoid any embarrassment to our country in his travels even in remote places. As to his loyalty there is no question.

Governor Stevenson was disturbed over organized gambling in Illinois. He believed in home rule, and did not think the state should interfere in a county unless local law enforcement had broken down entirely and the county asked the state for help. Nevertheless, he was seriously concerned about some counties where gambling had increased since he took office. He consulted with his top aides and the attorney general and they developed some ideas about what could be done if the situation worsened.

To Irving Dilliard

August 20, 1949

Dear Irving:

. . . The enclosed editorial was called to my attention yesterday. I only wish the local citizenry and officials would give us a chance to intervene in the gambling counties. . . . Just this week the Attorney General received — *confidentially* — letters from the Sheriff and State's Attorney of Lake County blandly advising him that they had received *no* complaints of gambling in that county, which I am sure is as bad as Madison [County]! In Lake County the structure of course is solidly Republican.

I would like to tell *you* in confidence what we are trying to do to get on top of this vexatious business in the open counties where we can get no cooperation from the local officials. What we are trying to do must be done quietly and without publicity or it won't work — and I am not sure it will work then. I will tell you about it when we meet and I hope there will be some progress to report.

Sincerely yours,

To Alicia Patterson [205]

August 20, 1949

. . . I'm off tomorrow morning for several days in Chicago and then

[205] This handsome letter is in the possession of Adlai E. Stevenson III.

on my "vacation" with Adlai until after Labor Day. I think I'll go either to Desbarats or to the Sidley's [206] ranch at Encampment, Wyo.

The bills are all signed or vetoed — 833 of them — and the State Fair is over. Things are still in a mess but if I'm ever going to have a breather this seems to be the best chance, so, pray God, I'll get off by the end of next week when Adlai gets back from British Columbia where he is now visiting the Kelloggs. . . .

Governor's Day at the Fair was a great success — Barkley,[207] Lucas [208] & Stevenson as the speakers. I made a good speech for a change. . . .

A

To Leonard Schwartz [209]

September 8, 1949

Dear Leonard:

Many thanks for the catfish. I will give them an expert's test very soon — but it doesn't take a test to induce me to go fishing! So please send me some spare time and we are off.

Sincerely yours,

Eloise ReQua, director of the Library of International Relations, in Chicago, invited Stevenson to the official opening of their new offices. He was a member of the board of directors.

To Eloise ReQua [210]

September 8, 1949

Dear Eloise:

I have your letter about the opening of the LIR's new quarters on September 29. I wish I could say with certainty that I could be there, but with the way things are accumulating I am afraid it may well be impossible to leave Springfield in the middle of the week. I will do the best I can but don't count on me too heavily.

As to publicity, you can, of course, do as you like, but please be forgiving if I can't make it.

Best wishes.

Yours,

ADLAI

[206] William D. Sidley, son of William P. Sidley, Stevenson's former law partner in Chicago.
[207] Vice President Alben W. Barkley.
[208] Senator Scott Lucas.
[209] The original is in the possession of Mr. Schwartz.
[210] The original is in the possession of Miss ReQua.

Archibald MacLeish wrote that he and his wife wanted to see Steven-son "here or there."

To Archibald MacLeish

September 8, 1949

Dear Archie:

I have read the piece.[211] I am deeply moved and aroused, but I don't know quite where to go. But I have read your letter. So I am going to Boston. What is your address? And would you consider exposing yourself to the Harvard-Princeton Football Game on November 5 if I were to provide the tickets; in the Princeton stands? How about Ada? [212] How about anyone else?

Yours,

In 1949, Vice President Alben W. Barkley, a distant kinsman of Steven-son, was courting his second wife, Jane Hadley of St. Louis. To avoid the publicity that would inevitably accompany visits to her, he found it convenient to accept many official invitations to Illinois. He was always a welcome house guest at the Governor's mansion in Springfield, and this enabled him to make a quiet stop in St. Louis before or after each of-ficial trip to Illinois. On September 8, 1949, he officiated at the unveiling of a statue of Benjamin Franklin for the Franklin Life Insurance Com-pany in Springfield, its home office. Governor Stevenson introduced him.[213]

More than a hundred years ago the black prairie soil of Illinois was the goal of a great westering migration along the wagon roads and rivers. They came from New England, they came from the South. Many of them came from the "dark and bloody ground" of Kentucky. Those hardy, proud settlers, my own ancestors included, nourished Illinois in its infancy. They broke the prairie sod, and they laid the foundations of the riches we in Illinois have inherited. They made only one mistake. They left Alben Barkley's for[e]bears home in Kentucky. Those Barkleys settled in Paducah, I suppose because that was as close to Illinois as they could get without deserting Kentucky!

Those pioneers from the South and the East who founded our great

211 "The Conquest of America," *Atlantic*, August, 1949.
212 Mrs. MacLeish.
213 The text is based on a carbon copy.

Illinois also established imperishable educational and commercial institutions, and, in a brief hour as history counts time, there sprang up
here on our rich prairie a fabulous agricultural, commercial and industrial civilization. The pioneering has never stopped in this bright land of
ours and here in Springfield the quiet, rural past has given way to great
industrial plants and businesses.

If a community is as great as its institutions, Springfield's distinction
and progress is in no small measure due to the Franklin Life Insurance
Company, whose phenomenal growth and strength is a measure of the
enterprise and foresight of its leaders, and I choose to think, of the invigorating environment of Springfield and Illinois. I think Benjamin
Franklin would be proud to be here today, not to witness the unveiling of
this splendid statue — he was far too modest a man for that — but to
witness what the hand of man and a kind Providence has wrought in the
unknown wilderness beyond the mountains.

And I think he would have been happy to meet here at this celebration of a great institution and this beautification of a great Illinois city
another American leader who believes that the destiny of man is freedom, justice and opportunity for all; another American who has proved
that thrift and honesty, conviction and courage, and boundless energy
will build enduring societies and enduring human institutions.

I am honored to welcome the Vice President of the United States to
Springfield on this significant September day. And I am honored even
more to welcome Alben Barkley of Kentucky who has long since taken
an exalted place among the inspired architects and incorruptible custodians of a people's government.

For thirty-five years a member of Congress; eleven historic years majority leader of the Senate — twice as long as anyone in history — he has
fought courageously, courteously, eloquently, in the best tradition of
our political institutions for his convictions, ever mindful that many
things are revealed to the humble that are hidden from the great. Like
Benjamin Franklin he has never lost touch with the humble while seated
with the great.

Ladies and Gentlemen, the Vice President of the United States, The
Honorable Alben W. Barkley.

Marshall N. Dana, editor of the editorial page of the Oregon Journal,
*wrote Stevenson on August 29, 1949, commending him on the July 7
speech at the close of the Illinois legislature, which Dana described as
being the height of frankness and picturesque phrase. He wrote that the
paper was commenting on it and enclosed the editorial page.*

To Marshall N. Dana

September 9, 1949

Dear Marshall:

I returned to find your good note and the very flattering editorial. I hardly recognize myself from my prose!

I hope some day you will be passing this way and will stop off for a visit with me in Springfield. I shall then have a proper opportunity to thank you properly!

Sincerely yours,

To Leonard Schwartz [214]

September 9, 1949

Dear Leonard:

I have read with great interest and satisfaction your report on the Department of Conservation as of July 31. I am particularly pleased with the elimination of additional automobiles and the personnel economies. I think we are a little alike — I am never satisfied either! As a wiser man once said, "It is well to be never dissatisfied but always unsatisfied."

I am most grateful for the copy of the operating plan for the Division of Forestry. It gives me a much clearer picture of what its activities are and I hope sometime that we can look at some of the reforestation activities in the submarginal areas with Mr. Nuuttila.[215]

Sincerely yours,

Prior to Vice President Barkley's visit to Springfield on September 8, 1949, he wrote Stevenson that his admiration and affection for the Governor increased with each visit.

To Alben W. Barkley

September 14, 1949

Dear Mr. Vice President:

. . . Let me say again what a joy it was to have you here, and I hope that Springfield will always be a stopping place on your travels. I hope the Democratic organization in Chicago didn't exhaust you. You refreshed them!

Yours,

[214] The original is in the possession of Mr. Schwartz.
[215] State Forester Eino E. Nuuttila.

To Alicia Patterson [216]

September 14, 1949

. . . Ellen leaves Sat for Boston to see the boys all put away in School & then back here the end of the month to pack up, close up the settlement & leave for the west — and there will end the first volume of two lives that could have been rarely happy & successful. Why did it end in Greek ghastliness? I don't know, in spite of borrowed hours of prayer & search. Am I mad? Is she? I don't know — but nothings left & the eyes are dry, and I'm staggering on & on in this fantastic routine without the faintest idea where I'm going or why.

Come when you can. I haven't been able to write anything sensible — sensible things all seem so senseless. There is much to say, but its no use & you know everything I'm *thinking* anyway. So its just day to day events, triumphs & failures, you don't know & those you can guess. . . .

A

To Mrs. Spencer Ewing

September 15, 1949

Dear Cousin Lena:

I noted in the Pantagraph that you are organizing a local committee to celebrate United Nations Day. I am delighted that interest continues active and that you are taking such a positive part in furthering it. If the United Nations were dissolved next week it would have to be reconstituted next year, as you so well know.

Warm regards to you and Cousin Spencer.[217]

Affectionately yours,

Stevenson throughout his administration continued to receive criticism from various sources about his handling of patronage. Dr. Sylvester Doggett, of Anna, Illinois, wrote Stevenson on September 8, 1949, that Paul Powell, speaker of the House of Representatives, was being criticized harshly by Democratic leaders for the Governor's slowness or "inaction" in dismissing Republicans from patronage jobs.

---

216 This handwritten letter is in the possession of Adlai E. Stevenson III.
217 Mr. Ewing, of Bloomington, Illinois, was a second cousin of Stevenson's father.

To Dr. Sylvester Doggett

September 15, 1949

Dear Doctor Doggett:

I have read your interesting letter, which I confess I don't fully understand. I talk with Paul Powell every few days and I think he realizes what I am afraid many people do not, that is, that we are ahead of either the first year of the Green administration, or the first year of the Horner administration, in the replacement of positions previously held by the political incumbents. Such a job can never be completed fast enough to suit some political leaders, but I have both considerations of time of the Directors [218] which can be devoted to patronage matters and also the considerations of efficient public service, which I am sure you appreciate.

I am grateful for your thoughtful letter.

Sincerely yours,

Mrs. MacLeish wrote Stevenson that she and her husband hoped he would stay with them during the Princeton-Harvard football game. She added that since her husband was extremely busy she was answering some of his correspondence.

To Mrs. Archibald MacLeish

September 20, 1949

Ada dear:

What a remarkable man he is! And with such a secretary he is even a more remarkable man than I thought. I hope the salary is substantial.

We will foregather for the game — and more details about place of residence later. I think I shall probably be staying, along with a couple of my boys, with their great aunt, Mrs. Kingsley Porter, who lives in the old James Russell Lowell house in Cambridge.

Love to you both.

Yours,

Judy Baumgarten was the daughter of the Reverend and Mrs. Martin D. Hardin, and cousin to Stevenson. The Governor wrote her on the occasion of the birth of the Baumgartens' youngest daughter, Ann.

[218] Of the code departments.

To Dr. and Mrs. Walter Baumgarten, Jr.[219]

September 29, 1949

My dear Judy and Walter:

I have the announcement and want to add another cheer for the latest Baumgarten — not to mention her enterprising parents.

My love to you all.

ADLAI

The National Council of State Governments sponsored a conference on state government reorganization in Chicago on September 29, 1949, at which Governor Stevenson was asked to speak.[220]

The proper management of the forty-eight American States is one of the major tasks facing the country. Taken together, these States spend about 6 billion dollars annually and employ almost one million people. Largely subject to State laws and partly subject to State supervision are in addition our 150,000 local governments which spend some 7 billion dollars more per year. Federal expenditures, it is true, far exceed these figures but if we exclude our military and other foreign commitments, our total Federal expenditures also added up to 13 billion dollars in the year 1947 and 14 billion in 1948. Fiscally and financially, therefore, the States together with their dependent cities share with the Federal government a vital responsibility for our governmental system and our national economy.

In spite of the growth of Federal and urban functions since the nation's beginning, the service and welfare functions of the States have also grown enormously. These functions show no promise of abating whether we decide to emphasize the welfare ideas or the enterprise ideas which our great political parties are contending with, or whether we continue to accept a healthy combination of the two.

The States in 1947 spent over one billion dollars for education and almost half a billion dollars for welfare. We may hesitate to call this the welfare state, yet we cannot deny that it is the embodiment of the service state. But the services the States perform are surely not limited to welfare. They make vast expenditures for highways and public works, for agri-

219 The original of this typewritten letter is in the possession of Mrs. Baumgarten.
220 The text is based on a mimeograph copy prepared by the Governor's office for release.

culture and resource conservation, for policing and military functions, for health and medical services. If our economic exigencies should require it, the States will be called upon to engage in additional public works expenditures, to encourage long delayed municipal reconstruction, and to handle the many social and economic emergencies that seem to have become their lot in both good times and bad.

No longer the constitutional repository of a somewhat evasive type of sovereignty, the American State has become the fulcrum of our political system, occupying a position midway between the Federal government with its responsibility for stabilizing our national economy and our local governments which deal largely with day to day community affairs. The State is now a vast public enterprise in its own right with a crucial responsibility in the political economy of the whole country.

How soundly, how efficiently, how economically, is this public enterprise being managed? For me, this is not merely an academic question of American administration. Every policy problem coming before me is accompanied by its associated problems of administration, organization and management. As these problems pile up, I find the following kinds of questions recurring:

(1) What reduction or consolidation can be made in the numerous departments and commissions which now report directly to me, and what new departments does the State government need in view of the additional functions that have been imposed on it since its last major reorganization during Governor Lowden's administration in 1917? [221]

(2) Should a particular function of government be undertaken or continued; should it be allocated to the State or to local governments, or to what particular department within the State? Frequently functions and programs have been undertaken and allocated upon the basis of a compromise of political or personal pressures of the moment. All of you can supply illustrations. Periodic review of decisions made under that sort of stress is necessary to prevent perpetuation of what may have been original errors.

(3) How effective are the so-called staff functions of budgeting and finance, of personnel and planning, which are used by members of my cabinet, by myself and my staff as devices for the executive management and the administrative control of the State government; how many of these staff procedures have become mere bureaucratic habits which no longer accomplish the results intended, and how can they be made more useful tools of management for a busy executive.

[221] During Frank Lowden's gubernatorial campaign in 1916 and his governorship he placed special emphasis on governmental reorganization. His inaugural address of January 8, 1917, contained a lengthy discussion of the need for streamlining the state government, and in his first term the Civil Administrative Code was enacted.

(4) How effective and efficient are our mechanics of government, our salary scales, our personnel practices, our classification plans, our administrative procedures, our space practices, etc., in State government, as compared with private business and especially as compared with other States. I am specially interested in the latter question because I suspect that Illinois does not rank as high among the States in various fields of public management as its hard-working population and its great enterprises deserve.

There are more questions of organization and management facing us in Illinois, but I do not wish to pre-judge the agenda of the promising Survey Commission on State Government in Illinois, which I am pleased to announce consists of Walter V. Schaefer, the Commission Chairman, who is participating in your deliberation here; of Lieutenant Governor Sherwood Dixon; Speaker of our House of Representatives, Paul Powell; Mr. James Knowlson, an outstanding Chicago business leader with experience in government management; Mr. Donald Funk, a leading downstate industrialist; Senators John Parish and Walker Butler; and House members James J. Ryan and Noble Lee.

As Governor of Illinois, I am not alone in raising these queries. The Governors of all of the States and particularly of some twenty States, most of which are represented here and which have recently created reorganization commissions or official survey agencies, are, I am sure, equally interested in these and many other related problems. We in Illinois are conscious of our history on this subject, for you will recall that 35 years ago Illinois did some pioneering in this field when it issued the so-called Lowden Report more than 30 years ago. At the time, there were also pending consolidation plans and proposals in one half the States. Today no single State can have a monopoly on sound management, for in the intervening years we have learned many lessons in this field and we have made some mistakes. But I have every hope that if we pool our tested experience as we now know how, through joint efforts like your own, we can make some marked and overdue improvements in the public management of our State governments.

In today's world this kind of undertaking has a new significance. Much more is involved than just our own convenience and the extent of our own willingness to tolerate inefficiency and waste. For our kind of government and way of life now stand on trial before many of the peoples of the world. And the degree of integrity and efficiency which we can achieve in governing ourselves will play no small part in shaping the future.

Stevenson wanted first-rate people at all levels of government and frequently interested himself in the choice of personnel where his participation was not essential.

To Fred K. Hoehler [222]

September 30, 1949

Dear Fred:

From my notes of last evening's discussion, I gather that you have at least the following possibilities for consideration as Executive Secretary of the Board of Public Welfare Commissioners:

    Mrs. Franklin Brown, Glen Ellyn;

    Mrs. Bowen Stephenson, McGraw-Hill Publications, Chicago;

    Mrs. Ralph Bettman, Chicago;

    Mrs. Wilbur, Champaign; [223]

    Mrs. Edgar Bernhard, Chicago suburbs;

    Mrs. Lloyd Lewis, Libertyville;

    Mrs. Preston Farley, Chicago.

I shall take the liberty of passing on any other names of really first class women who may occur to me in the Chicago area, and I assume Jane Dick will review all lists of active participants in her Women's Division.

Everything else being equal, I would, of course, like to see someone appointed who would do me some good.[224]

Sincerely yours,

When it became evident that the Governor and his wife could not avoid a divorce, it was their intention to make a mutually agreed-upon announcement. Because of the premature disclosure of their impending separation, the Governor issued a formal statement on September 30, 1949.

I am deeply distressed that due to the incompatability of our lives, Mrs. Stevenson feels a separation is necessary. Though I do not believe in divorce, I will not contest it. We have separated with the highest mutual regard.[225]

[222] The original is in the possession of Mrs. Hoehler.

[223] Unable to identify further.

[224] Marion Kirkland, who had acted as executive secretary of the Women's Division of the Stevenson Campaign Committee in 1948, received this appointment.

[225] In an interview with Walter Johnson on May 24, 1966, Carl McGowan said the divorce was catastrophic for Stevenson. McGowan went to Springfield as Stevenson's

To Mrs. Walter Baumgarten [226]

October 3, 1949

My dear Judy:

You were an angel to write me about my misfortune when you were in the midst of celebrating your good fortune!

It has been a harrowing and distressing interlude for me, and I feel bewildered and empty, but it must be for the best, and I found after long travail that there was really nothing else I could do in fairness to Ellen.

I am not coming to the Missouri-Pacific Railroad strike but I am sending someone else who knows more about it.[227] Hence we shall not meet now, but I will hope for a reunion soon. Perhaps you and Walter would come over and see me sometime. It would be a good lark.

Love,

ADLAI

To Joseph F. Bohrer [228]

October 3, 1949

Dear Joe:

You were good to write me. It has been a terrible ordeal on top of everything else, but I feel no bitterness — just bewilderment and great anxiety about Ellen and her future.

Yours,

ADLAI

To William I. Flanagan [229]

October 4, 1949

Yesterday I received a copy of the 31st Annual Report of the Department of Agriculture. This very fine and expensive book again reminds me

---

aide early in September, 1949, and the news broke on the thirtieth. During that time he lived at the mansion but Stevenson never spoke of it. Immediately after it became public, he and Stevenson were returning to Springfield from a trip to Chicago and McGowan felt constrained to say that he "felt badly about what I read." Stevenson replied that nothing could be done, that his wife felt she could not express herself in "this atmosphere. I don't know what she means." He never spoke a critical word to McGowan about his wife. But he took the divorce hard.

[226] The original is in the possession of Mrs. Baumgarten.

[227] During this forty-four-day strike, Governor Forrest Smith of Missouri asked the governors of other states affected by it — Arkansas, Colorado, Illinois, Kansas, Louisiana, Mississippi, Nebraska, Tennessee and Texas — to meet with him to discuss it. There is no record of whom Stevenson sent to represent him.

[228] The original is in the possession of Mr. Bohrer.

[229] The original of this memorandum is in the possession of Mr. Flanagan.

that we should review the whole scheme of format and expense in connection with these Departmental Reports. I know little about the extent to which they are read, but I must say this one seems to me a very extravagant job.

I should think we might try to work out some standardization for all the Departmental Reports on a more modest, inexpensive basis.

A.E.S.

Paul Powell, speaker of the House of Representatives, was an "old-line" Democratic politician from Vienna, Illinois, and must have found it difficult many times to support Stevenson's program in the legislature, but he was loyal and worked hard to promote the legislation Stevenson so ardently desired. He wrote Stevenson on October 5, 1949, enclosing a letter written to him by a Republican House member, Noble Lee, commending Powell on his performance as speaker.

To Paul Powell

October 7, 1949

Dear Paul:

I have read with interest this genuinely appreciative letter from Noble Lee. What he says has been echoed by many, but none have said it better. What's more, he means it. I think there is no doubt from all I have heard that you established a new level of performance, tempered by humility and humor — two virtues that have become all too rare in our public life. The Governor is proud and fortunate to be on the Speaker's side of the aisle!

Sincerely yours,

To Alicia Patterson [230]

October 9, 1949

Its Sunday night and all is still in my gloomy mansion after a frenzied, feverish week. I've read & reread your two letters. They were better than you think and gave me what I needed when I needed it most. Your mother [231] was an angel and I've just written her a note of thanks — and a fine paternal letter to Adlai who will be 19 tomorrow.

You must not grieve for me. . . . I was long since reconciled to it as

[230] This handwritten letter is in the possession of Adlai E. Stevenson III.
[231] Mrs. Joseph Medill Patterson.

I told you. There's much that I don't understand about life and human relationships, but there was little left for us, except the children, I know — whatever the reasons or the justice or injustice. I feel no resentment or bitterness or pain and as for the bewilderment, I've surrendered to the inscrutable. But I *am* troubled about Ellen & her future. She is in the East with her mother now and seeing the boys. She returns this week & the agreement will be signed over the week end, I suppose. Then she'll pack up for Reno, returning to the farm for the holidays with the boys — they'll be down here part of the time. After Jan. 1, she'll move to an apt. in town and start her life over. I had hoped she would go to Boston for a year, but she'll have none of that. She will have to live very carefully on her modest means — and so will I!

I'm so glad you think the press was OK. The Daily News & American strung it out for several days on the society page etc, but the news story was soon over and I'm so glad they treated it lightly in N.Y. Time & Newsweek were OK — altho the latter might have left out the picture.

The American had the story about 3 weeks ago — called Ellen about it in Boston and me here. They volunteered to say nothing until I was ready to issue a statement. But not so with the [Chicago] Tribune. Tagge [232] called me — . . . last Friday an hour or so after our talk, said he had the story and what did I have to say. I told him "I might have something to say next week and meanwhile would expect the same consideration from them I had from the American." He said he couldn't make any promises and hung up. About 1 AM — when the Tribune was on the streets in Chi the phone started and I didn't get to sleep again until 4:30. I don't believe Ellen got any sleep in Libertyville!

It was a "typical Tribune" performance, but I must say the story was good. Mulroy was in Chicago & they consulted him and rewrote it three times. Even Ellen was delighted with it — and all the others for that matter — thank God! Perhaps she thinks they've made her look like the shy, modest retiring little wife who can't bear publicity and me as an ambitious, ruthless politician.

Anyway the first ordeal is over and now if we can only finish it with dignity! . . .

A

P.S. This is the worst mess of all — I'm so tired I can hardly sit up. Why didn't I write this morning? I was playing golf in the beautiful warm Injun summer! So there!! . . .

---

[232] George Tagge, political reporter for the Chicago *Tribune*.

Senator Arthur H. Vandenberg, the Michigan Republican under whom Stevenson had served at the San Francisco Conference and the first UN General Assembly meeting, entered the University of Michigan Hospital on September 26, 1949. A week later he underwent serious lung surgery, and by October 9 the hospital reported that he was "comfortable and in excellent spirits." The following day, Stevenson sent him a telegram.

To Arthur H. Vandenberg

October 10, 1949

DEAR SENATOR —

YOU ARE IN MY PRAYERS. I WISH THERE WAS SOMETHING I COULD DO TO INSURE ABOUT 20 MORE YEARS OF USEFUL LIFE FOR YOU!

YOURS

ADLAI

Governor Stevenson took a special interest in the field of education. During the 1949 legislative session he proposed to spend some 61 per cent more on common school education than had previously been spent. After the war years, when all the states built up large surpluses, Illinois had a respectable balance in its treasury, but almost half was needed to cover deficiency appropriations of the prior administration and budget commitments already made. The General Assembly cut the amount Stevenson proposed for the schools, a move that Stevenson protested. "Although he had very progressive plans and the appropriations for schools in his budget were very liberal, there just wasn't enough money to cover everything. His own party leaders told him that all he wanted couldn't be done within the monetary limitations. They informed him that they were obligated to cut some of these to a level that the state could afford. Stevenson protested loudly, but his budget was cut, leaving him without his great improvements." [233]

Between 1907 and 1949, fifteen different legislative commissions had been established to study common-school problems, but they were primarily concerned with immediate problems and when they expired the state was then confronted with new ones. But the practice of using them seemed firmly established. The education leaders in the state could not agree on what needed to be done and each group functioned on a go-it-alone basis, introducing legislation it deemed most important through any

[233] Nicholas A. Masters, Robert H. Salisbury and Thomas H. Eliot, *State Politics and the Public Schools — An Exploratory Analysis* (New York: Knopf, 1964), pp. 144–145.

legislator who would sponsor its proposals. This produced an enormous number of bills each session, many of them on the same subject, and eventually the legislature found it could not handle them efficiently. A "reprieve" was granted during the war years, but after that hiatus the education leaders expected the legislature to act promptly on their problems which had by then grown so acute.

Although Superintendent of Public Instruction Vernon Nickell made studies and recommendations, the legislature for a variety of reasons, among them political rivalry and lack of support by education interests, paid little heed to his proposals.

Added to these problems was the enormous increase in the school population during the war.

The pressure for action from education groups was intense at the time Stevenson took office. He immediately, by executive order, created an advisory body to guide him in developing his education program (although no formal report was made). High on the list of this advisory committee was a recommendation to create a continuing commission to study full-time the problems of education. It was argued that such a commission would provide the legislature with the expert assistance it needed to meet current as well as future dilemmas.

The legislature was not convinced that such a commission was necessary, but the need for some kind of council, even a temporary one, was apparent, and late in the session it passed an act creating a commission "to survey and study the problems pertaining to public schools in the state," and to determine improvements necessary to "raise the educational standards of the public school to a desirable level." Between this first commission and the year 1957, three additional ones were created, substantially alike. In 1957 it finally became a permanent part of the decision-making process, known as the Illinois School Problems Commission.

"Although first established in 1949, merely as a temporary advisory commission for the legislature, the School Problem Commission today is actually the arena in which decisions concerning the state's role in education are made. It is uniformly regarded as the state's most powerful agency with regard to school politics." [234]

On October 11, 1949, Stevenson delivered a speech to a meeting of the Illinois Secondary School Principals' Association, in Champaign, Illinois, "to say some things I want to say about our public school situation in Illinois." [235]

[234] Ibid., p. 100. For a full discussion of Illinois school politics, see pp. 99–178.
[235] The text is based on a carbon copy.

I'm not sure just why I was invited here tonight. I do not know whether it was out of curiosity, or courtesy, to the new Governor, or whether there was some other reason. Possibly those in charge of your program thought it would be a good idea to get me over here and give me a little sales talk about the needs of the schools — for instance the financial needs of the high schools. You understand that is not an accusation; it is pure speculation.

Whatever the reason, I am glad to meet face to face with some of the real "working people" of our school system. I welcome this opportunity to say some things I want to say about our public school situation in Illinois. I intend to speak plainly, and I think I can do so because I am confident you know all about my friendship for the schools. That is to say, I don't believe I need to convince you I am well aware of the essential place of education in a free society. And I don't think I need to tell you I am aware of the fact that public education here in Illinois is going through a crucial transition involving many problems. Even if I were not aware of the problem before, I could scarcely be unaware of it now after living and sleeping with it ever since I took office last January!

In every profession, and especially in education, one must take directional bearings now and then. It is well to pause and consider where we are heading. In the case of the public schools it is essential in these periods of taking stock that we keep in mind always that free education was founded to promote the interests of our democratic society, rather than merely to serve the needs of the children as individuals. The early history of our State and nation, and the evolution of our school laws make it abundantly clear that the founders believed the primary function of education was to teach young people the fundamentals of good citizenship. They believed that only through free education could the continuation of free government be guaranteed.

The need for greater understanding has increased with the growing complexity of our society and with the mounting tensions and conflicts that have tormented this revolutionary age. Hence the growing insistence on better schools and a broader, richer, deeper curriculum. The pressures created by the eight or nine million children born during the post-war years have vastly aggravated the school plant and equipment needs. 250,000 new school rooms will have to be built in the United States, in addition to 200,000 rooms that will be needed to replace obsolete facilities. The estimated cost of this construction is nine billion dollars.

The demand for more and for better schools has made itself felt in Illinois, as elsewhere, in the form of ceaseless agitation for more money for the schools. As you all know, here in Illinois the current dissatisfaction has produced a variety of results — the extensive reorganization program of recent years, higher local taxes for schools, greatly increased state aid, and a new principal and Board of Education in Chicago. Nationally the demands were reflected in the drive in the Congress for federal financial aid to education. If the people at large had not thought that the schools needed a major overhauling, it would not have been possible to generate the widespread public support that was behind these movements.

The results of the public demand for better schools perhaps have been more striking in Illinois that anywhere else in the nation. We have cut in half the number of school districts in this state, where we had a staggering 12,000 districts five years ago. Hundreds of communities have raised their school tax rates with the approval of the voters. The legislature adopted my proposals and state aid to the common schools has just been raised to record high levels. And it has been recognized that this matter of better schools is not just a matter of more rooms and desks. We have made some real progress in increasing the attractiveness of teaching as a profession. Teachers' salaries have risen. Their training is improving and broadening.

We have through governmental processes brought about substantial improvements in the quality and the financing of the schools. That more, much more, can and must be done does not contradict the fact that much has been done. The question now is, where do the schools go from here?

The schools themselves now are on the spot. Having obtained a large part of what they asked from the people through their governments, state and local, the school administrators now are in the position of having to produce the kind of schools the people are being called upon to pay for. The people are going to be asking: "What are the schools doing?" rather than "How much is the legislature going to appropriate?" There is going to be a shift of emphasis from "How much money?" to "How much education?"

That is the challenge facing all public education in America. It applies particularly to education in Illinois, where the insistence upon more adequate school financing was so positive. It is a challenge which the teaching profession cannot ignore or defer.

I am not here to attempt to tell you how you should go about achieving results. The precise nature of the educational program should, of course, be determined by experts in the field of education. The function of government is to try to remove obstacles that hamper the achievement of the best possible type of education.

The state administration wants to work closely with you and the other educational organizations toward these objectives. There are several ways we can do this. One is through an understanding, sympathetic, cooperative attitude toward changing educational problems. Another is by providing good teacher training and lifting the prestige of the teaching profession. Still another is by maintaining a close liaison between the executive and legislative branches and the schools. And I don't mean just the liaison between pressure groups and politicians, which is all too common.

I am glad to say that the mechanics for healthy, effective cooperation have been set in motion in Illinois. They are in operation now. Just last week I appointed the five public members of the new School Survey Commission which was created by the 66th General Assembly on my recommendation, completing the membership of twelve. This most important Commission will, during the next two years, study various phases of the over-all public school problem and make a report to the Governor and the General Assembly by March 1, 1951, at which time the 67th General Assembly will be in session.

No doubt the reaction of some of you is: "So they are setting up another School Commission!" I know we have had a number of such commissions through the years, to the point where they have become somewhat suspect, but I also know that the informal Advisory Committee I appointed during the session last winter — including Dean Spaulding [236] here at the University of Illinois — did some very effective work in formulating positive and attainable goals for Illinois' schools. I have every confidence that the new and formally constituted commission will serve a highly useful purpose.

It has practically unlimited authority to make recommendations that will accelerate the reorganization, and perfect the financing of the schools. The commission will also study the distribution of school aid, and how to accomplish the construction of the many new school buildings that we need under the unit district program. And what is highly important, the commission will make a careful interim study of the amount of state aid that should go to the schools.

For the first time, therefore, we have an objective, qualified board to advise the Budgetary Commission, the Governor and the Legislature as to the amount of state aid that should be provided for the next biennium. I think you will all agree that such a step was long overdue. It is not a healthy condition when the amount of school appropriations is left to political pulling and hauling in the heat of a legislative session. In performing this part of its advisory function alone the new Commission will be doing a vital service for the people of Illinois.

There is a further word I want to say about the state's responsibility

[236] Willard B. Spalding, dean of the College of Education, University of Illinois.

for school financing. In the legislative session this year the General Assembly appropriated to the common schools, for all purposes, more than $126,500,000, or an increase of 52.7% over the previous biennium. The appropriation was three times as large as in 1943. It represents 22% of all the general revenue fund money which we expect — which we hope! — to collect during his biennium.

You are all familiar with the pattern of these appropriations, how they have increased in varying degrees from session to session. It was proper that these increases be voted, because the State of Illinois obviously has been far behind the procession in its support of the schools. Even as we have vastly increased the total amount per pupil spent in Illinois the State's relative position has fallen. In 1938 it ranked sixth in the nation in the total amount of money spent per pupil. In 1948 it ranked 22nd. With this year's large increases made locally and by the State the 1949 figures will show Illinois climbing back up the ladder again.

But money alone is not the measure of a successful school system. Money alone can never provide a substitute for or a guarantee of good teachers and an adequate curriculum. Moreover, we have reached the point where these huge increases in school appropriations cannot be continued indefinitely. In the first place, the Legislature will insist upon knowing that the present higher level of State aid is being properly utilized to really improve and equalize educational opportunities. In the second place, we are face to face with a grave financial problem in carrying on the essential services of State government.

This financial problem is not peculiar to Illinois. It is the same in most all the states. In the war years many ordinary expenditures were postponed because of the war and the shortage of manpower and materials. Now these demands — not only for schools, but for badly needed buildings, for highways, for relief, and for many other worthy purposes — have overtaken our income. We are living from hand to mouth.

The State Finance Department has just submitted to the Budgetary Commission of the Legislature a frank analysis of our situation. The Department points out that even if the level of State expenditures is NOT increased during the next biennium starting in 1951, it may be necessary to raise large additional revenues to sustain the present level of spending. Unexpectedly high state revenues during the boom period of the last biennium made available a surplus which has been appropriated in this biennium to meet the increased needs of the schools, the welfare institutions, for public aid, and for other necessary functions. Such a surplus will not be available again next biennium.

We are doing everything possible to conserve our resources. We have invoked administrative economies, we are holding construction to a bare minimum, and in all of the departments and agencies under the control of the Governor's office we have taken steps to hold expenditures in this biennium to a level 10 per cent below the sums appropriated by the General Assembly. This is being done as a precaution against the possibility of a sharp decline in business activity that would be reflected immediately in reduced state income.

This is prudent management, but it is not a total solution of the problem by any means. We cannot avoid the realities. The construction needs of our welfare institutions are staggering. We never know when the costs of relief and public assistance — now rising steadily — will shoot suddenly higher because of an economic decline. And it is well to bear in mind that the area in which we can exercise rigid controls is sharply limited. Only about one-third of the State's budget goes for all the operating functions of the executive, legislative and judicial branches. Two-thirds is for construction and distribution to local governments, over which we can exercise little control.

My problem and the Legislature's problem is to find money for each of the absolutely vital State expenditures and we can't dodge our responsibility by meeting one set of demands at the expense of others which are equally deserving. I regret to note that that kind of a solution has been suggested in the September issue of the magazine "Illinois Education." The statement is made that if the Legislature had acted on the school aid program earlier in the session the entire $112,000,000 which I originally proposed, could have been secured "at the expense of other items." At the last moment we had to cut down the State school aid program somewhat because the Senate defeated bills to provide additional revenue. Other deserving aid programs also had to be curtailed or eliminated, including some $5 million for buildings for the University of Illinois, in order to balance our budget.

No group can expect to continue getting bigger and bigger appropriations for the program it is interested in unless it will lend a hand in securing authorization of the necessary taxes. Unless a miracle happens it will be necessary in the next session to provide additional revenue to sustain even the present level of State aid for schools. The school people who are interested in sustaining such a state aid program should start right now to help us to formulate a suitable revenue program for the next session of the Legislature.

There are those who will say, of course, that the money needed for school aid and similar purposes can be made available by economies in other State expenditures. I am as strong for economy as anybody in this room and, what's more, I'm doing something about it. But, as I have said, we cannot overlook the fact that many of the biggest spending programs such as general relief, aid to dependent children, and old age pensions, are only to a very limited degree within the control of the state administration. The number of persons on the relief and aid to dependent children rolls has increased by 45,000 in the past year, an increase of approximately 33%. In order to try to make the appropriations for these purposes last, the Illinois Public Aid Commission made a 10% cut in relief allowances on September 1st, but the rise in the number of persons receiving relief was so rapid that total allocations for relief in the month following the 10% decrease actually increased and the same was true as to the aid to dependent children program. Nor can we overlook the fact that some expenses like tax refunds and the huge increase in principal payments and interest on the public debt, are fixed charges and beyond any control.

The financial problem is by no means the only one which will be considered by the new School Survey Commission. They will also study state aid for transportation, improvements in school budgetary accounting practices, and the possibility of the consolidation of the various school tax levies. They will tackle the extremely difficult problems of organization and financing of community or junior colleges and nursery schools. I talked to several delegations of educators last spring about state aid for junior colleges. It is just one more of those situations where we would all be glad to see some money allocated if it was available. The Commission will have to consider whether junior colleges, and perhaps nursery schools, should share such state aid moneys as Illinois can afford to appropriate.

The people look to the leaders of education for the intelligent direction of the creative service which will reassure them that their children are receiving the training they need to be good citizens of tomorrow's world. They will also look to them for a balanced, responsible recognition of the State's *total* responsibilities. They will wholeheartedly support that kind of leadership. They will support generously an educational program in which they have confidence. To merit that public confidence and support must be the continuing objective of the leaders of the great American system of free common school education.

As Thomas Jefferson said: "I look to the diffusion of light and education as the resources most to be relied on for ameliorating the condition, promoting the virtue and advancing the happiness of man. The basis of our government being the opinion of the people, the very first object should be to keep that opinion right. If a nation expects to be ignorant and free in a state of civilization, it expects what never was and never will be."

To Harry S. Truman [237]

October 13, 1949

My dear Mr. President:

The "Call to Action" which issued from your Conference on Industrial Safety held in Washington last March recognized the essential role of the States in accident prevention and recommended that each Governor convene a state conference on this vital subject. Among other purposes, it was thought that the holding of state conferences would further the achievement of the objectives of your own conference and provide some continuity of effort in the intervals between the annual meetings of your conference.

I am, therefore, pleased to advise you that I have concluded to respond affirmatively to this suggestion. A few days ago I announced that there will be held in Illinois, on April 19–20 of next year, a Governor's Conference on Industrial Safety. Plans for this conference are proceeding, and it is hoped that it will be an effective instrument for the advancement of the cause of accident prevention.

I have asked the Director of the State Department of Labor, Mr. Frank Annunzio, to take the lead in formulating plans for the conference. He advises me that, in the task of planning and organizing the work of the conference, the active assistance of the United States Department of Labor has been, and is being, given. This help is of great importance and value to us, and I am writing my thanks to Secretary [Maurice] Tobin today.[238]

Sincerely,

Hector McNeil, Under Secretary of the British Foreign Office and a member of the United Kingdom Delegation to the United Nations in New York in 1949, wrote Stevenson on October 10 that he expected to be in Chicago to speak at the Council on Foreign Relations on October 21 and would remain in Chicago for two days. He hoped to see Stevenson and suggested that his office get in touch with Louise Wright of the council as to his availability for "a drink or a coffee."

[237] The original is in the Official File, the Harry S. Truman Library.

[238] President Truman replied on October 31, 1949, that Illinois was to be congratulated for supporting the recommendations of the presidential industrial safety conference.

To Hector McNeil

October 13, 1949

Dear Hector:

I have your note, and I am distressed that I may miss you. I am obliged to be in Rockford, Illinois, dedicating a new — and very expensive — bridge, while you are speaking to the Council on Foreign Relations. Early Saturday morning I must fly to Connecticut and thence to New York. If there would any chance of seeing you Friday evening, I believe I could arrange to fly into Chicago. Please let me know what your plans are for Friday night.

I am sending a copy of this letter to Louise Wright against the possibility that she might know more about your plans for Friday evening than you do!

Warm regards.

Sincerely yours,

Catharine Hardin invited Stevenson to a cocktail party at her home in Rockford, Illinois, on October 21, to meet a group of supporters of his 1948 campaign, and to spend the night. Her husband, Dr. Parker Hardin, was Stevenson's cousin. She also wrote about Mrs. Martin D. Hardin that "Her visit with you made Parker's mother look positively radiant — almost girlish. She is so very proud of you, as are we all."

To Mrs. Parker Hardin

October 15, 1949

My dear Catharine:

I have your good note this morning. Unfortunately I am afraid I will have to leave Rockford in mid-afternoon to get back to Chicago for an engagement that evening with Hector McNeil, the British Under Secretary of the Foreign Office, who is going to be in town and wants to see me. My only chance is then because I will have to leave by seven o'clock the following morning for Connecticut.

All in all I see little prospect of taking advantage of your hideout — or cocktails!

Affectionately,

In 1947, Robert E. Merriam won a seat on the Chicago City Council representing the Fifth Ward. Stevenson was anxious that he run for the Illinois State Senate.

[167]

To Robert E. Merriam

October 19, 1949

Dear Bob:

I have a report from Donald Walsh [239] that you have finally decided not to run for the Senate. Of course, I am much disappointed, but I suppose if your political interests lie primarily in the city you are making the correct decision. All the same it would be a blessing to me to have you down here, and I think you would be an excellent addition to the ticket up there for the Legislature where we are so woefully weak.

Yours,

On October 19, 1949, Governor Stevenson addressed the Inland Daily Press Association, in Chicago.[240]

I have been Governor of one of the larger states for nine months. I came to this job rather suddenly after spending the war years in executive posts in the Federal government and the post-war years in the international field. I'm rapidly losing my perspective. Before it is all gone and my horizon has narrowed down to the borders of Illinois, I want to say some things to you newspapermen and publishers — whom I used to like to think of as my fellow craftsmen. I have no news for you and nothing spectacular or important to say, but my thinking, which for so long was preoccupied with the national and international scene, has, in these trying months, found a new, and, I think, a better balance.

At the risk of repeating what you already know so well, I want to say something about the Federal system, because I think it has some particular relevance to the great preoccupations of our day which are so largely national and international, and which, it seems to me, are threatening a rational perspective of our *total* problem.

I should not be surprised if some day at least an occasional historian referred to this revolutionary era among other things as the age of rediscovery — an interval in which we rediscovered and reexamined many of our concepts, discarded some, exalted others, and generally overhauled a political and economic system that has developed in the careless, expe-

[239] Mr. Walsh, on leave of absence from the Chicago *Herald-American*, was appointed by Stevenson as director of public safety. He remained in this position until 1950, when he returned to the newspaper as its circulation director.

[240] The text is based on a ribbon copy with pencil interlineations in Stevenson's handwriting.

dient, haphazard fashion that orders most affairs of men. If we do, I think we will have our two dread enemies to thank most — Russia and taxes. But more of that later.

Meanwhile, what of our Federal system and our States?

In 1787 one of the great documents of history, the Constitution of the United States, came into being, and with it a new concept of government, never before tried on such a vast scale. The Federal system was first propounded in detail in the *Federalist Papers,* those brilliant essays on the Constitution prepared by Hamilton, Jay, and Madison, and published in the New York press. Now, 162 years later, some 155,000 state and local governments have sprung up under this Federal system.

The first census of 1790 revealed that less than four million persons resided in the United States, not half the population of Illinois today. Now, with 150,000,000 population our problems have changed, multiplied and magnified. With a gross national income in the neighborhood of 200 billion dollars, and total governmental expenditures of 55 billion dollars, our problems are baffling. And yet we find that the remarkable flexibility of our constitution, its responsiveness to changing conditions, its reliance on dual national-state operations has weathered these fantastic changes.

The concept of federalism in this country has been largely unplanned, based primarily on the process of trial and error. This development of a dual governmental system has not been accomplished without its zig-zags and reversals of opinion. But my purpose is not to discuss the origin and philosophical background of the federalist concept.

Rather, I want to emphasize the *uniqueness* of our national-state government, and to remind you that we have successfully combined the need for a strong national government with vigorous state and local links. We have successfully found a way to establish national patterns with wide local participation and policy-determination. We have found a compromise between the over-centralization of a huge national government and the probable chaos of completely decentralized states. That there are duplications and waste we all know, that there are imperfections we are sure — government, after all, consists of human beings.

What we must determine is whether we are making the most of what we have, whether we as public officials — and responsible editors and publishers — can do more to make our democracy work, and work well, because if it doesn't work well and satisfy human needs and property rights it will not survive the winds that are blowing and will continue to blow for a long time.

Every national political campaign in the decades since the first World War has been full of political charges and counter-charges concerning the vaguely defined question of "states' rights." The "outs" generally have accused the "ins" of attempting to wreck our federal system, of concentrating all power in Washington, and most recently of leading the nation down the road to "statism." This phenomenon of our national political life has not been accidental. Nor has it been the exclusive property of any one side. The Democrats, whose patron saint is Jefferson, currently are accused of contributing most to this trend, contrary to true Jeffersonian principle. History shows us that the trend toward a strong federal government was first advocated by Hamilton, the great opponent of Jefferson, and sometimes considered to be philosophically the father of Republican policies. But Jefferson himself took one of the boldest presidential steps in our history when he agreed to the Louisiana Purchase.

In 1932 Franklin Roosevelt denounced the Republicans because they had committed "themselves to the idea that we ought to center control of everything in Washington as rapidly as possible." Yet I don't need to tell this group that in every campaign since then Roosevelt and Truman have been denounced for doing just that.

I cite these facts not to remind us of the inconsistencies of which we are all guilty, but to raise the question of where we go from here, and how we may analyze carefully and rationally this problem of an expanded federalism. In my opinion there is no point in belaboring the issue of "states' rights." Actually, almost all of us believe in the federal system. Some see less threat to states from federal encroachment than others, and detect less federal domination than others. Every state has profited from the federal grants-in-aid, but all sensible people know there must be some limits to the extension of federal programs. Those limits may well be determined by the taxpayers' pocket books more effectively than by frightened proclamations of states' rights.

The plain, hard fact is that the industrial age has created problems of health, housing, education, transportation and employment, which inexorably flow over state boundaries. No amount of talk can ever reverse this trend. But more than that, we must also face the fact that in many instances the states either would not or could not begin to cope with the many vast problems created by the industrialization of this country and the consequent complexities and stresses of modern life in the machine age.

The federal system with its 49 major governments, one national and 48 state, is the answer to the dangers of over-centralization in the United States. With 48 enlightened, progressive state centers there is little danger of too great consolidation of governmental authority. The 48 states in 1950 will spend something over six billion dollars for their operations.

Illinois' share of this total will run to over half a billion dollars. The area of Texas is larger than the combined areas of France, Belgium, Luxembourg, the Netherlands, and Switzerland; the population of New York State is more than that of Belgium and Switzerland combined. Can we possibly exaggerate the states' importance to our way of living and doing? Can we afford to neglect their management? And yet it appears to me that we are doing just that. It appears to me that here is one of the greatest threats to our federal system.

The states are the home of self-government — the states and their 150,000 local governments (counties, cities, schools, etc.), and the 1,000,000 elective officers within their borders.

Those who say that the state is out of date, or becoming so, have forgotten the facts of life about our country. Who organizes and operates our public schools? The states. Who provides protection for our health? The states. Who protects the persons and property of our people? In the main, the states.

One of the troubles with modern taxation is that the state does not share fully and effectively in our American system — to the great disadvantage of those who contribute the revenue for governmental functions. This is a major problem to which prompt attention should and must be given.

Within its constitutional field of action, the commonwealth for a century and a half has been free to work out laws and administrative arrangements adapted to the rich variety of interests and areas in the United States. If a state hits upon a good idea, it can quickly be adopted elsewhere, modified, or tried and found wanting. If a state wants to be dry, so be it; or wet, even so. One state even taxes the illegal sale of liquor. A state can have a community property law, or not, as it sees fit. It can experiment with various forms of local government in cities and schools, as it will, or deal with agriculture or business or labor within wide limits. The state can pass blue-sky laws or regulate public utilities as it sees fit, set up standards for state banks and insurance companies, and experiment with welfare plans. It is well to note that Wisconsin started the unemployment payments which were later adopted in revised form for the entire country.

This power to pass upon and decide local affairs is basic to our free society. It makes possible democratic participation at the grass roots of our human relations. If our 150,000,000 people did not have states, they would create them, rather than centralize all power at one central point, where congestion of authority would soon defeat the purposes and possibilities of democratic development and progress.

The founding fathers recognized the value of home rule on the one hand and national unity on the other, and in our federal system they built even better than they knew.

At the Governors' Conference in Colorado in June — the first I had attended — I was impressed by the range and importance of state problems, and by the capacity of the states for cooperation in state affairs. I was impressed too by the fact that the states are all facing the same budgetary problems and for the same reasons. More recently in this city, representatives of 22 states which have created so-called Little Hoover Commissions, met to discuss the tough problems of state reorganization for more effective, efficient administration.

States' responsibilities are as important as states' rights — responsibilities to aid in the work of government. The greatness of a state does not depend alone on its size, its wealth, its population, but upon the manner in which it helps to make good the ends of government. Nowhere are these purposes of politics more clearly stated than in the Preamble to the Constitution: common defense, tranquility, justice, welfare, and the blessings of liberty. (And in the current discussion of the proper limits of the welfare state, I have not heard anyone propose to strike "welfare" out of the preamble.) To these ends our commonwealths are dedicated. We have no quarrel with the national government; we are only in a friendly competition in promoting the pursuit of human happiness, in increasing our production, and in enriching the values of life for all our people.

Now I mention all these familiar facts and problems because even a few short months at the very trying job of being a governor of a great state has brought me a grave concern. It is not whether the national government is swallowing up the states, but rather how to glamorize the state sufficiently to lure at least a sidelong glance from the wandering eyes of a citizenry so fascinated with the national and international spectacle. I need not tell this group about the power and influence for better government and better public officials that lies in a vigilant, informed public and pitiless publicity.

But how do we go about interesting the generally disinterested citizenry in the all-important problems of our states? How do we arouse the kind of public concern which brings about effective action in state government? How, for example, do we in Illinois bring to the public an understanding of the problems of operating a 1950 government with an 1870 Constitution long since antiquated? How do we arouse concern about our welfare institutions, the condition of our roads, the pay we give those on relief? How do we reconcile the need for top-notch personnel to run a half-billion dollar yearly business with the salaries we pay? How do we persuade people to stop complaining about taxes and demanding new state services at the same time?

Most Americans know something of the workings of their federal government; in recent months additional interest has been aroused in the reports of the Hoover Commission on Reorganization, although twelve years ago many of the identical proposals were called another Roosevelt attempt to create a dictatorship. It isn't hard to stir up excitement about the Marshall Plan, the Atlantic Pact or the Steel Strike. But how many persons know what their state governments do for them? How many are interested in the problems of those governments? How many ask themselves what they would have to pay for the myriad social-economic tasks which the states, or their subdivisions, perform, if they had to go out and buy them on the market? How many have the faintest notion how many new state services have been added in the past 20 years? How does one create interest in the election of the all-important state legislators? *These* are today's problems in "states' rights."

Our great task is to make the 155,000 governing units of this country work, all the way from the mosquito abatement districts to the national government in Washington. Forty-eight of the 155,000 governments are states; the rest are subdivisions of states. That is where the decisions mostly lie. Here is where I suggest we must concentrate more attention. And here is where you publishers can exercise a great influence, because you will be talking about schools, roads, hospitals, police, courts and all the countless real and homely things the people confront from day to day.

We *can* make democracy work at all levels. We *can* get better government. We *can* do away with graft and corruption. As Elihu Root once said: "The true and only way to preserve state authority is to be found in the awakened conscience of the states, their broadened views and higher standards of responsibility to the general public; in effective legislation by the states, in conformity to the general moral sense of the country; and in the vigorous exercise for the general public good of that state authority which is to be preserved." That, not bitter recriminations, is the answer to those who fear the centralization of power in Washington. That, not speeches, is the answer to the gentlemen in the Kremlin. In a world plunged into a bitter war of ideas, the words and platitudes uttered by you or me today or our statesmen tomorrow won't have much effect. But what happens in each of those 155,000 governments in this country, in Chicago and Springfield, as well as in Washington, will have its effect, because the quality of democratic government can never be better than the average of its parts.

Perhaps what is needed is a new set of Federalist papers explaining state government to our people. But of one thing I'm certain. There *is* a quickening interest in government at all levels, due in part at least to the restiveness of the taxpayer. You have, it seems to me, an obligation to enlighten him about his local and state government — what it is spending and why, how well it is managed, and who and what kind of men the managers and legislators are.

I was much gratified to note that more reporters were assigned to cover the last session of our legislature than ever before and the news coverage was very extensive and good. I hear the same was true in many state capitals. But I was hopeful that some papers would make a serious effort to analyze and explain in simple terms the state budget of Illinois. I'm sorry to say that in Illinois there was little but the usual epithets and criticism of the budget increase which was actually less, proportionately, than in most states. There was the usual editorial approval for specific increases coupled with general criticism of the overall increase. Enlarged state aid for schools and tuberculosis control, for example, was applauded but the consequent increase in the budget was condemned. Last June a large Chicago paper ran an editorial denouncing the increase in the budget, and in an adjoining column another editorial demanded inclusion of several million dollars more for an additional state aid program. A large downstate paper damned the budget editorially and the next day with equal vigor demanded that the state subsidize the training of nurses.

Few, if any, Illinois papers took the trouble to point out that only about one-third of the budget is for the operating activities of the state government and two-thirds for construction, debt service, tax refunds and mostly for distribution to local governments for education, highways, welfare and relief over which we can exercise little if any control. So far as I know, none pointed out that the accumulated surplus which this state, like all others is currently spending, was an unexpected windfall due to a post-war business boom and inflation instead of a post-war recession.

What is true of Illinois is, I dare say, true in all the states here represented. What I say is not in criticism but in the earnest hope that you can do a better information job about state government. Generalized criticism is seldom as effective as pointed criticism. We in Springfield stand ready, indeed eager, to give you the information to help in every way we can to enlighten the people accurately. Indeed, I would like to arrange seminars and discussion groups about the various departments of state government for the Illinois press as we did for the State Chamber of Commerce.

I am sure the governors of other states are just as eager to stimulate the growing interest in the problems and programs of our states. And with the appalling increase in the cost of all government, it seems to me that the *news* value in state government is also increasing.

I know that government under our system can never be wholly

efficient. But I also know that it can be vastly better; indeed, it must be better. As Bryce said a long time ago, one of the greatest hazards of successful democratic government is excessive partisanship. But partisanship diminishes in importance as we descend from the national to the local level. There are very few issues which divide us into Democrats or Republicans at the state level. But unhappily the convictions of our national thinking often carry over to prejudice our political thinking in the local arena. All the same, the growth of political independence is marked, and the American press has had much to do with the rapid movement away from blind partisanship and toward a common concern for better government.

Now, I was asked to say a word about the foreign situation. It can be only a word; a relevant word, I hope. I said at the outset that if this proves, as I think it will, to be a very healthy era in American life in which we rediscovered and restated our principles; in which we demanded and got something cleaner and better in public management, we would have the Russians to thank for it. What I mean is this: The Soviet Union is not going to attack the Western world, nor are we going to attack them although they think we are when the capitalist cycle turns down to depression and unrest. But we *are* going to be incessantly engaged in an aggravating, exhausting cold war for longer than I like to contemplate. We have already been fighting this wretched war four years, a type of warfare with which Americans are unfamiliar, impatient and incredulous. Along with the troublesome irritations, the Red scares and the huge defense expenditures, I suggest, [it?] has produced some good.

It has caused the world to reexamine colonial policies and aspirations for freedom. It has drawn the Western community closer together for common defense and social and economic survival. It has kept the United States an alert and positive participant. It has even brought the dream of peace by world government closer to realization. It has made the United Nations and an international forum more imperative than ever. And, finally, it has caused us in the midst of all the ferment of ideological conflict and realignment to look to our own housekeeping.

While we have been loudly proclaiming the virtues of democracy and free enterprise, the Communists have been even more loudly calling attention to our failures and hypocrisies and, of course, to a lot of false failures as well. While polishing up the facade of our splendid edifice for all the admiring and envious of the world to see, we've also begun poking around among the long neglected fire hazards in our basement — and none too soon. And, of course, the Communists have been forcing us to spend money beyond our saddest dreams of precarious peace, with the result that the restive taxpayer is looking in the corners and under the rug for dirt and waste more diligently than he has for a long time — which is a very healthy thing.

All in all, this cold war and this relentless Communist pressure which is the strongest competition our Western individualism has encountered since the renaissance, has already and will continue to cause us to do all sorts of things and change all sorts of things, but in *our* own way, not *their* way. As Toynbee says, Communism is the catfish in the Western herring pond. It may eat a few herring, but it prevents all the rest from getting soft and stale. And of course if we can only keep fresh and alert like the herring bedeviled by a catfish; if we don't get rattled and can develop and improve our way of life by this self-examination and rediscovery, as we put our own house in better and better order, the less chance the Commies will have of imposing their way of life upon us. Indeed, our success will be their downfall, because it will have the slow, imperceptible effect on them they hope to have on us. *They* will be the converted, not us.

I'm not just trying to see the bright side of a dismal picture, but we all know that we achieve most under the pressure of necessity. And unless I read some signs, all too faint for certainty, quite incorrectly, we in the Western world who believe in individualism are moving into a fruitful period of housecleaning. And here in the United States, state government has a big part of the job to do. You — the press — can help us more than anyone by telling the *people* the facts, because governors are not commissars — thank God!

On October 24, 1949, Governor Stevenson appeared on the New York Herald-Tribune Forum, *in New York City. The program was broadcast locally by radio. Also appearing on the program were Dwight D. Eisenhower, then president of Columbia University, who spoke on "The Individual's Responsibility for Government"; Herbert H. Lehman, former Governor of New York; Federal Security Administrator Oscar R. Ewing; Senator Frank P. Graham (North Carolina); Senator Hubert H. Humphrey (Minnesota); Representative Franklin D. Roosevelt, Jr. (New York), Representative Howard W. Smith (Virginia), Representative Clifford P. Case (New Jersey); James G. Patton, president of National Farmers' Union; and Dr. Lindsay Rogers, Professor of Public Law, Columbia University. The subject assigned to Stevenson was: "What kind of Democrat I am." *[241]

[241] The text is based on a mimeograph copy.

"The kind of Democrat I am" seems to me most artfully, I might say diabolically, contrived. Had it been "why I am a Democrat,["] for example — I could have consumed my allotted time in threadbare but respectable generalizations about the party of Jefferson and Jackson and so on — all of which would have left neither you nor me any clearer as to just what I do think.

So I congratulate our program-makers on their cleverness, victim though I am. They have touched a great weakness in our political thinking — the reliance on labels, the lazy preference for catch phrases over the rigors of rational thought and self-analysis. I don't think that people in the mass really put much stock in labels, although they use them freely. As our distinguished visitor at the moment, Pandit Nehru, has wisely said: "People do not believe in 'isms.' They believe in their own individual lives." They judge men and measures by their impact on themselves. In the privacy of the voting booth at any rate, I think the images of both the donkey and the elephant are fading as infallible beacons on the path to truth.

"What kind of Democrat I am" makes me feel a little like the old lady who said she didn't know what she thought until she heard what she said. I'm not sure what kind of a Democrat I am, but I am sure what kind of a Democrat I am not. I'm not one of those who believes we should have a Democratic regime because it is good for the Democratic party. If the Democratic party is not good for the nation it is not good for me or for Democrats.

I have no fixed principles by which every issue is to be automatically resolved. I do not identify big government with good government. I entertain no ambition for the Democratic party to set the track record for President Hoover's mythical last mile. I think government should be as small in scope and as local in character as possible. But it is the job that needs doing that must shape and delimit the area of governmental activity. And I think any necessary task that cannot be done except by public authority should not be neglected because of any unyielding notions about the proper size or extent of government. And it is equally grievous error not to make the government we have as efficient as possible, because inefficiency in government as in business makes for size and waste.

Perhaps the best way to find out what one is is from what one does.

In Illinois I have tried to call a convention to modernize our 1870 Constitution which is a constant obstacle to more responsible, efficient government. I lost by a close vote but got a liberalized amending procedure as a consolation prize. If the people approve it in 1950 it should enable us to crawl out of our ancient strait jacket if we can't jump out as I had hoped.

Because there has been job discrimination in Illinois, because it is a great industrial state, because it has a huge population of Negroes and minority groups, and because I believed it neither just nor expedient to wait longer upon the slow processes of education to solve the problem, I proposed a Fair Employment Practices Law for Illinois. I don't believe a society is truly free where race, color or creed is a bar to equality of opportunity to earn a living. I failed again, by one vote.

Illinois has a long and stubborn tradition of spoils politics. Better personnel management is, of course, one of the imperative needs in public administration and nowhere more than in Illinois. We have abolished payrollers and part-time positions; eliminated and consolidated functions; restored the respectability of the Civil Service Commission, increased salaries; removed the State Police for the first time from political control and placed it under a merit system. We are making public service as a career more attractive to better people. Finally, without interference from the Democratic party organization I have been able to fill all major positions without regard to political labels.

By reforming purchasing and inventory control procedures and honest administration we are stretching the State's commodity dollar further. Last week we saved $500,000 on a coal contract alone over the previous year in spite of rising prices.

We have removed the Illinois Commerce Commission which regulates utility rates from direct political control by the Governor.

State aid for common schools has been increased 53 per cent and the state's support for the teachers' colleges has also been sharply raised. Money alone is not the measurement of a sound foundation educational program and we have taken several bold steps toward larger and therefore more economical and better grade and high schools.

During this session of the legislature we were able to bring about by agreement of labor and management large increases in Workmen's Compensation and Unemployment compensation rates which had fallen far behind wage scales and living costs. We also have the tools now, with labor's consent, to eliminate abuses by the unscrupulous in unemployment compensation.

We are, for the first time, giving state aid to the hard-pressed public tuberculosis hospitals.

I think we have the legislative machinery at last to reduce, at least, the absurd inequities and injustices in local property tax assessments.

We have tightened up the mine inspection service and eliminated the administrative causes for the Centralia mine disaster of 1947.

We have established a "Little Hoover" commission to survey the organization of our state government which has not been closely examined in more than 30 years.

We have not succeeded in increasing the gas tax to attack our shamefully neglected highway system. But we've tried and we are going to keep on trying until the people in the city and the country face the facts. Illinois has one of the lowest gas taxes in the country and the state's share is about the lowest, and in an agricultural-industrial state that depends on highway transportation. Meanwhile we are vigorously enforcing the truck weight laws for the first time and doing what we can to make the abuse of our roads hazardous and unprofitable.

In the mental hospitals and institutions we are putting more emphasis on career service, modernizing buildings, segregating the old and senile from those requiring more expert care and attempting to control intake by shifting the emphasis from state hospitalization to home care.

I vetoed some 60 bills, including a cigarette price-fixing measure, unnecessary appropriations bills, treasury raids, political bills, and the famous act to put cats on leashes!

As Governor of Illinois I can't shape any national or international policies, but I can improve the probity, the efficiency, and the moral tone of state government — or break my heart and head in the attempt; I can influence our policies in education, welfare, taxation and all the 101 housekeeping jobs, from grain inspection to police administration. If something needs doing that costs more money I can ask for it, as I have. If something costs more money than it's worth I can oppose it, as I have. If our old constitution makes for waste, law violation and injustice I can say so regardless of the opposition, and I have. In short, I can strive to improve the quality of my state government as I see it, and I will. "What man will not alter for the better, time — the great innovator — will alter for the worse," and the quest for good government cannot be confined to Washington. Some 155,000 units of government have sprung up under our Federal system and the quality of the national government is not going to be much better than the average of its parts. Moreover, I think the best government is the best politics — for Democrats and Republicans alike.

But does that superficial recitation of what I am doing in Illinois disclose what kind of Democrat I am? Or should I add that I'm an "internationalist" — no longer as rare a bird on the Illinois prairies as some of you think. I think that peace is the most important unfinished business of our generation; and that we are going to be in this brutal cold war for a long time to come and that we'd better win it if we want to preserve the Western idea of individualism and freedom which has been in the ascendancy so long.

I don't like doles. I don't like subsidies. I don't like any interferences with free markets, free men and free enterprise. I like freedom to succeed or to fail. But I also know that there can be no real freedom without economic justice, social justice, equality of opportunity and a fair chance for every individual to make the most of himself. And I know that there is little the man on the assembly line or the plow can do to affect the chain of events which may close his factory or foreclose his mortgage. Discontented, desperate men will sell freedom very cheap.

The basic political rift of our day in this country is by no means between those who favor individual liberty as against those who favor subjugation of the individual to the state. The rift concerns how far government is to go to attain the economic and social atmosphere in which the utmost individual liberty can thrive. Stated another way: how far government must impair some individual freedom to preserve more.

No one wants government to control every detail of human life and anyone who talks of a return to the good old days when government acted only as a policeman is on his way to a museum.

The real argument is between those who want government to do more at once and those who counsel caution lest we lose more of the Jeffersonian ideal of individual supremacy than we save. There are, of course, a lot of sideshows, posturing and windmill tilting to catch the crowd's fancy, but when the theatrical props are laid aside I can't see that the responsible "too muchers" are all agents of selfish interests, or the "not enoughers" agents of Moscow. The conflict is not going to be solved by epithets and slogans like "Communist," "Socialists," "statism," "welfare state," "Fair Deal," or "New Deal."

Somewhere in between lies the area where "welfare ideas and enterprise" ideas sometimes clash but more often merge. If we continue, as we have, with caution and thorough discussion; if we don't forget who or what we are trying to save — the American individual and his freedom — I am not worried about ruinous reaction on the one hand or radical misadventure on the other, because the American individual is a very sensible fellow.

Now if anyone can make out of all that what kind of a Democrat I am, I hope he'll tell me, because I don't know — perhaps just a "liberal," a label which has been appropriated by every politician of both parties, because it is the most fashionable and harmless nowadays.

William I. Flanagan sent the Governor a memorandum on October 24, 1949: "Attached is the new State Park booklet and a copy of the old booklet. Informatively, the new booklet cost $10,000 for 100,000 copies and the old booklet cost $25,000 for 100,000 copies."

To William I. Flanagan [242]

[no date]

Bill — I like this — I think its informative and adequate — and I like the economy!!

A.E.S.

On October 26, 1949, Governor Stevenson attended a dinner of the Chicago Council on Foreign Relations, in Chicago, where he introduced the guest of honor, Jawaharlal Nehru, Prime Minister of India.[243]

We live in an age swept by tides of history so powerful they shatter human understanding. Only a tiny handful of men have influenced the implacable forces of our time. To this small company of the truly great, our guest on this memorable day in Chicago and Illinois belongs.

He does us honor to come here and we pay him our *homage*, not just because he is the Prime Minister of India, but because he is a great and a good man. Pandit Jawaharlal Nehru belongs to the even *smaller* company of historic figures who wore a halo in their own lifetimes.

"The nation is safe in his hands." Those were Mahatma Gandhi's concluding words when he publicly chose Pandit Nehru as his heir and successor — because of his bravery, his prudence and discipline, his vision and practicality, his humility and purity.

Three hundred and fifty million of his countrymen love him, follow him, bless him for his brilliant leadership in their struggle for independence, and, some say, even more because of his character, spirit and sacrifice. Long ago he forsook ease and wealth and security, to risk life itself for his country.

A quarter of his life he has spent in prison for the same cause our own revolutionary ancestors pledged their lives, their fortunes and their sacred honor — freedom. Born to exalted station he knows the "art of being a king," yet he has a common touch that excites the devotion and understanding of all kinds and conditions of people, and he has a pen and tongue that stir the hearts of millions. In his address to Congress he said: "Even when preparing to resist aggression, the objective of peace

---

[242] This handwritten memorandum is in the possession of Mr. Flanagan.

[243] The text is based on a mimeograph copy prepared for release to the press by the Governor's Office. On October 27, 1949, Laird Bell, of Chicago, wrote Stevenson: "Your introduction of Nehru was perfect. It had dignity and appropriateness and real eloquence. It was another one of your masterpieces."

and reconciliation must never be lost sight of, and heart and mind must be attuned to this supreme aim, and not swayed or clouded by hatred or fear." So spoke our own Abraham Lincoln. These are words we understand, Mr. Prime Minister, and we are grateful for the reminder.

My friends, I bid you mark well what he says to us, for he is the voice of India — the home of a sixth of the human race and the largest stable, solvent democracy in the East. India can be the anchor of freedom in all Asia, but around it swirl dangerous currents and in it live millions in incredible poverty. Bedevilled with the infinite problems of national infancy, of the partition with Pakistan, of welding innumerable classes and minorities into a single Eastern state based on the liberal tradition of the West, his tasks beggar description.

Indeed I must acknowledge Your Excellency a personal debt. Whenever the problems of Illinois gets too oppressive I think of India and of you, Sir, and immediately I feel much better! We welcome you to Illinois.

To Harry S. Truman [244]

October 28, 1949

Dear Mr. President:

While in Chicago yesterday, representatives of the American Veterans Committee called on me to solicit my aid in endeavoring to persuade you to come to Chicago on November 25 to speak at their Fourth Annual Convention.

As you know, this is a relatively small veterans' organization, but they are bold enough to ask you to come to Chicago in view of the fact that you have spoken before the other veterans' national conventions.

Knowing your appalling burdens I am loath to urge you to accept, but I do feel that we have many friends in this organization and I am confident that you will give their invitation every consideration.[245]

Faithfully yours,

Representative Louis G. Berman, Democrat, from Chicago, sent Stevenson a gift of kosher salami which the Governor never received. On tracing the package it was found to have been delivered to the mansion, but it had been taken home by one of the servants. Representative Berman wrote the Governor on October 26 saying he was sending him another "yard of 'Kosher Salami' and hope they don't swipe this one."

[244] The original is in the Official File, Harry S. Truman Library.
[245] The President declined.

To Louis G. Berman [246]

October 28, 1949

Dear Lou:

The management around here informs me that the sausage did come although I have never seen it or tasted it. However, I am going to catch up starting tonight. I am mortified and most apologetic — and even more grateful! I will save some for you when you come to see me.

With warm regards, I am

Sincerely yours,

Paul S. Cousley, publisher of the Alton Evening Telegraph, *wrote Stevenson on October 26, 1949, complimenting him on his speech before the Inland Daily Press Association. "Perhaps, from remarks I heard afterward, it didn't set so well with the 'stuffier' members, but I think it was a clear-cut disempassioned statement of your ideas." He informed the Governor that the* Telegraph *was preparing pictures of scenes along the McAdams Memorial Highway. "Many of them are scenes beyond the end of the portion you so graciously and promptly got back into use last summer."*

To Paul S. Cousley

[no date]

Dear Mr. Cousley:

I was delighted to have your letter, and I am sorry if my remarks at the Inland meeting caused any displeasure. I was, as you know, pleading with them to take more interest, and more critical interest, in State government.

I was delighted with the pictures of the bluffs along the McAdams Memorial Highway, and I will look forward to others as they come along. You were good to think of me.

Sincerely yours,

On October 30, 1949, Governor Stevenson was asked to participate in the ninetieth anniversary of the Unitarian Church of Bloomington, Illinois. This had been his mother's church, and one to which he belonged all of his life. [247]

[246] A copy is in A.E.S., P.U.L.
[247] The text is based on a carbon copy.

The story of the founding of this church has been often told — based largely on the account left by Jesse Fell.[248] By 1859 Bloomington had grown to some 8,000 and there were already ten churches in the little community, including, interestingly enough, an African M.E. [Methodist Episcopal] church which had been established in 1847.

Most of the churches of that time were radically evangelistic in nature, and in a young community comprised of newcomers from the east and south it was natural enough to find in the Bloomington of that day and in the interpretation of religious belief a cross section of all the sectional prejudices. The clouds of disunion over the extension of slavery lay heavy on prairies in the summer of 1859, when a handful of men met in Kersey Fell's office. "To interchange views" in Jesse Fell's words, "And to consider whether any measures could be adopted for the establishment of a religious society on broader grounds and of a more progressive character than any existing in the city."

Jesse Fell, of course, was a Quaker from Pennsylvania and the 20 men who met that day were of all differing creeds. They organized what they called a "Free Congregational Society" to study and practice Christianity. As a Democratic Governor I can't overlook the fact that those 20 men, my own ancestors included, were all intimate friends of Abraham Lincoln and founders of the Republican party in Illinois! A few years later the Society's name was changed to the Unitarian Church of Bloomington.

It is interesting that out here on the prairies of Central Illinois a liberal religious movement sprang up entirely from the grass roots. So far as I can see no missionary activity from Chicago or the East influenced the organization of this church, which was open to people of all faiths. What's more, you could get *out* as easily as you could get *in!* The concluding sentence of the Declaration of Views prepared in 1861 is amusing and revealing — "There may be objections to this plan, as to every other, but thus far it has worked well, and it has the advantage of having open doors for going out as well as coming in."

Indeed, the church was commonly known as the "Broad Gauge Church" in the early days because all one had to do was to go into Dickinson's drug store and sign the book. It is reliably recorded that former Governor Fifer [249] once went in to order a ton of coal, but Dickinson handed him the Unitarian Church book instead of the coal order book

[248] Jesse W. Fell, Stevenson's maternal great-grandfather, who founded the Bloomington *Daily Pantagraph,* built roads, founded colleges and towns, and was a major power in central Illinois. He and his brother Kersey first proposed Lincoln as the Republican candidate for President. See Davis, *A Prophet in His Own Country,* for a fuller account of the Fell family.

[249] Joseph W. Fifer, Republican governor of Illinois, 1889–1893.

and Governor Fifer promptly signed. I don't know whether he got the coal — but he certainly got Unitarianism!

Among the most active participants in the early days of the society was Ezra Prince whose son Ed Prince has come back to be with us here today. Thanks to those famous brothers who had so much to do with the development of Bloomington — Cyrenius and Elisha Wakefield — the society for some nine years met *rent free* in Phoenix Hall. They were also important contributors to the building of this church in 1868.

Speaking of the financial fortunes — or rather misfortunes — of the church, I was interested in this item recorded in the account of the 50th anniversary in 1909:

"Miss Fannie Fell [250] reported that not a little of the success of the church socials introduced in the early days was due to the excellent waffles made by Mrs. McCann Dunn." Evidently the waffles warmed the heart of the Treasurer while they delighted the palates of the parishoners. . . .

But to go back: I've heard it said that Unitarians believe in the Fatherhood of God, the brotherhood of man, and the neighborhood of Boston! Be that as it may, Fell was commissioned by the founders to enlist as the first minister Charles Gordon Ames of Boston who had been sent out to Minnesota to convert the Indians. Let me hastily add that I find no connection between his mission to the Indians and the Bloomington Unitarians! Evidently the idea of starting out with a brand new liberal religious movement appealed to him and the famous Dr. Ames came and stayed in Bloomington until he was called back to a large parish in Boston.

In a letter written long afterward Dr. Ames speaks of that first meeting of the new church: "I looked down on the eager faces of a goodly congregation which included some timid sympathizers along with lovers of novelty." Apparently the "timid sympathizers" and the "novelty seekers" were afraid to join for we are told that the congregation used to number 150, but the membership was never as large as the congregation. And, sad to relate, what was true so long ago in this remarkable church is true today!

Now it's worth noting that the title of Dr. Ames' first sermon 90 years ago was "The Right and Duty of Private Judgment in Religion" — the right and duty of private judgment seems to me to express very aptly the idea of liberalism and individualism which is the first concern of *our* generation.

Can it be that a chief cause of discord in human affairs is not so much the undesirable nature of beliefs as it is the prevalence of com-

[250] Stevenson's great-aunt and daughter of Jesse Fell.

petitive indoctrination among them? Alfred Adler once offered the opinion that "it is easier to fight for one's beliefs than to live up to them." In effect this is what we have across the entire fabric of human affairs: rents and tears caused by the constant vendettas carried on by competing faiths: religious, economic, social and ideological.

If there is anything that the whole idea of liberalism militates against it is the notion of competitive indoctrination. And therein lies our potential strength in this current era of grace. When we start with the premise that we want human brotherhood to spread and increase until it makes life safe and sane, we must also be certain that there is no *one* true faith or path by which it may spread. We must forever banish the notion that there can be universal brotherhood just as soon as everyone gives up his faith and accepts ours. That day will never come. The richness of human diversity cannot be abolished. It can be resented and fought, but only at what an appalling cost. Difference is in the nature of life. It is part of our moral universe. It should be gladly and enthusiastically welcomed. There is nothing wrong with the fact of difference. What is wrong are our futile efforts to abolish it. Abolishing diversity is as frustrating a process as abolishing Mars or Jupiter.

Let us be sure, then, that we as Unitarians understand our proper role. Liberalism is our way of life. From our point of view it is spiritually healthy for us to nurture the attitudes and beliefs which we identify as our own. Let us feel very strongly that we have an important contribution to make, because we have. But let us make doubly sure we do not fall victim to the very practices and attitudes we deplore in more rigid and authoritarian groups. It is not impossible for a slow seepage of doctrinaire backwash to gather around the principles of liberal religion. Liberals are human, subject to the pressures of custom, parenthood and environment. It is perfectly possible for us to hold all our convictions, *except tolerance and open-mindedness,* in quite doctrinaire fashion. This is not only a philosophical problem but also a very practical one. If a liberal wishes to win friends and influence people (and what liberal doesn't) then one thing he cannot afford is the luxury of dogmatism. Of course, our reasonableness cannot be saccharine, but it must be reasonableness, and it must always be motivated by the urge to learn, to share and to find common ground.

There is much good, much sincerity, much altruism in any one of a wide variety of religious and ideological movements in our world. The common hysterical mistake of so many movements is in feeling that the good in something will be lost unless it is swallowed like a pill, whole and at once, with no questions asked. It is my own feeling that the unbending apparatus we have built about wholesale competitive indoctrination contributes much to discord and strife in human affairs.

To convince ourselves and others that there is nothing to fear in difference; that difference, in fact, is one of the healthiest and most invigorating of human characteristics, without which life would become lifeless is a great task. Here lies the power of the liberal way — not in making the whole world Unitarian; but in helping ourselves and others to see some of the possibilities inherent in viewpoints other than one's own; in encouraging the free interchange of ideas; in welcoming fresh approaches to the problems of life; in urging the fullest, most vigorous use of critical self-examination. Thus we can learn to grow together, to unite in our common search for the truth beneath a better and a happier world.

May I conclude, then, in the words of Galatians: "Stand fast therefore in the liberty wherewith Christ has made us free, and be not entangled with the yoke of bondage."

To Oscar F. Shepard [251]

November 1, 1949

Dear Mr. Shepard:

Thank you for your kind letter about John Fell. It is most encouraging.

I hope to be in Boston this week-end and to have an opportunity to visit the school on Sunday morning.

I have planned a reunion with all three of the boys at Adlai's rooms at Eliot House H-46, Harvard, on next Saturday morning, November 5. In the afternoon I intend to take them to the Harvard-Princeton game. If you could arrange to have John Fell at Eliot House by 11:30 Saturday morning I would very much appreciate it.

Sincerely yours,

Lady Mary Spears, wife of General Sir Louis Spears of London, was the sister of John Borden, Ellen Stevenson's father. Lady Spears was devoted to the Governor and kept in close touch with him throughout his life. She wrote from New York that she would like to visit him in Springfield.

[251] Dean of the Boys' School of Milton Academy, Milton, Massachusetts. The original is in the possession of Milton Academy.

To Lady Mary Spears

November 3, 1949

Dear Mary:

I have your letter today, and of course I would be delighted to have you come to Springfield. It would be good to have you and to have a talk, but unfortunately I am obliged to speak in Chicago to the Illinois Agricultural Association on the night of Wednesday, November 16, and in Peoria, Illinois, on the night of November 17. Would any other time be possible?

Affectionately,

To Leonard Schwartz [252]

November 3, 1949

Dear Lennie:

I think the best possibility of going down to Cairo [Illinois] with you for geese would be Sunday, November 13 and Monday, November 14. Perhaps I could arrange to fly down from Chicago Sunday, the 13th, and pick you up here in Springfield. We could fly on to Cairo in the afternoon, hold the plane, and return to Springfield Monday evening, November 14.

No hurry, but let me have your reaction at your convenience.

Sincerely yours,

Mrs. Edward F. Joyce wrote Stevenson to congratulate him on his introduction of Prime Minister Nehru. "Yours is a natural gift and many the democrat, like myself, was proud as punch of their Governor Stevenson."

To Mrs. Edward F. Joyce

November 3, 1949

My dear Mrs. Joyce:

I have not had a nicer letter since I have been sitting in this uncomfortable seat — and you were good to write me. Even if what you say is only half true I am still flattered.

And I will try not to forget that it is darkest before dawn.

Warm regards.

Sincerely yours,

252 The original is in the possession of Mr. Schwartz.

To William E. Stevenson [253]

November 3, 1949

Dear Bill:

Largely because my acquaintance in Ohio is so limited, and with no thought of seducing you from your tranquil Saturday afternoons, I am enclosing my tickets to the Ohio State game on November 12.[254]

If you can dispose of them to any advantage, please do so. They are probably very good ones.

In exchange all I ask is that you and Bumpy [255] come out and stay a night with me in my drafty old mansion in Springfield. I suspect she is neglecting the cornfields and I am sure you are neglecting your drinking!

Regards, etc.

Yours,

To Alicia Patterson [256]

[November 5, 1949]

. . . I'm madder than hell. I'm sitting in a hangar at Cleveland — for the past hour — while they get ready to wash the snow off this plane. Instead of being in Boston at 11 I'll be lucky if I'm there by 2 A.M. — and Archie and Ada [MacLeish] sitting up waiting for me.

I've read your letter again & I feel a little better — except that ludicrous D.A. God the people we elect to public office! Of course your right about the Commie advertising — as long as there's nothing treas[o]nous in the copy. The wretched little people that think freedom's a one way street for popular, majority opinions are enemies of freedom — like the fools that say Franco's fine because he hates Stalin! . . .

A

Friday night

Long before Governor Stevenson electrified so many people with his 1952 campaign speeches, he was already "talking sense" to the American people. He wrote "The Challenge of a New Isolationism" for the New York Times Magazine, *in which it appeared on November 6, 1949.*

[253] President of Oberlin College, Ohio. He and Adlai Stevenson were classmates at Princeton University. They were not related.

[254] Ohio State University's football team was scheduled to play against the University of Illinois that year at Urbana. The Governor was allotted a certain number of tickets to all the games.

[255] Mrs. Stevenson.

[256] This handwritten letter is in the possession of Adlai E. Stevenson III.

On a sticky, hot day in August, 1941, the tellers in the House of Representatives in Washington recorded a historic vote. The Selective Service Act, the first peacetime conscription in our history, was extended — by a margin of one vote. Poland and France had fallen, the Nazis were poised for the invasion of England and well on their way to Moscow — and Pearl Harbor was not four months away. Yet in such a perilous hour only one vote out of 435 saved our little draft-begotten army. Every Republican member from Illinois voted against extension.

How was it possible then? Could it happen again? That was but eight short years ago and some people say that already there is a rebirth of the old isolationist sentiment.

I don't think so. As a resident of a great Midwestern state once known for its supposed isolationist tendencies, I think old-fashioned isolationism is moribund. America has come of age, I believe, in these eight short years of toil and heartache. The misconceptions of adolescence, the care-free self-concerns of our youth vanished with the whirlwind that swept us to the center of the world's stage. And now we in the Midwest, like most of us everywhere, though bedeviled with the indecisions of a maturity that knows what it wants but isn't sure how to get it, have at least discarded some of the illusions which beclouded our earlier thinking.

When I venture the brave conclusion that "isolation" is a thing of the past, I mean the old traditional concept that America can live alone and like it; that we can live secure and prosperous behind our barricades of ocean and within our continent of plenty. The roots of that conviction were long and strong. Embedded in the Revolutionary struggle for freedom and a sturdy self-reliance, they were nourished by waves of immigrants who fled poverty and persecution in the Old World. Why worry about those unhappy peoples and their everlasting quarrels in which the poor man always suffered most, when there were new frontiers and untold wealth beckoning the strong, whatever his name and origin? The covered wagon was our symbol and the driver of the westering wagon had his back on Europe.

What's more, for nearly a hundred years little happened here in the Middle West to alter the old idea that to work hard and mind your own business was the sure formula for peace and prosperity for America and Americans. Besides, didn't George Washington say something like that, even if his light was a candle and his transportation a horse?

The first World War was a shock, but not a lesson. President Roosevelt's call for a "quarantine of the aggressors" on a wind-swept bridge in Chicago in 1937 was a voice in the wilderness. The munitions investigations, the Neutrality Act, the arms embargo, the pollsters, all showed that millions hoped and believed we could sit out World War II. Thousands of wishful thinkers rallied to the isolationist standard "America First." One vote saved the Selective Service Act when Europe was already in flames. And the record shows that a United States Senator from the Middle West was assailing the "warmongers'" notion that we were in jeopardy before an America First rally in Pittsburgh at the very moment the Japanese were bombing Pearl Harbor!

But in less than four years the United States had junked long-cherished concepts of neutral rights and the Senate had ratified the United Nations Charter! The reasons are as plain in the Middle West as elsewhere. Can a pilot who flew the ocean as casually as a mailman makes his route ever again believe that we can isolate ourselves? Do the millions of Americans who traveled to the ends of the earth and back during the war think of Paris or even Moscow as far distant? Like their parents they may wish it were so, but unlike some of their parents they know it isn't. How many people who saved sugar coupons for a birthday cake believe we are a self-sufficient world apart? Ask the Middle Western farmer what he has found out about his markets.

No, the impact of global war on our economy, on the millions of civilian soldiers and sailors who have lived and fought, sweated and shivered, laughed and groused in places they never heard of before, not only destroyed fascism abroad but a lot of isolationist notions here at home.

And since the fighting stopped still more water has rushed under the bridge of history. Four more years have passed in which we've been grappling with some hard, unpleasant realities of international life — mostly Russian. But this time we have not backed away. Instead, we've passed a second peacetime Selective Service Act, sent direct aid to countries far within the Mediterranean sphere, spent billions to rehabilitate Western Europe, ratified the first mutual defense pact in our history,[257] and participated positively and continuously in every activity of the United Nations.

Inter-continental defense machinery has been established and Congress has passed a peacetime lend-lease arms program. No responsible voices are clamoring for withdrawal from the United Nations or the conference tables. No one has suggested that we pull out of Germany, Austria or Japan. We were stirred as one by the magnificent feat of the airlift to Berlin. Indeed, the most insistent criticism has been that we failed to sustain China.[258]

[257] Direct aid was given to Greece and Turkey; the Marshall Plan provided billions of dollars in aid; and the North Atlantic Treaty Organization was the first mutual defense pact in U.S. history.

[258] Chiang Kai-shek and his Nationalist government fled the mainland of China to Formosa in 1949. Charges that the Truman Administration "sold out" the Nationalists to the Communists inflamed American politics for years.

While it is true that the Russian atomic explosion caused surprisingly little comment, it is also true that there has since been little criticism of the arms-for-Europe bill which Congress promptly passed.[259] No, I think that atomic energy, jet propulsion, radio and radar, and the debt, waste and blood of two world wars in a generation, have buried the whole ostrich of isolation. There are, of course, a few lonely voices echoing the old refrain, "The rest of the world be damned," but the people in the Middle West, as elsewhere, have abandoned that treacherous trail to security by insulation. Eight years after that dramatic vote in Congress, we have all come to realize that we are a part, a large, inseparable and indispensable part, of a larger world.

But the death of one discredited dogma does not preclude the rise of others. While we've abandoned the old road, we have by no means defined our goals or the means of reaching them. We have not found common ground nor taken the pledge of abstinence from our past vices of wishful thinking and cut-rate security.

While it can hardly be argued that there is much evidence of a resurrection of the body of isolation there is plenty of evidence of a reincarnation of its spirit. There is a conspicuous and growing tendency to be internationally minded in principle but not in practice, to favor international cooperation in the abstract while opposing concrete steps to make it effective. The thirteen Senators who opposed the Atlantic Pact for the most part professed their devotion to international cooperation. Just four years before only two opposed the United Nations Charter, a far more radical break with our traditional policy.

Another warning signal is the constant and alarming identification of our policy with the containment of communism. Does public support for the foreign aid program, for example, represent genuine recognition of global economic problems, or is it merely a reflection of the wide-spread fear of Communist Russia? Do people realize that some such program would have been necessary even if relations with the Soviet Union were the most cordial? Or have we merely created the happy illusion that we fully understand the economic realities?

Policy based on an anti-Russian crusade involves great dangers. Defense and economic aid might be sharply altered at the first sign of a truce in the cold war. If we wobble in accordance with the aggressiveness of their actions and pronouncements, the men in the Kremlin will exer-

[259] President Truman announced on September 23, 1949, the report that an atomic explosion had occurred within the Soviet Union, marking the end of American monopoly of atomic weapons. The Russians had rejected the UN Atomic Energy Commission's recommendations on atomic control two and a half years earlier, in March, 1947. The Mutual Defense Assistance Act, providing over one billion dollars of military aid chiefly for Atlantic Pact nations, was signed on October 6, 1949.

cise undue influence upon our policy. One who blindly opposes everything the Soviets favor and supports everything they oppose is just as much a stooge of Moscow as the most abject fellow-traveler. If our policy cannot stand on its own feet independent of the whims of the Kremlin we run the risk of withdrawing into economic isolation the moment the immediate military threat disappears. The Red scare and our preoccupation with Communists rather than the causes of communism are not reassuring.

While we have learned, I think, the military lesson of two wars in a shrunken world, have we learned the economic lesson? While we have learned that peace is indivisible, have we also learned that prosperity is indivisible?

I doubt it. While there is general agreement that winning wars is too expensive and that we don't want to have to win any more, it is hard for us to understand why winning peace in a world yearning for peace is so expensive, too. The "Economy First" people can't see why we should be scattering money all over the world when taxes are so high at home. "Participation? Cooperation? Sure — but not at the cost of our domestic economy."

The isolation of thought from action is a very common current "isolationism." Many people talk of international cooperation as the essential condition of peace, but they oppose tangible efforts to win the peace, without presenting any positive program of their own. They oppose the Marshall Plan because it's expensive and may not work, they oppose "involvements" and "new commitments" like the Atlantic Pact and the arms-for-Europe program. Many still oppose efforts to rationalize foreign trade like the Reciprocal Trade Agreements Act as harmful to some domestic producers. The implementation of President Truman's Point Four [260] seems to evoke little but critical cynicism.

As one who lives night and day with the problem of the rising cost of government, I am appalled and irked by the Federal drain on our tax resources, and I share the common conviction that the one clearly identifiable keystone of peace is a solvent, depression-free America.

But it is also apparent that peace and our domestic well-being depend on international conditions calculated to insure peace. To achieve those conditions is dangerously costly, and the demand for reduced government spending is growing more and more insistent. We must economize, but with most of the Federal budget devoted to defense and foreign aid,

[260] The "Point Four" program proposed in President Truman's inaugural address, January 20, 1959, was a worldwide, continuing program to help underdeveloped nations to help themselves through technical information and personnel. It became law on June 5, 1950.

any very large economies for the present, at least, cannot be effected without serious consequences to our foreign policies.

I suspect a large question mark for the future is whether we have learned or will learn in time that it is not economy but prodigality to save today's insurance premiums and pay for tomorrow's disasters. But in the past, democracies have usually preferred to save the insurance premiums and pay for the wars.

Then there are the imperialists, the zealous converts to internationalism, who talk defiantly about taking over the whole world and running it as we see fit, and, incidentally, to our advantage — somehow. Another group says "War is inevitable, so let's have it now." But this group is small and getting smaller, and includes few if any responsible leaders of our thought.

There are many more voices in the discordant chorus. At one extreme are the pessimists and skeptics who see no hope for peace and security and have already written off the United Nations and "cooperation" as a dismal failure. At the other, more hopeful, extreme are the world-government groups. Exploring uncharted seas, demanding more, not less, international cooperation, they have already enlisted the support of some twenty-nine Senators and over a hundred members of the House for various proposals leading toward the establishment of some form of actual world government.

Illustrations of the variations in our thinking could be multiplied. But from one end of the spectrum to the other no one, or almost no one, is preaching the old-fashioned isolation of eight years ago. Everyone seems to agree to some degree of world participation, some more, some less. Many a sturdy isolationist of yesterday is even in the world-government camp today. But more of them are viewing with alarm the relinquishment of an atom of "our sovereignty." Thus, it was on Constitutional grounds that the American Bar Association recently went on record against the genocide convention.[261]

Others view with even more alarm the appalling cost and the uncertain dividends from the billions we have invested in foreign aid and rehabilitation which are so badly needed at home. For example, a Republican aspirant for the Senate in Illinois,[262] who renounced his isolationism as a Congressman, has now denounced as a failure the Marshall Plan he voted for two years ago.

[261] In December, 1948, the United Nations General Assembly adopted a convention on the prevention and punishment of the mass killings of innocent peoples. This required ratification by member states. The American Bar Association, although declaring its repugnance to genocide, rejected the treaty in the belief that the international court, which was to be the judicial agent, would supersede the U.S. Constitution and endanger the self-governing powers of the American states.

[262] Everett M. Dirksen, who took his seat in the Senate in 1950.

So while I conclude that there is little indication of any revival of the pre–Pearl Harbor state of mind, it seems to me that there are dangers perhaps as great. An unscrupulous politician can play the whole keyboard. He can capitalize the fears of the apprehensive with dire warnings of national bankruptcy; he can gladden the hearts of the hopeful with visions of democracy and social justice; he can reassure the nervous with "in an atomic world no one will dare make war"; he can fortify the imperialists with threats to "unsound" governments to mend their radical ways.

He'll have the right line for the ladies' study clubs and the business men's luncheon clubs, and, of course, he'll have no convictions of his own. At least not until he sees which way the wind is blowing. If the going gets bad, business recedes, unemployment mounts, he'll be shouting for an end to this foreign aid at the expense of the hard-pressed American taxpayer. He will damn the "meddlers," the "spenders," the "theorists," the "one-worlders." He will demand expanded exports and diminished imports, which can only lead ultimately to catastrophe and the triumph of the Communists. But in the meanwhile he will be echoing popular attitudes and millions may follow into a neo-isolation — international cooperation by elocution. The words of high purpose and moral dedication — the verbal acceptance of the world's unity and brotherhood — will be there, but that's all.

Now I don't think this will happen, but it could; and if it should happen too soon, it could well be disastrous. It is the tragedy of democratic countries that foreign policy is always, in time of peace, sacrificed to domestic policy.

Britain, for example, could not institute conscription until the Nazi hammer had fallen because it took people out of private employment, interfered with personal freedom, etc. Of course, it should be just the reverse. Democratic countries are peaceful, and as peace is an external matter their external policy should be constant and firm. But unhappily the voters are more concerned with taxes, prices, wage rates and today's domestic concerns, and politicians are more concerned with today's votes than long-term policies.

Now my thesis is: There is no resurgence of blind, classical isolation in the Middle West, but there is a rapidly growing tax consciousness, and sooner or later we will have to face some stern issues. Can we, will we, pay the price of peace? Will we weary of the long ordeal? Will the disappointments, failures and frustrations light the fires of reaction? Is a neo-isolation in the making? Can a democracy hold fast to a long-term foreign policy of resistance and assistance? Or will popular short-term domestic policies carry the day? Can we make positive, progressive, forward adjustments as the war recedes in perspective and our war-born economy slows down? Can we steer a middle course between disillusioned pessimism and retreat on the one hand, and overextension and fiscal irresponsibility on the other?

We have identified our enemies since the war; we have hammered out by trial and error a policy of tangible cooperation to improve the lot of mankind within limited spheres; we have taken an oath of allegiance to the world; we have abandoned "live alone and like it"; we have embraced "live together or perish." But the going will get harder before it gets better, and the test of political maturity and consistency is still ahead of us. Hard-headed horse sense about the world, as about our business, is a prescription easy to write and hard to fill. The cost of peace insurance is very high in dollars and still higher in determination and applied democracy.

The first essential is leadership. The demagogues who say we can have our cake and eat it too are many and masterful. The hard way is never the popular way, but it is often the best way. One of the first steps is to do a better job here in our front yard. More than we realize, the future depends on the quality of government and public management right here at home in our cities, counties and states. Political corruption, extravagance, moral lethargy and expediency among our public officials are old but eradicable. If we can do a better and thriftier job of domestic housekeeping, we will have more confidence in ourselves, to say nothing of the confidence of others in our wisdom and purpose.

Is the circle vicious or can we break it? The people elect the leaders and the leaders lead the people. I choose to think that the whirlwinds of our generation have swept away some obscure, old cobwebs in the corners too, and that the greatest, oldest democracy is witnessing not the rebirth of isolation and obscurantism, but the birth of a new and wiser leadership in business, labor, agriculture — and public management which we call politics. The eagle, not the ostrich, is our national emblem.

To Robert M. Hutchins [263]

November 8, 1949

Dear Bob:

It occurs to me that it would be a wholesome experience for you and your lady not only to see me but a little of the prairie and some old fashioned college clamor. My proposal is that you come down to Springfield on the afternoon of Friday, November 18, have dinner with Mary

[263] The original is in the University of Chicago Library.

Garden [264] here at the Mansion, and Saturday morning drive over to Urbana via beautiful Allerton Park, have lunch with George Stoddard and go to the Nortwestern-Illinois football game. You can get back to Chicago by 9:40 P.M. that night very comfortably or stay overnight and go up Sunday.

Give this the most careful consideration, obliterate all conflicting engagements, and do the right thing for once in your life! [265]

Sentimental regards to your lady and my respects to you.

Sincerely yours,
ADLAI

While Governor Stevenson was in Cambridge, Massachusetts, early in November, he and his sons visited an old family friend, the former Mrs. Stanley McCormick of Chicago. The Stevensons were house guests of Mr. and Mrs. Archibald MacLeish.

To Katharine Dexter McCormick

November 8, 1949

My dear Mrs. McCormick:

It was good to see you again and our luncheon at your beautiful house was a fine experience for the boys. It was more important for me than you realize in the present confusing state of our domestic affairs. I am deeply grateful, and your sweet reverence [reference] to father touched me. He died before any of the boys were born.

Please don't forget that you have promised to come down to Springfield for a visit when you are in Illinois this winter. Until I find some place to stay on the occasional nights I am caught in Chicago, I can always be reached during the day either through the Executive Mansion or at my office in Chicago, 160 North La Salle Street, telephone Financial 6-2000, Extension 353.

Affectionately,

---

[264] The famous opera star, then in her seventies, who visited Stevenson at the mansion. She wrote him afterward that she had had a most wonderful time, and that she would never forget the kindness and charm of his invitation. She added that if he ever came to Aberdeen she hoped he would ring her doorbell.

[265] Hutchins, chancellor of the University of Chicago, replied that he and his wife had to be in Washington. "For the pleasure of seeing you in your new environment, I would be willing to go through a great deal, even Mary Garden and a football game." Hutchins abolished football at the University of Chicago in 1939.

To Mr. and Mrs. Archibald MacLeish

November 8, 1949

Dear Ada and Archie:

Please let me christen all your guest rooms henceforth. But of all the intolerables of this world I suspect literal minded guest room christeners must be the worst! Anyway, we had a better time than you can understand and I am eternally grateful. Not only did I want you to see the boys, but in the present state of our confusing domestic affairs it was very important for me to give them — John Fell, particularly — a more normal visit from father than [at] a hotel.

I am afraid we exhausted you both, but you made us all very happy and relaxed. God bless the MacLeishes of Louisburg Square!

Affectionately,

P.S. I am counting heavily on that visit in Springfield in February. Let me know the dates as far in advance as you can. I can send automobiles or the airplane for you anywhere at any time.

AES

On November 8, 1949, Lady Spears wrote that she was sorry she would not be able to see the Governor in Illinois and must postpone her talk with him to another time.

To Lady Mary Spears

November 10, 1949

Dear Mary:

I am distressed that our paths do not cross while you are in Chicago. I was anxious to see you and to hear all the news from England. If anything brings me to Chicago while you are there I shall call you on the telephone at least!

I understand perfectly your reaction to the domestic situation and it baffles me painfully, as you appreciate. But perhaps it is for the best. At least I must think so.

Affectionately,

The Governor's cousin Adlai S. Hardin and his family lived in Darien, Connecticut. His wife, Carol, wrote to Stevenson inviting him and his sons to visit them over the Thanksgiving holidays.

To Mrs. Adlai S. Hardin

November 8, 1949

Dear Carol:

I had all the boys with me in Cambridge over the week-end for the Harvard-Princeton game, and the Thanksgiving plans have now unfolded. Ellen feels, and I suspect she is right, that they should all go to Boston for Thanksgiving with her aunt, Mrs. Kingsley Porter. I am disappointed, as I had hoped that some of them could come to you, but Adlai must be in Cambridge on Friday and Saturday for classes, and it seemed a little complicated for them to try to foregather at your house. But I am sure there will be other opportunities, and I am hopeful that it won't be long before they have an opportunity to meet their cousins.

You were good to think of us and I am deeply grateful.

Affectionately,

P.S. Aunt Julia [266] is coming over from St. Louis to stay the night with me today on her way East. Her vitality and serenity and youth amaze me and I wish I could kidnap her for keeps.

AES

Urban Lavery, a Chicago lawyer, wrote Stevenson to congratulate him on his performance as governor during his first year. He wrote: "As a veteran observer and even friend of many statesmen and politicians. . . . I can see clearly that you will be facing grave decisions in the next six months or so. . . . I would tell you again . . . do what you want most to do and let the chips fall where they may."

To Urban A. Lavery

November 8, 1949

Dear Urban:

I am grateful for your kind and thoughtful and encouraging letter. I have not forgotten, nor will I, the simple, healthy advice you gave me, and I hope that this frightful pressure and tension will relax and we can have another talk sometime soon.

Sincerely yours,

---

[266] Mrs. Martin D. Hardin, Adlai Hardin's mother and a sister of the Governor's father.

To Alicia Patterson [267]

November 12, 1949

. . . I'm in the plane flying up to Chicago. My old friend Jimmy (Vincent) Sheean is with me. He came to Sp[ringfield] yesterday to stay the night with me and he talked long & interestingly of India and the orient. Its the first night I've broken the bound[a]ries of Ill[inois] never to return since I've been on this job. Now for some work in the Chi office, a football game with my classmate Ev[erett] Case, President of Colgate, a political dinner, a night in the country — the first in about 3 weeks — and down to Cairo tomorrow to shoot a goose Monday dawn, I hope! . . .

A

Mr. and Mrs. Archibald MacLeish accepted an invitation to visit Stevenson in Springfield.

To Archibald MacLeish

November 18, 1949

Dear Archie:

March 11th is on the calendar. The Gold Ball Room will be dusted and the musicians engaged. Don't fail!

Yours,

Olive Wakefield, sister of poet Vachel Lindsay, lived in the Lindsay house to the rear of the Governor's mansion. From time to time she gave Stevenson letters and poems written by her brother, as well as other papers she unearthed in the old home. She apologized in a note for the shower of papers and thanked Stevenson for inspiring her to get back to a book she had been writing, entitled "Stories for Betsy." (The book was never published.)

To Olive Lindsay Wakefield

November 29, 1949

My dear Mrs. Wakefield:

I have before me the material you have sent along for Aunt Julia. It

[267] This handwritten letter is in the possession of Adlai E. Stevenson III.

comes at a difficult time, but I am going to try and find some time to-night to look through it before I send it along.

I am glad that you have started on the "Stories for Betsy" again and I am sure you will finish "Your Wall" this time.

Aunt Julia's address is Mrs. Martin D. Hardin, Belleayre Apartments, Ithaca, New York.

Warm regards and my thanks.

Sincerely yours,

To Mrs. Martin D. Hardin

November 29, 1949

Dear Aunt Julia:

I haven't the faintest idea just what you did to stimulate Mrs. Wakefield into such feverish activity but this is the second deluge and evidently intended for you. So here it is.

I am fearful that I have not had an opportunity to look through it, but I shall put on a bold front should I encounter the author of "Stories for Betsy" on my midnight prowls about the streets. Meanwhile, I have no doubt you will absorb it word by word and pound by pound!

Devotedly,

Whitelaw Reid, editor of the New York Herald Tribune, *wrote to thank Stevenson for having participated in the newspaper's radio Forum in New York on October 24, 1949: "You not only did a superlative job in bringing people abreast of your own enlightened program for Illinois but concluded your talk with some wonderfully sage comment that goes across party boards. . . . If only the diehards in both Republican and Democratic ranks, and for that matter the radicals too, could take a leaf out of your book we would have far more sensible discussion on the crucial problem of government and how much of it we want."*

To Whitelaw Reid

November 30, 1949

Dear Whitelaw:

You were good to write me and you are most flattering about my remarks at the Forum. I enjoyed the evening enormously, although I can hardly agree that my contribution was important.

I have not forgotten that you promised to stop off for a night in Springfield when you are next at large in the Midlands. Don't forget!

Yours,

To the Reverend Preston Bradley [268]

December 6, 1949

Dear Preston:

I just want to say to you that I have never before heard as exquisite a funeral service as yours for Charlie Wheeler this morning. All of his friends are in your debt and my admiration for your restraint and the distinction is boundless.

With warm regards.

Sincerely yours,

On December 5, 1949, on the eve of his departure from New York for Brazil, the Honorable C. de Frietas-Valle, head of the Brazilian delegation to the United Nations, sent Stevenson a telegram reminding him of their common work at the meetings of the United Nations Preparatory Commission in London in 1945, and wishing him the best of success in his administration.

To C. de Freitas Valle

December 6, 1949

My dear de Freitas Valle:

I was delighted to have your wire today, and it reminded me of many happy and remote days in London when somehow the world looked much brighter. I am deeply disappointed that I did not have an opportunity to see you while you were in this country during the Assembly. I had only one visit to New York during the autumn — for the Herald-Tribune Forum — and could only stay overnight. Otherwise, I should have been in the gallery at Lake Success admiring the back of your large and well-groomed head! I hope another year when you are here that we can have a reunion.

Many, many thanks for your letter — and every good wish.

Sincerely yours,

To Alicia Patterson [269]

December 13, 1949

. . . Ellen got the divorce yesterday & I felt as thought [though] it

---

[268] Founder (in 1912) and pastor of the independent People's Church on West Lawrence Avenue in Chicago, popular religious speaker on Chicago radio and author of numerous inspirational works.

[269] This handwritten letter is in the possession of Adlai E. Stevenson III.

was the end of an era & a dismal failure for me — and all of us. The papers pressed me for a statement —

Love
A

To Stephen A. Mitchell [270]

December 23, 1949

Dear Steve:

You were more than good to send me the beautiful Atlas. But afflicted with all the instincts of a prowling dog, it won't make it any easier for me to stay at home!

My best to you and Evelyn [271] and a Happy New Year to you both.

Yours,

Dr. E. M. Stevenson, a cousin of the Governor, wrote to wish him a happy Christmas and to invite him to visit him in Bloomington in his new home.

To Dr. E. M. Stevenson

December 23, 1949

Dear Ed:

Many thanks for your very kind letter. It warms my heart and some day I hope I can take refuge with you.

Love to Sally [272] and the children and the best of everything for the New Year.

Yours,

To Alicia Patterson [273]

December 26, 1949

. . . Its been a glorious holiday. All three boys have been here, my sister & brother in law & their boy [274] — and Ellen *sent* them. I didn't beg — she said it would be dreary for them motoring into town for luncheon with Mr. & Mrs. Carpenter [275] — and Mr. in bed with a broken

[270] The original is in the possession of Mr. Mitchell.
[271] Mrs. Mitchell.
[272] Mrs. Stevenson.
[273] This handwritten letter is in the possession of Adlai E. Stevenson III.
[274] Mr. and Mrs. Ernest L. Ives and their son Timothy.
[275] Mr. and Mrs. John Alden Carpenter, of Chicago. Mrs. Carpenter was Ellen Stevenson's mother.

hip. So it all worked wonderfully & I've had 3 dream days — no work
and all play. Buffy did most of the appalling Christmas work. I don't
know what I'd have done without her what with all the presents, all the
traditional entertaining etc — and its not over yet. On Wed we're having
a dance! 30 young people from Lake Forest and 100 from Springfield,
Decatur, Bloomington etc. for Adlai & Borden. I'm getting a little
giddy! . . .

Forgive this wretched scrawl. John Fell is sitting on the desk & in
my lap mostly and wonders what I'm doing —

Love
A

Barnet Hodes was ward committeeman from the Fifth Ward in Chi-
cago. Stevenson appointed him chairman of the American Heritage
Commission, whose purpose was to educate people about their na-
tional heritage, a position Hodes held throughout the administration. In
December he sent the Governor a Christmas gift, a practice he followed
for many succeeding years.

To Barnet Hodes [276]

December 27, 1949

Dear Barney:

You were good to think of me and I am delighted to have Walter
Lippmann's new book.[277] I have known him well and for many years,
but I should never have gotten around to picking this up.

I hope we can see something more of each other in the year to come
than we have in the last. But I have not been unaware of all that you
have done for me and, believe me, I am most grateful.

Yours,

To Mr. and Mrs. T. Don Hyndman [278]

December 27, 1949

My dear Hyndmans:

I was conscious of some of your many talents but I had not realized
that cookie baking was among them! They are superb. We even deco-

---

[276] The original is in the possession of Mr. Hodes.

[277] Stevenson may refer to *Commentaries on American Far Eastern Policy* (New
York: American Institute of Pacific Relations, 1950).

[278] The original is in the possession of Mr. Hyndman.

rated the Christmas table with them — and then ate them! John Fell said that he never saw cookies that served both purposes.

Many thanks and my every good wish.

Yours,

Part Two

1950

A *t the end of his first year in office Stevenson became increasingly con-*
fident of himself as governor. Walter V. Schaefer, who served as the
Governor's chief aide during the 1949 legislative session, recalled that
Stevenson "worked like the devil," and by the end of the first session he
probably knew more than any governor ever did about Illinois govern-
ment.[1]

News commentator Eric Sevareid visited his old friend Stevenson in
Springfield during the spring of 1950, and in a broadcast over the Colum-
bia Broadcasting System on April 12, said: "He is that rare creature, a
reformer who was elected with the support of the hard bitten political
machine, which cannot abide reformers or reforms. And therefore his
position today is a rare one, exposed, dangerous and exhaustingly diffi-
cult. . . . He has failed on the big item of constitutional reform; he has
failed on a fair employment practices act, and a few other vital matters.
. . . But he has put through more than half of his major bills. . . . He
has begged and borrowed the ablest men he could for administrative
positions, and not all, by any means are from his own Democratic party.
Because he has chosen some Republicans, because he has refused to
throw out some 15,000 office holders overnight and turn the jobs over to
the organization faithful, he is now half blinded by a dark cloud of angry
political hornets buzzing around his head. They are not the hornets from
the Chicago-Cook County Democratic machine. . . . These are the
famished downstate hornets, who have found no honey, for lo, these many
Republican years. This is Stevenson's fundamental problem; therein his
political fate seems to rest. Reform governors, traditionally, have bucked
the machine and eventually been cut adrift; or, they have given in to the
machine, and been cut adrift by the people. Stevenson would seem to
have but one possible, winning tactic; that is to reform so fast and
effectively that he will bind the people to him; in other words, become

[1] Interview with Walter Johnson, April 5, 1966.

[*209*]

stronger than the machine. . . . Nobody is sure Stevenson can pull it off; he isn't at all sure himself. But meanwhile, it seems to this reporter, he is making the best college try in the league." [2]

Stevenson did feel that much of his strength lay with the ordinary citizen. He also felt that one of his principal duties as governor was to educate people about their state government. He made regularly scheduled personal appearances before organized groups throughout the state, explaining to a wide range of audiences his views on public affairs and his concern for good government. He believed if people understood they would support him regardless of political affiliation. He tried earnestly to inform, to interest, to educate, the citizens of Illinois.

For instance, on January 20, 1950, Stevenson spoke informally and off the record to the Law Club, a group of leading members of the bar of Chicago. Stevenson was a member of the club. The next day Stephen A. Mitchell wrote to James W. Mulroy, Stevenson's executive secretary, that "The Governor's speech . . . made a real hit, and I am convinced it was worth the very considerable effort it cost him. There was a capacity attendance made up largely of those lawyers who have direct or indirect part in shaping public opinion. I think they were thoroughly convinced of the size and complexity of the Governor's job and the important fact that is so clear to you and me that he has gotten a firm grasp on the many complexities and practicalities of the several important divisions of his job — not omitting the political side."

In a speech to the Illinois League of Women Voters on September 15, 1950, Stevenson said: "I sometimes think my biggest job is preaching, and my biggest problem is to find time to write, and travel and talk about state government. How does one interest people, masses of people, in their state government? How to keep them interested? Unless citizen interest is a continuing process, the government reforms we institute today will degenerate into bureaucratic habits of tomorrow."

During 1950, Stevenson made over a hundred speeches throughout Illinois. He also kept speaking engagements in the border states of Missouri and Kentucky. He addressed the Illinois National Guard and the 44th Division at Camp McCoy, Wisconsin; he appeared on the 4th Annual Forum of the Philadelphia *Bulletin*, and spoke in Washington, D.C., at the annual meeting of the American Bar Association Section on Criminal Law.

T. S. Matthews, Princeton classmate of Stevenson and former editor of *Time* magazine, wrote that Stevenson sent him copies of some of his 1948 campaign speeches and his inaugural speech and "perhaps one or

[2] From a copy of the typescript of the broadcast over CBS network, 10 P.M., E.S.T., April 12, 1950.

two others. [Later] when I went to visit him at the Executive Mansion in Springfield [October, 1950] he played me recordings of some speeches he had made on nonpolitical occasions: They were an extraordinary improvement on the campaign harangues and state papers he had sent me." [3]

Among the important problems Stevenson dealt with during 1950 were: amending the constitution by means of the Gateway Amendment; continued pressure for a fair employment practices bill; removal of the position classification service from control of the governor's office and placing it under the authority of the Civil Service Commission; continual study of the budget, taxes and state finances; law enforcement and commercialized gambling (the state police, now removed from politics, were used for the first time in the state's history to make statewide gambling raids); roads and highways, with study and constant political pressure for appropriate measures to be submitted to the 1951 legislature; housing (the legislature was called into special session for the primary purpose of extending rent controls); crime and juvenile delinquency; schools and education; public assistance; public welfare; mental illness; study of the reorganization of state government by the Schaefer Commission, responsible for the preparation of many related bills to be submitted to the next legislature; and a variety of other issues.

Stevenson spoke publicly about the measures he considered of first importance on many occasions, and touched on a great variety of other subjects as well. One of his constant themes was the importance of the individual and his contribution to government at the local level.

Herbert J. Muller wrote: "What makes Stevenson's governorship significant is that he faced all the problems obscured by the popular myths that state government is closer to the people than is the national government, that it takes care of their needs more cheaply and efficiently, and that the services it provides are somehow no such threat to their freedom as are services provided by Washington. He knew that in fact, most people paid little attention to state affairs." [4] *Nevertheless, throughout his term of office, Stevenson tried assiduously to interest people in their state government.*

Late in 1949 and throughout 1950 some of Stevenson's cabinet members resigned their posts, some to take more attractive positions, some to return to jobs from which they were on a leave of absence.[5]

[3] "Portrait with Scratches: Adlai Stevenson," *Vogue*, May, 1966, p. 238. He also expressed the opinion in this article that Stevenson "never became a great speaker, but he was now much easier and more gracious."

[4] *Adlai E. Stevenson: A Study in Values* (New York: Harper & Row, 1967), p. 63.

[5] Resigning in the 1949–1950 period were Walter V. Schaefer; Donald E. Walsh, director of Public Safety; Harry Hershey, director of Insurance; Richard J. Daley, director of Revenue; Frank Annunzio, director of Labor; George W. Mitchell, director

The Governor appointed his aide J. Edward Day as director of the Department of Insurance to fill a cabinet vacancy, and persuaded William McCormick Blair, Jr., a Republican,[6] of Chicago to come to Springfield to take Day's place as his assistant. Blair lived and worked at the mansion throughout the administration.

On January 2, 1950, Stevenson spoke by statewide broadcast about the accomplishments and defeats of his first year as governor. Because he reviewed again many of the subjects covered in his report to the people on July 7, 1949, only excerpts from his January 2nd speech are included here.[7]

One year ago next week I took office as Governor of Illinois. I want to extend my New Year's greetings to all of you and to review briefly the accomplishments and disappointments of my first year in office, and also my first year in politics! I want to tell about some of our plans for the new year, and to discuss frankly some problems that confront us.

Some people contend that it is a mistake for me to make these reports over the radio from time to time. They remind me that "what you don't say won't hurt you." But I find that one of our gravest problems is the lack of discussion, ignorance of the facts and the old reluctance to present and face problems of local and state government frankly and squarely. Many people seem to have forgotten the great role which their states play in our developing concept of government. We hear much discussion these days about the danger of concentrating too much power in Washington. I think the best antidote for this is effective, responsive, well-operated, state and local governments. Too many of the problems of states' rights have been created by states' wrongs. In the absence of

of Finance; Noble J. Puffer, director of Registration and Education; and William J. McKinney, state purchasing agent.

Schaefer returned to his teaching position at Northwestern University Law School and was replaced by Carl McGowan, also from that law school; Donald R. Walsh accepted a position with the Chicago *American* and was replaced by Michael Seyfrit, a Carlinville, Illinois, lawyer; Harry Hershey was elected to the state supreme court in 1951, being replaced by J. Edward Day. Richard J. Daley resigned to run for county clerk of Cook County, an office he won. He was replaced by Clifford E. Halpin. Frank Annunzio was replaced by Fern Rauh; George W. Mitchell returned to the Federal Reserve Bank in Chicago as vice president and was replaced by Joseph Pois, vice president of Signode Steel Strapping Company. Noble J. Puffer was replaced by C. Hobart Engle, an educator from Cuba, Illinois; and McKinney was replaced by Carl Kresl, a retired Sears, Roebuck official with long experience in purchasing.

6 Within a year Blair shifted his allegiance (and registration) to the Democratic party.

7 The text is based on a mimeograph copy prepared by the Governor's office for release to the press.

state action on many problems, the national government has stepped in to perform functions the people demanded which the states might have performed.

Our state is important to you because it is part of the great Federal system — the United States — which you believe in, and it is important to you because it spends a lot of your money. So I want to talk to you about Illinois a little. It's your state and your money and it doesn't belong to any group or political party. . . .

During the past year I think my biggest headache has been commercialized gambling. It's a stubborn problem because the profit is enormous — the tribute we pay to the slot machines runs into millions a year. Often they are not owned by the local tavern keeper but by powerful gambling syndicates. It's a difficult problem, too, because public gambling involves questions of morality about which there are a variety of opinions.

But it's against the law in Illinois, and it can only exist where local officials tolerate it, either because they are corrupt and profit from it, or because they think the people don't care or because it's politically expedient.

In several counties the local state's attorneys and sheriffs have lived up to their oaths of office and stopped it. Attorney General Elliott and I are most grateful to them. In other counties it stops for a while and then starts again. In others it never stops, and the state administration is under incessant pressure to come in and take over local law enforcement. It will cost taxpayers a lot more money to do what you are already paying your local officials to do. But even worse, it seems to me, is the idea that we should always look to higher levels of government — first to Springfield and then to Washington — to do what we should do for ourselves.

For the state to take over local police powers seems to me a dangerous acknowledgement of the failure of local government. But commercialized gambling with its attendant corruption and corroding disrespect for law is even more dangerous.

In Wisconsin and other states they ended commercial gambling at a minimum of expense by giving the Governor the power to remove any local official who tolerated it. But I have no such power. Nor have we the legal authority or the resources to take over local law enforcement on a widespread continuing basis.

The best way to end the social menace of wholesale commercial crime is to elect conscientious, vigorous officials and insist that they enforce the law. You can do it; you, the people, choose the officials and the people are still stronger than the gamblers.

It's a sad fact that more Federal taxes on illegal gambling devices are paid in Illinois than most any other state. Illinois is getting the reputation of a gambling state. For my part, while the law is on the books, we are going to do our best to see that it is enforced. We need the help of every good citizen who believes in law, order and public probity. And I don't believe you or anyone who knows the situation and loves Illinois is going to sit idly by while greed, corruption and indifference further damage Illinois' fair name for law-abiding decency.

For my part, I'll deal mercilessly with any state employee under my control who has any tainted association with commercialized gambling. Any community which seeks to clean its own house will meet no obstacle from the connivance, the purchased protection or the encouragement of any state official under my control if I can catch him.

. . . In allocating public funds, we have to ask not one question but two. Not only "what will a program cost?" but "what is the cost of not having it?" For example, the question is not simply "can we afford increased appropriations for schools and roads?" but also "can we afford inferior schools and bad roads?" If our school appropriation had been less, for example, you would have had to choose between inferior schools or higher local property taxes.

The State's other big responsibility is to maintain its physical resources, like highways and buildings. A farmer who doesn't keep his machinery in good shape isn't a good farmer. A man who refused to make urgent repairs on his house, with the result that in a few years he had no house, would be a fool. Just how much of a fool a governor can't say on the radio, though the President of the United States might get away with it!

In the same way the State of Illinois must maintain and renew the facilities by which it serves the public. We have held down expenditures for construction to a minimum. But there is one place where we cannot delay indefinitely, and that is the immense task of restoring our highway system. Every year we delay rebuilding, the cost of upkeep will go higher and the amount left for new roads will be less. We are already spending almost as much for maintenance as for construction.

We are getting more for our road dollar. Since the last half of 1948, construction costs have been reduced 17.6 per cent. Better ways of handling construction contracts have saved some $3,000,000. But the needs are so great that savings alone cannot do the job. Engineers say we should spend $211,000,000 a year to put our highways in shape. But we were able to award only $30,000,000 in contracts from State and Federal funds.

Some 28 other states, facing a similar problem, have increased their gas taxes since the war, and not one of them has a tax as low as Illinois. . . .

The problem is not simply one of raising the tax. A more difficult hurdle is the division of the tax between the state, the cities, counties and rural road districts. That was our principal obstacle in the last session. But the time has come to give and take; the time has come to consider each other, to consider Illinois. I look forward with hope for a more understanding view of the total problem in the next session of the legislature.

. . . So far we have been able to keep the budget balanced by economies and by utilizing reserves left over from easy money days, when the State could depend upon income far in excess of its needs. But the reserve won't be there next time, and the legislature may well have to find substantial new revenue for the two years beginning in 1951. And further cutting administrative costs won't bridge a large gap between income and outgo. Even if you could eliminate all the administrative expenses to every agency responsible to me you would have less than 10 per cent of a budget of a billion of state funds.

Talking about the budget is tiresome, I know, but it is very important to you who have to pay the bill. I think we have done a pretty good job of putting first things first where we can control them. And I get some satisfaction out of the fact that in spite of huge increases for schools, the universities, public assistance and welfare, public health and salaries, our appropriations from state funds are up 12 per cent while the average for all the states is about 22 per cent.

But the old adage "never dissatisfied, always unsatisfied" describes the way I feel. I am sure there is more we can do and we will keep everlastingly at it. But I don't propose to achieve a record for economy by neglecting fundamental needs, nor by dodging today's problems, and letting them grow into bigger headaches for future governors.

Perhaps it isn't "good politics" to talk at such great length about all these problems. But they're not just my problems; they're your problems. Socrates said the unexamined life is not worth living. We who believe in democracy may just as truly say that the unexamined government is not worth having.

We hear much talk about the democratic form of government. But democracy is more than a form. It is a process — the process by which the people collectively endeavor to meet their collective problems. It avails little for the form of government to remain intact if the process stagnates. If public officials become unresponsive to public needs, if government becomes so paralyzed by the pressures and counter-pressures of special interest groups that it is unable to act for the general welfare, if elected officers hesitate to take needed action for fear they will be misunderstood by an [un]informed electorate, if the people fail to recognize and to face their problems — then the democratic process has failed.

Politicians often speak of "giving" the people good government. But one can't really give good government to the people. Good government is not a gift; it is an achievement. It has a price — the price that must be paid in time and energy and mental sweat in order to understand and to inform others of our problems; the price of examining all sides of public issues; the price of subordinating your own immediate interest to the long range welfare of the whole people.

That's the price of good government. But the price of poor government is infinitely higher.

I would ask you all to abandon any narrow, partisan, selfish view of our state government, and to help us put Illinois back on the map as one of the most progressive, efficient, well-run of the 48 states.

Finally, I want to thank the thousands of diligent servants of Illinois who are helping us realize that ambition, and who really are the state government. I have never been in politics or elected office before. This has been a new experience for me. I am grateful for the help and the loyalty of many new-made friends who have eased my path. And I want to thank hundreds of unknown friends who have somehow sensed what we are trying to do and have sent me encouraging letters. I am full of gratitude. I like my job — it's worth all the painful sacrifices.

I wish you all a happy New Year — prosperous in material things and blessed with the things of the spirit.

When Stevenson's sons were in Springfield during the holidays, a picture of them with their father was published. Mrs. Stevenson objected to it because she was fearful that public exposure would be harmful to the boys.

To James W. Mulroy and William I. Flanagan [8]

January 2, 1950

During the holidays our photographer took a picture of the three boys and myself by the Christmas tree. I gather it was subsequently released to the press, and I would earnestly request to be consulted about any

[8] The original of this typewritten memorandum is in the possession of Mr. Flanagan.

releases involving the children. They always present acute difficulties for me with Mrs. Stevenson.

A.E.S.

To Mrs. Edison Dick [9]

January 5, 1950

. . . What was wrong with the speech? [10] I've been expecting to hear. Too dreary, too pious, too self-righteous, no humor, too hurried, no spirit???

. . . How about coming down Sunday. I'll be back from Missouri and Buffy is arranging an informal supper party for some local obligies, Bishop O'Connor [11] etc. Monday & Tuesday are also fine & of course the only way to learn the Dept. of Welfare is to work around it & know the people. . . . [12]

On January 7, 1950, Governor Stevenson was the main speaker at the annual Jackson Day dinner at Springfield, Missouri. [13]

I come here tonight as an ambassador from Springfield, Illinois, to Springfield, Missouri — an ambassador from the Illinois Democrats to the Missouri Democrats. I'm told the latter have increased rapidly in the last few years. Well, so have the Illinois Democrats — in the past year. How loyal Democrats multiply following a successful election seems to me a singular and little noted phenomena.

After my visit to you, to even things up, a lot of you are going to have to visit Springfield, Illinois. You'll get a warm welcome. We've some new management over there now and you will even find some Democrats around for the first time in a long while. Indeed, if you find anything but Democrats I'll be disappointed. . . .

Last week one of the big St. Louis dailies [14] was good enough to publish year-end statements by your distinguished Governor [15] and myself. While writing that statement I was forcefully reminded of the mutuality

[9] This handwritten letter is in the possession of Mrs. Dick.

[10] His January 2 radio report to the people.

[11] William A. O'Connor, Roman Catholic bishop of the diocese of Springfield-in-Illinois.

[12] Mrs. Dick was a member of the Board of Public Welfare Commissioners.

[13] The text is based on a mimeograph copy prepared by the Governor's office for release to the press.

[14] The St. Louis *Post-Dispatch.*

[15] Forrest Smith, governor of Missouri, 1949–1953.

of interest that exists between Missouri and Illinois. St. Louis newspapers make public opinion in a great section of our State. Large numbers of people who work in Missouri live in Illinois (of course, one would prefer to live in Illinois!) and, as I have discovered from following developments in your state government and your state legislature, you are struggling with many of the very same problems with which we are concerned. . . .[16]

I suppose that all governors find themselves, as I do, participating in and sponsoring all sorts of non-partisan committees and commissions. In Illinois we have our non-partisan committee on constitutional reform, on crime prevention, on highway safety, government reorganization, and a lot of other subjects. But it's a relief now and then to be able to meet with a group like this where the emphasis is not particularly non-partisan! For example, if I should express some views here about Representative Dewey Short [17] I assume you would not be offended if they were not strictly non-partisan! What's more, I trust I won't be criticised if I point with pride to the tremendous part which the Democratic party and its great leaders have had in shaping the destiny of the United States in the most notable half century in the history of the world.

Perhaps at the halfway mark of this spectacular, revolutionary century in which we are privileged by Providence to live, we can properly look backward for a moment along the path from our national and political infancy to our full manhood.

Jefferson once said that a democracy should stage a revolution at least every twenty years. But we have found a gentle medium by which to accomplish the same results. Our revolutions are fought with weapons forged by constitutional processes, through freedom of the press and freedom of expression. We fix our aims and when we decide upon a change we bring it about in a twelve-hour march to the polls. Our party has, since 1800, been in every one of the 37 classics called national elections, and it has won 22 of them — won 22 and lost 15. We have met all comers in the long span of time that runs from one great Democrat, Thomas Jefferson, to another great Democrat, Harry Truman. In these 37 engagements we have met Federalists, Whigs and Republicans, one after another. The opposition changes its uniform every so often — we stay the same. It looks as though the Republican party was molting right now!

Over the years of our national life why have we Democrats had the people's confidence the bulk of the time? Why latterly — in this critical

[16] The three paragraphs omitted here summarize points made by Stevenson in his January 2 radio report to the people of Illinois.
[17] Republican congressman from Missouri.

century — has our destiny been directed most all the time by Democrats — Woodrow Wilson, Franklin Roosevelt and Harry Truman? I think it's well for us as party men not just to do and die but to reason why. As we look forward into a future that may be dark and ugly or bright and golden, we Democrats better pause a moment and reflect on what we are, where we are and how we got here. If you know where you've been it's easier to decide where you're going. As somone said, wisdom doesn't always consist in knowing what to do ultimately so much as it does in knowing what to do next.

I think our success in the past may have two main reasons — we can thank ourselves and we can thank the Republicans. We can thank the Republicans because their principles, if any, are archaic, obsolete and don't work. We can thank ourselves because we are wedded to a great principle that works. When we lose it, when we stray from the true faith, when we embrace false gods, we are doomed. So it has been and so it will be.

The Republicans found a great principle in the Civil War — national union and human freedom. Afterward they embraced the principle that what was good for business was good for the nation. Business was protected by tariffs and from cutthroat domestic competition. They passed the Homestead Act, distributed free land, and pensions to soldiers. The era of development was on and they won election after election. As Walter Webb [18] says: "What could you do with a party that had emancipated the slave, saved the Union, given everybody a bounty in land or tariff, assured businessmen of prosperity and poor men of a full dinner pail."

But by the turn of our century the Republican party had lost its bearings; it had made its choices, and cast its lot with power, money, big business and the employer. There was no place at the table for the farmer who had to buy in a protected market and sell in a free market. One by one the Republican party deserted the farmer, the working man, the small businessman; they deserted the people, and at last the people deserted them. Then came Woodrow Wilson and the New Freedom, Franklin Roosevelt and the New Deal, Harry Truman and the Fair Deal, and through them all runs the long, strong cord of faith in the Jacksonian-Jeffersonian principle that in a people's government the people are sovereign; that our strength and well-being don't trickle down from the overflowing cup at the top, but rise up the mighty trunk from the myriad roots that are the people.

I don't know what direction the Republican party of the future is go-

[18] Professor of history, University of Texas, 1933–1963; Harmsworth Professor of American history, Oxford University, 1942–1943; author of many books and articles.

ing to take. At the moment it reminds me of the Missouri mule who starved to death standing between two stacks of hay trying to make up its mind which to eat.

Confused, leaderless, torn with irreconcilable conflicts between the vaporous yearning to retreat to a dear, dead past, and the yearning to restate and reassert the great liberal principles of its birth; rudderless between forthright conservatism, hopeless reaction and expedient "metooism," the people have said to the once great, proud party of Lincoln and Teddy Roosevelt in the words of Revelations: "I know thy works, that thou art neither cold nor hot; I would thou wert cold or hot. So then because thou art lukewarm, and neither cold nor hot, I will spew thee out of my mouth."

And in November a year ago, in spite of all the prognoses, diagnoses and psychoses, they spewed mightily and embraced a game little guy who looked more like David than Goliath. But Harry Truman did not win last November by sweeping the people off their feet with the mere spectacle of his intrepid courage. That helped — but the real reason he won was because, in that final blast of Jacksonian candor and horse sense, he opened the eyes of the people to the solemn fact that the benefits that had come to them under the Democrats were in danger.

When they saw that, and remembered how the Democrats had saved their homes, their jobs, and extended their rights and privileges and made the nation strong where it had been weak, confident where it had been despairing, they rushed to the polls and voted to keep the same old team in uniform — and the same little Missouri quarterback calling the signals.

No, the American people didn't vote for Harry Truman because they were sentimental about a game little guy fighting out there all alone — they selected him because he went back and put on the armor of Andy Jackson and Franklin Roosevelt and spoke the old Democratic gospel of protecting the typical American against privilege and monopoly.

He won because he started to preach the old-time religion of the Democratic party — to preach the Democrats' traditional faith in the typical American citizen.

And as the days go by, it is interesting to see President Truman take on more and more of the characteristics of that lodestar of the Democratic heavens to whom our compasses ever turn — Andy Jackson. We see in Truman the same strength, the same fearless stand for enforcing human rights. We see in him the same impulsiveness — even to the point of using some of Old Hickory's cuss words in a blaze of indignation. We see in him a Jacksonian candor which lets the chips fall where they may. Harry's heart is in the same place Jackson's was — and the people know it.

Let's not forget that our Democratic Presidents have each in his time captured the imagination of the voters not by artifices of the theatre — none of them ever had a professional coach to teach him elocution. All of them won because they were the apostles of a great principle and because they wrote or talked straight to the heart of the typical American voter. They got their strength from the mass of the people — they reflected the hopes and wishes of the people — they stood by the people — and they worked for the people.

Our party's great leaders have seen through the hypocrisy of those who oppose change on the ground that confidence must not be shaken. They have unmasked the selfishness and greed of groups who always want government to stand still, who want the status quo undisturbed.

. . . Our great leaders have never yielded to the temptation to resist imperative change; we have met the challenges of our history. We have clung fast to our principles; and we must never forget that change is the order of life, that "what man will not alter for the better, time, the great innovator, will alter for the worse."

But our work is not finished, and the very weakness of the Republican party is a danger to us. Through our two party system we are, or should be, assured always of a responsible party in office and a powerful opposition party, alert and watchful, ready to expose the errors of the ruling party and to urge its overthrow. For party divisions are inseparable from free government, as Edmund Burke said. Too many parties, which results in diffused responsibility, was a potent contributor to the cataclysm that struck the unhappy continent of Europe. But even more dangerous than too many parties is too few. When political division appears, when one party becomes all powerful, democracy is dead and tyranny and dictatorship is the master even though they may masquerade in benevolent disguise for a long time. Arbitrary power can exist nowhere in a democracy — not even in a majority. And a government "can remain free only so long as party peddlers cry their wares of principles, of personalities and even patent medicines."

So while we celebrate our victories, while we pay reverential respect to our political antecedents, while we proudly proclaim our achievements, let us also not forget that pride goes before a fall. And let us be thankful for the Republican party, and the two party system, a manifestation of political genius unequalled and indispensable.

In the present critical days when so much of the world's destiny depends on our being right it is important that there be a strong opposition party which can contribute to the solution of our problems at home and abroad more than epithets and witch hunts. So, I was going to express the hope that the Republican party will rapidly recuperate. But I'll amend that; not too rapidly! They're doing all right as it is, and I don't think we Democrats are dangerously threatened with over-confidence — or dangerously threatening ourselves, the people, with tyranny or dictatorship.

You know, I sometimes think that the failure of my many Republican friends to evolve a program which would contribute to this country's forward and upward march may be due in part to bitter disappointment. They predicted dire consequences for this country upon cessation of hostilities. It didn't happen and they can't forgive the Democrats for it. They predicted unemployment of 15,000,000 men following the war. That prophecy failed to materialize. About 60,000,000 are gainfully employed and the Democratic Party is happy to be blamed for that disappointment. They predicted a depression within a year or two after the war. It didn't happen — again the fault of the Democrats. They predicted that high taxes would bankrupt the country. Instead we find that the income of this country, after taxes, in 1948, and again in 1949, was four times as great as the income under the last Republican administration and at least double the amount of the gross income in the golden years of the 1920's. They predicted that the New Deal and the Fair Deal would bring socialism to this country and we find ourselves more sheltered against the inroads of socialism than ever before. They almost seem disappointed that disaster hasn't overtaken us while the Democrats are in office.

The facts are plain to see. We have in the United States today, after 17 years of Democratic rule, by far the soundest, most free economy of any highly developed nation in the entire world. Those who are more concerned with the nation's health than they are with some stubborn doctrine of bitterness and criticism, can see very readily that the case for pessimism about our country is persuasive but superficial and misleading.

I was very much interested in an article by Professor Sumner Slichter in the Atlantic Monthly.[19] . . . In the United States and in most countries of Western Europe, he says, the first half of the 20th Century has been an age of remarkable moral progress, with great concern for human well-being and a growing capacity on the part of the community to deal with its problems. When there is so much pessimism, as many forebodings, so many predictions of disaster, it is well to count our blessings, and Professor Slichter's article reminds me of the Army story about the Indian in New Mexico who was smoke signalling love messages to his Indian sweetheart a few miles away. Right in the middle of it the atom bomb test went off, covering the sky with smoke for miles. "Gosh," the Indian muttered enviously, "I wish I'd said that."

The statistics on our progress in this 50 years in which our party has done most of the planning are impressive. For example, in 1890 only one

[19] "Better Than We Think," *Atlantic*, January, 1950.

out of 14 children between the ages of 14 and 17 was in school. Today the proportion has grown to four out of five. The number of high school graduates has been increasing since the turn of the century about thirteen times as fast as the population and the number of college graduates six times as fast. Only 20 years ago this country had fewer than 500 private pension plans and no public social insurance schemes except Workmen's Compensation laws. Today we have over 9,000 employer initiated pension plans, many plans negotiated by unions, a scheme of Federal old age pensions which covers about three workers out of five, and a system of unemployment compensation which covers about seven workers out of ten. We spend about $12 billion a year on public assistance to those in need. Through collective bargaining a framework of rules by which the rights of employees are protected has been developed. Thus at the very time when some governments have been going to extremes in asserting the claims of government against the individual, the United States has been helping millions of individuals to acquire important new rights.

We have emphasized a new liberty, freedom from want. We have set a goal of full employment and today we have 60 million people gainfully employed. Only a few years ago when there was talk of having 60 million workers in this country, the idea was ridiculed. It was ridiculed by some of those same people, who, you may remember, made such sport of President Roosevelt's promise that we would turn out 50,000 airplanes a year, which turned out to be very conservative.

I confess that I don't know whether we can afford all the things we would like to do to improve the lot of the average man. Obviously national solvency and individual incentive are still the first condition of a successful free economy and free society. But these anguished cries of "statism," "welfare state," and particularly "socialism," have a strangely familiar ring. We heard it all before, 15 years ago when Roosevelt was proposing price supports for agriculture, regulation of securities, social security, collective bargaining, etc. — policies that no Republican proposes to repeal. Indeed I am reminded of the so-called radical proposals that were being made at the time of the Haymarket incident in Chicago in 1886. One of the union's insistent cries at that time was for an eight-hour working day. The opposition termed the demand "a body blow to the American way of life."

Of course, in some circles these epithets and catch-words always meet with response. I saw a cartoon the other day showing some vestrymen in the church vestibule counting the money in the well-filled collection plates. One was saying to the other: "That jab at the welfare state certainly paid off."

The current cry of "socialism" looks a little incongruous against the background of national income of over $220 billion a year, corporation profits at new peaks, the stock market industrial average over 200, and savings of more than $150 billion. The average American receives 86 per cent more dollars in his pay envelope than he did in 1929, which is more than twice the percentage increase in prices during that period.

These are not the statistics of socialism and collectivism. These are not the results of neat socialistic plans calculated to enable everybody to eat well, work four hours a day and retire at 60. They are the accomplishments of a government which says that the people flourish or we all perish; a government that puts the public welfare first but which knows that a free market, subject only to essential controls, is the best way of providing the good things of life for the great mass of the people. As we see it, in short, the role of government is to lay down the rules of the game, not to play it. And if that's socialism then my dictionary is obsolete. Someone, maybe a Republican, must have rewritten it. I'm reminded of the frantic young husband who was working on his budget and complained that every time he was about to make both ends meet his wife moved the ends.

I would like to talk a bit about the welfare state we are hearing so much about. As someone said, it's not the "welfare" state but the "warfare" state for which we're paying such high taxes. Moreover, amid all the clamor I haven't heard anyone proposing to cut our investment in human values — in aid for the needy, the old, the unemployed, the homeless.

Then there is "statism," but the dictionaries are not in agreement as to what that means. And, besides, since its full scale run in the November's New York senatorial elections we haven't heard much more about "statism." [20]

No, we must not be deterred by epithets. If our great leaders, starting with Thomas Jefferson and Andrew Jackson, "had been frightened by epithets, the great program which has made this nation strong would never have been accomplished." Those are recent words of a wise, courageous, beloved American who also came to Missouri for inspiration — Alben Barkley. And I might add that if epithets and mistrust had paralyzed him, Abraham Lincoln's tomb in Springfield, Illinois, would not be a national shrine.

But there is one thing that I'm sure we can all agree upon from President Truman on down — Republicans and Democrats alike — and it poses a formidable responsibility for our party. If we can't balance our national budget now, when will we? And I hope and pray that history will never record that the Democratic Party after leading America

[20] Republican John Foster Dulles was defeated by Herbert H. Lehman, a Democrat.

boldly, wisely, courageously, through two world wars and the most extensive social revolution in the shortest period of time in history, foundered on the rocks of fiscal irresponsibility.

And there is something more in connection with all this talk about the welfare state we who are proud and happy to carry the ball into the unknown last half of this dramatic century dare not forget. "Man does not live by bread alone." There are needs beyond physical needs — emotional and spiritual needs that will not be satisfied by social security programs and the iron uniformity of legislation and central power. May we who believe in the individual never crush his self-reliance, his instinct for self-help, mutual aid, and responsibility beneath the heavy hand that feeds him — beneath a monster state that loves him but doesn't know him. Welfare, yes; usurpation, no. For the only thing worse than neglect and too little government is paternalism and too much government. Welfare is an instrument of social justice, but it can be an instrument of power too, and "power corrupts the giver and the gift."

There is much to say about the management of our foreign affairs by Democratic leadership; there is much to say about Communism's cold, implacable contest for men's minds and hearts that will plague our times for years to come. But I have kept you too long.

Let me conclude with the suggestion that the advent of this New Year — the halfway mark in the 20th Century — is a time for reflection, for self-examination, for trying to get the sights trained on future targets — for political parties as well as individuals.

The first 50 years of this century constitute a period of scientific and material progress without parallel in the history of man. And the same period has seen a comparable advance on the moral front. We have altered and revised our economic and social arrangements in the interest of a greater equality and a fuller life for all. We have dared to face up to political tyranny wherever we have found it. We have struggled to make men free at home and abroad, and we have realistically recognized that freedom is compounded of economic as well as political elements.

I make no claim that the Democratic Party is responsible for all these accomplishments in the first half-century, but I would ask all to consider what these 50 years would have lacked had there been no Woodrow Wilson — his New Freedom and his agonizing first steps in the direction of American participation in world affairs; no Franklin Roosevelt — his New Deal and his grasp of the interdependence of free men everywhere; no Harry Truman — his Fair Deal and his readiness to mobilize the resources of this country in opposition to the spread of the police state? The Democratic Party can claim a major share of participation in the

20th Century's contributions thus far to human betterment. The Democratic party is fulfilling its mission gloriously. It has given reality to the dream of Thomas Jefferson and new vitality to the triumphs of Andrew Jackson. It has answered the prayers of Woodrow Wilson.

But what of the future? What of the fateful 50 years we are now beginning? Our tasks are not finished. There is much to be done — many dark and ominous difficulties to be overcome.

There is the overshadowing need to find enduring foundations for world peace. There is the necessity of maintaining our economy at high levels of production and employment, in order that the paralyzing threat of economic stagnation may be frustrated. There is the age-old problem of dividing the fruits of capital and labor fairly and equitably, of providing reasonable security for those who must live by their own labor, of making available to all the benefits of our increasing knowledge. And we must break down the ancient barriers which have been falsely founded upon distinctions of race, color and religion.

When we remember that in the second half of our century these objectives must be sought not only for the United States alone but for a large part of the earth's surface and for millions of its inhabitants outside our own country, tomorrow's job emerges in all its sobering immensity.

That job can only be done by boldly setting our goals for the future, not by timid, wistful looks toward the past. It will not be done by any omniscient dictator or demagogue; it will not be done by class struggle. It will be done by free men with common purpose.

Let us resolve that our party shall not swerve from the path it has followed, that we will not trifle with the ideals that have brought us to our present position, that we shall continue to find our leaders among men whose wisdom comprehends the simple truth that the dignity of individual men — all men — is the fundamental basis of any good society.

The sunrise of our century was bloody. God willing, the sunset will be golden.

Stevenson invited George Young, a young Chicago lawyer (and a Republican) and his wife to the Lincoln's Birthday ceremonies in Springfield and suggested they spend the night of February 11 at the mansion. Also invited were Bill Blair and Kathryn Lewis.

In accepting Stevenson's invitation, Mr. Young wrote that he hoped the Governor could come to a dinner party in Chicago — "a reunion of some of the younger Stevensonians" and added that "even Republicans can, and do, admire what you're doing."

To George Young

January 9, 1950

Dear George:

I was glad to have your letter and I shall look forward to seeing you in February. I hope you will stay over for the Lincoln doings on Sunday the 12th.

I am leaving town for a few days, and unhappily will not be able to meet with the "younger Stevensonians" at your apartment on the 13th. I hope Friday, the 13th, has no significance!

You were good to think of me — and warm regards to Mary.[21]

Sincerely,

To Mrs. Lloyd Lewis

January 10, 1950

Dear Kathryn:

I have your letter and you are invited for Lincoln's Birthday — breakfast, lunch and dinner. Indeed, I suggest you come the night before. I think young Bill Blair and some of his Republican friends will be here and there will be other attractions no doubt.

Love,

To Mrs. Edison Dick [22]

January 11, 1950

. . . I'm off early in the morning to Cincin[nati] — with the Ives, thence to Georgia . . . to shoot quail with the Guggenheims [23] for a few days, and back here next Monday — then to Chicago for Thurs. Fri. Sat. & Sunday. . . .

There is much to report — difficulties here — a gratifying *triumph* in Springfield, Mo. — and not the least — a thorough physical exam to satisfy Buffy. Blood, urine, teeth, heart, chest etc etc — and I'm sound as a nut except for a "low grade, chronic, bronchial infection" and 15 lbs overweight. I'm starting medication, penicillin inhalation etc for the former, dieting for the latter, an exercise regime and cutting down if

---

[21] Mrs. Young.

[22] This handwritten letter to Mrs. Dick was probably written in Springfield. She says it was mailed from Cincinnati, Ohio.

[23] Alicia Patterson and her husband, Harry Guggenheim. They owned a large estate near Kingsland, Georgia.

not out on smoking. . . . Indeed I'm going to be so virtuous I'll soon be insufferable — and for what I'd like to know!

Do you like this:

I cannot praise a fugitive and cloistered virtue, unexercised and unbreathed, that never sallies out and seeks her adversary, but slinks out of the race, where that immortal garland is to be run for, not without dust and heat.

Well, you should. Its John Milton — and it reminds me of you and your virtuous friends in L.F. [Lake Forest] and all over this land — fugitive, cloistered friends. I choose to think they really envy you some dust and heat. But is the garland good enough — its mortal.

Hermon D. Smith, Louis A. Kohn and Stephen A. Mitchell, three of the original founders of the 1948 Stevenson for Governor Committee, sent Stevenson a telegram on the occasion of his first anniversary in office.

To Hermon D. Smith [24]

January 11, 1950

Dear Dutch, Lou and Steve:

Your wire was the first reminder of my anniversary and I am glad you hadn't forgotten — even if I had! We must have a reunion soon. Meanwhile my warm thanks and everlasting gratitude for all your help — before and after!

Yours,
ADLAI

To Frederic Woodward [25]

January 16, 1950

Dear Fritz:

As my life becomes more normal I am thinking about some old friends whom I hope to induce to come to Springfield to visit me sometime. I live in a state of solemn and solitary grandeur, and I hope you and Mrs. Woodward will take a night off and spend it with me here at the Mansion.

Word comes from Kathryn Lewis that you have been ill. I hope it is

[24] The original is in the possession of Mr. Smith.
[25] Owner of the University Book Store, near the University of Chicago campus.

nothing serious and that we can inspect the Lincoln shrines together before very long.

With every good wish, I am

Sincerely yours,

On January 13, 1950, former Secretary of State James F. Byrnes wrote Stevenson that because the press had carried a garbled report of his speech to the Conference of Southern Governors he was sending the Governor the full text of the speech.

To James F. Byrnes

January 16, 1950

My dear "Mr. Secretary": [26]

I was delighted to have your note and the enclosed copy of the speech. I saw the newspaper account at the time and will read it with much pleasure and profit.

Today I read that you have announced for Governor.[27] As a veteran of one year in that appalling office I don't know whether to say "Hooray" or suggest a psychiatrist!

My affectionate regards to Mrs. Byrnes.

Faithfully yours,

Richard Bentley, a Chicago lawyer and an old friend of the Stevensons, represented the Governor in the divorce suit instituted by his wife. The Governor did not contest her action but the settlement preceding the action was complicated and delicate.

To Richard Bentley [28]

January 18, 1950

Dear Dick:

I enclose my check in payment of your statement, and also, for your information, a copy of my letter to Mr. Merrill.[29]

[26] While Byrnes was Secretary of State, Stevenson had served under him as chairman of the U.S. delegation to the United Nations Preparatory Commission in London in 1945, and in New York at the UN General Assembly in 1946.

[27] He was elected governor of South Carolina and served from 1951 to 1955.

[28] The original of this typewritten letter is in the possession of Mr. Bentley.

[29] Charles M. Merrill, of Reno, Nevada, where the suit was brought, who was named in the divorce decree as appearing as attorney for Stevenson in that city.

Sometime I will have an opportunity to thank you personally for handling this difficult matter for me, which I am sure was no joy for you. . . .

I shall hope for a glimpse of you over the week-end.

Yours,

ADLAI

Miss Martha Love, of St. Louis, wrote Stevenson on returning from a trip to Europe to express her regret about his divorce. She also wrote that he had many admirers in Missouri.

To Martha Love

January 19, 1950

Dear Martha:

You were sweet to write me and I was so glad to hear from you again.

It is all very sad and I find it difficult to understand, but we have to asume that everything is for the best.

I envy you your trip abroad and there are moments when I wish I were on a remote island in the South Pacific without telephone or radio!

Do come over and see me some time when you have an opportunity.

Yours,

John Nuveen, a Chicago businessman, wrote Stevenson from Brussels, where he was serving on a special mission of the U.S. Economic Cooperation Administration to Belgium and Luxembourg. He had talked with visiting newspapermen in London and heard them express the opinion that the Governor was doing an excellent job — about which, he added, he had no doubts himself but he was happy to have it confirmed by the reporters.

To John Nuveen

January 23, 1950

Dear John:

I was delighted to have your letter, and the thought of a ski vacation in Switzerland leaves me fidgeting with envy in the cold winter fog of Springfield.

I hope very much that if you get back this spring you will let me know, and, if possible, spend a night with me down here. I am eager to get a first-hand report from abroad, and your axis is pretty extensive by this time. I would be still happier if you were about to come back here and go to work for the state!

But, thank God, you are where you are!

Yours,

On January 20, 1950, Stevenson spoke to the Law Club of Chicago about the problems of state government. The speech is not reprinted here since it covered the same material contained in speeches already published in this volume. Thomas W. Mulroy (brother of Stevenson's executive secretary) wrote him on January 23, 1950: "It was the finest thing of its kind I have ever heard. But more important than my own reaction, are the comments which I have heard from every single member of the Law Club with whom I have talked since last Friday. Those comments without exception have been extraordinarily complimentary to you. In short, you took the staid, old Law Club by storm!"

To Thomas W. Mulroy [30]

January 24, 1950

Dear Tom:

I am much encouraged by your letter. I felt that it was a clumsy, disordered, ill-prepared and tiresome talk. The only thing worse than speaking badly is speaking too long. I did both. But you reassure me mightily. Thanks!

Sincerely yours,

Kenneth F. Burgess, one of Stevenson's former law partners in Chicago, made a contribution to the fund out of which Stevenson supplemented the salaries of some of his assistants and cabinet members who came to Springfield at considerable financial sacrifice.[31]

To Kenneth F. Burgess

January 24, 1950

Dear Kenneth:

This is a better day than I had expected! Your generosity touches me

[30] A carbon copy is in A.E.S., P.U.L.
[31] An explanation of this fund will be found in the introduction to Part One of this volume.

deeply. I am not only more grateful than I can tell you for the money but for what lies behind it. I was distressed about my clumsy, unprepared and disorderly talk at The Law Club. The only thing worse than talking badly is talking too long. I felt guilty of both sins and you have comforted and reassured me.

I also have your letter regarding Secretary Johnson's [32] speech at The Commercial Club on March 17. I shall certainly be there.

Many, many thanks.

Yours,

To Mrs. Edison Dick [33]

January 29, 1950

. . . I'm in Phelps Kelley's apt.[34] — deserted by even the dark skinned Virginia — purring peacefully after a hot bath and a freezing cold day on the moors of Du Page County — Good shooting with stiff fingers and liquid eyes — 23 pheasants for 7 guns in a couple of hours of tramping. I doubt if I hit any of them but they were polite and 5 beautiful plumed cocks are lying in mortuary splendor in a box outside the door. I would have driven back to L.F. [Lake Forest] & left you some but providence made other provision. Now they'll go to Gertrude [35] — for the birthday guests and to . . . [a powerful Democratic boss] in lieu of "compromises" as a peace offering!

. . . I'll call the guests tomorrow A.M. & recommend either the 8:25 A.M. Alton [Railroad] Saturday or the 4:50 P.M. Friday. The Smith's [36] take a midnight train from Cincinnati to St. L[ouis]. Friday night & an early Alton train from St. Louis Sat. A.M. — which means that the mine inspection [37] will leave for lunch in Taylorville near the mine late Sat. A.M. . . .

---

[32] Secretary of Defense Louis Johnson.

[33] This handwritten letter is in the possession of Mrs. Dick.

[34] Stevenson's house at Libertyville was rented. At this time the governor's suite in the penthouse of the State of Illinois Building in Chicago had not been completed. When Stevenson remained overnight in Chicago he stayed with various friends, among them Mr. Kelley, who maintained a bachelor apartment on the Near North Side.

[35] The cook at the mansion in Springfield.

[36] Mr. and Mrs. Hermon D. Smith.

[37] On his birthday, Stevenson took his guests to visit a coal mine near Taylorville, about thirty-five miles from Springfield. See his letter to Alicia Patterson, February 18, 1950, below.

To Alicia Patterson [38]

[late January, 1950]

. . . I went pheasant shooting Sunday in sub zero temperature and 7 guns got 23 in a couple of hours — near Elgin. I think my shooting was about as usual — o. But they were very courteous to the Gov. & I brought home 5 — with becoming embar[r]assment & protestations.

Added to some more I have we'll have a pheasant dinner Sat when the McDougals, Oates, Derns & Smiths [39] come down from Chi to celebrate my 50th birthday. Horrors what a thought — 50! Where have I been & what have I been doing all this time. Life is ⅔ gone & I don't know what its all about yet or what I want or am trying to do. . . .

A

To Ronald Tree [40]

January 31, 1950

Dear Ronnie:

I am distressed that I missed you in Chicago. I had hoped that you and Marietta [41] would have inspected the Governor's Mansion in Springfield long before this, and I will be disappointed if you don't arrange to do so on your next trip to Illinois.

With affectionate regards to you both.

Yours,

To Paul Powell [42]

February 1, 1950

Dear Paul:

I have read with much interest and profit the attached speech [43] and, as the girl said, I am blushing all over, about the nice things you had to say about me.

I am constantly baffled about the "Republican holdovers" I hear so

[38] This handwritten letter is in the possession of Adlai E. Stevenson III.

[39] Edward D. McDougal, Jr., James F. Oates, John Dern and Hermon D. Smith and their wives. McDougal, Oates and Dern were former partners of Stevenson in the Chicago law firm.

[40] The editors were unable to locate any message to Stevenson from Mr. Tree. It is likely that he telephoned Stevenson's office in Chicago and left a message for him there.

[41] Mrs. Tree.

[42] Democratic speaker of the Illinois House of Representatives.

[43] The editors were unable to locate a copy of Mr. Powell's speech.

much about.[44] I wish the people who complain could be more specific and point at individuals by name and address and position. Whenever they complain to me I ask for specific names. Occasionally I get one and have managed to remove several that way. More frequently I hear nothing more about it.

Regards.

Sincerely yours,

To Alicia Patterson [45]

February 1, 1950

. . . Will you admit this is a *really* silly edit[orial], or must I convince you. Do you *really* think the French who have been fighting the commies in Indo-China for 7 years don't "realize that is one more step on road to world conquest"; or that the British who have been fighting 6 yrs in Malaya don't understand the score. I marvel — and so does most of the rest of the world — at the smug asininity of Americans and especially American editors who didn't know Viet Nam from Kuala Lumpur two or three years ago and are now telling the Br[itish] & the Fr[ench] who have been there 100 yrs all about the importance of S.E. Asia and the menace of comm[un]ism that they were fighting before most of our editors could find Korea on the map.

Some editorials *begging* the Fr to give these people total, unequivocal independance and *begging* them to go on fighting would be more helpful.

Ho Hum — Sorry — But I'm depressed with everything that comes out of Wash[ington] & most everything that comes out of our newspapers. I was going to add that this one is almost bad enough for the Pantagraph!

Love

A

On February 4, 1950, Stevenson celebrated his fiftieth birthday (which was the following day) at a party for which three of his former law partners, James F. Oates, Edward D. McDougal, Jr. and John Dern — and their wives — were responsible. It was a casual affair at the mansion in Springfield, attended also by the J. Edward Days, the Loring Merwins, James W. Mulroy, Jane Dick and the Hermon D. Smiths. Mr. Smith recalled later: "It was an evening to be long remembered, and it was

[44] There were continual complaints from the Democrats, particularly those from downstate, over Stevenson's handling of patronage, which the Governor was never able to satisfy.

[45] This handwritten letter is in the possession of Adlai E. Stevenson III.

remembered in a series of annual birthday parties. . . . Following his move to New York, the party was held several times in the embassy in the Waldorf Towers. . . . The 1965 party was arranged by the James Oates at the River Club, with much brilliant and original poetry recited. . . . Adlai mentioned late that evening that he felt this party should be the last, and even entreaties of some of us to come back to Lake Forest in 1966 appeared futile. It was the last of a remarkable and truly unique series of parties!" [46]

On January 31, 1950, Edison Dick wrote the Governor expressing regret that he could not be on hand for the party. He said he was sending Stevenson a printed copy of hearings held the previous October before the House Foreign Affairs Committee that included a resolution stating that a fundamental objective of U.S. foreign policy was to support and strengthen the United Nations.

To Edison Dick

February 1, 1950

Dear Eddie:

Many thanks for your letter. We will miss you at the Half Century activities!

I will look forward with interest to the testimony, although I wish I could find a little more time to do it — and a lot of other things — justice. Certainly it illustrates the deplorable paucity of reporting in the Chicago press. I was hardly conscious that the hearings were in process.

Yours,

On Stevenson's fiftieth birthday, George Mitchell, director of Finance, sent the Governor a handwritten letter:

I was early indoctrinated with the Christian virtue. But my intellectual awakening was accompanied by a concentration of study in the social sciences. This, as you may surmise, added up to a matured state of cynicism about most affairs — certainly public affairs. My association with you has taught me that intelligence, humility and sincerity can provide leadership — the only kind of leadership that even counts or ever helps. It matters very little that I have seen you demonstrate this — it matters a great deal that many others have observed the same phenomena and have really felt the irresistable

[46] "Politics and R & R," in *As We Knew Adlai: The Stevenson Story by Twenty-two Friends,* edited and with preface by Edward P. Doyle, foreword by Adlai E. Stevenson III (New York: Harper & Row, 1966), pp. 36–37.

[sic] pull of sincerity in a political leader. Fewer have seen you as one who could have relied on his own completely adequate competence humbly seeking help from others or refusing to compromise the public interest with mercenary or mean political ends. Faith in others is most important in this world perhaps in part because what we have always seems to be disappearing. To create faith in a political leader is the hardest job I know of. You are doing it and in that knowledge I hold you in highest respect and admiration.

To George Mitchell

February 6, 1950

Dear George:

I have read your letter and reread it. There is little I can say, but I can feel deeply. Did it ever occur to you that the virtues you recount are less the positive product of "intelligence crossed with humility and fired with sincerity" than the negative result of a careless courage born of confidence? And where, pray tell, does the confidence come from? It comes, of course, from the outside, not the inside; it comes from others who know what is right, what is wrong; what is wise and what is stupid. Pick the men — then listen to them.

I picked you — forever, I hope.

Thanks. I will keep it always.

Sincerely yours,

Governor Stevenson's staff at the capitol building presented him with a tennis racket as a gift for his fiftieth birthday.

To James W. Mulroy, Lawrence Irvin, Bette Figueira, Naomi Dunn, Mary Leggett, Virginia Sterrenberg, Anne Alexander, Jane Paxton, Anne Risse, Don Hyndman, Dorothy Wallace, Margaret Munn, Josephine Maloney, Walter R. Coon and Albert Smith [47]

February 6, 1950

My dear friends:

I was delighted with the splendid tennis racquet, evidently selected by that crafty old player, Don Hyndman.

You were more than good to send me anything — let alone anything so useful. To be sure, some visitors remarked that my contours are the

---

[47] The original is in the possession of T. Don Hyndman.

best reason for your extraordinary thoughtfulness and generosity. But I am sure that never occurred to you!

Many thanks.

Sincerely yours,

On February 7, 1950, Governor Stevenson was awarded an honorary degree by Centre College and delivered the commencement address.[48] *Accompanying him was his sister, Mrs. Ernest L. Ives, who wrote:*

> The trip I enjoyed most while Adlai was Governor was to Danville, Kentucky, to see him receive an honorary degree at Centre College, where our Great-grandfather, Reverend Lewis Warner Green, had been president before the Civil War. During that visit, my brother and I went to see Waveland, the beautiful brick house built in 1797 on the Wilderness Road by our Great-great-grandfather, Willis Green, after he married Sarah Reed — some say the first marriage of white settlers performed in Kentucky. It's now a large dairy farm, and the owners were extremely nice about letting us go through the fine old house. . . . Having been brought up on our Stevenson grandparents' tales of Kentucky, we were thrilled to see the places they'd loved." [49]

Centre College has many intimate associations for me. I believe it was Gladstone who said: "No greater calamity can happen to a people than to break utterly with its past." In coming here to Danville, to Kentucky and to Centre College, I have a sense of continuity with my family's past which I could not have in the same degree anywhere else. What's your Commencement is my Homecoming. Each of us, then, will have ties of sentiment with this day which can never be forgotten.

My grandfather Stevenson was a student at Centre College almost 100 years ago. He was born in the district known as the Pennyrile, in Christian County. Whether it was because the tobacco crop failed, as the story goes, or for some other reason, in 1852 his family moved to central Illinois, a month's journey by wagon and horseback. As Governor of Illinois of course I always say I can understand why they moved from Kentucky to Illinois, but in a few years he came back to Kentucky to Centre College. I have often thought that it was here at Centre that his flair for politics and his good judgment of people was clearly fore-

[48] The text is based on a mimeograph copy.
[49] Elizabeth Stevenson Ives and Hildegarde Dolson, *My Brother Adlai* (New York: William Morrow, 1956), p. 237.

shadowed. For here he courted and won none other than the daughter of the President of the College — always sound strategy for a struggling student.

My great grandfather, the President of the College at that time, was Dr. Lewis Warner Green. He was born and raised near Danville at "Waveland," his father's plantation. An ardent Union sympathizer, he evidently suffered greatly over the divided loyalties and broken families of the Civil War. He was a college president in the great 19th Century tradition — a classical scholar, an ordained and gifted minister of the Presbyterian Church, an intellectually and spiritually whole man. I often wish I had inherited more of his characteristics!

So you will understand why my attachment for Centre is so great. Indeed if it wasn't for the romantic qualities of this ancient campus I would not be here today. I would not be at all!

Curiously enough, when my other, my maternal, great grandfather first came to Illinois in 1832, his path at once crossed that of Centre College. The letter of introduction which he brought from Pennsylvania to the new country was addressed to John Todd Stuart, a member of the Centre graduating class of 1826, Abraham Lincoln's first law partner and a cousin of Lincoln's wife, Mary Todd.

Apart from family ties, Centre has come actively to my attention in at least one other way. During the war my closest associate in the Navy Department in Washington was a man [50] who had the misfortune to be the captain of the Harvard football team on that golden day in 1921 when divine intercession proved as potent on the gridiron as the T-formation or the forward pass. My old friend has spent much of his time since that day brooding on his failure to devise some earthly stratagem which would have held Providence in check, on at least the one yard line. His unhappy experience on that occasion has at any rate, I can report, made him a life-long believer in the power of prayer — and the power of the "Praying Colonels." [51]

I know something, then, of your College's glorious past. But I am more interested at the moment in your own future, and that of the society in which you live. I should like to fix your attention upon the close relationship between the two — your education and the future.

[50] R. Keith Kane.
[51] "The Praying Colonels of Centre College came to Soldiers Field for the second time on October 29, 1921 and handed Harvard its first varsity defeat since its loss to Yale in 1916. Their strategy directed by Bo McMillin, the Kentuckians won by 6 to o and accomplished something no other college had been able to do in the previous forty years — defeat Harvard in an intersectional game." Morris A. Bealle, *The History of Football at Harvard, 1874–1948* (Washington, D.C.: Columbia Publishing Co., 1948), p. 243.

In his "Imaginary Conversations," Walter Savage Landor characterizes a man as "an example that a liberal education is peculiarly necessary where power is almost unlimited." I suggest to you the transparent truth of this observation and its relevance to the times in which we find ourselves.

The power, for good or for evil, of the political organization which goes by the name of the United States of America is virtually beyond measurement. The decisions which it makes, the uses to which it devotes its immense resources, the leadership which it provides on moral as well as material questions, all appear likely to determine the fate of the modern world.

Consider, if you please, the reports which the newspapers bring us of the decision to proceed with the construction of the hydrogen bomb. Even with the substantial discount always to be made in the case of unofficial rumor, this weapon is apparently the most awesome instrument of destruction yet contemplated.

The resolution of this question has momentous consequences for all mankind. The corresponding responsibility carried by those in whose hands this decision rested is virtually immeasurable. In terms of power lodged in a few — perhaps only in one — over the destinies of millions of fellow human beings, the prospect is staggering.

Your generation will, I greatly fear, be called upon to make many similar determinations. Everyone of you will certainly be called upon to make many decisions in your lives, some of them perhaps massive in scope, commensurate with your power and responsibility — all of them far-reaching in effect on you and others.

By what road should you seek the wisdom and judgment which must always underlie your great decisions if you are to lead a happy life, a satisfying life, a good life?

Having asked the question philosophers have asked for all time, I will not attempt to answer it, except to say this: good judgment is a quality of heart as well as mind, informed not alone by cool intelligence and practical experience, but also by those warmer perceptions which are of the spirit and which search the ultimate ends of our existence on earth.

It would be presumptuous and out of character for me to lecture you about your spirit. That I must leave to wiser, better men. But perhaps you'll forgive me if I draw on my own desultory, haphazard experience in business, in law, diplomacy and government to say a word about intelligence and experience as attributes of good judgment — good sense, if you please.

Don't be afraid to learn; don't ever stop learning because at the very best you can know very little. And don't be afraid to live, to live hard and fast; not dissolutely and badly, but hard, fast and fearlessly. Because it is not the years in your life, but the life in your years that count[s]. You'll have more fun, you'll do more good and you'll get and give more satisfaction the more you know, the more you've worked and the more you've lived. For this is a great and glorious adventure at a stirring time in the annals of man. Take it standing up boldly, not sitting down complaining, yawning and waiting for a pension.

You have a better chance than many to give a lot and, therefore, take a lot out of life. If we can't look to people like you for leadership, for good judgment, for wise directions for yourselves and the convictions of our society, where can we look? For here at Centre which for 130 years has transmitted from one generation to the next the riches of Western civilization you have gotten some grasp of the basic principles on which our cultures is founded — the concept of supremacy of the individual, the worth of the individual human being and the necessity for a climate of freedom in which these values may find means of expression. You have the basic core of a liberal education which can convert the possession of the influence and power you attain into a beneficent force instead of an evil one.

But you are not educated. You have a good start. That's all. And most of you will have to carry on by yourselves. The important thing is to carry on, in order to make the most of the components of character which you have and which will make your successes meaningful and enable you to bear your failures philosophically.

Parenthetically, I know it is not fashionable to talk of failure to a graduating class. Indeed, the very last precaution a commencement speaker takes is to examine his text carefully for any guilty word or phrase which might even suggest the possibility that each bright young person before him may not become either President of the United States or Chairman of the Board of General Motors.

But, at the risk of being unorthodox and of never being asked back to Centre, I venture to point out that there will not be enough openings in these or comparable jobs to accommodate all of you. Some of you may come to feel that, through no fault of your own, you have not achieved that rung in the ladder which your talents and your industry warranted.

This dissatisfaction will not result in merely a problem of personal adjustment. For Hitler's brown shirts, I remind you, covered many who knew better and who were merely venting their spleen upon a world which had failed to supply sufficient notice or reward. Arnold Toynbee has noted that one of the danger signs of a disintegrating civilization is a restless intellectual proletariat — persons whose economic status and opportunities for utilization of their special skills are not proportionate to their educational development.

There is, thus, not only the problem of education for success but also of educating for failure or disappointment. Fortunately the same kind of education achieves the desired results in both situations. There is the curious paradox that the man who is big enough to exercise wisely the power that comes with success is often also the man with the inner resources to lead a happy, useful life in obscurity. In either role he will be contributing to the well-being of his time and place — a fact which I am encouraged to believe that we have once again come to appreciate after a long period of worship of false and deceiving gods.

Granted then that you have the necessary fundamental equipment of good judgment and wise decision; spiritual depth and discernment, a basic liberal education, eagerness to learn, and courage to live boldly, what then?

I have dwelt on the importance of the equipment for sound judgment because you are destined to live at a dramatic, critical interval in history as citizens of the most powerful country in the world. As such you will be participating in decisions affecting the future not alone of yourselves but of the whole world. Your collective might can tip the scales for very much better or infinitely worse in the last half of the 20th Century.

Did you know that our century dawned in optimism and America seemed to be on the threshold of a century of unprecedented peace and progress? The Spanish-American War had been gloriously concluded. The United States had reached its present continental limits and was extending its hand across the sea. American imperialists, chanting Kipling's refrain of "the white man's burden," were casting covetous eyes across the Pacific and south of the border. The nation was prosperous. The western farmers had started to make money and were beginning to give some thought to the amenities of life. The old sod house of the Great Plains was being superseded by frame dwellings. The scars of the Civil War were healed. Cotton had become a profitable crop again. The South had reached a degree of stabilization unknown since ante-bellum days. The railroads earned more money in 1899 than in any previous year.

Well, half of that century is gone, and with it much of our complacent optimism. Our time on earth has been the bloodiest, most disordered and violent since the Renaissance illuminated the Dark Ages. Two world conflagrations and two economic convulsions have taken a savage toll in physical suffering and spiritual disillusionment. Today's mood is one of anxiety. People are apprehensive about tomorrow. Some even ask: "Will there be a tomorrow?" This is the Anxious Age.

The specter of Communism, which a century ago Marx and Engels boastfully proclaimed to be "haunting Europe," today actually stalks the world, and with it are the twin specters of war and depression.

What will the next half century be like? Will it bring a repetition of the frustrations and disasters of the last 50 years on a more appalling scale? Or will we somehow find a way to break the wretched cycle of wars and depressions and end the 20th Century in a golden, peaceful sunset? Will we take advantage of the great moral, social and scientific advance of the last 50 years to set at rest anxiety and fear?

We should not let the wide gulf between the hopes of 1900 and the fears of 1950 fool us into thinking that the last half century was a period of unrelieved retrogression. It may well be that when the definitive history of the 20th Century is finally written it will record as the most significant development of the first half of the century not the two World Wars, nor the great depression, not the Russian Revolution, nor the rise and fall of Hitler, not even the atom bomb, but rather the expansion of the intellectual and moral horizons of millions of people, an expansion that has been evidenced in America by two striking developments. First a recognition of our responsibility as a nation in the world community, and, second, an appreciation of our individual and collective responsibility to alleviate human suffering — a recognition of the correlative truths that we are our brother's keeper and that all men are our brothers.

In the United States, and most of Western Europe, the first half of the 20th Century has been an age of remarkable moral progress, with great concern for human well-being and a growing capacity on the part of the community to deal with its problems.

The statistics on our progress in the last 50 years are impressive. Education furnishes but one example. In 1890 only one out of 14 children between the ages of 14 and 17 was in school. Today the proportion has grown to 4 out of 5. The number of high school graduates has been increasing since the turn of the century about 13 times as fast as the population and the number of college graduates six times as fast. Social security and public assistance for the unfortunate have expanded beyond the wildest dreams of 50 years ago. Through collective bargaining, a framework of rules by which the rights of employees are protected has been developed. The attitude of government toward its people has come a long way since Marie Antoinette said of the poor who had no bread: "Let them eat cake."

We have, in short, made enormous economic and social advances in this past half century. Yet we seem to be more moved by anxiety and fear than by faith and hope. We are doubting our beliefs and believing our doubts. What is the explanation of this curious timidity at the very pinnacle of our national strength, prestige and affluence? Why is this the age of anxiety, the anxious age?

The reasons are many; two are large and obvious. The memory of the great depression and the emphasis on economic security for the individual in late years have increased our misgivings about our free capitalist system at home, and a new, powerful, aggressive idea has emerged abroad to challenge dangerously the democratic idea which has been in the ascendancy for so long.

The competition in armaments between East and West is merely a symptom of an underlying antithesis compounded of many elements in addition to differences of opinion as to the proper economic organization of society. We are confronted with a reactionary imperialism which is a baffling blend of medievalism and an ends-over-means type of advanced humanitarianism.

The preservation of the free world hangs upon our ability to win the allegiance of those millions and millions of people throughout the world who have not yet made their choice between our democratic system, on the one hand, and the promises which Communism offers, on the other. That choice will be mainly shaped by our own performance. It will turn upon such things as our ability to avoid the disruptions of depression, to guarantee equality of opportunity, to narrow the gulfs separating economic status, to preserve freedom of thought and action, to make democracy accord in practice with its premises and professions of faith.

We won't resist the Soviet impact on the Western world with a schizophrenic society which protests its devotion to democratic ideals while it indulges in undemocratic practices, or which recoils in horror from an alien materialism but, blinded by its own material accomplishments, loses sight of its spiritual heritage. If Western civilization is to save its body, then it must save its soul too.

In the words of Dr. Charles Malik, the Delegate of Lebanon to the United Nations: "If the Western world can show a way to eradicate the shame of poverty, of exploitation, of oppression, of greed, without resort to social revolution and class struggle and dictatorship, if it can place these material values within their proper place within the context of a mighty spiritual movement which will be revolutionary without being subversive and which will draw its substance from the infinite riches of the Western positive tradition, then communism will vanish, and the specter which now walks the earth will be laid forever."

I say to you, my young friends, that you cannot, you must not, stand aside from the great, the continuous, decisions in your time, in your

country, and in your world. You are the inheritors of a tradition of
freedom which is the fruition of centuries of pain and effort. Unlike
many of your generation, you have been privileged to receive the best
gift that tradition has to offer — a liberal education. You and many more
like you will be called upon to make the decisions and man the defenses
of the humane individualist concept against its avowed opponents and
its covert foes — indifference and ignorance. You have the components
of good judgment and wise decision. Many of your decisions will be
executed throught the instrument of government, and of one thing I can
assure you. If responsible citizens like yourselves don't make that government good government, responsive government, there will always be
irresponsibles, and worse, ready to usurp the positions and leadership
which should be yours by every consideration of intelligence and integrity. For these tasks and these exciting opportunities, use the equipment that God and this college have given you, and that your own industry each day improves. Use your heart and your head, and not your
prejudices. Even if you are among the fortunate who inherit their prejudices and don't have to acquire any you are more than the social animal
Seneca spoke of. Man is a moral agent with the power of making choices
affecting not only himself but countless others. And man can hope.
Not animals, only mankind, can hope. It is because we are more than
animals that we can blow ourselves off the face of this planet in the next
fifty years. But it is also because we are more than animals that we can
make this world a better place than it has ever been before.

And be not afraid. Fear God and nothing else. But if you have to
fear, be afraid of fear! Don't worry about what might happen, and start
thinking now about what you are going to help make happen.

To Amelia Craig Riker [52]

February 10, 1950

My dear Cousin Amelia:

Perhaps Buffy or Ernest [Ives] have reported to you our harrowing
adventures in the air after we left Lexington. We finally landed in black
fog on a radar ground approach without ever seeing the ground until
we struck it in Chicago — too late to catch the train to Springfield! But
there is always some consolation, and we saw "The Red Shoes," which
otherwise I am sure we should never have seen.

My little glimpse of the Blue Grass has agitated my appetite for Kentucky. Or was it your charming home, hospitality — and self! I hardly
know. But anyway, I had a lovely visit and I am deeply grateful to you.

Yours,

[52] A distant relative of Stevenson who lived in Harrodsburg, Kentucky.

To Walter Lippmann

February 10, 1950

Dear Walter:

The Chicago Council on Foreign Relations has just informed me that you are going to speak there on February 22. I wish I could be there to hear you, but it is almost impossible for me to get up to Chicago during the week. However, I am hopeful that you may be able to come to Springfield either before or after for a visit. I hope and pray that you will not be on a one-night stand lecture tour and that it may be possible for you to come down Thursday. There are several excellent trains on the Illinois Central and the Alton Railroads, and I could give you full information if there is any possibility. I would like to offer you my plane, but unfortunately it has just gone into the shop for a three-weeks overhauling.

My best to Helen.[53] I hope she will be with you.

Yours,

To Mrs. William R. Odell [54]

February 10, 1950

Dear Ginc:

I have received "Richer by Asia," [55] and I am impressed by your extraordinary memory. I can't remember of anybody else who ever promised to send me a book who remembered it. My only problem now is to find time to read it, but I shall do so — and I hope I remember to return it to you!

Affectionately,

Alfred MacArthur, friend and Libertyville neighbor of the Stevensons, wrote the Governor on February 3, 1950, "Black Republican that I am . . . I am willing to concede that you are doing a pretty good job." And, "If by any chance you should be able to get away for a little while . . . and could use Cuernavaca in the immediate future or Desbarats this summer, it can be arranged."

---

[53] Mrs. Lippmann.
[54] The Odells were Lake Forest friends of Stevenson.
[55] Edmond Taylor, *Richer by Asia* (Boston: Houghton Mifflin, 1947).

To Alfred MacArthur

February 11, 1950

Dear Alfred:

I was enchanted by your letter, although I wish people like you wouldn't constantly remind me that there are tranquil places like Cuernavaca and Desbarats! But as long as you have gone and done it I may have to yield to my natural disposition and take advantage of yours. So look out!

You do a Democratic politician more than justice, and I wish there were more Republicans like you.

Yours,

To Joan Pirie

February 16, 1950

Joan dear:

Could it be — that my lovely Joan has sent me a valentine? At all events, one has arrived curiously anonymous and inscribed with a very distinctive and attractive handwriting that Miss [Carol] Evans says bears a striking similarity to yours! If it is yours, I am very happy — indeed a little giddy. If it is not, I love you all the same — and I'll just have to guess who my secret admirer in New York is. But that's fun too!

Affectionately,

Egbert White, publisher of United Nations World, *a monthly magazine dealing with international and regional affairs, sent Stevenson an advance copy of their February issue. He expressed his high regard for Stevenson's journalistic achievements and wrote that he would be honored to have the Governor's opinion of the magazine.*

To Egbert White

February 16, 1950

Dear Bert:

I have your letter of January 25, and I am most happy to receive the advance copy of the February issue of your magazine.

I congratulate you on the commencement of your fourth year of publication, and I wish for you many, many more years of similarly successful effort. I personally have been an enthusiastic reader of your magazine from the beginning, and, although I do not have the time to devote to matters of this character which I should like to have by reason of the involvements in which I presently find myself, I expect to continue to look at it regularly in the future.

I think you have done an excellent job of putting out a highly readable journal in a most important field, and I am sure that your influence is commensurate with the excellence of your endeavor.

With best personal regards, I am

Sincerely yours,

To Alicia Patterson [56]

February 18, 1950

. . . And speaking of mines, I've never told you about *"the birthday"* which you were good enough to remember both by wire and a brave, good letter which made me feel useful and significant — for a few hours. Well, anyway, 5 couples of friends arrived from Chicago to help me celebrate — invited themselves — and we had 24 hours plus of undiluted merriment. First we all went down to Taylorville — changed into miners clothes accompanied by the usual confusion and female cackles & excitement. After a really fascinating exhibition of most modern electrical equipment at a coal [illegible] 5 miles from the [illegible] of the shaft we had "lunch" — at 4 PM at the Peabody executives club — fried chicken, baked beans and all the usual with liquor, wines and speeches. Back to Sp[ringfield]. in time for an elegant dinner preceded by songs around the piano written for this momentous, historical celebration extolling the virtues of "that wonderful, that wonderful etc. guy, Illinois' governor." I took it with becoming dignity — I hope — covered with confusion and full of bursting heart. To finish the evening we all ended up at a night club to hear Hildegarde. And she was superb — even treated me with gentleness. Sunday we went to church, lunch & they headed back to Chicago leaving me very happy, surrounded with my letters, telegrams and presents from the Democratic faithful. . . .

A

On February 20, 1950, Francis J. Loughran, an attorney from Joliet, Illinois, wrote the Governor that in the selection of the state candidates in 1948 he was the first downstate committeeman called who proposed Stevenson's name for governor, Paul Douglas for U.S. senator, and Edward J. Barrett for Illinois secretary of state. He felt he had made no mistake in his proposal.

[56] This handwritten letter is in the possession of Adlai E. Stevenson III.

To Francis J. Loughran

February 27, 1950

Dear Mr. Loughran:

If I said I was grateful for your letter I would be understating it. You are a good politician, a good guy — and a good friend.

Sincerely yours,

February 27, 1950

To All Directors of All Code Departments and Heads of Commissions

I have agreed to serve as Chairman for the State Government group for the Red Cross fund raising campaign which will begin on March 1, 1950.

I will appreciate it if you will designate someone in your Department to handle solicitations and various problems in connection with this Drive. Will you kindly send the name of the person designated in your Department to the Co-Chairman, Richard J. Daley, Director of Revenue, in Chicago and Charles P. Casey, Director of Public Works and Buildings, in Springfield, as soon as possible.

Thank you for your help and cooperation in this very meritorious work.

Sincerely yours,

Mrs. Helena McEvoy served as a volunteer in Stevenson's 1948 campaign. After an illness she wrote the Governor to say if any of the old campaign workers were near she hoped he would give them her love. She expressed the opinion that perhaps it was the harmony Stevenson himself engendered that "won the battle." She hoped he would be active in another campaign in 1952.

To Helena Mitchell McEvoy

February 27, 1950

My dear Mrs. McEvoy:

We were delighted to have your letter. "We" includes Miss [Carol] Evans and Mr. [James] Mulroy — about all that is left in the immediate vicinity of our "valiant little band" from 7 South Dearborn Street.[57]

I am sorry to hear that you have been ill and we all hope that we will see you out here one of these days. I have a strong feeling that — in

[57] Stevenson's 1948 campaign headquarters in Chicago.

[*248*]

spite of your good wishes and ardent support — come '52 I shall be delighted to see somebody else moving into my uncomfortable chair!

With warm regards and happy memories, I am

Sincerely yours,

To J. W. Mulroy and Wm. I. Flanagan [58]

February 27, 1950

Please make an announcement in the March 13 papers that Dick Daley retires as Director of Revenue March 15 and that Ernest Mahron has been designated as Acting Director of the Department of Revenue.

I should like to say something a little special about Dick and if you will work up something I will check it over at your convenience. I believe he plans to have a report of what he has done to reorganize the department, which could be released simultaneously and to which I could refer in my statement.

Mrs. Edward F. Joyce, of Chicago, sent Stevenson a copy of a newspaper article recounting his experience of delivering a message to President Roosevelt in 1941. On leaving the President, the article stated, "he walked ker-smack into a closed door and suffered a broken nose!" Mrs. Joyce said she had twice suffered a broken rib, once on Roosevelt's first election as President and again when he was elected four years later. On both occasions she was being helped over a mud puddle by Judge Cecil Smith. "So, since these things run in cycles, isn't it good you do not have two noses!" She observed, "You probably can use a chuckle now and then."

To Mrs. Edward F. Joyce

February 27, 1950

My dear Mrs. Joyce:

Well, I got a chuckle all right. Indeed, I almost got a broken rib! Little did I know what an awful price you had paid for your politics or what an exceedingly selective gallant Judge Smith was.

What do you say that we go puddle-jumping together the next election eve? I will gladly match you a nose for a rib!

My affectionate regards and thanks,

Yours,

[58] The original of this typewritten memorandum is in the possession of Mr. Flanagan.

On February 22, 1950, the Progressive Mine Workers of Illinois pulled approximately ten thousand miners out on strike for higher wages and additional fringe benefits. The United Mine Workers of America had already been on a nationwide strike for several weeks and the Illinois miners of that union numbered about nineteen thousand. Illinois's coal production was reduced to about 5 per cent of normal by the combined strikes. Many schools were forced to close, hospitals and other institutions would have to operate with heatless buildings unless an early settlement was reached, and a "dimout" of downtown Chicago was ordered by the Commonwealth Edison Company.

During the Illinois strike, the Chicago Daily News *said in an editorial: "So far the governor has done nothing about it. The best that can be said of him is that unlike the President, he has done nothing to aggravate the situation. . . . All that is required is a governor who puts his duty to all the people above the political fervor of a minority that is conducting an economic insurrection."*

The Chicago Tribune *called on the Governor to either call a special session of the legislature or call out the state militia.*

Meanwhile, at the urging of the Governor, talks continued between the union and the coal operators association. An agreement was reached within a week that the contract then in effect be extended while negotiations between the union and mine operators continued. The Progressive Mine Workers returned to work; and, in addition, some six thousand United Mine Workers went back to the mines under independent contracts.

On March 1, Stevenson made a public announcement of the strike settlement.

I want to take this opportunity to say publicly over the radio how much I appreciate the spirit of give and take and compromise of the leaders of the Progressive Miners and the operators of the Illinois coal mines employing Progressive miners.

They have today announced the settlement of a strike which commenced a week ago Tuesday. As these Progressive mines produce normally about 1,200,000 tons of coal a month, the prompt resumption of this production should enable us to meet the most pressing demands for coal in Illinois.

After the strike commenced last week, I met with the leaders of the Progressive Union and the operators' association and urged them to resume negotiations at once, pointing out the human distress, the industrial stagnation and economic loss involved in the loss of this coal — the last that was being produced in Illinois. This was an Illinois problem exclusively — involving only Illinois mines and an Illinois union, and it seemed to me it should be settled in Illinois without waiting for a national settlement. It has, and I am very grateful to the leaders of the Union and to the operators for promptly resuming negotiations which culminated in the settlement announced today. I think it is a fine example of what both labor, management and the public want — industrial peace and the prompt settlement of disputes of which all the people are the victims. And I am confident that the Progressive miners will resume production at once — production which is vitally necessary to relieve human distress and the acute coal shortage which is paralyzing the whole state.

Because the needs of hospitals, nursing homes and institutions caring for the helpless, the old and the infirm come first, along with essential public services for water, light, sewage disposal, transportation, etc., we are establishing a state Emergency Coal Committee to obtain coal for these high priority needs.

The operators of the mines, through the President of their association, Mr. Walter Gill, and Mr. [John] Marchiando, the President of the Progressive Mine Workers, have assured us of cooperation in this voluntary plan of priority allocation. We have no legal authority in Illinois to impose a rationing plan, but with the cooperation of the mines I think this Committee can help a lot to see that these highest priority needs for the care of the sick and for essential public services are met.

The State Emergency Coal Committee will be headed by Mr. Walter Eadie, State Director of the Department of Mines and Minerals, and it includes Vernon Nickell, State Superintendent of Public Instruction, Walter Fisher, Chairman of the Illinois Commerce Commission, Dr. Roland Cross, Director of the Department of Public Health and George Mitchell, Director of the Department of Finance.

The committee will assemble current information on production and available supplies of coal and, with the cooperation of the mines, will do its best to insure the minimum needs of hospitals, public service plants and similar highest priority users. The Committee will be instructed to cooperate with the local emergency coal allocation committees which have been established by Mayor [Martin] Kennelly in Chicago and in other municipalities and communities throughout the state.

I am sure everyone realizes that with the limited supplies available and the numberless demands, this Committee must confine its efforts to serving only those most essential needs. So I must urge everyone to limit requests addressed to the State Emergency Coal Committee, Department of Mines and Minerals, Springfield, only to hospitals, nursing homes, similar institutions, and public utilities.

The balance of the production of the Progressive Mines, together with any additional coal which becomes available pending the settlement of the national strike, will doubtless flow into the normal channels of commerce, and should help to relieve the needs of individuals and industrial plants who are suffering for lack of coal.

Let me say again, as your Governor, that I am grateful for the spirit of conciliation, the good faith, and the determination to reach a settlement which has animated these successful negotiations, and I am happy that Illinois has been able to resolve a wholly Illinois problem promptly and without further aggravation of the coal shortage which is paralyzing the nation.

Production of coal is a huge industry in Illinois on which the welfare of thousands depends. All of us want to see this industry flourish — operators, miners and the public, and, like you, I hope and pray that it will not be long before the loss and suffering occasioned by the national strike is at an end. Meanwhile, I know that every conscientious citizen will do what he can to save coal and to save electricity in order to stretch our meager supplies as far as possible.

The sick must be cared for, public services — from streetcars to water pumping — must go on. We must all pitch in and share our inconveniences in this national crisis which, happily, has been much relieved in Illinois today.

Mrs. Joseph T. Bowen gave Bowen Hall to Hull House and the Bowen Country Club, a summer camp for underprivileged youngsters which was then located in Waukegan, Illinois. (The camp has since been moved to Wisconsin.)

At the request of Governor Stevenson, State Architect Herrick Hammond was able to persuade two independent companies to donate enough cement to the camp for a swimming pool.

To Mrs. Joseph T. Bowen

March 1, 1950

Dear Mrs. Bowen:

We have a tardy birthday present for you!

Mr. Herrick Hammond has just told me that he has arranged for a gift of sufficient cement to build the pool at the Bowen Country Club. He has made the arrangements with Mr. Deknatel [59] and the suppliers

[59] William Deknatel, a Chicago architect, who was on the board of trustees of Hull House. His parents had lived at Hull House, his mother being a teacher there and his father a social worker. Mr. Deknatel was born there.

are Universal Atlas Portland Cement Company and the Marquette Cement Company. The arrangements at the former were made through Mr. A. C. Cronkrite and through the latter with Mr. S. L. Cribari.

Now let us know what you need for your 92nd! [60]

Affectionately,

Stevenson spoke at the Masaryk Centennial Celebration at Cicero, Illinois, on Sunday, March 5, 1950.[61]

I am honored to have a part in your program today. I sense in this meeting more than the routine recognition of the hundredth anniversary of the birth of a great statesman. To me it is an evidence that the ideal of political freedom of which Thomas Garrigue Masaryk was such a brilliant symbol has, in the minds and hearts of his American countrymen, been etched in even sharper outline by the events recently occurring in your unhappy homeland. I think it is a demonstration — inspiring and significant — that they are determined to do everything they can to bring back into the family of free nations the republic that Masaryk founded in 1918, only to be twice ruthlessly crushed in the last decade.

It is not surprising that this demonstration should occur in metropolitan Chicago. It was here that so many men and women of Czech and Slovak origin found the free life and the unlimited opportunities for themselves and their children which first beckoned them to these shores. It was here that they found the individual liberties that were denied them in the Czechoslovak lands of Imperial Austria, and here that they helped to build the America we know today. It was here that they learned the real meaning of Western individualism and democracy.

It was not my good fortune to know Thomas Masaryk personally. But I did know and greatly admired his son, Jan, whose death in a Prague courtyard was one of the most tragic events of the tragic postwar era.[62] Jan Masaryk's death, by what means we cannot be certain, was a loss to the entire western world and a blow to the cause of democratic government everywhere. Yet it served to bring out in crystal clarity the true import of the Communist coup of two years ago; it was dramatic testimony to the world that the new regime in Prague meant oblivion

[60] Mrs. Bowen replied: "As to your question of what I need for my ninety-second birthday: if I live that long, it will be to have in the government more men of integrity and ability and human interest toward our people. In fact I hope they will be just like you."

[61] The text is based on a carbon copy.

[62] In March, 1948, President Eduard Beneš was forced to agree to a predominantly Communist regime in Czechoslovakia. That same month Foreign Minister Jan Masaryk was reported to have committed suicide.

for the Czechoslovakia his father had wrought, and the silence of death for the voices of freedom. But his broken body on the stones of the courtyard broadcast the message that he tried to bring to his people in life — that the destiny of his homeland lay on the side of the democracies and that death was not too high a price to pay for freedom.

He was my friend of 20 years. He stayed in my house. I stayed in his. We collaborated in late years in the formation of the United Nations at San Francisco, London and New York. Jan Masaryk was a kind, wise, gay, earthy man. In those wild years of war and peace, of hope and despair, he was the most trusted Central European. No man saw better, perhaps none as well, the import of the developing conflict between East and West. With the great [President Eduard] Beneš he fought a long, resourceful, forthright battle to help his country steer a middle course — hoping, preaching, pleading that the Soviets and the democracies would learn to live with each other in peace, and that their beloved Czechoslovakia, the bridge between east and west, retain her freedom and sovereignty. When Masaryk's hopes faded and the iron curtain rolled ruthlessly down upon his people, he preferred death to servile silence. To me he will always be one of history's heroic figures — a martyr to the cause of Czech freedom for which his father also gave his genius, energy and life.

Thomas Masaryk's life, spanning the years from 1850 to 1937, embraced a period of manifold and dramatic changes in the destiny of Czechoslovakia. At 65, after a full life of service to his nation at a time when many retire weary and broken, Thomas Masaryk set out to do the greatest of all the tasks he had undertaken. Risking his life and reputation, leaving the family he loved so well, he entered upon the great struggle from which emerged the Czechoslovakian republic. He was 70 then, yet full of vigor and purpose he served his country for 17 years more as President, an office in which he served longer even than Franklin Roosevelt! During his lifetime he became a legend to his people. There is no doubt that in the annals of history his will always stand out as one of the most purposeful, idealistic and fruitful lives fate ever granted to mortal man.

Thomas Masaryk was a humble man, as most great men are. "The lonely Slovak," who, as an Austrian writer described him in 1909, seemed to be "a mixture of Tolstoy and Walt Whitman," turned out to have some of the qualities of Abraham Lincoln as well. Indeed these great leaders had much in common. They placed above all else the interests of their country and the welfare of the people. Both had a consuming sense of social justice and a deep moral conscience. Both possessed the courage, the vision and the qualities of leadership that enabled them to bring their respective infant republics through periods of trial and stress. Both considered individual freedom to speak and worship and to determine one's own life to be the greatest goal toward which men could strive, the richest of human possessions.

I think it can be said that Masaryk was more than a great leader of his people. He was a rare combination of thinker and man of action — as a scholar unusually sensitive to some of the modern implications of social and economic change, and at the same time deeply aware of the ultimate dependence of all political and cultural achievement upon the strength of the ethical and moral foundations of public action. He was a perfect link between the Slav peoples and the English speaking world, and his influence as a teacher reached deep into the Balkans among the Croats and the Serbs. He was the builder and the symbol of the cultural and intellectual bridge between Czechoslovakia and America.

But that bridge was broken by the shameful betrayal of Munich — the lowest point in the curve of democratic disintegration.[63] And today even the ruins of the beautiful bridge are obliterated by the fundamental and irreconcilable differences on the nature of man and the meaning of history which divide us from the closed society of Russia.

Today we are told that there is no freedom as we understand it in Czechoslovakia. There is only the long night of repression, with no promise of dawn in the eastern sky. We are told that the concentration camp and the secret police haunt and silence those who would protest against the new regime. In recent weeks the press reports the regime is even busily attempting to wipe out the memory of the names of Masaryk and Beneš from the minds of the Czech people. Postage stamps bearing the likeness of Masaryk have been invalidated. Pictures of Masaryk and Beneš have been banished from schools and other public buildings. Textbooks have been rewritten to picture Masaryk and Beneš as enemies of the Czech people.

Time and events will disclose whether this kind of repression can destroy the democratic traditions of your countrymen. In the light of history, which records the relentless and everlasting struggles of the Czech and Slovak peoples against oppression, it is hard to believe that the love of freedom ever can be stamped out by a policeman's boot or a censor's pen. History offers the more logical hope that in another time, under other circumstances, a new Masaryk will arise to lead your people to a happier destiny.

That is the hope which I know fills your hearts as you celebrate this anniversary, and the hearts of all Americans who know that we are all

[63] At the Munich Conference in 1938, the British and French governments met with Adolf Hitler and agreed to the dismemberment of Czechoslovakia.

part of one another — politically, economically and morally. Americans cannot by nature be oblivious to human oppression, and they have learned by bitter experience that the rise of totalitarian power anywhere is a threat to freedom everywhere.

Czechoslovakia's plight has helped bring home to us the real issues in the cold war. It has helped arouse the free world to its new danger; it has clarified our concept of responsibility as a world power, and it has unified the democracies in the measures they are taking to check the spread of Soviet influence.

None can foretell when or how the freedom and independence of Czechoslovakia can be restored, but the spiritual kinship between our countries is close and will endure. It was from the example of this republic that Thomas Masaryk drew spiritual inspiration and constitutional guidance. It was in Independence Hall in Philadelphia that he proclaimed the establishment of the Czechoslovakian republic. Its constitution is patterned after our own. Its ambitions, its ideals, parallel ours. Its leaders, like Masaryk, father and son, and Beneš, have become an integral part of the tradition and the heritage of the democratic world.

Here in Chicago, and in Illinois, we are especially conscious of these close relationships. We see on every hand the rich contributions which the various national groups have made to American life. Illinois has one of the largest populations of foreign born citizens to be found in any of the states. Chicago is the second largest Czech city in the world. The estimated two hundred thousand men, women and children of Czech ancestry living here are exceeded in number only by the population of Prague itself. Many have contributed notably to the advancement of our arts, sciences, professions and public life. You have helped fight our wars; you have grown with your adopted country; you have become a part of America and its traditions.

In a large sense, that is the essence of the American success story. We have learned to live together here, the men and women of all nationalities. We have become the world's great sanctuary for those fleeing from oppression and tyranny, and we have gained new vitality from this flow of immigration from overseas.

For some the struggle has not been easy, just as life itself is not easy for many of us, but we may be proud of the fact that there are no restrictions here upon the foreign-born whose ambitions and talents qualify them for high places in our society. I like to recall that before me only three members of my political party have been elected Governor of Illinois since the Civil War, and all were men of immigrant stock. John Peter Altgeld was born in Germany. Edward F. Dunne was only one generation removed from Ireland. Henry Horner's father was a native of Bavaria. It is also significant to note that Governor Altgeld was a Protestant, Governor Dunne a Catholic, and Governor Horner a Jew. Here indeed is the American story written in the last half century in our own City of Chicago and in our own Illinois, by these men of diverse religions and nationalities, who brought to us so much and left behind them such a rich legacy.

Today America has again became the land of sanctuary for thousands of Europeans displaced from their homes by the recent great war. And I am proud that Illinois is playing her part in the process of providing this haven for worthy people who need us and whom we need too.

I know there are those who say that sentiment has no place in the ugly realities of this tormented world. I know there are those who say we should bar our doors to further immigration in our own "self interest." I disagree vigorously with that contention. I believe that America will gain new vigor, greater understanding, greater tolerance, a keener awareness of the blessings we enjoy in this free rich land if mercifully we open our golden doors to worthy refugees from the cruelty, oppression and tyranny we despise.

These are anxious, clouded days and the future is obscure. But I believe our course is clear: We must cling to our ideals, we must hold fast to our faith in freedom and the individual. When our ideals, our faith, our freedom suffer abroad, we suffer here — you Americans of foreign ancestry — and we who have lived here longer. For names and national origins have nothing to do with our common faith and our common struggle to preserve and protect that faith in freedom everywhere.

A half century ago Thomas Masaryk asked his people the question: "When we recall our numerous struggles for existence in the past, such as our uprising at the White Mountain, which ended in defeat; our fall; our rebirth during the French Revolution and the enlightenment of the eighteenth century; the Revolution of 1848; the Polish rebellion, we, as thinking Czechs, are forced to decide: shall we choose violence or peace, the sword or the plow, blood or labor in the sweat of our brow, death or life?"

And his answer was: "Not violence but peace, not the sword but the plow, not blood but work, not death but life for the sake of life; this shall be the answer of the Czech spirit, this is the meaning of our history and the bequest of our great forebears."

That was the philosophy of Thomas Masaryk. Today, his abhorrence of war and his patient faith in ultimate justice, are the most meaningful parts of the legacy of wisdom and truth we have from him. With his courage and honesty, and his firm faith, we must strive on resolutely to find peaceful means of solving the issues dividing the two worlds in which we live.

So doing, we shall be true to the memory of Thomas Masaryk, whom an English scholar said was the nearest historical example of Plato's ideal of the Philosopher-King. So doing, we shall be true to the great traditions of Western civilization he did so much to advance. To those traditions, let us fervently hope, his people can one day return.

To Alicia Patterson [64]

March 5, 1950

. . . I'm back from a ghastly ordeal. Friday night Boyle — Nat Dem Ch.[65] — called from Washington to insist that I had to pinch hit for [Vice President] Bar[k]ley at a gigantic Jefferson-Jackson Day fiesta in Indianapolis. He trapped me after prolonged negotiations. I doctored up a speech and flew over there last night — and it *was* a gigantic thing with all the trimmings including Tommy Dorseys band. The speech went OK; at last the pols cleared out of my hotel quarters & I fell into bed at 1:30. No sleep; up at 6 to fly to Chicago to dedicate the new Sinai Temple on the South side. 2½ hours of that — another speech — also OK. Then a luncheon party — then out to Ciccro for the Centennial celebration of Thomas Masaryk's birth in the Czech colony. Another speech — also OK (Doing well!) Thence back to the Stock Yards to show off at the great International Outdoors show, then back to Municipal Airport & finally Springfield — and my lonely room in the deserted Mansion. . . .

Mrs. Edward F. Joyce sent Governor Stevenson a telegram on March 17, 1950: "Tis a great day for the Irish when their great Governor joins them. Tis sorry I am that you are at one shindig and I at another." [66]

To Mrs. Edward F. Joyce

March 20, 1950

Dear Mrs. Joyce:

Your telegram was the best thing that fell on my plate during the Irish Fellowship Banquet Friday night. The party would have been just

[64] This handwritten letter is in the possession of Adlai E. Stevenson III.

[65] William Boyle, chairman of the Democratic National Committee.

[66] Although Mrs. Joyce and the Governor exchanged letters on several occasions, they never met.

a little better, however, if you had been there. I don't mean on my plate!

Many, many thanks and my best wishes always.

Sincerely yours,

Donald J. Walsh served as director of the Department of Public Safety from March, 1949, to March, 1950, when he returned to Chicago to join the staff of the Chicago American. *Stevenson relied heavily on Walsh for information and advice not only during the year he served in the cabinet, but throughout his administration.*

To Donald J. Walsh

April 4, 1950

Dear Don:

I am afraid I will have to decline Mr. DeWitt's [67] invitation to speak at the Tournament of Orators [68] on Thursday, May 4. As I must be in Springfield the preceding day and the following day it would necessitate a special trip. I am sure you appreciate my predicament and I hope you will make my apologies and express my thanks — eloquently and vigorously!

Yours,

P.S. How I miss you!

Mrs. Wallace Irwin, a friend of Mr. and Mrs. Ives who lived in Southern Pines, North Carolina, wrote Stevenson to congratulate him on his Centre College speech.

To Mrs. Wallace Irwin

April 5, 1950

My dear Mrs. Irwin:

Please consider that this is *not* an acknowledgment. Otherwise you may not write again. And, though I can't keep a tune, I like music and your letter was music to a distracted Governor.

Warm regards.

Sincerely yours,

[67] George De Witt, managing editor of the Chicago *Herald-American.*
[68] The Hearst Newspaper Tournament of Orators.

L. D. Mallory, counselor of the U.S. embassy in Argentina, had known Stevenson since 1933. He wrote that he hoped the Governor was enjoying his duties — and that he had not lost the few remaining hairs on his head.

To L. D. Mallory

April 5, 1950

Dear Les:

I was delighted to have your letter, and it reminded me of that hot summer long ago when we first saved the world. I have run across your tracks from time to time through foreign service officers during my postwar tour of duty in the State Department and United Nations, and I hope that it won't be long before I can see you in the flesh. As for my hairs, there are hardly enough left to identify. But I have acquired a politician's coarse contours! And, pray tell, how do you look after sixteen years of eating your way around the world at the end of a cable?

Warm regards and many thanks for your letter.

Sincerely yours,

Stephen E. Hurley was chairman of the City of Chicago's Civil Service Commission, an agency over which the Governor had no control. This letter was marked "Personal and Confidential."

To Stephen E. Hurley

April 5, 1950

Dear Steve:

I tried to call you on the phone while in Chicago on Monday but I missed you.

I came to know during the campaign a policeman attached to Commissioner Prendergast's [69] office named Cornelius A. Ryan and developed the utmost liking for him, both as a companion and as a diligent and shrewd officer. He came in to see me the other day to report that he took the examination for sergeant in 1948 and is, of course, most hopeful that he will obtain a promotion when the list is published.

I merely wanted to say a good word for him for what it is worth.

Sincerely yours,

[69] John C. Prendergast, chief of the Chicago police.

Timothy Read Ives, the Governor's nephew, was the only son of Mr.
and Mrs. Ernest L. Ives. Because his father's work in the foreign ser-
vice took the family to many different countries the boy's early formal
education suffered. He did not receive his diploma from the Univer-
sity of Virginia because he failed languages. He worked for the Eco-
nomic Cooperation Administration in Vienna in the summer of 1950.
He returned to the University of Virginia that autumn, but enlisted in
the Air Force in June, 1951.

To Timothy Ives

April 5, 1950

Dear Tim:

I am reminded that your birthday is Easter Sunday, and I wish I
could be there to congratulate you and to have another taste of that
southern sun!

I think you have made *extraordinary* progress in the past few years.
Considering all the difficulties you have confronted it seems to me you
have come along rapidly and well. The most important qualifications
for a full and useful mature life are character and health. Those you
have. And if you have had some difficulty with school work it can be
remedied, and, with application, will be. I would rather have a man
with character, devotion and diligence than the brightest erratic and
irresponsible man in the world on my team.

Don't be too worried or depressed about not getting your diploma.
You can go on to law school here or elsewhere, I should think, if you
wish to, although I am not fully informed about all the requirements.
Your father told me about the arrangements with Ambassador [John
George] Erhardt in Vienna and I think it should be a wonderfully
informative and useful experience. I much admire your anxiety to
"work" during the summer, and I could imagine no better combination of work, pleasure and experience than a few months with him in
Vienna during the Joint Occupation.

With all my love and admiration, I am

Yours,

Stevenson took time to read the galley proofs of Lloyd Lewis's book,
Captain Sam Grant, *on which Lewis was working at the time of his*
death. They were sent to Stevenson by Little, Brown and Company,
who asked for his comments to be used in sales promotion of the book.

To Dudley Frazier [70]

April 6, 1950

Dear Mr. Frazier:

I apologize for neglecting to acknowledge receipt of the galleys of CAPTAIN SAM GRANT. I have had an opportunity to read the first chapter and I am bewitched! Indeed, I am afraid Captain Sam has interfered with the public business of Illinois!

I don't know just what you want but I shall try to send a few lines of comment soon.

Sincerely yours,

Harley Notter, adviser to the Assistant Secretary for United Nations Affairs, Department of State, wrote Stevenson that he was sending him a copy of Postwar Foreign Policy Preparation, 1939–1945.[71] *He hoped Stevenson might become more prominent on the national scene, but the first and most important business was for him to do a good job in Illinois.*

To Harley A. Notter

April 10, 1950

Dear Harley:

I was so glad to have your letter and I hope to find a moment more sometime to look through "Postwar Foreign Policy Preparation," which I have received. I earnestly hope that factual historical narratives of this kind can induce a little more popular writing and perspective. I tried to do something of the kind about "Isolation" in an article that the New York Times asked for which was published in the Magazine Section in September.[72]

I have seen Eddie Miller [73] occasionally but my contacts with the State Department have been all too few. I was under the impression that internally, at least, things were better and the Department was clicking well in spite of the asinine attacks that seem to be its destiny.

[70] Member of the advertising department of Little, Brown and Company, in charge of publicity and promotion.

[71] Department of State Publication 3580, General Foreign Policy Series 15 (Washington: Government Printing Office, 1950).

[72] "The Challenge of the New Isolationism" was actually published in the November 6, 1949, issue.

[73] Edward G. Miller, Jr., Assistant Secretary of State.

I have been as busy as a bird dog here and see little prospect of any marked relaxation in my predicament. As to what I have been doing, I am bold enough to enclose a copy of a talk summarizing my objectives and experiences during my first year, which I am sure you should *not* read!

Please let me know if you pass this way.

Warm regards and many thanks.

Sincerely yours,

Francis T. P. Plimpton wrote Stevenson on April 8, 1950, urging him to attend their Harvard Law School class reunion on April 28 and 29.

To Francis T. P. Plimpton

April 11, 1950

Dear Francis:

It was good to hear from you again, and I had expected you and Pauline [74] would be out here to inspect my Mansion long before this. I still stand ready to give you an elementary course in the realities of politics on the prairie whenever you are available.

As for New York, I was there in the autumn for the Herald-Tribune Forum, for one night, and have no further prospects in the early or remote future, in spite of the blandishments of various organizations thereabout who are evidently thirsting for my wisdom!

I have not overlooked the Law School doings in Cambridge on April 28 and 29, but I am so submerged here the possibility is fading rapidly.

Sincerely yours,

Stevenson's old friend Thomas K. Finletter was appointed Secretary of the Air Force on July 1, 1950.

To Thomas K. Finletter

April 14, 1950

Dear Tom:

That this is delayed only confirms what you note — that I am perpetually behind schedule.

Perhaps it is a good thing to lie out on the grass a bit now and then, graze and contemplate the total scene. I feel less and less aware after so

[74] Mrs. Plimpton.

many years of concentration on segments — and for that reason, full of admiration for your techniques. But I am mighty glad you are back in the line at such a level, in such a place. God bless you!

Yours,

During the weekend of April 14–16, 1951, historian Arthur Schlesinger, Jr., visited Stevenson in Springfield. Mrs. Harry Neuberger, of Red Bank, New Jersey, and Mrs. Edison Dick were also mansion guests. The Governor took his guests on a picnic to New Salem State Park to show them some of the "Lincoln country," a twenty-mile drive from Springfield.

Mr. Schlesinger recalled that the spot chosen by the Governor was off limits and a state trooper who failed to recognize the Governor ordered them to the approved picnic ground.[75] Mrs. Dick's recollection was that "we didn't comply but sat right in front of the museum on a lovely patch and as people walked in and out they were astonished to have the Governor pointed out to them munching a sandwich, as oblivious to the public gaze as if he had been sitting on the banks of the Des Plaines [River]." [76]

To Arthur M. Schlesinger, Jr.

April 17, 1950

Dear Arthur:

I enjoyed your visit but failed to ask you to inscribe a copy of "The Vital Center," [77] which I had set aside on my desk. It will remain there until you return!

I was disappointed that I didn't have more opportunity to pick your brains — thanks to the lively ladies that surrounded us. But your interest was flattering.

I am enclosing a copy of a statement I issued following the first Collier's article,[78] and also, for no reason whatever, copy of a radio talk I made the first of January which briefly summarizes something of what we have been doing in the first year.

Next time you had better bring your wife and all the little Schlesingers and we will properly commence their Lincoln indoctrination with a picnic in a better place at New Salem.

Yours,

[75] Letter to Carol Evans, February 21, 1969.
[76] Letter to Carol Evans, April 5, 1969.
[77] Boston: Houghton Mifflin, 1949.
[78] Mr. Schlesinger does not recall what the statement or the *Collier's* article were about. Letter to Carol Evans, February 21, 1969.

When Stevenson was assistant to Secretary of the Navy Frank Knox, from 1941 to 1944, he became acquainted with Captain W. D. Puleston. Captain Puleston wrote Stevenson commending him on his work as governor, adding that he deserved to be President, and he hoped this would come about in the not too distant future.

To Captain W. D. Puleston

April 19, 1950

Dear Captain:

I was delighted to hear from you again and more than a little flattered by your very generous and encouraging remarks. It has been a difficult and at the same time fascinating experience. Rubbing shoulders day and night with the hard realities of politics and human nature at this level is quite a different thing from my prior experience as you well know. Indeed, I am afraid that one of the by-products is a rapidly diminishing ambition for much more of it.

I know that we have made conspicuous progress, and I feel that we can make some more but its price is "eternal vigilance" and unremitting work, with a disquieting suspicion that party, press and people are mostly looking for mistakes and errors rather than solid achievements.

But I am really not a pessimist as you know! I hope some day you will find Illinois on your itinerary and stay with me in my fine, old Mansion.

With every good wish and warm thanks, I am

Sincerely yours,

Irving Dilliard, editor of the St. Louis Post-Dispatch, *conducted an editorial crusade to allow Ellen Raphael Knauff, German-born war bride of a U.S. Army combat veteran, to be admitted to the United States as a prospective citizen. It was reported in* Time *magazine April 17, 1950.*

To Irving Dilliard

April 19, 1950

Dear Irving:

I ran across the *Time's* story about the case of *Ellen Raphael Knauff* which reminded me that I had intended before this to express my admiration — again — for the Post-Dispatch and for Irving Dilliard!

Yours,

Before Stevenson's living quarters were completed in the State of Illinois Building in Chicago he availed himself many times of the hospitality of Mr. and Mrs. John Paul Welling, who had an extra room in their spacious Chicago house. Mr. Welling was an invalid and confined to his home.

On receiving an invitation to attend a reception at the Democratic Cook County headquarters on May 13, that included his "wife or lady friend," Stevenson added a handwritten note to the form letter and sent it to Mrs. Welling.

To Mrs. John Paul Welling

May 9, 1950

Harriet —

I think this is a buffet business for the visiting Democrats. Will you be my "lady friend"!

ADLAI

Let me know when I come up — probably Thursday night.

To Dudley Frazier

May 9, 1950

Dear Mr. Frazier:

I am mortified that I have only now found an opportunity to look through Lloyd Lewis' remarkable book.

"Sam Grant" is more than a biography; it is the moving story of the lusty, earthy infancy of the middlewest. Here is no fine philosophical writing but a gripping panorama of the men, manners and events of that fateful era from Andrew Jackson to the Civil War, against a faithful background of rivers, wilderness, heartaches and the smoking guns of the Mexican War.

"Sam Grant" is history written with high-hearted sensitivity and intuition. No one of our time can write that way of the youth of men and nations like Lloyd Lewis. That he could not live to finish this brilliant beginning is a sad loss to the literature and the annals of the pioneer midwest of which he, like the strange, somehow tragic Grant, was so much a part and a product.

Again my apologies for my tardiness.

Sincerely,

Harry Wood, an Illinois artist who painted Stevenson's portrait late in the year 1949, wrote the Governor from Italy in May, 1950.

To Harry Wood

May 9, 1950

Dear Mr. Wood:

I was delighted with your charming letter, and your little portrait of George Santayana [79] persuades me that you are as good on paper as on canvas!

Don't be homesick for Illinois. It has been the most miserable spring and winter I can recall. At the moment it is cold and raining — and the United Mine Workers and Progressive Mine Workers are at war again.

I shall look forward to hearing about your adventures when you come back, and I hope you succeed even in getting the Pope to sit still.

Warm regards and many thanks.

Sincerely yours,

Dorothy Fosdick met Stevenson when they both were on the United States delegation to the United Nations Conference in San Francisco in 1945. She sent the Governor a number of releases from the Department of State denying charges by Senator Joseph McCarthy that the department was "thoroughly infested with Communists."

She mentioned that Mrs. Quincy Wright, executive secretary of the Chicago Council on Foreign Relations, was trying to work out some speaking engagements for her in Chicago. "This doesn't let you out, however, of popping in on your next Washington visit, and if possible letting me feed you from my new store of skills at French cooking!"

To Dorothy Fosdick

May 11, 1950

Dear Dorothy:

Send me more, not less! It all transports me to another world, albeit harassed and difficult even as mine.

May the negotiations with Louise Wright prosper — and the Mansion brighten therewith.

The next Washington trip seems to be scheduled for June 6 for a speech at the President's Safety Conference with the probability that I

---

[79] The Spanish-born philosopher, who died in Italy in September, 1952.

shall arrive in the morning and fly back in the afternoon — and you won't have to get out your cook book. But I will hope for better things.

Love,

P.S. I think the atmosphere is improving daily in regard to McCarthy and the State Department, and if the timing is propitious it should be an asset rather than a liability for Lucas.[80]

After Stevenson's election, and on his initiative, a Patronage Committee was formed as part of the Democratic State Central Committee, to which all job applications from various county Democratic organizations were submitted by county chairmen. It handled most of the paper work and contacts with county organizations, but its main purpose was to determine the political worthiness of job applicants. The staff consisted of Paul Madison, of Table Grove, and several others.

An Advisory Committee was also created to review recommendations from the Patronage Committee and to pass on applicants' qualifications, particularly for higher-level jobs. Members of the committee were Paul Madison, State Chairman George Kells, Secretary of State Edward J. Barrett, State Auditor Benjamin Cooper, and several others. Lawrence Irvin represented the Governor's office.

It soon became obvious that the committee was used only by the Governor to fill jobs. The other elected state officials handled their own patronage distribution without consulting the committee. They used it, however, to strengthen their own personal organizations.

After much urging, Stevenson finally disbanded the committee and delegated full responsibility for distribution of patronage to Irvin. Irvin felt the damage had already been done — that some of the other elected officials had already installed their own people in key jobs that should have gone to candidates selected by the Governor.[81]

When Mr. Madison submitted his resignation to Governor Stevenson as secretary of the Advisory Committee he wrote to express his gratitude for the friendship the Governor had always extended to him, and pledged his continued loyalty and support.

[80] Scott Lucas, of Illinois, was up for reelection to the U.S. Senate on the Democratic ticket in 1950. There was concern that the anti-Communist, "brass-knuckle" tactics used by Senator McCarthy would be harmful to Lucas's campaign. He was defeated by Everett M. Dirksen.

[81] Letter to Carol Evans, February 25, 1969.

To J. Paul Madison

May 11, 1950

Dear Paul:

I want to make some formal note of my personal appreciation for your loyal and intelligent service to me and to the party on the Screening Committee during this past trying year and a half.

I do not for a moment expect that our contacts or your usefulness ends with the reorganization of the State Committee and the patronage management. However, it is not often that one finds in this difficult field of conflicts, aggravation and self-interest, service as patient, wise and devoted as yours has been. I for one am most grateful, and I am sure there are many others.

Sincerely yours,

To John C. Martin

May 11, 1950

Dear John:

With the meeting yesterday, the reorganization of the State Central Committee and the election of new officers, I am reminded of your long, wise and devoted service to the Democratic Party. Even though you are no longer the official Treasurer, I know that you will not lose interest in the party's and my administration's fortunes, and I shall confidently count on your advice and help.

The old-timers who have seen us through thick and thin and who have such an accumulation of wisdom and experience become more valuable to me as my own experience and difficulties increase.

I hope you will not come to Springfield without calling on me, which will also afford another opportunity to express one Democrat's thanks and respect to you.

Sincerely yours,

To George Kells

May 12, 1950

Dear George:

With the reorganization of the State Central Committee and the conclusion of your service as State Chairman, I want to say again that which I have attempted to say so often. Your encouragement, loyalty and constant concern for my personal interest, my political interest, and a better quality of public service for the people, has been both more gratifying, sustaining and comforting than I have been able to tell you.

I wish you well, and I wish there were more like you! And don't think for a moment that you have escaped the constant harrassment of a babe in the woods!

Sincerely yours,

One of Stevenson's severest problems was that of commercialized gambling. During 1950 he spoke about it publicly many times, most notably in his Report to the People on January 2. In Collier's magazine, April 15 and 22, 1950, articles appeared about the "Illinois Shakedown," deploring the seeming lack of active attention to the problem by Stevenson and Attorney General Ivan Elliott. The following statement by the Governor was issued to the press: [82]

The Collier's article correctly quotes me as having said during the campaign that I would keep the state administration free of gambling taints. I say the same thing now, and I have done what I said.

The enforcement by local officials of the gambling laws is better now than it has been for a long time. Had Collier's wanted the facts — and to know what the Attorney General and I have done — its reporter could have come to Springfield and talked with us. He didn't.

Stevenson received much mail on the subject of gambling. Included was a letter of May 2, 1950, from Paul Simon, the young editor and publisher of the Troy Tribune, *Madison County, Illinois. Mr. Simon said, "It seems to me your extremely able administration should not be hindered by attacks of failing to act in the gambling situation."*

James W. Mulroy replied to Simon's letter on May 4, saying that much thought had been given to the suppression of open syndicated gambling and the efforts of the Governor and the Attorney General had met with success in a "great number of counties. . . . I am told that Madison County is still open in some respects but I am of the considered opinion that in a comparatively short time the better known gambling places in your county will be closed either due to action taken by your own authorities or by some other type of action which might have to be taken in the future."

On May 12, 1950, the state police were used to raid Madison County,

[82] The text is based on a carbon copy. The release is undated.

much to the surprise of the gamblers and the local officials. Simon said, years later: "It is impossible to gauge the long-range improvement that [suppression of gambling] has brought to many of our communities, but it is tremendous. Instead of endless arguments, token raids, and corrupting influences, many of our local governments are discussing things they should have been long ago: whether they should have a detention home for juveniles, whether they need a park and recreation program. In areas where gambling money flowed freely to the treasuries of both parties, happily we are relatively free from these gifts which were always given only at a terrible price." [83]

After the initial raid in Madison County, the state government continued to use state police to break up gambling interests in other counties where local officials refused to act.

Stevenson himself said of the gambling situation: "While Governor, after reorganizing and decontaminating the State Police in 1949 and giving them the security of tenure and merit advancement, I had an instrument with which I could reliably enforce the gambling laws if the local officials wouldn't. After personal talks with the law enforcement officials of some of the worst counties and plenty of notice to clean house, I started raids by the state police in 1950 for the first time in the history of Illinois. And the first county we hit — Madison — was a Democratic county. Raids continued all over the state until commercialized gambling and slot machines had virtually been eliminated from Illinois. This attracted much press attention at the time." [84]

At the time of the May 12 Madison County raids, Stevenson issued this statement to the press.[85]

I have today, in association with Attorney General Elliott, used the State Police against commercialized gambling in Madison County.

For more than a year Attorney General Elliot and I have attempted to stop commercialized gambling by several methods. We have found our direct talks with local officials of offending counties the most effective method. Because it is a local responsibility, commercialized gambling should be suppressed locally. Local authorities have cooperated with us

[83] Mimeograph copy of the first annual Adlai E. Stevenson Memorial Lecture, delivered at the Unitarian-Universalist Church, Bloomington, Illinois, October 22, 1965.

[84] Handwritten letter to Kenneth S. Davis, March 19, 1957, in the possession of Mr. Davis. Mr. Davis had just completed the draft of his book *A Prophet in His Own Country* and sent the manuscript to Stevenson, then vacationing in Barbados. Stevenson's long letter made various comments and corrections in the manuscript.

[85] The text is based on a carbon copy.

in many cases. In others we have been successful only temporarily or in part or not at all.

On the whole the results have been gratifying. Commercialized gambling is at the lowest ebb in Illinois in many years.

I have stated repeatedly that the state would intervene if necessary in cases where commercialized gambling persists in spite of all our efforts. Hence today's raids. The evidence is being turned over to the State's Attorney.

The State Police will be used again if need be to stop persistent, defiant violation, although the force is still in process of reorganization and has all it can do to patrol the highways, enforce the truck weight laws and discharge its regular duties.

But Illinois is not and must not be a "gambling state." The local citizenry and their elected officials can stop commercialized gambling with its attendant corruption and lawlessness. I hope they will, and that Illinois will not contribute further to the abdication of local government and local responsibility.

On May 15, 1950, Illinois Democrats gathered at the Chicago Stadium to celebrate the 150th anniversary of the election of Thomas Jefferson to the presidency. The guest of honor was President Harry S. Truman. Governor Stevenson delivered the address of welcome.

Mr. President, we welcome you to Illinois which gave Abraham Lincoln to the world — and many other men and women who have added luster to our nation's history — including the majority leader of the United States Senate [86] who is here tonight. But I dare not call him by name lest it be thought that there is something political about this celebration!

We are proud that Illinois and Chicago could be host to this celebration in honor of the immortal philosopher of democracy — Thomas Jefferson — for whom liberty meant not only freedom of the person, but freedom of the mind and spirit as well.

To do our reverent honor on the 150th anniversary of his election to the presidency, we meet in this hall which has witnessed in our time so many fateful events in American history — including a hot night just six years ago when a senator from Missouri was nominated to be Vice President of the United States.[87] We are proud it happened here!

[86] Scott Lucas.
[87] The Democratic National Convention of 1944, held in Chicago, had rejected Vice President Henry Wallace and chosen Mr. Truman as President Roosevelt's running mate.

And, Mr. President, while we refresh our memory of Jefferson's firm faith in the people, in life, liberty and the pursuit of happiness for all alike, may I remind you that until two years ago only three men of the political faith of Jefferson had been elected Governor of Illinois since the Civil War. The first was John Peter Altgeld — the eagle forgotten — a German immigrant; the second was Edward F. Dunne, but one generation removed from the old sod of Ireland; the third was Henry Horner, son of an immigrant and beloved in the memory of all those here tonight. May I remind you, Mr. President, that John Peter Altgeld was a Protestant, that Edward F. Dunne was a Catholic, that Henry Horner was a Jew.

That is the American story; that was the dream of Thomas Jefferson. And here, Mr. President, in the City of Chicago, on the prairies of Illinois, his descendants believe in human freedom; we believe in equal opportunity for all; we believe in special privilege for none; we believe in the democratic institutions; we believe in our chief executive; we believe in you, Mr. President!

In the age old struggle against tyranny over the bodies and minds and souls of men we know there can be no respite, no rest for you or for us. For:

> "On the plains of hesitation
> Bleach the bones of countless thousands
> Who, on the eve of victory, rested —
> And resting, died." [88]

As each day, in the tradition of Jefferson, you forge a broader shield for free men everywhere, we join our prayers to yours that out of the ugly clamor and conflict there will come your heart's desire and ours — peace on earth.[89]

---

[88] Stevenson received many inquiries about this verse. On diligent research it was discovered to have been written by George Cecil, vice president of N. W. Ayer & Son, Philadelphia, who used the name "William Lawrence." It was first used in an advertisement of International Correspondence Schools, Scranton, Pennsylvania, under the title "The Warning of the Desert."

[89] Stevenson received a cordial letter from President Truman, dated May 20, 1950, stating that his visit to Chicago was a memorable one, and continuing with high words of praise for Stevenson's speech at the Chicago stadium. He expressed his appreciation for the Governor's personal welcome to him and the warm hospitality of his entire visit, and commented that such evidences of loyal support were a challenge and an inspiration.

To James W. Mulroy, William I. Flanagan,
J. Edward Day and Carl McGowan [90]

May 16, 1950

If I am going to make a radio report the end of June, Bill Flanagan should assign someone to gather the material and we should not overlook what we have done about Career, Merit, Civil Service Systems; State Police, Commerce Commission, Welfare Department, Civil Service exam program.

We are going to get no credit from the pols for what we have done so we better get all the credit we can with the people.

A.E.S.

To Ivan Elliott, Baird Helfrich,[91] Murray Milne,[92]
Thomas J. O'Donnell,[93] James W. Mulroy, William I. Flanagan,
Carl McGowan and J. Edward Day

May 17, 1950

I think in the "public relations" in connection with the gambling raids, several points should be emphasized which seem to be distorted in the press:

(1) The Attorney General has been at work incessantly for more than a year on local officials to enforce gambling laws. In other words, there is nothing new about the recent and more spectacular use of the state police.

(2) Neither the Attorney General nor myself ever promised to close up gambling at the county level. What we did promise was that there would be no connection between the state administration and commercial gambling and that we did use our best efforts to restore law and order in Illinois. That is precisely what we have been doing for more than a year.

(3) We have deliberately avoided publicity to enable local officials to take full credit for law enforcement. The results have been gratifying. Long before the raids in Madison County there was far less commercial gambling in Illinois than in many years.

---

[90] The original of this typewritten memorandum is in the possession of Mr. Flanagan.
[91] Special assistant attorney general, who led gambling raids in several counties.
[92] Of the attorney general's staff.
[93] Acting director of public safety.

To Walter V. Schaefer [94]

May 18, 1950

Dear Walter:

. . . I have been planning to talk with you for some time about the possibility — however remote — that I could induce *you* to become Director of Insurance. I have discussed it at various times with Harry Hershey,[95] who, as you know, is anxious to retire. I know from many members of the industry that we have made as important progress in that Department as any in the past year and a half and I am anxious not to lose the impetus or public esteem, in the industry at least, that Hershey has generated. Also, of course, it would strengthen my whole picture enormously if you could be blasted out of the [Northwestern University] Law School.

Looking at it from your point of view and ultimate objectives, I also don't think it would hurt. As for knowing anything about insurance, Hershey has persuaded me that the important thing is intelligence and character rather than technical proficiency. Please let me know if you think it is even worth talking about.

Sincerely yours,

ADLAI

P.S. Of course, there is also the Department of Public Safety, which is a monstrous and difficult job but might leave you a little less freedom than Insurance.

A.E.S.

The Public Administration Clearing House, at 1313 East 60th Street in Chicago, consisted of a number of specialized agencies in the field of government including the Council of State Governments. Herbert Emmerich was the director of "1313."

To Herbert Emmerich [96]

May 19, 1950

Dear Mr. Emmerich:

For a long time I have intended to tell you how useful the Public Administration Clearing House has been to me and to others in the state

[94] The original of this typewritten letter is in the possession of Mr. Schaefer.

[95] Director of the Department of Insurance from 1949 to September, 1950. Stevenson finally appointed J. Edward Day to succeed Hershey.

[96] The original is in the possession of Mr. Emmerich.

administration of Illinois, and how valuable I consider to be the work being done by the agencies associated with the PACH.

The organizations at "1313" have become a national center to which public officials, at all levels of government and without regard to political affiliation, look for information and guidance in dealing with administrative problems. Nowhere else that I know of is it possible to get such prompt, informed, objective and practical information and suggestions for dealing intelligently with governmental questions of procedure and policy.

I have the feeling that if we are to succeed in improving the efficiency and probity of government we shall do so not only by electing better qualified men and women to public office, but through the greater utilization of the research and technical facilities available through the Clearing House. I think your organizations have made substantial progress in this direction in a comparatively short time, and that if given the means will make much more in the future.

Thank you for your generous cooperation and all good wishes for continued success.

Sincerely,

Stevenson, on May 24, 1950, ordered that all leases for concessions in Illinois State Parks contain the following paragraph:

The concessionaire agrees that no person shall be denied or rejected full and equal use of accommodations or facilities on account of race, color, or religion.

To Marnie Dick [97]

May 26, 1950

Marnie dear

And I too wish it wasn't so far to Baltimore — and your graduation.[98] I'd like to kiss the girl graduate — sweet and lovely as she is!

This is an important milestone (as the sobersides say!) for you. It will feel good to have "school" behind you and the larger, freer vistas ahead. But, too, you'll hate to feel the cover closing on a chapter and the parting will be hard. Its all part of the emotional pattern of life — and the more

[97] This handwritten note is in the possession of Mrs. James T. Last, the Edison Dicks' elder daughter.
[98] Miss Dick was about to graduate from boarding school.

you "feel" in life the *harder* it will be, but the *more* you'll get out of it. And you're going to get a lot!

Congratulations & best love.

THE GOV.

Governor Stevenson visited his home in Bloomington over the Memorial Day weekend in 1950, where Dr. Watson Gailey kept his eye clinic open for the purpose of testing Stevenson's eyes. He wrote the Governor on June 6, 1950: "The dark heavy weight pair of frames are to be worn for reading only — for the old bedroom type of reading. The light colored heavy weight pair of bifocals are for your desk and the light weight bifocals having a longer range are to be used for your public speaking engagements."

To Dr. Watson Gailey

June 8, 1950

Dear Dr. Gailey:

The glasses have arrived and I am almost submerged in equipment! I find the bifocals hard to use but I am going to institute a course of self-training. The horn rimmed pair is comfortable and I have been using it most of the time, taking it on and off as in the past. I presume I should discontinue using the old ones.

I enjoyed my visit to your superb clinic, but the inconvenience I caused so many of your charming and efficient entourage on a holiday has embarrassed me ever since.

Warm regards.

Sincerely yours,

To Alicia Patterson [99]

June 13, 1950

. . . I'm in the dumps again, tho I've reread your letter & feel a little better. I've had or rather am having another very difficult affair with [Mayor Martin] Kennelly & the Chicago boys. Without any warning & just as Congress renews rent control & I breath[e] a great sigh of relief they insist on a special session of the legislature anyway for aid to Chicago. Its maddening & I'm having a harder time than ever before keeping calm & my temper under control. It will most surely end up in

---

[99] This handwritten letter is in the possession of Adlai E. Stevenson III.

more recriminations and more trouble for all of us in a campaign year. . . .

A

Stevenson gave the commencement address on June 18, 1950, at the University of Illinois, at Urbana, where he was awarded an honorary degree.[100]

On July 19, 1950, James Colvin, editor of the Illinois Alumni News, *wrote from Urbana to Stevenson's aide Don Hyndman: "You know that I'm not the kind of guy who writes fan mail to state officials but, by Gosh, I can't help saying that Governor Stevenson's address over here at commencement time was magnificent. . . . There was a veritable wave of enthusiasm here because the speech was meaty, wonderfully well written and well delivered. When there's really something in a commencement speech, that's news."*

I am going to let you in on a secret I have discovered. All commencement speeches evolve the same way and always have and probably always will. The speaker says to himself: "I'm not going to tell them how fortunate they are and what they should do with their hard-won educational disciplines; I'm not going to tell them that the old order is changing, that the sky is overcast, visibility low, and that in their still soft hands lies the making of a better morrow. I'm not going to repeat any of those old platitudes. I'm going to be different!" Having made that splendid resolution he seizes his pen and with solemn innocence proceeds to use every one of those old platitudes — and so will I!

Of course the old order is changing. It always is. Of course the future is obscure and full of forebodings. It always is, especially on Commencement Day! Change is the order of life. Change is disturbing. It always seems to be for the worse. We talk of the good old days. (When someone sighed that Punch wasn't as good as it used to be, a wiser man replied that it never was!)

I graduated from college and you were born in another hour of change, and a much happier hour than this one. A savage war to make the world safe for democracy had ended victoriously. A noble concept, the League of Nations, had emerged from the chaotic aftermath of the elemental struggle. It was the twilight of kings and the dawn of world-wide democracy. Optimism was boundless, and people proclaimed that we were

[100] The text of this speech, "The Responsibility of the College Graduate," was published in *School and Society*, Vol. 72, No. 1872 (Nov. 4, 1950), pp. 289–292.

on the threshold of the new era of universal and perpetual peace and prosperity.

It did not turn out that way. It was not a threshold after all. A bitter young man, Lawrence of Arabia, wrote: "It felt like morning, and the freshness of the world-to-be intoxicated us. We were wrought up with ideas inexpressible and vaporous, but to be fought for. We lived many lives in those whirling campaigns, never sparing ourselves any good or evil: yet when we achieved and the new world dawned, the old men came out again and took from us our victory, and remade it in the likeness of the former world they knew. Youth could win but had not learned to keep, and was pitiably weak against age. We stammered that we had worked for a new heaven and a new earth, and they thanked us kindly and made their peace."

No, there really was not much change. It was not the dawn after all — those twenty-odd years between wars. Before you could add and subtract, the bountiful earth was paralyzed with unemployment, and poverty stalked through fields of plenty. And by the time many of you were ready for college, they handed you a gun and told you to fight for your life.

Surely there is something fateful about a generation that was born in the era of flappers, Freud, bathtub gin, ostrich politics, and "everlasting prosperity"; that was raised in economic agony and then had to fight its way out. Had to fight its way out — to what? To mountainous debt, strikes, inflation, quarreling, and politics as usual at home; to hunger, fear, and political unrest abroad; and to cold war and the hydrogen bomb! Surely this is a doubtful inheritance; surely we are a long way from the four freedoms; surely these graduates are not to be envied, the orators are saying.

No, those decades between the wars were not an entrance to the new, but they were an exit from the old. And you are going to live and work and play, I hope, in a new dimensional world. Great, restless forces are at work — spiritual, philosophical, scientific, economic, and political. The remotest corners of the earth feel the ferment.

Canning said he called the New World into existence to redress the balance of the Old. The Jinns of Science and the Four Horsemen of the Apocalypse have called a new dimensional world into existence not to replace the balance of the old, but to replace the old.

Electronics, jet propulsion, atomic energy, social security, collectivism, ideological conflict, spiritual reawakening, and a hundred other products of the thinking and anguish of our times urgently beseech us to find the discrimination to develop what is good in the new and to keep what is better in the old.

It is all a little confusing to your elders, even if it is not to you who are young and unafraid and see things better because you do not see so much. You know that the world is a tenement with many families. Some are jealous, some ignorant, some ambitious, and so on. They have different ideas about how to keep peace in the house and how to promote their welfare and the welfare of the other tenants. There has been everlasting trouble in this house.

Some of the tenants believe in Capitalism, some in Communism, some in Socialism. In the American family we believe in tolerance — live and let live. Others do not. They feel that discord and distrust will always poison the house until everyone thinks alike — thinks as they do. The tension will be acute for a long time. We live in one house, but not in one time. Ann O'Hare McCormick [101] put it this way: "The primeval tom-tom still beats while the atom bomb ticks. Russia is straddling the centuries, in victory more than ever pounding backward to Peter the Great and racing to overtake Henry Ford and Henry Kaiser before she has caught up with Thomas Jefferson. The clocks of Europe are turning back and the clocks of Asia are turning forward. And there are places where time stands still because the night does not lift and there is no tomorrow."

Now you are about to come in from the school yard and take an active place in this house. You will live in the best apartment. You will have the best food, the best furniture, the best plumbing, the best of everything. The others will envy you, which does not make it easier for you. But you cannot escape. We have found that out at the price of two wars. You will live with your family, but you will also live with all the other people in this crowded house.

Some of you may be a little confused by the complexity of it all, by the discord, by the conflicts of opinion that pull you this way and that, by the clocks that are out of time and the voices that are out of tune with the bright new world we promised you yesterday.

If you feel all these misgivings do not be alarmed. You are quite normal, because today's mood is one of anxiety. This is the Anxious Age. We are moved more by anxiety and fear than by faith and hope. We are doubting our beliefs and believing our doubts.

Walt Whitman said. "There is no week nor day nor hour when tyranny may not enter upon this country, if the people lose their supreme confidence in themselves — and lose their roughness and spirit of defiance — tyranny may always enter — there is no charm, no bar against it — the only bar against it is a large resolute breed of men."

But, my young friends, we are not behaving like a resolute breed of

[101] Correspondent and member of editorial board of the New York *Times;* author of *The Hammer and the Scythe.*

men. We are behaving more like nutty neurotics. We are more concerned with pensions and personal security than personal achievement; we are nervously looking for subversive enemies under the bed and behind the curtains. We exchange frenzied, irresponsible accusations of disloyalty. "Guilt by Association" has been added to our language. The slanderer is honored. The shadow of a nameless fear slopes across the land. There is talk of thought control among Jefferson's people. Fear, not freedom, seems to be our portion on the very morrow of our greatest victory, at the very pinnacle of our strength, prestige, and affluence.[102]

Why? Why is this the Anxious Age? Why do we behave like nutty neurotics instead of a "large resolute breed of men"? The answer, it seems to me, is compounded of many factors. Industrialization and standardization have improved our living standards and culture, but they have also organized us in herds with little control over our destiny, apprehensive of our future as anonymous social-security numbers. Our splendid industrial civilization has exacted a heavy price in the comfort of neighborliness and the fulfillment that people once got from working for themselves as part of a community. Politically, new, powerful, aggressive ideas have emerged and reemerged to challenge the democratic idea which has been in the ascendancy for so long. Our free society has been buffeted by the hammer blows of Communism, Fascism, and their autocratic antecedents for a generation and we are a little rattled. We are a little rattled because democracy, freedom, and unrestricted inquiry mean tolerance, consent, persuasion, and diversity. They are the antithesis of iron conformity, hero worship, ritual, and fanatic obedience. Our values are rational and peaceful. Totalitarianism, on the other hand, cultivates a passionate, fighting, political religion.

When freedom did not exist it, too, was a fighting faith that men would die for. But now that it does exist it looks a little pale and gentle and lacks the appeal to the militant, irrational sentiments once mobilized by conquering religions and now by totalitarianism.

But totalitarianism resolves no anxieties. It multiplies them. It organizes terror. It is without spiritual content or comfort. It provides no basic security. In the long run it cannot cure the disease of the Anxious Age. But its short-term methods are grimly effective as we have seen. We cannot sit still and wait for the fever to run its course, passively protesting our devotion to democratic ideals while indulging in undemocratic practices. A schizophrenic society which recoils in horror from a godless materialism, but, blinded by its own material well being, loses sight of its spiritual heritage will not long hold out against the subtle

[102] Stevenson refers to the charges of Senator Joseph McCarthy and others that the U.S. government was infiltrated by Communists.

poison of doubt and fear. If Western civilization is to save its body, it must save its soul too. It must resolve the anxieties of mass civilization. It must awake again the emotionalism, the confidence, the defiant faith of a resolute breed of men to whom democracy and freedom mean something positive every day — not just when war has reduced us to the stark issue of self preservation.

It is easy to care mightily then; it is hard now. It is easier to fight for principles than to live up to them. But now is the time that a confident, fighting faith in freedom counts if we are to avoid another war, and if we are to avoid the greater menace of bloodless surrender to our own anxieties.

So I urge you to act like the resolute breed from which you are sprung. Do not stand aside afraid of the great continuous decisions of your time. You are the inheritors of a great tradition born and nurtured in centuries of pain and effort. You have received here its best gift — an education. Man the defenses of the humane individualist tradition against its avowed enemies, its covert foes — indifference and ignorance — and its frightened friends who would surrender it to save it. You have the components of good judgment and wise decision. Many of your decisions will be executed through the instrument of government. Of one thing I can assure you. If responsible citizens like yourselves do not make that government good government, responsive government, there will always be irresponsibles, and worse, ready to usurp the positions and leadership which should be yours by every consideration of intelligence and integrity. And remember that if you fail to do the chores of organized society the power of the state will expand. As it does it beckons to the dictator, the demagogue, to come and organize its vast intricacy. For us — or for him?

For these tasks and these exciting opportunities, use the equipment that God and this great university have given you, and that your own industry each day improves. Use your heart and your head, and not your prejudices. You are more than the social animal Seneca spoke of. It is because we are more than animals that we can blow ourselves off the face of this planet in the next fifty years. It is also because we are more than animals that we can make this world a better place than it has ever been before.

I cannot close without reminding you of the high purposes of the institution from which you are graduating today. "University" is a proud and noble word. Around it cluster all of the values and traditions which civilized peoples have for centuries prized most highly.

The idea which underlies this university — any university — is greater than any of its physical manifestations: its classrooms, its laboratories, its athletic plant, even the particular groups of faculty and students who make up its human element at any one time. What is this idea? It is that the highest condition of man in this mysterious universe is freedom of the spirit. And it is only truth that can set the spirit free.

The function of a university is, then, the search for truth and its communication to succeeding generations. Only as that function is performed steadily, conscientiously, and without interference, does a university realize its underlying purpose. Only so does a university keep faith with the great humanist tradition of which it is a part. Only so does it merit the honorable name it bears.

As it is sometimes difficult to see the forest for the trees, so it has perhaps been difficult for you, in the excitement of a happy and busy student life on this large campus, to grasp and to comprehend fully the elemental motivation of this great university, the close relationship it has to the eternal aspirations of mankind for emancipation from the slavery of ignorance.

As you depart, then, from this campus that you have known and loved, I bid you to fix your thoughts increasingly upon its inherent ideas and purposes as its outward trappings recede. Do not forget that it is a university, as well as your university; and that it has obligations to the whole of mankind which it can neither ignore nor shirk, and which cannot, consistently with its honorable name and place in the community of scholarship, be sacrificed to passing passions or prejudices. As members of the alumni family, be alert to its needs, but keep always in the forefront of your vision the realization that the single greatest need of any university, as of any seeker after truth, is not money, not expensive libraries and laboratories, but freedom — freedom to do its work, to pursue its inquiries, to conduct its discussions, to extend the limits of learning.

See to it that no one, for whatever reason or in the service of whatever interest, diverts this university from its basic objects or sets its sights lower than those of any other university in the civilized world. As its graduates, as individuals who have made in it an investment of the golden and irretrievable years of youth, you cannot, I suggest, do less to pay your debt. And carry always with you some part of this wise serenity, of the timeless courage, the unhurried objectivity, which is the atmosphere of this university and which represents the collective imprint of its founders, students, and teachers who have gone before you.

And do not be afraid. Do not worry about what might happen. Start thinking now about what you are going to make happen. It is a good time to be alive — and awake! It is exciting. It is your time, and you can say with Emerson:

If there is any period one would desire to be born in — is it not the age of Revolution; when the old and the new stand side by side, and admit of being compared; when the energies of all men are searched by fear and hope; when the historic glories of the old can be compensated by the rich possibilities of the new era? This time, like all times, is a very good one, if we but know to do with it.

During the summer of 1950, the Illinois State Museum sponsored an exhibition of paintings by Illinois artists, and Stevenson purchased one by Robert Hooton, of Bloomington. Mr. Hooton wrote to express his pleasure, and commented that every artist thinks the person who buys one of his paintings must have excellent taste.

To Robert Hooton

July 3, 1950

Dear Bob:

Many thanks for your letter. I am delighted that you, as its creator, thought well of "Pensive Girl." The comment has all been ecstatic. I only wish I felt I could have had some more of your things.

With warm regards — and stop in to see me when you pass through Springfield.

Sincerely yours,

Director of Public Welfare Fred Hoehler informed Stevenson that he intended to leave for London and Paris for a meeting of the International Conference of Social Work. He concluded his letter: "I have had an interesting time over the past seventeen months although it was not always too smooth, nor was my patience always at its best. For the years ahead, if I last, there are plans of which I am convinced we can both be proud. . . . Most of these were prompted by your encouragement and faith."

To Fred K. Hoehler [103]

July 11, 1950

Dear Fred:

I shall be waiting eagerly your report on the great world when you get back. And I need hardly say that I wish I was stowed away in your luggage somewhere.

[103] The original is in the possession of Mrs. Hoehler.

I shall do nothing about designating any acting Director unless something unforeseen overtakes us.

Only today I saw your memorandum of July 5 to the Superintendents about the budget situation [104] in the Department of Public Welfare. I hope and pray that they cooperate or the situation may become embarrassing.

Have a good time — and find time to have a good time!

Yours,

ADLAI

In July, 1950, political writer and radio newscaster Raymond Swing visited Stevenson in Springfield. He wrote later to say how much he had enjoyed it and how deeply impressed he was with the work being done by the Governor.

To Raymond Swing

July 13, 1950

Dear Ray:

I was delighted to have your letter and also the reprints from the NATION, which I hope to read — some night very late!

I am sure your visit was more of a tonic for me than for you, and you can't come back too soon.

Yours,

The Dick family vacationed at Ephraim, Wisconsin, in July, 1950. Mrs. Dick invited Stevenson and his executive secretary, James W. Mulroy, to join them there.

To Mrs. Edison Dick [105]

July 13, 1950

My fat friend Mulroy agrees that we should move the seat of your troubles and our pants from Springfield to Ephraim Tuesday for a couple of days if your invitation was really serious. Hope nothing interferes from Korea [106] or Illinois and will wire or telephone you Monday time

---

[104] The editors were unable to locate a copy of this memorandum.

[105] A telegram.

[106] On June 25, 1950, North Korea invaded South Korea. On June 27, the United Nations Security Council adopted an American-sponsored resolution calling upon all member nations to render assistance to South Korea.

of arrival at Sturgeon Bay Tuesday afternoon. Suggest as little publicity as possible promotes more peace and better fishing or what have you. Love to all.

ADLAI

Mrs. Nevile Gardiner wrote Stevenson from The Hague, Netherlands, where her husband was serving as commercial secretary to the British embassy, suggesting that the Governor arrange to meet the new British consul general in Chicago, Mr. Berkeley Gage.

To Mrs. Nevile Gardiner

July 21, 1950

Dear Madeleine:

I was delighted to have your nice thoughtful letter, even if the news about the Gardiners was a little sparse.

Berkeley Gage has called on me and I have had several opportunities to talk with him — socially and professionally — and I have tried to give him some suggestions. He is a delightful man and he will be a great improvement in the British representation in the shadow of the Chicago Tribune. What's more I really think he likes the post — or at least dissimulates admirably.

And speaking of posts, I suspect you are to be envied. Our bright new world looks horrid again, but I am sure all is in order at The Hague.

Affectionate regards.

Yours,

Dorothy Fosdick, while on a speaking tour in the Midwest, stopped in Springfield to visit Stevenson. She wrote him after returning to Washington.

To Dorothy Fosdick [107]

July 21, 1950

Dear Dorothy:

I am back today after a couple of days holiday visiting friends up in northern Wisconsin, and find your letters awaiting me — for which I am profoundly grateful! I am glad you got a little of the Lincoln infection while here and I hope it at least neutralized a little of the [Chicago]

[107] A carbon copy is in A.E.S., P.U.L.

Tribune infection! I shall read your St. Charles speech with the usual profitable results — and plagiarism!

But now I have another request. I enclose copy of a letter from a friend [108] in California, with the hope that you can refer me to some published report or something which will give him the whole story of the evolution of the veto for the permanent members of the [United Nations] Security Council. I really haven't the time to try to piece it all together myself. What's more, it would be wrong.

Forgive me for imposing on a busy policy planner [109] — and don't decline any invitations to speak in Illinois. You are good for my horizons.

Yours,

The publisher of a downstate Illinois newspaper was attempting to lure Lady Nancy Astor, onetime Member of Parliament, to the United States, and more specifically Illinois, for a speech. Lady Astor wrote Stevenson that she might come; that if she did come she would surely visit Springfield — not to speak but to see him. She invited him to England for a holiday.

To Lady Nancy Astor

July 24, 1950

My dear Lady Astor:

I was delighted to have your charming letter and to know I had such an eloquent champion in England of good or at least better government, but I am afraid I need you in Illinois!

I wish I *could* fly over for a holiday. Instead I shall be flying in a few minutes to the Menard Penitentiary, and for at least a couple of years to come there will be no vacations abroad — or even vacations, I am afraid.

With affectionate regards, I am

Sincerely yours,

In considering an offer to join the Governor's staff, Porter McKeever wrote that he had one reservation: "the question of whether or not the Korean crisis spreads out into general war. If that should develop, I imagine all of us will have to make sharp readjustments in our plans." He

[108] Actually Stevenson's cousin Davis Merwin.
[109] Miss Fosdick was a member of the Policy Planning Staff of the Department of State.

added that he expected to come to Illinois for the State Fair, and, "I told Dicky [Dorothy Fosdick] that your price for staying at the Executive Mansion was her entry into the greased pig contest."

To Porter McKeever

July 25, 1950

Dear Porter:

Thanks for your letter. By all means plan to come out on August 11 and witness the opening chaos at the State Fair and the confusion of the Governor.

I am sending a copy of this to Dorothy and I hope she can contrive to come with you, as you suggest. Nothing would please me more, and I will see that she is entered at once in the greased pig contest and also the gander pulling contest, which, of course, she has to do in a polka-dot dress mounted on a Dalmatian dog.

As to our business: In view of the developments I am tempted, reluctantly, to concede that you better stay by your post until the atmosphere clears a little to the eastward. I should hate to ever feel that I had robbed Austin [110] to pay Adlai — at such a time as this. As to next January, it is, of course, difficult for me to see that far in advance as to what my circumstances will be but we can talk more of that when you are here.

Yours,

Stevenson took a keen interest in the State Fair and was distressed that it did not pay for itself. The Schaefer Commission, an agency to survey the structure of the state government, in its report to the legislature disclosed that the fair had sustained an operating loss of two and a half million dollars for the five-year period 1946–1950. The commission, of which Walter Schaefer was chairman, made a number of recommendations to the General Assembly for cutting or meeting this loss.

To Walter V. Schaefer [111]

July 27, 1950

Dear Wally:

I read this report last night — at last! [112] I think it is very good and

[110] Warren R. Austin, U.S. ambassador to the United Nations.

[111] The original of this letter is in the possession of Mr. Schaefer.

[112] The editors were unable to locate a copy of this report, by Ralph Ammon, one-time director of Wisconsin state Department of Agriculture, about the operations of

forthright, but of course tells us little that we didn't already know. Actually much of the report and its recommendations will be obsolete by the time this summer's Fair is over.

I can disagree only in a few minor respects with Mr. Ammon's conclusions. For example, I can hardly agree that "Republican and Democratic Days are evidence of political infestation and have no place in a State Fair." It seems to me this conclusion overlooks one purpose of a Fair, which is educational. Certainly there is, at least theoretically, no more important aspect of education than citizenship, public issues, candidates and the democratic process, if you please. Many of the people coming to the Fair are country folk who have little chance to see and hear politicians hawking their wares.

Be that as it may, and I don't feel strongly about it, I am inclined to think that the report might, if any report is to be issued before this year's results and resumes can be surveyed, well be confined to the comparative costs and emphatic recommendation that the Illinois Fair be put on a self-sustaining basis at least by increasing revenue from the gate and grandstand and by more thrifty and competent management, with a view to early elimination of any operating appropriation.

Yours,

A.E.S.

Stevenson, who was a member of the U.S. Delegation at the founding of the United Nations in San Francisco in 1945, was asked by his cousin Davis Merwin to explain exactly how the veto power for members of the UN Security Council came to be written into the articles.

To Davis Merwin

August 2, 1950

Dear Dave:

I have hastily put together and am sending you under separate cover, some material relating to the veto. It is a long, complicated story which I cannot take the time to attempt to recite, nor could I do it accurately without a lot of reference reading at this late date.

In addition to what I have sent, you will find more about it in "Post-

---

the Illinois State Fair. The State Fair report that the Schaefer Commission used was a condensation of one written by a management firm into which some items of the Ammon report were inserted. Letter from Jack F. Isakoff to Walter V. Schaefer, April 9, 1969.

war Foreign Policy Preparation in 1939–1945" by the State Department in 1949.[113] This book is doubtless available in any library and will describe something of the development of the principle and the unanimity of the great powers in concept at Dumbarton Oaks, the Yalta Conference and San Francisco.

What none of the books will disclose is that an American veto over the use of our armed forces was always considered a condition precedent to ratification of the charter by the United States Senate. "What, send our boys to war without our consent! Never!!" That was the state of mind I think, as you will well recall. In addition to that was the virtual Russian refusal to cooperate without some assurance that the "three great powers" would always have to act in concert. France and China were later added to the three great powers. It all seems a long way off from Springfield!

Sincerely,

Under the established patronage system, applicants for jobs were subject to a long and cumbersome method of investigation before approval. After submission to a political screening committee their names were sent to the Governor's office, which checked on their experience and qualifications.

On February 8, 1950, Lawrence E. Irvin, the Governor's aide in charge of patronage, made suggestions as to how he thought it could best be handled. He stated that "the handling of patronage, or to use what I think is a more appropriate term — the recruitment of personnel, is a definite function of state government and should be treated and supported as such. . . . I believe the average voter would recognize the forthright and basic honesty of such a step and could be educated to understand the need for it." He suggested that such a program could give the Governor more personal control over recruitment policies, strengthen his political effectiveness by developing a better appreciation of the fact that jobs of a patronage nature stem from the Governor and not from other sources, and eliminate the slow and complex method by which all patronage jobs had been filled.

To Walter V. Schaefer [114]

August 4, 1950

Dear Walter:

I hope you can find the time to examine carefully the attached mem-

[113] Department of State Publication 3580, General Foreign Policy Series 15 (Washington: Government Printing Office, 1950).

[114] The original of this letter is in the possession of Mr. Schaefer.

orandum from Lawrence Irvin dated February 8, 1950. I have been meaning to talk to you for months and have overlooked it. It seems to me to have much merit.

We know quite well that employment in the service of the State of Illinois will for many years to come include a large number of so-called patronage positions. The whole method by which this is traditionally handled has been rather disillusioning to me. Certainly it is unscientific. Certainly it is cumbersome. Certainly it is no secret. And certainly it is and will be for a long time to come a function of state government which will have to be performed either furtively or honestly. I think the honest approach would be not only the best but would also yield better results in personnel screening and selection than the old-fashioned wire-pulling.

I am not sure what the Schaefer Commission proposes to recommend with respect to personnel management generally. However, it would seem to me to be both sensible and realistic to recommend, if nothing more basic or comprehensive is contemplated, that henceforth there be established in the Governor's Office an Assistant for Personnel and that funds be provided by appropriation for his work.

This may sound a little extreme, but on mature thought I believe you will recognize its honesty and merit and possible major contribution to better personnel practice in a state which is still so largely under the spoils system.

Sincerely yours,
ADLAI

Stevenson liked to have his official cabinet members mingle with the Democratic politicians and their wives after the Governor's Day ceremonies at the State Fair. The weather was usually hot and dry, and a reception was held on the spacious lawn of the mansion where the guests found cool drinks and cookies.

To Leonard Schwartz [115]

August 7, 1950

Dear Director Schwartz:

Following the Governor's Day program at the State Fair on Thursday, August 17, we are to have an informal reception at the executive mansion for visiting Democrats from all parts of the state, including

[115] The original is in the possession of Mr. Schwartz.

the county chairmen and chairwomen, state committeemen and committeewomen, the ward and township committeemen, and various others.

I would appreciate very much your serving as a member of a small reception committee for this reception, which will be between 3 and 5 P.M. standard time. The affair is to be quite informal, and we don't plan to have a reception line. My hope is merely to greet personally as many of the guests as possible and visit briefly with them.

If you can arrange to assist me in welcoming the guests at the reception, I shall be grateful.

With every personal good wish,

Sincerely,

Don Hyndman wrote drafts of speeches from time to time and Stevenson then reworked them into his own style.

To Don Hyndman

August 10, 1950

I wish you could draft something for me for Governor's Day at the State Fair. I hope to find some time to work on it Tuesday if you could have something in my hands by that day. I should think not more than 1500 words — humor — a word of pride and thanks about our administration — big plug for Engle, Smith, Howlett — ending on a solemn note about war and peace and Lucas' great services as helmsman of U.S. Senate.[116] I think, in short, this being a campaign year, I should put the emphasis on the need for a Democratic legislature and the state ticket. I believe I am supposed to introduce [Vice President] Barkley, and there may be something suitable in the speeches of last year and the year before.

To Harry S. Truman [117]

August 18, 1950

My dear Mr. President:

Because the problem is not a local one, I have followed with close in-

[116] C. Hobart Engle was the Democratic candidate for superintendent of public instruction. Since Ora Smith's term as state treasurer was for only two years and he could not succeed himself, the candidate for that office was Michael Howlett and Smith ran for clerk of the Supreme Court. Scott W. Lucas was up for reelection to the U.S. Senate. All four were defeated.

[117] The original is in the Harry S. Truman Library, Independence, Missouri.

terest the progress of Secretary Chapman's [118] efforts, in line with the general policies you have laid down, to combat racial discrimination in the use of the recreational facilities under his jurisdiction, notably the public swimming pools in the District of Columbia. I note in the newspapers that the results in this instance are proving to be very satisfactory indeed, and it appears to be the general opinion that the manner in which this situation has been handled is most creditable.

I am somewhat more familiar with the situation than I might otherwise be because one of the persons whom I have persuaded to serve the State of Illinois, Mr. Joseph D. Lohman, Chairman of the Illinois Board of Pardons and Paroles, was a consultant to the Department of the Interior in this connection and played an important part in the training of the police and park attendants in the District for the particular assignment which they are carrying out so successfully. It is another example of how the most difficult of problems can be made to yield to careful preparation.

I write only to say that I feel that Secretary Chapman and his associates are entitled to a large measure of credit for the manner in which they have put into practice a principle which, in the context of the times, is of the greatest importance to all of us, as you have been among the first to recognize.[119]

Sincerely yours,

On Sunday, August 20, 1950, Stevenson visited the Illinois National Guard summer encampment at Camp McCoy, Wisconsin, to review the 44th Division. From there he and his three sons flew to Wyoming for a vacation. En route he wrote to his executive secretary, James W. Mulroy.

To James W. Mulroy [120]

Tuesday afternoon [August 22, 1950] [121]

Dear Jim:

Just passed Omaha — so far so good!

The trip to McCoy was a major disaster — an hour and 40 minutes late to the reviewing stand and you can picture the state of mind of the

[118] Secretary of the Interior Oscar Chapman.
[119] The President's response to this letter was perfunctory.
[120] This handwritten letter is in the possession of Mrs. Helen Kaste.
[121] Carol Evans's desk calendar for 1950 showed that he and his sons left for the Grand Tetons in Wyoming the Tuesday following his appearance at Camp McCoy on Sunday, August 20, so presumably this letter was written on Tuesday, August 22.

troops & spectators. General Allen [122] was very upset and insists on an "investigation." Evidently the instructions to Dan Smith [123] were to go to Sp[ringfield] the night before. He didn't — and due to engine trouble we were about ½ hr. late in starting. Then we had to stop in Chicago to pick up the other passengers — and refuel! Head winds all the way. Instead of being faster the plane was slower than mine; [124] to get there at 10:30 I should have taken off at 8 instead of nine even without the misfortunes. If Smith is responsible Gen. Allen talked as though he would insist on relieving him of his command. If he made any mistakes, they are Dan's first and I hate to see him severely punished. He said something to me this morning that sounded as tho he blamed Bill Blair for fixing the departure time and not notifying him that we would have to land in Chicago on the way to pick up additional passengers. But I don't see how Bill could have decided the plane speed & proper time for departure.

I'm telling you this as you may hear something about it & the investigation. The press made inquiries and I told them that we were delayed at take off by engine trouble; that I notified Gen. Bolen [125] from Chicago that we would be late and assumed they would go ahead with the review on schedule without waiting for me.

I have told Geo. Mitchell that I wanted to replace McKinney [126] this fall in a manner calculated to do the least injury to McK. Of course if another job could be found for him in private business he could resign for that reason & it would be the best way "out." If he's told now that the date is Oct. 1 or something he might get mad, start to feather his nest or do something rash. On the other hand, if he is not told now he won't have an opportunity to look for another job.

I've talked it all over with Mitchell & he *agrees*. He will talk to you about timing and replacement. I've mentioned Cummings [127] & Miller [128]

[122] General Frank Allen, commander of the Illinois Air National Guard.

[123] The Governor's plane pilot, a major in the Air National Guard.

[124] The plane officially assigned to the Governor for his use was a twin-engine Beechcraft. Apparently another plane was used on the trip to Camp McCoy.

[125] General Harry L. Bolen, commander of the 44th Division, Illinois National Guard.

[126] State Purchasing Agent William J. McKinney. His position fell within the Department of Finance, headed by George Mitchell. As a source of graft the office of state purchasing agent was one of the most vulnerable in the state government. Stevenson took great pains before appointing McKinney to be sure he had someone who was completely honest as well as knowledgeable and efficient. McKinney resigned not long after this letter was written.

[127] David Cummings, a Peoria businessman. Cummings agreed to fill the position temporarily. Later Carl Kresl, a retired Sears, Roebuck official with many years of purchasing experience, was appointed.

[128] William S. Miller, a businessman of Ottawa, Illinois, who helped form the Good Roads Association at Stevenson's suggestion.

to him, with a preference for the former only because of Miller's Good Roads Assoc[iation]. connection. Also I told him I thought Steere [129] should go in with the new director [130] as his personal assistant. I agree with you that Steere looks fine. I talked with him yesterday. But he's too inexperienced & unsure for the top job yet.

I suppose we should do nothing about the replacement until I get back unless you want to make a deliberate canvass of the whole state govt. with George. I'm coming more & more around to the view that honesty, intelligence, hard work, judgment & "savvy" are more important than technical knowledge of purchasing, particularly if we can add a couple of technically competent people to the staff — an expert textile buyer for example — which George plans to do anyway. As you know, I think very well of Baird Helfrich & would like to use him in a more conspicuous spot. Also he's a good investigator & *might* be able to run an organization, altho I am less confident on that score tho he did have considerable organization experience in the war. There may be others that should be considered before we settle on Cummings. If you and George conclude that C[ummings]. is the best bet perhaps you will think it best to warn him about what I have in mind so that he can be thinking, *very confidentially,* about timing and a replacement on the Police Board. *
I would like to make Kiner [131] Ch[airman]. of the Bd. but Gardner [132] told me he too would like to resign — embarrassed over taking pay while on the U[niversity]. of I[llinois]. faculty. I hope I can talk him out of it. Anyway, we will have to make at least one Democratic appointment and I want to find a really high class man. A good retired Army officer, if we had any among the deserving, would be fine. How about Tommy Tomlinson? Ralph Hawthorn? Dan McMullen (??),[133] Hemphill.[134] Maybe Larry [Irvin] will have time to assemble all the top brass names we have for me.

I talked with Nelson [135] — suggest Sec'y of Liquor Com[mission] or our Sp. office. He now gets 5400 & makes 1500–2000 on the side writing briefs etc. He seems to prefer the Sp. job, but will take the other, which I suggested to him in the greatest *confidence.* He is going to talk to

* Also he might have some ideas as to where McKinney could be placed.
[129] Robert Stierer, who joined the staff of the Department of Finance and remained until the end of the Stevenson administration.
[130] Stevenson was anticipating the resignation of Director of Finance George Mitchell, who was on leave from the Federal Reserve Bank in Chicago.
[131] Charles Kneier, professor of political science at the University of Illinois.
[132] Henry A. Gardner, a Chicago lawyer, chairman of the State Police Merit Board.
[133] Democrats and downstate businessmen.
[134] Judge Victor Hemphill, of Carbondale.
[135] Richard J. Nelson, who joined Stevenson's staff in Springfield. Soon afterward he was elected president of the Young Democrats of America.

Wirtz [136] whom he knows & will also talk again to you. He would do his Young Dems job better from a Sp. base than Chicago, would be a good greeter, could quickly pick up much substantive usefulness, but I doubt if he is "senior" enough or politically wise enough to be much of a liaison man. But I should think he could quickly relieve you of a lot of corres. etc. If we take on Porter McKeever too — how about budget and office space? Can't we move the budgetary Commission? [137]

Please write up & send the attached letters.

Yrs
AES

P.S. . . .

John S. Miller and his wife, Catherine, old Chicago friends of Stevenson, presented him with some binoculars before he left on a vacation in the Grand Tetons in Wyoming with his three sons. Stevenson had appointed Miller a member of the Chicago Transit Authority.

To John S. Miller

September 5, 1950

Dear John:

Four Stevensons have alternated with the binoculars for two weeks inspecting moose, deer, elk, mountain sheep, trumpeter swans, coyotes and mountains — thanks to the Millers.

It was a splendid present and the boys have abruptly developed a great regard for the Millers who must be "very different politicians"!

And I am grateful to you also for reclaiming my pajamas; also for laundering them; also for sending them to me; also for a bed in which to wear them!

Indeed, I am very, very grateful all around.

Yours,

In the fall of 1950 rumors abounded that Secretary of State Dean Acheson would resign his office, and there was much speculation that Stevenson would be appointed to that post. On September 11, 1950, the

[136] W. Willard Wirtz, then a member of the Illinois Liquor Commission. In 1962 he became U.S. Secretary of Labor.

[137] The office of the Budgetary Commission adjoined the Governor's office in the capitol building.

Chicago Daily News *ran an editorial stating, in part: "Mr. Stevenson is highly qualified and experienced for diplomatic service. But we would not recommend him for this post. Among his qualifications are a keen intelligence, a wide knowledge of the world, a pleasing personality and a gift for expressing himself well orally and in writing. . . . Why do we not recommend Mr. Stevenson for Secretary of State? The answer is that his chief difficulties as governor have come from indecision and vacillation. . . . When the 1949 legislature was in session Gov. Stevenson didn't know for sure whether he wanted a higher gasoline tax or not . . . even in the recent special session, he invited the legislature to consider financial aid to cities without submitting a program of his own to achieve the purpose. He went into the session with Mayor Kennelly undecided on a program of HIS own. . . . Stevenson is by no means the worst possible choice for that great place in the cabinet. He may well be better than what we will get. . . ."*

On September 11, 1950, a letter protesting this editorial appeared in the Chicago *Daily News "Letters to the Editor" column. Although it was signed by Hermon Dunlap Smith, the letter was originally drafted by Stevenson himself. This letter is reproduced here as Stevenson originally composed it, to show how sensitive he was before 1952 to the charge of vacillation.*[138]

Whatever Governor Stevenson's qualifications for Secretary of State, I want to emphatically disagree with your editorial statement of Sept. 11 that as Governor he has been guilty of indecision and vacillation. If he has been you picked two very poor examples to prove it.

On the issue of the gasoline tax increase in the 1949 legislature you seem to forget that both Republicans and Democrats joined in the legislative Commission's recommendation for an increase. The big dispute was not the increase but how the tax was to be allocated between the state, the cities, counties and rural roads. As many can testify Stevenson worked incessantly and adroitly for months to reconcile the sharp conflicts in these groups. Had he personally endorsed an allocation scheme while there was still a chance for agreement he not only would have wasted his bargaining power, but would have turned the argument into one between Republicans and Democrats in that badly divided legislature.

Perhaps you could have criticized his estimate of good strategy, but a mistake in technique is no proof of vacillation. And I hope the Daily

---

[138] The text of the letter used is the original handwritten draft by Stevenson. It is in A.E.S., P.U.L.

News does not consider it vacillation for a Governor to try to keep public questions from degenerating into partisan conflicts.

Your other example of "vaccilation and indecision" seems no better. Aid to cities was included in the special session at the request of Chicago as everyone knows. Mayor Kennelly was very frank in admitting that he had no recourse but to come to the Republican Senate hat in hand. And he came with a program of general licensing first, or an increase in the peg levy second. That the Mayor's program was defeated does not mean that he had no program or that Governor Stevenson was vacillating.

While citing examples of Gov. S's vacillation and indecision, I think it could properly comment on a multitude of examples of his courage and decision in the face of every kind of pressure. Has he been indecisive or vacillating in his appointments of qualified men; on padded payrolls; on civil service reform. What does the Daily News think about law enforcement under Stevenson — gambling, liquor, trucks, etc? How about his reform of the state police; of the Commerce Commission? Did he wobble about const[itutional]. reform, about the Crime Commission bills; about FEPC or aid to schools?

I think the DN could afford to reappraise its examples of indecision & vacillation and perhaps admit the possibility that they represented a sincere effort to achieve not mere shouting — but results.

Before the advent of Governor Stevenson, state employees, whether under civil service or holding patronage jobs, were expected to contribute a percentage of their salaries to campaign coffers. In his campaign in 1948 Stevenson castigated the Green administration for "destroying the security and morale of civil service employees" by using "civil service and the merit system to build up a political machine instead of a career in public service. . . . I shall insist that the civil service and the merit system be respected." [139]

After Stevenson took office, and after careful deliberation, it was decided that although no assessment would be made of any state employee, civil service or patronage, voluntary contributions would not be turned aside.

On September 9, 1950, Mr. M. B. O'Hara, of the Illinois State Penitentiary Menard Branch Employees Union, inquired of the Governor whether Civil Service employees should pay a campaign contribution; that those in his union thus far had refused to pay. Lawrence Irvin, of the Governor's office, drafted a reply, dated September 11, 1950, sending it to Stevenson for his approval with the suggestion that "we will handle

[139] Speech to the Young Men's Club, Bloomington, Illinois, October 26, 1948.

future correspondence relating to the same subject in a similar manner."
In his reply to Mr. O'Hara, Irvin said: "The Governor's attitude in this
matter is well known. You are undoubtedly familiar with his numerous
public statements about the solicitation of campaign funds from civil
service employees. I can assure you his attitude has not changed and
that no state civil service employee will be discriminated against because
he did or did not contribute to a poltical campaign fund." Stevenson
added the following handwritten note to Irvin's memorandum.

OK — Perhaps you better send copy of his letter & your reply to
Warden Robinson,[140] informing him that Civil Servants should not be
"slugged" — that it must be made clear to them they can contribute but
no recrimination if they don't.

AES

Mr. and Mrs. William E. Stevenson sent the Governor a postcard from
England.

To Mr. and Mrs. William E. Stevenson

September 11, 1950

Dear Stevensons:
   Your postcard from Cambridge filled me full of jealous, bitter, hateful
envy! My horizons grow closer and closer, and a trip abroad seems to
me for wastrels and academics only.
   Why don't you come out here and stay a night with me and see something of the rude realities of life in the Western world?
   My love, and thanks.

Yours,

To Alicia Patterson [141]

September 11, 1950

I tumbled down the last weary mountain Sat afternoon. Sunday we
all spent a hilarious day motoring thru the Yellowstone & Monday we
flew back to Springfield — brown, burned, fit, lean, happy. It was
glorious — the boys all to myself for the first time for almost 2 whole
blessed weeks. Marvelous scenery, superb fishing in Bridger Lake, perfect
weather, good food, a fascinating old cook, fine guide & jolly wrangler

[140] Browning Robinson, warden of the state penitentiary, Menard branch.
[141] This handwritten letter is in the possession of Adlai E. Stevenson III.

— and no misfortunes — *except* — saddle sores on poor little John Fell's rump that looked like the black plague. But he didn't seem to mind & I daubed him dutifully & lovingly with zinc ointment which he promptly rubbed off. We caught countless big, fat cutthroat trout and smoked a lot of them in an improvised smoke house.

Back here a day — wriggled thru the accumulated mountain of work & I felt I had never been away. The boys took off to Chicago and Ellen & I was desolate again.

Its Sunday night and the week-end has been a horror. Flew to Chi Friday morning for a conference of Governors; spoke before the American Legion convention in the afternoon; Introduced Trygve Lie at a huge to do in the evening; met with [Senator] Lucas, [Jacob] Arvey et al early Saturday; flew to Nauvoo for 5 hours of drives, parades, speeches, dedications; then to Bloomington 2 hours late for a big party at my sisters house; and off this morning by auto & airplane (foul weather) for southern Ill. and another speech; winding up with one last feeble despairing oratorical effort over the telephone and broadcast to 200,000 faithful democrats in Riverview Park in Chi; then back to Sp[ringfield]. by air & my empty lonesome mansion and groaning desk — and the Nth rereading of your letter. What a life! . . .

The Secretary-General of the United Nations, Trygve Lie, spoke to the Chicago Council on Foreign Relations on September 8, 1950. He later wrote Stevenson to thank him for his generous introductory remarks and to say how much he enjoyed his visit to Chicago.

To Trygve Lie

September 14, 1950

Dear Trygve:

You should not have written me — I should have written you, to tell you of the many people who are very grateful for your visit to Chicago. And I can safely say that you did more good where it was needed than you probably realize.

With affectionate regards and great respect, I am

Sincerely yours,

On September 14, 1950, Stevenson sent the following letter to various outstanding citizens of Illinois.[142]

[142] This copy is in the possession of Mrs. John Paul Welling.

I am writing to enlist your help and cooperation on behalf of United Nations Day, October 24. The General Assembly of the United Nations has designated October 24 as United Nations Day and has asked its member governments to encourage appropriate observance of this day by their citizens.

United Nations Day provides an opportunity for citizens to review the aims and achievements of the United Nations and to dedicate their energies to a truly constructive program for a free and peaceful world.

As Governor of the State of Illinois, I shall shortly issue a proclamation honoring United Nations Day and urging both citizens and public officials to participate in appropriate observances. It is expected that the President will issue a proclamation calling upon the American people to observe United Nations Day. The United States Government intends to present these official proclamations to the United Nations.

An Illinois committee of representative citizens is being formed to assist in arranging State and local observances. I hope it will be possible for you to serve on this committee.

A National Citizens' Committee for United Nations Day 1950 has been established and is responsible for the national program. Mrs. Franklin D. Roosevelt is serving as Chairman. This committee, with headquarters at 700 Jackson Place Northwest, in Washington, will be a source of information and assistance to state and local committees.

Please advise me as promptly as possible if you can accept this appointment as a member of the Illinois Committee for United Nations Day.

Sincerely yours,

W. Irving Osborne, Jr., a friend of Stevenson's from Lake Forest, took some snapshots of Stevenson while he vacationed in Florida in the spring of 1950. Osborne sent them to the Governor with a note saying he thought it well to send them to him personally lest they fall into unknown hands.

To W. Irving Osborne, Jr.

September 20, 1950

Dear June:

They have come, and I am prepared to submit to any blackmail you suggest. How much is the negative of that fat, white worm on the mat worth? And how many Republicans have already seen it?!

Yours — with many thanks.

To Alicia Patterson [143]

September 25, 1950

. . . I'm in the air en rout, Chi[cago]-Sp[ringfield]., flanked by Mr. Daniel Longwell of Life (why I don't know) and madder than ten snakes! Attached is your distinguished cousin's latest editorial assault on me,[144] & I'm also sending the speech it refers to [145] — marked in red are the passages about the Hiss deposition — to save your lovely eyes from unnecessary scrutiny of Stevenson literature.

I think this is the lowest of all — to damn & impugn a man for telling the truth, rather than taking the easy, timid, safe way out by refusing to testify. But I guess there are neither rules nor morals in Bertie's ugly book and look.

I've just finished two hideous weeks — 8 spee[c]hes this week — on my own job & trying to help Lucas a bit, & so it is for another fortnight. I've just scanned the nasty schedule. On Oct 1 — Sunday I leave Chi at 10:30 AM (with T. S. Matthews of Time) for Chanute Field at Rantoul for luncheon, air show, troop review and the inevitable damn speech. . . . Tuesday I head north to Rockford, Dixon, Ottawa, etc. ending up back in Sp. on Friday Oct. 6. The next day — Sat — I go to Champaign for the Ill[inois]-Wis[consin] football game — back to Sp that night with Marshall Field Jr & new wife & 4 other house guests and on Sunday to Lewiston to speak at a Dem[ocratic]. fish fry. . . .

To Mrs. Edison Dick [146]

September 25, 1950

. . . En route to Sp[ringfield]. in the plane — Monday afternoon after a morning of elaborate atomic bombing exercises at the Theatre in the Field Museum. And next to me is Dan Longwell of Life whom I should talk to but after reading dear Bertie's editorial of this AM I don't trust myself to speak aloud — yet!

James L. Houghteling, of the Civil Service Commission in Washington, sent Stevenson a postcard from Ireland.

[143] This handwritten letter is in the possession of Adlai E. Stevenson III.
[144] The Chicago *Tribune* editorial, headlined "Gov. Stevenson and Alger Hiss," maintained that Stevenson "could not deny and the people of Illinois will not forget that he arrayed himself willingly beside Alger Hiss."
[145] The editors are unable to identify this speech.
[146] This handwritten letter is in the possession of Mrs. Dick.

To James Lawrence Houghteling

September 25, 1950

Dear Lawrence:

I was delighted to have your postcard from Killarney. In my present predicament I wish I were lying on one of those purple hills listening to the linnets sing at noonday!

It was good to hear from you and I am delighted that you and Laura [147] had such a good summer. I hope my path may cross yours soon.

Yours,

Although the Governor did not make a secret of the fund with which he supplemented certain administration salaries, neither did he issue a press release announcing it, so that during his years as governor its existence was generally not known. The fund was added to from time to time through the efforts of Stevenson's friends, most notably Hermon D. Smith, Stephen A. Mitchell and Louis A. Kohn.

To Hermon D. Smith [148]

September 29, 1950

Dear Dutch —

I think it better to write this in long hand. For your personal information, the supplementary payments last year were about as follows:

Schaefer	1000
Day	1000
Hoehler	1000
Mitchell	1000
Mulroy	5000
McGowan	500
Irvin	500
	13 500

I say "about" because I don't find that Mulroy took this much. But I've talked to him and he says his understanding has been that he is entitled to $14,000 a year which means an annual supplementation of about $6000 on his present salary. Maybe I can do something to adjust this salary up or his supplementary down.

In addition there are Xmas distributions & presents to office staff, house-

[147] Mrs. Houghteling.
[148] This handwritten letter is in the possession of Mr. Smith.

hold staff, police, party for the Springfield children, uniforms for the Governor's female and male bowling teams etc. that aggregate $2500–4000. Contributions to charities, buying pages in charity programs, tickets to benefits, flowers to sick people we have handled very closely. There seems to be *literally* almost no limit to what one can spend this way.

This year I would very much like to increase some of my supplementations. Schaefer will be off, but McGowan should get $1500–2000, and there are one or two I would like to add. One I will *have* to add to the extent of about $2000.

In short $20–25 000 a year should enable me to do what we have talked about with[out] robbing the children! [149] — or for that matter, embar[r]assing me by tapping our meagre "political" funds collected in the political ways which the State Central Committee always needs and which *I* will need like the devil if I ever run again, or want to help others.

I hope this will give you something of what you need for the purposes we discussed the other morning, and I would be glad to have you show or send this letter to John Miller who has the same problem of explaining what its about — and that it is not to help Truman or the Democratic candidates.

Yrs
A.E.S.

P.S. As I write I think of others — for example, last year I gave Bob Merriam [150] $250 for helping me with some speeches — out of my pocket; $100 to George Nichols [151] for some research and writing.

To W. Emery Lancaster [152]

September 29, 1950

Dear Mr. Lancaster:

Maude Myers [153] tells me that you have some Dalmatian puppies and have offered me one. I am most grateful, but I have one full-grown Dalmatian, which seems to be a little more than I can handle properly here at the Mansion.[154] If we added some puppies I think it would be a question of the puppies — or the Mansion!

149 Stevenson's three sons.
150 Robert E. Merriam, alderman of the Fifth Ward in Chicago.
151 Of the attorney general's office.
152 An attorney in Quincy, Illinois, who had served as chairman of the Civil Service Commission in the administration of Henry Horner (1933–1937).
153 The president of the Illinois Civil Service Commission, who lived in Springfield.
154 The Governor had brought his Dalmatian, "Artie" (King Arthur), to Spring-

Adlai Stevenson in 1951.

*Governor Stevenson in his statehouse office, inauguration
day, January 10, 1949.*

*Governor and Mrs. Stevenson at the inaugural ball,
Springfield, January, 1949. Directly behind them are Mr.
and Mrs. Ernest L. Ives.*

Governor Stevenson's Libertyville home.

MERCURY STUDIOS, SPRINGFIELD, ILLINOIS.

*Governor Stevenson looks at a painting of his Grandfather
Stevenson in his mansion office. This life-size portrait
was unveiled by Stevenson in Bloomington when he was 14
years old.*

Governor Stevenson at the opening game of the Springfield Brownies, 1949. Edison Dick is to the right of Stevenson; behind him is Captain Van Diver, the Governor's chauffer. The two boys to the left of Stevenson are his son John Fell and "Little Eddie" Dick.

Executive Department—Memorandum *Telegram*

Senator Arthur H. Vandenberg
Grand Rapids, Mich.

Dear Senator —

You are in ~~the prayers of~~
~~many people~~ my prayers.
I wish there was something else
I could do to insure about
20 more years of ~~your~~ useful
life for you!

yours

Adlai

Oct 10, 1949

71562 26

Draft of a telegram to Senator Arthur H. Vandenberg,
who was ill. Senator Vandenberg died on April 18, 1951.

Governor Stevenson with his sister, Mrs. Ernest L. Ives,
his Aunt Julia (Mrs. Martin D. Hardin), and Mrs. R. O.
Wills, of Bloomington. The occasion was a tea given by
Mrs. Ives to D.A.R. members at the mansion in Springfield.

Governor Stevenson with his sons Borden, Adlai III and
John Fell at the Harvard-Princeton football game,
Cambridge, Mass., 1949.

*Governor Stevenson with President Truman and Martin Kennelly,
mayor of Chicago, at Shriners Convention in Chicago, 1950.*

The Executive Mansion, Springfield.

*Governor Stevenson with members of his family and staff,
Christmas Day, 1950, at the mansion.* Back row, *left to
right: Adlai E. Stevenson III; Borden Stevenson; Timothy
R. Ives; Louis Livingston and his wife, Marietta; J. Edward
Day and his wife, Mary Louise; Carl McGowan; Loring C.
Merwin and his wife, Marjorie; James W. Mulroy.*
Second row: *Carol Evans, Amanda (Jill) Merwin; Mrs.
Carl (Jody) McGowan.* Third row, seated: *Mrs. James W.
(Helen) Mulroy; Susan Merwin; Mrs. Ernest L. Ives;
Governor Stevenson; John Fell Stevenson; Mr. Ernest L.
Ives.* Front row, seated: *Geraldine Day; Mary McGowan;
Molly Day; Rebecca McGowan.*

*Vice President Alben Barkley, Stevenson and Illinois
Senator Scott W. Lucas, Springfield, probably in 1951.
The Governor's executive secretary, James W. Mulroy, is
in the front seat.*

*The Governor with his two secretaries, Carol Evans and
Margaret Munn, Governor's staff party, at the mansion
Christmas party, 1951.*

*Governor Stevenson with his three sons, Christmas 1951,
in Springfield. From left to right: John Fell, Borden
and Adlai III.*

Governor Stevenson with "Artie" in his mansion office,
1951. In the background is a portrait of Stevenson's
father, Lewis Green Stevenson.

WESTERN UNION

W. P. MARSHALL, PRESIDENT

The filing time shown in the date line on telegrams and day letters is STANDARD TIME at point of origin. Time of receipt is STANDARD TIME at point of destination

SA126 PA229   DEC 7 PM 9 44

P.PSA050 NL PD=PRINCETON NJER 7=

HON ADLAI STEVENSON=

    GOVERNOR OF ILL EXECUTIVE MANSION SPRINGFIELD ILL=

IN LIGHT OF REPORT IN NOW. 24 "QUICK" THAT YOU WILL BE
CONSIDERED FOR NEXT PRESIDENT OF PRINCETON BY UNIVERSITY
TRUSTEES AS WELL AS RUMORS FROM OTHER SOURCES WOULD YOU
REPLY TO FOLLOWING QUESTIONS BY WIRE COLLECT?

    ¶ HAVE YOU BEEN OFFERED PRESIDENCY OF PRINCETON?

    ¶ TO YOUR KNOWLEDGE, ARE YOU UNDER CONSIDERATION FOR
THIS POST?

¶ WOULD YOU ACCEPT PRINCETON PRESIDENCY IF OFFERED YOU?=

    JOHN A CORRY   CHAIRMAN, DAILY PRINCETONIAN=

Re your telegram I know nothing whatever of the matter you mention and I do not accept or decline proposals I have not received

Regards

Adlai E Stevenson

Draft of a telegram to John A. Corry, chairman of the Daily
Princetonian, *December 7, 1952.*

Dear Mr. Turner — It has just come to my attention that you have presented to the Illinois Historical Library a fine letter of Elizabeth Edwards to her sister, Mary Todd Lincoln.

I am most grateful to you, and also for the part you played in the formal presentation several weeks of the Oliver Barrett material to the Library. With this acquisition our Library will house the greatest collection of Lincoln manuscripts material in existence, enriched by your fine and thoughtful gift.

With gratitude and good wishes,

Cordially yours,

Adlai S. Stevenson

Springfield, July 17, '52

Letter to Justin G. Turner

Governor Stevenson with members of his staff at the mansion office, January, 1952. From left to right: Carl McGowan; William McC. Blair, Jr.; Lawrence Irvin; Governor Stevenson; J. Edward Day; Richard J. Nelson; William I. Flanagan; Don Hyndman.

Governor Stevenson pheasant hunting with Michael Seyfrit, Director of Public Safety, at the Virginia Hunt Club, Virginia, Illinois, March 15, 1952.

I still look forward to that long deferred visit with you, and I hope you will let me know a day or so in advance if you are ever coming to Springfield.

Warm regards.

Sincerely yours,

Dorothy Fosdick sent Stevenson a foreign policy statement by Senator Tom Connally, chairman of the Senate Foreign Relations Committee. She added that the Policy Planning Staff, Department of State, had received a large document on foreign policy and someone innocently asked whether the various policy recommendations had been coordinated. "One of the wits of the Staff replied, 'Yes, coordinated by stapling.'"

To Dorothy Fosdick

September 29, 1950

Dear Dorothy:

Many thanks for your letter and Senator Connally's statement. Lord knows when I will have a chance to read it but it will be a useful "reference work."

I am happy to hear that coordination in the State Department is by stapling — as usual. There has been no change in Illinois either.

I hear indirectly that you may be sent out to the frontier for some more speaking and I hope you will not overlook Springfield, its Executive Mansion, and its Governor!

Affectionately,

Porter McKeever visited Springfield several times and talked with Stevenson about joining the Governor's staff. Several obstacles arose in their negotiations, the chief ones being the low salary and a possible misinterpretation of McKeever's presence on the local scene. In a letter of September 28, 1950, James W. Mulroy brought up these difficulties:

> First, let me tell you that I do not see any way in which we can get
> more than eight thousand dollars per year for you. . . . If the Gov-
> ernor is willing and able to supplement your salary, whatever he
> could give you would, of course, be in addition to the eight thousand
> dollars. I must say that he is not overloaded with funds but he prob-
> ably could get you some additional money and it could be worked

---

field from his farm at Libertyville. Artie, who was accustomed to seventy acres for roaming and chasing rabbits, adjusted to mansion life with difficulty.

[305]

out all right. . . . I am not so sure that you will like having to stay in the background for several months. To be quite frank about it, there is, in my opinion, a very real danger that some newspapers and some politicians may feel that the Governor has brought on a friend from the State Department to help him set his cap for the White House or Acheson's job etc. etc. They are likely to set up a great hue and cry as only the Chicago Tribune can and as only some of our "distinguished" legislators can. I would not be loyal to the Governor if I didn't tell you that I don't want to see him take this sort of "heat" until such time as his legislative program has a decent chance to be presented and passed by the legislature.

To Porter McKeever

September 30, 1950

Dear Porter:

Jim Mulroy has shown me his letter to you. I think it states the apprehensions that have been developing of late. However, I need the help and you want to come, so I am quite reconciled to taking such heat as the situation may generate. If we handle it well and you stay in the background for a few months, I think it will work without too much embarrassment.

As I have said before, writing — good writing — and saying something thoughtful and coherently is my greatest problem. I simply *can't* use the conventional banalities of politicians, even if I should. On the other hand, speech-making will decline sharply in the spring due to the pressure of the legislature, but there will be a large grist of research and writing all the same. We are not without talent or competence, but I can't afford to have too much of Carl McGowan's time given to creative writing when his substantive load cannot be neglected and is bound to increase.

I hope the salary that Mulroy mentioned will suffice. There is the usual budget problem, but the future should hold some promise of improvement.

As to timing, you can write your own ticket.

I have been following the [United Nations General] Assembly avidly, and I sometimes wonder how anyone could leave that happy, exciting turmoil for this! But there are compensations here too — perhaps!

Warm regards.

Yours,

To Frank Annunzio [155]

October 2, 1950

Dear Frank:

Some months ago I told you that I wanted a reduction in the Department of Labor, and I believe you agreed to review the situation. I have heard nothing about developments and the matter appears again on my calendar. Please let me know what has been done.

Also, I wish you would have Mr. Bernstein [156] review for me the reasoning which underlies the provision of the Illinois statute forbidding disclosure of the names of unemployment compensation recipients. I am informed that an all-out campaign for modification of the Illinois law is incipient and I shall doubtless be confronted with the necessity for taking a position on this matter before long. I am informed that there is no federal law prohibiting such disclosure.

Sincerely yours,

To William I. Flanagan [157]

[October 2, 1950?] [158]

Mr. Flanagan —

I have told Annunzio that I want him to review his information officers with a view to cutting from 7 to 4. I suppose I'll have a report from him saying why its difficult but I'll follow thru and I think he'll try to co-operate. If you hear nothing please remind [me] again in a month.

AES

To Leonard Schwartz [159]

October 6, 1950

Dear Lennie:

Miss Evans tells me that you have had 15 pounds of catfish delivered to me, and I am full of gratitude. Soon, I will be full of catfish! Many thanks.

Sincerely yours,

[155] Director of the Department of Labor. A carbon copy of this letter is in the possession of William I. Flanagan.

[156] Samuel C. Bernstein, commissioner of unemployment compensation.

[157] This handwritten note is in the possession of Mr. Flanagan.

[158] Although undated, this note was probably written at the same time that Stevenson wrote to Annunzio on October 2, 1950, when Flanagan was trying to take some of the surplus press officers off the payroll of the Labor Department.

[159] The original of this note is in the possession of Mr. Schwartz.

To Mrs. Edison Dick [160]

October 6, 1950

Dear Jane:

I have just seen your letter about your mother's emergency operation.[161] I pray and hope and know that all will be well, and my heart is very much with you.

Please keep me informed about the progress as I should like very much to send her a little "bunch" at the right time — something old-fashioned, like me — but not like her! And give her my love and all good wishes.

Yours,

P.S. The matter of Russell McWilliams [162] I will take up with Joe Lohman [163] on Monday. I will be speaking in St. Louis that night and he will go over it with me.

P.P.S. A few more speeches like the enclosed by Lottie Holman O'Neill [164] and the Democrats will have little to worry about in Illinois!

A.E.S.

To Mrs. Edison Dick [165]

October 8, 1950

. . . Flash! Bulletin! — Extra!

Joe Lohman reports Parole Bd will rec[ommend] executive clemency for R. McWilliams! — which means he could apply for a parole on next Board docket — i.e. next month. Careful now! This is confidential until papers received & approved by a flinty hearted Governor who is

---

[160] The original of this letter is in the possession of Mrs. Dick.

[161] Mrs. Dick's mother had cancer.

[162] In 1931, Russell McWilliams was sentenced to death for robbery and murder. Many people were shocked by the severe sentence because of his youth (he was under eighteen) and his previous good record. Mrs. Dick became involved through Mrs. Harry Neuberger, a member of the New Jersey Prison Board, who took an interest in the case. In April, 1950, the two women went to Springfield and talked to Stevenson about it. McWilliams was a model prisoner. He was paroled on January 31, 1951, and discharged by expiration of sentence on February 6, 1956. After his parole he was employed by a large wholesale greenhouse in Massachusetts. He later married and acquired his own business. Letters to Carol Evans from Mrs. Edison Dick, March 10, 1969, and Illinois Parole and Pardon Board, May 7, 1969.

[163] Chairman of the Parole and Pardon Board.

[164] Mrs. O'Neill, an extremely conservative Republican, represented the 41st District in the Illinois State Senate.

[165] This handwritten letter is in the possession of Mrs. Dick.

now being charged by Republicans with having cut old age pensions. And him — an old man himself. . . .

To Mrs. Quincy Wright [166]

October 9, 1950

Dear Louise:

Miss Patricia Milligan, Springfield correspondent for the International New Service, tells me that she has been talking to you about a job with the Council. She is a bright, alert, tough-minded girl, whom I have seen since I have been in Springfield at press conferences. I think she evidently feels thoroughly frustrated in her present work and would make a financial sacrifice to get out of this journalistic "dead-end."

I know nothing about what you have discussed or her personal circumstances, but I know she is able, industrious, humorous, and "conditioned" in a hard school in competition with bright boys on the way up the wire service ladder.

This is gratuitous.

Yours,

To Robert M. Hutchins [167]

October 11, 1950

Dear Hutchins:

The Governor is not ashamed to be seen with the President of that subversive institution,[168] and if you and your lady have a similar liberal attitude, you would be most welcome on Friday, October 20, followed by the University of Washington v. University of Illinois football game at Urbana on Saturday, and conversational and intellectual exercises with the Governor on Sunday.

The telephone number here is Springfield 4604.

Yours,
ADLAI

Charles Becker, president of Franklin Life Insurance Company, with its home office in Springfield, gave Stevenson a chair that jiggled when

---

[166] Executive director of the Chicago Council on Foreign Relations.

[167] The original of this typewritten letter is in the Robert M. Hutchins collection at the University of Chicago Library.

[168] The University of Chicago was undergoing an attack from State Senator Paul Broyles and others for being a hotbed of radicalism.

plugged into an electrical outlet. It was supposed to be soothing as well as weight-reducing. (Stevenson did not use it often.)

To Charles Becker [169]

October 19, 1950

Dear Mr. Becker:

The "agitated" chair has arrived, and I have enjoyed some tranquil moments of agitation sitting in it! I can't say I have seen any perceptible diminution of my waistline, but I am hopeful.

I tried to reach you on the phone today to get you and Mrs. Becker over for dinner and an exhibition. Let me know when you get back to town and we will arrange a convenient date for an expert demonstration.

Many, many thanks.

Sincerely yours,

Stevenson's former law firm, Sidley, Austin, Burgess & Harper, was one of Chicago's largest and maintained a staff of approximately half a dozen "messenger boys." They were usually young men working part-time while attending college. Richard Uckena, who joined the messenger service, was an older man already retired from business but wanting to be partially active.

To Richard C. Uckena

October 20, 1950

Dear Mr. Uckena:

I understand that you called at my office the other day and I am most disappointed to have missed you. I remember so well all the encouragement you used to give me for getting into politics. Sometimes I would like to wring your neck!

With warm regards.

Sincerely yours,

Edward J. Kelly, mayor of Chicago from 1933 to 1947, died on October 20, 1950. Stevenson took part in a memorial radio broadcast on that date.[170]

[169] A copy is in A.E.S., P.U.L.
[170] The text is based on a carbon copy.

The names of some men and women live long after they are gone. Edward J. Kelly is such a name, and it will be remembered for years to come in the company of those who built and embellished Chicago — the second city of the United States and the crossroads of the modern world.

His origins were humble. Born in the tumultuous stock yards district, the melting pot of Chicago, he was typically American, a product of the tumult and struggle of growing cities forever bursting their seams.

He was raised in a hard, practical, realistic school, and he rose to great eminence and influence in the public life of his county. But he never rose above the common people he loved so well; he never lost touch with them and their trials and hopes and fears. He never forgot that the little people are the only important people, and somehow he seemed to know that many things are revealed to the humble that are hidden from the great.

Like so many public figures who must take positions, who *have* responsibility and must *exercise* it, who must manage men to attain ends, who must *do,* not *talk,* he was and he will be a center of controversy for a long time. We would be bold and foolish to assign his place in the history of Chicago and of our troubled times.

But of one thing we may be sure: Here was a leader! — Strong, adroit and tireless, he guided the destiny of Chicago as its Mayor longer than anyone in history. He loved Chicago as few men love their home towns, and its splendid lake front will be his enduring monument.

Never too busy to help in charitable enterprises and the inspiration of many, a champion of civil rights, of social justice, better living conditions, of all the humane causes of his time upon our stage, he will be mourned by thousands. And he will be studied by students of American politics as a leader who was never afraid to lead. We will miss Ed Kelly.

The legislature during Stevenson's administration was dominated by downstate representation as the result of a failure to redistrict the state properly. In addition, politicians from rural downstate Illinois bore a traditional suspicion and distrust of "big-city" Chicagoans. In order to better his performance with the legislature in 1951, Stevenson asked the advice of many people, including Lieutenant Governor Sherwood Dixon, who wrote him at length on the subject on October 19, 1950. Dixon expressed his exasperation at the "inadequate way some of our people presented their cases [to the 1949 legislature]. Often they knew so little about the bills they were plugging that they could not answer simple

*questions put to them from the floor." He suggested that the Governor
choose the bills that would constitute the heart of his program and select
the man he expected to rely on to carry each one through the legislature
so that those who introduced the bills would have time to educate themselves on their assigned subjects. He pointed out that "nearly every downstate member of both houses appears to be suspicious of well dressed
strangers," especially from Chicago. He confessed that he had no idea
who might be acceptable. "But if you can do so I would certainly urge
you to hire a legislative liaison man who has had experience in either
house, who has some native shrewdness and diplomacy, and who wears
a celluloid collar and a made up tie and who reeks of the barnyard."*

To Sherwood Dixon [171]

October 23, 1950

Dear Sherwood:

Many thanks for your letter. It is helpful. But where, oh where, do I
find that paragon of simplicity and shrewdness, the diplomat in a
celluloid collar? I will hope for a miracle.

Yours,

ADLAI

To Mrs. Ralph Hines

October 27, 1950

Dear Betty:

I am *hoping* to come East for the Harvard-Princeton football game on
November 11. If by any chance the boys can get off,[172] and I likewise,
what prospect would there be for the four of us having dinner with you
on Friday night, November 10, in New York?

I am getting so old and irresponsible that I even thought it might be
fun if we all went to the theater, which in these parts means only South
Pacific. If you can join up in this important project and could make a
theater suggestion I [will] have my "contacts" get the tickets, but I
should proceed at once.

Love,

---

[171] The original of this typewritten letter is in the possession of Mr. Dixon.

[172] During the school year 1950–1951, Adlai III was a student at Harvard University, Borden attended the Choate School, Wallingford, Connecticut, and John Fell
was at Milton Academy, Milton, Massachusetts.

To Adlai E. Stevenson III

October 27, 1950

Dear Bear:

It occurs to me that it might be fun — if my schedule permits — to pick you all up in the plane on Friday afternoon and fly into New York in time for dinner with Aunt Betty (if she is available) and go to the theater together that night.

Could you let me know PROMPTLY what time you could be free Friday afternoon. Also, please be good enough to call up someone at Milton and find out if John Fell could get off in time to meet me with you ,at the Boston airport at, say, three or four o'clock Friday afternoon. We could fly down and pick up Borden at Meridon [Meriden] or Hartford and get on into New York in time for dinner.

It would be a great convenience to a busy "statesman" if you could check into this and let me know promptly. I believe I can arrange it with Borden's school but I don't want to proceed unless I know you and John Fell can do it.

If this is unsatisfactory I shall probably arrive in Boston Friday evening and we will start out Saturday morning, pick up Borden and fly direct to Princeton.

Love,

Benjamin P. Thomas, the well-known Lincoln scholar, and Stevenson were friends of long standing and renewed their close ties when Stevenson moved to Springfield, Thomas's home. He and Mrs. Thomas were frequent guests at the mansion, and the two men spent hours discussing matters of mutual interest. Through Mr. Thomas, Stevenson added to his store of knowledge not only of Abraham Lincoln but of the history of Illinois.

To Benjamin P. Thomas [173]

October 31, 1950

Dear Ben:

On Sunday, November 19 the Chicago Historical Society is opening an exhibit of all the copies of the Gettysburg Address on the "Four Score and Seven Years Ago" Anniversary of its delivery. Evidently I am expected to make a short speech — perhaps 10 minutes or more. I am a

[173] The original is in the possession of Mrs. Benjamin P. Thomas.

little vague on what I should attempt to talk about, but I presume Lincoln, the Gettysburg Address, Illinois, war and peace would not be wholly inappropriate!

If by any chance you have any ideas whatever that you could put to paper that I could hold in my trembling hand, I would be fortified — not to mention grateful!

Very truly yours,

To Alicia Patterson [174]

[probably Sunday, November 5, 1950]

. . . Its Sunday morning and I'm back in Sp[ringfield]. for the first time in a solid week — and off the "hustings" for the first time in two weeks — of hell! Four performances in Rock Island last night — three in Bloomington noon & afternoon etc. They may not like me too much but the politicians can't say that I haven't done my bit for "the ticket" & then some, but they probably will! One day this week I spoke 8 times between 10 AM & midnight in Chicago and suburbs — and now, thank God, its all over but the shouting and I can get back to my regular job full time. Indeed I'm at it right now & find in the pile your precious note & the clips from Newsday. . . .

I thought we had a little excitement built up here in Ill. but from what I hear about N.Y. state & city, Ill must be a wake. I hope you can get Macy; [175] he's the kind of character that louses up this political business and freezes the bright young hopefuls out. But I suspect its like trying to knock the GOP out of Lake County, or the Dems out of Chi. But who am I to be complaining about machines & bosses, me "the creature of Kelly, Nash, Arvey et al"!! . . .

To John Fell Stevenson

November 5, 1950

Dear John Fell:

I have your letter today on my return to Springfield after a week of campaigning around Chicago. I was glad to hear you had a pleasant visit and the theater with Mrs. Mitchell.[176]

This afternoon I talked to Dr. Perry [177] on the telephone and he tells

[174] This handwritten letter is in the possession of Adlai E. Stevenson III.

[175] W. Kingsland Macy, Republican congressman from the 1st District of New York. He was defeated for reelection in 1950 by Ernest Greenwood, a liberal Democrat.

[176] The William H. Mitchells, of Lake Forest, were old friends of the Stevensons. Their son attended Milton Academy at the same time as John Fell.

[177] Arthur Perry, headmaster of Milton Academy.

me you cannot go to Princeton because they have a rule forbidding boys to take a week-end more than a hundred miles from school. Evidently it makes them so tired it affects their work over the following week. Moreover, I understand your work has not been good of late. Dr. Perry tells me he has had a talk with you, and I hope you realize what a serious business school is and that after the trouble you had last year you will get to work now and "hit the ball" hard and straight.

I am fearfully disappointed to miss this chance to see you, and I suppose I will have to wait now until the Christmas holidays.

Mother tells me she is planning to come to have Thanksgiving with you all, and I wish I could be there too. Meanwhile, you may be sure that Princeton will demolish Harvard with the greatest ease.

Now get to work!

Love,

To Borden Stevenson

November 5, 1950

Dear Bordie:

I have written Mr. Steele [178] as per the enclosed, telling him I hoped you could get into New York by Friday evening, November 10, by 7:00 o'clock. Please go to Aunt Betty's apartment . . . where Adlai and Tim [Ives] and I will meet you. We will have dinner together and go to the theater and go down to Princeton Saturday morning. You can stay overnight there with me and I will get you back to New York in time to catch a train to Wallingford, or New Haven, at whatever time you have to be back to school. Unfortunately, Milton will not let John Fell leave because of a rigid rule they have there, and I hope the same does not apply in your case. Adlai will be coming down by airplane from Boston Friday afternoon, and I believe Tim will come by automobile.

I hope the work is going well and that your heart and mind are at Choate and not Farmington! [179]

Love,

To Adlai E. Stevenson III

November 5, 1950

Dear Bear:

I have just talked with Dr. Perry at Milton and he tells me that he

[178] Associate headmaster and dean of students at the Choate School.
[179] Borden was interested in a girl attending Miss Porter's School at Farmington, Connecticut.

cannot let John Fell off this week-end. They seem to have, as your letter suggested, a rule forbidding boys to go any such distances for a week-end because they come back invariably too tired and it impairs the work the following week. He said he could make no exceptions, so I guess I have to swallow my medicine although it is most distasteful and irritating. I suppose there was some such rule when you were there, although I don't recall hearing about it before.

I wish you would plan, therefore, to catch a plane to New York Friday afternoon in time to be there for dinner. Go to Aunt Betty's apartment, which is 237 East 61st Street (Telephone Templeton 8-8170), and tell Tim [Ives] to do likewise. I will see what I can do about Borden, and we will all go to the theater and down to Princeton on one of the special trains Saturday morning. I will be able to put up Borden with me for the night and I presume you can sponge on one of your friends on the campus. Perhaps you better get a reservation returning to Boston from New York late Sunday afternoon, and we will get back to town somehow in time for you to catch your plane. I expect to stay in New York over Monday to visit the United Nations and my old friends and do some errands, returning to Chicago Monday afternoon or Tuesday morning.

Love,

P.S. Tell Tim that he can use John Fell's ticket to the game and won't need one for himself.

To Benjamin P. Thomas [180]

November 6, 1950

Dear Ben:

I have just read Stevenson's best speech! I wish you could be there on November 19 to hear it, the shattering applause and to witness the orator's unctuous modesty. But even here in Springfield perhaps you'll hear his unspoken, fervent thanks to a ghost among ghosts!

Yours,
ADLAI

To Mr. and Mrs. Hermon D. Smith

November 7, 1950

Dear Smiths:

It is my understanding that Mr. and Mrs. Smith and son, Farwell, will

[180] The original is in the possession of Mrs. Benjamin P. Thomas.

arrive in Springfield Friday afternoon, November 17, at 2:50 P.M. or 8:00 P.M. (as they wish), and that on Saturday we will drive to Champaign, lunching with Dr. [George] Stoddard before the Illinois–Ohio State game. Afterward instead of returning here we will go on to Chicago and have dinner with Marshall Field, Jr., and thereafter attend the Sun-Times Festival — whatever that is.

If there are alterations in the foregoing, please inform me at your leisure.

Sincerely yours,

P.S. I find I have also invited the Keith Carpenters [181] and I *believe* they have accepted.

A.E.S.

Thomas S. Matthews planned to attend the Harvard-Princeton football game with Stevenson and his sons on November 10 at Princeton. Mr. and Mrs. Lewis B. Cuyler, relatives of Matthews, who lived in a large house in Princeton, offered to take in the overflow of guests.

To T. S. Matthews

November 7, 1950

Dear Tom:

The horizon is bright and the prospects good that the Governor of Illinois, accompanied by two sons and one nephew (one son detained at Milton by travel rules) will arrive at Princeton by special train from New York in time for the game Saturday, and are still counting on a couple of beds with you and Buz Cuyler Saturday night. If the latter proves inconvenient to the Cuyler establishment, please advise and I will canvass other possibilities.[182]

Yours,

To Alicia Patterson [183]

[probably November 9, 1950]

. . . Bruised but not bloody, I take my pencil in hand to report that

---

[181] Friends who lived in Lake Forest, Illinois.

[182] Matthews wrote Stevenson on November 19, 1950: "Margery [Cuyler] liked you very much indeed, and in fact regards you as a kind of surprise I sprang on them; why hadn't I told them what an intelligent and understanding person you were?"

[183] This handwritten letter is in the possession of Adlai E. Stevenson III.

[317]

the Dems got the pants trimmed off 'em here.[184] If my life's been hell so far, I've seen nothing yet, when that Rep[ublican]. legislature goes to work on me in Jan. Ho Hum — guess I asked for it, and no complaints. Sorry to lose Lucas & I'll hope for the best from Dirksen who can probably reverse himself again & make some sense — but for how long with your esteemed kinsman [185] pulling the wires?

. . . The scribble is worse than usual. I'm on a train en route to Chi for a midnight meeting with Arvey, Paul Douglas for breakfast & then Mayor K[ennelly] — I'm going to begin asserting myself a little & see if I can't get a decent guy, *my* guy, in as County Ch[airman]. in Cook County & start rehabilitating that organization. Arvey stubbed his toe badly & must quit anyway on account of his health. Douglas will go along with me & if that pompous Mayor will step down from his icy, lonesome throne we'll get a new shake & a new look in that groggy outfit — but I'll have to strike quickly. Then I'm going to jump on a plane & go East — gather up the boys & take them to the Harvard-Princeton football game — keep out of town & out of reach a couple of days & let the dust settle — I hope! I'll probably come back surreptitiously, but if [I] stay over Monday — to fill a long deferred date at the UN — I'll try to reach you by phone.

That testimonial to Newsday was fine and you have a right to be proud & happy — So am I! And a Dem. said it!! Must be a good sort.

I thought Lucas was going to win & you thought Dewey was close.[186] Great pair of political prophets.

A

A survey of the normally Republican precinct where Dixon State Hospital was located showed that the Republicans had retained their voting strength there. Fred Hoehler, director of Public Welfare, with Stevenson's consent, had kept on many of the capable Republicans in patronage jobs in the hospital, hoping it would influence their votes. It had not.

---

[184] In the November elections, Everett M. Dirksen defeated U.S. Senator Scott Lucas, and both houses of the Illinois General Assembly went Republican.

[185] Robert R. McCormick.

[186] Thomas E. Dewey was defeated by President Truman in 1948 by slightly over 3 million votes out of more than 48 million cast. Opinion polls had indicated that Dewey would win.

To Fred K. Hoehler [187]

November 10, 1950

Mr. Hoehler —
   I'm discouraged!

A.E.S.

*In 1949 the 66th General Assembly established a commission "to sur-
vey the entire structure of state government and of the organization,
functions and interrelationships of all units thereof, including advisory
and non-executive bodies." This was patterned after the Hoover Commission on the national level; in Illinois it became known as the
"Schaefer Commission," after its chairman, Walter V. Schaefer, appointed
by the Governor.*

*Toward the end of 1950 the commission had all but completed its
recommendations for changes in the state government to be submitted to the legislature the following year.*

*On November 13, 1950, John Stuart, of Chicago, wrote Stevenson that
Kendall I. Lingle, executive vice president of the Citizens Public Personnel Association, of Chicago, had informed him that studies of the commission covered many of the same problems as those of the Hoover Commission and suggested that the two efforts might be merged instead of
setting up two organizations in the state. Stuart suggested that if Stevenson thought anything would come of a combined effort he would get
his group together and they could discuss it.*

To John Stuart [188]

November 15, 1950

Dear Mr. Stuart:
   I am taking the liberty of passing along your letter of November 13
to Walter Schaefer, the Chairman of our "Little Hoover" Commission,
against the possibility that you might find a mutually convenient time
for him to tell you something about the work of his Commission and
perhaps make some suggestions as to how a citizens committee for the
Hoover report in Illinois could help with our program for reorganization

---

[187] The original is in the possession of Mrs. Fred K. Hoehler.
[188] A carbon copy of this letter is in the possession of Walter V. Schaefer.

of the state government. I am sure we are going to need all the help we can get!

With all good wishes and my warm thanks for your continued interest and support.

Sincerely yours,

To Walter V. Schaefer [189]

November 15, 1950

Note the attached correspondence. If you could find time to have lunch with John Stuart sometime I think he might be helpful in organizing public support for the Schaefer Commission recommendations. You ought to know him anyway.

A.E.S.

In a letter to the Governor dated November 17, 1950, Hugh L. Moore, of Columbia, Missouri, wrote that he could not support Truman again since he was against a third term for any President. In addition, he felt the Democratic party was in need of new ideas, and he wondered if Stevenson might consider the nomination for President in 1952. Moore also recalled meeting the Governor's Grandfather Stevenson in 1892.

To Hugh L. Moore

November 22, 1950

Dear Mr. Moore:

I am more than a little flattered by your kind letter and much touched by your happy recollections of my grandfather.

I am so preoccupied with my job here that I have entertained no thoughts of further political activity. I have no objection whatever to your interest in me, as you can well understand, but I really think I have found the measure of my competence here in Illinois — and then some! What's more, my ambitions are sharply limited. But I felt I should take the opportunity to serve my state as my family have for three generations before me.

With my thanks and kind regards, I am

Sincerely yours,

Stevenson addressed the Chicago Historical Society on November 19, 1950, using the draft that had been written for him by Mr. Thomas.

[189] The original of this memorandum is in the possession of Mr. Schaefer.

To Benjamin P. Thomas [190]

November 22, 1950

Dear Ben:

I am sure you heard the reverberating applause on Sunday for the voice of Stevenson and the words of Thomas Copy as delivered is enclosed for your ghostly scrap book. And a thousand thanks.

Yours,

ADLAI

During Stevenson's Harvard Law School days he was a frequent visitor at the home of the Loring Underwoods, of Belmont, Massachusetts. The Underwoods had three young charming daughters, Lorna, Nina and Esther. Lorna, who was a particular friend of Stevenson's, later married George Sagendorph. When Stevenson was in Princeton for the Harvard-Princeton football game he unexpectedly met Lorna, who lived there. He had not seen her in many years.

To Mrs. George Sagendorph [191]

November 26, 1950

Lorna dear —

I'm sorry we got away from the Cuylers too early for your call. I rounded up the boys on the campus, went to chapel, took them to call on Pres. Dodds,[192] had a good walk about the campus . . . & back to N.Y. in time to ship them off to school. It was a good lark — and not the least of it was the glimpse of you and the enchanting Lorna.[193] It all compensated for the accumulated horrors that awaited me here.

I hope I can come back to Princeton, but God knows when. You've chosen wisely to go there. You've been lost too long in the "Valley." Be calm, serene and beautiful as you are & life will bring you much thats good —

Love

AD

Work on the budget to be presented to the 67th General Assembly in 1951 continued through the intersession. In July, 1950, Stevenson re-

[190] The original is in the possession of Mrs. Benjamin P. Thomas.
[191] This handwritten letter is in the possession of Mrs. Sagendorph.
[192] Harold Dodds, president of Princeton University.
[193] Mrs. Sagendorph's daughter.

quested agency and department heads to hold their operating expenditures to the level established in the fiscal year 1950, or less. That level generally was 10 per cent under the appropriations made for the 66th biennium. He also requested early and advance approval for new programs and capital outlays before they were incorporated into formal budget requests. Budget requests had come in slowly, and most of the major departments had yet to submit their requests. Stevenson was fearful that the Republicans would take advantage of this tardiness to accuse him of wild spending and take credit to themselves for his economies.

To George W. Mitchell [194]

November 27, 1950

I wish you would drop what you are doing, if possible, long enough to draft a further letter to each of the Code Directors and Department heads, with copies to the elected officials, reiterating my determination to hold the operating budgets down to the irreducible minimum in the next biennium, and referring to the letter of July.

This letter should summarize our expenses during the past biennium, pointing out the favorable features of our control and the explanation for increases where there have been increased expenditures.

I should also like to point out in this letter that in view of the national tax burden I am determined to avoid, if possible, any tax increases in the next biennium and including something to indicate that that is entirely possible.

The purpose of this letter is publicity. I see no reason for sitting here any longer and letting the Republicans take the leadership in economy when we have been practicing it for so long. I think you will see the point and the necessity for getting out something before they start issuing statements that they are going to force me to economize and frustrate my plans for additional taxes and more spending.

Sincerely yours,

A Princeton classmate of Stevenson wrote the Governor that his son expected to be a part of the entourage of the Princeton Triangle Club in its annual show in Chicago on the first of January, 1951. He suggested if Stevenson went to the play that he go backstage to meet his son.

---

[194] This memorandum was marked *"Personal and Confidential — Read and Destroy."* Carbon copies were sent to William I. Flanagan and James W. Mulroy. A carbon copy is in the possession of Mr. Flanagan.

To Mord M. Bogie

November 29, 1950

Dear Mord:

So the Bogies are invading Illinois again. I will alert the State Police and stand at the bridge myself, at least long enough to be sure that is is Mord Bogie III and his father.

You were good to warn me, and I hope I can get to Chicago for the Triangle show for a glimpse of your young man. The latter you could readily arrange if you were to call on the Governor with him some dark or sunny day. Indeed, you could stay the night and make the Governor very happy.

Yours,

The following letter was sent out to agency and department heads.[195]

December 7, 1950

Except for meeting our highway needs, I do not wish to ask for new taxes in the next session of the Legislature.

Thanks to the economies you have already made and to increased revenue collections, the state's finances are better than we anticipated earlier. Even with higher costs and some large unavoidable new expenditures, the state's present services can be maintained without new taxes — but only with your *very positive cooperation.*

Granting the extreme urgency for many further expenditures, I think we must put first things first — and *mobilization for national security is now our first obligation.*[196] Faced with steep increases in Federal taxes, with more inflation and controls, no dollars should be spent at this time which can be saved, no buildings built which can be deferred, and no manpower used which can be conserved.

By my order of July 1949, operating expenditures of the agencies under my control were fixed at 10 per cent less than the appropriations voted by the legislature. This precaution has proved very helpful and I am grateful for your cooperation.

In July 1950, I wrote you that the policy to be followed in budget requests for the next biennium was the reduction of spending to the absolute minimum.

[195] This copy is in the possession of Miss Maude Myers.

[196] U.S. armed intervention in Korea had been ordered on June 27 by the President, and on the same day the United Nations invoked military sanctions against North Korea.

I expressly requested you to do two things:

(1) Hold your operating expenditures to the lowest possible level, and generally not to exceed that of the fiscal year 1950.

(2) Omit from your budget requests all new programs and capital outlays not approved by me in advance.

From the budget requests filed thus far, it is apparent that this policy is not being strictly observed. This is a reminder to those who have not yet submitted their budgets. To those who have, it is a request that they be promptly re-surveyed if they do not now comply.

While uniform limitation of expenditures is not possible, I am depending on *you* to know how you can best adjust your operations to the overall policy.

In this administration we cannot measure accomplishment solely by comparisons, however favorable, with past history. Our problem is the present. It is not enough that we are doing better than has been done before. We must be doing the *very best* we can.

Sincerely yours,

Fred K. Hoehler, director of the Department of Public Welfare, appointed Miss Dora Somerville as a social worker at the Geneva School for Girls. Lawrence Irvin, who handled patronage requests, wrote Stevenson on November 22, 1950, that he had just learned of the appointment: "I would like to know if you have an understanding with Director Hoehler which authorizes him to employ such professional personnel without approval from our office. If such is the case it is certainly agreeable with me as long as I understand your arrangements with the Director. All other departments automatically clear such matters with our office."

In response to Irvin's memorandum, Hoehler on December 2, 1950, wrote the Governor: "I am not interested in Miss Somerville's political background . . . but I am terribly concerned for fear that, if we did clear this and anybody talked to her, we might lose Miss Somerville as we have some other professional people. I am sure that [she] is loyal to you because one of her reasons given in accepting this position was that she was satisfied that under your leadership work could be done without too much interference of various kinds. This is the only explanation I have to offer, and this position classification is listed with a group of professional jobs on which I asked that we be allowed to make placements without clearance."

Irvin pointed out to the Governor: "It just seems to me you could have made a little 'political hay' with someone like Senator [Christopher C.]

Wimbish, or Representative Corneal Davis,[197] *etc., on an appointment such as this without jeopardizing the department!"*

To Lawrence Irvin [198]

December 9, 1950

RE: Miss Dora Somerville

I have authorized Director Hoehler to employ specialized professional personnel without the approval of the patronage office. But I have asked him, as a result of this case, to try to bear in mind the possible political advantage of prior information to us about prospective employment and he assures me that he will keep it in mind hereafter. Should similar cases arise I hope you will use your judgment about letting me know in advance so that I can mention it to members of the legislature who might be concerned. I think your point is very well taken and so does Director Hoehler.

A.E.S.

John S. Miller took on the task of helping to raise money for the Stevenson for Governor Committee Fund. He was given some assistance by another Chicago attorney, Clarence Ross.

To John S. Miller

December 15, 1950

Dear John:

Many thanks for the checks. They will help a lot. Your contribution to the Stevenson for Governor Committee fund will clear this month.

I am glad that Clarence Ross is going to do a little canvassing. It is hard to get any money from the usual sources except during campaign times, but I think the non-political people who are not concerned so much with winning or losing as they are the quality of the service could well be approached most any time.

I hope to see you soon.

Yours,

P.S. And Merry Christmas!

---

[197] Miss Somerville, Senator Christopher C. Wimbish, and Representative Davis were Negroes.

[198] The original of this typewritten memorandum is in the possession of Mr. Irvin.

*Robert M. Hutchins resigned as chancellor of the University of Chicago
to join the Fund for the Republic, Inc., in Pasadena, California.*

To Robert M. Hutchins

December 20, 1950

Dear Bob:

Well, as long as no one has asked me to comment I will say merely
that I think it's a contemptible trick — walking out on Chicago, its great
University, its lovely climate, its fascinating Governor — and just as we
were about to enjoy those long, tranquil evenings of good conversation;
I mean Vesta and me.[199]

Merry Christmas — you louse!

Yours,

P.S. Pasadena — phooey!

*Kent Chandler, who lived in Lake Forest, Illinois, made a half-hour
drive to and from his work each day, a trip he found boring. He told a
friend, who also knew Stevenson, that he had fallen into the habit of
counting the number of trailer trucks going both ways and making a
record of them when he got to his office. The friend suggested humor-
ously that the Governor should bestow a title on Chandler.*

To Kent Chandler

December 21, 1950

Dear Mr. Chandler:

This Christmas season is the more joyous for me because I can now
officially designate you "Chief Official Spotter of Trucks Northeastern
District of Illinois." I have followed for many months your exemplary
work in this all important field which is so heavily freighted with the
hopes of all mankind. And it is with no small satisfaction that I can
now, without further hesitation, bestow the title of Chief Official Spotter
upon you in recognition of your brilliant service. I shall ask nothing in
return — except a continuation of your devotion to the same enlightened

[199] Mr. Hutchins replied to Stevenson's letter on December 27, 1950: "That's why
I'm leaving — I fear those conversations between you and Vesta [Mrs. Hutchins]. I
have gone, like John the Baptist, to prepare the way for your coming in '52. We are
reserving a rocker on the porch for you. Please come to visit *us* — soon."

work — until it has completely absorbed you. When that day of utter bliss arrives you may be sure that we have a nice warm bed awaiting you in the Disturbed Ward at Elgin [200] with six whole inches on each side — plenty of interesting company — and even a toilet on the same floor.

Congratulations! And carry on my dear colleague!

Sincerely,

All three of Stevenson's sons were with him during the Christmas holidays in 1950, and the old mansion was aglow with lights, laughter and parties.

To Mrs. Edison Dick [201]

December 26, 1950

. . . Christmas 1950 — is a delirious day for me — all the boys, gay, handsome, happy — . . . from the words of the Prophet — I *have* seen the goodness of the Lord in the land of the living . . .

Maybe it isn't such a bad and ugly world after all. Maybe Christmas 1950 was the *best* Christmas!

. . . The enclosed was written by two [of] the newspaper correspondents — both girls! — stationed here in Spfd [Springfield] & sung by the multitude today — much to my surprise and pleasure. It reminded me of a birthday once upon a time . . .[202]

---

[200] Elgin State Hospital for the Insane.

[201] This handwritten letter is in the possession of Mrs. Dick.

[202] The enclosure, entitled "A Christmas Cantata," was written by Miss Patricia Milligan, of the International News Service, and Mrs. Millicent Lane, of the Associated Press. The recitative was a takeoff on "The Night Before Christmas." The lyrics, set to the tunes of songs popular at the time, reflected many of the Governor's troubles. It ended:

The Governor shouted, "Enough is enough!
Why, not even Truman gets all of this guff!"
And he ran to the window and, hands over face,
He cried: "Farewell, world!" and leaped into
   space.
He felt himself falling, but to his surprise,
He seemed to be floating. He opened his eyes.
'Twas morning and Christmas and over his bed,
To his stocking was fastened a greeting which
   read:

"Here's hoping for a white Christmas.
"Here's hoping things will come your way.
Though you may be weary,
Things aren't so dreary,
So have a happy holiday.

"Here's hoping for a good new year,
In everything you plan to do.
May your skies be shining and blue,
And may all your hopes and plans come true."
"MERRY CHRISTMAS!"

Part Three

1951

E arly in January, 1951, the Illinois General Assembly met again in regular session, this time with a Republican majority in both houses. Although this did not seem at first to hold out much promise to Stevenson for passage of his legislative program, in actuality he fared better than in 1949, when he had had a slender Democratic majority in the House and a Republican Senate. By 1951 he was more skillful with the legislature. In addition, some of the more enlightened Republicans were helpful to him.

Highlights of his legislative program included adoption of a tax on cigarettes imported into the state, which yielded much-needed revenue; establishment of a civil defense agency; repairs to existing highways and construction of new roads, payment for which was to come from proposed truck license fees and an increase in the motor fuel tax; proposals for amending the constitution under the Gateway Amendment as suggested by the Schaefer Commission; a proposal for a single board of higher education; authorization for the Welfare Department to charge patients or their families, where they were able to pay, for cost of care and maintenance in the state's hospitals; extension of research in mental illness at the Galesburg hospital; city aid and home rule, especially for Chicago; extension of the grand jury in Chicago; redistricting of the state from twenty-six to twenty-five congressional districts; and revision of mining laws and parole laws.

The most important legislation passed, and that for which Stevenson fought hardest and longest, was the increased gasoline tax and truck license fees. Part of this was the result of a campaign to educate the public and of many private sessions spent with representatives of the transportation industry. Almost unanimous newspaper support was also extremely effective.[1]

[1] For an account of this legislation see Kenneth S. Davis, *A Prophet in His Own Country: The Triumphs and Defeats of Adlai E. Stevenson* (New York: Doubleday & Company, 1957), pp. 352–353.

Although Stevenson considered a new mining code of great importance, he was unable to rally support from those it would affect and the senators from the mining districts.

Of the 166 bills introduced to carry out the proposals by the Schaefer Commission for reorganizing the state government, 78 were passed, and about a dozen other bills growing out of its findings were also enacted. However, no legislation basically affecting the code departments was passed.[2]

Of the total of 1,040 bills passed by the legislature, Stevenson felt compelled to veto 134. The most important veto was that of Senate Bill 102, the so-called "Broyles Bill," making it a crime to advocate overthrowing the federal government, defining "subversive" organizations and making them illegal, and requiring public officials to sign a loyalty oath.

During World War II many state and local governments accumulated sizable treasury surpluses. Because the greater share of building materials was diverted to the war effort, most states, including Illinois, had fallen behind in public construction, and all were faced after the war with bursting demands for public services, long neglected. In 1949, when Stevenson took office, he found a surplus in the state treasury, about half of which was already earmarked for deficiency appropriations and items already committed in the 1949–1951 budget. The balance was used mainly for education and welfare services, aid to municipalities and soldier bonus payments.

When budgeting began for the 1951–1953 biennium, Stevenson was faced with an extremely tight financial situation. He ordered his department heads to keep their costs to 10 per cent below the 1949 appropriations and to include no new programs or capital outlays without his approval. The major increases in the 1951–1953 budget were for common schools and higher education, additional aid to local governments, the Department of Public Welfare, increases in salaries of state employees, and disability assistance. There was no room in the budget for additional appropriations unless corresponding cuts were made in the Governor's recommendations.

During 1951 Stevenson made over fifty speeches, straying from the borders of Illinois only a few times. He attended and spoke at the Annual Governors' Conference at Gatlinburg, Tennessee; the National Convention of Young Democratic Clubs in St. Louis, where his aide Richard J. Nelson was elected president of that organization; the Wisconsin Democratic State Convention in Wausau, Wisconsin; and the 88th Anniversary of the Battlefield at Gettysburg, Pennsylvania.

[2] Mimeograph memorandum by J. Edward Day, "The Stevenson Administration — The First Three Years," May 7, 1952, pp. 36–37.

Chicago's mayoralty election fell on April 3, 1951, and Mayor Martin H. Kennelly was up for reelection. Stevenson supported his campaign with money and also made a "nonpartisan" radio address on behalf of the mayor.

In March, 1951, Stevenson appointed his former aide, Walter V. Schaefer, to the Illinois Supreme Court to fill a vacancy caused by the death of one of the justices whose term was due to expire in June of that year. Schaefer, who ran for the next full term during the early spring and summer, was given wholehearted support by Stevenson, and won the election.[3]

As part of the Lincoln's Birthday ceremonies in 1950, Stevenson attended a meeting of the Old Salem Lincoln League at Petersburg. At the meeting he suggested that the league sponsor a Lincoln play at New Salem State Park, Lincoln's home as a young man. The league made the suggestion a reality and the first performance was given on June 30, 1951. The drama was an excellent one, but the weather was rainy and the crowds disappointing. The play, according to Mrs. John Whitaker, a member of the league, could never have been staged without Stevenson's great interest and cooperation and that of his brother-in-law and sister, Mr. and Mrs. Ernest L. Ives.[4]

The year 1951 was not without its difficulties.

In July, when a Negro, Harvey Clark, and his family attempted to move into a white neighborhood in Cicero, near Chicago, a crowd gathered to protest. The Clarks left the building, but some of the young people in the crowd entered their apartment and tossed all the furniture into the street, where it was burned by the mob. Cicero police failed to disperse the crowd and called on Cook County Sheriff John Babb to help. The sheriff dispatched some police to the scene but the disorder continued, and finally, at the sheriff's request, Stevenson ordered National Guard troops to preserve order and prevent further mob violence.

On August 23, 1951, a story broke in the Chicago *Daily News* that eight state legislators and four state employees were stockholders in the Chicago Downs Association, which operated harness racing at Sportsmen's Park, near Chicago. Among those listed was Stevenson's executive

---

[3] At the Governor's urging, Richard J. Daley undertook the task of persuading the Cook County Democratic organization to make Schaefer the candidate and then to deliver the votes. Carl McGowan wrote: "The whole story is really one of what the combination of a strong Governor standing firmly for a good man, and a powerful and highly organized political organization, can do in combination. It was the power of the Organization to do good things like this under enlightened leadership that always made Adlai loath to get unnecessarily at odds with the politicians and also caused him to respect them greatly." Letter to Carol Evans, April 14, 1970.

[4] Letter to Carol Evans, July 4, 1968. Mr. Ives raised funds for the production and Mrs. Ives persuaded Kermit Hunter to write the play, *Forever This Land*.

secretary, James W. Mulroy, who held one thousand shares. The track had been used for running races until 1949 when the legislature gave the Illinois Harness Racing Commission authority to approve trotting races at regular racetracks. The twelve people listed as holding stock, the Daily News stated, had paid ten cents a share for the stock. The first dividend, in 1949, paid $1 a share; in 1950, $1.75 a share.

Mulroy declared that he knew nothing about the legislation until after it was enacted; that the stock had originally been offered to House Majority Leader Paul Powell after the track was in operation, with the suggestion that he sell the stock to his friends. Powell denied that the stock was a payoff. Mulroy in a letter to Hermon D. Smith on September 6, 1951, declared that he would welcome an investigation but that it would never happen "because no law had been broken." He also stated that he had had an opportunity to keep his name out of the papers when the story broke but he had declined because he knew he had done nothing wrong. Mulroy resigned as Stevenson's executive secretary on October 22, 1951.

On Saturday, December 22, 1951, an explosion occurred at Orient Mine No. 2 at West Frankfort, Illinois, in which 119 men were killed. Stevenson had made a serious attempt to get a revised mining code through the legislature, but on being assured that he would have no support from the unions, the operators, or the senators from the coal mining districts, he abandoned the measure for the 1951 session, hoping agreement could be reached on a program to be presented at the next session of the legislature.

In December, 1951, Stevenson revealed that the state had lost approximately ten million dollars in tax revenue when cigarettes with bogus tax stamps began to appear in the Chicago market following the theft of four tax metering machines. (Cigarette stamp counterfeiting was not unique to Illinois.) Raids by the state police resulted in seizure of half a million packages of cigarettes with fraudulent tax stamps. The police also found the four tax metering machines. No state employee was found to be guilty of collusion with the distributors of the cigarettes bearing the fraudulent tax stamps. The investigations by Stevenson and his special assistant attorney general, Ben W. Heineman, and his aide Carl Mc-Gowan, were conducted with the utmost secrecy, thus insuring success of the raids. Had Stevenson announced the theft of the machines at the time they were taken and his intention to catch the thieves, his efforts would likely have been doomed to failure, although he would have been praised publicly. Stevenson and his aides considered the solution of this crime to be a real coup, but during his campaign for the presidency in 1952 he was to hear much Republican oratory about the scandals of his administration, including this one.

During 1951 Stevenson received increasing attention by the press, both locally and nationally, as being an outstanding governor and qualified for high political office. In November a reporter from Time *magazine spent several days in Springfield and Chicago interviewing Stevenson and his aides and department heads for a cover story on the Governor, which appeared in the January 28, 1952, issue of that publication. He was also interviewed several times by Edwin A. Lahey, of the Chicago* Daily News *Washington bureau.*

Stevenson's relationship with President Harry S. Truman during the first three years of his administration was formal but cordial. His letters to the President consisted mostly of state business and invitations to appear and speak in Illinois. At the request of political friends he made a few suggestions to the President for appointments to offices, and, during 1951, he requested aid for havoc created by Illinois floods.

By the end of 1951 Stevenson still had made no announcement as to his political plans. He was displeased with John S. Boyle, state's attorney for Cook County, who had not handled well the cases involving the Cicero rioters. In addition, Boyle had been widely criticized for his handling of cases involving the Chicago syndicate gamblers, a murder committed by one of his own policemen, and several other incidents. Stevenson let the Cook County Democratic organization know that he preferred to run with someone else on the ticket and withheld his statement until after its choices were made. When Judge John Gutnecht was picked as the candidate for this office, Stevenson made his announcement — but not until after the first of the year.[5]

On January 3, 1951, Governor Stevenson addressed the 67th General Assembly in joint regular session.[6]

We meet today in joint session in accordance with the constitution. It is an ancient and agreeable parliamentary custom. It affords the Governor not only the rare privilege of entering this chamber in your presence, but an opportunity to do all the talking!

You are here as the representatives of almost nine million inhabitants of Illinois. For the confidence our sovereign, the people, have placed in you, I congratulate you. Those who are here for the first time I welcome to a public service both exacting and satisfying. On the veteran members whose influence rests upon experience and familiarity with our problems, falls the heaviest burden of leadership.

The executive branch will be at your service. The good that is done

[5] John Bartlow Martin, *Adlai Stevenson* (New York: Harper, 1952), pp. 113–114.
[6] *Message of Governor Adlai E. Stevenson to 67th General Assembly, January 3, 1951* (printed by the State of Illinois). Governor Stevenson repeated many of his statements and recommendations in the message in a radio report to the people on January 11, 1951. Because of the duplication of much of the material, the radio report is not included in this volume.

here for Illinois and the nation will profit all of us; the evil, none of us. While we will not always agree on details, I do not believe we will disagree on major objectives. By intelligent joint effort we can find common understandings and therefore common solutions of our problems. So it is my purpose to bring about the kind of teamwork and mutual understanding between the legislative and executive branches that the constitution intends and urgency demands.

Actual accomplishments, however, will rest largely with you. The Governor can *propose;* but only the legislature can *dispose.* It is upon performance that the people will judge and history evaluate what can be the most productive session of the General Assembly in modern times.

We meet in a critical hour. I am told that the Chinese character for "crisis" is compounded of the two characters meaning "opportunity" and "danger."

The *opportunity* is before this 67th General Assembly of Illinois to reorganize our governmental machinery, to modernize our constitution, to restore our highways, and to push forward with dispatch in many directions. Seldom has a General Assembly had such an opportunity.

But *danger* surrounds us too. Two years ago I said to you that we faced "a long trial of strength between individualism and collectivism — a trial of strength not limited to military and economic potentials, but also to moral and spiritual actualities." The pace has accelerated. What was apparent then is insistent now. The shadow of the antagonist is creeping over Asia. Our forces are engaged in unequal combat. Our public opinion is confused and divided. The free world's hope for peace hangs by a slender thread.

The spread of the highly communicable disease of communism can be arrested, the scales can be weighted toward the west, only by quickly achieving a preponderant balance of power that will dishearten the predators.

The effort will itself be dangerous. Inflation already threatens our economy. Controls will threaten our liberties. It will all be very expensive and very inconvenient.

But strength does not come by miracle or accident and we must make the effort with all our might and main, with all the courage and conviction of a faith more precious than life — faith in the free man. Armed with that unconquerable principle we can be of good heart because the enemy dreams of world conquest by stealth and strength; an ancient dream that always destroys the dreamer.

It is against that backdrop of opportunity and danger, of crisis if you please, that I shall make some suggestions about the public affairs of Illinois at the threshold of its 67th General Assembly.

State Finances

Illinois is only one of the 48 states. But our production potential, our energy and resources, constitute a large part of the strength of America and the free world. Our task is to so manage our affairs that the necessary functions of state government can be carried on, come what may, so that Illinois may contribute fully to the national struggle. That struggle will affect the state in many ways — tax revenues, operating costs, personnel. It will shape the decisions we must make in almost every state activity.

Among the first major decisions I think we should make is to ask for no additional tax revenue, aside from meeting our highway needs which I will mention later.

Can we do it? I think we can. The state's finances are healthy. Thanks to a high level of business activity, revenues have exceeded somewhat the estimates made two years ago. The same favorable conditions have reduced relief demands. Appropriations for building construction will not all be spent. Other expenditures have also been deferred, and the order I issued in July of 1949 to hold operating expenditures 10% below appropriations has yielded substantial savings. It appears that we should finish this biennium on June 30, 1951 with an unencumbered balance of at least $50 million in the general revenue fund.

Forecasting revenue receipts two years in advance is hazardous at best. It is even more so now. Any sharp reduction in retail trade due to Federal restrictions would affect our calculations adversely and immediately. The necessity for any large emergency expenditures, for example for civil defense, could do likewise.

The careful study of our needs which the Budgetary Commission has been making has been complicated by manifold uncertainties. But even with the certainty of higher costs and some large, unavoidable new expenditures, it appears that the State's present services, except for highways, could be continued through the next biennium without additional general purpose taxes.

I *hope* this can be done. But I *know* it can be done only if we continue to adhere strictly to the course of prudence and economy; and only by the exercise of Spartan self-control by legislators and administrators alike.

Many demands for appropriations will be made upon you. Many will be meritorious. But all should be appraised in the setting of national emergency. Projects with a high priority in peacetime may well fail to meet the test of today.

In short, I think we must put first things first. Our job is to aid wherever possible in shoring up the nation's defenses. Faced with steep increases in Federal taxes we also have a responsibility to the taxpayer. So I would emphatically recommend that no state dollars be spent at this time which can be saved, no buildings built which can be deferred, and no manpower used which can be conserved. Our job is to hold the line.

After further scrutiny by the Budgetary Commission and the Executive Offices I will submit to you in detail the State's financial position and a proposed budget for the next two years based on these fiscal policies.

While, as I have indicated, no more taxes should be needed to maintain present services, we must protect revenue yields from the taxes now in effect. There is widespread evasion of our cigarette tax by the importation of non-tax paid cigarettes from out of the state. Our losses in cigarette tax revenue are estimated at as much as $5,000,000 per biennium. There is also the question of fairness. Those who do not evade the cigarette tax are entitled to insist that others pay the same as they do.

Therefore, I recommend the adoption of a use tax calculated to stop this evasion and subject every package of cigarettes to the same tariff.

Civil Defense

The imperative necessity for protection of our civilian population and industrial production from enemy attack has become starkly evident and urgent. Chicago is the hub of the nation's transportation system. It has one of the largest industrial concentrations in all America. It is our prime potential target, but not the only one.

Most national defense planning must be on a national scale. But the responsibility for leadership and supervision of civil defense planning within their borders has been delegated to the states.

I have taken steps to meet that responsibility in Illinois. Today I can give you but the barest outline. Five months ago I appointed Major Lenox R. Lohr state director of civil defense and established an interim office of civil defense. A small but experienced staff has been recruited. Private individuals and organizations have most generously contributed their help. Basic plans have been formulated to minimize the effects of enemy attack.

These plans have been widely distributed. They give complete autonomy to local authorities in the development of local defense plans. It is not contemplated that the state office shall be a super-agency to manage every phase of civil defense. Rather it will advise local defense committees and coordinate local plans within a statewide pattern.

Our constitution places major responsibility for the protection of the civilian population upon the Governor, but his powers are not clearly defined. Hence I shall place before you shortly specific proposals for legislation to support a permanent civil defense program for Illinois. It will reflect extensive study in an unexplored field of state action where our necessities must be conjectural at best.

The appropriation required to maintain the state civil defense program on a continuing basis is one of the unavoidable new expenditures. On the basis of our present planning the cost of the state office will not be large. It is very unlikely, however, that we could undertake large civil defense expenditures for extensive bomb shelter construction, for example, without new revenues for that purpose.

Closely related is the formation of a reserve militia to take over, if necessary, the vital functions of home security now performed by the National Guard. In forming the Illinois State Guard I followed the recommendation of an advisory committee of civilians and ranking officers of the National Guard. Whether or not either of the two divisions of the Illinois National Guard will be called into federal service remains uncertain, but we must be prepared for that possibility.

While referring to the National Guard let me also say that I hope to submit during the session a complete revision of our Military and Naval Code. Adopted some 80 years ago, it is both obsolete and inconsistent with modern practices and needs.

Highways

If civil defense is a new problem, our highways are an old one. While we must hold the line on other state expenditures, I don't think we can defer any longer a positive approach to highway restoration. We have delayed too long as it is.

I shall not linger on familiar facts. Every year our primary system deteriorates further. Pavements wear out faster than we can rebuild them. To postpone the necessary rebuilding is not economy; it is gross extravagance.

More people use our roads than any other state facility. Moreover in times like these good highways are indispensable to the system of production and transportation which is America's great non-secret weapon.

Our paved roads were financed originally through bond issues. Some argue that we should follow the same course now. But we still are paying off the original bonds; we already have the second largest debt of all the states; and further borrowing would only increase the ultimate cost of the job that must be done.

I think we should pay for our roads as we build them, and I propose that it be done by increasing both the gasoline tax and truck license fees. Only three other states have gasoline taxes as low as Illinois. Our truck fees are about the lowest in the nation. Yet Illinois has the largest primary system of rigid roads in the country.

While the necessity for more highway revenue is generally recognized, there is a wide disparity of views as to its allocation among the various units of government. To bring our thinking down to specifics and promptly, I propose the following:

(1) Truck, bus and trailer license fees should be equalized on a ton-mile basis with the fees and taxes paid by passenger cars.

(2) The motor fuel tax rate should be increased 2 cents per gallon.

(3) The 5 cent per gallon tax resulting from this increase should be distributed:

40% to the state;

30% to the cities;

30% to the counties, of which one quarter shall be spent on township roads for not to exceed three years pending consolidation of local road districts.

I need not belabor the first point of this program. Trucking is a major and essential industry, but the heavy trucks do the most damage to our highways, while the heaviest taxes are paid by the light vehicles which do the least damage. Common fairness demands that heavy vehicles share our highway costs equitably with the small car owners. The ton-mile equalization method of fixing license fees would assess heavy trucks the same proportionate sum as passenger cars.

It seems to me a reasonable and just distribution of the burden, and it will help to close the inexcusably wide gap between the taxes we now charge and those imposed by other states. It will help to end an unfair and unnecessary subsidy of the heavy trucking industry at the expense of the rest of Illinois' motoring public. And it will still leave the Illinois truck fees well down the list of states.

In this same connection, I urge you to examine and correct our existing laws on penalties for overweight violations. The cynical impudence of the chronic violator should be curbed and the expense of enforcement reduced. Specific proposals to this end will be presented to you.

With respect to the gas tax, Illinois has lagged far behind other states in gearing the rate to the needs. The 5-cent tax has become the rule rather than the exception. Many states charge more. With one of the largest primary systems of all, with the cities and other units of government in acute need of funds, we must face unpleasant facts.

Of a 5-cent total tax I suggest 2 cents, or 40%, go to the state for the primary system which carried 75% of the non-urban traffic and is the state's sole responsibility. Forty per cent is low in relation to the 48 states which receive on the average more than 60% of their gas tax revenues. But other political subdivisions of the state have needs as well, and, together with increased license revenue, 40% would enable the state to match all Federal aid funds and make considerable progress on our most pressing construction needs.

The state has long wanted an exact definition of those needs. The Division of Highways will shortly publish maps and reports disclosing in detail the 10-year needs of the primary and secondary systems.

It is apparent from these maps that, whatever funds are likely to be available, they cannot meet all of our enormous and growing needs. In my opinion our funds must be spent only in accordance with demonstrable traffic requirements on existing roads, and we should enlarge a primary system already far too large for our resources only with the utmost caution.

I believe we have done too much road work to serve political rather than public needs, and you will also receive a report on the priorities which should be observed in future road work based on traffic needs. It will be the first of a series of annual programs of work determined in terms of urgency by the application of a formula which has been worked out for this purpose.

From these two reports the legislature will be able to tell what the basic needs are for the next ten years, and also the immediate programs which the state intends to follow to meet those needs.

It is apparent that all the funds the state will have can be most advantageously spent on the principal thoroughfares for some years to come. From what information we have there is no present likelihood of any Federal restrictions on reconstruction and repair of major highways. I think we should, therefore, proceed on the basis of our clear and present needs. If conditions should change, the remedy always rests in your hands.

The allocations to the cities, counties and rural roads represent, frankly, what seems to me the best reconciliation of all the conflicting interests. The needs, the equities, of each level of government cannot be disputed. None can be wholly satisfied. But with restraint and in a spirit of conciliation for our common welfare we can and must find an acceptable solution. The division suggested affords, I believe, a basis for sound action. Certainly it reflects long and prayerful study and consultation.

A final word about the township roads, which many people feel should not participate in motor fuel taxes because of their light traffic loads. Aside from the importance of many of them as feeder roads in our commerce, in the last five years consolidations have reduced by more than 7,000 the number of rural school districts. The number of rural pupils relying on bus transportation has increased tremendously. During the winter and spring pupils are often unable to reach school. In too many cases schools have to close because of impassable roads. Such conditions demand a remedy.

Most all students of our road situation seem to agree on the obvious need for better financing and management of local roads and that the solution lies in the contraction of our 1,600 township road districts into larger, more efficient units.

I believe gas tax aid for local roads is justified not only by needs, but also if it will bring about such consolidation. Although I much prefer voluntary consolidation, conditions and difficulties vary, and financial inducements provide a compelling incentive. Hence, I am suggesting that one-quarter of our gas taxes allocated to counties be used by them on local roads for a period of three years. During that interval surveys could be completed and referenda held with respect to consolidation on a minimum mileage basis, or, preferably, on a county-wide basis within the county highway organization, as the legislature sees fit. Where townships do not choose to consolidate then I suggest the money revert to the common pool.

As we must act to protect the physical condition of our highways, we cannot overlook the protection of the people who use them. My own shock and dismay at the frightful toll in death and injury on our highways resulted in the convening of a statewide conference on traffic safety last spring. Ways of improving traffic safety, including legislation, were diligently explored. A number of things can be done, such as strengthening drivers' license requirements, clarifying responsibility for enforcement, and related matters. Specific proposals in this area will be presented to you.

I have outlined a possible solution of as important and complex a problem as you will confront — our highways. I believe it is fair and reasonable. I urge its adoption.

Constitutional Revision — Governmental Reorganization

Circumstances sometimes combine to offer the General Assembly an opportunity to enact historic legislation. Such an opportunity is presented to this General Assembly by the Gateway Amendment to the constitution and by the reorganization proposals made by the Commission to Study State Government created in the last session.

The report of the Commission is not Utopian. It is severely practical. It recommends only changes which in the opinion of the Commission are necessary to give Illinois the kind of government it should have.

There will not be universal agreement as to all the Commission's recommendations. That was to be expected, and I am reliably informed by members of the Commission that no process of divine inspiration guided their deliberations.

What you have before you is the product of more than a year of intensive work by an experienced committee of private citizens and legislators, aided by an exceptional staff working with the assistance of experts in special fields.

We have not had a comprehensive survey of our state government since the Administrative Code was adopted in 1917. And into that short span of 30-odd years have been compressed more dramatic changes in the scope and tempo of government in all the states than occurred during the entire preceding century and a half.

The Commission's work has already produced substantial values. There is hardly an agency in the executive branch of the government which has not, within the last 18 months, made a critical appraisal of its own internal organization and operations. Many changes resulting therefrom are already in effect or in process. I propose to put into effect other recommendations of the Commission by administrative action. But to secure for the state the major benefits from the Commission's study, legislative action is necessary.

Senate Bill 652 creating the Commission to Study State Government had bi-partisan sponsorship. It passed the Senate with only two dissenting votes. It passed the House unanimously. The membership of the Commission is bi-partisan. The entire operation to date has been bi-partisan, and I trust it will continue that way.

It was important to put our house in better order when the 66th General Assembly provided for this study. The dissipation of energy or money in inefficient government is even less excusable today.

I urge you, therefore, to give earnest consideration to bills which will be introduced to implement the Commission's report. If major decisions on the report could be made at an early date, the biennial budget, now being prepared, could reflect any changes and economies involved.

The adoption of the Gateway Amendment represents the longest stride toward constitutional reform in Illinois in a half-century. The overwhelming popular vote for it has dispelled the idea that the average citizen is not interested in constitutional improvement.[7]

The best way to give effect to the people's will is now of first concern. The import of constitutional revision is too great, the effect upon the

[7] In November, 1950, the voters approved the Gateway Amendment, which provided that up to three articles of the state constitution could be amended at the same election. Moreover, the Gateway Amendment provided that future amendments to the constitution required only a favorable vote of two-thirds of the electors actually voting on the proposition or of a majority of those voting in the election, whichever was less.

people too widespread, the subject matter often too complex and technical to be dealt with in any but the most orderly and considered way.

So I recommend that you promptly create a special commission, representing both Senate and House, to study the many amendments which will be proposed, to hold public hearings and to recommend to the General Assembly which amendments should be submitted to the voters at the election of November, 1952.

By diligent application and by taking full advantage of the less active early weeks of the session, I believe such a commission could submit its report prior to the usual date of adjournment. But if further time should be required, the General Assembly could continue in session or recess until a later date for action on the constitutional questions.

With amendment to three articles now possible, the opportunity for extensive revision is before you. I earnestly hope that out of your mature consideration will emerge agreement on some of the major constitutional changes we need so badly and that this session will not be content with only minor revisions.

Education

The 66th General Assembly took a notable forward step toward equalizing educational opportunities throughout the state and assuring a good common school education for every boy and girl. We are fortunate to have in this session the findings of the School Problems Commission established by the last legislature to study the problems of our common schools, including state aid.

Few legislative commissions have produced more thoughtful and useful work. Under the chairmanship of Representative W. O. Edwards, this Commission's findings should largely eliminate the pulling and hauling and haphazard approach to school legislation of many past sessions. It has defined for us the goal of a "foundation" program which is nearly within our reach, and told us what it will cost. We know now precisely where we are trying to go and we can measure against our other needs the steps we can take to get there.

With a gratifying concern for the state's financial condition as a whole, the Commission recommends a continuation of the present equalization rate of $160 per pupil. With larger enrollments and to pay claims in full at that rate would increase the common school distributive fund appropriation about $24 million. Such an increase in school aid is in my judgment consistent with sound policy and the "first things first" yardstick, and I believe the money will be available on the basis of our present calculations.

In higher education we have made distinct progress in meeting the expanded academic requirements as well as building and housing needs of the state colleges and universities. Our future policies in these respects must be dictated by our resources. The postwar peak in enrollments appears to have passed. Some essential capital improvements have been started and must be completed. But further building which can be deferred must be deferred.

The most urgent need now is to establish a better overall administration. Three separate boards now divide control over the six state universities and colleges. There is little coordination. Confusion and rivalry complicate just and wise decisions on appropriations and other legislation related to higher education.

With a view to possible improvement in this situation the United States Office of Education has, at my request, examined the administration of tax supported higher education in this state during the past year. In the report of its study which will shortly be made available to you it did not attempt to say what plan of coordination Illinois should adopt, but it offers several alternative plans to improve the present disorderly system.

For this biennium you appropriated over $128 million for our state supported institutions of higher education. A public service so expensive and competing with privately supported higher education should be considered as a single program and coordinated on a statewide basis. The budget requests of the several institutions should be equitably appraised on the basis of relative needs. There should be some competent overall determination of the curriculum, the degrees offered, and the research programs at each institution. There should be a continuing evaluation of the operations at each, and a continuing study of the state's needs for tax supported higher education.

If these controls are not exercised how can we assure the taxpayer his money's worth out of this costly service? And how can the legislature deal fairly, prudently and intelligently with such intricate problems at six institutions? I hope that here again the 67th General Assembly will attack disorder and disintegration boldly and decisively.

Welfare Services

The state's welfare services, including public assistance, represent its largest and most expensive responsibility. Although the public assistance load has been lightened by full employment in the past few months, the Public Aid Commission informs me that it will have to request a deficiency appropriation for general relief, and that all its services to the needy have been handicapped by insufficient funds.

Legislation will be required to take advantage of recent changes in the Federal Social Security Laws, including the creation of a new category of permanently and totally disabled. This new category will relieve somewhat our state burden for general relief.

The agreement between the Department of Public Welfare and the Public Aid Commission to merge their local county offices is a notable achievement in cost control. Also by better operating practices the Welfare Department has reduced the cost of meals while food prices were going up. But now we are confronted with still higher prices for everything we have to buy.

In an effort to check the steady growth in our hospital population the transfer of patients to their own or foster homes has been accelerated, and local mental clinics have been encouraged.

But Illinois must do a better job of caring for its wards, and we have inaugurated a carefully conceived long range plan for expanding the facilities of the state mental hospitals. In a further effort to improve its services the Welfare Department will propose to you a codification of our mental health laws to bring our hospital administration up to the most modern standards and practices. This legislation will include authorization to charge patients or their families, where they are able to pay, for the cost of care and maintenance in our institutions. Illinois is the only state which does not provide by law for voluntary payments. Most states not only make such provision but require payment in cases where the financial circumstances of the patient or his family permit.

I urge the General Assembly to adopt a plan by which the growing cost of state hospital operation could be shared by those receiving its benefits. Such a plan would not, of course, deny care to persons unable to pay for it, or affect in any way the quality of service rendered. But it would yield substantial revenue and enable Illinois to move forward more rapidly toward our goal of better facilities, care and treatment.

At our new Research Hospital at Galesburg we propose to sponsor a research center in diseases of the old. We also have a committee at work developing programs of training for reemployment and recreation for people over 65, who have increased 25% in the past 10 years. Aggravated by pension and retirement plans based on age the time may soon come when the legislature will have to give serious attention to a human problem which is growing to enormous proportions.

City Aid and Home Rule

In June of last year I convened a special session of the 66th General Assembly to consider, among other urgent questions, the adequate financing of city governments in Illinois. At that time I told the General Assembly: "It is fundamental to orderly government that our cities be given the tools to meet their responsibilities. If they cannot properly finance even their historic functions we can hardly expect to resist pressures for the state to take over more and more of their duties."

Several proposals were presented to permit cities a wider latitude in local taxation, but none found favor with the General Assembly. Meanwhile, the plight of Chicago and some other Illinois cities has not improved. In some instances fire, police, and health protection have been impaired and are threatened with even more serious curtailment. Necessary salary raises and the added expense of civil defense preparation have further complicated the problem.

The need for prompt, positive action is manifest. The cities look to the legislature for relief. In the most critical cases they have exhausted their local limitations and have nowhere else to turn.

In general, the plea of the cities is not for aid in the form of outright grants from the state treasury. What the cities do ask, and should have, is authority to meet their own obligations locally. They ask only to be allowed to help themselves. The General Assembly should thoroughly re-examine the restrictions upon local taxing authority which are at the root of this difficulty. The problem is a challenge to our capacity to apply democratic processes to changing needs and conditions in local government.

In addition, I propose an affirmative step which would help the city of Chicago meet its especially critical problem. Under present laws the state assumes the necessary expense of hospital care for the indigent sick in downstate counties. In Chicago, the County of Cook bears this expense for indigent patients in the Cook County Hospital. I recommend the adoption of legislation that will accord the city of Chicago and the County of Cook the same treatment and on the same terms as is now provided for the rest of the state.

Many students of municipal government in Illinois conclude that the problems of our cities would in some instances be lessened by the city manager method of operation. Existing laws permit a city manager only in towns of 5,000 population or less. Larger cities in other states have found the system effective. As a step in the direction of greater home rule and increased flexibility, I believe the legislature could well offer to all cities of under 500,000 population the additional option of the council-city manager form of government to be adopted by referendum.

Law Enforcement

Law enforcement is another field which merits the earnest attention of the General Assembly. The growing evidence of the magnitude of organized crime in America, its wealth, power and sinister ramifications, is revolting and alarming. An outraged public is demanding better law enforcement loudly and insistently.

Commercialized gambling has been commonplace and widespread in Illinois. I was reluctant to use the limited personnel of the state police to do a job local officers are elected and paid to do. The Attorney General and I appealed to local officials to enforce the law, in some cases with success, in others with none. Where enforcement was not forthcoming I directed the state police to act. I am satisfied the effort has been worth while in terms not only of the suppression of commercial gambling, but in revival of public respect for law enforcement in Illinois.

But the permanent and proper remedy lies not in the assumption by the state of local responsibility, but in local officials who will be faithful to their oaths and enforce the laws. And secondly, it lies in strengthening certain of our state laws relating to gambling.

Other states have dealt with commercial gambling effectively by insisting that licenses to sell liquor be conditioned upon strict observance of the anti-gambling laws. Wisconsin, for example, quickly eliminated a very bad situation indeed by this approach.

No reasonable person can, I think, object to a requirement that a person who has sought and received the privilege of selling liquor should obey the gambling laws as well as the liquor laws. I shall submit proposals to you for the strengthening of the powers of the State Liquor Control Commission in this respect. By so doing the greatest stride could be taken to rid Illinois once and for all of the evils of widespread gambling.

The Congress has recently prohibited the shipment of slot machines and similar gambling devices in interstate commerce. If Illinois effectively prohibited the manufacture of gambling devices we would strike another mighty blow against organized crime, because Illinois is the center of the manufacturing industry.

In the field of law enforcement generally, I urged the General Assembly two years ago to enact, among others, the so-called grand jury and immunity bills sponsored by the Chicago Crime Commission. There is no justification for the present limitation of thirty days upon the life of a grand jury in Cook County when the limit is ninety days to six months in other counties of the state. Cook County is certainly entitled to the same if not greater power to fight crime as other counties.

The immunity bill would enable the court to require a witness to testify in return for immunity from prosecution for any felony or misdemeanor revealed by his testimony. It will be of help to all State's Attorneys throughout the state, and it also should be added to the people's arsenal of weapons against crime.

I believe the people have a right to expect the legislature of Illinois to join vigorously in the national crusade against crime and corruption.

Labor

The General Assembly two years ago increased the scale of benefits under the Workmen's Compensation Act. There remains, however, the need to simplify this statute. We should have a statute covering both workmen's compensation and occupational disease that the average layman can read and understand. Many months ago I asked the labor-management committee which drafted the amendments adopted at the last session to simplify and clarify the entire act. When the committee's work is completed I trust you will give it careful consideration.

Benefits payable under the Unemployment Compensation Act also were liberalized at the last session. However, the Illinois law still discriminates against employees in establishments hiring fewer than six persons. Most states have brought such workers under the provisions of the unemployment compensation law. I believe Illinois should do likewise.

I urge also that you consider the desirability of providing a system of temporary disability insurance. A worker and his family, deprived of income over a considerable period of time by illness or non-occupational disability is as much in need of assistance as a worker who loses his job. Such a program would also ameliorate our relief costs by shifting many people from the general assistance rolls to the protection of insurance.

The related functions of unemployment compensation and the state employment service should be more closely integrated. They are operated now as separate agencies except at the top level. I believe this involves needless confusion, rivalry and expense. I recommend now, as I did two years ago, the closer coordination of the two services by legislative authority.

If the principle of a minimum wage is a sound one, as I believe it is, I think the legislature should give attention to broadening and strengthening our present law which is cumbersome and obsolete. And I also request your consideration of better machinery for the enforcement of the prevailing wage rate law.

Discrimination in employment on racial or religious grounds continues. Some employers and employer organizations have recently taken vigorous and intelligent steps to solve it, including effective educational campaigns and special recognition for employers who eliminate discrimination in their own business.

I hope there will be more efforts of this kind and that labor unions which practice discrimination will follow suit. Voluntary action is always better than laws. But the process of education and persuasion is slow and uncertain and our sins are old. Two years ago I said to you: "Prejudices can no longer find safe refuge in rationalizations. How we deal with this subject is intimately related to the world conflict of ideologies which is the battle for tomorrow." I believe events only affirm that judgment. In our present peril we look to *all* the people to join in the common defense. If we do not discriminate in sacrifice we cannot discriminate in opportunity. So again I bespeak your sympathetic consideration for fair employment practices legislation in Illinois.

Margarine Law

Our law requires the distinct labeling of margarine sold in package form. Since 1897 Illinois has also prohibited the sale of margarine in colored form, and limited its use in state institutions to 25 per cent of their food fat needs.

Most of the states which had laws similar to Illinois' have repealed them. Thirty-four states now permit the retail sale of yellow margarine, including Ohio, Michigan, Indiana, and Missouri.

While it is argued that the law protects the dairy industry, only 16 per cent of Illinois' milk production went into the manufacture of butter in 1949, and butter represented only 11 per cent of the dairy cash income.

Moreover, Illinois has become the leading state in the manufacture of margarine, and soybean oil is one of the principal ingredients. Illinois outranks all other states in soybean production.

The repeal of this law would leave intact ample state and federal laws to protect the consumer. Margarine would have to be distinctively labeled to avoid confusion with butter.

Hence I urge the General Assembly to repeal the laws prohibiting the sale of margarine in colored form and restricting its use in state institutions.

Reapportionment

The returns in the recent federal decennial census indicate that the number of Representatives from Illinois in the Congress will be reduced from 26 to 25. This will impose upon you the burden of redistricting the State into 25 congressional districts which, in the language of the federal statute, must be "composed of . . . contiguous and compact territory, and containing as nearly as practicable an equal number of inhabitants."

The need for congressional redistricting and the passage of the Gateway Amendment also suggest the problem of reapportionment with respect to this legislative body. The present constitutional provision obviously has not been acceptable to the General Assemblies for 40 years.

The fact that the constitution has not been respected in this matter is, I am sure, repugnant to all of us. Therefore, I presume that in your consideration of amendments to the legislative article of the constitution you will give high priority to an equitable plan of representation, with due concern for the diverse, if not necessarily conflicting, elements in our State community.

Elections

After long experience with the separate party primary ballot and the registration requirements incidental to its use, many competent observers have concluded that it has not proved effective. That only about one-third as many people vote in a primary election as in a general election is a negation of the great purpose which the primary was designed to serve.

I think the legislature should, therefore, consider substitution of the consolidated primary ballot for the separate ballots now required by law. While recognizing that the consolidated ballots can be abused, on balance it appears to be better calculated to encourage public participation in the elective process and the cause of good government than the present system.[8]

Another defect in our system is the large number of elective offices. Even under our present constitution the legislature could sharply reduce this number. Aside from other advantages, a shorter, simpler ballot would make intelligent voting easier.[9]

Supervisor of Assessments

The 66th General Assembly took a great stride forward in improving the administration of property taxation by adopting the county super-

[8] Justice Walter V. Schaefer, of the Illinois Supreme Court, wrote to Carol Evans: "One of my law clerks spent some time checking in the journals for the 1951 legislative session and was unable to find any message from the Governor relating to a 'consolidated primary ballot.' The reason that I asked him to check is that I share your uncertainty as to what was meant by 'consolidated primary ballot.' If it means (and this is the only possible meaning that occurs to me) a primary at which members of one party may vote for a candidate of the other, I would be surprised that Adlai supported the notion. We had such a primary in Illinois this past spring, . . . and enough Republicans crossed over into the Democratic primary to defeat Paul Simon, the present Lieutenant Governor, who was seeking the Democratic nomination for governor. . . . The Second Circuit Court of Appeals, which includes New York, held unconstitutional a primary which permitted crossing over party lines. (*Rossario* v. *Rockefeller*, C.A. 2d, April 7, 1972)." Letter to Carol Evans, July 6, 1972.

[9] The offices of attorney general, secretary of state, auditor of public accounts and superintendent of public instruction were all elective in Illinois. Stevenson felt they should be filled by appointment.

visor of assessments bill.[10] But the Supreme Court of Illinois has held it unconstitutional. The acute need for county-wide uniformity in property taxation is, therefore, with us again.

I urge the legislature to explore all possibilities for replacing the invalidated bill by a new measure drafted to meet the Court's objections to the old. While we have suffered a setback, the effort to rationalize our property tax procedures must not end.

Mining Laws Revision

An important segment of our statutes which needs to be thoroughly revised and modernized is the coal mining code. A comprehensive and skilled effort to this end has been under way for many months at my request, and I shall present the results to you for what I hope will be your favorable action.

Parole Laws Revision

Not content with the operation of our parole system, last June I appointed an Advisory Committee on Parole Legislation to examine into the parole laws and their operation here and elsewhere and to make recommendations for their improvement. This committee has not completed its inquiry but upon receipt of its report I shall transmit to the General Assembly any recommendations I may have upon this important subject.

Conclusion

I have outlined a formidable program. And it is only a part of your load. But our needs are formidable; our times are anxious. We can strengthen or weaken self government by what we here do, or fail to do. With God's help we can serve a great tradition greatly. The people ask no less.[11]

In reply to Stevenson's letter of December 21, 1950, Kent Chandler wrote the Governor an amusing letter on January 3, 1951, thanking him for the title "Chief Official Spotter of Trucks, Northeastern District of Illinois." He concluded that while he appreciated the Governor's suggestion about Elgin he had a better idea: that a lighthouse in the middle of the Hudson River had always intrigued him and that it would be fun to

[10] The purpose of this bill was to standardize tax assessment methods within counties under 500,000 population. A similiar bill introduced in the 1951 legislature failed to pass.

[11] For a review of Stevenson's successes and failures with his legislative program, see his report to the people, July 15, 1951, below.

retire to that lighthouse and count the boats going up and down the river.

To Kent Chandler

January 5, 1951

Dear Kent:

What! Desert Illinois for New York? Never!! For such as you we'll build a house — with lights — in the Illinois River, complete with barred windows and padded walls. We too have boats, fish — and ducks! We'll provide you a pea shooter. We'll even provide you with company — me! Indeed I'll be waiting for you.

So long now, and keep the lint out of your navel.

Hoopla!

An editorial appeared in the December issue of the American Bar Association Journal, *in which it was stated: "Governor Adlai E. Stevenson, of Illinois, whose address to the section of Criminal Law appears elsewhere in this issue, gives an example of public service of which his fellow members of this Association may well take note." It cited the Governor's declaration of "war upon organized commercialized crime, using the reorganized State Police to attack this cancerous growth with its attendant corruption of minor officials." It also called attention to the Governor's statement that "government should be as small in scope and local in character as possible." It concluded: "In what Governor Stevenson unassumingly says and does is apparent a fundamental belief in the importance of economy in government and the responsibility of citizenship. His type of statesmanship, which lawyers generally must approve, is all too rare in public life today."*

Stevenson, who realized that his political fortunes lay with the voters even more than with the political "pros," was eager to get as widespread publicity as possible on such gratuitous approbations. He sent copies of the editorial to James W. Mulroy and to William I. Flanagan, suggesting various editors and publishers of newspapers in Illinois that the editorial might be sent to.

To James Mulroy and William I. Flanagan [12]

By some devious method the editorial about me at page 1018 of the December 1950 edition of the American Bar Journal should be brought

[12] This handwritten memorandum is in the possession of Mr. Flanagan. It is not dated, but was probably written about January 5, 1951.

to the attention of Akers, Field OR Reynolds, A. T. Burch, Don Walsh, Ed Lindsay, Barney Thompson, Carl Slane, Irving Dilliard, Loring Merwin, McNaughton and the man in Danville.

It might be a good idea to get it to Tom Matthews also — [13]

AES

Walter V. Schaefer commended Governor Stevenson on his message to the 67th General Assembly.

To Walter V. Schaefer [14]

January 8, 1951

Dear Walter:

Thanks for them kind words — and whenever you're ready to quit loafing and move down here for a couple of months and work please let me know.

Yours,
ADLAI

Edison Warner Dick, thirteen-year-old son of Mr. and Mrs. Edison Dick, visited the mansion in Springfield during the holidays at Christmas. When he returned to school after the first of the year in 1951 he wrote the Governor a thank-you letter for "the swell time you gave me while I was in Springfield . . . I'm hoping the senate & house will agree to your ideas."

To Edison Warner Dick [15]

January 10, 1951

Dear Eddie:

I enjoyed your letter very much. You write very well indeed. Not only can I read it easily but you have something to say, which is more than most people have!

[13] Those named in the memorandum were Milburn ("Pete") Akers, Marshall Field, and Thomas F. Reynolds, all of the Chicago *Sun-Times;* Donald J. Walsh, of the Chicago *Herald-American;* Edward Lindsay, Barney Thompson, Carl Slane, Loring Merwin, and "the man in Danville," all newspaper people in downstate Illinois; Irving Dilliard, editor of the St. Louis *Post-Dispatch;* Frank McNaughton, with *Life;* and Thomas S. Matthews, editor of *Time,* in New York.

[14] The original is in the possession of Mr. Schaefer.

[15] The original is in the possession of Mrs. Edison Dick.

Be sure to come and see me again and I will tell you how I am getting along with the Senate and the House.

> Sincerely yours,

Louis Ruppel, editor of Collier's, *wrote Stevenson on January 3, 1951, that he had enjoyed a* Collier's Weekly *of September 1, 1900, with a one-page article by former Vice President Adlai E. Stevenson. Ruppel thought Stevenson would like to have a copy in case the family archives did not have an original of the magazine itself.*

To Louis Ruppel [16]

> January 10, 1951

Dear Louis:

And what, pray tell, were you doing fumbling around in Collier's Weekly of 1900! At all events, your research was very profitable for me and I am deeply grateful for "Stevenson on Vice Presidents." The archives are empty and this constitutes a major acquisition.

Many thanks.

> Sincerely yours,

Adlai E. Stevenson III, while a student at Harvard University, lived at Eliot House, named after Charles W. Eliot, president of Harvard from 1869 to 1909. The master of that house, Professor John H. Finley, Jr., invited Governor Stevenson to be the main speaker at the celebration on March 19, 1951, of the "great occasion" of the house, President Eliot's birthday.

To John H. Finley, Jr.

> January 10, 1951

My dear Mr. Finley:

I have been trifling with your letter of December 20 long enough! Nothing has bedeviled me more. I want to come; I am honored, flattered, indeed eager, even without the remotest idea of what I could talk about that could be of lively interest to the undergraduates. However, my second son's spring vacation commences on March 15, and my third son's on March 17, and the mayoralty election in Chicago is on April 3, for which I will have to do a little campaigning to maintain

[16] A carbon copy is in A.E.S., P.U.L.

my cordial relations with the Democratic organization in Cook County. In short, I suspect that my only chance of seeing the other boys will be the first part of their vacation and therefore I should not commit myself to be in Cambridge on March 19. It is all very complicated, but I feel that I dare not risk it what with vacations, legislatures and campaigns. All the same, I am deeply grateful and I very much wish that Dr. Eliot had chosen another day!

I hope very much to find some opportunity to get to Cambridge during the spring for a glimpse of Adlai — and I hope of you and Mrs. Finley.

With warm thanks.

Sincerely yours,

To Alicia Patterson [17]

January 11, 1951

. . . The opening of the legislature is over, the message written and delivered — and received very well on the whole. The Tribune score so far is 2 approvals & 1 disapproval out of some 20 proposals. Top marks from St. L. P-D [St. Louis *Post-Dispatch*] & a few others & the usual erratic behavior among the downstate papers. I'm always interested by the way one editor can be enthusiastic about something and the editor in the next town equally disapproving — and generally neither of them know much about it or evidently make any effort to find out. Do editorial writers work hard? I should like to know because in the smaller papers their work seldom shows it. Also why the hell do they presume to express considered views on *everything?* How refreshing it would be to read in the Mat[t]oon, Ill. paper some morning that the editor *just didn't know* the answer to Korea, China, or what have you.

I'm en route to D.C. — civil defense, lake filtration plant etc. . . .

You flatter me . . . that I could tell *you* about the international situation. But I could tell you about Illinois' roads & what should be done about them! And the only consolation I have is from the Arabic — "Its a wise man who knows what he doesn't know." But of this I'm sure — that cowardice or timidity never saved man or nation. . . .

A

Richard L. Neuberger, a member of the Oregon state senate, wrote Stevenson that he had written an article on the antiquated Oregon constitution and that he had quoted one of the Governor's "excellent

[17] This handwritten letter is in the possession of Adlai E. Stevenson III.

speeches" on the need for modernizing the Illinois constitution. Stevenson and Neuberger shared a love of the out-of-doors and of the Rocky Mountains in particular.

To Richard Neuberger

January 19, 1951

Dear Dick:

I was delighted to have your letter and it reminds me of some of my happiest hours — both in the forest and out!

Please give Maurine my love, but I can hardly congratulate her for getting into this tumult.[18] I should think one in the family was enough!

Please don't neglect me if you come this way.

Yours,

To Mrs. Franklin D. Roosevelt [19]

January 19, 1951

Dear Mrs. Roosevelt:

I am distressed that I cannot come to the Roosevelt College dinner on Friday, February 16, but I am hopeful that if your schedule permits you will come down to Springfield the following day and "rest up" over the week-end in my nice old house.[20]

I will promise not to plague you with *my* troubles but I will want to hear all about *yours*.

Faithfully yours,

To Fred K. Hoehler [21]

January 20, 1951

Dear Fred:

I have your letter of January 16. My suggestion that someone might travel about contacting the political organizations in the counties in which institutions are situated did not relate to community-institution relationship as much as it does to political relationships. What I think we must have is a little bit more positive talk to the political leaders in an effort to explain to them the problems in our institutions regarding our program for their management. The only sort of person who

---

[18] Mrs. Neuberger had just been elected to the Oregon House of Representatives.
[19] The original is in the Franklin D. Roosevelt Library, Hyde Park, New York.
[20] Mrs. Roosevelt declined, saying that she had to return to New York immediately.
[21] A carbon copy is in the possession of Lawrence Irvin.

can talk with authority to the politicians is a politician, but he must understand and be sympathetic with what we are trying to do to mollify demands and gripes.

Sincerely yours,

On January 28, 1951, Governor Stevenson delivered an address at Northwestern University's Founders' Day Convocation honoring the university's 100th anniversary. Stevenson was asked to deal with world affairs generally, in order to establish a framework for the speeches of George F. Kennan (then at the Institute for Advanced Study at Princeton) and theologian Reinhold Niebuhr, who had been asked to speak on specific subjects.

Late in November, 1950, Chinese forces in large numbers had crossed the Yalu River and over the next weeks the United Nations forces in Korea were driven south of Seoul. All through these weeks a great debate raged on foreign policy. On December 15, 1950, Senate and House Republicans demanded the dismissal of Secretary of State Dean Acheson. Five days later, former President Herbert Hoover proposed that America should "hold the Atlantic and Pacific oceans with one frontier on Britain (if she wishes to cooperate); the other on Japan, Formosa and the Philippines."

On January 5, 1951, Senator Robert A. Taft stated: "In the first place, we should be willing to assist with sea and air forces any island nations which desire our help. Among these islands are Japan, Formosa, the Philippines, Indonesia, Australia and New Zealand; on the Atlantic side, Great Britain, of course." Taft strongly objected to an announcement by President Truman that additional troops were being dispatched to Europe to increase the strength of the North Atlantic Treaty Organization.

"There Are No Gibraltars" [22]

Some five years ago this University, for reasons best known to its trustees, conferred an honorary degree on me. Having thus honored me I suppose the least the Governor of Illinois could do in appreciation was to decline President [Roscoe] Miller's and Mr. [Kenneth] Burgess' invitation to speak at this hundredth anniversary convocation. Instead I accepted, after the manner of insensitive and egotistical politicians. I apologize.

Because there are others who can speak with authority about the

[22] The text is taken from *Vital Speeches of the Day,* Vol. 17, Feb. 15, 1951, pp. 284–288.

founding of Northwestern University, I am, with, I am sure, your enthusiastic approval, going to resist the temptation to tell you of the faith and convictions of the founders who stood here 100 years ago and dreamed of "a university of the highest order of excellence." All that we see about us testifies that they founded well and that their successors have wrought well upon those foundations. In the 100 years the dream by the Lake here in Dr. Evans' town [23] has become one of the world's large and honored communities of scholars.

Early Illinois was notoriously inhospitable to higher education and I recall the remark of a lusty legislator who said in opposition to a bill to charter the first three Illinois schools that he was "born in a briar thicket, rocked in a hog trough and never had his genius cramped by the pestilential air of a college."

Northwestern, too, was born upon a scene on which the light of higher education shone but fitfully. But in our time one never sees a considered catalogue of the assets of Illinois that does not always proudly list its universities at the top.

I once heard it said that Massachusetts Institute of Technology "humanized the scientist" while Harvard "simonized the humanist." Just what Northwestern does I don't know; perhaps both. But at all events its contributions to the sciences and the humanities and also to the wholesome goodness and gaiety we associate with American student life have brought to this campus imperishable distinction and affection.

Thanks to Northwestern, its neighbor, the University of Chicago, the great State University, and many distinguished lesser institutions, Illinois and particularly this section of the state, is now one of the treasure houses, one of the major repositories, of the Western world's culture.

It is proper, therefore, that we pause to note the 100th birthday of this proud university; that we pause a moment in our feverish defense preparations to recall what we are defending. Certainly one of the things we are defending is the future security and health of privately supported universities such as Northwestern. In turn we confidently expect them to defend for generations to come the spirit of free inquiry and fearless scholarship which is a basic condition of free men. For that protection and for the contribution of the universities to "a large resolute breed of men" which Walt Whitman called the only bar against tyranny, we will have to trust to the future; we will have to trust that the guardians here and elsewhere of the riches of our learning will never forget what the treasure they guard is, what it is composed of. We will have to trust that the guardians of Western thought will never permit its vitality and

[23] Evanston, Illinois, is named for Dr. John Evans (1814–1897), who took an active part in the founding of Northwestern University.

beauty to be smothered by strong, arrogant men who burn books and bend thought to their liking, nor obscured by timid men trembling in the darkness of anxiety.

The continuity of our heritage of scholarship, both bold and free, which is the peculiar and priceless possession of the university, must, then, be entrusted to the future. But what of the present which has such a bearing on the health and strength and continuity of the custodians of our culture?

Are the universities to be stripped of students in order to defend our cultural heritage? The young of college age are the seed corn of a society and a nation. To survive must we eat our seed corn? And if we do, can we survive? We must and we will, I think, find at least a partial answer to that disturbing question. And we will find it in calm deliberation, not in frantic fright.

Then, like you, after some experience, I have made the disturbing observation that absence of thought in war seems to be mandatory. And, of course, total abstinence from thought is very agreeable for most of us, and a uniformly popular condition among adolescents. But is it necessary in mobilization, in half war, if you please? Perhaps we have something to think about here as we enter the new and unexplored era of the garrison state.

Again, I must ask with a shudder if it will be largely women who enjoy the benefits of more advanced education in the new era? Is the ancient tradition of masculine primacy in jeopardy? Heaven forbid! And I should think a little reflection on this appalling possibility by the male leaders in all countries could do more to insure peace than a balance of power in the world. It is high time, it seems to me, that we males begin to think of survival in terms of gender as well as nationality and ideology.

There is another problem of which you are all soberly mindful. How are the privately endowed universities to survive financially; how can inflexible income meet flexible costs — costs that "flex" in only one direction? What will be the further ravages of inflation, of ever higher income taxes and sharply diminished student population and student fees? How will President Miller balance his budget? Actually I really don't feel very sorry for him because he can always tell the trustees to raise more money. But if I can't balance the budget of Illinois you'll tell me to find another job!

But there must be survival for the privately endowed institutions. By virtue of their very independence, they are indispensable to the kind of survival we are all talking about. We have long since accepted as right and just publicly supported primary and secondary education for all. But is that the destiny of higher education too? I hope not. It will be an ominous day indeed when all higher education is government subsidized. Yet simple economies point that way and already most of the great private universities must rely more and more on government subventions, whether it be GI tuition or scientific research projects.

And in this connection we could well afford to examine critically the relative growth of the tax dollar and the private dollar contributed to higher education.

There are masses of statistics but let me just refer to the immediate situation in our Illinois. As taxpayers you support six state universities and colleges. For this two years period the legislature appropriated $128 million for them. In all of them tuition is but a fraction of the fees charged by private institutions. Three separate boards of trustees, elected or appointed, now divide control over these institutions. There is little coordination. Confusion and rivalry complicate just and wise decisions on appropriations and other legislation.

With the hope of improving this situation, I asked the United States Office of Education to survey the situation in Illinois. This week I published its interesting and informative study which does not attempt to say what plan of coordination Illinois should adopt, but offers several alternative plans to improve the present disorderly system.

With what emphasis I can command I say that a public service so expensive and competing with privately supported colleges should be considered as a single program and coordinated on a state-wide basis. The budget requests of the several institutions should be equitably appraised on the basis of relative needs. There should be some competent overall determination of the curriculum, the degrees offered, and the research programs at each institution. There should be a continuing evaluation of the operations at each, and a continuing study of the state's needs for tax supported higher education.

If these controls are not exercised how can we assure the taxpayer his money's worth out of this costly service? And how can the legislature or the executive deal fairly, prudently and intelligently with such intricate problems at the six institutions.

I believe the time has come and gone when Illinois should attack disorder and disintegration in a major and expensive state service boldly and decisively, and with a considerate view to the plight of those private institutions of which the state is so proud.

Northwestern was born here in a quiet village on Lake Michigan by a burgeoning city a hundred years ago. That too was a time of revolution abroad and of transition here. In 1851 Illinois was filling up with immigrants from the south and east. A steel plow to cut the tough prairie sod had been invented. The reaper had come to our prairies. On plank roads Illinois was rising out of the mud. A railroad was pushing westward. Europe was in political and economic ferment. The Irish and the Germans were coming in search of something better and more hopeful for the average man. With not 30,000 souls Chicago was struggling out of the swamps. Illinois was passing from the log cabin frontier era and shouldering its way into the new industrial day that was breaking upon the Union.

A hundred years have passed; a hundred years which have seen the culmination of a great historic expansive movement of peoples from Europe to the West, and the conquest, development and integration into the world community of the two great American continents, severed by revolutions but tied by cultural inheritance to their western European roots.

At the same time there came another great expansion — from West to East. The Slavic peoples and culture pushed through the Ural Mountains, across the vastness of Siberia to the Pacific and on across the Bering Sea to Alaska and our own West Coast. The Russian tide collided with the Japanese, just emerging from the hermits' hut with vaulting ambitions too. There it stopped — for a time — but the land mass over which the Russian expansion surged has for the most part remained firmly in Russian hands, while the European overseas expansion created a new and independent center of power here on our continent.

Twice in 25 years our new center of power, stretching from the tropics to the Arctic and facing both the Pacific and the Atlantic, has been compelled to intervene to redress the balance of power in the world. And now with Britain and France enfeebled by these wars, with the German and Japanese power crushed, the United States and Russia, which have risen from the mists of these short hundred years, even as this university, stand face to face, with the other nations polarized around them, drawn by the gravitational pulls of proximity, coercion, self-interest and kinship.

Believing as we do in a community of free nations and free peoples acting peacefully and responsibly through governments freely chosen, we conclude at last that we cannot live in comfortable security with a great imperial power which has seen the barriers to its expansion collapse and is on the move again, taking here, probing there, and pressing relentlessly against the uncommitted, discontented millions. Capitalizing [on] the ancient racial zenophobia and the messianic zeal to missionize the world of the Russian people, the leaders of the new Russia, armed with force and the old weapon of fomented revolution, use the seductive new weapon of communism to soften their victims. But whatever the trappings, the methods, the weapons, the objective is domination — imperialism. I often think it would be both more accurate and more effective if we talked less of communism with all its appeal for ignorant, miserable peoples and more of imperialism which threatens the freedom and independence of everyone and has no appeal. Communism can be a fighting faith, but imperialism is subtle slavery.

So, as Northwestern enters its second century, America, rich, peaceful and undisciplined, finds itself face to face across both the seas with an inscrutable, ruthless conqueror, strong, cunning and armed with an egalitarian idea that has great appeal for the miserable masses of humanity. No longer is there anyone to protect us. No longer can we sow when and where we are certain to reap. There is no safe investment, no certain harvest any longer. We cannot even measure the price of saving ourselves. Indeed, we seem to be in some doubt as to whether we should save ourselves at all; whether we are worth the cost!

The quiet past in which this great university grew to manhood is no more. Our bright land is troubled and sorely tried. Things are badly out of balance when we spend $230 million for one aircraft carrier, four times the endowment of this university. Its future is in doubt. Our future is in doubt. Some say fight now. Some say despotism is the wave of the future. Some say abandon Asia. Some say abandon Europe. And worst of all, everybody says something — including me!

In our time peace has become as abnormal as war used to be because this is the revolution. And revolution is extremely irritating, vexatious and bewildering to a prosperous, peaceful, contented people that want nothing except to be left alone.

How have we reacted to this condition of perpetual danger? It seems to me that for five years we have suffered from the confusion and distraction of alternate moments of illusion and despair. Hoping always for a cheap and painless escape from the realities of a distasteful destiny, aided and abetted by politicians who will say anything to be popular and by editors either myopic or worse, public opinion has moved in violent pendular swings between optimism and pessimism, between the mountains of complacency and the marshes of despair.

In fatuous haste to be shut of war, worry and expense, we obliterate our power and leave it to the United Nations to keep a peace that never existed. When things go right we gush paeans of praise for the United Nations; when they go wrong we damn it and even propose to forsake the good because it is not the perfect. In fear we overestimate the danger; imperil our liberties, exaggerate the foe's cunning and strength; even demand a showdown as though the certainty of doom were preferable to the uncertainty. Again, perpetual danger invites the complacency of status and we underestimate the peril by overconfidence in our virtue and power, as though that were enough in a moral contest. But the self hypnosis of loud and repeated talk about our righteousness and freedom will rally no allies nor blow the Kremlin walls down.

And now as things get tough and we find we can't buy, threaten or preach our way to peace, we are menaced by amateur strategists. Even the isolationists have reappeared, flexing their muscles, or rather their tongues, and proclaiming "Let the whole world go. We should worry. We can defend ourselves with a strong navy and air force." Haven't they heard about Pearl Harbor or the atom bomb? Was the last war all in vain? Haven't they heard that we are not self-sufficient? Won't a garrison state become a police state? And do they forget that nothing succeeds like success? If they do, conquerors don't. I suppose any moment even America First may emerge full blown again, except that I hope this time it is more properly entitled America Last — last on the Kremlin's list.

The reemergence of the straight isolationist doctrine — the same people saying the same things we heard before the whirlwind a decade ago —is to me the great regurgitation. They remind me of Charles Lamb's remark: "I cannot make present things present to me."

But fortunately the great debate about foreign policy, which was mostly a debate about military strategy and not foreign policy, appears to be about over. And, none too soon, it appears that we have about made up our mind to stop fighting each other, gather all the like-minded allies we can find and settle down seriously to the very serious business of getting stronger than the brigands that are preying on the world.

Perhaps an occasional national debate like this one is a healthy thing. It clears the air, releases tensions, focuses torpid attention on great issues, and melts divisionist controversy into a mould of common conviction.

Maybe we have about reached a common conviction that peace through power is our salvation. Maybe we have decided that only by once again redressing the balance of power in the world and confronting Russia with a preponderance of force can we thwart an imperialism more sinister than the world has ever seen.

But we should profit from an experience like this, because it won't be the last time we get rattled; it won't be the last time we doubt our beliefs and believe our doubts.

I suppose, for example, we will have to assume that the isolationist argument will have at least nine lives, for the very human reason that it pleases the average man because it spares him any immediate inconvenience or sacrifice, and it flatters his sense of power to feel that America can live alone and like it.

And have we learned that while the whole nation may debate the broad policy of whether to defend or not to defend, whether to defend alone or with allies, the details of the where, when and how we will defend are sometimes questions of military, political and diplomatic strategy which cannot be settled safely or wisely by public debate? Nor can they be wisely settled by men who behave, to borrow a line from King Lear, "as if they were God's spies," but who are neither military strategists nor geopoliticians.

Have we learned that what 160 million Americans know about our plans the enemy knows too? Have we learned that hunting scapegoats is not a foreign policy?

Have we learned that our mission is the prevention, not just the survival of a major war? Have we discovered that there are no Gibraltars, no fortresses impregnable to death or ideas, any more?

While the debate talks incessantly in terms of our national crisis and our national survival, it is not just our crisis, it is the crisis of the whole free world. Have we learned that making domestic political capital out of world crisis is not the way to win friends and influence people? Do we realize that the Russians have already gained a portion of their objective by using our indecision and moral confusion to weaken our leadership in the free world? The Russians know the value of even reluctant allies in this final struggle for power. Do we? Or are we going to risk the slow strangulation that comes from whittling away the friendly world?

If we have not learned that having the most to lose we have the most to save, then, I say, let us pray.

But if we have, if the immensity of the responsibility and the stakes has dawned upon us, then the great debate has been a great blessing and we are on the way to thwart this latest greatest threat to all this university symbolizes.

Why should we be poor in spirit? The task is great, the price is high, but the prize is better than life. With Europe and its great industrial concentration and forward bases shored up and steadfast, with access to the tin and rubber of south Asia, middle eastern oil, African manganese and uranium, the scales are still weighted to the west, and the waves of the future are still free. Aggression must be called aggression in the United Nations. But in insisting on no equivocation about the legal and moral position, we dare not forget that the allegiance of India, uncommitted to East or West, is the ultimate objective of both East and West in the orient. And we dare not fall into the trap, the oubliette, Russia has prepared for us in China. War there will drain our resources and at the same time make China completely dependent militarily on Russia. With every Russian jet at least six Russians go along. A weakened China means a stronger Russia pressing from behind against Hong Kong, Indo China, South Asia, and finally India. Hounded by people of small vision and great emotion it will not be easy to withstand the pressure to help solve Russia's problems with China. And with us mired in the morass of the China mainland the Soviet could turn next summer to some unfinished business with Tito in Jugoslavia.

Pray heaven we can remember amid the discord and chagrin of defeat that military force alone cannot win the day for us in Asia. Our moral authority there is low because we are white and Asia is colored. Desperately poor, struggling to shake off the shackles of white colonialism, Asia is just now passing thru the era of revolution, independence and self-determination that swept the western world long ago. It will take great patience, great insight, great restraint for us who see the whole world in our own image and likeness to win confidence and faith in the great uncommitted areas of Asia. It can't be done with the white man's sword. But it can be done; they can be convinced that communist imperialism is not liberation but a more deadly enemy of normal aspirations for freedom and social justice than colonialism.

Are we, I wonder, moving as a nation from our Greek period to our Roman period; from a period in which the validity of our ideas was the important consideration to one in which their effectiveness is crucial? Good intentions and reliance on the rightness of our cause will avail us little against an enemy that cares nothing about validity and is concerned only with effectiveness. The Greeks were right, but they died.

A danger greater, it seems to me, than Germany or Japan in the last war, or communist imperialism now is moral fatigue, disintegration, half loyalty, timid faith — the "weakening of the central convictions to which Western man hitherto has pledged allegiance."

When freedom didn't exist it too was a fighting faith that men would die for. But now that it is old, it looks a little pale and gentle and lacks the appeal to the militant, irrational sentiments once mobilized by conquering religions and now by imperial communism.

But communism resolves no anxieties. It multiplies them. It organizes terror. It is without spiritual content or comfort. It provides no basic security. In the long run it cannot cure the disease of this anxious age. But its short term methods are grimly effective. We can't sit still and wait for the fever to run its course. Without combative faith in our spiritual heritage, we won't long hold out against the subtleties of selfishness and fear. If Western civilization is to save its body, it must save its soul too. It must awake again the emotionalism, the confidence, the defiant faith of a resolute breed of men to whom liberty and justice mean something positive every day — not just when war has reduced us to the stark issue of self preservation.

It's easy to care mightily then; it's hard now. It's easier to fight for principles than to live up to them. But now is the time that a passionate belief counts if we are to avoid another war, and if we are to avoid the greater menace of cowardly surrender to our own doubts and fears.

Don't the universities have a large, indeed the leading, role to play in articulating the purpose and the combative faith of a great people in this era of convulsive transition and this hour of discord and doubt? Don't they know best what we stand to lose?

We have proclaimed our military weakness, our vacillation, our hesitation, our fear. Enough of that! The test of a nation is defeat. The time has come to proclaim our faith in all its might and majesty. History will go on and "The Forfeiture of Freedom" would be a sorry title to this chapter; rather the historian must write that in arousing America to re-define and defend its ideals the ugliest despotism dug its grave in the twentieth century.

It was in 1776 that Tom Paine wrote: "The heart that feels not now is dead; the blood of his children will curse his cowardice, who shrinks back at a time when little might have saved the whole."

To Alicia Patterson [24]

January 31, 1951

. . . I've sent you copy of a speech I contrived amid the alarums and confusion for the Centennial of Northwestern — which expresses with, I hope, becoming restraint some of my rattle brained views on the foreign business. I would rather tell you about them. But how can I when I don't even know if you're alive! At which point some ladies say bitter things, but not suave politicians — diplomats. . . .

P.S. . . .

P.S.S. Like a wiser man than I am, I don't prophecy [prophesy], but if you were to ask me I would have to say that Stalin is right and no war with Russia is in sight. But as for the Rep[ublican]. party — how Hoover & Dewey can ever find common ground I can see, but meanwhile Taft will be floundering around doing his intellectual contortions somewhere between them capitalizing [on] every discontent, proposing everything and nothing, and acting like "Mr. Republican" for sure, and they call that leadership!

A

In 1948, G. Merle Bergman, just after his graduation from North-western University Law School, had volunteered his services in Steven-

[24] This handwritten letter is in the possession of Adlai E. Stevenson III.

son's campaign for governor. In 1950 he was called to active duty as a reserve officer in the Air Force during the Korean War.

At the urging of Louis A. Kohn, Stevenson wrote Thomas K. Finletter, Secretary of the Air Force, on behalf of Mr. Bergman.

To Thomas K. Finletter

January 31, 1951

RE: G. Merle Bergman, First Lieutenant, AO 971203, 437th Supply Squadron, 437th Troop Carrier Wing, APO 929, Unit 1, % Postmaster, San Francisco, California

Dear Tom:

Please refer this letter to the proper person for consideration of the reassignment of an officer to the Judge Advocate's Department, and read no further yourself — if you have read this far!

G. Merle Bergman is a rather brilliant young man, who was a student of mine [25] at Northwestern University Law School some years ago and who has done some work for me from time to time subsequently. He was called to active duty several months ago as a reserve officer in the Air Corps under the impression that he would be assigned to the Judge Advocate's Department to do legal work. Instead he was assigned as Adjutant to the above unit and is now on duty in Japan. Friends of mine in Chicago have suggested that I should make his rather unusual qualifications known to the Judge Advocate of the Far Eastern Air Force in Tokyo against the possibility that he might find him more useful in legal work than in his present administrative work as Adjutant.

Sincerely yours,

Mrs. Marjorie Grigsby devoted many long hours as a volunteer in the Women's Division of the Stevenson for Governor Committee during the 1948 campaign. After Stevenson's election she was assigned a position with the Industrial Commission. On January 31, 1951, she wrote the Governor to thank him for approving the commission's action in appointing her secretary.

To Mrs. William A. Grigsby

February 2, 1951

Dear Marjorie:

Many thanks for your thoughtful letter. I believe *I* should be thanking

25 See *The Papers of Adlai E. Stevenson*, Vol. II, p. 517.

you—for a personal loyalty and a quality of service that makes me feel that I *have* added a little something to state government.

Good luck!

Sincerely yours,

Governor Stevenson celebrated his fifty-first birthday on February 5.

To Mr. and Mrs. Edison Dick [26]

February 6, 1951

My beloved Dicks:

The birthday festivities finally terminated late after a final and happy fling by the office staff down here.

The skies this morning are weeping but I am not! Indeed, my spirits are on a permanently elevated plane — thanks largely to the enchantments of our evening at your house. You made me very happy and I'm afraid I made you very tired.

Love,
ADLAI

Walter V. Schaefer wrote Stevenson that he had heard the Governor was thinking of proposing a Department of Personnel, to be headed by a single director. At a meeting of the Schaefer Commission, attended by legislative leaders as well as regular commission members, Schaefer said he had set forth vigorous arguments for a departmental form of organization, but there was "absolutely no indication of any favorable response from any of the legislators who were present." As a result of the discussion at that meeting, the commission decided to make no recommendations concerning a change in the structure of the Civil Service Commission.

To Walter V. Schaefer [27]

February 17, 1951

Dear Walter:

Many thanks for your discouraging comment on the Department of

[26] The original of this typewritten letter is in the possession of Mrs. Dick.
[27] The original is in the possession of Mr. Schaefer.

Personnel idea. I guess that one goes on ice along with other "best laid plans." [28]

> Yours,
> ADLAI

Mrs. Forsyth Watson, a childhood friend of Stevenson and his sister, Mrs. Ives, wrote reminding him of summers long ago in Charlevoix, Michigan. She added that he was a governor with many good works and she heard his name often mentioned with the greatest admiration.

To Mrs. Forsyth Watson

February 22, 1951

Dear "Gladys":

It was wonderfully kind of you to write to me from that cherished past of our childhood Charlevoix days. I have shown your note to Buffie, who is visiting us here, and together we recalled the old board walk and the playmates on the "grounds of the Belvedere resort."

I am glad to know you keep one foot and finger on Illinois, and I'm doing my very best to be a good servant to her and her people.

> Very sincerely yours,

To Mrs. Edison Dick [29]

February 22, 1951

Dear Jane:

I have been wanting to talk to you about Senator ——— [30] . . . He is, as you know, one of the very best in the legislature — in spite of his party! Some years ago he and his wife adopted a baby, now four years old, and they are *intensely* eager to adopt another. He has sought my assistance with the Illinois Children's Home and Aid Society. I am mortified that I am so out of touch with the ICH&A [31] that I must turn to you for some information as to the routines, the prospects, etc. I am sure he and his wife, whom I have met, could stand the Society's most searching scrutiny as adoptive parents. When you are down here next

---

[28] In 1957 the 70th General Assembly established a Department of Personnel with a single director.

[29] The original of this letter is in the possession of Mrs. Dick. The main body is typewritten, but the paragraph at the end is in Stevenson's handwriting.

[30] Mrs. Dick asked that this Republican senator's name be withheld.

[31] Stevenson was for many years a member of the board of trustees of the Illinois Children's Home and Aid Society. He resigned from it and many other organizations when he became governor.

time I hope you will bear this in mind and perhaps a little talk with him if the legislature is in session. I am, of course, eager to help him. . . .

I wish I could sit by little Eddie's bed a bit and listen to that enchanting cracked voice & watch those curious inquisitive eyes.[32] Maybe I will! . . .

To Alicia Patterson [33]

February 20, 1951

. . . I've been in hell again for the past 3 weeks with this dam[n] legislature, a schedule always too crowded, no serenity, no peace, no thought. . . . I saw Charlie Murchison [34] in the D.C. airport while he was waiting for a N. Y. plane & I for a Chi plane Tues. I had 24 hectic hours there on civil defense, lunch with Marshall,[35] Bradley [36] et all [al.] on manpower & Nat. Guard, then Truman, then Edgar Hoover, then more conferring with the Governors — etc.

. . . As to Eisenhower & Stevenson — I've heard of the former, but whose [who's] the latter? How about resigning as Gov. and being Chancellor of U[niversity] of C[hicago]? That's more my alley I think! . . .

A

On February 26, 1951, Stevenson spoke in Chicago at a meeting of the American Association for the United Nations.[37]

. . . there is pending in the Illinois legislature at Springfield a resolution calling on the United States to withdraw from the United Nations.

Now what accounts for this violent distaste for this best and only hope for collective security and peace in the world? What accounts for the unhappy fact that there are evidently thousands of adult, sober Americans whose disappointment with the Korean war and the continued tension in the world prompts them to cut off their nose to spite their face, to throw out the *baby* with the *bath*, to destroy the *good* because it is not the *perfect?*

It was only a few years ago that people were clamoring to bring the

[32] Edison Warner Dick was thirteen years old and his voice had just begun to change. He was ill at the time of this letter.

[33] This handwritten letter is in the possession of Adlai E. Stevenson III.

[34] A Washington lawyer and chairman of the executive committee of Capital Airlines.

[35] George C. Marshall, Secretary of Defense.

[36] General Omar N. Bradley, chairman, U.S. Joint Chiefs of Staff.

[37] The text is based on a mimeograph copy prepared by the Governor's office for release to the press. Stevenson's introductory and closing remarks have been omitted.

boys home, liquidate the war and leave it all to the United Nations. It was only a year ago that the country was ringing with demands for lower taxes and less defense spending. It was only a few months ago that the time changed and they began hurling epithets about unpreparedness and demands for more defense spending. And now, after some reverses in Korea, there is a clamor to junk the U. N. because there is no peace in the world.

We are a volatile people. Our consistency in the long run is the product of compensating peaks and valleys of inconsistency in the short run. Opinion tends to drift with the erratic winds of our fortunes. Today we clamor for this, tomorrow for that with noisy self confidence, but without consistency, conviction, vision — and most of all understanding.

But I did not come here to psychoanalyze my fellow Americans, nor have I any professional qualifications for such a diagnosis. Yet this sort of erratic impatience following on the very heels of last summer's applause and approval of the U. N. after the intervention in Korea reflects, at least to me, an alarming national instability that I can only charge to ignorance about our progress toward world order largely under American leadership.

Be that as it may, we quickly learned some years ago that the premise of the U. N., the common consent of the great powers, to underwrite peace and security was a false premise, and that Russia did not in fact consent. So for the past four or five years we have been connoting a system based on consent to a system based on force. And despite limited resources, public indifference, to put it mildly, and strong indigenous communist influences in Europe we have made impressive progress in this conversion both in and out of the U. N. toward the organization and preservation of the free world. The stop gap Greek-Turkish aid program led directly to the Marshall Plan which all concede has reduced the communist menace in Europe, raised the standard of living and re-established confidence and hope. The Council of Europe, the Consultative Assembly, manifestations of political renaissance and unity in Europe, have been fortified by the North Atlantic pact and the arms program.

But aggression came not in Europe but in Korea where we had no like minded allies. Yet 53 out of 59 members of the U. N. promptly endorsed resistance and many have contributed military and material aid to this bloody battle for peace and security — the greatest experiment of its kind in history.

Now it seems to me that all these are no inconsiderable steps toward the goal of peace and security thru the U. N., where possible, and outside the U. N. where necessary, by consent where possible, by force where necessary. These anxious years have demonstrated the U. N.'s virtues, flexibilities and also its deficiencies — deficiencies which were patent for all to see when the basic premise of sincere consent by the great powers was sabotaged by imperialist communism. And we should not forget that we helped to make the charter of the U. N. a limited instrument; that it has failed to do only what it was never given the power to do because the world was not ready to give it that power, including ourselves. But we do not say that the Constitution of the United States has failed because there is Jim Crow in the south, and gambling and lawlessness everywhere.

Is there an explanation of our failure of comprehension and our impatience in our long tradition of approaching international issues on idealistic and moralistic bases? Internationalism began here as a moral movement. Most of the public support for the U. N. has been of this character.

The idealist-moralistic approach to the U. N. has been useful in overcoming public inertia and in launching the organization, but it is now high time the public matured its thinking about the U. N. The lack of such maturity may account for much of the disillusionment today, and from time to time in the past, which has been expressed in despair and rejection of the U. N. because of its failure to relieve the growing world tension and because it has not by some miracle proved a full-blown, effective collective security system able to maintain peace in a world divided by the ruthless ambitions of a strong and stealthy conspiracy. This frustration and disappointment has also been expressed at the other end of the spectrum by its most passionate friends in frustration and disappointment that so much international business is conducted outside the U. N. Again it is express[ed] in petulance about disagreements; the idea that the U. S. must always be right and that all states should look at issues from the same viewpoint that we Americans do and always vote with us; in short, the concept of one world — in our own image and likeness.

But internationalism is now a life and death matter; not a matter of good will and idealism. We should look at the U. N., as we look at other political instruments, and see what it is *not*, disabuse ourselves of any illusions and recognize how useful it has been, is and can still be.

Of course, the U. N. is not a full-blown collective security system and it is dangerous to think of it and operate within it as if it were. It's a council table, not a police force.

We all know that the disarmament provisions of the charter and the military contingents contemplated by Article 43 have never been implemented due to Russian intransigence. In short, the U. N. operates in a balance of power world, half of which is massively armed and the other half only beginning to arm. At best the organization now has only limited capabilities available from the free world. These must be developed and deployed and applied intelligently, flexibly, and not rigidly and dogmatically.

When one part of the world rejects the principles on which the U. N. is founded while retaining its membership, its role is inevitably modified. Increasingly it is becoming a political framework through which a broad coalition of the free world operates. A bridge to the Soviet Union is useful — indeed, when we cease to talk we will probably start to fight — but the U. N. cannot solve the Soviet problem. It is vital to our security to have this political framework as the maintenance and development of the coalition of the free world is our chief political task today. And if it did not exist it would have to be created even today.

I hope I've made it clear that the task of this organization, the American Association for the United Nations, is depressingly large: education and understanding of what's being done and why so that with each change in the mind [wind] public opinion is not diverted. This is a conference on "Our responsibility for world leadership." But how can America lead if America doesn't understand? . . .

In 1950 and 1951, Senator Estes Kefauver, as chairman of a Senate committee, investigated the corrupt relationship between politicians and organized crime. Many of the sessions were televised. In the course of a year the committee examined more than five hundred witnesses, including political leaders, gamblers and racketeers. Professional gamblers were found to have a total gross income of some $20 billion on which they paid only a tiny fraction of the income taxes due. Gamblers maintained close relations with political leaders, and were able to avoid prosecution by bribing public officials.

Stevenson did not appear before the committee, but he recorded a statement for veteran newscaster Edward R. Murrow's Hear It Now *program.*[38]

No, I don't think gambling should be legalized. But I am not one of those who thinks that gambling can be wholly suppressed. It is instinct in humankind and as *old* as humankind. But we also know that gambling is not always a harmless pastime; that too often it becomes a vice, en-

[38] The text is based on a mimeograph statement prepared by the Governor's office for release to the press. It bears no date other than "March 1951."

riches only the professional gamblers and impoverishes everyone else. So it has been the settled public policy of this country to outlaw gambling, not to legalize it and thus increase the temptations by increasing the opportunities, too often of those who can least afford it.

Moreover, to legalize gambling sounds easy, but someone has to be licensed to operate the gambling establishments, and what reason have we to think that the same racketeers and gamblers who monopolize illegal gambling by bribery, intimidation and political corruption would not end up as the licensed operators of *legal* gambling? I think they *would* and so do they! If bribery and political corruption are effective in securing protection *from* the law, they are also effective in securing favors *under* the law.

I am not impressed with the familiar argument that legalized gambling would provide the states a new source of revenue. God forbid that government in this country should ever be supported by chance and the misfortunes of a few for the benefit of the many.

Should the Kefauver Senate Investigation Commission continue its work? Certainly. It or some similar investigation should continue to reveal to the people the sinister enormity of this shadowy, super government of crime and corruption that debauches public officials, mocks the laws of the land and fattens off the weak and the foolish. Commercial gambling with its enormous profits is the keystone of the arch of crime over the United States. We have cleaned it up pretty well in Illinois in the past two years. But it's hard work, expensive work. If the people understand what's going on they can do the job, elect honest officials, and knock out the hoodlums, the racketeers, yes, and their allies, the corrupt politicians. I think Senator Kefauver's committee has performed a great service of enlightenment to the complacent American people — and in a people's government public understanding is the first step to public action.

William B. McIlvaine, Jr., a Chicago lawyer and Princeton classmate of the Governor, wrote Stevenson that a Mr. Kirkpatrick, of the Chicago Tribune, *had telephoned him saying they were thinking about writing some articles about Stevenson and wanted to interview Mr. McIlvaine.*

To William B. McIlvaine, Jr.

March 1, 1951

Dear Bill:

I am a little bewildered by your letter and the call from Mr. Kirkpatrick, whom I don't know. At the moment I don't know whether to fear the dishonesty of the Tribune or the honesty of McIlvaine most! I remind you that I have always been a serious, conscientious, sober and diligent barefoot boy from the prairies struggling up the ladder of success — wrong by wrong! In short, the less you remember the better. There — my fortunes are in your tender hands, and if they want any more horrid details I suppose Jim Oates and Ed McDougal are equally untrustworthy.

Yours,

Republican charges that Dean Acheson was to blame for the collapse of Chiang Kai-shek's government — that he was "soft on Communism" — became a bitter and divisive political issue. Elmer Davis in an article in the March, 1951, issue of Harper's *magazine compared Acheson with some of his predecessors, defending and, for the most part, praising his actions and policies.*

To Elmer Davis [39]

March 12, 1951

Dear Elmer:

Yesterday I read your piece on Dean in Harper's. You have done what has needed doing so desperately and for so long. If it is *late,* I get some comfort out of the fact that it is *better* than anyone else could have done it. I only wish it could get a thousand times the circulation and I propose to make it my business to see that it gets at least a little more.

Warm regards and all good wishes.

Sincerely yours,
ADLAI

To Mrs. Edison Dick [40]

March 20, 1951

. . . Three days of rest [41] . . . We've done *everything* — except hunt possum — and that will happen any night. The boys are fine and Borden's prospects for Harvard and Dartmouth bright — the latter, by the way, is a beauty spot too many haven't seen. Each evening there's always time for at least one story from the volume of Irish ghost stories you sent the Ives and then we shudder and shake off to bed — leaving

[39] The original is in the Elmer Davis collection, Library of Congress.
[40] This handwritten letter is in the possession of Mrs. Dick.
[41] Stevenson was on a brief vacation at Southern Pines, North Carolina, with Mr. and Mrs. Ernest Ives.

the ghost of Charley Wheeler mumbling contentedly by the fire place with the Dicks, while Tagge and Dreiske take off for the Dunes Club! [42] It all seems so long ago — and I wish you were here, even if it made the possum hunt more inevitable!

I'll be back amid my horrors in Chicago next Sunday night. Bring the children down to Sp[ringfield]. any time during the holidays you want to. My boys are going on to Fla. to join Ellen [Stevenson] on Saturday. . . .

P.S. "Jane & Eddie" — the twin mulberry bushes are flourishing in a clearing in the pine forest. Ernest acts like a man about to bring in an oil well!

To Mrs. Franklin D. Roosevelt [43]

March 22, 1951

Dear Mrs. Roosevelt —

My office in Springfield informs me that you are speaking in Centralia [Illinois] on March 31st. If a visit to Springfield fits into your schedule I would be glad to send a car or an airplane to Centralia to pick you up.

I am spending a few days here at my sister's place with my sons during their spring vacation and will return to Illinois on Sunday.

Please don't bother to acknowledge this and you can let me know at the very last moment if Springfield fits into your itinerary.[44]

Faithfully yours –

Porter McKeever decided not to join Stevenson's staff in Springfield, and wrote the Governor a memorandum on March 17, 1951, raising the question whether the Governor was willing to become a figure on the national scene. "Until you answer that question yourself . . . the question of who helps you and what they do is secondary, if not academic." He concluded: "I only hope you will remember that there are two causes I am interested in promoting: one is selling the United States and what it stands for to the rest of the world, and the other is selling Adlai Stevenson

---

[42] After the election in 1948 Stevenson had spent a few days with the Iveses in Southern Pines. The Dicks accompanied him. Assigned to cover his activities were Charles Wheeler of the Chicago *Daily News*, George Tagge of the Chicago *Tribune*, and John Dreiske of the Chicago *Sun-Times*.

[43] This handwritten letter is in the Franklin D. Roosevelt Library, Hyde Park, New York.

[44] Mrs. Roosevelt informed Stevenson in a handwritten note that she was compelled to cancel her trip to Centralia because she came down with the "grippe."

and what he stands for to the United States. And the latter also includes the former because it is one of the best ways I know of expressing and demonstrating the greatness of this country."

To Porter McKeever

April 2, 1951

Dear Porter:

I have been under such a mountain of work since I returned from my little holiday that I have had no proper opportunity to digest your impressive and penetrating memorandum, but I am sure you were 100% right about what we need to do to make the most publicly in this administration. And because we have no one who can think and execute in those terms is precisely why I have wanted you to join me.

As to a deliberate determination about the future, I confess that is much more difficult for me and I am afraid, as in the past, that I will probably drift with the winds which is doubtless the disadvantage of having no fixed ambition.

I cannot quarrel with your decision, of course, but in turn I see little prospect of articulating a future course until I can first feel the wind. In short, I never have cared to overestimate my abilities or prospects, and I hate to fail at anything I undertake. The result is that I tend to measure objectives one at a time and conservatively. Does the chicken come before the egg or vice versa.

Should this make any sense to you I should be surprised. I am disappointed that we did not have more of a talk when you were here and I hope the trip was not too tiresome for you.

My love to Sue.[45]

Sincerely,

To Alicia Patterson [46]

April 7, 1951

. . . It's midnight & I'm back in the Mansion after a hasty trip to Jacksonville [Illinois] to "address" the annual banquet of the State Employees Association — 1500 pension enthusiasts. Its been a hideous week trying to find time to put my budget message in shape for the printer. But I finally collapsed & sent it in late this afternoon. Tomorrow we'll have an "editorial" conference over the galley proofs & Tuesday I'll

[45] Mrs. McKeever.
[46] This handwritten letter is in the possession of Adlai E. Stevenson III.

deliver it to a joint session — thanking God all the while that I'm done with the ordeal for 2 yrs — or forever! But it will call for no new general taxes & less total expenditure than last time. And if the people and the press don't like it I can only weep the salty tears of ingratitude — because they should! We've done an amazing job of cost control here for the past two years — thanks largely to George Mitchell, my Director of Finance, who now has to leave me to go back to the Federal Reserve Bank [of Chicago].

My major triumph of the session — if any — came at 2:20 AM one night this week when we reached a compromise on the division of the gas tax. I kept the warring wolves here in the Mansion 6 hrs and 20 minutes straight. Exhaustion overtook them & they began to crack. We had arranged to have the press — 15 of them — on hand and they stood by all night. Before anyone could leave I called them in and announced the terms of the agreement before any of the conferees could reverse himself! The exhaustion technique I learned from the Russians and it seems to work just as well in Springfield as in London. . . .

Life is tough but I think I'm seeing the light at last — even enjoying my job more — . . .

A

To Mrs. Edison Dick [47]

April 8, 1951

. . . After the guests left last night I sat up until 2 AM and finished the damn budget message. I'm afraid its disorganized, discursive & ineffective, but I'm afraid it will have to do. So get ready to like it! . . .

I've been checking the calendar. I think I'll come up Thurs, go to [Walter] Paepcke's party for [Robert M.] Hutchins, spend the night in L[ake]. F[orest]., go to dentist Friday AM, work in town Friday, spend Fri night in L F & see the wretched man again Sat AM & then come back to Spfd. to work on that double damned radio speech which I have to record Monday night the 16th. Then there is the mental health speech the next day. How & when I'll put those bright touches in I don't know. . . .

But the bad news is the 24th. The Mansion is yours but I find I have to speak at the Marquette Univ. Law School in Milwaukee that night! Horrors!! Indeed I thought I might come up Sunday Ap 22 & stay there Mon & Tues going to Milwaukee Tues. night and returning here Wed for the 25th for my dinner for the Senate that night.

What a life. . . .

[47] This handwritten letter is in the possession of Mrs. Dick.

Mrs. Margaret Munn, one of the mansion secretaries, was in the hospital for surgery. Stevenson sent her some flowers and wrote her a note.

To Margaret Munn [48]

April 9, 1951

Dear "M M"

Courage! All is not lost — just some dispensables. You'll be on the mend in no time — and meanwhile you are missing nothing here except budgets, budgets, budgets —

With these flowers you will have more spring in the room than you'll find outdoors —

We have a candle in the window for you!!

Good luck and all good wishes —

AES

On April 10, 1951, Governor Stevenson delivered in person his budget message to a joint session of the legislature.[49]

Mr. Speaker, Mr. President and the Honorable Members of the Sixty-seventh General Assembly:

Last week Mr. Charles E. Wilson, Director of Defense Mobilization, said with respect to the next two years: "The nation demands, and must be given, the same degree of support by its citizens now, in a period of peace, that it would receive in a war. The times are no less challenging."

On January 3, I said to you that we must put first things first; that our job is to aid wherever possible in shoring up the nation's defenses. I said then, and repeat now, that we should impose no additional general purpose taxes; that we should hold the line; that we should spend no state tax dollars at this time which can be saved, build no buildings which can be deferred and use no manpower which can be conserved.

The financial plan for the next two years which I am proposing has been prepared in accordance with these principles of rigid control. But it reflects, as it must, the unhappy fact that costs have increased sharply over the past two years; wages are higher, commodities are higher, equipment and building are higher. The average increase of all costs is well over 10%.

The budget is in balance. It calls for no new general purpose taxes.

[48] This handwritten note is in the possession of Mrs. Munn.

[49] The text is based on a carbon copy. The Governor in a radio report to the people broadcast on April 22, 1951, repeated much of the budget message. The April 22 message is therefore not included in this volume.

It reflects only a 3% net increase in general fund appropriations, in spite of certain major increases of almost $86 million. Grand total appropriations of new money from all sources are about $1,206,000,000, or less than the $1,221,000,000 of new money available during the present biennium.

Public assistance to the needy, the old and dependent and grants to local governments — "distributive" payments — account for 45% of the total; operating expenditures 38%; capital outlay 10%; and debt service and tax refunds about 7%.

The balance is precarious; there are no hidden reserves, and careful legislative scrutiny might well cause some alteration for still greater prudence.

How the Budget Was Prepared

How is it that Illinois can weather another biennium without new or increased general purpose taxes when all the large states have found more such revenue necessary in the past five years of rising prices?

Confronted with a threatening recession, in July 1949 I ordered expenditures in the agencies under my control to be held 10% below appropriations. In July 1950, after Korea, I requested all agencies to hold their budget requests for the next biennium to the expenditure rate for 1950 and to include no new programs or capital outlays without my prior approval.

By close control of expenditure and expansion, by reduction of our building construction program, and thanks to a sharp increase in tax receipts occasioned by the menacing inflation since Korea, we can make both ends meet for another two years, in spite of the increased cost of everything we build and everything we buy from hospitals to handkerchiefs.

Briefly, the major increases in appropriations from General Revenue which I feel we should include in this budget are:

	INCREASE OVER 1949–51 IN MILLIONS
Common Schools	25.7
Higher Education — operations	9.7
Additional aid to local governments	19.0
Department of Public Welfare — operations	10.7
Salary adjustments	14.0
Disability Assistance	6.5
	85.6

You will note that these new needs, which I feel must be met, are largely for distributions to local units of government, and to meet the increased cost of commodities and to adjust salaries to the higher cost of living.

As in past budgets, virtually all anticipated resources are appropriated. And this time they can and probably will be spent, which would leave us almost no treasury balance at the end of this unpredictable biennium. We have included little or nothing which may not be spent. Moreover, we believe our calculations are realistic within the limits of the present uncertainties. We are not underestimating probable income to give us a hidden cushion of safety, nor are we underestimating expenditure needs in order to keep the budget total down to create a good if misleading impression. In spite of the unexpected sharp rises in commodity and relief costs during the past two years, we have but $15 million of deficiency appropriations this year as against the $65 million I inherited in 1949. I think the contrast is evidence of the candor and soundness of our calculations.

It is apparent, therefore, that there is no room in this budget for additional appropriations unless there are corresponding cuts in my recommendations. I know that there are many other worthy expenditures you will want.

But if we are going to hold the line, if we are going to conduct this government prudently, with a view to paramount national concerns and with considerations for a taxpayer hard pressed by Federal and local governments, we will have to forego much and risk the displeasure of the disappointed. So I bespeak your rigorous restraint; I must ask you not to add to this budget without also subtracting from it.

Revenue and Expenditure Estimates

Our budgetary problem relates, of course, wholly to the General Revenue fund. This budget, as all present day budgets, ties in closely with economic conditions. On the income side the retailers' occupation tax, the mainstay of the Illinois revenue system, follows closely the trend of consumer spending.

On the expenditure side some of the State's largest items of cost drop when tax revenues decline, but unfortunately others rise in depression. If the level of employment drops as it did, for example, in the summer and fall of 1949, public assistance costs soar in the face of a decline in tax revenues.

If the economy experiences a sharp inflationary spurt, as it has since Korea, the cost of commodities used by our institutions skyrockets, and the cost of providing the accepted standard of living to the aged, to the unemployed, and to dependents follows suit, but in this case tax yields also increase.

The course of the next two years is as unpredictable as any period in American history. Yet this budget, as every one before it, has to be predicated upon certain assumptions.

We can assume with reasonable accuracy a treasury balance, or surplus, on July 1 of $60 million in General Revenue. As to future tax collections and costs, the assumptions I have adopted reflect today's consensus of opinion.

We assume the tremendous national production effort will require full utilization of our manpower and industrial resources during the two-year period for which we have to plan. Full use of our productive resources will generate a high level of personal income and, in turn, a high rate of consumer expenditure.

Therefore, we are assuming, as are most states, a continuation of the current high price levels and the current high rate of consumer expenditures. Tied to consumption taxes as Illinois is, we are, accordingly, projecting general revenue receipts for the next two years at the current rate of income, or $615 million, as against estimated receipts for this biennium of $563.5 million.

The spending plan I propose contemplates a decline in the public assistance rolls, due both to the removal of employables from general assistance and to rising family income, which will thus enable more self-help to the aged and to dependent children.

Consistent with the policy of only the most essential construction and also in view of the anticipated shortages of manpower and materials, we have sharply reduced capital outlay for construction. With respect to wages of state employees, the detailed figures in the budget are based upon existing levels, but a lump sum is included to compensate for the changes in the cost of living and in wage patterns generally since 1949.

In view of the possibility of further upward pressure on the price level, I invite your consideration of a reserve appropriation to enable us to promptly adjust salaries and payments to public assistance recipients, and also to meet the increased cost of commodities throughout the government. Although it might seem imprudent to assume such a contingent liability, yet, if prices rise, so will tax receipts and costs, and such additional revenue might be appropriated in advance to meet these higher costs. It is possible to equate the increase in the State's resources with the increase in its liabilities and to use the augmented tax yields to meet the higher costs without waiting until the next biennial session to make the adjustments.

Education

More than one out of every three dollars of the State's General Revenue goes to the support of education — schools, colleges and universities. The total expenditures of new money for this biennium will be about $245 million.

Two years ago we adopted as our equalization goal in the common school distributive fund the level of $160 per pupil.

The Commission you created at the last session to advise the legislature on the problems of our schools has, in my judgment, made a very important contribution to the orderly discharge of the State's responsibility to our common school system. While recommending the attainment of a "foundation" education for every child in the State "as soon as possible," its report points out that on present costs such a program would require State aid of $178 million.

But in view of our financial condition and the present difficulty of increasing further the local property tax qualifying rate, the Commission feels that for the State to pay school claims in full on the basis of the $160 equalization level would be a satisfactory step in the next two years toward the ultimate attainment of the foundation goal. To pay the claims at that rate in full will require $24 million more in the next biennium because of the large increase in enrollment.

Notwithstanding the severe strain on our resources, I am recommending this large additional appropriation and this further step toward the constitutional goal of "a good common school education" for all the children of Illinois.

Adding the appropriations recommended by the Commission for pupil transportation, the excess cost of educating the physically handicapped, vocational education and the school lunch program, brings the total proposed appropriations for State aid to common schools to about $150 million.

I am also including in the budget $1 million for reimbursement at $400 per year per full time pupil at the Chicago Teachers College. The School Problems Commission recommended somewhat more State aid to the Chicago Board of Education, which for years has operated this teacher training institution solely at local expense although it performs the same function as the teachers' colleges which are supported wholly at State expense.

As to higher education, I am budgeting a total of $78.6 million from General Revenue for operation and maintenance, not including new buildings, of the University of Illinois, Southern Illinois University, and the four teachers' colleges — an increase of $9.7 million over comparable expenditures for this biennium.

But with three separate boards of trustees, with no coordination of program or objective, with strong regional pressures and loyalties, I point out again the imperative necessity for a State-wide control and coordination of tax supported higher education which is rapidly becoming one of our major costs. While we talk about reorganization and greater integration of State government, the trend in our higher education is toward disintegration.

Welfare and Health

Even more costly than education are welfare and health. Almost half of all we spend from General Revenue goes for public assistance to the needy, for tuberculosis and mental hospitals, and for a wide variety of welfare and health services.

Net total operating increases out of General Revenue budgeted for the next biennium are $15 million for the Public Aid Commission and the Departments of Welfare and Health. The cost of operating the new State tuberculosis hospitals at Mt. Vernon and Chicago is $3.2 million, and $11 million more is included for the Department of Welfare. The latter has recently or will open in the next biennium many new or rehabilitated buildings, including the large new hospital at Galesburg.

Notwithstanding the large increase in staff personnel in the mental hospitals in the past two years, the ratios of doctors, nurses and attendants to patients are still very unsatisfactory. Illinois is still near the bottom of the list of comparative salaries for doctors. Hence, the budget contemplates higher salaries and the recruitment of more professional personnel, particularly doctors, nurses and therapists where we have had our greatest difficulty.

Overcrowding is an acute concern and in this fiscal year alone the net population of the welfare institutions will increase some 1500. We have little control over commitments by the courts, and you know the appalling cost of a gigantic building program. But with more and better staff we can reduce the hazards of overcrowding, improve care and treatment and thereby accelerate cure and discharge.

I am gratified by improved cost controls in the Welfare Department. In this biennium commodity costs will be $2 million less than in the previous two years when prices and population were lower. I hope you will not again limit such expenditures to 75% in the first 18 months. That limitation forced us to postpone purchases last year and pay much higher prices this year.

By passing the pending limited licensure bill you can help us to recruit doctors. And by other pending legislation you can help to distribute the ever rising cost of state hospital care among those beneficiaries of that care who can, and in my judgment should, pay for it at least in small part.

A new program included in this budget is $18 million of General Revenue to pay the State's share of the cost of caring for the medically indigent of Chicago on the same basis that the State contributes to similar costs downstate. I believe it is now generally agreed that this unequal treatment should be remedied. If the State assumes that burden it would enable Cook County to reduce taxes and hard pressed Chicago to raise taxes by the same amount, with no additional cost to Chicago taxpayers and a saving to Cook County residents outside of Chicago.

The only other new spending program in the field of welfare and health is a proposed appropriation of $6.5 million to meet the State's share of the cost of aid to the permanently and totally disabled which the Congress last year added to the social security system. In the long run this program is calculated to shift to the Federal government part of the cost of relieving many people now on the general relief rolls and wholly at State and local expense.

Civil Defense

Another cost of State government which appears for the first time is $500,000 for the operation of the State Civil Defense office. This is the total appropriation I am recommending for State civil defense at this time, although it is small in comparison with civil defense appropriations in the other large states.

Civil defense against atomic attack is without precedent. Organization and planning to enable us to marshal the resources of the State and its cities quickly and smoothly is urgent. The State Civil Defense office which I created last summer has been living in borrowed quarters, staffed in part by borrowed personnel. Its comprehensive plan is largely completed. The appropriation proposed should enable it to continue the state-wide planning function, the communications center and the promotion and coordination of local civil defense planning and organization.

But I am making no provision for State stockpiling of equipment or for matching Federal funds. The sums involved are so enormous and the intentions of Congress still so unclear that I am proceeding on the assumption that in the event of necessity I could use any departmental appropriations and then ask the legislature for approval and to make good any deficiencies.

Highways

I shall not dwell on the familiar and deplorable condition of our highways or pending legislation to assist all levels of government. But I must point out that due to the destruction and decay of the primary system, aggravated by a severe winter, I am obliged to recommend an increase for maintenance and patchwork from $35 million to $61 million for 1951–53.

Construction

The construction or capital budget includes some $40 million of new money from General Revenue, as against $76 million in this biennium. The bulk of this money is for repair, rehabilitation and minor construction that can no longer wisely be deferred. Consistent with the policy of deferring all but the most essential construction there is included but $12.3 million for new construction of major projects. The largest is the long awaited and critically needed Pharmacy Building at the Chicago campus of the University of Illinois Medical School. I recommend $6.3 million for this building at this time only because more doctors and pharmacists are so sorely needed.

There is also included $5 million for further development and construction at the new Tinley Park Mental hospital near Chicago, the only new facility which will provide material relief from the serious overcrowding in state hospitals in the northern part of the state. When completed Tinley Park will accommodate 3,750 to 4,000 patients.

Employee Compensation

This budget includes personal services appropriations to cover payroll costs at the levels established by the 66th General Assembly and merit increases for all employees who have not reached the maximum of their range. An additional $14 million of General Revenue is included to cover cost of living increases to state employees, other than employees of the University of Illinois which makes its wage policies independently.

The consumers' price index now stands at 184 compared with 169 in the spring of 1949. With prices continuing to advance, it seems likely that by the time the new biennium begins the index will have increased by about 10 per cent in the past two years. I believe that a compensating adjustment is imperative and I so recommend.

In view of present inflationary trends we might be well advised to apply an escalator provision to the compensation of State employees if the legislature makes a reserve appropriation of income in excess of estimates. It should be of assistance in reducing the growing employee turnover and providing a measure of flexibility the next two years.

Also of payroll significance is the position classification system, which affects about 18,000 employees. By repeated amendment it has become cumbersome and unwieldy. When adopted in 1943 some thirty-two job levels were established. The number has now risen to forty-two, and the maxima and minima are obsolete.

The Position Classification Act should be amended to reduce and simplify the number of ranges and to raise the maxima and minima in each. The budget figures would be inadequate only to the extent that no provision is made for increases for persons at the top of their present range. I propose that such increases be absorbed through reduction in the number of positions and the better utilization of personnel. In terms of overall cost the state would be far better off with a higher average rate of compensation and a smaller, more stable staff.

Conclusion

Finally, let me express my thanks to the members of the Budgetary Commission for their tireless patience and assistance in preparing this very difficult budget. That no general purpose tax increases are necessary and that it has been possible to reduce total expenditures is gratifying. That General Revenue costs are up only 3% without sacrificing any services and actually increasing grants and salaries is even more gratifying, considering the rise in all costs.

In my budget message two years ago I promised you relentless effort to eliminate every unnecessary job and every wasteful practice. On closer examination of this budget, you will notice that before salary increases we have held the line or actually reduced appropriations for most of the executive departments and agencies, in spite of inflation and the tendency of governments to grow toward ever wider and more costly horizons of service. If our housekeeping has been good, I am proud, but the credit goes to my directors and a multitude of loyal employees.

Although our State government costs the citizen of Illinois much less than the average for all the states, we will not be able to sustain even our present level of services and grants much longer without additional revenue for our general purposes. Inflation cannot save us forever; indeed, it can only destroy us all.

On the executive side we must and we will continue to live frugally and search relentlessly for ever better government. On the legislative side, I ask, in conclusion, what I asked at the outset: that you guard

the delicate balance we have struck; that you do not add without subtracting — that Illinois may be an example of thrifty management in a
time of fiscal peril.

*During the Korean War, General Douglas MacArthur disagreed re-
peatedly with the policies of President Truman. MacArthur did not hesitate to make his views public. On April 5, 1951, for instance, he sent a
letter to U.S. Representative Joseph W. Martin, Republican minority
leader, rejecting the concept of limited war and calling for bold measures
and a decisive victory on the battlefield. On April 10, 1951, the President
relieved General MacArthur of his command. The President announced
that MacArthur "is unable to give his wholehearted support to the policies of the United States Government."*

*Stevenson had many requests from the press for a statement, and is-
sued the following on April 11, 1951.*[50]

No one has done more than MacArthur to preserve and protect our
system of government — but it is a system in which civilian control of
the military is basic.

As a great military leader his apparent departure from the fundamental
principle of obedience is hard to understand.

Our only compensation for a great loss is the reaffirmation of a great
principle.

To Mrs. John Paul Welling

April 10, 1951

Dear Harriet:

Jane Dick was here the other day and told me that Paul [Welling]
had broken his hip. I am distressed and horrified. I hope you will give
him my love and best wishes — reserving appropriate quantities of
both for yourself.

Affectionately,

P.S. I had expected to be camping on your doorstep long before this,
but what with the budget and the legislature I have found Springfield
my perpetual home.

A.E.S.

[50] The text is based on a carbon copy.

To T. S. Matthews

April 10, 1951

Dear Tom:

Isn't it time for you to come back to see the Illinois Legislature in action — and to hold the Governor's hand and conscience!

Yours,

Mr. Matthews replied on April 13, 1951: "I take it kindly that spring-time, which starts the crocuses and other evidences of hope brings thoughts of me. I suppose you are worn to the nub by a hard winter's work, and are wishful to relax in an evening conversation — cosmic complaints not loud but deep." He declined because he was going to England with his son, saying he might come later. "You don't mention them — no doubt from shyness — but if I bring the [Lewis B.] Cuylers with me, will you give a ball?"

To T. S. Matthews

April 19, 1951

Dear Tom:

Of course I will give a ball if you bring the Cuylers. It is possible that they might not identify it as such.

I remember the time you took me to England.[51] I hope your son profits more than I did. I will be awaiting your return, conserving my cosmic complaints.

Yours,

To Mrs. Walter P. Paepcke

April 19, 1951

Dear Pussy:

Your party for the Hutchins was my only escape from my hideous routine in a long while. I am sure I had a better time than you, Bob, Vesta,[52] or anyone else. And, if I must, let me repeat in writing my invitation to the Paepckes to come to Springfield — soon, I hope. Next week-end, April 28 or 29, would be fine!

Yours,

[51] Stevenson, Matthews, and several other Princton classmates toured England in 1920. See *The Papers of Adlai E. Stevenson*, Vol. I, pp. 78–85.
[52] Mrs. Hutchins.

On April 12, 1951, Basil L. Walters, executive editor of Knight Newspapers, Inc., which published the Chicago Daily News, wrote Stevenson:
"I was delighted to read your good words of wisdom on the MacArthur
matter. As I have told you before, I have the feeling that you have a
true sense of the fundamentals that have made this a great nation. . . .
It is of course most essential that civilian control of the military be
maintained."

To Basil L. Walters

April 19, 1951

Dear Stuffy:

God bless you for that letter. It diluted a deluge of rattle-headed,
abusive mail. No, it didn't dilute — it obliterated!

I thought you might be down to see me for a "quiet" evening long
before this. I am still hoping.

Yours,

In a long letter setting forth some political and philosophical views,
Stevenson's friend John Monroe of Boston wrote that he was sure the
Governor was the best presidential timber in either party; that it was
unfortunate Stevenson was not in the Republican camp for there was no
Republican who could match him; that on his first meeting with Stevenson he was filled with an admiration that only increased with the passage
of time.

To John Monroe

April 19, 1951

Dear John:

I have just finished reading your very interesting and thoughtful letter.
It has given me much food for thought, and I shall expect to see an
article any day now in one of the better magazines! I think you are right
that the old life is cracking up a bit. Frankly, I rather like what I see in
some directions. But the current emotional binge seems to me not only
unwholesome but dangerous.[53]

[53] There was an outburst of emotion after President Truman removed General
Douglas MacArthur. Republican congressional leaders insisted on an investigation of
the Administration's foreign policy. On April 19, 1951, General MacArthur addressed
a wildly applauding Congress.

Your flattering remarks about myself are warming, but not persuasive. I am afraid my horizons and ambitions are limited.

With thanks and kind regards, I am

Sincerely yours,

To Mrs. Edison Dick [54]

April 25, 1951

Dear Jane:

I have read with literal fascination Titia's adolescent creations.[55] What a girl! I was moved to write her myself and the inadequate letter is enclosed. Please observe that I have protected the parent from the customary charge of press-agenting.

I hope and pray that all goes well and if I can steal a moment from MacArthur I shall call from Chicago tomorrow to inquire about your mother.[56] Do come down if you can this week-end or let me know if you think of anyone I should invite. The Odells [57] are coming and Alan Cranston.[58]

Yours,

ADLAI

To Letitia Dick [59]

April 25, 1951

My dear Titia:

There has come to my hands the April issue of "The Full Cry," and I have you to blame for keeping me awake for several nights. I think you have done a bit of fine writing in "The Furnace," but my sins are catching up with me and I feel closer to the furnace door every night! The poem is lovely and I think you have great depth.

Affectionately,

P.S. Don't blame your mother. She didn't give it to me. I have my secret agents!

[54] The original is in the possession of Mrs. Dick.

[55] Mrs. Dick had sent Stevenson some writing done by her daughter, a student at Garrison Forest School in Garrison, Maryland.

[56] Mrs. Dick's mother was seriously ill. Stevenson was expected to attend a large parade, in his official capacity as governor, scheduled for General MacArthur in Chicago.

[57] Mr. and Mrs. William R. Odell, of Lake Forest, Illinois.

[58] Alan Cranston, of California, was later elected to the U.S. Senate from that state.

[59] This handwritten letter is in the possession of Mrs. Edison Dick.

Stevenson in his official capacity as governor attended the parade in Chicago for General Douglas MacArthur.

To Mrs. Edison Dick [60]

April 26, 1951

. . . I have today witnessed one of the appalling experiences of a full life. I arranged to ride in a separate car with the Ill[inois]. Nat. Guard Generals & kept in the background in the chaos at the airport. After 23 miles thru a wall of yelling humanity I could take no more and vanished from the Stevens [Hotel] to Meigs field, the plane, Spfd and fresh air. I think at last I can understand something of the mass incitations in Rome and Berlin. But what does this mean? Are we yelling for more war or less. Is it a man? Is it synthetic? is it an idea? what idea? . . .

To Fred K. Hoehler [61]

April 30, 1951

Dear Fred:

I seem to be in political trouble again due to the reemployment of Burley Orrison, as an Account Clerk at Manteno [State Hospital]. I don't know what can be done now, but I hope in view of his former Republican political leadership in Piatt County that no advancement or other recognition will be accorded him until we have some opportunity to review it.

[Lawrence] Irvin tells me that the committee was requested to fill the job Orrison is on at a salary of $190 per month. They were unable to furnish a qualified candiate at this rate, though Irvin points out that after the job was "released" Orrison was employed at $270 per month. Undoubtedly the committee could have uncovered a qualified candidate at the higher rate.

I am told this is a ruse often used to circumvent the committee and it does not seem fair. As another example, Irvin mentioned the case of a Republican Maintenance Worker at Lincoln [State Hospital] who was discharged for political reasons. The committee was asked to replace him at a salary of $125 per month. When they were unable to furnish a candi-date the same Republican was rehired at $193 and the committee again felt that they could have located a candidate at the higher salary.

All of this suggests to me the desirability of having another three-cornered talk with Irvin sometime soon about the patronage situation.

[60] This handwritten letter is in the possession of Mrs. Dick.
[61] A carbon copy is in the possession of Lawrence Irvin.

Approaching a campaign year you will understand that I must give more and more attention to that constant problem, consistent with the general policies we have agreed upon.

Sincerely yours,

In the spring of 1951, Walter V. Schaefer was running for the office of Justice of the Illinois Supreme Court, which he won.

To Walter V. Schaefer [62]

April 30, 1951

Dear Walter:

I have asked Jim [Mulroy] to scratch the barrel, and I am enclosing a personal contribution of $1,000.00. I think it best to send it to you to use as you see fit.

Sincerely yours,

ADLAI

State Senator Peter J. Miller told General Douglas MacArthur that Stevenson approved President Truman's dismissal of him and that the Governor had ripped the General "up the back." The Chicago Tribune's *editorial was entitled "The Party of Acheson, Stevenson, and Hiss" and stated that New Dealers would not give up Alger Hiss but "have no faith in an American of Gen. MacArthur's unchallengeable patriotism."*

To Alicia Patterson [63]

May 1, 1951

. . . My miseries are many even as yours. But we're making a little progress in spite of the level of politics that prevails in this sovereign state, paced by the Chicago Tribune. Its latest contribution is enclosed. I issued a statement on MacArthur, copy enclosed, and this imbecile Miller who belongs to the Tribune body and breeches told MacArthur that I had "ripped him up the back." Ho! Hum! Its a grizzly life. . . .

A

[62] The original of this letter is in the possession of Mr. Schaefer.
[63] This handwritten letter is in the possession of Adlai E. Stevenson III.

To Mrs. Edison Dick [64]

May 2, 1951

. . . I wonder what the news is this morning & its all I can do to resist the telephone. . . .

I wish there was something I could do or say or think or pray that would help in your agonizing vigil. . . .[65]

I'll reread your letter & the report from street corner & feel better and better about the state of the world and the state of the nation & the state of the gov. But how about the state of J?

If Taft hasn't destroyed his position yet, I tremble. But the U.S. Chamber of Commerce rose and cheered.[66] What goes on? Could it be that 99% *are* unbalanced after all?

Anyway the N[ew] Y[ork] Post reports that the escaped insane man who did such a good job of impersonating a Senator from Maine may be committed to the Ohio Legislature!!

Now laugh!!!

P.S. I leave Friday for Louisville & will stay Friday & Sat nights with Barry Bingham — and the Duchess of Windsor! Sunday I will fly, God willing, to St. Charles [67] to dedicate the chapel and then back to Spfd for Carl McGowan's birthday party.

Chins up! . . .

During the latter part of April, 1951, state Representative G. William Horsley, Republican from Springfield, in a letter to Governor Stevenson, called for an investigation of what he termed wrongful and wasteful expenditures of state funds. The story, including Stevenson's letter dated May 3, 1951, appeared in the Illinois State Journal *on May 4, 1951. Highlights of Stevenson's reply follow.*[68]

---

[64] This handwritten letter is in the possession of Mrs. Dick.

[65] Mrs. Dick's mother was dying of cancer.

[66] In a speech before the annual convention of the Chamber of Commerce of the United States in Washington, D.C., on April 30, 1951, Republican Senator Robert A. Taft talked about the Korean War. He deplored the indefinite stalemate of the war and recommended that the policies of General Douglas MacArthur be adopted: the use of Chiang Kai-shek's troops on the Chinese mainland and Korea, the bombing of Manchurian bases, and the blockade of Communist China.

[67] The Illinois State Training School for Boys was located at St. Charles.

[68] The text is based on the *Journal* story of May 4.

To G. William Horsley

May 3, 1951

. . . You have made some useful comments regarding printing practices. However, they are not new and the matters you discuss at length were studied by the staff of the Schaefer commission more than a year ago. Indeed, H. B. 585, calculated to remedy at least to some extent a statutory situation that has existed for many years, was introduced three weeks before your letter. I should be glad to have you take an interest in that bill. The law must be revised to eliminate the present schedule of maximum prices established in 1915 and not substantially changed since then.

You are incorrect in your statement that Mr. [Leo] Pflum, the state printer, is under the misapprehension that he can ask for bids only every two years. Mr. Pflum has been in the division of printing for 18 years in both Democratic and Republican administrations. But in a period of constantly rising prices it will probably serve little purpose to ask repeatedly for bids to establish basic maximum prices. Indeed, under present conditions, when we have to wait for deliveries from three months to a year for some items, quarterly bidding might be not only impossible but very expensive. A carload of mimeograph paper today, for example, costs $6800. Purchased in smaller lots the cost would be $9000.

You imply that some bidders receive the bulk of office supply orders through political influence, but you cite no case in which a higher bidder was accepted because of political favoritism. Nor can you find one. Are you proposing that we reject the lowest bids in such cases?

Although you state with bold assurance that "the spirit and the letter of the law is being violated" by the division of printing, the only case you present in five pages, single spaced, is the purchase of magazines and books for the state institutions and departments from the Hanson Bennett Magazine agency. This company is one of the largest in the country and the state has been doing business with it for 25 years. I am informed that no other agency in the state is equipped to handle the business, but in view of your complaint I will direct an inquiry of the possibility of reducing current costs by some other form of contracting.

I do not understand the relevance of your paragraphs about the purchase of shale to mend roads at the fairgrounds from a Mr. Ziller in the amount of $100.50. As to the mysterious piece of equipment which you say was loaned to him by the state, you are right that Mr. [Roy E.] Yung, director of agriculture, knows nothing about it, nor can I find any department head that does.

Your next complaint refers to state owned automobiles and their use.

You state that there has been an increase in state owned cars. On the contrary, in the agencies of the state under my jurisdiction, there has been a reduction of 216 in the number of passenger vehicles since January, 1949.

Anonymous letters about accidents and the improper use of state cars are of no value to me. And perhaps you are unaware of what we have been doing for the last two years to stop improper use of vehicles by repeated departmental orders and instructions. Moreover, commencing with 1950 I ordered all state cars to carry M license plates so they could be distinguishable, except cars used by investigators and top executives.

As you must know, complaints calculated to discredit in general terms are the familiar weapon of disappointed salesmen who no longer have things their own way.

But as for the letter you cite from a Chicago attorney who complained about a contract for processing and packaging butter at $4000 above the low bid, the fact is that this contract was not let by the division of purchases, but by the Illinois public aid commission which has given me a fully documented and valid explanation of it.

Your informant, I am told, is a disgruntled former employe of the department of agriculture, who resigned before charges were filed against him. While ostensibly working full time as an inspector for the department during the prior administration he defended as a private lawyer 10 or 15 prosecutions by the federal food and drug officials.

If you would like to know more about the source of your information, we can give it to you. We can also provide some interesting information about our progress in the protection of the public from impure and adulterated foods.

I say again that I appreciate your efforts to find something either wrong or wasteful, but on the basis of your information and misinformation, I think you will have to agree that your charges, orally and in writing, are more colorful than factual, and hardly constitute a reasonable basis for another unlimited legislative investigation at the taxpayers' expense.

My objective has been to clean up and tighten up our housekeeping all along the line. That many improvements have already been made I assert with confidence. That more can and must be made I have often repeated. I welcome, indeed I count upon, the assistance of all the members of the General Assembly in achieving economies wherever possible.

On May 2, 1951, Representative Horsley wrote Stevenson that official Illinois stationery was being used by a California bookie to solicit bets.

In his letter he said that it merely pointed up the fact that if an immediate investigation were made of state purchases it would disclose the various loopholes by which the state was being milked of large sums of money each year. After Stevenson's reply the issue died a natural death.

To G. William Horsley [69]

May 4, 1951

Dear Mr. Horsley:

Your letter of May 2 asks for a prompt reply. You could have had a more prompt reply if you had called me by telephone but I suppose you cannot release telephone calls to the press.

The bond paper bearing the State seal watermark was purchased from the Birmingham & Prosser Company and manufactured by the Fox River Paper Company, Fox River, Wisconsin. In the manufacture of such papers there are often "over-runs." Such "ends," or "culls," are sold by the mill to the Fort Dearborn Paper Company, Chicago, a paper dealer which also sells job lot ends, rejects and imperfect papers. This company has an office in California, which probably explains how this stationery reached California.

There is nothing, I am informed, in the statutes, which prohibits private sale or use of paper rejects bearing a watermark of the State seal.

I will not ask you what you mean by "these various loop holes by which the State is being milked of large sums of money each year," because you do not know yourself. But your taste for unverified accusations reminds me of the lawyer who said to the jury: "These are the conclusions on which I base my facts."

Sincerely yours,

To Edward D. McDougal, Jr.[70]

May 7, 1951

Dear Ed:

I have your letter. May 18 I will be at home and the schedule indicates that the [Kenneth F.] Burgesses will probably be staying here that night. You would be most welcome. May 19 I have to go to Chicago in the afternoon and to Danville to speak on Sunday, May 20. If you wanted to come down the 18th you would miss the legislature, but I could take you back

[69] The text is based on a mimeograph copy prepared by the Governor's office for release to the press.
[70] The original is in the possession of Mr. McDougal.

to Chicago with me by plane the next day. Or you could stay over here and make yourselves at home.

If you want to see the legislature, which is getting pretty warm, you would have to be here Monday afternoon, Tuesday, Wednesday or Thursday — preferably Tuesday or Wednesday!

Yours,

ADLAI

P.S. Walter Schaefer needs help anywhere he can get it and I am sure you could pass the hat for him a bit or talk it up; particularly to get suburbanites to vote would be helpful.

Paul Simon, editor and publisher of the Troy Tribune, was about to serve in the Korean War. He appeared first on Stevenson's horizon in 1950 when he wrote the Governor urging him to crack down on gambling in Illinois. Mr. Simon noted years later: "I was 22 years old when he sent me this [letter]. Rather a remarkable thing for a governor to take this much interest in a 22-year old." [71]

To Paul Simon [72]

May 7, 1951

Dear Mr. Simon:

I hear today from Carl McGowan that you are shortly to be inducted into the Army. I find myself of two minds: I am delighted on the one hand that you are going to be serving in the armed forces, and disappointed on the other hand that your emphatic and clear voice is going to be stilled hereabouts for a while. I hope it will not be long before you can resume your very important and helpful contribution to the revival of interest in law enforcement in Illinois.

With all good wishes and my regards, I am

Sincerely yours,

Stevenson wrote to Mrs. Edison Dick, consoling her on the death of her mother.

---

[71] On December 9, 1965, Mr. Simon sent Walter Johnson copies of his correspondence with Governor Stevenson. This comment was attached to the letter of May 7, 1951, by Mr. Simon.

[72] The original is in the possession of Mr. Simon.

To Mrs. Edison Dick [73]

May 14, 1951

. . . When my mother and father forsake me, then the Lord will take me up. For in the time of trouble he shall hide me in his pavilion: in the secret of his tabernacle shall he hide me; he shall set me up upon a *rock.*

I shall be glad and rejoice in his mercy: for he has considered my trouble; he has know[n] my soul in adversities. . . .

Stevenson asked Mr. Gail Borden, of Chicago to serve as his military aide. Aside from accompanying Stevenson to the Governors' Conference in Colorado Springs in 1949 he had not performed any service. In May, 1951, he wrote Stevenson that he was a poor excuse for a governor's military aide, that he never got to Springfield, rarely saw the Governor in Chicago, and felt he should resign. He concluded: "You are doing one grand job with that crowd of people's choice in the Legislature."

To Gail Borden

May 14, 1951

Dear Gail:

I decline to accept the resignation of my "military aide." Aside from our happy journey to Colorado Springs long ago I have had no need for "aideing," but should the time come I will call upon you.

I am delighted to hear that things are going well for you and I wish I could say the same. Your comforting remarks about the public job I appreciate. But the fiscal price is high!

My best to you and Betty.[74]

Yours,

The explosion of a coal mine at Centralia, Illinois, in 1947, in which 116 miners were killed, was an important issue in Stevenson's campaign in 1948. In 1949 he recommended a complete reorganization of the Department of Mines and Minerals, and the legislature acted to improve the mining laws. Afterward Stevenson asked Dr. Harold Walker, head of the University of Illinois Department of Mines, who had served as

[73] This handwritten letter is in the possession of Mrs. Dick.
[74] Mrs. Borden.

director of the Illinois State Department of Mines and Minerals at Stevenson's request during the first months of his administration, to make a complete recodification of the mining laws. It was Stevenson's intention to have the revisions introduced into the legislature in 1951. He was unable to get support from the Mining Investigation Commission, the unions, the operators or the senators from the mining areas. Rather than risk the failure of other important items in his legislative program, Stevenson abandoned his plan to introduce this mining legislation.

On May 16, 1951, he wrote to Sam Cape, chairman of the Mining Investigation Commission, on the subject, and also issued a general statement of his views, both of which were released to the press.[75]

To Sam Cape

May 16, 1951

Dear Mr. Cape:

In my opinion the Mining Laws of Illinois are in many respects ambiguous, obsolete, or both, and the provisions governing mine safety urgently require clarification and strengthening. I believe the coal mining industry, and everyone for that matter, agree that the State should do everything it can within reason to prevent mine disasters which have cost so many lives.

To that end I recommended and the Legislature enacted at the last session a reorganization of the Department of Mines and Minerals and removed ambiguous lines of authority and responsibility in the administration of our laws.

While our mine safety record is now the best it has been in many years, I believe we all agree that there is much room for improvement in our laws. I had hoped to make further progress in this session by comprehensive codification, simplification and improved safety requirements. Accordingly, I am disappointed to hear that the mine unions and the operators have "unanimously rejected" the draft bill codifying, modernizing and strengthening our laws which I submitted to the Mining Investigation Commission for consideration on January 10, 1951.

I have conferred with the legislative leaders from the coal mining areas and they advise me that in view of the opposition of both operators and unions the draft legislation we have so painstakingly prepared for the past year has no chance of passage at this session.

I gather that the industry wants additional time to consider such legislation. Hence, I will not introduce the bill at this time. Meanwhile, I

[75] Only the text of the letter is published here, since the general statement repeats the same points that are made in the letter.

earnestly hope the industry will prepare and present such mine safety legislation as can be agreed upon at this session if possible, and if not, may I urge the Commission to take the initiative in preparing a comprehensive legislative program for introduction at the next session. And may I also suggest that the draft bill the administration has prepared and submitted might serve as a suitable basis for consideration.

I am sure we all agree that in view of the importance of our coal mining industry, there is no reason why Illinois should not have the best and most up to date mining laws. To that end I stand ready to assist now and in the future in any way I can.

For their information, I am sending copies of this letter to the other members of the Mining Investigation Commission and to the officials of the mine unions and operators listed in your letter of April 3, 1951.

Sincerely yours,

By the summer of 1951 the Korean War had moved into a deadlock, where decisive victory for either side seemed impossible without a wider conflict. President Truman, distracted by the war and a difficult Congress, nevertheless was faced with a campaign year in 1952 and some fence-mending in 1951. Or at least, so thought Governor Stevenson in asking him to come to Illinois.

To Harry S. Truman [76]

May 26, 1951

Dear Mr. President:

It is with much hesitation that I have concluded to even suggest that you speak at the Illinois State Fair on Democratic Day, which is on Thursday, August 16.

I think I fully appreciate the futility of requests this far in advance, but it has occurred to me if you were going to do some speaking this summer, as the newspapers indicate, this would be a good place and a good time. I think you can be confident of a minimum of 15,000 to 20,000 people in and adjoining the grandstand if the weather is fair.

Vice President Barkley has spoken here for the last three years, and we hope, of course, to have him again if you are unable to come. The state of mind is rapidly improving here in spite of the long shadow of the Chicago Tribune, but I hardly need add that the effect of a personal

[76] The original is in the Harry S. Truman Library, Independence, Missouri.

appearance and a foreign policy pronouncement would be tremendous. With heartfelt best wishes — and prayerful hope! [77]

Faithfully yours,

To Mrs. Edison Dick [78]

June 11, 1951

. . . Why, oh why haven't you ever shown me thru this collection.[79] I feel neglected; indeed hurt! Am I *only* a politician or even a statesman — without literary perceptions, tastes, appreciations. Ho Hum — maybe you're right, but it wasn't always thus — nor will it always be thus!!!

I'm back from my wanderings and Borden's in Harvard — thank God.[80] What a relief to have that minor crise over. He really did very well this last year. Adlai's going to Europe, Borden may go, the Dicks are going, John Fell's going to the ranch & what the hell am I doing here! I can't wait to talk about your trip — but what have I to say that's wise & helpful — I'll be up this weekend. . . .

After a visit with Averell Harriman, who was assisting President Truman in the White House, Stevenson wrote him a letter with further suggestions as to how Secretary of State Acheson might go about educating the public about the Korean War. A copy of the letter was sent to Mr. Acheson.

To Averell Harriman

June 11, 1961

Dear Averill:

I have been thinking a little more about our conversation of Saturday. I agree emphatically that Dean [Acheson] should, if he can possibly contrive it, take the initiative and exploit the advantage. If he could do but a few discussions, commencing shortly after Labor Day, if not before, I am sure it would help immensely. As I told you, I think the formal speech and repetition of familiar positions less effective than informal

[77] The President replied on June 6, 1951, saying he could not give a definite answer until he was aware of what Congress would do. Later he declined.

[78] This handwritten letter is in the possession of Mrs. Dick.

[79] Mrs. Dick had an especially fine collection of works by Katherine Mansfield, including first editions and manuscripts.

[80] Stevenson had just visited the East Coast. His second son, Borden, had been admitted to Harvard University.

discussions, with questions and answers, with smaller groups of editors, publishers, educators, commentators, and what I believe the Department calls "public opinion forming groups." I feel that the important thing is not so much a "speech" and a headline as it is genuine information and respect for the policy and its symbol, the Secretary. I hope you can persuade him to try something of this kind and somehow make the time and find the energy to do it.

Warm regards and my thanks for your hospitality.

Sincerely yours,

Laird Bell, a member of the board of trustees of the University of Chicago, was interested in a bill to consolidate control of six state institutions of higher learning under a single state board of education. The bill was sponsored by Stevenson in the 1951 legislature. Bell had found it impossible to attend the legislative hearing on the bill.

To Laird Bell [81]

June 11, 1951

Dear Laird:

I was delighted to have your note. Perhaps it was just as well you didn't come to the hearing on the Higher Education bill because they disposed of it adversely after hearing only two witnesses. The vote was 11–8 and the opposition was led by Senator Peters who signed the "Works Bill" in 1945, as Chairman of a legislative commission which made an almost identical report and recommendation.[82] Ho hum!

But I would like to talk with you about this sometime, because I think it has important implications for the taxpayer and the privately endowed universities. Moreover, I *know* something of this kind will be done in Illinois ultimately.

[81] The original of this letter is in the possession of Mrs. Laird Bell.

[82] Senator Everett R. Peters, Republican, of Champaign, was chairman of a commission created by the 1943 legislature to survey higher educational facilities and resources in Illinois. In 1945 Peters sponsored Senate Bill 260, containing the commission's recommendations, including a provision for a state board of education to govern the University of Illinois and other state-controlled institutions of higher learning. The bill was tabled. In 1951 a proposal (Senate Bill 720) to create a state board of education to operate the state-controlled universities was adversely reported by committee and subsequently tabled.

In 1961 a state board of education was created to analyze the requirements of higher education in Illinois, prepare a master plan for its development, and make budget proposals to the governor. Senator Peters was a cosponsor of the bill (S.B. 766).

I have had no opportunity to tell you how deeply I appreciate your help for Walter Schaefer. He deserved it, and in your case he got it. It was a great comfort to him.

Yours,
ADLAI

P.S. Should you and Mrs. Bell care to witness any of the Legislature's expiring weeks I hope you will come down.

A.E.S.

The legislature passed bills involving approximately twenty million dollars for the building of roads, bridges and other public works. Stevenson felt obliged to veto some of these bills.

*To the Honorable, the Members of the Senate of the
Sixty-seventh General Assembly* [83]

June 15, 1951

I herewith return, without my approval, Senate Bill No. 3, entitled "An Act making an appropriation to the Department of Public Works and Buildings for constructing a certain highway bridge and road project in the City of Kankakee, Illinois."

I veto and withhold my approval from this bill for the following reasons:

The bill appropriates $750,000 to the Department of Public Works and Buildings for the construction of a highway bridge across the Kankakee River at Third Avenue in the City of Kankakee.

I have repeatedly expressed my conviction that special highway appropriations are bad in principle. The General Assembly long ago established the desirable policy of leaving the details of the expenditure of funds upon highway improvements to the Department of Public Works and Buildings. Under existing laws, the time, manner and place of construction of roads and bridges are rightly left to the determination of the expert engineers of the Division of Highways. All our road and bridge needs cannot be met at once, and special bills like this one deny to the engineers the discretion they should exercise on the basis of scientific traffic counts and professional methods of ascertaining priority in the spending of available funds.

[83] *Messages of Adlai E. Stevenson, Governor of Illinois, on Senate and House Bills Passed by the 67th General Assembly of Illinois* (published by the State of Illinois, 1951), p. 7.

I have also repeatedly said that Illinois has suffered too much in the past from the construction of highway projects on a political basis; and that these special bills cause a reversion to log-rolling and political back-scratching.

These considerations apply with peculiar force to Senate Bill No. 3. It is an aggravated case of the evil to be avoided because not only does it appropriate for a special project, but it goes further and specifies the exact location of the bridge itself. I believe the Department should determine the location on the same basis of scientific and non-political considerations which should determine whether a bridge should be built at Kankakee at all. I have been gratified by many communications from the residents of Kankakee who share this view.

Further, the location at Third Avenue appears to be objectionable to many local residents and organizations who are interested in the civic betterment of Kankakee and it does not, so I am advised, square with the long-range plan for the development of Kankakee formulated by local planning authorities. Whatever the respective merits of local differences of opinion about the location of the bridge, the very fact that there are differences is all the more reason why it is sound practice to leave the selection of the location to the impartial judgment of the Department in consultation with all the local interests in Kankakee.

The need for a new bridge at Kankakee is clear. Indeed, a million dollars is provided for a new bridge at Kankakee (in addition to the outer belt line bridge) in the Department's published construction program for the next two years. Regardless of any legislation, the department intends to proceed with this project during the next biennium if adequate funds are available. Gasoline tax and truck license fee bills to provide such funds are now under consideration by the legislature. The future of the Kankakee bridge and other sorely needed bridges elsewhere in the state depends on the Department's available funds, not on spending authorization which already exists.

All that Senate Bill No. 3 accomplishes is to tie the hands of the Department in selecting the location best suited to the needs of the community.

Respectfully,

On June 15, 1951, Governor Stevenson was the commencement speaker at the graduation exercises of the professional schools of the University of Illinois.[84]

[84] The text is based on a mimeograph copy released to the press.

. . . Commencements are traditionally, perhaps even properly, a time for viewing with alarm, for oratorical anxiety over these tender young things about to attack the grisly old world in search of a secure foothold. And then the orators inevitably end up on a note of rugged confidence and spiritual exhilaration. Distasteful as it may be to both of us, I shall probably do the same, but with, I suspect, somewhat more disorder and confusion of thought than is conventional on such solemn and orderly occasions.

I am so old I can even remember when ministers had text for their sermons. My text is from King Henry IV, Part I, Act II, Scene 3, where Hotspur says:

> "But I tell you, my Lord fool,
> out of this nettle, danger,
> we pluck this flower, safety."

In the nettle, danger, lies the flower, safety. Can we pluck it out? Can we identify the nettle? The flower? Can we agree what the danger is; can we agree what safety is; can we agree where it lies? Perhaps it has never been more difficult. But we must try, and keep on trying to identify our dangers and our goals. If most of us can't agree what's good and what's bad then our destiny is not nobility and peace but impotence and disaster.

Perhaps you in the health professions who have an urge to cure the ills of man and an education to identify the nettles, the dangers, in the human body are well equipped to press the search for the nettles and flowers of humanity as well as humans. And that — the quest for truth — after all is the essential purpose of all education.

But are you educated? Are you without precocity on the one hand and backwardness on the other? Are you balanced mortals? I know you will shortly hold diplomas and graduate degrees from one of the great universities of the modern world. But I remind you that John Milton's test of complete education — "that which fits a man to perform justly, skillfully and magnanimously all the offices, both private and public, of peace and war" — is as good today as it was 300 years ago.

Because the business of growing up as a whole, rather than in parts; because the business of education "to perform all the offices both private and public, of peace and war," has become so infinitely difficult in this age of vocational specialization in everything from lobotomies to law, I am bold enough to suggest that the first nettle, the first danger, for all of us is to miscalculate the meaning of education and the quality of our own education. Just as legality is not a synonym for morality, just as compliance with the letter of the law is not always compliance with its spirit, so graduation is not always the equivalent of education. Indeed there are many who say that the growing emphasis on the pragmatic disciplines, on specialized training and vocationalism, on the exaltation of the sciences at the expense of the humanities is, if anything, diminishing our perceptions, our horizons and our philosophical aptitude for the good life and the understanding heart — for civilized living, if you please.

And because there are few really educated, complete, balanced people on earth; because there are few specialists with the versatility of Leonardo da Vinci, or Thomas Jefferson, I am bold enough to suggest that you professional people especially should beware of any complacent idea that to know your own field well is enough. Unfortunately an education, so called, which should be only an introduction to humility and further inquiry is too often an introduction to pride and mental paralysis.

So, with that brief plea for restless, unsatisfied mind always open to everything except fear and prejudice, which, so far as I've been able to detect, is the only remedy for the humanist deficiencies of scientific education, I would like to mention some other nettles and dangers in which lie sorrow and safety alike. And at this point I'm sure you expect me, like all harrassed public officials, to talk about that nettle, more taxes, and beguile your unwilling hearts with the promise in exchange of that flower, security and better government. But you're wrong, although I confess I would like to say something about the way the Illinois Legislature applauds a spartan budget one day and then gaily appropriates additional money that doesn't exist. I feel like the young bridegroom who said that every time he was about to make both ends meet his wife moved the ends.

But back to our nettles — which don't all grow in Springfield. Has something happened to our morals and ethics? Is this the century of cynicism? Has the black bag with the payoff money become the national emblem? Is the fix more influential than the Bible? It begins to look that way. Of course, having lived only one life of which I have any distinct recollection, I have no basis of comparison and I don't know whether things are any worse than they used to be. But I do know they are pretty bad. We have heard much about the alliances of crime and politics. Hoodlums and racketeers dominate whole sections of our cities. Public officials are corrupted for protection of gambling. By muscle and money racketeers take over legitimate businesses and ruin honest men. The revelations of the Kefauver investigations [85] about the extent and power of organized crime shocked many of us. Evil influences creep into high places. The shake-down is a commonplace. For a little money a busi-

[85] The Senate Crime Investigation Committee, under the chairmanship of Estes Kefauver of Tennessee, set forth before rapt television audiences the connections between politics and organized crime in big cities.

ness man can save a lot of trouble. Lobbies for every special interest, good or evil, are an institution in all legislative halls. Gamblers bribe college athletes to fix games. Colleges hire athletes who are not bona fide students. Two-legged jackals peddle narcotics to children on our street corners. Respectable citizens protest loudly about lawlessness and venality but don't hesitate to fix a traffic ticket or buy a black market steak. A lot of overweight trucks are punishing our roads this very day because it pays to violate the law. Tomorrow someone will commend my efforts to enforce the gambling laws, but, he will add, of course the private clubs and lodges should be exempted. And then there are the unscrupulous for whom anything goes if it is within the letter of the law, or not too far outside; the numerous kind to whom legality and morality are the same. The defiant, "well, ain't it legal!" has become a part of our language.

I could go on and on, and so could you, adding to the evidence that something has happened; that the distinction between right and wrong is blurred; that cynicism and materialism are eating away at morals and ethics. I made no pretense of being a moral philosopher, nor do I know, as I say, if we are getting worse or better. In the field of government indeed we have seen nothing as shocking as the Teapot Dome Scandal. Nor have I forgotten the Seabury investigation of corruption in New York, nor the insurance scandals at the turn of the century.[86] I have even recently refreshed my recollection of what Paul said to the Corinthians about their morals. Indeed I have even earlier evidence of the malaise now current. This was written on an Assyrian tablet 4700 years ago: "Our earth is degenerate in these latter days; bribery and corruption are common, children no longer obey their parents; every man wants to write a book, and the end of the world is evidently approaching."

So maybe things are not as bad as they seem. At least everyone doesn't want to write a book nowadays. Rather since the advent of television, I'm beginning to wonder if anyone even wants to read one! But we will have to concede that things are pretty bad and getting worse after the ultimate evil of two and a half wars and all the historians have taught us that societies like human beings can sicken and die.

Unless you and your likes all over the country resist the corruption and corrosion of our times you will pluck no flowers of safety from this ugly nettle of moral danger, because whatever the apostles of the easy way, whatever the heralds of cynicism say, the inexorable law, the inescapable fact, remains that whatever we sow we reap. And no man, nor nation, nor civilization has been able to beat that rap yet — if I may use a vulgarism in such exalted company.

And speaking of moral fatigue and nations, let me also view with

[86] In 1905 a New York legislative committee investigated the New York insurance industry and exposed the cutthroat competition and shady finances of the industry.

alarm the hosts of political charlatans and false prophets who promise us painless solutions of the painful problems that bedevil our world. Of course there are no painless solutions to war, inflation, revolution, communism, imperialism, hunger, fear and all the diseases of a world in convulsive transition. But the political mountebanks blithely assure us that there is a better way to meet these challenges with less or no inconvenience — particularly to the group they happen to be talking to at the time. They remind me of the man who said he hoped we would soon get back to normal. I asked him for his definition. "That's a condition," he said, "where you have 1951 income, 1932 costs and 1911 taxes, all at one time."

Inflation is a case in point. Everyone applauded inflation control because everyone knows that inflation can ruin us quicker than Stalin. Well what happened? You know. Labor wants controls, but not on wages; farmers want price control but not on farm products; merchants want to halt inflation but no credit restrictions, etc., etc. Congress joins in the run-around by hesitating to raise taxes to soak up the excess purchasing power, and the easy way-out boys utter their soft words about no controls, no tax increases, just cut out the unnecessary spending. But they don't say where, and assuming 5 or 6 billion can be cut from the Federal budget, is it going to arrest this menacing inflation when the current rate of spending for goods and services is $316 billion?

And now the self same groups that have been most angrily isolationist and parsimonious about our defenses have overnight become the loudest voices demanding bigger military adventures. Incidentally may I remind you that Japan tried to conquer China in 1931. They called it an "incident." Fourteen years later they were still conquering China.

All your life I suspect you will hear the siren songs about easier, less painful, less costly solutions of everything. You will have to identify the dangers in these popular and seductive proposals. For years to come perhaps your greatest danger and ugliest nettle will be Communism. And you won't pluck the flower safely from that nettle by anything as easy as elocution, laws, or firing a few public officials. For Communism is far more dangerous than all our familiar authoritarian enemies, Kaiserism, Fascism and Nazism, because Communism is the corruption of a dream of justice. That dream is politically powerful, particularly among the miserable masses of the Orient who know nothing of the great Western liberal tradition and are only now catching the first intoxicating fragrance of the freedom of the Occident. But how fragrant are moral laxity and crumbling standards of responsible citizenship?

That's a job you have to do; restore our perfume! And another is to thread your way between imperialism and isolationism, between the disavowal of the responsibilities of our power and the assertion of our power beyond our resources. And always include, if I may offer you a bit of neglected advice, in any calculation of our resources, our moral resources. The power of a nation or an alliance consists of other factors than its military strength. Military power without a moral base is always intolerable. That's something people seem to overlook, particularly about Asia which is in the throes of a vast social convulsion and resentful of the white man's arrogance. You cannot reduce the struggle in Asia to purely military proportions, and the sooner we realize that the better it will be for us.

I have only touched on the myriad paths you will be summoned to follow. It won't be easy to find your way. The baffling difficulty of it all may explain one of the most unwholesome manifestations of our current disorder — which is called "McCarthyism." Perhaps this hysterical form of putrid slander not only escapes tar and feathers but actually flourishes because it satisfies a deep craving to reduce the vast menace of world Communism to comprehensible and manageable proportions. If the danger is only a local conspiracy and not a global challenge then we can meet and beat it by the arts of the prosecutor and politician which we understand. And of course that's another easy way, but a sad miscalculation of the perils we face. Indeed the apoplectic quality of our anti-Communism, its very violence, makes it the more difficult for us to analyze and understand its attractive power, and thus to combat it by eliminating the social conditions and resentments which Communism exploits.

I promised not to detain you long. So I conclude this botanical walk by reminding you that there are flowers of safety among the nettles of danger I've mentioned. The breadth of your education you can enlarge; our morals you can raise; our national wisdom and purpose you can improve.

Because the dangers are many it is a good time to be alive. Pitch in and enjoy it. Be an active part of your world, not just part of your profession, and, who knows, the golden promise of this bloody century will yet be fulfilled. Meanwhile, you will earn a living in the most satisfying field of man's endeavor — by relieving human suffering. You are very fortunate, and I wish you Godspeed.

Fred Young, of the Bloomington Daily Pantagraph, *wrote Stevenson on June 21, 1951: "The most intelligent story I have ever read on politics came to my attention today from the pen of Edwin Lahey in the Chicago Daily News. . . . I can say* AMEN *to every word he wrote. You have done a hell of a job, I must say, in tackling the toughest job in these great hours of trial and tribulation. It's grand to even know a guy like you, Adlai."*

To Fred Young

June 25, 1951

Dear Fred:

Your letter touched me deeply. I hope sometime we can have a talk and that you will not hesitate to let me know when you are hereabouts or would care to come down for an evening. Our philosophical observations are parallel, but I find it very hard to come by the "peace of mind" which we all seek.

Lahey's article pleased me, of course. But I had to read it twice to be sure who he was writing about!

Yours,

One of the best-known and most controversial of Stevenson's vetoes was that of Senate Bill 102, sponsored by Senator Paul Broyles, a Republican, from Mt. Vernon, Illinois. The purpose of the bill was to "protect against subversive activities" and required all public employees and officials to take a loyalty oath. It was enacted against a background of the national hysteria of "McCarthyism" — a fear of Communism in general and specifically of Communists in government. In Illinois this legislation was promoted by the American Legion and some newspapers, notably the Chicago Tribune *and the Chicago* Herald-American. *Stevenson vetoed the bill when it was politically dangerous — and correspondingly courageous — for him to do so.*

In 1966 Carl McGowan recalled:

In those days the attention of each legislature was diverted unnecessarily by proposals to set up machinery to flush out the Communists assertedly hiding behind every barn and silo on the prairie. In due course bills were passed which created a state instrumentality to chase subversives, and appropriated funds to support it. This kind of thing was anathema to Adlai for lots of reasons, including his sense of the efficient distribution of governmental functions. . . . But he wanted to be sure that his bias was not getting in the way of the public interest. So he took time out of his busy schedule and went to Washington to talk the matter over with the FBI.

There Stevenson learned

that about the only trouble the FBI had encountered in infiltrating the Communist Party completely was an occasional arrest or subpoenaing of one of its undercover agents by a state agency on the hunt for *bona fide* subversives. . . . The Governor . . . was not encouraged in this private inquiry to permit the creation of still another set of local watch dogs. Thus . . . [he] came home and wrote a veto message in which he took the full responsibility for nullifying the legislative decision to put the state in the subversive business at a time when many other problems pressed urgently upon its attention and resources.[87]

Since the legislature was not to adjourn until June 30, the Senate had a few days in which to override the veto. On June 28, three Republicans joined sixteen Democrats in the Senate to uphold the Governor's veto. The Nation *wrote: "A sharp reversal for the witch hunters and demagogues, the vote to uphold the veto illustrates what courageous leadership can accomplish against what seem to be heavy odds."* [88]

To the Honorable, the Members of the Senate of the Sixty-seventh General Assembly [89]

June 26, 1951

I herewith return, without my approval, Senate Bill No. 102, entitled "An Act to protect against subversive activities by making it a crime to commit or advocate acts intended to effect the overthrow of the Government of the United States or the State of Illinois or of any political subdivision thereof by violence or other unlawful means, or to attempt or conspire so to do, by defining subversive organizations and making them illegal, by establishing procedures to insure the loyalty of candidates for public office and of public officers and employees, and providing for the enforcement of the provisions of said Act, and providing penalties for the violation thereof."

I veto and withhold my approval from this bill for the following reasons:

The stated purpose of this bill is to combat the menace of world Communism. That the Communist Party — and all it stands for — is a danger to our Republic, as real as it is sinister, is clear to all who have the slightest understanding of our democracy. No one attached to the prin-

[87] Speech to the Law and Legal clubs of Chicago, March 11, 1966.
[88] *Nation,* Vol. 173, July 7, 1951, p. 1.
[89] *Messages of Stevenson, 67th General Assembly,* pp. 14–17.

ciples of our society will debate this premise or quarrel with the objectives of this bill.

Agreed upon ends, our concern is with means. It is in the choice of methods to deal with recognized problems that we Americans, in and out of public life, so often develop differences of opinion. Our freedom to do so is a great source of strength and, if not impaired by mistakes of our own, will contribute greatly to the ultimate confusion of the enemies of freedom.

The issue with respect to means raised by this bill has two aspects. One is the question of the need for it in relation to existing weapons for the control of subversives. The other is whether this addition to our arsenal may not be a two-edged sword, more dangerous to ourselves than to our foes.

Were the latter alone involved, I should hesitate to impose my judgment upon that of the majority of the General Assembly. But it is precisely because the evil at hand has long since been identified and provided against that we here in Illinois need not now do something *bad* just for the sake of doing *something*.

What are the facts with respect to need? On June 4 last, the Supreme Court of the United States affirmed the conviction of the twelve top leaders of the Communist Party in the United States. They were indicted under the provisions of an Act of Congress (the so-called "Smith Act") for conspiring (1) to organize as the Communist Party a society for the teaching and advocacy of the overthrow and destruction of the government of the United States (which by definition in the Act includes the governments of the states and their political subdivisions) by force and violence, and (2) to advocate and teach the overthrow of the government of the United States, as so defined, by force and violence. Close upon the heels of this opinion, the Federal government has moved to indict twenty-one more known Communist leaders. It is, of course, no secret that the Federal Bureau of Investigation has identified and has under observation virtually every member of the Communist Party and every serious sympathizer, and is prepared to take such persons into custody on short notice.

But Senate Bill 102 is unnecessary not alone because of the Federal anti-subversive law and activity, but because under the existing laws of Illinois it is now, and has been since 1919, a felony for any person to advocate the reformation or overthrow, by violence or other unlawful means, of the state or federal government, or to assist in the organization, or to become a member of, any organization dedicated to that objective. Our laws also prohibit the compensation from state funds of subversive employees or members of subversive organizations.

Indeed, it is ironic that the Ober law of Maryland, on which Senate Bill 102 is patterned, was itself an effort to make Maryland's sedition laws as comprehensive as Illinois'!

Senate Bill No. 102 makes it a felony to commit or attempt any act intended to overthrow by force the federal or state governments, or any of their political subdivisions; to advocate or teach the commission of such acts; or to have any connection with an organization devoted to such an objective. This approach parallels and duplicates criminal statutes of both the federal and state governments already in effect. Nor am I aware of complaints by any State's Attorneys throughout Illinois that our present sedition laws are insufficient.

Not only does Senate Bill No. 102 appear wholly unnecessary, but I agree with the Bar Associations that if the present sedition laws could be strengthened by expressly prohibiting the commission of acts as well as the advocacy thereof, this could best be accomplished by amending the existing laws rather than enacting new and more laws. Criminal laws, especially on subjects of vital importance, should not be confused by patchwork and duplication.

But it is in the enforcement provisions that I find this bill most objectionable. The Attorney General of Illinois is directed to appoint a Special Assistant Attorney General who must assemble and deliver to the State's Attorney of each county *all* information relating to subversive acts or activities within such county. The local State's Attorney then must present this matter to the Grand Jury. The Assistant Attorney General in Springfield must maintain complete records of all such information which may, with the permission of the Attorney General, be made public.

This transmission of such information and the subsequent presentation of it to the Grand Jury is mandatory under the Act — and covers in terms all information, however inconclusive or insignificant. I know of no precedent for any such interference with the normal discretion accorded to a public prosecutor. One of the important responsibilities of State's Attorneys and one of the greatest protections of the citizen is the exercise of sound judgment in sifting the many rumors, charges and countercharges which come to State's Attorneys' attention. This is true in the operation of the criminal laws generally, and it must, of necessity, be even more true when we are dealing with criminal laws relating in large degree to the state of men's minds.

I can see nothing but grave peril to the reputations of innocent people in this perpetuation of rumors and hearsay. When we already have sedition laws prohibiting the offenses of which these provisions relate, I see more danger than safety in such radical change in the administration of criminal justice.

Other substantive provisions in the bill are intended to assure the loyalty of the employees of the state government and its political subdivisions. All agencies of government must establish procedures to ascertain that there are no reasonable grounds to believe that any applicant for employment is committed, by act or teaching, to the overthrow of the government by force or is a member of an organization dedicated to that purpose. Thus, one who wishes to work for the state or to teach in a school must himself carry the burden of proving the absence of any reasonable grounds for belief that he is subversive or even belongs to a subversive organization. The bill does not even require that the applicant for employment know the purpose of such an organization.

Provisions as to those already employed also shift the burden of proof to the employee. With all the multitude of employing agencies throughout the State, each establishing its own rules and procedures for the enforcement of these provisions, it is easy to see what variations there might be and what possibilities for discrimination depending upon the wisdom and fairness of the particular employer.

By such provisions as these, irreparable injury to the reputation of innocent persons is more than a possibility, it is a likelihood. If this bill became law, it would be only human for employees to play safe and shirk duties which might bring upon them resentment or criticism. Public service requires independent and courageous action on matters which affect countless private interests. We cannot afford to make public employees vulnerable to malicious charges of disloyalty. So far as the employers are concerned — heads of departments and of schools and so on — the only safe policy would be timid employment practices which could only result in a lowering of the level of ability, independence and courage in our public agencies, schools and colleges.

Lastly, the bill provides that candidates for public office, other than offices for which an oath is prescribed by the Constitution, shall file an affidavit that he is not a subversive person. The Attorney General informs me that, despite the exception made, this requirement is of dubious constitutionality.

Does anyone seriously think that a real traitor will hesitate to sign a loyalty oath? Of course not. Really dangerous subversives and saboteurs will be caught by careful, constant, professional investigation, not by pieces of paper.

The whole notion of loyalty inquisitions is a natural characteristic of the police state, not of democracy. Knowing his rule rests upon compulsion rather than consent, the dictator must always assume the disloyalty, not of a few but of many, and guard against it by continual inquisition and "liquidation" of the unreliable. The history of Soviet Russia is a modern example of this ancient practice. The democratic state, on the other hand, is based on the consent of its members. The vast majority of our people are intensely loyal, as they have amply demonstrated. To question, even by implication, the loyalty and devotion of a large group of citizens is to create an atmosphere of suspicion and distrust which is neither justified, healthy nor consistent with our traditions.

Legislation of this type, in Illinois and elsewhere, is the direct result of the menacing gains of Communism in Europe and Asia. But it would be unrealistic, if not naive, to assume that such legislation would be effective in combatting Communist treachery in America. Such state laws have nowhere uncovered a single case of subversive disloyalty.

Basically, the effect of this legislation, then, will be less the detection of subversives and more the intimidation of honest citizens. But we cannot suppress thought and expression and preserve the freedoms guaranteed by the Bill of Rights. That is our dilemma. In time of danger we seek to protect ourselves from sedition, but in doing so we imperil the very freedoms we seek to protect, just as we did in the evil atmosphere of the alien and sedition laws of John Adams' administration and just as Britain did during the Napoleonic era. To resolve the dilemma we will all agree that in the last analysis the Republic must be protected at all costs, or there will be no freedoms to preserve or even regain. But if better means of protection already exist, then surely we should not further imperil the strength of freedom in search of illusory safety.

We must fight traitors with laws. We already have the laws. We must fight falsehood and evil ideas with truth and better ideas. We have them in plenty. But we must not confuse the two. Laws infringing our rights and intimidating unoffending persons without enlarging our security will neither catch subversives nor win converts to our better ideas. And in the long run evil ideas can be counteracted and conquered not by laws but only by better ideas.

Finally, the states are not, in my judgment, equipped to deal with the threat of the world Communist movement which inspired this bill. Communism threatens us because it threatens world peace. The great problems with which Communism confronts us are problems of foreign relations and national defense. Our Constitution wisely leaves the solution of such matters to the national government.

In conclusion, while I respect the motives and patriotism of the proponents of this bill, I think there is in it more of danger to the liberties we seek to protect than of security for the Republic. It reverses our traditional concept of justice by placing upon the accused the burden of proving himself innocent. It makes felons of persons who may be guilty more of bad judgment than of anything else. It jeopardizes the freedom of sincere and honest citizens in an attempt to catch and punish subversives. It is unnecessary and redundant.

I know full well that this veto will be distorted and misunderstood, even as telling the truth of what I knew about the reputation of Alger Hiss was distorted and misunderstood. I know that to veto this bill in this period of grave anxiety will be unpopular with many. But I must, in good conscience, protest against any unnecessary suppression of our ancient rights as free men. Moreover, we will win the contest of ideas that afflicts the world not by suppressing these rights, but by their triumph. We must not burn down the house to kill the rats.

Respectfully,

Lieutenant Governor Dixon's wife wrote Stevenson on June 26, 1951, that their son Henry was unlucky in finding summer work until made an offer at a state park where they really needed help. He took the job. She was sure the Governor would not mind but she wanted him to know.

To Mrs. Sherwood Dixon

June 27, 1951

Dear Helen:

If you were in the state government I would have a much better idea who my employees are! I am delighted to hear that Henry has a job at the Pines State Park. I wish I was working along side of him!

Yours,

To Alicia Patterson [90]

July 1, 1951

. . . The legislature has adjourned thank God. I've recorded my 6 mos. report to the people (65 stations). The party for the descendants of the Governors is over [91] — and a succes faux too. The tumult & the shouting has died & all I have is a neglected mountain of work, 6 house guests — including Ray Swing who is doing a piece for the N. Y. Times magazine on me [92] — and a date to make a speech at Vincennes [Indiana] celebration on July 4. So with clear skies I plan to be in Chi, Libertyville or Lake Forest Thurs Fri & Sat nights (Sunday I must go to Camp

[90] This handwritten letter is in the possession of Adlai E. Stevenson III.

[91] On the initiative of Stevenson's sister, Mrs. Ernest Ives, the descendants of former governors of Illinois were invited to be house guests at the mansion for several days. The party was a great success and received statewide publicity.

[92] This article was evidently never published.

McCoy, Wis. to the 33rd Division) & . . . I was hoping you might be out to see you[r] mother or something. . . .

Isn't it possible that you[r] dear Uncle Bertie [McCormick] & your pals on that wretched rag [93] need to see you Thurs, Fri or Sat?? . . .

Irving Dilliard sent Stevenson copies of items from the editorial pages of the St. Louis Post-Dispatch: *one quoting in full his veto of the Broyles Bill; the other entitled "Up in Kelso Hollow," lauding the play* Forever This Land. *Kelso Hollow was in the Lincoln Village State Park at New Salem — "a place that a lot of highways ought to lead to these July and August nights."*

To Irving Dilliard

July 3, 1951

Dear Irving:

That you would have commented on my veto in an editorial was more than I had expected; that you would have quoted it so extensively contributes dangerously to my inflation! I am delighted and flattered!

"Up in Kelso Hollow" is a honey and a much needed boost. I saw the play Sunday night and was deeply impressed, as I gather you were. I think it can be shortened a little and a few costumes altered to make it even better, but the crowds are very disappointing and the financial situation will be acute in a few days. Your editorial has done much to encourage them.

I am sorry to have missed you the other night, but I was so tired I thought I'd better get to bed with a 24-hour day ahead of me — and that's what it was.

Yours,

To Mrs. Edison Dick [94]

July 9, 1951

All went well, except that Danny [95] refused to land at Meigs — too rainy to see well!! — and I had to go to Municipal [airport] & take a cab. And how about you & the adorable Titia? [96] You're at home now — asleep

[93] The Chicago *Tribune*.
[94] This handwritten letter is in the possession of Mrs. Dick.
[95] Captain Dan Smith, Illinois National Guard, who piloted Stevenson's plane.
[96] Mrs. Dick's daughter Letitia.

with weariness and well being I hope — safe & sound & without mis-
adventures on the road.

The speech [97] was a great success — stood & clapped until I took a
modest bow, and then sat down to fall asleep with my eyes open —
great talent that for banquets, conventions, etc. etc. . . .

Say with me (and Shaft[e]sbury!)

"Strengthen us in the work we have undertaken; give us counsel and
wisdom, perseverance, faith and zeal, and in Thine own good time, and
according to Thy pleasure, prosper the issue."

THE SIGHTSEER

*On July 15, 1951, Stevenson made a radio report to the people on the
accomplishments and failures of the 67th General Assembly.*[98]

The legislature of Illinois has completed an eventful and in some respects an historic session. I'm happy to say that in the main the results
are highly gratifying and encouraging. The decisions reached will have
a profound effect upon you and your state government for many years
to come. And, thanks to many radio stations, I have this opportunity to
tell you something about important things the General Assembly did and
didn't do during the six months long session.

This report is in keeping with my policy of reporting at regular intervals on the progress of the administration of your affairs at Springfield.
I am aware that just now almost everyone is preoccupied with developments in Korea, or at least with the White Sox. And may I leave Illinois
long enough to urge every one of you who read and hear so much about
Korea to bear in mind that its really great historic significance is not
that it has proved conclusively that collective security works, but rather
that our joint action there prevented the Communist alliance from proving that collective security does not work. But Korea was only the first
round and by no means alters the necessity for building our own and
the free world's defenses against Communist aggression. So we must
continue to gear our activities to the national effort, to hold the line on
state expenditures, and to so manage our affairs as to make the maximum
possible contribution to the unity, the physical, and the moral strength of
the nation.

It was against this background of national peril that the legislature

[97] Stevenson spoke at a dinner meeting of B'nai B'rith in Chicago.

[98] The text is based on a mimeograph copy prepared by the Governor's office for
release to the press.

met early in January. A record total of more than 1,000 bills were passed, so I am compelled to confine this report only to the most important. In the aggregate it was unquestionably one of the most productive sessions in the history of Illinois. The new laws enacted to rebuild our highways, to reorganize some of the agencies of state government, to improve our schools and the administration of our welfare institutions, to modernize municipal government, and the initial steps taken in the direction of constitutional reform all were notable accomplishments.

The achievements were all the more remarkable considering the dire prophecies that a Republican legislature and a Democratic state administration would quickly deadlock and produce nothing but bitterness, frustration and paralysis. But that was not the case; political partisanship was subordinated for the most part to the public interest and I think the people fared very well. . . .

For the first time in more than 20 years we now have a highway reconstruction program that bears some resemblance to our needs; after 36 years of effort and failure cities can now experiment with a City Manager; for the first time in more than 40 years we have a bright prospect of amending our rigid old constitution. That these and many more old issues have been met and mustered in spite of all the political hostilities speaks well of Democratic government.

Early in the session I proposed an entirely new approach to the problem of truck license fees. In total taxes — gasoline and license fees — the passenger car has been paying far more than the trucks for the maintenance of our roads and of course does little or no damage. Along with many others I felt this grossly unfair advantage that the trucks have enjoyed should be corrected. So we worked out a formula to equalize the cost to the passenger car owner and the truck owner to push a ton of weight 1,000 miles across our roads.

Illinois is the first state to adopt this principle of equal treatment for passenger cars and trucks, and I have high hopes that it may serve as a basis for greater uniformity among the states where there is so much variation now. In dollars it means that starting January 1, 1952 truck and bus license fees will be increased by about 20 million dollars a year, and on January 1, 1954 they will advance another 8 millions a year. When that level is reached the trucks and buses will for the first time pay the same relative taxes for the use of our highways as passenger cars.

After the avalanche of votes and the lobbying that defeated any truck legislation in the last session I am particularly elated that we have this vexatious problem solved at last — and solved fairly to the passenger car owner. I doubt if it would have been possible had it not been for the persistent pressure and constant scrutiny of many private organizations, and notably the newspapers of the State.[99]

They also helped immeasurably in the passage in the very last hours of the session of new gasoline tax legislation which in time will enable Illinois to put all of its roads and streets in a respectable condition.

Starting August 1 this year the gasoline tax will advance from 3 to 4 cents a gallon, and effective January 1, 1953 the rate will go to 5 cents. As most of you know, I recommended that the nickel gas tax be made effective immediately. The Senate adopted that recommendation by an overwhelming vote, but the Republican leaders in the House insisted on deferring the 5-cent tax until after the 1952 elections. The result is that the full benefits of the highway restoration program will be delayed at least a year. Some may consider this delay a political victory of some kind, but not for the people who pay the bill because delay in beginning the rebuilding program can only be more costly in the end. Moreover the distribution of the gas tax revenue for the next year and a half is unfair because 40 per cent of it will go for roads carrying only 12 per cent of the traffic.

But after January 1, 1953, when the five cent tax becomes effective, a fairer formula for distribution will be established. Thirty-five per cent of total gas tax income will go to the state, 32 per cent to the cities, 11 per cent to Cook County, 12 per cent to the other counties, and 10 per cent to the townships for farm roads.

While the full effect of the road legislation adopted in this session will, therefore, not be felt until 1953, the Division of Highways will move ahead as rapidly as the increased funds become available on the program of rehabilitation and construction which we published some time ago. Likewise you can look forward to better city streets and county roads. And something entirely new introduced by this legislation will in time go a long way toward the improvement of our 75,000 miles of farm or township roads, many of which are in a deplorable condition. Now for the first time in the history of the state the rural roads will receive a substantial share of the income from the gas tax. And another enactment should encourage the consolidation of township road districts of which we have too many, into more efficient county units. That overdue reform will now be possible where two-thirds of the townships in any county approve by vote of the people.

Another highly important bill passed by the legislature increased penalties for truck overweight violations, and provided that fines for such violations shall be paid into the state treasury rather than into

[99] The truckers were extremely dissatisfied with this legislation. In the 1953 legislature they lobbied successfully for adjustment of these increases.

county treasuries as in the past. Under this new law we will be able to crack down more effectively on the unscrupulous truckers who habitually violate the weight limit laws because it pays to cheat.

Before I leave the highway subject I want to say that I am vetoing the many millions of dollars which the General Assembly voted by special bills for the construction of various bridges and roads throughout the state, because I think the experts — the engineers of the Division of Highways, should decide where bridges and roads should be constructed to best accommodate the traffic demands. Some of the bridges involved are already included in the construction plans of the highway division, and will be built anyway. Illinois is cursed with too many "political roads" already and special appropriation bills, passed on a political log rolling basis, would only divert our precious road funds and handicap the road construction program which should be designed to meet traffic needs, not political needs.

So much for the highway program. It alone would make this a memorable session and, after my failure to get anything done in the last session, I am well content that during my administration Illinois has taken a long stride toward restoring its once proud highway system and catching up with the other large states.

There was not much fanfare about school legislation during the session, and such publicity as there was, was largely confined to the increase of 24 million dollars in the state distributive fund to aid local school districts. I proposed this increase in keeping with the recommendations of the Schools Problems Commission created at my instance during the 1949 legislative session.

But a great deal more legislation was passed to clarify and modernize our school laws, to raise minimum wages for teachers, etc. I hazard the guess that there has never been a more productive session in school legislation, and it was accomplished without bickering, lobbying and pressure. I am personally as much gratified by the achievements in this field as in any other — accomplishments due in a large measure to the work of this excellent Commission which I am happy to say will be continued for another two years. We are bringing order out of chaos, defining our goals sharply in education with relation to the state's resources, and that we have almost doubled state aid for schools during my administration will be an everlasting source of satisfaction to me and I hope to all who have made it possible.

First proposed in 1915 we have enacted in Illinois at long last and in spite of the political divisions an enabling law which I recommended in January under which any city, except Chicago, can adopt the city manager plan of municipal government. After many failures in former years, the legislature has subordinated the mistrust of politicians and at last recognized that the people should be entitled to experiment with non-political business management in search of better, more efficient and economical city government. Certainly this is a milestone in home rule for the cities of Illinois.

Out of this session too there came a measure of financial relief for distressed cities. Legislation which I recommended last January transferring to the state the cost of care of the medically indigent in the Cook County Hospital, on the same basis as in the downstate counties, was passed. This will give Chicago some 4 million dollars a year for other essential needs, although it will cost the state some $10 million a year net, and I am disappointed that Chicago will not profit more from this large new state expense. The state has also assumed for the first time part of the cost of operating the Chicago Teachers College.

In addition, the legislature lifted the so-called "pegged" levy for Chicago and substituted a higher tax rate authorization that will yield the city several millions more in yearly revenue. Also passed were bills to authorize the Chicago city council to raise the city vehicle license tax.

As far as downstate cities are concerned, the principal enactment was to raise by about 10 per cent the taxing authority of city governments. Here again, as in the case of the bills affecting only Chicago, this legislation is at best a temporary remedy. It has not corrected the old and complex fiscal troubles of our cities, rooted in antiquated revenue systems and legislative and constitutional restrictions. But the legislature also created a commission to explore every phase of this question and present its findings to the General Assembly in 1953. Certainly this problem will never solve itself, and it must be solved if we are to insure the stability and responsibility of our local governments.

In the field of constitutional revision, some of you will recall that in my message to the legislature in January, I recommended the immediate creation of a commission of the Senate and House to consider all proposals for amendments to the constitution, to take full advantage of the Gateway Amendment that the voters approved in the election of 1950.

But the legislature rejected that suggestion. As a consequence there could be no thorough, selective consideration of the many constitutional amendments that were introduced by individual legislators. Only one constitutional amendment proposal of any significance was adopted — the proposed change in the revenue article. Although I do not consider the proposed revision wholly satisfactory, it at least represents an improvement and you will have an opportunity to approve this long needed reform at the elections in November, 1952.

A major failure of the session was the old problem of legislative reapportionment. The General Assembly did enact a Congressional redistricting plan as it was required to do since Illinois will lose one representative in the House of Representatives at Washington after next year. But it again ignored the constitutional edict that the state shall be reapportioned legislatively every ten years. It failed even to create a commission to study this question before the convening of the 68th General Assembly two years hence.

And now a word about appropriations. I proposed a very tight budget, less actually than for the biennium 1949–51, and no increases in general purpose taxes in view of the crushing burden of Federal taxes. I cautioned the legislature that the budget balance was precarious and that they should not add without subtracting. Well what happened? They added $50 million and subtracted $300 thousand. And that was subtracted from the $500 thousand I recommended to operate our State Civil Defense office, the lowest civil defense appropriation by far of any of the large states. I question the thrift or wisdom of that cut. And we all pray that the legislature is right in its apparent confident conclusion that we will not be attacked from the air.

With respect to the millions of appropriations in excess of the budget, I may say that I have already vetoed many of these appropriations, and I expect to veto more of them. If I have any paramount responsibility it is to keep the state financially sound and to protect the hard-pressed taxpayer wherever I can, regardless of the political consequences. At least that's the way I see it.

There is nothing unique, of course, about the tendency of legislatures to approve appropriations that people want and at the same time to oppose the taxes to pay for them. I feel a little like the harassed young husband who was worrying about his household budget and complained that every time he was about to make both ends meet his bride moved the ends. And it is always difficult for me to reconcile such irresponsible conduct with the self-righteous protestations of economy and charges of extravagance that come from Republican leaders with such fervor and frequency. Yet as a politician, albeit a new one, such inconsistency doesn't worry me much anymore because I'm convinced that the great majority of people are fed up with words; what they want is performance, not rhetoric.

I think one of the cruelest examples of fiscal irresponsibility in this session was to increase old age and blind pensions by a flat 10 per cent, without even an accompanying pretense of raising some $14 million of necessary additional revenue. What's more the Republican leaders who sponsored this transparent political gesture omitted the dependent children and the recipients of general relief because, I'm told, the children and relief recipients are not organized politically.

Actually the law already requires the Public Aid Commission to adjust old age and blind pensions and other public aid grants upward or downward as living costs fluctuate. If living costs continue to rise the IPAC will adjust payments accordingly under existing law. But to raise the hopes of many old people living on the very edge of want that they would receive a 10 per cent increase regardless of cost of living fluctuations without providing the money seems to me the height of political cynicism. And if it was intended to intimidate me it didn't work. I vetoed it as I had to, and I will veto any fiscal foolishness like it as long as I'm Governor.

From the standpoint of its long range importance, the proposals for reorganizing the state government which were advanced by the Commission to Study State Government, the so-called "Schaefer Commission," constituted one of the biggest subjects on the legislative calendar.

One hundred sixty-six bills were introduced to improve the structure of our cumbersome government. Of these 78 were passed and many of them I have already signed. In addition about a dozen other bills resulting from the Commission's findings were passed. I think the total result is highly gratifying. Some of the "Little Hoover" Commissions in other states have produced no affirmative results whatever, or very few. In Illinois the $50,000 spent by this Commission already has been saved several times only just by recommended administrative changes. While I am disappointed, of course, that the legislature did not see fit to accept more of the major suggestions of the Commission for fundamental departmental rearrangement, these recommendations remain for further consideration at later sessions and I am well content with the face-lifting operation Illinois has started.

I can't possibly list everything that the legislature did on the credit side, but I do want to point out that the half-century old restriction against the sale of colored margarine in Illinois was finally removed. The cigarette use tax was passed, eliminating an inequity through which millions of dollars of cigarettes purchased outside the borders of Illinois escaped the state tax. The unemployment compensation and workmen's compensation laws were altered to increase benefits and reduce abuses. The public aid program was broadened to include the new federal-state category of totally and permanently disabled persons. Disabled people who up to now have had to rely primarily upon general relief for survival will now receive aid in part from federal and in part from state funds. State grants to tuberculosis hospitals will be continued so that there will be no retreat in our effort to rid Illinois of this dread disease.

Salaries of most all state employees were increased to compensate for the increased cost of living in the past two years. The state should save a couple of million dollars a year as a result of the Welfare Department's new authority to charge patients who can pay for care and treatment in our state hospitals.

And now, very briefly, I would like to mention some other results of the session which were disappointing. Higher education is rapidly becoming one of our largest areas of expenditure of your money. We now have three separate boards of trustees administering the University of Illinois and the five state supported colleges and universities. It has become apparent to me that some coordination of their policies, curricula, expenditures, the division of educational responsibility and the like, on a state-wide basis is essential if we are going to get our money's worth out of this state-wide service. There is too much duplication of effort, too much rivalry and competition for appropriations, all of which is costly and wasteful. I had a careful study of our situation made by the U. S. Office of Education without cost to the taxpayer, and, with the help of Senator Mac Downing of Macomb and other leading Republican and Democratic Senators, proposed a single board of higher education. But it was defeated in committee, I'm sorry to say. I hope there will be a great deal more discussion and consideration of this question before the 68th General Assembly convenes two years hence because some such reform must come in time and the sooner the better.

I was disappointed also that the General Assembly again refused to enact the so-called FEPC [Fair Employment Practices Commision] bill, although I am gratified that the legislative consideration of this question during the past two years has stepped up interest in it and has aroused considerable voluntary action to eliminate discrimination in employment which FEPC is aimed at correcting.

Still another disappointment was the failure of the new supervisor of assessments bill, to replace the 1949 act held invalid by the Supreme Court. The purpose of the supervisor of assessments act was to eliminate the gross inequities that exist in property tax assessments within counties. The legislature also failed again to consolidate the administration of unemployment compensation and the free employment service. It seems apparent that the same agency that pays unemployment compensation should also have a close check on whether recipients are really trying to find employment.

One of my greatest disappointments was the defeat of the bills designed to improve law enforcement. As you all know I have been struggling for a long time to suppress commercial gambling in Illinois and, thanks to the state police, with great success. But we are under-manned as it is and the state police should not have to do that work. Congress has forbidden the shipment of slot machines in interstate commerce and it is difficult to comprehend the General Assembly's refusal to enact the bill that would have prohibited their manufacture in Illinois, and also the bill to strengthen the powers of the Liquor Control Commission to halt gambling wherever liquor is sold. Together these bills would have dealt a body blow to commercial gambling in Illinois. But they were defeated, with the help of some legislators who, at the same time, clamored for the appropriation of public funds for a commission to "investigate" crime.

Two notable law enforcement bills were passed, however, one the bill that allows longer grand jury sessions in Cook County, and the bill sponsored by the Crime Prevention Council to provide severe penalties for the contemptible creatures that peddle narcotics even to children. Both of these measures will be positive aids to criminal law enforcement, particularly in metropolitan Chicago.

I could mention some other minor disappointments, but as I said in the beginning, the good far outweighs the bad and this was certainly the most productive session of the legislature in many years.

Illinois is now in a position to move forward in many directions — highway building, improving our schools, improving our state hospitals, modernizing our constitution, and improving the efficiency of government at all levels.

All of these are urgent tasks for the future. We will apply ourselves to them, and we propose also to keep on working for some of the gains which weren't achieved in this session. For example, we now have the best mine safety record in the country and I wanted to protect and improve it by enacting a new mining code for Illinois in this session, to simplify and strengthen our laws for the protection of coal miners. For some reason the unions and operators opposed it. But we intend to keep working at it until we get the most up-to-date and thorough code of mining laws to back up our non-political inspection service.

Even though the legislature failed to do anything about legislative reapportionment steps could be taken to get an expression of public sentiment on this question in the general election next year. Under our law such public policy questions can be submitted to the voters upon a petition of 12 per cent of the registered voters of the state. It might be worth considering, for such an expression of popular sentiment would undoubtedly be a strong influence in favor of affirmative action on this old and vexing problem.

Enduring progress in government and in the quality of public administration requires constant sustained interest and effort on the part of citizens as well as conscientious officials. We have made much progress in Illinois of late only because we have had a great deal of public interest and support.

For that support and encouragement I am deeply grateful, and I look forward to its continuation to consolidate our gains and to press on to other goals in the public interest. To the extent we suceed all of the people of Illinois will profit, because the major problems of state government are not partisan problems.

And, with the conclusion of this eventful session, I wish to express my gratitude also to the Democratic leaders in the Senate and House, Senator William J. Connors of Chicago and Representative Paul Powell of Vienna in southern Illinois for their indefatigable effort and brilliant leadership. To the many Republicans, who controlled both houses of the legislature and honored me by adopting most of my proposals, I am indebted as Governor and, like you, as a citizen convinced that good government is not a matter of party, it's a matter of will, and where there's a will there is always a way. We are on the way to something better in Illinois.

Mrs. John Paul Welling congratulated Stevenson on his veto of the Broyles Bill, and also commented on the legislative session: "In case that you feel you have failed in working all you wanted out of a hostile majority, I hope you remember that when the session started it was common gossip that whatever legislation passed or failed was a minor consideration compared with getting your scalp. I am delighted to see that it is still firmly in place, alas for all to see, and even more delighted when one considers your record as governor to see that it is they who failed and, that abysmally."

To Mrs. John Paul Welling [100]

July 16, 1951

Dear Harriet:

Thanks for your note. My scalp *is* firmly in place — as all can readily see, unhappily!

You were good to write me, and I had hoped that long before this I would have seen you in the Executive Mansion. May I hope?

Yours,

ADLAI

P.S. I am distressed that Paul [101] is still in the hospital. Is there anything I could do? Could I go to see him sometime when I am in Chicago and have a spare half hour?

AES

[100] The original is in the possession of Mrs. Welling.
[101] Mr. Welling.

To Alicia Patterson [102]

July 16, 1951

. . . As for me — I came through the legislative session with colors flying, all of my budget and most of my formidable program adopted by a Republican legislature. Now I'm gasping under the legacy of more than 1000 bills to dispose of, and I've already established a new high for vetoes. Each one loses a few more organized votes so, in spite of the laudatory press, I suspect my political fortunes are fading. But I don't mind & I'm having some fun. If only somehow, sometime I could get the day cut from 16 to 10 hours I'd really be happy in this job at last. But I can't seem to do it & still do things the painstaking way I like to do them — only way that gives me any satisfaction.

On top of the legislative aftermath, scores of difficult appointments to make we've had race riots in Cicero and a small scale insurrection against the Chicago Transit Authority to bedevil me. Uncle Bertie [McCormick] continues to howl about paroling convicts from the penitentiaries having, I choose to think, nothing else to attack me for. And so it goes — with the pressure gathering already to run again. Chin up & good cheer. . . .

A

On May 26, 1951, Senator Paul H. Douglas, amidst mounting attacks on Secretary of State Dean Acheson by Republican leaders, stated that Acheson had become a "casualty of war" and "a political liability." Edward G. Miller, Jr., Assistant Secretary of State, wrote the Governor that he felt it was tragic for the Democrats to give in to the Republicans, and even Douglas must realize that Acheson, with his personal qualifications, would be almost impossible to replace.

To Edward G. Miller, Jr.

July 16, 1951

Dear Eddie:

Thanks for your letter.

As for our friend PD, the story is long and baffling and has caused me acute embarrassment. Frankly, I can't make him out. Either there is a fire in his belly or mighty vistas in his head.

I think it seems obvious that most thinking people realize that Dean's

[102] This handwritten letter is in the possession of Adlai E. Stevenson III.

departure at this time would be political capitulation and the result in unity be more confusion and recrimination.

I wish I saw you occasionally.

Yours,

Miss Lila Ives, Ernest Ives's sister, wrote Stevenson on July 8, 1951, to express her pride in the Governor and to say that it brought her happiness that he and her brother were congenial friends.

To Lila E. Ives

July 16, 1951

My dear Lila:

You were an angel to write me, although I don't [sic] think my press agent, Ernest, has a way of doing me more than justice!

And I wonder if anyone has told you what a really extraordinary job he has done, not just for me, but in inspiring, promoting and managing this gigantic undertaking "Forever This Land." Had it not been for his persistence, resourcefulness and quiet confidence, the project would never have started, let alone come to pass. How he does it, I don't know. I'm sure I would have despaired and given up at any of the many crises, but not Ernest!

Somehow you must contrive to come out here for a visit to see it — if a good old Confederate like Ernest can promote a Lincoln play, his sister can enjoy it too! So come, and meanwhile, my love and thanks.

Yours,

John Paulding Brown wrote Stevenson on July 13, 1951, saying he hoped his letter would arrive at the time Mr. and Mrs. Edward D. Mc-Dougal were still in Springfield. Mr. Brown, a Republican, and an ardent horseman, sent snapshots of himself, one on horseback and another with a donkey. "The horse is a noble fellow, powerful and alert and playful. . . . The Scicillian jackass is a great friend of mine. He is intellectually brilliant and if we can get him into Princeton this fall I feel he will go far. Perhaps you could find a place for him, later on, with one of the State Commissions? . . . With warmest regards, dear Oblomoff. . . ." [103]

[103] This letter is in the possession of Edward D. McDougal.

To Edward D. McDougal, Jr.[104]

July 16, 1951

Dear Ed:
   This arrived with your departure. I thought it would amuse you.

Yours,

AD

To John Paulding Brown

July 16, 1951

Dear John:
   Your letter arrived too late for the McDougals but I am forwarding it to Ed together with the photographs which will probably impress him as much as they did me. I am delighted that you are mounted again and well mounted! Ed had already told me that you were consorting with donkeys which gives me some hope for your political redemption. And by the way, we call them donkeys not jackasses!
   I am distressed to have missed you again and Oblomoff awaits his loyal servant's return. Be quick about it!

Yours,

Lucy Williams, an old friend from Bloomington, wrote Stevenson commending him for his veto of the Broyles Bill and his performance as governor, expressing the wish that he might someday be President.

To Lucy P. Williams

July 16, 1951

Dear Miss Lucy:
   You were sweet to write me and your letter is more comforting and encouraging than you know. Our oldest friends know and judge us best.

Affectionately,

All records of the state's financial transactions were kept in the Department of Finance, and the director of that department was in a position to know a great deal about the activities of the code departments under

[104] The original is in the possession of Mr. McDougal.

control of the governor. Stevenson wanted to make sure the director had full communication and cooperation with the various department heads.

To Leonard Schwartz [105]

July 17, 1951

Dear Director Schwartz:

The effectiveness with which the Department of Finance functions is dependent to a large degree upon maintenance of close working relations with the various State agencies. Such relationships would undoubtedly be facilitated if the Code Department Directors, or their representatives, met together regularly with the Director of Finance to discuss such matters as budgetary planning and control, purchasing administration and over-all management problems.

I have, therefore, requested the Director of Finance to arrange for such interdepartmental meetings which would be attended by the Code Department Directors or by representatives of such Directors as are unable to personally be present. As the meetings progress there will undoubtedly be matters which are of concern to only several departments and in those cases it would be appropriate to have special meetings attended only by representatives of the departments concerned.

It is not feasible to outline in detail how these meetings will be conducted but I am confident that they can do much towards improving management of the State's business. I hope you will be prepared to comment on this proposal at a Code Directors meeting with me which I will call as soon as I can clean up the bills.[106]

Sincerely yours,

Kermit Hunter, who wrote the drama of Lincoln and New Salem Forever This Land, *wrote Stevenson on July 23, 1951, to express his appreciation for the Governor's thoughtfulness, friendliness and confidence.*

To Kermit Hunter

July 24, 1951

Dear Kermit:

Your letter touched me deeply. I wish I could say in reply just what

[105] The original is in the possession of Mr. Schwartz.

[106] Stevenson was still in the process of signing and vetoing bills passed by the legislature.

you have said. Perhaps we can both hope and wish each other "that final great success" which, in your words, is "peace of mind and heart."

Yours,

Stevenson liked and respected Barnet Hodes, one of the powerful figures of the Cook County Democratic organization. Mr. Hodes's wife had been extremely ill.

To Barnet Hodes [107]

July 26, 1951

Dear Barney:

I am not up to date on your wife's condition, but I hope and pray that all goes well. In any event, if you and Scott [108] would like to spend a night with me during the Fair, August 10 to 20, so that he can have a look at it you will be most welcome.

Sincerely yours,

Mrs. Walter T. Fisher, formerly president of the Illinois League of Women Voters, wrote Stevenson on July 26, 1951: "You are undoubtedly familiar with the volume 'The Dissenting Opinions of Mr. Justice Holmes.' [109] I hope that some day there may be a companion volume 'The Vetoes of Governor Stevenson.' The two would have in common not only clear thinking and expression but would ring with the same courage and integrity. That is just another way of saying Hurrah for you! Hurrah for your intrepid veto of the Broyles bills."

To Mrs. Walter T. Fisher

July 27, 1951

Dear Katharine:

If that is another way of saying hurrah for me, it is the most flattering way I have yet heard. Holmes and Stevenson! I tremble!!

You were good to write me and I only wish the vetoes elicited more vocal approval instead of howls of protest. However, I will content myself

[107] The original is in the possession of Mr. Hodes.
[108] Mr. Hodes's son.
[109] Oliver Wendell Holmes, *The Dissenting Opinions of Mr. Justice Holmes* (New York: Vanguard Press, c. 1929).

with the thought that there are others. Meanwhile, your letter helps me mightily.

Yours,

Former Secretary of the Interior Harold L. Ickes congratulated Stevenson on his veto of the Broyles Bill. He wrote that he hoped the Governor would join him for lunch when he was next in Washington.

To Harold L. Ickes

July 28, 1951

Dear Harold:

I was delighted to have your letter, and very much flattered by your thoughtfulness and flattering remarks about the Broyles bill veto. Copy is enclosed. As for vetoes, I seem to have long since established an all-time high.[110] I am afraid I am a little punch drunk and enjoy vetoing more than signing! I hope I have some friends left after the last of the bills is cleared away, but I very much doubt it — unless it is Harold Ickes!

I am going to file your letter in my "Eastern File" against the possibility that I may be in Washington and can take advantage of your invitation. I hope very much that we can meet again before too long.

Warm regards.

Sincerely yours,

Stevenson was able to spend a few days at the camp of the Hermon D. Smiths in Canada. Miss Dorothy Fosdick accompanied him.

To Mr. and Mrs. Hermon D. Smith [111]

August 2, 1951

Dear Dutch and Ellen:

All's well! I am behind the mountain of villainy again — but my skin is pink, my forehead peeling and I am in a state of well being that no

---

[110] Stevenson was under the impression that he had established a record for the number of vetoes signed. However, the percentage of vetoes as related to total number of bills passed by the legislature during the years 1937, 1939 and 1941 exceeded Stevenson's vetoes. See Gilbert Y. Steiner and Samuel K. Gove, *Legislative Politics in Illinois* (Urbana: University of Illinois Press, 1960), Table 3: "Executive Action on Bills Introduced in Legislative Sessions, 1937–1959."

[111] The original is in the possession of Mr. Smith. The postscript is in Stevenson's handwriting.

one can identify, thanks to your extraordinary therapy. It was an exquisite idyll — and just in the nick of time.

A thousand thanks, and my love.

ADLAI

P.S. Dorothy had the time of her life and "loved" the Smiths — old & young. Don't we all! You were angels to let me bring her. Most any night except Wed. Aug 15 will be OK for the Fair (Aug 10 to Aug 19 both incl.)

Ralph J. Bunche, then director of the Trusteeship Division of the United Nations, wrote Stevenson on August 2, 1951, commending him for calling out the National Guard to restore order after a white mob in Cicero had sacked the apartment of a Negro family. Mr. Bunche said: "My sole source of information was the newspapers and the only bright spot in the sordid picture appeared to be your action. That did not surprise me at all, however, for I well know how you think and feel about such matters. Still, I am not unmindful that decisions and actions of this kind are never easy."

To Ralph J. Bunche

August 4, 1951

Dear Ralph:

You were good to write me about the Cicero incident. We have a lamentable situation here and the end is not in sight. But with restraint, some judicial fearlessness and prompt police action we should be able to master it bit by bit. Meanwhile, the restraint and constructive attitude of the Negro leaders is one of the most encouraging and hopeful aspects.

I am still hoping that our paths will cross one of these days.

Sincerely yours,

To Marquis Childs [112]

August 4, 1951

Dear Mark:

That I have not written you before does not mean that I have overlooked your very, very, indeed *very* flattering remarks about me in a recent column.[113] I only wish I possessed a fraction of the good qualities you suspect.

[112] The original is in the Childs collection at the Wisconsin State Historical Society.
[113] The editors could not locate this column.

The record here *has* been good, but still far from as good as I would wish and as I shall continue to try to make it.

I am somewhat dismayed by the confusions and conflicts in the Democratic party. With so little to look forward to from the Republicans I feel the more concerned by our deficiencies.

I hope our paths will cross, and I am sure you will let me know if you pass this way.

With kind thanks for your flattering words, I am

Sincerely yours,
ADLAI

To Mr. and Mrs. Edison Dick [114]

August 5, 1951

My dear Dicks —

Heartfelt thanks! Adlai [III] reports from Paris that he has had enough to eat at last — thanks to the Dicks! As for his itinerary, I'm bewildered — except for his trip to the Left Bank, which I hope the girls found more exciting than I ever did.

I journeyed to Detroit for its 250th birthday celebration and took great pleasure in presenting the felicitations of its older brother — Cahokia, Ill! From there to Desbarats for a couple of beautiful blue and white days with the Smiths at familiar Thorne Camp — which seems to get more dilapidated and comfortable each visit. Then to Libertyville to greet John Fell in cowboy hat, blue jeans and a professional swagger. He placed 4th in the Jackson rodeo horse race — No, there were 9 horses in the race, not four! Thence chez Dick for the night, to find Mary [115] in fine spirits, in spite of a house full of plumbers. You were good to arrange it for me and your hearth seemed tranquil, serene and very orderly. I wish mine was — the well gave out — something I gather the Marshall Fields are not accustomed to. But they're off to Hawaii now and Frank, the gardener, says he takes too many baths anyway! [116]

Alicia Patterson was here for the weekend en route back to Wyoming and Josephine's [117] ranch in good spirits and full of Bertie's madnesses. Garbed in Ernest's underpants, my shirt and Buffy's shoes we took her up to the Drakes [118] to play tennis yesterday and to "Forever This Land"

[114] This handwritten letter is in the possession of Mrs. Dick.

[115] The Dicks' housekeeper.

[116] Stevenson used the Dicks' home occasionally while they were away. Mr. and Mrs. Marshall Field IV were occupying his house in Libertyville.

[117] Miss Patterson's sister, Mrs. Ivan Albright, who owned a ranch near Jackson Hole, Wyoming.

[118] Mr. and Mrs. William Drake, who lived near Elkhart, Illinois, about fifteen miles from Springfield.

last night. She was profoundly impressed and no little irked when an innocent producer informed her that "a Tribune man" had been out there all day, but didn't stay to see the performance!

The weather is insufferable and whatever the climate in Italy you're lucky to be there — at least today. I'm still struggling with the bills, but the end is in sight and the vetoes won't be equalled for years to come. Having lost all restraint and balance I veto now by preference — its great fun, altho not recommended for ambitious politicians I'm told. The Douglas-Truman fuss over the judges has become a national spectacle without apparent solution, but I don't even care about that!! [119]

Much has happened, but the troops are out of Cicero, the floods have subsided and my clipping bureau has broken down — and besides nothing is as important as sightseeing. I'll be waiting for the photographic exhibit. Meanwhile all *I* have to offer is enclosed. I hope the nude on rock passes the Italian censor!

ADLAI

Stevenson vetoed Senate Bill 504, "An Act prohibiting the sale or exchange of motor vehicles on Sunday."

To the Honorable, the Secretary of State [120]

August 7, 1951

. . . I veto and withhold my approval from this bill for the following reasons:

This bill makes it a criminal offense for any person to sell a motor vehicle on Sunday.

The Attorney General advises me that this bill is unconstitutional, and I append hereto a copy of his opinion to this effect.

I cannot forbear to add that this is one case in which the constitutional objection and sound policy clearly coincide. Under this bill anyone who chooses to sell his automobile on Sunday could be imprisoned for as long as ninety days. Surely our public officials charged with law enforcement

---

[119] Senator Paul H. Douglas asked President Truman to appoint William H. King and Benjamin P. Epstein as U.S. District Court judges in Chicago. Truman instead named his own appointees, Cornelius J. Harrington and Joseph H. Drucker. The Senate Judiciary Committee, after some maneuvers by Douglas, refused to report favorably on the President's nominations, although they did not report unfavorably either. The President said he was satisfied with his original choices, that the appointive power was his, and the Senate must take the responsibility for the continued judicial vacancies. The issue between Douglas and the President was never resolved, and the vacancies were allowed to exist until after the 1952 elections.

[120] *Messages of Stevenson, 67th General Assembly*, pp. 36–37.

have more important tasks than to seek out and prosecute persons engaging in such transactions. If such a restriction on Sunday trade is sound for automobiles, why should it not be extended to newspapers, groceries, ice cream cones and other harmless commercial transactions? Carried to its logical extreme, any business group with sufficient influence in the legislature can dictate the hours of business of its competitors. And if hours, why not prices?

Under our free enterprise system government should not interfere by regulatory or prohibitory laws in the business field except (1) where the activity in question is directly related to the public health, safety, morals or welfare, or (2) to *enforce* competition. Traffic in automobiles does not qualify under the one, and, so far as the latter is concerned, its only purpose and effect are to *restrain* competition.

Surely such restrictive legislation as this is not compatible with our earnest convictions and constant proclamations about the merits of free enterprise.

Respectfully,

Stevenson's aide Lawrence Irvin, in a memorandum dated August 7, 1951, pointed out to the Governor that it was time he began making plans and adopting some sort of policy to be used in selection of the delegates to the Democratic National Convention in 1952, as well as the State Central Committeemen in the various districts. Stevenson responded in a handwritten note at the bottom of Irvin's typewritten memorandum.

To Lawrence Irvin [121]

[no date]

Larry —

I agree that I must give some thought to this. Could you discuss it with Mike Seyfrit [122] and then let's talk it over. I'm a novice and have no idea how to proceed.

AES

During Stevenson's visit to Russia in 1926, he traveled from the Caucasus to Moscow by train, and on this journey met Miss Anna M. Graves, of Green Spring Valley, Maryland. Miss Graves wrote him on July 30,

[121] The original is in the possession of Mr. Irvin.
[122] Director of Public Safety Michael F. Seyfrit, a member of the Democratic State Central Committee from the 21st District.

1951, to remind him of their travels. In her letter she called herself a "complete pacifist," but thought Stevenson was right to send the National Guard into Cicero. She recalled that the famous Negro scientist Dr. Percy Julian was refused admittance to a luncheon at the Union League Club of Chicago because of his color, which she considered more outrageous than the teenagers who drove a colored family from their home in Cicero. She commented that the members of the Union League Club knew they were not doing a dangerous thing, that the National Guard would not be sent to prevent their act of insult, but that they, being members of the intelligentsia, must have known that acts such as theirs were the causes and excuses of such acts as those of the teenage gangsters.

She added that a Mr. and Mrs. Hague, her neighbors, were from Illinois, and that Mrs. Hague's father admired the Governor and felt he was honestly trying to make Chicago "better."

To Anna M. Graves

August 9, 1951

My dear Miss Graves:

I was delighted to have your letter. I remember so well our journey in the autumn of 1926 and your many kindnesses to an inexperienced traveller in the Soviet Union.

You will be pleased to hear that the Union League Club has been roundly criticized for its treatment of Dr. Julien [Julian]. I am afraid, however, that your assumption about their understanding of the effect of such discrimination is wrong. Unhappily, I am fearful that many of the instances of intolerance which afflict our country spring from people who should know better and who themselves would be the first victims of a mass intolerance.

I hope you will express my gratitude to Mr. and Mrs. Hague and her father for his confidence and encouragement. It is a difficult job as you well know.

With warm regards and my thanks for your thoughtful letter, I am

Sincerely yours,

To Mrs. Edison Dick [123]

August 9, 1951

Dear Jane —

Many thanks for your splendid report on the innocents abroad — the

[123] This handwritten letter is in the possession of Mrs. Dick.

gentlemen on the Lido and the ladies on the Arno.[124] I've been having difficulty deciding which I should join, but your depressing account of war ravaged Florence has at last sent me to the Adriatic sands — even if I have to ride in a gondola by moonlight with Eddie! I'm glad I was spared a look at Florence after the war, but I saw the south from Sicily to Casino just behind the guns and that was enough.

But it will all be different in Ireland where "noonday is a purple haze and the evening full of linnets wings" — as we Irish poets are so fond of saying.

What an adventure you must be having and lest I swoon with envy I've consoled myself with the enclosed piece by Francis McFadden [125] that Ellen[126] sent me. Curses! I've carelessly thrown away the first page and her immortal photographs on the student ship. But even this remnant will give you and Eddie a good chuckle.

But you aren't the only awed sightseers, because tomorrow the Fair opens and the wide eyed Governante will start once more his piligrim-mage among the pigpens, cattle barns and rabbit hutches spreading cheer, perspiration and love with winsome and weary indifference as he wanders thru the wonders — dreaming of far away places and faces — the Dicks! executing an envelopement of a ruin, a shop, a museum, with Everreddie [127] leading the charge!

My portrait is finished,[128] the bills and veto[e]s are finished — and so am I! "Forever This Land" is doing well however. John Fell is with me; Borden comes next week: Hord, Oates', Kelly etc. arrive today & all's well on the San Gamon.[129]

ADLAI

In signing Senate Bill No. 679, providing that state-owned motor ve-hicles be identified with appropriate markings, Stevenson wrote the following message.

---

[124] Mrs. Dick and her daughters went sightseeing and shopping in Florence, while her husband and young Eddie went to Venice and the Lido.

[125] Miss Frances McFadden, an old friend of Stevenson's from Chicago.

[126] Mrs. Hermon D. Smith.

[127] Governor Stevenson's affectionate nickname for the Dicks' son, Edison Warner Dick, who at the time of this trip was thirteen years old.

[128] Joseph Allworthy, a Chicago artist, had just finished an oil portrait of Stevenson. It is now in the Adlai E. Stevenson Memorial Room, Illinois State University at Normal.

[129] Stephen Y. Hord and Mr. and Mrs. James F. Oates, Jr., of Lake Forest; Phelps Kelly, of Chicago. "San Gamon" is the Sangamon River that flows near Springfield.

*Statement by Governor Adlai E. Stevenson
on Signing Senate Bill No. 679* [130]

August 10, 1951

The Commission to Study State Government [Schaefer Commission] included in its report a recommendation that state-owned motor vehicles be identified as such by appropriate markers. The Commission prepared and introduced Senate Bill No. 679 for the purpose of carrying out this recommendation. It applied in terms to all of the agencies of the state government.

This bill was amended before passage to limit its application to the code departments alone. I am at a loss to understand the motives or justification for this astonishing change. If it is sound to label vehicles as state property, it should apply to all state agencies inasmuch as the taxpayers own all of the state motor vehicles no matter which agency uses them.

I have no hesitation in approving this bill even though it is limited to the departments under my jurisdiction. But in approving it I wish to say that "what is sauce for the goose is sauce for the gander"; what is good for my departments is good for all. If politics underlies this curious distinction it is poor politics and the people should know about it.

All bills passed by the Illinois legislature technically are to be signed or vetoed by the governor "within ten days." They first must go to the attorney general, who passes on their constitutionality. Since most of the bills are passed during the last days of the session it would be an almost impossible task for the governor to sign or veto the hundreds of bills within such a short time. If the attorney general's office is cooperative it holds up some of the bills to insure a more even flow into the governor's office, which eases his burden greatly.

To Ivan A. Elliott [131]

August 10, 1951

Dear Ivan:

Now that the bill signing ordeal is practically over, I want you to know how much I appreciate the great service which you and your office have rendered me. Examining and preparing legal opinions was a more arduous undertaking this year than ever before because of the greatly in-

[130] *Messages of Stevenson, 67th General Assembly*, p. 120.
[131] The original is in the possession of Mr. Elliott.

creased number of bills which were passed. But I must say that you and your office did the job with dispatch and care. I am full of admiration and you and your staff have my warmest thanks for this invaluable co-operation.

Sincerely yours,

To Mrs. Edison Dick [132]

August 13, 1951

Dear Jane:

Here are some more [newspaper clippings] — But you asked for it!

The Fair — so far — is a triumph, appalling crowds, heat, cloudless skies, perspiration — and all the inverted attributes of success in this queer business. Ah for a cool English day — a tranquil eve in Eire! But Desbarats [133] is coming and I've resisted [James F.] Oates' blandishments to join his yacht and fish for salmon north of Vancouver. . . . And back to the fair to present the awards to the best marching teams, bands, etc., in front of 12,000 veterans and their wives whose pet bills I've vetoed 100%! But 60 leaders came to lunch, and not one unpleasant word — indeed respectful congratulations from some. Is this the calm before the storm?

This afternoon the beauty queen contestants for tea in the garden and not a one of the lovelies as lovely as Marnie or Titia [Dick] — or for that matter — the Welfare Commissioner!! [134]

Love to you all
THE GUV

Victor C. Leiker, editor of the Christopher Progress, *Christopher, Illinois, wrote Stevenson congratulating him on the splendid job he was doing and encouraging him to give serious consideration to the next campaign. He wrote that his hopes and predictions were (1) that Stevenson would be reelected governor; (2) that he would take on Senator Everett Dirksen in 1956; and (3) that he would be elected President in 1960. He concluded that there were many who looked forward to having a fearless and courageous leader in Stevenson.*

[132] This handwritten letter is in the possession of Mrs. Dick.

[133] Mr. and Mrs. Edward K. Welles had invited him to their camp at Desbarats, Ontario.

[134] Mrs. Dick.

To Victor C. Leiker

August 18, 1952

Dear Mr. Leiker:

I have never read a more friendly, comforting and encouraging letter. You were good to write it. If your ambitions for me are a little above my merits and capacity, your good will and loyalty are only the more reassuring.

It is a struggle day and night, as you know, but the progress is my satisfaction and my reward.

I hope you will let me know whenever you are in Springfield.

Sincerely yours,

To Leonard Schwartz [135]

August 22, 1951

Dear Leonard:

I am told that two fine lake trout have arrived at the Mansion from you. Many, many thanks. You know my weaknesses.

Sincerely yours,

Historian Allan Nevins was obliged to decline an invitation by the Governor to come to Springfield, but hoped to come another time. He remarked in his letter to Stevenson that he had spent a few days in Big Sur, California, and that people there thought General Dwight Eisenhower would be the Republican candidate for President in 1952. He added that he was pleased to hear Stevenson spoken of as one of the best possible men for the Democratic nomination.

To Allan Nevins

August 27, 1951

Dear Allan:

This is your raincheck and there will be a welcome awaiting you at the Mansion the end of September.

I am bewildered, as always, by your vitality and velocity — California, Canada, New York and now Illinois — I hope!

With warm regards.

Yours,

[135] The original is in the possession of Mr. Schwartz.

To Ronald Tree

August 27, 1951

Dear Ronnie:

Looking through some old papers of my grandfather's yesterday in search of something else, I ran across the enclosure, evidently written by your grandfather to mine in 1903. I presume it refers to a note of sympathy at the time of your grandmother's death.

It occurred to me that perhaps you might like to have this among the other correspondence of your grandfather.

We still live in hopes that you and Marietta [136] will find your way to the Executive Mansion in Springfield one of these days. Last week I had lunch in Chicago with Anthony Eden and he spoke of you fondly.

Yours,

To David Davis [137]

August 27, 1951

Dear Dave:

The other day the State Historical Library acquired the correspondence of General L. B. Parsons who was in charge of transportation for the Union armies of the West during the Civil War. Among this correspondence were several letters he exchanged with my grandfather and I thought the enclosed copy of a letter of 1876 and the reference to Judge David Davis would interest you.

Warm regards.

Sincerely yours,

To the "Voice of the People," the Chicago Tribune [138]

August 27, 1951

The attached editorial [139] says I told a lie with respect to the reputation of [Alger] Hiss. This is a serious charge and what is more it is a lie. I have always assumed that *The Tribune* does not lie deliberately.

During the time that I met him at occasional meetings in Washington in the spring of 1945, and in London in 1946, no question of his loyalty

[136] Mrs. Tree.

[137] A lawyer in Bloomington, Illinois, and a great-grandson of Judge David Davis (1815–1886), a friend of Jesse W. Fell, Stevenson's maternal great-grandfather.

[138] This letter was published in the Chicago *Tribune* on August 31, 1951.

[139] The editorial appearing in the *Tribune* on August 18 was entitled "We're Glad You Brought It Up, Governor."

and integrity ever reached my ears. This was some 7 or 8 years after the acts for which he was accused. The question asked me was not even my opinion of him, but his reputation based on what others said. I replied that it was "good." It was, and anything to the contrary would have been a falsehood.

I can hardly believe *The Tribune* is recommending that politicians protect themselves in unpopular situations by lying. Nor can I believe that you would discourage citizens from testifying honestly in a criminal case for fear the defendant might later be convicted.

To James W. Mulroy [140]

[no date]

Mr. Mulroy —

[Carl] McGowan is utterly indispensable to me. He has said nothing, but with a 3rd child about to arrive I don't know how much longer he can afford to stay with me.[141] What more can I do for him in salary in his range and grade? I would like to make a substantial increase effective Sept. 1.

AES

Meyer Kestnbaum, president of Hart, Schaffner & Marx, invited Stevenson to attend a banquet honoring Samuel Levin, who was retiring as head of the Chicago Division of the Amalgamated Clothing Workers Union of America.

To Meyer Kestnbaum

September 12, 1951

Dear Kesty:

I have your letter about the testimonial dinner for my dear old friend, Sam Levin, on October 24. I find I have a speaking engagement in Wisconsin on the 22nd and one here in Springfield on the 23rd before the Sangamon County Bar Association. I am afraid the return to Chicago the next day would be zigzagging a little too fast even for this agitated Governor.

I am distressed. I can think of few people here or elsewhere in whose

[140] This handwritten memorandum is in the possession of Mrs. Helen Kaste. It was probably written in August.

[141] Mr. McGowan's third child, John, was born on October 22, 1951. Presumably some adjustment was made in McGowan's salary; he remained with the Governor until the end of his administration.

honor I should prefer to dine than Sam Levin. Actually, I am not sure why I feel that way because his incessant pressure over a period of years had as much to do with my being in politics as anything — and can I thank anyone for that! I don't dare ask whether *you* could thank him!

But even if I have suffered, thanks to him, and even if many would compare him unfavorably with the Earl of Warwick, I still love him as a citizen, a humanitarian and a wise man and dear friend whose counsel and encouragement has been a blessing of mine for many years.

I hope you have a good time at the dinner and that Meyer Kestnbaum doesn't do all the talking and gives Sam a chance. It is a good thing for both of you that I can't be there.

Warm regards and my thanks for your thought of me.

Sincerely yours,

Stevenson's Libertyville neighbor Alfred MacArthur, after a holiday in the wilds of Desbarats, Ontario, wrote the Governor of the "great interest I had in getting Helen Hayes [his sister-in-law] acquainted with the somewhat primitive ways of the Desbarats Cult." He also said he would like to order a pair of cotton pants for Stevenson and asked the Governor to have his tailor send the proper measurements. The choice of colors, he wrote, was red and black or green and white. He added: "Even though I am a Republican you can accept them because I do not think even the Tribune would accuse you of selling out for a $5 pair of britches. . . . Anyway it is up to you to show people that 'striped pants' might mean something other than what Mr. Orr is trying to insinuate." [142]

To Alfred MacArthur

September 13, 1951

Dear Alfred:

Your letter has enlived the gubernatorial gloom more than a little. So much so, in fact, that I have stretched a tape measure about my center, my rear, and the length of my extremities. The results are something as follows:

Waist 42

Hips 47

[142] *Chicago Tribune* cartoonist Carey Orr during the campaign in 1948 and after depicted Stevenson as a "striped-pants" diplomat, unable to cope with Illinois politics.

Trouser length measured on the inside seam — 29½
As for a tailor, you flatter me. Besides, he is in Chicago, and as his prices rise I neglect him more and more.

I am torn with indecision between red and black and green and white. Having seen the latter, however, on your long, lean and lovely legs, I am tempted to play safe.

As for the rain check on the Mansion, I might insist that you and Mary [143] deliver the trousers in person and we will rehearse my visit to Mr. Orr's office. Bring Helen Hayes if she is about. You can assure her that I don't have a canoe in Springfield, or a sailboat, not even water.

Thanks.

Yours,

Mr. and Mrs. Ronald Tree planned to join a duck-hunting party a short distance from Springfield in November. They hoped to visit Stevenson in Springfield.

To Ronald Tree

September 13, 1951

Dear Ronnie:

I am delighted to hear that you are going to be out here in November. I am planning to go East for the Harvard-Princeton football game with my sons on November 10, but we must foregather in Springfield some time when you are here. Indeed, I might join you on the banks of the Illinois River with a gun in my hand!

Love to Marietta.

Yours,

Harry Green, of Chicago, wrote the Governor on August 31, 1951, that Vice President Stevenson was "prominently described in all of Kentucky's official archives, including their beautifully done large folder, of which I attach herewith Page 41. . . . Publication of the folder ended the Civil War officially and irrevocably. The reunion is clearly established when one peers at your grandfather's picture using a bright light in back, showing the image of Jefferson Davis on reverse side."

---

[143] Mrs. MacArthur.

To Harry G. Green

September 13, 1951

Dear Mr. Green:

I was delighted with your letter, as always. And that my grandfather has been rediscovered by Kentucky is no minor satisfaction either! Certainly the proximity of Stevenson and Jefferson Davis must have some amicable significance below the Mason-Dixon line — or, as somebody has said, the Smith and Wesson line!

Speaking of grandfather, you will be amused by an excerpt from a letter from Mrs. David Davis to Judge David Davis in 1879, which was sent to me the other day. Mrs. Davis writes the Judge: "Mrs. Stevenson called on me today and asked me to ask you if Mr. Stevenson took wine at the President's dinner. I told her that you probably took so much wine yourself that you were not a reliable informant."

With my warm regards and very best wishes, I am

Cordially yours,

Mrs. Paul Scott Mowrer expected to be in Illinois for a niece's wedding. Mr. Mowrer wrote Stevenson that he could not come as he would be in Maine on a fishing trip. Mrs. Mowrer added a humorous note about her husband's hesitation in letting her visit Springfield alone.

To Mrs. Paul Scott Mowrer

September 14, 1951

Dear Hadley:

I can understand perfectly why Paul is anxious to protect you from the aggressive Governor of Illinois. However, I suggest we conspire to thwart his protective instincts. Besides, if he feels that way he could forego a little fishing for a little lickering with that exemplary public servant!

Now do your best, and don't you dare show him this letter.

Affectionately,

To Alicia Patterson [144]

September 14, 1951

. . . I've had my holiday — lovely days with Borden & John Fell

[144] This handwritten letter is in the possession of Adlai E. Stevenson III.

visiting the [Edward K.] Welles in Desbarats and now I'm back at the crisis corner — with new and better crises all about. [James] Mulroy, the damn fool, put $100 in the Chicago Downs race track & of course told me nothing about it. Now there's hell to pay with lurid suggestive stories of corruption and influence — 9 members of the legislature are stockholders *and* the Gov's [executive] secretary! In addition I now find he bought a house from a man who is a big contractor with the state. That may break tomorrow. Nice eh! And the worst of it is that Mulroy is guiltless of any wrong doing — other than enormous stupidity. But they'll have a field day with it at my expense. Yet I haven't summoned the courage to fire him and the hotter it gets the more embittered and stubborn he gets about resigning. What a job!

No — the copy of my letter to Bertie *didnot* carry the "cc" to you.[145] So have no fear that he suspects any collusion. The SOBs sequel is enclosed.[146]

. . . I was in Wash[ington] early this week but I see no prospect for N.Y. I wanted to go down to meet Adlai who arrives from Europe Monday, but John Fell goes back to school that day & I'm going up to see him a bit over Sunday. Adlai will come out here for a few days before he has to be back at Harvard — A Senior! It startles me somehow to [realize] that he's grown up & will be of age this fall — when only yesterday — But such reflections do no good and for me are very painful. Did I ever tell you that I'm a sickly sentimentalist and that I love my boys so that it literally hurts. Perhaps that's why I haven't been a better father. . . .

A

Early in September, 1951, Stevenson vacationed for a few days with the family of Harry Emerson Fosdick on Mouse Island, Boothbay Harbor, Maine. The Fosdick grandchildren, Patricia and Steven Downs, aged ten and eight, respectively, returned to school the morning he arrived. Before they left they buried a "treasure" and drew a map on a partly burned piece of paper. They saw the Governor only briefly and no mention was made of the surprise that awaited him.

Mouse Island is about sixteen acres of fields and pine forest with typical Maine inlets and promontories.

145 That is, the copy sent to the *Tribune* did not indicate that a carbon copy was being sent to Miss Patterson.

146 After Stevenson's letter of August 27 appeared in the *Tribune* on August 31, the newspaper denounced him again in an editorial, saying among other things that it was possible he was "innocent or naive," or that he was "color blind and could not see Red."

September 17, 1951

Dear Stevie —

I found a bit of old rolled and partly burned paper hidden in my bedroom at Mouse Island, tied with a red ribbon. Opening it only long enough to see that it was an old map, I hastily secreted it carefully. Then at night when every one was in bed and the house still I turned on my bed lamp & examined it carefully. Yes, it *was* a map and evidently a map of the very legendary treasure you and Patty had searched for on Mouse. It even bore the signature of Captain *Kidd* himself! But never having seen the signature of Capt. Kidd how could I be sure it was authentic; how indeed could I be sure the map itself was not a forgery and a hoax, planted by somebody to divert me from the rest I had promised myself at Mouse?

Well I couldn't be sure, but it was clearly worth investigating. So the next day I made some casual inquiries about the roll of paper — if anyone had misplaced it, etc. No one seemed to know or care about it, and of course I was at some pains not to reveal its contents. What to do? I was determined to search for the treasure in the brief time I had — but alone! — lest I be too chagrined if it was a hoax, or the family, if *I* found a treasure after their long years on the island.

So in the afternoon I stole away, ostensibly to take a nap in the sun. Following the shore line I made my way by a strange and beautiful path to the far side of the island to a spot marked on the old chart with the word "keys." And there — to my dismay and acute embarrassment — I found your Aunt Dorothy! What's more she had already found the keys, rusty keys. There was nothing for it but for both of us to confess and join forces. By long and forced marches, with only occasional stops to rest and study Spanish moss we made our way toward the Spanish treasure marked on the map on a remote promontory. At last we found what appeared to be the spot, passing an abandoned camp on the way, doubtless once the abode of disappointed seekers of this same treasure. But were we to be disappointed too? I wondered.

While Dorothy dug rather aimlessly I thought, I closely examined the place and the old chart. Finding what must be the exact spot I started to work among the roots of a mighty pine. After digging furiously, alternately dripping with sweat and shivering with excitement — and east wind — I suddenly struck a metallic object. Dorothy joined me with, I thought, rather unbecoming cupidity — In a moment it was out — a

147 This handwritten letter is in the possession of Mr. Downs.

small metal chest, wired and padlocked. In a jiffy I had the lock open with the old rusty key — only to find that the lock was a ruse and the box opened by itself — revealing to our blood shot eyes — What! With hands trembling from fatigue we lifted from the chest the dried and hideous face of a pirate — dried as dry as paper, — the old villain's hat, even now in good repair, his cutlass, his compass, a wicked looking old knife, a bottle of ancient liquor that I at first mistook for mosquito repellant — and a bag of coins, curious old coins!

With his unsheathed cutlass in one hand, his knife in my teeth, his face draped over mine, his hat on my head, and the treasure clutched in the other hand I fairly ran all the way back to the house without stopping, using the compass as my guide. Dorothy came panting behind as fast as her short, but sturdy!, legs could carry her and with the bottle in one hand, open, I'm sorry to say! We were *so* eager to escape from that grisly place and to examine and exhibit our extraordinary find with the family and that celebrated old explorer and navigator, Dr. Fosdick, the scourge of Boothbay Harbor.

But, horrors!, I had not reckoned with my terrifying appearance. As I rounded the corner of the house at the gallop the family were all sunning on the lawn. With a blood chilling shriek the women all fainted instantly and simultaneously. Dorothy put the liquor to good purpose to revive them, while I, shedding my ghastly accoutrements, took off after Dr. Fosdick who was racing down the path to summon Wesley [148] and reinforcements.

Contrite, mortified by the havoc I had wrought, I betook myself to my room — with the bag of coins, you may be sure! And here is one for your microscopic examination, evidently an ancient Russian gold rouble. It is probably of even greater value as a collector's item than as gold. So guard it well, study it carefully, make discreet inquiries, never reveal its origin, and let me have your opinion. I will reward you well — and I know you need money to pay for that hike [bike?] — indeed if the treasure is of the value I suspect, I will divide with you, after, of course, deducting the portion that Dorothy claims as joint finder. You know how girls are.

Yours,
ADLAI E. STEVENSON
[sketch of skull and crossbones]

In his reply to Stevenson's letter of September 13, 1951, Harry Green wrote: "The amusing letter from Mrs. David Davis to Judge David

[148] Wesley Barrett, the caretaker who lived on Mouse Island all year.

Davis reminds me that Grandfather Stevenson was at a social affair during his campaign for governor [1908] and a much bourboned gentleman kept assuring the former Vice-President that he was good as elected. The Vice-President was heard telling him: 'Shall I take the oath of office here and now?' "

Mr. Green also sent Stevenson a copy of a letter from former Secretary of the Interior Harold L. Ickes.

To Harry G. Green

September 19, 1951

Dear Mr. Green:

Sometimes I suspect that humor is the indispensable element in the survival of a public official. I remember they used to say in Washington during the war that you would develop one of three things: ulcers, galloping frustration or a sense of humor. Thanks to you my flame still flickers.

I am returning Walt Whitman Ickes' letter. I enjoyed it. Thanks.

Sincerely,

Herbert King, of New York City, a former classmate of Stevenson, motored through Illinois and wrote to commend the Governor on the roads. During his trip he questioned people about Stevenson's performance and was impressed by the responses he received. He thought Stevenson might be President someday and pledged his support.

To Herbert G. King

September 19, 1951

Dear Herb:

I was delighted to have your letter and more than a little flattered and comforted by your research in Illinois. I had concluded that complaint, criticism and abuse was about the only reward, and I feel better. Indeed, I suggest you take up your voting residence in Illinois!

As for your larger ambitions for me, I am afraid I shall have no trouble disappointing you.

With all good wishes and many thanks, I am

Sincerely yours,

The Governor went to Washington, D.C., to try to persuade the federal government to buy Illinois coal for export to Europe. The Chicago

Tribune, *September 20, 1951, charged that he did it to win the votes of the coal miners. In addition, the editorial denounced New Dealers like Stevenson for wasting natural resources and the taxpayers' money.*

To Alicia Patterson [149]

September 20, 1951

Alicia —

I've written your mother & I'm counting on your arriving Friday afternoon or evening or Sat AM. I really hope she comes to[o].

Here's the SOBs latest. I go to Wash. to plead for help for the depressed Ill[inois]. mining industry (biggest drain on relief funds is down there) and say nothing to anyone about what I'm doing — no publicity and no one asked me to go. Then when I get back the Tribune man asks me what I did in Wash. & I mention this among other things — and then this edit[orial]! . . .

A

General George C. Marshall had just announced his resignation as Secretary of Defense and his retirement from public service. Robert A. Lovett was appointed as his replacement in that office.

To General George C. Marshall

September 26, 1951

Dear General:

May I add a small voice to the national chorus of thanks to you. Your retirement is, of course, a disappointment because there are never enough men in exalted positions only because of their selfless distinction and the public's respect and confidence. Few, if any, Americans have epitomized that disinterested devotion as you have, but some of us at least know at what a price in health, convenience and peace of mind.

I hope you can find now what you want and need and have earned long since.

And if we are not too happy about your retirement, I am sure Mrs. Marshall and you are!

Faithfully yours,

[149] This handwritten letter is in the possession of Adlai E. Stevenson III.

To Robert A. Lovett

September 26, 1951

Dear Bob:

Reading the report of your admirable cautionary press conference this morning reminded me how grateful I am to Providence that you were there to pick up the beloved General's burdens — or rather, add to yours! If there is such a thing in this tormented, bewildered country as faith and confidence in a leader, you have it in full measure. I don't envy, but I bless you.

With warm regards and my prayers, I am

Sincerely yours,

Stevenson appointed his aide J. Edward Day to head the Department of Insurance in 1950. Both Day and the Governor were anxious to appoint the best qualified people to positions in that department.

To Stephen A. Mitchell [150]

September 27, 1951

Dear Steve:

I enclose a confidential memorandum. The short of it is that we need to employ a lawyer to head up the Liquidation Division of the Department of Insurance. For many reasons that I shall not attempt to go into, this is a conspicuous position in the industry and we must fill the vacancy properly. It is also a plum.

Ed Day has talked to Dick Daley [151] and I would be delighted if you had any really first-rate suggestions. The industry will be watching carefully in view of Frank Bartsch's long service and general popularity. Do not hesitate to talk to Dick Daley if you care to, but any general news about the vacancy would invite pressures that I would like to avoid.

Sincerely yours,

ADLAI

Stevenson attended the annual Governors' Conference, held in 1951 in Gatlinburg, Tennessee. The New York Times, *October 7, 1951, stated: "With both party conclaves still nine months away, the big question at*

150 The original is in the possession of Mr. Mitchell.
151 County clerk of Cook County.

Gatlinburg has been less 'Who will win the election?' than 'Who will be the nominees?' . . . One Democrat — Stevenson of Illinois — suggested that Ike's nomination would split the G.O.P. wide open" on the issue of foreign policy.

To Mrs. Edison Dick [152]

October 2, 1951

. . . Guess where I've just been — a square dance in the Smoky Mts after a ponderous banquet (never learned to write with a pen) at which Foster Dulles told us all about the Japanese Peace treaty.[153] The Conf. has not been spectacular to date altho the press have turned out from all over the country — even San Francisco. I presided this morning with Gen. Marshall, Charley Wilson [154] & Gov. Caldwell [155] (Civil Defense Man) as features and they all talked so long the Governors never had a chance to discuss the questions. I had to submit to a brutal press conference where they pitched every possible curve at me. All the press seemed to be interested in Presidential politics and they asked me not a single question about state govt. . . .

In the fall of 1951, Harry S. Truman had not yet removed himself as the Democratic candidate for President in 1952. Gregg M. Sinclair, president of the University of Hawaii, wrote the Governor on September 26, 1951, that it would give him much pleasure to see Stevenson occupying the position once held by his "distinguished grandfather," Vice President Adlai E. Stevenson.

To Gregg M. Sinclair

October 4, 1951

Dear Dr. Sinclair:

I was so glad to have your letter, but I am disappointed that your journey on the mainland will evidently not bring you to Springfield.

As to my political future, I am afraid your proposals do not coincide

[152] This handwritten letter is in the possession of Mrs. Dick.

[153] Dulles, special representative of the President with rank of ambassador, negotiated the Japanese Peace Treaty in 1951, and the Australian, New Zealand, Philippine and Japanese security treaties in 1950–1951. He was appointed Secretary of State in 1952.

[154] Charles E. Wilson, director of Defense Mobilization and former president of General Electric.

[155] Millard F. Caldwell, Jr., governor of Florida, 1945–1949, Civil Defense Administrator, 1950–1952.

either with the realities here or my own ambitions. I have found Illinois about as much as I can handle, and then some!

It was good to hear from you, and I am deeply gratified by your encouragement and support.

Sincerely yours,

Samuel Cardinal Stritch, archbishop of Chicago, wrote Stevenson inviting him to a fund-raising dinner on behalf of Loyola University Medical School and Lewis Memorial Maternity Hospital in Chicago on November 15, 1951. He concluded his letter by saying that only a few failed to appreciate the Governor's high right principles and unswerving loyalty to his honest convictions.

To Samuel Cardinal Stritch

October 10, 1951

My dear Cardinal:

Your very gracious and flattering invitation for Thursday evening, November 15, comes to me just after I have written Steve Mitchell telling him that I cannot get up to Chicago that night due to an obligation I have long since contracted at Southern Illinois University in Carbondale the following day. I am disappointed because I remember so well the Loyola dinner two years ago, and also because the welfare of the Medical School is of such great consequence to the State — indeed, to the Middle West. What is more, I do not forego an opportunity to meet and to hear you lightly. I only wish that the opportunities were more frequent, and I wish very much that I could come up and dine with you again at your residence, if you ever have a free dinner hour. May I submit some dates when I may be in Chicago?

Your concluding words about my feeble efforts are as gratifying as anything that has happened to me in the past three years.

With profound respect and affection, I am

Faithfully yours,

In 1951 the legislature extended the responsibilities of the Illinois Interracial Commission and renamed it the Commission on Human Relations. The first meeting of the new commission was held in Springfield on October 11, 1951, with Stevenson delivering the following speech.[156]

[156] The text is based on a mimeograph copy prepared by the Governor's office for release to the press.

Our strength stems less from our material and technical attainments as a nation than from our historic record in securing and broadening the rights of our people. From the earliest settlement of this country, America has been a symbol of hope wherever men have aspired to be free and stand erect.

We have learned from the past, and more recently in the bitter experience of two World Wars, that today human freedom is indivisible. We have come to know that the basic human rights we cherish are linked with the fate of even the most humble and remote peasant. Whenever fundamental human rights are denied, freedom everywhere is threatened, whether it be in far off Korea or in Cicero, Illinois.

In our time science and technology have made the world so small and intergroup contacts so numerous and involved, that otherwise normal human relations have become fraught with tension. Racial friction has become a major threat to the peace and security of all mankind. While the Cicero events have tragically exaggerated our shortcomings, we must not underestimate their importance. We can ill afford to exhibit to the world either incompetence or injustice in dealing with the relations of racial groups. Bigotry and violence contradict the sincerity of the principles which have been our greatest contribution to human history. And today they are a visible encumbrance which weakens America's moral leadership in world affairs.

There must be no doubt that here in Illinois we are committed to the protection of all citizens, irrespective of race, color or creed, in the enjoyment of their rights. Furthermore, there must be no doubt that the laws which guarantee these rights will be enforced impartially in Illinois.

Whatever our personal prejudices and shortcomings, problems in human relations cannot be solved by violence. If they are, it means only that law and order have capitulated, and that we have cheaply surrendered to the enemies of democracy.

The Illinois Legislature has recognized how important it is to protect and re-emphasize the American tradition of tolerance and good will. During the past session of the legislature, the Illinois Interracial Commission was renamed the Commission on Human Relations and its responsibilities extended to include the "promotion and encouragement of interfaith and interracial harmony and good will."

The creation of this new Commission on Human Relations is timely. It comes when we are struggling to restore the housing lost to us because of the priorities of war production, and now again of defense. Deep beneath the Cicero disorders and the breakdown of local law enforcement, lie the fears, the alarms, the pressures, and tensions of the continuously critical housing shortage. Notwithstanding the tremendous technical advances of the past two decades, America is currently confronted by what can very well become a dangerous threat to the integrity of our free society.

Large numbers of the low income groups, and among these large numbers of the so-called minority groups, are inadequately housed, rigidly segregated and confined to slums and deteriorated residential areas. The demoralizing effects of overcrowding, of substandard housing, inadequate sanitation, illegal building conversions, and a host of resultant social evils, are placing a severe strain upon the whole range of state and municipal welfare services.

This is the root of the Cicero affair — the grim reality underlying the tension and violence that accompany the efforts of minority group members to break through the iron curtain which confines so many of our fellow citizens.

We must remove fear and prejudice. We must destroy the myths which gnaw at our vitals. And as ever, it is in public enlightenment and understanding that we must place our trust. An informed public opinion is the only condition in which our way of life can flourish. If the relevant facts and information are supplied, the public can be trusted to create a climate of reason and order in which we can go forward to the solution of our difficulties.

Our shortcomings are dramatized at the very center of our power as a nation, in the great metropolitan centers of commerce and industry. The symbolic significance in the whole life of the nation of our great cities such as Chicago, Detroit, New York, Los Angeles and Washington cannot be gainsaid. It is unfortunate that social tension was focussed at these centers of our power and prestige.

But there it is, and we must produce the facts before we propose the solutions. We must study this urgent problem of human relations — sanely, soberly, intelligently. And I know no better place to start than right here in Illinois. So it seems to me imperative that a group of representative citizens from the Chicago Metropolitan area undertake such a study. I think the study should be under the auspices and direction of private citizens rather than an official governmental body. And I think it should be financed with private, not public, funds. I am sure they can be obtained.

I am hopeful that a very responsible citizens' committee can be assembled to make such a study and to issue its findings and recommendations to the public. There is something wrong and it is time we had an honest and expert diagnosis.

To Harry S. Truman [157]

October 12, 1951

Dear Mr. President:

I take the liberty of enclosing a resolution adopted by the Democratic State Central Committee of Illinois. They are very anxious to hold a large Jackson Day dinner at the Armory here in Springfield in January, and, of course, they are intensely eager to have you present for a brief speech, if at all possible.

I understand your predicament and I appreciate that it is impossible for you to foretell at this time your circumstances in January. But your presence would be of enormous encouragement to the Democrats in Illinois, and many others besides. Should you "feel a speech coming on" at that time, we hope you will give some thought to the possibility of Springfield.[158]

I send to you the good wishes, warm respect and admiration of the Democratic State Central Committee of Illinois — not to mention the Governor!

Respectfully yours,

To Mrs. Edison Dick [159]

October 15, 1951

. . . I will spend Thurs & Fri nights in my eyrie [160] and Sat night with the Fields,[161] leaving Sunday at 10 for Wausaw, Wis. to speak again — God help me — and so on and on and on – – –

We glory in tribulations, knowing that tribulations maketh patience, and patience, experience, and experience, hope.

Hope — in His good time . . .

To Barry Bingham

October 16, 1951

Dear Barry:

Thanks for the clipping of the editorial on gambling and the very

[157] The original is in the Harry S. Truman Library.
[158] President Truman finally declined the invitation.
[159] This handwritten letter is in the possession of Mrs. Dick.
[160] The governor's suite on the top floor of the State of Illinois Building in downtown Chicago.
[161] Mr. and Mrs. Marshall Field IV.

flattering reference to "Governor Stevenson of Illinois." [162] Our statistics are interesting actually. We have virtually eliminated the slot machine as an instrument of commercial gambling in Illinois outside of Cook County. It still persists, however, in the fraternal organizations, servicemen's posts and clubs. I have been disturbed, and I am a little shocked, at the apparent reluctance of the good people to comply with the law themselves while bellowing denunciations of the unhappy state of public morals.

However, considering our plight three years ago in Illinois, we have made most gratifying progress. But it is an endless job and until the local citizenry demand local enforcement and stick to it, it will never be solved. I have disliked using the State Police and coercion from Springfield to force local officials to do what the law requires. Moreover, I don't see why the taxpayer should have to pay for the same service twice. But the taxpayer seems curiously indifferent about his front yard.

All good wishes to you.

Sincerely yours,

To Alicia Patterson [163]

October 16, 1951

. . . Here I am violating all the rules — writing you in mid morning, when I should be at work. Such is my irresponsibility! I have no transcript of the press conferences at the Gov's Conf. Indeed I doubt if one is made. Ike would, of course, be a very strong candidate. By saying that he would divide Reps. I didnot say that he would lose. The point I was trying to make in answer to their devilish questions was that Taft vs Truman would present the foreign policy issue much more clearly than Ike vs HST. The Bertie [McCormick] wing of the Reps on this issue would have no where to go if Ike vs Truman. That issue which has been so confused by Taft, MacArthur, McCarthy, Dirksen, Wherry, Malone, Jenner et al *must* be settled again in this election, if we are going to present any unified, confident, strong and certain leadership, I think you'll agree. Perhaps Ike vs Truman settles it also, but by elimi[n]ating it rather than voting on it.

---

[162] The Governors' Conference in Gatlinburg, Tennessee, had just passed a resolution that the prime responsibility for suppressing organized crime rested with local law enforcement officers. The editorial agreed, saying that although a governor may exert influence for ill or for good, if the people themselves do not insist that their officers enforce the laws, gambling and other evils would continue to exist. It referred to Stevenson's "clean record" in Illinois. Louisville *Times*, October 5, 1951.

[163] This handwritten letter is in the possession of Adlai E. Stevenson III.

As to whether Ike could beat HST, yes I think he would, but perhaps not as overwhelmingly as one would surmise in the present state of Trumans popularity. Its hard — evidently impossible for me — to make these things in the black and white colors the newsmen want. Likewise as a politician it puts you in an uncomfortable spot to prophesy the defeat of your party.

I strongly suspect: Taft can't be stopped among the regulars and I would feel much better about the future if he is not and the Dems. could nominate Ike — thus presenting the only really important issue in clear colors and letting Harry off. As you know he really does not want to run & takes very seriously the *principle* of the 2 term constitutional limitation on presidential terms. But I suppose that is too much to hope for. In re Taft, while Gov. [Walter J.] Kohler of Wis. came out emphatically for Ike in Tenn., a week later the Rep. state chairman & most of the Wis GOP leaders called upon Taft to run and pledged their support. Thats the way it is in the regular GOP organizations elsewhere I suspect. The likely Cook County GOP candidate for Gov of Ill. — [William] Erickson — has pledged for Taft already doubtless at Bertie's insistence, because I'm sure he has no views of his own other than political.

As for me, I don't want any national business, nor do I intend to run for re election *unless* I can be sure that the Dem. organ[ization]. in Ill & Chicago will give me a really good candidate for states atty of Cook County, and some more things I will have to insist upon to make 4 more years of this hell endurable. I believe you'll agree that I should use the large bargaining power I now have to the utmost to accomplish some of the less conspicuous and more important long range objectives I have — i.e. better people in this business to make it a better business. I've done it in the administrative branch, with great difficulty, and before I get out I would like to help the party save itself and the system, at least in a small way.

The Tribune is stepping up its fantastic dishonesties & I wonder if the press can be kept free and dishonest at the same time. I never thought of freedom as license for *individuals* — Can it be for *institutions* — public institutions?

I must to work. . . . I enclose a piece that may interest you on the race business. There are so many things that need doing I'm distracted and feel futile & ineffective all the time. And out doors the soft indian summer sun is shining, the skies are blue and all I want to do is roll in the leaves — . . .

On October 13 and 14, 1951, Stevenson and U.S. Senator Paul H. Douglas met and came to an informal understanding about delegates they would support for the 1952 Democratic National Convention. The conflict that subsequently arose between the two over the agreement was never fully resolved.

To Lawrence Irvin [164]

October 18, 1951

Mr. Irvin —

Paul Douglas has promised me a list of suggestions for delegates by Nov. 1. We should have some suggestions for him. I think we can work together on this.

AES

Mrs. Dick served as chairman of the Board of Public Welfare Commissioners' Volunteer Service Program. On October 19, 1951, she sent the Governor the program's first monthly report covering four of the state's psychiatric hospitals.

To Mrs. Edison Dick [165]

[October 22, 1951?] [166]

Dear Mrs. Dick —

I have read the report and am very much impressed. I had no idea how much thought, work & progress had already taken place. Bravo! Well Done!! Bravissima!!! I'm your debtor — again.

Sincerely yours,

Three speeches in Chi — horrors what a flannel mouth I've turned into — Sat. night with Kay & Marshall [Field] — Sat morning tennis on my court with Marsh, Ruth [Winter] & Ginc [167] — warm sun, soft wind and golden trees. I almost cried — Off at 12 for Wausau, Wis. only to be grounded 50 miles from my destination and have to turn back, to the delight no doubt of the Wis[consin]. State Democratic Convention!

And what of the children. . . .

[164] The original is in the possession of Mr. Irvin.

[165] Stevenson wrote this note by hand on Mrs. Dick's typewritten letter to him of October 19, 1951, beginning at the bottom of the page and continuing on the reverse. The original is in the possession of Mrs. Dick.

[166] The note is not dated. Stevenson was scheduled to speak in Wausau, Wisconsin, on Sunday, October 21, and it was probably written the following day.

[167] Mrs. William R. Odell.

To Mrs. Carl McGowan [168]

October 27, 1951

Jodie dear —

Don't worry about climbing trees, fireworks & football *yet*.[169] In between you have cuts, bruises, roller skates & whooping cough. And after football there's *girls!*

I can't wait to see him —Is it McGowan or Perry [170] — or wait and see? With *two* older sisters my heart goes out to him!!!

Take it easy — the old man has completely recovered.

Love —
ADLAI

The merchants in Springfield annually conducted a contest at Hallow-
een when young people in the city were encouraged to paint shop
windows with water paints instead of engaging in the more traditional
destructive activities associated with this festival. Donna, the young
daughter of Stevenson's aide Don Hyndman, won first prize for her
painting.

To Donna A. Hyndman [171]

November 2, 1951

My dear Donna:

Although your proud father would never have told me, one of my spies uncovered the fact that you had won the first prize in the Hallow-e'en window painting contest. I am delighted, and I hope you make every effort to cultivate your art work. It is a wonderful talent and a great lesson for you in many ways.

With my congratulations and affectionate best wishes, I am

Sincerely,

William Stevenson wrote that he and his wife had been to Illinois but
had to rush back to Ohio without seeing the Governor.

---

[168] This handwritten letter is in the possession of Mrs. McGowan.
[169] The McGowans' third child, a son whom they named John, was born on October 22, 1951.
[170] Mrs. McGowan's maiden name was Josephine Perry.
[171] The original of this typewritten letter is in the possession of T. Don Hyndman.

To William E. Stevenson

November 2, 1951

Dear Bill:

So you have been in Chicago, Decatur and Bloomington! I was never more irked. And I have instructed my agents to watch our borders carefully. Should you cross them again the State Police will escort you directly to the Executive Mansion in Springfield. How much nicer and more dignified if you and Bumpy [172] were to come quietly!

Yours,

Roger Lane, political reporter for the Associated Press in Springfield, wrote to the editor of the Atlantic *that he would like that publication to request Governor Stevenson to write an article on one of his favorite themes — citizen responsibility in a democracy. He enclosed a copy of a speech Stevenson gave before the Sangamon County Bar Association in Springfield on October 23, 1951, together with a press account of the affair. He wrote that he thought the Governor had much to say and a rare gift for saying it effectively, and compared Stevenson favorably with Thomas Jefferson. The* Atlantic *asked Stevenson to contribute an article, and he adapted the October 23 speech for that purpose. It appeared in the February, 1952, issue under the title "Who Runs the Gambling Machines?"*

To Roger Lane

November 2, 1951

Dear Roger:

One of my espionage agents has sent me a copy of your letter to the Atlantic suggesting that Thomas Jefferson Stevenson do a piece for that austere journal. To say that I am flattered would be to say the obvious. To say that you do me more than justice would be to say not half enough.

Anyway, I like it — and how!

Sincerely yours,

Dr. John Finley, master of Eliot House, where Stevenson's eldest son, Adlai III, lived while attending Harvard University, renewed his invitation to Stevenson to speak at their "Eliot Dinner" in March, 1952.

[172] Mrs. Stevenson.

To John H. Finley, Jr.

November 9, 1951

Dear Dr. Finley:

That you could ask me twice is due to the fact that you haven't heard me once! This time I would really like to come, in spite of possible campaigns and all the horrors hereabouts, particularly to keep in touch with my Freshman son, Borden. However, I find that the vacation of my youngest son, John Fell, who is at Milton, and the vacation period of Adlai and Borden do not overlap. Accordingly, I shall probably come East the latter part of March to spend a little time with John Fell and then see the others.

In short, to take advantage of your invitation would mean a special trip, and all things considered I am afraid I had better not risk that much time off just then.

You were good to think of me and I am immensely flattered.

With warm regards to you and Mrs. Finley, I am

Sincerely yours,

P.S. I shall hope to see you this week-end before this letter even reaches you. I am planning to be there for the Harvard-Princeton game and have Sunday with the boys.

P.P.S. Having read your commencement address at Smith I think it is all the better that I cannot come!

A.E.S.

After spending the weekend of November 10 and 11, 1951, with his three sons in Boston, Stevenson wrote to Mrs. William H. Mitchell, a family friend living in Lake Forest, Illinois, whose son, Teddy, roomed with John Fell at Milton Academy.

To Mrs. William H. Mitchell

November 13, 1951

Dear Ann:

I spent the weekend in Boston with the boys and Teddy came along with John Fell. He seemed very well and I was not a little impressed to find him sitting in his pajamas writing to you Sunday morning while the Stevensons were still asleep!

He is a charming, well-mannered, alert and bubbling boy. Also, I wish John Feil were as well-mannered.

> Yours,

The Democratic National Convention was scheduled to be held in Chicago in July, 1952, and Stevenson's friend Louis A. Kohn was beginning to think about arrangements for Stevenson, who, as governor of the host state, would be called upon to play an extraordinarily active role.

To Louis A. Kohn

> November 14, 1951

Dear Lou:

Thanks for your letter and the enclosures. I think from now on you are my "convention coordinator," and some time you should tell me in detail what you have in mind that I should do. I think I could probably borrow someone's apartment in town, which, together with my office, should make a hotel suite unnecessary.

By all means tell Mr. Bressler [173] he may use my name as one of the Honorary Chairmen for the dinner for Judge [Harry] Fisher.

> Sincerely yours,

P.S. I hope you can come to Gettysburg.[174]

To Stephen Y. Hord [175]

> November 17, 1951

Dear Steve:

Would it flatter your vanity and improve your public position to accompany me to the Illinois v. Northwestern football game on Saturday, November 24? We would have lunch beforehand with President [Roscoe] Miller of Northwestern, and I should be glad to provide transportation in [and?] my engaging company. If you have any carousal in contemplation for the evening I might even bless Lake Forest for the night.

> Yours,
> ADLAI

[173] Unable to identify.
[174] Stevenson was scheduled to speak at ceremonies marking the anniversary of Lincoln's Gettysburg Address on November 19.
[175] The original is in the possession of Mr. Hord.

On November 9, 1951, Stevenson made a radio report to the people about their state government. Edward McDougal wrote the Governor that while listening to the speech he was reminded of a verse:

"If you would make a speech or write one,
Or get an artist to indict [indite] one,
Think not because 'tis understood, by men of sense, 'tis therefore good,
Make it so clear and simply planned no block head can misunderstand."

He added: "You presented those facts so beautifully and very impressively and made them so clear that even a blockhead could get the point."

To Edward D. McDougal, Jr.[176]

November 17, 1951

Dear Ed:

Thanks — and thanks again — for that engaging little verse. It has a moral that I have never mastered. I sometimes think my success as a speaker is largely due to the fact that most of my audiences *don't* understand me. Indeed, the unhappy truth is that I probably don't understand myself half the time. You remember the one about the old lady from Vermont who said she didn't know what she thought until she heard what she said!

Thanks again for your charity about the radio speech. Maybe I expect a little too much from the Guv.

Love to Kate.[177]

Yours,
ADLAI

On November 19, 1951, Governor Stevenson spoke at ceremonies on the occasion of the eighty-eighth anniversary of Lincoln's Gettysburg Address.[178]

We are met here today on the field of a bloody, shattering battle. And we meet in reverence for the tall, gaunt man who, standing here 88 years ago, mindful of the dead and the cause for which they here died, phrased in words, clean of all ornament, the duty of the living to con-

[176] The original is in the possession of Mr. McDougal.
[177] Mrs. McDougal.
[178] The text is based on a mimeograph copy prepared by the Governor's office for release to the press.

tinue the struggle. The struggle did continue, the high fever that was Gettysburg passed, and the democratic experiment survived its mortal crisis.

More than the survival of the American Union was at issue here at Gettysburg. Upon the fate of the Union hung the fate of the new dream of democracy throughout the world. For in Lincoln's time the United States was the only major country of the world that enjoyed the democratic form of government, the only land where government was of, by, and for the people. America was democracy's proving ground. The masses of other lands looked to us with hope. If our experiment proved successful, they too might win self-government. But the cynics and the privileged, regarding our experiment with foreboding, identified it with mob rule and lawlessness, sneered and prophesied its doom. When civil war broke out they said: "We told you so."

But Lincoln saw the war in its global dimensions. He was a man of peace, yet even the horror of a brothers' war was not too great a price to save the Union and to demonstrate the viability and the superiority of government by the people.

As Lincoln saw it, the Confederate States had rejected two fundamental precepts of democracy. First, in refusing to accept him as their President and making his election their justification for withdrawing from the Union, they had violated the first rule of democratic government, the obligation of a minority to abide by the result of an election. Without such acquiescence democracy would not work. The Union must never be dissevered for any such reason as this.

Second, in making slavery the foundation stone of their new government, the Confederacy was renouncing the doctrine of the equal rights of man in favor of the creed of the master race, an idea that Lincoln abhorred. "The last, best hope of earth," in his view, was to be found in our Declaration of Independence which affirmed that all men are created equal, that they are endowed by their Creator with certain inalienable rights, among which are life, liberty, and the pursuit of happiness.

Here, in fact, was the whole pith and substance of Lincoln's political philosophy. Here, in his deep reverence for the rights of man as proclaimed in our American charter of freedom, is to be found the explanation of most of his political actions. "I have never had a feeling politically," he said, "which did not spring from the sentiments embodied in the Declaration of Independence." It was these principles, Lincoln believed, that would lift artificial weights from men's shoulders, clear the paths of laudable pursuit for all, and afford everyone an unfettered start and a fair chance in the race of life.

When we realize that Lincoln saw the dissolution of the Union as a threat to democratic aspirations throughout the world, his words at Gettysburg become more meaningful. Chancellorsville, Antietam, Chickamauga and Gettysburg were deciding more than the fate of these United States. Americans were dying for the new, revolutionary idea of the free man, even as they had died at Bunker Hill and Yorktown. They were dying to save the hope of all people everywhere.

So when Lincoln was asked to speak at the dedication of this cemetery, he welcomed the chance to tell the people what those three days of bloody battle meant and to explain what those men died for, as he saw it.

His thoughts went back four score and seven years to the revolutionary founding of this nation, conceived in liberty and dedicated to the proposition that all men are created equal. Then his mind came back to the war being fought to determine whether that nation, or any nation conceived in revolution and dedicated to such radical principles, could long endure — whether the people were capable of shaping their own destiny. He thought of the heroic dead, and of what the living owed them for their sacrifice. Mere words could not express it. The world, he thought, would little note nor long remember what was said that day. Then he looked ahead — not merely to the tomorrow, but into the far distant future, as he said: "It is for us, the living, rather to be here dedicated to the great task remaining before us . . . that these dead shall not have died in vain."

The war ended. The nation, reunited, once again offered hope for liberal yearnings everywhere. Inspired by the example of America, democracy made striking headway throughout the world, even among the so-called backward peoples of the earth. It seemed that the principles for which Lincoln fought and died would win world-wide acceptance. America took it for granted. To us it became merely a question of when and how. Busy building up a rich continent, America lost sight of its mission.

Then came the shock of World War I. But with victory, democracy took up its march again. Russia, most reactionary of all European countries, was in revolt against autocracy. Germany, Austria, Czechoslovakia, became republics. Woodrow Wilson, who, even as Lincoln, saw the fate of democracy as the prime issue of the war, went to Europe with a purpose to mark out new boundaries which would express, as nearly as possible, the people's will. Democracy was again in the ascendant. But America, mindless of her mission, following the soft voices of men of little vision, shrouded herself in isolation.

The rest is within the recollection of us all. Adolph Hitler resurrected the malevolent doctrine of the master race, and poised its ghastly death's head over Europe. And now comes imperial Communism, stalking freedom throughout the world.

The struggle for human liberty goes on. The great bearers of our tradition have believed in it not because they were born in it, but because they saw despotism as we have seen it and turned from it to rediscover the American faith in the free man.

The struggle must be re-fought by every generation and democracy is threatened not alone by hostile ideologies abroad, but by fear, greed, indifference, intolerance, demagoguery and dishonor here at home. Little men spread mistrust, confusion, fear. Careless inquisition and irresponsible accusation increase tensions, and tensions, repressions. The tyranny of organized opinion lifts its ugly head to mock the faith of the American Revolution.

No, Lincoln's fight is not finished. The far future into which he looked is here, and we are now the living. Eight and eighty years after he uttered here those immortal words, it is for us, the living, to be re-dedicated to our democratic faith; to be here dedicated to the great task, the same task, remaining before us. The fight goes on. Cemetery Ridge is shrouded in the mist of history. But American boys are dying today on Heartbreak Ridge far away for the last, best hope of collective security, of peace and of freedom for all to choose their way of life.

Proud of the past, [im]patient with what Washington called "the impostures of pretended patriotism," it is for us, the living, to rekindle the hot, indignant fires of faith in the free man, free in body, free in mind, free in spirit, free to hold any opinion, free to search and find the truth for himself; the old faith that is ever new — that burned so brightly here at Gettysburg long ago.

To John Parish [179]

November 23, 1951

Dear John:

You are a good guy, as usual, to write me about my "effort" at Gettysburg, and if you don't look out I'll send you a copy and you will be obliged to read it in toto!

I wish you would come in to see me at the next opportunity. I cannot accept without further protest your decision not to run again.[180] Being

---

[179] Democratic state senator from the 42nd District. The original is in the possession of Mr. Parish.

[180] Stevenson was eager to have Parish run for the state Senate again. He also offered to appoint him director of revenue, saying he wanted Parish in Springfield to

in such an uncertain state of mind myself it is easy to try to persuade others!

The sheets are clean and the meals on time at the Mansion!

Yours,

To Alicia Patterson [181]

[late November or early December, 1951]

. . . I'm in dreadful travail about politics. I literally don't know whether I could physically survive another campaign and 4 more years. Yet if I slow up as everyone advises, I dread the possibility of the administration slipping back, losing the momentum and the public confidence I've gained. And it all seems to depend on me — the pace, the tone, the everlasting pressure, and the public preaching about state govt. and good govt. Moreover if Ike runs and it turns into a landslide as well it might I'm not sure I could win against the deluge. If I quit now the record would be excellent and how many politicians quit at the peak of popularity; I might save not only the record, but my health and even make some money somehow which I've neglected for 10 yrs plus, or be available for some other govt. service. Meanwhile I'm playing strong and silent, and turning on the pressure for good candidates which, if I get them, will prove my theory that men can influence political organizations, no matter how big and powerful, rather than the converse — and you don't have to be a political "boss" to do it. All of which is another way of saying that the people — which means public opinion, which means the "press" can still run the democratic system and run it right if it is fair and honest. But that's oversimplifying. On a grander scale Ike illustrates the point, but more due to historical accident, than the day to day problem of how to make political organization serve the purpose for which it was intended, rather than the mercenary purpose of the political managers. But I'm wandering!

I wish we could discuss the Ill. situation — you are so wise and intuitive — for I'll have to make up my mind before long or else I'll drift into a position I can't get out of gracefully without doing the party grave injustice. I have to confer with the State Dept. Tuesday — then back to Spfd — but I don't think I'll call on Truman, although to put him in a position of asking me to run [for governor] might have future value.[182]

---

consult with him and give him advice. However, Parish declined both suggestions and returned to his business affairs in Centralia. Letter, John Parish to Carol Evans, December, 1967.

[181] This handwritten letter is in the possession of Adlai E. Stevenson III.

[182] Stevenson announced his intention to run for reelection on January 5, 1952.

But the press & therefore public reaction would be "pledging support" etc. which wouldn't do me any good in Ill. among the people, where he is hardly popular to say the least. . . .

A

Many festivities clustered around the Governor's mansion during the Christmas season, among them a party for the Governor's personal staff, with a separate party during the afternoon hours for their children. The Governor's sons always visited him during the holidays and the highlight of the Springfield social season was a ball held for their young friends.[183]

To Mr. and Mrs. T. Don Hyndman [184]

November 26, 1951

Dear Don and Anna Louise:

I want very much this year to entertain the members of my staff and their families at a Christmas party at the Mansion, and I hope you can come on Friday afternoon, December 21. The time 4:30 to 5:30 is being reserved for the special entertainment of the young children, and as many of the grownups who want to come at that time are welcome also. There will be a Christmas tree and Santa Claus for the children and some other entertainment.

As for the adults, we expect to make merry from 5:30 on. There will be a punch bowl and buffet supper — so please make your arrangements now for the baby sitter!

Sincerely yours,

On November 19, 1951, Senator Estes Kefauver wrote Stevenson a sympathetic letter, saying that Henry Crown had told him in Chicago the week before that Stevenson was ill in the hospital.

To Estes Kefauver

November 27, 1951

My dear Estes:

Many thanks for your thoughtful letter. I am afraid Colonel Crown

[183] For a good account of the Christmas holidays in Springfield, see Elizabeth S. Ives and Hildegarde Dolson, *My Brother Adlai* (New York: William Morrow, 1956), pp. 232–235.

[184] The original is in the possession of Mr. Hyndman.

somewhat exaggerated the state of my health since I haven't been in a hospital for twenty years — although I sometimes feel like crawling in one to hide! The fact of the matter is, I am fine and there is nothing the matter with me that a good long rest could not cure. I suspect the same goes for you.

Do let me know when you pass this way again.

Sincerely yours,

Louis Brownlow, former director of the Public Administration Clearing House, wrote Stevenson that someone had given him a pamphlet containing the Governor's veto messages. He loaned it to so many people that eventually it was lost, and he asked for additional copies. He added that his friends, not only his dispassionate academic acquaintances but others who in his opinion had some political sense, told him that Stevenson was just about Illinois's best governor.

To Louis Brownlow

December 4, 1951

Dear Brownie:

I was enchanted with your letter. We must have that conversation soon, and I am confident that suitable conspiracies will result.

Why not let me know when you are going to be in Chicago and come down to Springfield for a night with me? My time there is usually dreadfully engaged, but the Mansion is warm, quiet, and full of good food, etc. Please don't fail me.

Yours,

P.S. I believe the pamphlets have already been sent to you. What you say about the veto messages inflates me dangerously.

Francis T. P. Plimpton wrote Stevenson that he would be in Chicago for a meeting and free from Saturday afternoon, December 8, until Monday morning, December 10.

To Francis T. P. Plimpton

December 4, 1951

Dear Francis:

I am back from Chicago today and find your letter of November 30. You *must* come down Saturday, as early as possible. It is the first week-end I have been here in months, and there will be other guests.[185] Somehow we will contrive to have a good time — I hope! I am afraid I will have to leave Sunday afternoon for Washington.

I enclose the transportation schedule from Chicago to Springfield. I wish you could get the G.M. & O. [Gulf, Mobile & Ohio Railroad] at 11:45 A.M. If not, you must get the 4:50, which doesn't get here until 8:00 o'clock. However, we can hold dinner, and will exempt you from a dinner coat.

Yours,

P.S. You would be infinitely more attractive if accompanied by Pauline.[186]

Stevenson's second cousin, Mrs. Carl Vrooman, and her husband spent Thanksgiving day with the Governor at the mansion in Springfield.

To Mrs. Carl Vrooman [187]

December 8, 1951

Dear Cousin Julia:

Your sweet letter wasn't necessary, but it pleases me mightily!

I am sure I enjoyed Thanksgiving more than anyone and your love, confidence and encouragement is a mighty tonic.

Affectionately,
ADLAI

In November, 1951, Frank E. McKinney, chairman of the Democratic National Committee, innocently touched off a minor fracas between Stevenson and Robert R. McCormick, publisher of the Chicago Tribune, *when in a speech he devoted a portion of his remarks to the biased reporting of the* Tribune. *The paper retaliated by calling McKinney a "crook" and printed a collection of complimentary statements by many Illinois Democrats testifying to the* Tribune's *objectivity. But Stevenson observed: "The Tribune is entitled to its views of the world but pray God they don't prevail now any more than they did in 1863, when the publisher* [188] *said we could not win the Civil War." [189]*

[185] The other guests were Miss Judith Montagu, of London, a niece of Winston Churchill, and Mr. and Mrs. Ronald Tree, of New York.

[186] Mrs. Plimpton.

[187] The original is in the possession of Mrs. Vrooman.

[188] Joseph Medill, McCormick's grandfather.

[189] Press release, undated.

On November 23, 1951, the Tribune *in a scathing editorial commented on Stevenson's November 19 speech at Gettysburg, concluding that "Gov. Stevenson cannot have understood the Gettysburg address itself if he is incapable of noticing the nationalism it breathes." The final paragraph concluded: "Well, we should not have expected Adlai to understand Lincoln very well — not when his Democratic grandfather stumped the state of Illinois for Gen. McClellan against Lincoln in 1864."*

Harry G. Green, of Chicago, with whom Stevenson had had a lively correspondence since 1949 about the Governor's forebears, wrote on November 29th, that he was half blind from "re-wading through all the Lincolniana," and had found not a scrap of evidence that Grandfather Stevenson had campaigned for McClellan.

To Harry G. Green [190]

December 8, 1951

Dear Mr. Green:

I was delighted, as usual, with your letter. I too have done a little research of late, and my Aunts likewise, to see if Grandfather Stevenson ever campaigned for McClellan. We can find nothing whatever. At that time he was State's Attorney of Woodford County and he didn't move to Bloomington until 1868. If he was doing any campaigning it was not from "one end of the state to the other," but in the immediate vicinity of Metamora and nowhere else. Moreover, had he campaigned for McClellan I can hardly believe that the hot Lincoln Republicans of Bloomington and vicinity would have elected him to Congress as a Democrat in 1871 [1874], which they did.

And speaking of grandfathers, and such, the "morning colonel" overlooks that my great grandfather, Jesse Fell, had as much and probably a little more than anyone else with Lincoln becoming President. Nor did he lose faith in him in 1863 as Medill did when he wrote to Washburn.

Should you run across Lincoln's criticism of Medill which Harold Ickes refers to I would prize a copy for possible reference in my everlasting and not wholly displeasing skirmishes with the Napoleon of the Tribune Tower.

With best regards, I am

Sincerely yours,

p.s. I return Mr. Ickes' letter herewith.

[190] A carbon copy is in A.E.S., P.U.L.

In a December 17, 1951, column, Colonel McCormick charged that Grandfather Stevenson had put in only thirteen days of military service during the Civil War and then hired a substitute to take his place in an Illinois regiment. The story, he said, was based on an affidavit filed by a Metamora, Illinois, preacher in 1908. The column also declared that Grandfather Stevenson was affiliated with the Knights of the Golden Circle, a notorious pro-Confederacy movement that advocated armed resistance to the Union — also proved by affidavit — and that he had stumped Illinois for McClellan. To which Stevenson replied: [191]

The campaign smear against Grandfather Stevenson in 1908 was refuted by *responsible* affidavits at that time which the Tribune story overlooks. The Tribune also overlooks his election to Congress in 1874 in the hot Lincoln Republican country around Bloomington, Illinois — as a Democrat! The smear of 1908 resembles the Tribune's tactics against Senator Tydings in Maryland last year.[192]

As for his "stumping the state for McClellan against Lincoln in 1864," as the Tribune says, I doubt if he ever got out of Woodford County, where he was the very young State's Attorney at that time. While digging up very old dead cats, the Tribune said of Lincoln after the assassination: "Johnson's little finger will prove thicker than were Abraham Lincoln's loins." [193] Can they find any similar estimate of Lincoln by Grandfather Stevenson? No. Quite the contrary.

And speaking of Lincoln and the Civil War, there is much the Tribune could write about my *great* grandfather, Jesse Fell, and his long association with Lincoln. Will it?

Miss Eunice Stevenson, of Galesburg, Illinois (no relation to the Governor), in a letter to Stevenson warned him that the more successful he was the more criticism he should expect, and because he was still young

[191] A carbon copy is in A.E.S., P.U.L.

[192] Senator Millard Tydings was defeated in a campaign of abuse and implied disloyalty. Not only the Chicago *Tribune* but Senator Joseph McCarthy participated actively in the campaign to defeat Tydings. See Richard Rovere, *Senator Joe McCarthy* (New York, Harcourt, Brace, 1959), pp. 160–161.

[193] The *Tribune* on April 18, 1865, expressed its satisfaction with President Andrew Johnson's desire to punish Confederate leaders whom Lincoln had intended to treat leniently, and this metaphor was meant to indicate the consequences to the South of the assassination. The editorial continued: "While he [Lincoln] whipped them gently with cords, his successor will scourge them with the whip of scorpions." Quoted in Philip Kinsley, *The Chicago Tribune: Its First Hundred Years*, Vol. II (Chicago: Chicago *Tribune*, 1945), pp. 5–6.

he should not duck every time a brickbat sailed through the air in 1952.
She requested an autographed photo of him "to put on her dresser."

To Eunice Stevenson

December 18, 1951

My dear Miss Stevenson:

I was delighted to have your letter, and I am sending the inscribed picture, which, I am afraid, has graced few ladies' dressers!

What you say is most encouraging to me. Perhaps you are right and at least the philosophy of gratification and abuse would be a mighty weapon in a politician's armory.

With all good wishes to you, and my thanks, I am

Sincerely yours,

To Alicia Patterson [194]

December 19, 1951

. . . I've been in fiendish travail trying to decide what to do. The party wants and needs me desperately this time. But where does it all lead? Four more years of this and, if I'm still alive, where am I? 4 yrs older, feebler, completely out of touch with the international field, no job, no security (damnable word), and no use, except in politics for "higher office," which I don't want. In short, it would seem to me that now is the time to get out and during the remaining year of my term when my availability would be known look about for something else to do.

However I'm sure to succumb to the immediate I suppose. Meanwhile I'm using my bargaining power for all it's worth to get as good candidates as I can — particularly in Chicago. As to the national, Tafts professional political backing seems to be growing apace, and Ike is in the unhappy position of coming back, changing clothes, and at once losing much of his reverential following or staying in Europe awaiting the draft that may never come, especially as the word gets around that Truman won't run. If I were Ike and wanted the nomination I would stay in Europe, keep up the impression that Taft can't win & hope the hungry leaders would ditch Taft at the convention to be sure of a winner.

That lousy Tribune has now and for the third time taken to attacking Grandfather [Stevenson].[195] The absurd charges in this story which were

[194] This handwritten letter is in the possession of Adali E. Stevenson III.

[195] In a news story on December 17, 1951, the Chicago *Tribune* declared: "Gov. Stevenson, a self-confessed believer in Alger Hiss, convicted traitor, is the grandson

trumped up in the 1908 campaign were all disproved then which the Tribune overlooks now. They have also carefully overlooked any mention of Jesse Fell who probably had more to do with Lincoln's nomination for the President than anyone else. Nor have they published letters of protest in the Voice of the People, copies of which have come to me. However I've become so serene and indifferent I don't react any more — probably because I don't care a damn about this job, but more perhaps because I'm now convinced from many incidents that the Tribune really has little vitality politically any more. Its extreme, unbalanced, dishonest partisanship has paid off like a boomerang at last. All the same one worries about the effect on newspapers, freedom of the press, etc, of everlasting distortion. . . .

A

On Saturday, December 22, 1951, an explosion occurred at Orient No. 2 coal mine at West Frankfort, Illinois, in which 119 men were killed.

During the 1951 legislative session, Stevenson had presented a modern mine safety code, representing months of work by experts, but neither the unions, nor the operators, nor the senators from the Illinois mining districts would support it.

Orient No. 2 was considered to be a "model" mine; no complaints had been made to the Governor's office, to the Department of Mines and Minerals, or to the inspectors. The mine was checked officially by an inspector ten days before the blast and was also approved as safe by a group of miners acting as examiners only a few hours before the explosion. There was no evidence that any inspector had neglected his duty.

After the explosion Stevenson flew to the disaster area to confer with officials directing the rescue operations. On December 22, while in West Frankfort, he made an extemporaneous statement to the press that he later set down in writing.[196]

This is a sad Christmas. I came down to West Frankfort to see if the state is doing all it can to help. All of the state's trained rescue teams are on the job and the rescue work is proceeding as rapidly as possible, I am told. There is no shortage of men and materials. I wish there was something I could say or do to help the men and the families. But I guess all I can do is pray. I hope people will send me contributions for the

---

of a pro-slavery, pro-southern Democrat who was shown to have been an Illinois Copperhead and member of anti-northern secret organizations in 1863 and 1864." *Newsweek* in its January 7, 1952, issue summarized the "Battle of the Grandfathers."

[196] The text is based on a carbon copy.

dependents of the dead and the injured at this Christmas season. I have already solicited and received three.

Illinois was on the eve of a national all time safety record — only one fatality per one and a half million tons of coal mined this year.

The cause of the explosion must have been gas, but the place was inspected in usual routine only an hour and a half before the accident took place. The state inspected this mine only 10 days ago and reported the ventilation "good" at that time.

I hope the disaster was not due to anything a modern mine safety code would have prevented. I presented one — the work of months — at the last session of the legislature, but neither the unions, the operators nor the Senators from Southern Illinois would support it.

It is a very sad Christmas here in Southern Illinois. I hope the fortunate everywhere will temper their rejoicing at this glad season with a prayerful thought for the soldiers in Korea — yes, and for the miners who work in constant peril too.

After the explosion at Orient No. 2, state and federal investigations got under way to determine the cause of the disaster. Stevenson made this statement on December 24, 1951.[197]

As soon as all the men are removed and the ventilation is restored the State of Illinois will institute a searching investigation of this horrible disaster. The state investigation will be headed by Walter Eadie, Director of the Department of Mines and Minerals, and he will be assisted by selected examiners from the staff of the Department. I have asked Dr. Harold Walker, head of the Department of Mines at the University of Illinois, to assist with the investigation on my personal behalf but not as a member of the state investigation team.

The State and Federal investigations will proceed concurrently. I suppose the Federal and State findings of fact will be compared as the examination of the mine proceeds and that the State and Federal investigators will compare their evaluations and conclusions. No pains will be spared by the State, nor the feelings or interest of anyone, to determine the probable causes. Such a ghastly tragedy must be used to the fullest to enlarge our knowledge of mining hazards and their remedy. These men must not have died in vain.

Our purpose in this investigation will not be to find a scapegoat. We will not approach it with any spirit of vengeance or punishment. But it

[197] The text is based on a carbon copy.

must be as thorough as our scientific knowledge and the human resources of the State and Federal governments permit, and negligence, if any, will be held to sharp account. Illinois had the best safety record in the nation in 1950. We were on the eve of establishing the nation's all-time record in 1951 — one fatality per one and a half million tons of coal mined in this calendar year.

Our hearts go out to the families of the dead and injured at this Christmas season. I hope people everywhere will send to me at Springfield donations for distribution among the many widows and dependents of the men who died in this frightful holocaust on the eve of Christmas. I earnestly plead for a generous response to this appeal.

Until we know more about the causes, or probable causes, it would be impossible to speculate on responsibility or remedy. At this time the important useful thing to do is to exhaust every possible means to find out what happened and why. God has seen fit to leave us no witnesses apparently. After the investigation will be the proper time to assess the blame and take the steps by law or regulations that may be necessary to eliminate or at least reduce the danger of recurrence. I say "reduce" because from what I have learned there does not appear to be any absolute safety in coal mining.

To Letitia Stevenson [198]

December 24, 1951 [199]

Dear Aunt Letitia:

Many thanks for the clipping from the old paper. I shall read it with interest and hope for some enlightenment. I enclose a clipping from the Chicago Tribune last week about the charges that were made against Grandfather in the campaign of 1908. If you and Aunt Julia have any recollections about the incident and what was done to disprove the charge that he was a member of the Knights of the Golden Circle, it would be very helpful. I remember Father talking about these scurrilous attacks and I think there were a multitude of affidavits from responsible people procured at the time disproving them, but I find it impossible to run anything down in what files I have.

As this is my only copy of the Tribune clipping I wish you would return it.

In spite of the ghastly weather, the West Frankfort tragedy, and other headaches, we had a fine Christmas, with a lot of children to enliven

[198] A carbon copy is in A.E.S., P.U.L.
[199] This letter seems to be misdated. Stevenson in the last paragraph refers to Christmas in the past tense. It was probably written December 26 or 27.

things. My boys will be down at the end of the week to stay with me over New Years.

With very best love to all.

P.S. I have just run across your letter enclosing a contribution to the miners' relief fund. Many, many and heartfelt thanks.

AES

To Mrs. Ronald Tree

December 24, 1951

Dear Marietta:

Many thanks for your sweet letter. I felt our brief visit was all too brief.

I should love to stay with you when I am in New York on January 21, but I think I have already made a tentative commitment with Betty Hines, my former sister-in-law. But if things do not work out I shall take advantage of your everlasting charity.

With affectionate regards to you both, and with every good wish, I am

Sincerely yours,

Stevenson was invited to speak at ceremonies honoring Lincoln's birthday in Springfield in 1952.

To Benjamin P. Thomas [200]

December 24, 1951

Dear Ben:

I have your letter and I am stricken with apprehension about February 12. I see little hope of finding time to do much by way of preparation, and I am hoping, praying and pleading, that somehow you can get to me some suggestions as to what I should do or be prepared to do on that austere and scholarly occasion.

I am writing Allan Nevins and T. V. Smith [201] inviting them to stay here if they care to do so. Perhaps we could arrange a festivity in more tranquil circumstances for the evening before or after, depending on everyone's circumstances.

Yours,

ADLAI

[200] The original of this letter is in the possession of Mrs. Benjamin Thomas.
[201] Maxwell Professor of Citizenship and Philosophy, Syracuse University.

To Allan Nevins

December 24, 1951

Dear Allan:

I understand that you are coming out for Lincoln's Birthday. By all means plan to stay with me if it is convenient. I shall also ask T. V. Smith. You know the situation here and you can stay as long as you like — the longer the better!

With all good wishes, I am

Sincerely yours,

Adele Smith, daughter and youngest child of the Hermon D. Smiths, was responsible for the Smith family's Christmas card in 1951.

To Adele Smith [202]

December 26, 1951

My dear Adele:

I think quite the nicest Christmas card I had this year was the splendid photo, splendidly inscribed from the "Hermon Smiths." If, as seems likely, you had anything to do with this I want to be among the first to thank and congratulate you. I have known about your talents in the dining room, on the dock, on a horse, and skipping rope, but this adds one more! Woe to the girl who has too many talents; but I hope one such girl at least will not forget an old and very admiring friend.

Love,

Mrs. Charles S. Bromwell, Stevenson's second cousin, wrote him on December 18, 1951, that she had heard he had announced that he did not intend to run for governor again. She recalled his big victory in 1948, and was extremely eager to hear more about his decision. She expected her daughter, Lady Mildred Bailey, from England to join her in Palm Beach, Florida.

To Mrs. Charles S. Bromwell

December 26, 1951

My dear Cousin Lettie:

I was so glad to have your good letter. You sound very much alive

[202] The original is in the possession of Hermon D. Smith.

and I only wish there was some prospect of a visit with you this winter. I am afraid I shall have to be here most of the time whether I run again or not. Actually, I suspect I will, but for many reasons I should like to get out of "combat" politics while there is yet time to do something else.

I do hope that when Millie comes this winter we will have a glimpse of her here in Illinois.

Meanwhile, my best love to you.

Yours,

To Mrs. Franklin D. Roosevelt [203]

December 26, 1951

My dear Mrs. Roosevelt:

I seem to be incessantly plaguing you with invitations to speak in Illinois. Please forgive me if I must add one more.

On May 1, 2 and 3 we are planning to hold an important Conference on Youth and Community Service in Illinois. This is a field in which we have been attempting to do something really effective, and, of course, it would be a godsend to all of the people who have taken an interest in the work if you could be here on any of those dates to speak, quite informally and in what vein or direction you choose.

I suspect your calendar is hopelessly congested, and if it is anything like mine I could imagine how aggravating it is to be asked to make a decision for such a remote date. If you feel you cannot accept safely now, why not carry it on your file of "possibles" and let us hear later? [204]

With affectionate best wishes, I am

Cordially yours,

General George C. Marshall sent Governor Stevenson his Christmas greetings in a handwritten note. He wrote that he had gone to Pinehurst, North Carolina, early in November to spend the winter, where he had had some fine shooting.

[203] The original is in the Franklin D. Roosevelt Library.
[204] Mrs. Roosevelt again felt obliged to decline.

To General George C. Marshall [205]

December 26, 1951

My dear General:

I was deeply touched and flattered and pleased by your note. I hope and pray that you are having, at last, the relaxation and "fun" which has been so long denied you. The shooting expeditions make me acutely jealous!

My sister and her husband, Mr. and Mrs. Ernest Ives, join me in heartfelt good wishes to you and Mrs. Marshall.

Cordially yours,

By the end of December, 1951, Stevenson still had made no announcement of his political plans. Lieutenant G. Merle Bergman, stationed in Japan, wrote that he had read in the Chicago Daily News *that Stevenson possibly would not run again for governor, and he agreed with such a decision for two reasons: (1) good government could not depend upon a single man for its accomplishment, and (2) an elected official reached a point of diminishing returns in political office after the first term.*

To Lieutenant G. Merle Bergman

December 27, 1951

My dear Merle:

I was glad to have your letter. Evidently you are one of the very few who sense some of my reasoning about not running again. However, I suppose I will capitulate — and probably live to regret it.

Our Christmas here was white — indeed, so white that the city is virtually paralyzed, and many of the highways are impassable. Moreover, Illinois has just suffered a ghastly mine disaster at West Frankfort — 119 dead. If there is any consolation, I can find it in the fact that we took the Department of Mines and Minerals out of politics in 1949, and last session attempted very vigorously to adopt an entirely new mining code. The unions and the operators and Senators from the mining districts, however, turned it down.

However, all goes well with you I hope; and I am deeply grateful for your thought of me at the time of this difficult decision.

With affectionate regards, I am

Sincerely yours,

[205] The original is in the possession of the George C. Marshall Research Foundation, Lexington, Virginia.

At the time of the West Frankfort mine disaster, state Senator John Parish was in Washington, D.C. "Knowing how terrible the Governor would feel," he wrote later, "and fearing that he would be blamed for not getting legislation which would have prevented this disaster I called him to offer my help in explaining what he had tried to do. Fortunately the press didn't blame him, and I thought it best not to issue a statement for it would only have hurt several Senators and they were victims of their own constituents." [206]

To John Parish [207]

December 28, 1951

Dear John:

God love you for that Christmas present written on December 25. I have been miserable since the disaster and never felt more futile. Your check for the relief fund is also most gratifying.

What you say about the incidents of last spring confirms my recollection, but you say it with far too much charity for me I'm afraid. Actually, I should think that you might issue a statement, for what it is worth, confirming my efforts to gather sponsorship and support for my bill after the Mining Investigation Commission had turned it down but that the senators from the mining districts would not support it and unanimously urged me not to introduce it, with no prospect of success.

However, you will be the best judge of what to say and how to say it, and when and where. I have already told the [St. Louis] Post-Dispatch and the Chicago Daily News that you volunteered to introduce the bill but that it seemed utterly futile to you and to me, and to everyone else, in view of the unanimous opposition.

I had wanted to see you long before this. Could I make one final plea to you to run again? I am not sure yet what I shall do myself. It depends a good deal on the Cook County ticket, of course. If I announce that I am a candidate for re-election, as I may, I would feel a lot more comfortable about things if I thought you were coming back. Please give it some thought — consider your nation, your state — yes, me!!

Happy New Year, and many many thanks.

Yours,
ADLAI

---

[206] Letter to Carol Evans, December, 1967.
[207] The original is in the possession of Mr. Parish.

Part Four

1952

*T*he year 1952 found Stevenson embarrassed by and struggling to right the scandals that beset his administration in 1951. He was to be visited with yet another — the so-called horsemeat scandal.

To avoid any possibility of corruption in an area where it was traditional, Stevenson was extremely careful in his selection of the superintendent of Foods and Dairies, choosing Charles W. Wray, a man with an impeccable reputation for honesty and ability. During the summer of 1951, it was rumored that horsemeat was being mixed with hamburger in Illinois, with the knowledge of state meat inspectors. Stevenson called on the superintendent of Foods and Dairies to make an investigation, and Wray reported that he found nothing wrong. In December, federal investigators for the Office of Price Stabilization reported to Stevenson that something was wrong, and they were sure that some investigators were bribed to overlook the adulteration. In January, 1952, after an investigation conducted by the Governor's office, the superintendent confessed that he himself had taken a bribe from Joe Siciliano, a Cook County gangster. He was fired and indicted on charges of bribery and conspiracy. Siciliano was indicted, tried, and convicted.

Kenneth S. Davis wrote: "No event in Stevenson's administration struck harder at his confidence in human nature than this one. His immediate response was stern. He pressed for a thorough investigation of the inspectors . . . with the result that a dozen of them were fired or suspended. He enlisted a senior FBI agent to be his special personal investigator. He called his department directors to his State House office and there lectured them on their responsibility for the wrongdoing of their subordinates in so far as they failed adequately to supervise those subordinates. He said flatly that the 'calm confidence' he had theretofore had in the men under him was being replaced by 'an eager persistent surveil-

*lance.' Thereafter . . . his faith in the essential decency of human beings
was qualified by a greater awareness of human weakness."* [1]

*Early in January, 1952, Stevenson announced publicly that he would
seek reelection as Governor of Illinois. After his overwhelming victory in
1948, his name was mentioned for high national office, including that of
President, and by the time of the Democratic National Convention in
1952 he had received widespread publicity. If his thoughts turned toward
the presidency they did not contemplate the year 1952.*

*In mid-January, 1952, Stevenson was scheduled to attend meetings in
Washington, D.C., in connection with the federal investigation following
the West Frankfort mine disaster. Shortly before he was due to leave the
city he received a telephone call from President Truman asking him to
call at Blair House. He spent about two hours with the President on the
evening of January 22. President Truman recalled:*

> I told him that I would not run for President again and that it was
> my opinion he was best-fitted for the place. He comes of a political
> family . . . had made an excellent Governor of Illinois. When I
> talked with him, I told him what I thought the Presidency is, how
> it has grown into the most powerful and the greatest office in the his-
> tory of the world. I asked him to take it and told him that if he
> would agree he could be nominated. I told him that a President in
> the White House always controlled the National Convention. . . .
> But he said: No! He apparently was flabbergasted. [2]

*Toward the end of 1951, Time magazine sent one of its top reporters
to Springfield and Chicago for the purpose of interviewing Stevenson,
his principal aides, cabinet members, and various friends of the Governor,
for the publication of a "cover" story. Stevenson was scheduled to address
the National Urban League in New York City on January 21, and Time's
editors decided to "peg" their story on the speech. However, after Stevenson's long secret conference with the President, Time decided to write
the story around that event. A few days later, the January 28, 1952, issue
of Time appeared on the newsstands, and Stevenson's life was changed
forever. The concluding paragraphs of the article asked these questions:*

> Last week President Truman summoned Governor Stevenson to
> Washington. Why? Did he want Stevenson to run as Vice President?

---

[1] See Kenneth S. Davis, *A Prophet in His Own Country: The Triumphs and Defeats
of Adlai E. Stevenson* (Garden City, N.Y.: Doubleday, 1957), pp. 364–365; John
Bartlow Martin, *Adlai Stevenson* (New York: Harper, 1952), pp. 134–137.

[2] *Memoirs by Harry S. Truman, Vol. II: Years of Trial and Hope* (Garden City,
N.Y.: Doubleday, 1956), pp. 491–492. For a later version of the meeting and Tru-
man's attitude toward Stevenson, see Margaret Truman, *Harry S. Truman* (New
York: William Morrow, 1973), pp. 527, 530–533.

That was one rumor. Or had Truman decided not to run at all, and to ask Stevenson to head the Democratic ticket? That was another rumor. Or was the oldest, biggest pol of them all turning to Sir Galahad for advice on how to win? That seemed hardly likely.

Whatever the truth behind the rumors, this much was evident: in a cold season for the Democrats, Adlai Stevenson is politically hot, and Harry Truman feels the need of a little warmth.

After his conference with the President and after the Time *article, Stevenson was besieged constantly by newspaper and magazine reporters, publishers, radio and television newscasters, government officials and just ordinary citizens and friends who wanted to know his plans and to urge him to seek office at the national level — or to run again for governor.*

On March 20, 1952, Stevenson attended the annual Illinois Jackson Day Dinner in Springfield and introduced the main speaker, Senator Hubert Humphrey. He included this statement in his remarks: "I intend to be brief. I am also going to be frank. This is the season of our political cycle when men dream dreams and see visions — mostly of the White House. Well, I'm not one of them. I want to run for Governor of Illinois — and that's all. And I want to be re-elected Governor — and that's all. And I want to finish some work we have under way here in Illinois — and that's all."

Still rumors abounded and the pressures grew. When he was not answering the vastly increased correspondence, the long-distance telephone calls, and the requests for interviews, Stevenson tried to conduct the business of the State of Illinois as usual.[3]

The Illinois primary fell on April 8, 1952. Stevenson, not wishing to appear presumptuous that the Democratic nomination was his for the asking, waited until after the primary to make a further statement. On April 16, he reiterated his intention to run for governor, adding: "I could not accept the nomination for any other office this summer."

The next day Stevenson attended a political dinner in New York honoring his friend Averell Harriman. His short speech there brought forth a spontaneous and exuberant response from the New York Democrats — and the race was on again.

Stevenson spoke outside Illinois several times during the first six

[3] Following are examples of the national interest in Stevenson: *Life,* March 24, carried his picture on its cover along with Senator Estes Kefauver, Senator Richard Russell, and Senator Robert Kerr. The April issue of *Harper's* magazine ran a story entitled "Stevenson and the Independent Voter," by Bernard De Voto; *Newsweek,* April 14, carried his picture on the cover and published a three-page story on his career; *Collier's,* April 19, published a story entitled "Democrats' Dark Horse"; and the *Saturday Evening Post,* June 28, published "He'd Rather Not Be President," by Joseph Alsop.

months of 1952. In April and May he spoke in Texas and Oregon, and in California, where he reviewed the 44th Division, Illinois National Guard, which was there awaiting shipment to Korea. All the engagements were made before his meeting with President Truman on January 22, and after he announced his intention to run again for governor. In June he gave the commencement address at Hampden-Sydney College, in Virginia, of which his great-grandfather the Reverend Lewis Warner Green had been president. He also wrote three articles for publication. "Who Runs the Gambling Machines?" appeared in the February issue of the Atlantic, *and "Korea in Perspective" appeared in the April issue of* Foreign Affairs. *On June 3,* Look *published his article "The States: Bulwark Against 'Big Government.'" Meanwhile, the April 25 issue of* U.S. News & World Report *carried a question-and-answer interview with Stevenson covering a variety of subjects.*

On January 5, 1952, Governor Stevenson announced that he would seek another four-year term of office.[4]

After long and prayful consideration I have decided to be a candidate for re-election as Governor in 1952.

That office, like many others, has its heavy burdens. But the burdens are also opportunities to give Illinois the kind of government it ought to have.

I have tried to do that. And I take great satisfaction in the progress we have made since 1949. But I have learned that the road is long and we have far to go before any of us, myself included, can in good conscience stop and rest.

I invite the Republican party to nominate the best man it can find. It is of little importance whether the next Governor of Illinois is named Adlai Stevenson; but it is of the highest importance that he finish what we have started. No matter then who loses, the people will win.

That is the kind of an election Illinois needs and deserves. I am gladly and proudly ready to take part in it.

After his announcement that he would seek reelection, Mrs. Anne Risse, who supervised his staff at the capitol, sent Stevenson a campaign contribution.

[4] The text is based on a carbon copy.

To Anne Risse [5]

[no date]

Mrs. Risse —
Bless your heart — and my thanks!

AES

Edward D. McDougal wrote Stevenson, congratulating him on his decision to run again.

To Edward D. McDougal, Jr. [6]

January 9, 1952

Dear Ed:
Thanks for your note. I certainly *am* a glutton for punishment, and I wonder if I have done the right thing. I can only hope for the best and try to deserve the encouragement of my dearest friends.

Yours,
ADLAI

In 1947, Sir Saiyid Fazl Ali, judge of the Supreme Court of India, served as a delegate to the United Nations, where he met Stevenson, one of the U.S. delegates. On January 4, 1952, he wrote Stevenson that he had retired from the court. He mentioned that he had met United States Ambassador Chester Bowles.

To Sir Saiyid Fazl Ali

January 9, 1952

My dear Fazl Ali:
I was delighted to hear from you again. It brought back memories of many interesting and crowded days together. I too feel exceedingly remote from the United Nations after some four years of "isolation" in Illinois.

I am so glad to hear you have met Chester Bowles and I am sure you could be of service to him in his enormously responsible job. I think nothing concerns us more in this country nowadays than proper mutuality

[5] This handwritten note is in the possession of Mrs. Risse.
[6] The original is in the possession of Mr. McDougal.

of understanding with India. We Americans know so little of the Orient and are so prone to think of others, their ideas and traditions and aspirations in terms of ourselves. Surely we must strive to find some way to interpret America's very genuine basic concern with the hopes and aspirations of the Eastern peoples in a manner that they can understand and believe.

I am sorry to hear you have retired from the Supreme Court but I am confident you will never be inactive.

With best wishes and my warm thanks for your thought of me, I am

Sincerely yours,

On January 10, 1952, Stevenson made his radio report to the people for the year 1951.[7]

. . . It has been a crowded, eventful year, for you and for me. If I could be granted a single wish for the new year it would be for more time. The days are so short and there is so much to do. But I suspect many of you suffer from that same feeling.

But happily, it has been a good year — filled with many blessings — for most of us, including myself. . . .

But our blessings and triumphs have not been unmixed. There has been anxiety and tragedy . . . anxiety over rising living costs and the menacing peril of inflation; anxiety for our fighting men in Korea, and tragedy in the homes of those who have given their lives and blood in the nation's service in this great crusade for peace and security in the world.

And in the last days of the year tragedy in another form struck at our very heart — tragedy that came with cruel suddenness at the height of the joyous Christmas season. 119 men died in the ghastly explosion in the New Orient Mine No. 2 near West Frankfort.

Seldom have the sympathies of the American people poured out more generously, more universally and spontaneously, than they did to the families, the widows and the children, of the victims. Hundreds of people, rich and poor, and many organizations, have contributed thousands of dollars to help ease the financial plight of the families that lost their chief support in this hideous holocaust. It was another heartwarming demonstration of the inherent compassion and generosity of Americans. And I want to thank you again, everyone who responded to my appeal

[7] These excerpts are from a mimeograph copy prepared by the Governor's office for release to the press.

for relief funds. I have received many thousands of dollars. More would be welcome, until January 15, when the funds should be distributed through a local committee set up to supervise the equitable disbursement of contributions from all private sources.

But that the Workmen's Compensation Law, the Union Welfare Fund, and the open hearted sympathy and gifts of many, have much better provided for the sufferers than in similar accidents in the past, is, at best, small comfort to them.

If any lasting good is to come from this frightful misfortune it can only be positive, forthright measures to further reduce the hazards of coal mining. I say reduce, because from what I personally saw and heard at West Frankfort and from what I've learned during the past few years, it seems apparent that there is no such thing as absolute safety in coal mining. Besides, the element of human failure, human mistakes and carelessness, is an ever present hazard in this perilous occupation.

I do not presume to know whether this accident was preventable or whether some human failure was to blame. Only the federal and state investigators can speculate responsibly on that. Perhaps we will never know for certain. But we do know that stronger safeguards against its repetition can and must be established.

As to responsibility, there should be no buck passing by the state, the company, or the union. If the state's inspection system is inadequate I want to know it, and how it can be strengthened. Already Walter Eadie, the Director of the State Department of Mines and Minerals, has issued an order to the state inspectors requiring more frequent testing of the combustion content of coal dust in the mines. Electricity or matches can ignite dangerous gases in mines. The law forbids carrying matches or cigarette lighters into the mines, but that law is hard to enforce and is frequently broken.

Presently we have both federal and state inspection of coal mines. But the federal and state laws are not the same, and the federal inspectors cannot enforce the stricter federal rules in the states. The state, of course, has enforcement powers, but only as to its own laws. The companies also have their own mine examiners, who are union members, and who go into the mine just before each shift starts work to check for gas or other hazards. Only a short while before this explosion occurred these examiners made such an inspection and reported no abnormal conditions. The last state inspection, completed less than two weeks before the accident, referred to ventilation in the mine as "good" at that time and the rock dusting to prevent coal dust explosions as "fair."

I mention these things only to show that in spite of existing safeguards, the explosion did occur and with terrible consequences, which seems to me to only emphasize that either present safety measures are not enough or their enforcement by the industry and the state is not good enough, or both.

As a result of this disaster there will be renewed demand in this session of Congress to make the federal mine safety code compulsory. People ask me what I think of that, and I'll tell you precisely what I think. I think that unless the coal states enact modern and adequate mining laws and enforce them effectively with the full cooperation of the industry and the unions, then Uncle Sam should and will take over. But personally I deplore the tendency of the states to abdicate their responsibilities. I deplore the concentration of power and authority in Washington, not because Washington wants it but because the states have defaulted. And this is only another example in that trend.

Moreover, I don't concede that because the states have not done the job properly, they can't do it. I think we can do it right here in Illinois, and I don't think we should contribute by our failure to do it to the further centralization and growth of our Federal government that is already so big it is almost unmanageable.

In Illinois we have already made a lot of progress since the Centralia disaster in 1947. The Department has been reorganized by law to remove the former ambiguities and to clearly fix the lines of authority and responsibility. The mine inspection service has been wholly divorced from politics and placed under a merit system. Witness the fact that although I am a Democrat there are far more Republican than Democratic inspectors on the state inspection staff. The frequency of inspections has been increased, the rules tightened and other safety precautions have been written into the law.

What's more, after the 1949 session of the legislature we commenced work on a comprehensive codification and revision of our patchwork old laws to make them comprehensible and to stiffen and clarify the safety requirements. It was the painstaking work of many months, and exactly a year ago today, at the beginning of the last session, I submitted this new mining code to the Mining Investigation Commission, a permanent agency created by the legislature back in 1909 to recommend mining legislation. They called in many representatives of the industry, both operators and unions, and finally rejected it unanimously on April 3. I then submitted it to the senators of both parties from the large shaft mining areas, but in view of the opposition they would not support it either. So I then expressed my disappointment to the Commission and requested them to prepare a new and comprehensive code of their own. They agreed to do so.

I don't believe the elaborate bill I proposed a year ago would have prevented this disaster, but it would have given Illinois a strong, up-to-date and understandable state law. However, that's past and the important thing now is to take advantage of this new experience to get something done. I hope the Commission can agree upon a strong, streamlined, modern mining code for Illinois. As I told them last spring "there is no reason Illinois should not have the best and most up-to-date mining laws." Certainly the sooner it is done the better, and I would not hesitate to call a special session of the legislature to consider it.

For myself I would like to see Illinois do something besides complain about the concentration of power in Washington. If we don't we better stop complaining and admit that "we asked for it."

Ironically, the accident at West Frankfort shattered a record for mine safety which, up to that time, was the best ever made by any state. There had been in Illinois mines only one fatality for every million and one-half tons of coal mined in 1951. In 1950 Illinois had the best safety record in the nation. In 1951 we were doing even better.

In another field of state activity, a record of another sort was established in 1951. The vast new program of highway reconstruction and repair which the legislature authorized last June was set in motion, and detailed plans completed for the first major attack on our huge highway problem since the hard roads were originally constructed.

But here again, careful planning suffered a setback in the form of lawsuits by truck operators against the new truck license fees. I am hopeful that there will be an early decision by the Supreme Court, in order that we may know where we stand. If the decision comes early enough and the law is upheld, the progress of the highway program in 1952 will not be seriously affected. If the decision is adverse we will lose some $20 million this year alone, and the program to restore our worn out roads will be badly crippled. . . .

There are many other developments that I should like to mention. But a word about the State's general financial position. It is good. Revenues are running at about the levels we estimated at the time the budget for this biennium was drafted over a year ago. It is a very tight budget and contemplates a continuation of a high level of business activity and employment. It is confined to basic essentials; makes no provision for large expenditures for construction, other than highways, and neither does it include many other increased expenditures which I felt could be deferred when people are being called upon to bear the heavy new burdens of federal taxation for national security.

Illinois is pioneering in the field of governmental financial reporting by issuing for the first time in any state a simple, quarterly report on state finances. We are applying the practice of large business firms to the state government. There should be no mystery or misinformation about the state's financial affairs. Yet there is much misunderstanding, usually created deliberately for political purposes. The Taxpayers' Federation of Illinois is cooperating with the Department of Finance in the distribution of this quarterly report. The more people know the essential facts about their state's needs and resources, the better our state government is going to be. . . .

These are only examples of more recent administrative steps to improve the quality and integrity of our public administration within the whole structure of our state government. This is not a simple task; it can't be accomplished overnight. In an enterprise of this magnitude and complexity you achieve better results step by step, sometimes by trial and error. I get frustrated and impatient sometimes, and so would you. . . .

The new year is always a time for looking ahead with confidence and fresh resolution. And so it is with 1952. It will be a political year, with all of the distractions that go with the free choice of a President, a Governor and other officials. I hope that partisanship and the intemperance which is so characteristic of campaigns will not obscure truth and the broader interests of the nation and of Illinois. Who holds any office of responsibility and trust seems to me less important than what he stands for — his competence, courage and honesty. No matter who loses, the people must win.

If you are troubled and have misgiving about what lies ahead in the new year perhaps you will find, as I have, some comfort and strength in these imperishable words: "I stood by the gate of the year and asked of one standing there: 'Give me a light that I may see the way.' He answered: 'Go forth. Put your hand in the hand of God. Then you will need no light or a known path.' "

Shortly after the public announcement of his intention to run for reelection as governor, Stevenson formed an independent campaign committee.

To Stephen A. Mitchell [8]

January 11, 1952

I SHOULD ESTABLISH PROMPTLY A PLANNING GROUP TO ORGANIZE AN INDEPENDENT CAMPAIGN COMMITTEE. PLEASE ATTEND IF POSSIBLE A LITTLE MEETING IN MY CHICAGO OFFICE MONDAY MORNING AT TEN OCLOCK. REGARDS.

[8] The original of this telegram is in the possession of Mr. Mitchell.

Beginning late in 1951 and continuing through the early months of 1952, many newspapers gave General Dwight D. Eisenhower enthusiastic and unreserved support for the nomination for President on the Republican ticket, without fully knowing his views on important domestic and international issues.

To Irving Dilliard

January 12, 1952

Dear Irving:

Thanks for your kind editorial about the two Governors. I have also been much interested in your admirable editorial about Eisenhower. Although I am tempted to think he offers by far the most on the Republican side, I have been a little surprised by the impetuous endorsement of so many newspapers.

I wish we could have a good sober talk about the mine business one of these days. I am afraid there is considerable misunderstanding as to how we make progress legislatively in Illinois. My experience here has certainly been a revelation, and particularly latterly.

Yours,

On January 12, 1952, Governor Stevenson sent the following letter to the chairman of the Illinois Mining Investigation Commission about the West Frankfort Mine disaster. At the same time his office released the letter to the press.[9]

To Sam Cape

January 12, 1952

My dear Mr. Chairman:

The United States Bureau of Mines and the Illinois Department of Mines and Minerals have now submitted reports on their respective investigations of the New Orient Mine No. 2 disaster at West Frankfort, Illinois, on December 21 last. Those reports include, among other things, recommendations for future action.

Of course I am not in a position to appraise technically the significance of those reports, and I am sure that many other citizens are in the same position. In any event, the reports raise questions of substance with respect to the laws and practices which have governed the mining of coal

[9] The text is based on a copy of the press release.

in Illinois in the past, and suggest possible improvements in both. I think it important that these reports, together with all other relevant facts and circumstances related to this explosion in particular and to the safety of coal mining in general in Illinois, be the subject of open and adequate examination by a qualified official agency possessed of the powers requisite to the conduct of a thorough inquiry. As Governor I do not possess the power to compel the attendance of witnesses by subpoena nor the giving of testimony under oath. No special commission created by me could exercise such powers without legislative authority and the General Assembly is not in session. Under existing laws, not even the Illinois Department of Mines and Minerals is vested with these powers for the purpose of conducting the kind of inquiry needed.

The statute creating the Mining Investigation Commission provides that it

> . . . shall have power and authority to investigate the methods and conditions of mining in the State of Illinois with special reference to the safety of human lives and property . . .

That statute also provides that, in any such investigation, your Commission shall have the power to compel the attendance of witnesses by subpoena; and this power, coupled with certain other references, appears to justify the inference that the testimony of such witnesses may be taken under oath.

In short, the legislature has given your Commission the powers necessary to conduct an inquiry into this case, and also an appropriation. Indeed, under the Illinois laws relating to coal mining your commission appears to be the only agency equipped and intended by the legislature to act in this instance.

I suggest, accordingly, the prompt initiation by your Commission of a full and complete inquiry, including the taking of testimony in public hearings, into the causes of the New Orient No. 2 explosion, the responsibility therefore, and the steps which should be taken to prevent or reduce the hazard of a recurrence of such tragedies.

In this last connection, of course, the question of the modernization of the laws relating to coal mining is of key importance. I do not need to remind you of the history of the effort which was made to accomplish this objective during the regular session of the General Assembly from last January to July. That history is set forth in my letter to you of May 16, 1951. On June 19, 1951, you replied to my May 16 letter and stated that it would be the purpose of the Commission to undertake immediately a comprehensive revision of the mining code which would command the agreement of unions and operators alike and would achieve the objectives in which we are all interested. You asserted that the Commission had been assured of the "immediate and complete cooperation" in this task of the unions and of the operators; and that you "should have an agreed program available for introduction in the next session of the Legislature." The making of such recommendations for legislative improvements is, as you recognize, a principal function of your Commission under the statute.

I feel sure the Commission agrees with me that the explosion at New Orient Mine No. 2 has accelerated the urgency of improving our mining laws. Even if the Federal and State investigations and hearings held by your Commission do not reveal legislative changes which could have prevented this explosion, there is, I believe, common agreement that our present mining laws need extensive revision and modernization. I do not feel that we can afford to contemplate the possibility, however remote, of other accidents which might be prevented by changes in the law and its administration.

The hearings into the New Orient Mine No. 2 explosion, which I suggest, could be held promptly and would, I believe, contribute to your ultimate end of presenting an agreed mining code which would place Illinois legislatively in the forefront of the coal mining states.

With the benefit of the information derived from this additional and tragic experience and the comprehensive draft law submitted for your convenience a year ago, I should think the Commission might well complete in the near future the task undertaken in your letter to me of June 19, 1951. Yours is the agency created by the General Assembly for the very purpose of aiding it to discharge its general responsibility of enacting adequate and forward-looking mining legislation which represents the views of the miners themselves and those who have the responsibility of ownership and management.

I have little doubt that when your Commission is prepared to present such a legislative program the General Assembly will enact it without delay. I hope that you will be able to present such an agreed program soon, and I would gladly convene a special session of the 67th General Assembly to consider it because the next regular session of the General Assembly does not convene until January 1953.

For your convenience, I am sending copies of this letter to the other members of the Commission.

Sincerely yours,

Archibald MacLeish urged the Governor to deliver the Phi Beta Kappa address at Harvard University.

To Archibald MacLeish [10]

January 14, 1952

Dear Archie:

Since I became a big-time politician my ego has been subjected to a variety of inflationary attacks. But yours is the worst. Me, address the Phi Beta Kappa! Something is wrong and I must tread carefully. Any real danger, however, is resolved by the fact that my son graduates on the 19th and I hope to go down to witness the event, which will make it impossible for me to come back again on the 23rd or 24th.[11]

Ho hum! What a relief! Anyway you were good to think of me and I shall be at pains to tell everyone that the Phi Beta Kappa Society at Harvard sought me as a speaker, without revealing the sinister influence of MacLeish.

Thanks. Many, many thanks.

Yours,
ADLAI

To Alicia Patterson [12]

January 15, 1952

. . . Christmas chaos, politics, decisions, explosions, crises, presents, children — and now a horse meat scandal! Ugh! (as the cartoonists used to say). And me asking for 4 more years of it. I must be nuts — which will be no surprise to you!

I'm coming to N.Y. to speak at the Urban League banquet on Jan 21, the following day I must spend in Wash & perhaps part of Wed. . . . Its been unshirted hell here for a month but things are unravelling slowly — the tickets in Cook County and the State have been chosen etc etc. and in the process I've become something of a boss they say, altho I didn't know it and don't feel any different. . . .

I have a piece in the Atlantic for Feb [13] — out the middle of Jan — which will doubtless give you an exhilarating few minutes & Time has been shaking all the family skeletons for a cover piece for end of Jan.

[10] The original is in the Archibald MacLeish collection in the Library of Congress.
[11] Adlai Stevenson III graduated from Harvard College on Thursday, June 19, 1952. The Phi Beta Kappa exercises, a traditional feature of Commencement Week, were held that year on Monday, June 16. The editors are unable to explain the discrepancy with the later dates mentioned in Stevenson's letter.
[12] This handwritten letter is in the possession of Adlai E. Stevenson III.
[13] "Who Runs the Gambling Machines?" *Atlantic,* February, 1952.

which gives me the willies. And here I am, just minding my own business. . . .

A

On January 21, 1952, Stevenson spoke at a meeting of the National Urban League, in New York City.[14]

I count it a privilege to have this opportunity to pay my respects to the National Urban League which for forty years, with moderation and reason, has reminded us that the American Negro needed not alms but opportunity. The progress toward his fuller participation in American life in that interval must be very gratifying to many of you who have been in the forefront of the struggle for so long. The pattern has changed spectacularly in those years, in the South as well as in the North. Indeed, I often think that the progress in the South over ancient, solid walls of tradition is too little noted and appreciated. From what I hear I think, indeed, that some of us in the North may be more intemperate than informed about the South and the evolution of its racial problems.

Yet the problem still remains, both North and South. Indeed our illiteracy in human relations is, I think you will agree, perhaps our foremost domestic problem. And now, suddenly, it has been further magnified. Perilously challenged on both flanks, with the totalitarian roadways to the right and to the left of us more heavily traveled, the hostile world has rudely exhibited for all to see this fire hazard in the basement behind America's golden doors.

So suddenly we are reminded, and it is well we are, that America's position of leadership in world opinion rests only in small part upon our industrial "know-how" or our material strength. Still less are we measured by our numbers. It is the historic record in securing and broadening the rights of our people that has earned us the respect and admiration of the peoples of the world. From the earliest settlement, America has been a symbol of hope wherever men have aspired to be free and stand erect.

But today the great American experiment encounters those who manipulate and toy with the symbols of democracy, who would undermine our prestige, who in the hot war of ideas offer up as a program the paradox of democracy through dictatorship, liberty through repression, justice through tyranny, and freedom through thralldom.

Paradox, yes. A conspiracy disguised as a state, yes. But there are listeners everywhere. And I believe that the effectiveness of the Soviet

[14] The text is based on a mimeograph copy prepared by the Governor's office for release to the press.

Union has been chiefly due to one thing: it has made the miserable everywhere conscious of their misery. It has given distorted impetus to the newborn urgings and aspirations of oppressed and subjugated peoples. And it has stuck a mischievous finger into almost every country, including this one.

Both East and West vie desperately with each other to win the allegiance, faith and confidence of the miserable millions of Asia, Africa and South America. Each displays in advance of its battle legions, the banner of freedom, of hope and of an ever-expanding democracy.

An inventory of our strengths and weaknesses is not my job here tonight. But we know that racial bigotry and violence are mute denials of the sincerity of the principles emblazoned on our banners, principles which have made of us in truth the last, best hope on earth. And a democracy qualified by color will win no hearts in Africa and Asia. The ramparts of democracy are not only in Korea, nor along the Western European defense line — they are right here in Cicero, Illinois, in Miami and Birmingham. Bigotry, intolerance, race violence and the social tensions they engender are not only serious handicaps upon our strength and unity as a nation, but they are a visible encumbrance on America's leadership in the world, where we must lead or lose. And to lead we will have to tell the world what we are for, not just what we are against.

But enough of that. We know it all too well and it is easy to dramatize and also to exaggerate our failures and our dangers. Nevertheless, we can ill afford to exhibit to the world either injustice or incompetence in securing the rights of every citizen or in dealing with the relations of all racial groups, because what we do speaks much louder than what we say.

But honesty is always the best policy, for nations as well as men. And only within a democracy is there the courage, the nobility of candid self-criticism, which could produce such a document as the report of the President's Committee on Civil Rights.[15] We have laid before all the world a forthright picture of the disparity between democracy as we would have it, and as it stands.

The American dream belongs to every American. The Negro-American wants it no less than any other. But the Negro-American, more than any other, has reason to regard it as more a promise than a reality. Nevertheless, the confidence of the Negro in our expanding democracy is as one with that of every other American, for he too has enjoyed the good fruit of our progress in strengthening and extending democracy in every corner of the land.

[15] Charles E. Wilson, Chairman, *President's Committee on Civil Rights* (New York: Simon & Schuster, 1947).

Self-criticism is democracy's secret weapon. It enables us to periodically re-examine our successes and our failures, our advances and our retreats, on the road toward the fuller expression, and the maximum employment of all our human resources.

Since the inception of our nation we have moved steadily toward the extermination of stubborn prejudices. Sharp changes in attitudes have marked the past — toward the Irish, the Poles, the Italians, the Germans, the Orientals, the English, and even the American Indians. What's more Baptists and Methodists are speaking to each other. I'm told, indeed, and it's very comforting, that even Unitarians are no longer suspected as infidels and heretics!

In spite of all these advances in tolerance during the past century, I think it fair to say that we have made even greater progress in securing the rights of our people during the past decade than has been made since the Civil War. Notwithstanding the stress of war and chronic world crisis, we are brushing aside the racial myths which have held us fast — myths which obstruct democracy, frustrate the yearnings and hopes of all men, and give credence to the siren propaganda of those who traffic in hunger, oppression, and disillusion.

Long ago science laid low the myth of the master race. Adolf Hitler resurrected it, and civilization trembled before that myth could be interred.

But, ghost-like, the malevolent myth of racial inferiority returns to plague us. Ancient, rigid beliefs persist among many of us who have had only limited opportunity for actual contact and communication with members of other racial groups. But we are learning rapidly it seems to me. The desperate war years produced a myriad of new associations, both under arms and in the defense industries. Experience has done more to expose the nonsense of racism than generations of formal education and earnest elocution.

Yet the myth of racial inferiority is only one of the popular delusions we still have to overcome. The truth, of course, is that men do not feel or believe as they do about other races merely because of ignorance or error. From whence these beliefs come, and why they hold so fast, is a riddle for the scholars. It is problem enough that for too many of us they have the force of etiquette and custom, even of law.

But at long last, these giant fables are becoming suspect. Not alone science and scholarship, but experience as well, are exposing them for what they are — not truths to be reckoned with — but dangerous misbeliefs.

At the turn of the century, our highest Court held in the case of Plessy vs. Ferguson [1896], that laws requiring segregated rail facilities were not in conflict with the equal protection clause of the Fourteenth Amendment when equality of accommodations was guaranteed.

And for half a century, the doctrine of "separate but equal" has been taken for granted as a self evident truth. It remained for the Supreme Court to expose the myth in its notable decisions on higher education and interstate transportation.[16] The doctrine on which rests the case for racial segregation is being severely scrutinized by courts and legislatures.

Other significant changes in the status of the Negro are being affected, not only in the North, but in the South as well. The idea, widely entertained in the North, that the South is unyielding in its opposition to changing the status of the Negro is itself a myth. The evidence is the contrary, in spite of the contradiction of barbaric incidents. Progress against prejudice and passion is never passive.

Southern states are unmasking the Klan and extending the suffrage. When the Urban League was founded, less than a quarter of a million Negroes voted in the primaries of southern states. Four times that number, about a million, voted in 1948, and there are signs that this figure will be more than doubled in the election this year.

The experience of the South has been instructive to us in the North. Too many of us believe that the general public will not be persuaded to grant equal status to the Negro until individual bigotry and prejudice have first been wholly exterminated by education. The myth of unyielding prejudice boasts a host of related fallacies: "That it is premature" — "That the time is not ripe" — "That it will take a hundred years, or even a thousand" — "That legislation is futile." But these myths are disintegrating under our day-by-day experience.

In industry, residential communities, public recreation, the schools, the defense establishments — the average American is accepting all of his fellow Americans. The real spectre is doubt and fear, bred of dogma and misinformation. So long as we serve the myth that progress must wait upon prejudice, so long will prejudice sit in judgment.

There is another aspect of our human relations which is [a] disturbing one also shrouded in myth, and in some respects the most dangerous myth of all. In our time, science, technology and crowded cities have necessitated intergroup contacts so numerous and involved that otherwise normal human relations are fraught with tension. Fearfully, some among us have ignobly surrendered to the threat of violence.

[16] The Supreme Court in *Sweatt* v. *Painter,* 339 U.S. 629 (1950), and *McLaurin* v. *Oklahoma,* 339 U.S. 637 (1950), and other cases, ordered Negroes to be admitted to hitherto white institutions of higher education. With this barrier breached, the National Association for the Advancement of Colored People brought cases attacking segregated public schools. The Supreme Court in *Brown* v. *Board of Education of Topeka* (1954), held that segregated schools were unconstitutional.

There are those who assert that progress comes only by violent means. There are others who insist that violence inevitably accompanies any adjustment in racial relations or the traditional status of racial groups. These strange bedfellows offer us only the counsel of despair.

But our civil authorities must not be misled; there must be no doubt about the protection of all citizens, irrespective of race, color, or creed, in the enjoyment of their rights. There must be no doubt that the laws which guarantee these rights will be enforced impartially.

Whatever our personal prejudices and shortcomings, problems in human relations must not be solved by violence. If they are, it means only that law and order have capitulated, and that we have cheaply surrendered to the enemies of democracy. More disturbing, in this connection, than the incident at Cicero is the fact that similar incidents could take place, given a little encouragement, in scores of American communities.

This catalogue of mythology could be extended, and the Negroes are by no means the only victims of the lingering remnants of once larger, more formidable and extensive myths. But our progress has been good, spectacular, and probably without current equivalent in the world or historical counterpart.

Freedom and justice have found their greatest and fullest expression within our shores, and as an American, I am proud of our record in securing and broadening the rights of man. And I, like you, believe passionately and proudly in the way of life that has been fashioned here out of many peoples, colors and creeds. I think we have found the closest approximation of the good life that Providence has vouchsafed to mankind.

But it is because we believe in America and what it stands for that we deplore the more acutely its every imperfection. We must destroy the lingering myths that gnaw at our vitals because they are gross imperfections, because intolerance is spiritual sickness, because it is a contradiction of our profession of faith in liberty and equality, and because it is an ugly enemy weapon.

The answer to communism is democracy; not less democracy, or just enough, but more. And democracy is color blind.

While we are defining with increasing preciseness the legal responsibilities of government for protecting the citizenship rights of all Americans, we must also spread, patiently and tirelessly, everywhere and at every social and economic level a clearer understanding of the common responsibilities that life in a democratic country imposes upon us all.

That is why I am here tonight, because the Urban League is defining the citizens' obligation to one another, as well as government's responsibility for our common protection. There is no better way to learn and appreciate these obligations and responsibilities than by working together in their execution. That's the way the Urban League does it.

After the January 28, 1952, issue of Time *magazine devoted its feature article to him, Stevenson wrote to his Princeton classmate T. S. Matthews, editor of* Time.

To T. S. Matthews

January 28, 1952

Dear Tom:

I am tardy but my thanks for the friendly and flattering article are none the less emphatic and genuine. Most of all I was touched by your personal concern.

There are some inaccuracies, of course, but they are not too important and my larger dismay is the flurry of national interest to which the article has contributed. I feel as though I was shrinking as the interest enlarges!

Yours,

P.S. I was flattered by your presence at Lloyd Garrison's luncheon on such a busy day for you.

A.E.S.

John Madigan, of the Chicago Herald-American, *started a daily column as a political reporter for that newspaper just before this letter was written.*

To John Madigan [17]

January 29, 1952

Dear Mr. Madigan:

I see your face plastered all over the Herald-American trucks and as a fellow sufferer from recent public exposure I welcome you to these dizzy heights. May I say also that I welcome the lively and literate interest of the Herald-American in the local political scene — thanks to you.

Sincerely yours,

[17] The original is in the possession of Mr. Madigan.

To Alicia Patterson [18]

January 29, 1952

. . . Never did disaster befall an innocent bystander quite as abruptly as it did me last week. After a day and night of frenzy and speeches and parties in N.Y. I went to Wash on Tuesday, saw John Lewis [19] in the afternoon and the Pres. in the evening, and then the heavens opened. On Wed. I spent 4 solid hours on the telephone at one stretch and most of the day dodging around from hotels to houses to clubs trying to avoid all my "dear old friends" of the press who began coming thru the walls and over the transomes. Then things broke in Spfd & there was nothing for it except to get home as fast as I could.

So, instead of the black river [20] . . . I have miseries here compounded of mines and horsemeat . . . and great distress of soul and mind about this sudden clamor about the Presidency — in which . . . even Newsday has joined. The phone rings from near and far, newspaper characters are arriving and asking hideous questions and departing with crumbs. Instead of a rest I've an advanced case of traumatic exhaustion — and what's more I don't know what the devil its all about. If its true and Eisenhower is a lost cause and the only hope of the rationals is Stevenson, we're in a hell of a fix. Besides Stevenson wants nothing except to be Gov. of Ill. again — and his heart won't break if the people deny him that. But I suspect it will all blow over and I can relax a little before long. . . .

I must to bed — with a prayer that you can forgive my last minute "chucking" as the English say — and thanks for the best editorial I've seen regarding that remarkable, virtuous, fraud, the Governor of Illinois — who really does know his own measure and has no illusions.

ADLAI

In the January 24, 1952, issue of the New York Times, *Arthur Krock devoted his column to Stevenson's deposition concerning Alger Hiss. Among other things, Mr. Krock observed that "as a lawyer, to give such testimony in a criminal trial was a matter of principle with Mr. Stevenson; as a*

18 This handwritten letter is in the possession of Adlai E. Stevenson III.

19 President of the United Mine Workers of America.

20 Stevenson had planned to go to Miss Patterson's estate near Kingsland, Georgia, on the St. Mary's River, the dividing line between Florida and Georgia. Locally it was called the Black River because of the dark color of the water caused by mangrove roots.

citizen he felt it would be cowardice not to do so on the possibility that the accused might be proved guilty as well as a block to due process where a man's liberty was at stake. For him there was no choice between telling the truth and bearing false witness."

To Arthur Krock [21]

January 29, 1952

Dear Arthur:

I have read your piece on my deposition in the Hiss case and I am delighted. I think you handled it perfectly and I am most grateful for something in print on my side.

I have reviewed the file. I was asked to testify as a character witness by counsel for Hiss in the first trial. I was unable to do so and thereafter the trial judge approved interrogatories propounded by Hiss' counsel and cross-interrogatories for the prosecution. The United States Commissioner took my deposition here in Springfield on June 2, 1949. A copy is enclosed, which tells the whole story, omitting some minor details, such as:

At San Francisco I was in the Fairmount [Fairmont] Hotel with the [United Nations] Delegation and he was down town with the Secretariat. We saw each other hardly at all at that time. Back in Washington after the Conference in early July I worked with him several different days preparing questions and answers for the [State] Department's witnesses on the ratification of the Charter. I resigned and returned to Chicago and my law office the end of July or August. Secretary Byrnes [22] sent for me after he returned from Potsdam in late August, I believe, and asked me to go as Deputy to Stettinius [23] on the Preparatory Commission. I finally accepted, and left with Byrnes by ship early in September for London. Hiss was Director of the Division of Special Political Affairs in the Department and backstopped our Delegation in London. You will recall that Stettinius fell ill in early October and I took his place as Chief of our Delegation. I had no personal contact with Hiss, however, until he arrived in January with the American Delegation to the first session of the General Assembly. During that interval, which lasted a month or six weeks, I saw him a lot in the American Delegation offices and meetings. Following that Conference, in February 1946, I did not see him

[21] The original is in the possession of Mr. Krock.

[22] James F. Byrnes, Secretary of State. He resigned on January 20, 1947.

[23] Edward R. Stettinius was Secretary of State from November, 1944 to June, 1945. In 1945 he became head of the U.S. delegation to the Preparatory Commission of the United Nations in London. See *The Papers of Adlai E. Stevenson,* Vol. II.

again until the General Assembly in New York in 1947, when he was Director of the Carnegie Foundation for International Peace. At that time I saw him once or twice in my office when he called to discuss the budget of the UN for the following year, a representation chore that Senator [Arthur] Vandenberg had passed along to me.

Following a particularly nasty editorial in the [Chicago] Tribune on Saturday, August 18, 1951, I wrote Colonel McCormick as per the attached copy.

Further deponent saith not — except thanks to Krock and love to Martha! [24]

Yours,
ADLAI [25]

To T. S. Matthews

February 1, 1952

Dear Tom:

That distinguished journal, the Chicago Tribune, today reports me as saying that the Time article had "too many inaccuracies." For your information what I said was that there were two inaccuracies: my ex-wife's family was not the Borden Milk Company family, and my brother-in-law Ernest Ives is a retired U. S. diplomat but not a wealthy one. As for Ernest, the facts seem to be that the Ives' family fortune went with the wind in the Civil War — if not the Revolution!

But now see what you have done! The telephones clatter incessantly, gentlemen appear from all over the country, the mail has us swamped, and the Rabbit [26] is behaving with all the confidence, composure and courage of a rabbit.

---

[24] Mrs. Krock.

[25] Mr. Krock responded to Stevenson's letter on January 31, 1952: ". . . The deposition itself completely sustains the conclusion I advanced as a fact. I decided to write the piece after one or two intimates of the President said something to me about a fear that the Hiss deposition was 'poison.' I notice that, despite your very effective letter of August 27, 1951, The Tribune continues to misrepresent the facts of the deposition. . . ."

[26] The *Time* article reported that "A Princeton roommate recalls Stevenson as 'a nice, harmless, pleasant guy' whose personality got him the nickname 'Rabbit.'"

In a handwritten memorandum, undated, and written some time later to his press secretary, Stevenson commented: "Mr. Flanagan — Forgive my self consciousness, but the nickname Rabbit was at college — so far as I can recall — was used only by a couple of roommates and referred to my taste for salad. Reading these articles it seems to have assumed some other significance. My nickname at college was always 'Ad' — AES." The original memorandum is in the possession of William I. Flanagan.

Anyway, experts on Time assure me that you have treated me far beyond my deserts, and they can pick no quarrel with me on that.

Sincerely yours,

The Time cover story greatly increased Stevenson's mail. Some letters were from those who remembered his grandparents. One such letter, from Ernest B. Forbes, of State College, Pennsylvania, recalled his boyhood in Bloomington, Illinois, when he broke several ribs and was taken care of by a Dr. Elder. Stevenson's great-grandfather Jesse Fell stopped by the boy's home carrying a live turkey in each hand, "and for my entertainment, put them on my bed. Fortunately, no untoward happenings ensued. In this incident Jesse Fell revealed himself the gentleman that he was, kindly, and of simple habits to which he adhered to the end of his days, often to the distress of his more fastidious women-folk."

To Ernest B. Forbes

February 2, 1952

Dear Mr. Forbes:

I was enchanted with your letter about my great grandfather Fell and the turkeys on your bed. I am glad they behaved, although I suspect your mother felt that he didn't! Your mention of Dr. Elder also evoked memories of that name which was so familiar in my family in my childhood. I wish you were still living in Illinois!

With my warm thanks and every best wish, I am

Sincerely yours,

To Douglas Fairbanks [27]

February 2, 1952

Dear Doug:

I was delighted to have your letter and I hope I shall have an opportunity to see you in Chicago next week. As of now, however, it looks as though I shall be out of the state.

With much of what you say I agree. The impression is widespread in professional political circles that Ike has little chance of the nomination, hence the anxiety about [Robert A.] Taft and the necessity for the Democrats making the best fight possible to save the things we believe in.

There is another point with respect to Ike that the newspaper men in

[27] The original is in the possession of Mr. Fairbanks.

Washington do not overlook: the preponderance of isolationists in the leadership of the Senate and the House who would be more powerful politically than the General.

How to evaluate these things I don't personally know, and all I am interested in is running for Governor of Illinois again.

It was good to hear from you and I envy you your travels. My horizons have been the Wabash and the Mississippi all too long.

With every good wish, I am

Sincerely yours,

ADLAI

Stevenson celebrated his fifty-second birthday in Lake Forest, Illinois, at the home of Mr. and Mrs. James F. Oates, Jr.

To Mr. and Mrs. James F. Oates, Jr.[28]

February 6, 1952

Dear Oates:

I can't speak for the birthday girls, but the birthday boy had the time of his life — and also his birthday — including the chicken patty and green pea era.

How I contrived to have such dear, good and gifted friends I don't know. But I thank God for them, and pray that somehow their charity and loyalty to me can be rewarded.

With love and thanks.

ADLAI

H. Hamilton Hackney, who raised purebred cattle, was a Princeton classmate of Stevenson. He wrote the Governor while on a "bull-selling junket" in Florida that he had read in the Time *story that Stevenson played a fair game of tennis. "I do want to note a hearty exception to that silly phrase about a fair game of tennis — you never did so play, and I doubt if you do now." He added: "Didn't I name you Rabbit?"*

To H. Hamilton Hackney

February 6, 1952

Dear Hacker:

I have your screed, illegible, insulting and distasteful as usual. As for

[28] The original is in the possession of Mr. Oates.

my tennis, I am prepared to meet you under any terms and conditions and for any stakes. Unless you are more of a man than I think you are I would recommend that you default.

It must be agreeable to spend your winters in Florida but you don't need to explain to me that you are trying to sell bulls. But go ahead, I will save the country while you languish on the beaches.

My affectionate sentiments to your wife.

Yours,

P.S. Yes, you did give me the name of "Rabbit" and you put it in Time magazine. Otherwise Matthews did all right by me.

A.E.S.

After the election in 1948, Stephen A. Mitchell, one of the original members of the Stevenson for Governor Committee, helped to solicit funds to cover the campaign deficit. In taking this action it was rumored that he was a spokesman for the Governor. He was careful to avoid any action that might give color to another such charge, and annually sent the Governor the auditor's report on his law firm that included the names of clients and amounts of fees received of $500 or more. Mitchell noted that "I never got any clients or did any work for pay that related in any way to the State or the governor." [29] *He sent the Governor the 1951 audit just prior to the following letter.*

After Stevenson announced early in January, 1952, that he would run for reelection, Mitchell agreed to serve again on the Stevenson for Governor Committee.

To Stephen A. Mitchell [30]

February 6, 1952

Dear Steve:

Mitchell, Conway and Bane looks like a spectacular success and if you are really having some fun and enjoying your prosperity then I *know* it is! [31]

Many thanks for the clipping about "cousin Oscar." [32]

I am enclosing the check which we discussed to create a working fund for the Stevenson for Governor Committee. [33] I should like to be included

---

[29] Letter to Carol Evans, July 23, 1969.

[30] The original is in the possession of Mr. Mitchell.

[31] Mr. Mitchell and his partners had formed a new law firm in 1950.

[32] Oscar Ewing, Federal Security Administrator, 1947–1952. Mrs. Ives thinks they were distantly related.

[33] Stevenson enclosed a check for $5,000.

among the signatures which the bank will honor on this account, and I assume the account will be opened at the Chicago National Bank after explaining the situation to Lester Armour.[34] If Ed McDougal would prefer to put it in the Northern Trust Company where his brother Dave is a Vice President it would be entirely satisfactory with me. I will be sending Ed McDougal or whomever he designates miscellaneous contributions that come in from friends of the independent kind. Such a contribution from Lawrence B. Perkins [35] is enclosed. I have acknowledged and endorsed it and I assume a record of it will be kept here.

Sincerely yours,

ADLAI

To the Governor's Staff, Mansion and State House [36]

February 8, 1952

My dear friends:

I am overwhelmed as usual by your generosity to me on my birthday. The pen set is a dandy and while I found no guarantee attached that it will make me any more literate I am hoping for the best. At any rate, with a little practice, there will be no excuse for illegibility!

With grateful thanks, I am

Devotedly yours,

THE "GUV"

Stevenson again participated in the annual Lincoln's birthday ceremonies in Springfield. On February 12, 1952, he made an address at the annual meeting of the Abraham Lincoln Association in the Historical Library of the Centennial Building.[37]

Lincoln as a Political Leader

A man in public office can find no surer guide than Lincoln. Personal integrity, surpassing love of country, the loftiest idealism, faith in the people and a passion to serve them well, far-ranging vision, these were the qualities by which he commands our homage, and to which every public leader should aspire.

But how does one gain these qualities? How does he rise above the

[34] President of the Chicago National Bank, of which Stevenson had been a director before taking office as governor.

[35] A Chicago architect, member of the firm of Perkins & Will and a personal friend of Stevenson. He had donated $100 to the campaign.

[36] The original is in the possession of Lawrence Irvin.

[37] The text is from the *Abraham Lincoln Quarterly*, June, 1952, pp. 79–86.

gloom of personal defeat that may come any time in politics and that came so often to Lincoln? Where can he find the courage to persist when measures which he knows will serve the people meet rejection? How does he preserve his faith in human nature when it is betrayed and so often sternly challenged? How does he throw off, or suffer in silence, the dishonest or unfair personal and political attacks that sometimes become his lot? How can he learn to lead, and where to lead, and when to lead, and how to wait in patience? How may it be given to him to know, to understand, to sympathize?

These are but a few of the questions one might ask. Lincoln was faced with every one of them and many more besides. While the problems that confronted him are different from our own, still, the lessons of history, the courage to persist, the faith in truth, the soul searching, the idealism, those same inner resources that he commanded, can also be our reliance. He cannot solve our problems; but in the record of his striving and his victory are lessons not only for the man in public office but for all of us.

But Lincoln is a mystery, someone may say. He was unique. Even his closest friends confessed that they could not always understand him. We cannot learn from the inscrutable.

Of course, to reduce the area of the inscrutable about Lincoln is a major reason for this Association's embarking upon the project of publishing his *Collected Works*. It has been a primary inducement to the Rockefeller Foundation, and to generous individuals, to aid the project financially. For before we can solve the riddle of this man we must have the facts in hand — all the facts that can be gathered, reliably presented, with whatever clarification the best of scholarship can give them. Then will come the scholars' further task of helping us to draw richer meaning from these facts.

Scholars must help us, yet these books should not be solely within the scholar's domain. Lincoln belongs to everyone. Any of us will be privileged to delve here for the flashing epigram, the tight-knit argument, the homespun figure of speech with which Lincoln could so graphically illuminate this meaning, and for the wisdom as valid now as it was then.

The true function of a political leader in a democracy is not to impose his will upon the people but to aid them in making proper choices. Harder than charting the course of public policy, harder even than converting generalities into details, is the indispensable task of explanation; indispensable because the political leader only proposes but the people dispose. He must explain and try to lead them to the truth. A large part of Lincoln's first inaugural address was devoted to explanation. "Physically speaking, we cannot separate," he said, ". . . the different parts of our country cannot do this. They cannot but remain face to face, and intercourse, either amicable or hostile, must continue between them. Is it possible, then, to make that intercourse more advantageous or more satisfactory after separation than before? Can aliens make treaties easier than friends can make laws? Can treaties be more faithfully enforced between aliens than laws among friends? Suppose you go to war, you cannot fight always; and when, after much loss on both sides, and no gain on either, you cease fighting, the identical old questions as to terms of intercourse are upon you again."

Throughout his presidency Lincoln was constantly trying to clarify the choices the people must make. In his letter to James C. Conkling of August 26, 1863, which was meant to be read at a great mass meeting in Springfield, he wrote: "There are those who are dissatisfied with me. To such I would say: You desire peace, and you blame me that you do not have it. But how can we attain it? There are but three conceivable ways: First, to suppress the rebellion by force of arms. This I am trying to do. Are you for it? If you are, so far we are agreed. If you are not for it, a second way is to give up the Union. I am against this. Are you for it? If you are, you should say so plainly." The third choice was compromise, which was clearly impossible.

Lincoln adjured the people to speak plainly, because he recognized that the final choice lay with them. If a majority, both North and South, had come to favor disunion, he would have negotiated a peace on the basis of Southern independence. Because, as Lyman Bryson of Columbia University, has said: "The purpose of political action and the opportunity of free political life is to allow the people ultimately to determine their own destiny, and — after they have the chance to learn — even to make their own mistakes." Lincoln must have realized that to deny the people this privilege is to look upon government merely as an agency to solve political problems rather than as an instrument to perform the people's will. The conception of a government which gives the people what it thinks is good for them, whether they want it or not, is not democracy but authoritarianism.

Lincoln had no sympathy with authoritarian concepts. He was determined to keep the South in the union with every power at his command, because, he said: "The chief magistrate derives all his authority from the people, and they have conferred none upon him to fix terms for the separation of the States." But he added, and this is most significant: *"The people themselves can do this also if they choose;* but the executive, as such, has nothing to do with it. His duty is to administer the present government, as it came to his hands, and to transmit it, unimpaired by him, to his successor."

Such willingness to allow the people to make what he holds to be mistakes puts an awesome responsibility upon the democratic leader. It means that his faith in the people must surpass his faith in himself. Lincoln had such self-denying faith, for he went on to say: "Why should there not be a patient confidence in the ultimate justice of the people? Is there any better or equal hope in the world? . . . If the Almighty Ruler of Nations, with his eternal truth and justice, be on your side of the North, or on yours of the South, that truth and that justice will surely prevail by the judgment of this great tribunal of the American people."

An informal speech that Lincoln made at Springfield at the end of his campaign against Stephen A. Douglas in 1858 might well adorn the office wall of every public man. Yet I believe it is not too well known. For almost four months the rivals had spoken nearly every day to large crowds in the open air, often under a broiling sun, now and then in rain. Between engagements they had traveled constantly by rail, river-boat, or horse and buggy, putting up at wretched country inns, where food was often poor and ill-prepared. The issues were momentous, both for the contestants and the nation. Lincoln knew that the outcome hung in a delicate balance. Out of what must have been an utter weariness, he said (and I quote him only in part):

"My friends, today closes the discussions of this canvass. The planting and the culture are over; and there remains but the preparation and the harvest.

"I stand here surrounded by friends — some political, all personal friends, I trust. May I be indulged, in this closing scene, to say a few words about myself. I have borne a laborious, and, in some respects to myself, a painful part in the contest. Through all, I have neither assailed, nor wrestled with any part of the Constitution. . . . To the best of my judgment I have labored *for,* and not *against* the Union. As I have not felt, so I have not expressed any harsh sentiments towards our Southern brethren. . . . I have meant to assail the motives of no party, or individual; and if I have . . . I regret it. . . . Bespattered with every imaginable odious epithet . . . I have cultivated patience, and made no attempt to retort.

"Ambition has been ascribed to me. God knows how sincerely I prayed from the first that this field of ambition might not be opened. I claim no insensibility to political honors; but today could the Missouri restriction be restored, and the whole slavery question replaced on the old ground of 'toleration' by *necessity* where it exists, with unyielding hostility to the spread of it, on principle, I would, in consideration, gladly agree, that Judge Douglas should never be *out,* and I never *in,* an office, so long as we both or either, live."

Would that every candidate could make such a statement on the eve of our elections. For in such an avowal as that is, a man in public office, or anyone who aspires to office, can find a creed: no personal or party malice; fairness in tactics; toleration of opponents; respect for honest difference of opinion; devotion to country; honest ambition; but utter subordination of self to principle.

But in speaking of Lincoln's greatness of soul I am stating nothing new. Others have discussed with eloquence or written with practiced pens of his surpassing human qualities. We know his virtues. His great accomplishment at Gettysburg is familiar to every schoolboy, although too few of us truly understand how skillfully he linked the everlasting traditions of our past with the vast future of mankind that he envisioned.

For in our rededication and faithfulness to our national ideals, such as he pleaded for at Gettysburg, lies an unleashed power sufficient to frustrate and humble any Fuehrer, any Duce, any Commissar, and to make government of the people prevail throughout the world.

But if we do not fully understand the wisdom that this man tried to bring us, at least we see in part, and know in part. Lincoln's most moving passages are emblazoned on the walls of great memorials and public buildings. His achievements, his traits of character have inspired great books, and offer lessons that we seek to take to heart. But how much better to know, also, the why and wherefore of these things. How did Lincoln gain and perfect these rare qualities? How did he cherish them in failure and success? For with this knowledge we also may gain them, each according to his own capacity. And it is only from a record such as this association has prepared, "not in idolatry but in honest fact," as the editor has stated in the foreword to it, only from such a record may we beguile these secrets.

Lincoln was a profound student of history. As a boy, reading Parson Weems' *Life of Washington,* he pondered on the deeper meanings of the American Revolution and wondered what great principle it was that kept the soldiers faithful to a painful task. He spent hours of research in preparing his Cooper Union speech in order to prove that the framers of our Constitution had planned for the containment and ultimate end of slavery. In writing his first inaugural address he studied the Constitution, the events of the Nullification crisis of 1832, and Webster's reply to Hayne. His letters and speeches are studded with historical references.

He concluded that all through human history runs a struggle between right and wrong, which is destined to endure, perhaps, to the end of time. Historians during our materialistic years disavowed this theme. But now in our age of anxiety and time of testing, they are bringing it again within their purview. Arthur Schlesinger, Jr., recently stated: "If historians are to understand the fullness of the social dilemma they seek to reconstruct, they must understand that sometimes there is no escape from the implacabilities of moral decisions"; while Allan Nevins notes with approval the emergence in historical writing of "a deepened moral sense much needed in our troubled age." So two, at least, of our most thoughtful present-day historians accord a degree of validity to Lincoln's view of the theme of right and wrong in history.

If the record of man's progress, or lack of progress, is the chronicle of everlasting struggle between right and wrong, it follows that the solutions of our problems lie largely within ourselves, that only with self-mastery can we hope for peace and contentment. This would seem to be confirmed by the fact that the scientific mastery of our environment brings us not tranquillity but rather unrest and new fears. Knowledge alone is not enough. It must be leavened with human benevolence before it becomes wisdom.

Lincoln's life story is the record of a great unfolding, of a marvellous growth of mind and character largely through self-teaching. He handled political problems astutely because he was thoroughly and completely the politician — almost his whole adult life had been spent in political activity and in political reflection. He could give utterance to everlasting words when moved by inner emotion because through resolve and long practice he had learned to draw beauty from language as well as meaning.

It has been largely lack of facts or our inability to draw full understanding from them that has cloaked Lincoln in mystery. Now, with the preparation of this record, we may expect to see him as much less of an enigma but an even better, wiser, therefore greater, man.

We can all be thankful that Lincoln is not regarded as a perfect man. The very fact that he shared some of our frailties encourages us to try to improve ourselves just as he did. And in the record of his life, as set forth in his *Collected Works,* is inspiration for the lowliest, the humblest, the most discouraged among us.

T. S. Matthews wrote Stevenson that he wanted to come to Springfield on February 26 because "under my arm I'll have the original portrait of you that appeared on TIME's cover, beautifully framed. I should like to present it to you with a bow — and perhaps an appropriate toast."

To T. S. Matthews

February 13, 1952

Dear Tom:

On February 26 the Governor of Illinois is obliged to speak at the Belleville Rotary Club at noon and at a Jackson Day Dinner in East St. Louis in the evening. In short, the Governor is in a hell of a fix on that day. He will be back in Springfield either late that night or the following morning, depending on whether T. S. Matthews can come down to Springfield on the afternoon train from Chicago arriving here about eight o'clock and stay the night and a bit of the following morning.

Certainly I cannot permit that picture to get to Illinois — and out again!

Yours,

With pressures mounting daily, Stevenson was happy in February to escape on a brief holiday. On the eve of his departure for a visit with Mr. and Mrs. Marshall Field III at their home in South Carolina, he wrote to Jane Dick.

To Mrs. Edison Dick [38]

February 13, 1952

. . . The pressures are APPALLING. Some samples from this mornings mail enclosed. I've positively declined to the Sec[retary] of Int[erior]. who came out for the night; but no one will take no for an answer. Now for the rest & reflection you suggested. . . .

Carl & Jodie [39] will probably come tomorrow. I'll be back early next week I think — unless I get shot by a quail or drowned by a crocodile, which would be too good to happen. . . .

To Lawrence Irvin [40]

February 20, 1952

It has come to my attention that some state employees under my jurisdiction are doing personnel work at the [Democratic] State Central Committee headquarters. While I fully appreciate that personnel re-

[38] This handwritten letter is in the possession of Mrs. Dick.
[39] Mr. and Mrs. Carl McGowan.
[40] The original is in the possession of Mr. Irvin.

cruitment, call it patronage or what you will, is a necessary function that must be performed, and performed well, I disapprove assigning secretaries from their Departments to the State Committee offices to do it.

Please see that these people are severed from the state payroll promptly.

For a long time I have been concerned with the whole policy of personnel recruitment, and I think I have discussed with you a frank and candid approach to the problem by the creation of an overall personnel agency or Department of Personnel, which will include a Civil Service Commission for protection of the merit principle. The state hires people through political party patronage, and probably always will, and also hires people regardless of party affiliation. The recruitment problem — the simple necessity of finding the people to fill our large personnel needs — is difficult, and patronage sources must be used along with non-political sources. The important thing is that sound standards of selection be applied to all persons recruited from all sources. I see no reason why this recruitment process should not be treated professionally as a state function, and a very important one.

This whole subject of personnel management deserves more of the study which we commenced a couple of years ago. You will recall that we considered it in connection with the Schaefer Commission and its agenda. I think you have considered this yourself at length and we should discuss it more and more.

A.E.S.

Stevenson spent a few days of vacation with Mr. and Mrs. Marshall Field III at Chelsea Plantation, their estate at Ridgeland, South Carolina.

To Marshall Field III

February 21, 1952

Dear Marshall:

That glimpse of another world — a tranquil, relaxed world — lifted me so quickly and so far from present ugly realities that it is hard to assume the debate "to be or not to be." Quail seem so much more important than politics! My perspective is better, mind clearer, and Chelsea was Nature's sweet restorer. I am most grateful to you for that magic interlude. Besides, talking with you in that peaceful environment, and with Marshall and Kay,[41] for whom I have long since added respect to affection, was more helpful than you can realize. I don't know whether

41 Marshall Field IV and his wife.

it is your gentle, diffident way of talking, intuition, or just great "understanding," but it has always been the same and I come away from a talk with you wiser, surer and *very* thankful!

Yours,

Ellen Stevenson's aunt, Lady Spears, wrote the Governor that comment about him over the British Broadcasting System and in the British press was "always appreciative — never anything but good is said of you — and whatever comes of it I do want you to know that the Spears family are backing you heart & soul from a distance."

To Lady Mary Spears

February 21, 1952

My dear Mary:

I was enchanted with your letter. It was more than good of you to write me, and I also had a very welcome letter from Louis.[42]

The loyalty and affection of the Spears family means much to me and I only wish that our paths could cross again, and soon. Life here has become all the more complicated for me with the recent clamor about running for President. Actually, I will continue in this job if the people will let me, and I find it the full measure of my capacity.

We have followed avidly the grief and joy that has been England's lot of late. Certainly the devotion of the people seems to have grown, if anything, with the years, and the absorption of Americans with the King's death and the Queen's accession to the Throne has been most interesting to note. I think democratic America finds some comfort in the stability of an institution in these trying and anxious times.

There has been little untoward or critical comment in our press — even the Chicago Tribune.

With affectionate regards to you both, and every good wish, I am

Sincerely yours,

On February 15, 1952, Arthur Krock, of the New York Times, *an old friend of both Stevenson and his former wife, wrote the Governor: "I don't know whether you know it or not but Ellen has been talking very foolishly in these parts about the reasons given in TIME, and pieces by [Marquis] Childs and me, for the divorce. She wrote TIME a letter denying every statement made. . . . Now she has threatened to write*

[42] General Sir Louis Spears, Lady Spears's husband.

some letter to the Chicago papers on the subject. . . . I find that what she wants published is that, because of 'incompatibility' (asinine word!), she was going to divorce you anyhow and your entrance into elective politics did not affect the decision one way or the other. If it is added that you never wanted the divorce, the foregoing is utterly harmless, so I am not worried about it any more."

To Arthur Krock [43]

February 21, 1952

Dear Arthur:

Many thanks for your letter. I have heard about Ellen's talking of late from other quarters and it is all very disturbing. Her sister has called me from New York and I think she may be able to do something through the children.

I only wish I had the opportunity to tell you the background because the case is really not too complicated and the element of *l'amour propre* is, I think, evident to you. She does not wish to be publicly portrayed as a bad sport.

Perhaps it is a disguised blessing and will add another cogent reason why Stevenson should not be considered for President! I only hope it isn't a sufficiently cogent reason to eliminate him for Governor too!

Sincerely yours,

ADLAI

George W. Ball spent many hours by telephone and in person trying to persuade his friend Stevenson that he should run for President. On February 20, 1952, Mr. Ball wrote the Governor at length from Washington:

You asked me in Springfield if I thought you were the indispensable man. I told you I wouldn't put any money on such a contention. It did seem to me, however, that, in order to fulfill a kind of personal sense of adequacy, everyone had to utilize his own talents in the way in which he judged they could be most useful to the world. . . . On further reflection I think that what I said was not a very good answer. "Indispensable" isn't an absolute term; it must be defined in terms of alternatives. . . . On the basis of these available alternatives, the word "indispensable" takes on real meaning as applied to you. I can tell you, with no sophistry whatever, that I do consider you indispensable.

[43] The original is in the possession of Mr. Krock.

Mr. Ball sent with his letter a copy of an article by Bernard De Voto, scheduled to appear in the April issue of Harper's *magazine, saying that an interview by Joseph Alsop would appear in the* Saturday Evening Post *at about the same time and that a* Look *picture story on Stevenson's family would probably appear early in April.*[44] *In closing his letter, Ball said: "Please let me know if at any time I can help either by doing a useful chore or by just keeping my damned mouth shut, leaving you alone and tending to my law practice. Believe me, you have my prayerful and affectionate sympathy in the decision you are facing and my full understanding whatever that decision may be."*

To George W. Ball

February 27, 1952

Dear George:

I have your letter and have marked it well. I am sorely troubled. My heart is here and my head not far behind. We will see.

I know I have your prayers and affectionate sympathy, and that helps mightily.

Yours,

P.S. The De Voto article is altogether too good. If I could suggest a single change to make it a little more responsive to the technical facts it would be in the second and third sentences of the second full paragraph on galley 3C. They could read as follows:

"For nearly a year he was American Minister in London and Chief of the U. S. Delegation to the Preparatory Commission that drew the ground plans for the UN. His work there was widely applauded, and in 1946 and 1947 he was a U. S. Delegate to the General Assembly, practicing law in Chicago in the intervals."

This is not important but straightens out some ambiguities.[45]

A.E.S.

[44] The article in *Harper's,* by Bernard De Voto, appeared in the April, 1952, issue under the title "Stevenson and the Independent Voter." Joseph Alsop's article appeared in the June 28 issue of the *Saturday Evening Post,* entitled "He'd Rather Not Be President." *Look* did not publish the story referred to by Ball. However, the July 21, 1952, issue of *Life* published a photographic essay entitled "Adlai Stevenson — Democrats' Best Foot Is Reluctant to Put Himself Forward." The pictures included Stevenson and his immediate family, his aunts, Mrs. Martin D. Hardin and Miss Letitia Stevenson, then living, and others of his forebears.

[45] The article as published incorporated the change substantially as suggested by Stevenson.

In April, 1951, Stevenson entertained reporters representing the foreign press at a luncheon at the mansion. Among them was Jean-Claude Servan-Schreiber, of Les Echos, Paris, France, who wrote the Governor early in 1952 that he had reported in his country that Stevenson would inevitably be President of the United States; that his efficiency, capacity and honesty were bound to lead him there; and that he knew of Stevenson's deep interest in foreign affairs and his friendship for the French Republic.

To Jean-Claude Servan-Schreiber

February 28, 1952

Dear M. Schreiber:

I was deeply touched and pleased by your thoughtful letter. I had not realized that the Presidential clamor had penetrated to France. I wish it had not even penetrated to Illinois! Actually, all I want to do is to be re-elected to the governorship of this state and carry on some work I have barely commenced. All the same, I am deeply flattered by your encouragement and confidence and good will.

I hope our paths will cross again.

Sincerely yours,

Rexford G. Tugwell, an original member of Franklin D. Roosevelt's "Brain Trust" and Under Secretary of Agriculture, 1934–1937, wrote Stevenson: ". . . You must not let a very natural modesty . . . govern certain of your actions in the coming months. . . . I feel that I may write you because I have seen what it means to move from a governorship to the larger Federal area. When President Roosevelt was anticipating such a possibility . . . he discovered that his mastery of state affairs . . . was of amazingly little help as he contemplated national leadership. Of course, if elected, he would have a depression to fight: but our next President will have something even worse — guidance toward coexistence with a ruthless, powerful and almost inscrutable equal power in the world. . . ."

To Rexford G. Tugwell

February 29, 1952

Dear Dr. Tugwell:

I have read and re-read your letter many times. I have received few that summarized the hazards more eloquently. My modesty is not false.

I just feel that the difficulties are beyond my limited capacity, and moreover, I have become so preoccupied with this job, which seems to me of worthy magnitude, that I am loathe to leave to go to sea without a chart.

You were good to write me.

Cordially yours,

Archibald MacLeish was vacationing in the West Indies when he wrote Stevenson on February 21, 1952: "A man's friends . . . do for a man what he can't rightly do for himself: to help him to see himself from the outside in a just perspective. . . . The sincerity of your modesty makes it difficult for you to see your real proportions. . . . The thought that you might be president of the republic seems to you . . . a grotesque halucination [sic]."

To Archibald MacLeish [46]

February 29, 1952

Dear Archie:

Your phrase "grotesque hallucination" is better than any I have been able to contrive, and I wonder if you really do see me in a "just perspective." I cannot find it myself. The next President will have something worse to face than most any predecessor — guidance toward co-existence with a ruthless, powerful, hostile, inscrutable, *equal* power in the world. What to do about agriculture and the management of industries? Emergency measures must give way to something more permanent and tolerable. Can inflation be controlled and social security measures protected? How to balance groups that each may contribute what the others need and the whole be kept in effective operation. What of the revolution in all of the underdeveloped areas of the world? Our policies are neither firm nor wholly well conceived.

I shudder. And what's more, I am a candidate for re-election as Governor of Illinois, and how can I in honesty run for two offices? Moreover, how can I neglect this brutal job and find the time for the other, if I had the heart and the confidence?

But you try me sorely, and I never want it said that "he was a coward."

My love to Ada,[47] and may the sun shine and the poems bloom.

Yours,

ADLAI

[46] The original is in the Archibald MacLeish papers in the Library of Congress.
[47] Mrs. MacLeish.

To Mr. and Mrs. Carl Vrooman [48]

March 5, 1952

My dear Cousins:

I have your letters and they comfort me in this difficult ordeal. There is nothing I want to do besides get in a few more licks in Illinois, but the pressures are extreme. I think I can escape, however. After all, a man can't run for two jobs!

Certainly "wisdom" comes in an infinite variety of packages, including many nicely wrapped counterfeits.

Affectionately,
ADLAI

P.S. I look forward to the stories.[49]

On October 13 and 14, 1951, Stevenson and Senator Paul Douglas had met at the home of Clifton Utley to discuss plans for the forthcoming campaign year.

In a long memorandum, undated, Douglas set forth his version of the meetings and subsequent developments. According to Douglas, he and Stevenson were to submit lists of names to each other and agree on various candidates. The names were to be submitted to Fred Cain, chairman of the Democratic State Central Committee, who was to see that the slate was nominated. The Governor was to urge a slate of better candidates from Cook County for the legislature, and Douglas was to furnish names for this also. It was agreed that Douglas's aide, Douglas Anderson, and Stevenson's representatives, Lawrence Irvin and Richard Nelson, would meet and work out the details and mechanics of the understanding. Douglas claims to have been in touch with Cain and Irvin from time to time and was reassured by both that "everything was all right." Finally, Douglas says, he learned in February, 1952, that very few of the names they had agreed upon as delegates had been filed and even fewer of those agreed upon as alternates; and also that nothing was done by the Governor to get improved candidates for the state legislature.

The slate sponsored by the Democratic State Central Committee to run for state offices in the 1952 primary campaign was made up of Stevenson for governor, Sherwood Dixon for lieutenant governor, Ivan A. Elliott for attorney general, Benjamin O. Cooper for state auditor, Edward J. Barrett for secretary of state, and Fred Cain for state treasurer. The candi-

[48] The original is in the possession of Mrs. Vrooman.
[49] Not known what stories Stevenson refers to. Mrs. Vrooman's letter was not available to the editors.

dates were those supported by the Central Committee in 1948, with the exception of Ora Smith, who under the law could not succeed himself for another term as state treasurer. All these candidates won in the 1952 primary election.

To Fred Cain [50]

March 10, 1952

Dear Fred:

I am obliged to be in Washington on Tuesday when the County Chairmen meet with you here in Springfield. I am a member of a small subcommittee of the Governors' Conference on Federal-State relationships and meetings with Congressional leaders have been scheduled for Tuesday and Wednesday, which I cannot in good conscience miss. I hope you will explain my absence to the County Chairmen and make my apologies.

I had wanted especially to attend this meeting to discuss the approaching campaign, and also to emphasize to the party leadership the importance to me, as Governor, and to the administration as a whole, of the nomination of Ivan Elliott as Attorney General at the primary. I have worked with him for more than three years now with the utmost confidence and respect. He has given me invariable and invaluable cooperation and assistance. If re-elected, I want to continue to be able to count him on our team, along with Sherwood Dixon, Eddie Barrett, Ben Cooper — and Fred Cain!

I think the County Chairmen will understand how indispensable a like-minded Attorney General is to a Governor, and, therefore, why I attach such importance to his nomination, while not in any way deprecating the other candidates for that post.

I wish you would also tell the County Chairmen for me that my name was entered in the Oregon Presidential Primary, without consultation with me and without my approval, either directly or indirectly. I wanted to say to them what I have said frequently in the past few weeks: that is, that I want to run for Governor and be elected, with their help, and that's all!

Sincerely yours,

To Paul H. Douglas [51]

March 10, 1952

Dear Paul —

I've heard from Dick Nelson & Clifton Utley that you were disap-

[50] A carbon copy is in the possession of Ivan Elliott.
[51] This handwritten letter is in the possession of Lawrence Irvin.

pointed about the way the delegate business worked out. I confess I
didn't follow it personally, but turned it over to Irvin to arrange with
Anderson. I asked Irvin in Spfd yesterday — Sunday — to give me a
memo on what happened and here it is.[52] I'll hope to see you about it
in Wash[ington] this week —

Yrs hastily —
ADLAI

*On March 11, 1952, Stevenson traveled to Washington, D.C., to attend
a meeting of the Committee on Intergovernmental Relations of the Governors' Conference. He was able to spend an evening in Cambridge,
Massachusetts, with his sons Adlai III and Borden, students at Harvard
University. After this reunion, he and his youngest son, John Fell, a student at Milton Academy, proceeded to New Smyrna Beach, Florida, to
spend a brief holiday with their cousin, Mrs. Edward L. Ayres, the
former Hester Merwin. Wherever he went, members of the press dogged
his footsteps.*

To Alicia Patterson [53]

March 13, 1952

. . . I was so upset and bewildered by your note about [Bernard]
Baruch that I stopped in N.Y. en route to Boston to see the boys and
went to see him this morning at his apt. Obviously it was a good thing to
do anyway. I didn't let on that you had suggested I come to see him and
was entirely innocent of any activity on your part for me politically —
except that we were old friends from Chicago. He mentioned a man
named Lubbell[54] as a very smart man whom he understood I was trying
to get as a publicity man evidently thru you. I casually remarked that I
had never met, indeed never heard of Lubell, which is the simple truth
and that was the only mention of you in the conversation. . . .

[52] In his memorandum to Stevenson dated March 8, 1952, Irvin said he "thought it
was clearly understood that we could merely suggest these 'agreed' names to the
various state central committeemen. We felt neither you nor the Senator would want
us to 'pressure' or demand that our recommendations be followed to the letter. . . .
There were innumerable factors and practical reasons as to why many of our original
suggestions were not or could not be followed."
Irvin later wrote: "We were all a little naive in believing we could dictate to the
political leaders in the various congressional districts, as to who could or could
not file, as delegates to the nominating convention." Letter to Carol Evans dated
June 30, 1970.
[53] This handwritten letter is in the possession of Adlai E. Stevenson III.
[54] Samuel Lubell, author of *The Future of American Politics.*

I spent an hour and a half with Baruch, mostly his interesting reminiscences and little of value in the present situation, except that he seemed confident Truman would now want to run after the licking in N.H.[55] and in his judgment might still beat Taft in spite of the South.[56] This view, however, is not shared in Wash where I spent Tues night & Wed re a Governors' conf[erence]. job and was assaulted from all sides by the same people plus some more who have been pressing me to tell HST that I would run. N.H. only stimulated their pressures and I escaped in utter exhaustion and mental distress. I just don't want to go out for it; I wouldn't be honest with myself if I did and I attach importance to the inconsistency of being a candidate for Gov. of Ill. and publicly or even privately running for Pres. I just can't seem to get over that hurdle which no one seems to understand — even if I wanted to run for Pres. which I don't.

Boston below: and now to see the boys and then gather up John Fell tomorrow — Friday — when his spring holiday begins and — if things in Spfd permit — take him down to stay with my cousin Mrs. Edward Ayres, New Smyrna Beach, Fla., for a few days and then back to Chicago, with my resolve boldened, I hope, that I will keep out of this thing and concentrate on *being* and *running* for Gov. unless the Democratic convention should nominate me which would seem very unlikely. . . .

A.

To Mrs. Edison Dick [57]

March 14, 1952

. . . I had not a moment to report from D.C. It was a worse holocaust than the first time I was there if possible. I finally escaped to N.Y. for a session with Bernie Baruch & now I'm in Boston after a wonderful evening with Borden & Adlai and an Irish political party in Dorchester!

I must run now — the press are in the lobby — horrors — Gov. Devers [58] car is waiting. Adlai is impassive! But very strongly & deftly persuading about running for Pres. I'm off at 1:40 with John Fell for New Smyrna Beach until next Wed. then home. . . .

---

[55] In the New Hampshire presidential primary, held on March 11, 1952, Senator Estes Kefauver had defeated President Truman, 19,800 to 15,927.

[56] Ohio Senator Robert Taft had lost the New Hampshire primary to Dwight D. Eisenhower by 46,661 votes to 35,838. However, because Taft was a conservative, he was expected to fare better in the South.

[57] This handwritten letter is in the possession of Mrs. Dick.

[58] Paul Dever, governor of Massachusetts, 1949–1953.

To Mrs. Edison Dick [59]

March 15, 1952 — en route to Florida.

. . . I "reported" to you yesterday morning very hastily from Cambridge amid some disorder — and then carried the letter about all day after my custom! Finally John F deposited it for me in Phila airport en route Boston-Wash. The signals were changed at the last moment while I was in Gov. Dever's office in Boston due to a plea from Key West to come to D.C. en route to Florida for another secret conf. — this time with Murphy [60] — not HST. I obeyed — like a docile servant — and spent another evening on the griddle. The situation now seems to be that the Pres. just wants to know if I will accept the nomination if it comes to me. Evidently his long anxiety to withdraw — he wrote a statement 2 yrs. ago — has now reasserted itself with probably renewed pressures. My only escape — aside from flat refusal — now would appear to be to deflect the attention to [Averell] Harriman. But it probably won't arouse much party enthusiasm. In short the hour of decision seems to be approaching with inexorable certainty just when I thought it was all settled & he was going to announce on Mar. 29. [61] I'm in sore travail — torn between the clear desire to escape — at least this time — and the uniform and utter impossibility of practically everyone to believe that I would not accept a nomination I did nothing to get — did not want — with all there is at stake in re Taft.

Well enough of this everlasting & tiresome soul searching. At last John F. & I are side by side on our holiday together and appro[a]ching Fla. and a little peace, I hope. When he asked me this morning what I had said last night to "the men" I told him I had wriggled out again. In his simple direct way he said you did the right thing for *us*, but the wrong thing for the country — and that was that! I love him so I positively ache.

We'll be leaving the Ayres' on Wed. to fly back to Illinois. I wish I didn't feel like a condemned [man] with the noose tightening around my neck. I know more about those wretched people whom I reprieve from time to time while the law grinds on to their final doom. . . .

While in New Smyrna Beach, Florida, Stevenson wrote to Charles S. Murphy. Murphy was then with President Truman at the U.S. Naval Base, Key West.

[59] This handwritten letter is in the possession of Mrs. Dick.

[60] President Truman was in Key West, Florida, and Stevenson talked with his special counsel, Charles S. Murphy, in Washington, D.C.

[61] On March 29, 1952, President Truman announced for the first time publicly that he would not be a candidate for reelection. Stevenson on March 15 apparently thought the President would announce that he *would be* a candidate. See his letter to Charles S. Murphy, March 17, 1952, below.

To Charles S. Murphy [62]

March 17, 1952

Dear Mr. Murphy:

I have been thinking about our confused talk the other night. Let me try to summarize the situation as I see it.

1. I donot want to be a candidate for the nomination. I do not want to run for President, and I donot want to be President at this time. Ihave been in "politics" only three years; while Ihave learned a great deal, Ihave a great deal more to learn.

2. My ambitious program in Illinois is well under way, but there is much still to be done. I should like to do it, or at least *try* to do it, if the people of Illinois will let me.

3. Iam the unopposed Democratic candidate for reelection, and I am loath to abandon an objective I *do* want to work for one I *donot* honestly want.

Even if I did want to run for President (because of the extraordinary circumstances) I would find it uncomfortably difficult to carry water on both shoulders and run for the nomination for President while ostensibly running for Governor. What's more, I think the inconsistency and insincerity of my candidacy for Governor would be quickly apparent. Hence the only honest thing to do would be to resign my candidacy, either now before the Illinois primary or just afterward, with attendant political confusion in the Ill. Democratic ranks, yes, and loss, I'm afraid, of considerable personal following based on convictions about my dedication and suitability for the Illinois job. (Perhaps I should inject here that I will be a much stronger candidate for Governor of Illinois than for President, due to large independent and Republican support for Governor)

4. To the foregoing I could add misgivings about my strength, wisdom and humility to point the way to co-existence with a ruthless, inscrutable and *equal* power in the world. That I am, aside from the President, the best available man to assume this monstrous task seems to *me* grotesque. But I will quickly concede that *that* decision is for the President and those who have written and talked with me and share his view.

5. To the foregoing I *must* add, however, that my children seem to me altogether too young and undeveloped to subject to the pityless exposure of a national campaign, let alone the Presidency. Nor do they have the security and advantage of a stable family life.

You will see, then, that there are many considerations which inhibit me at this time — without mentioning the burdens of the Presidency now-

[62] This handwritten letter is in the Charles S. Murphy collection, the Harry S. Truman Library, Independence, Missouri.

adays which challenge human endurance and so few people comprehend.

Another four years, I hope as Governor of my beloved Illinois, and many of these obstacles will have vanished. As a more seasoned politician with my work in Illinois behind me, creditably, pray God, I might well be ready and eager to seek even the Presidency, if I then had anything desirable to offer.

But you will say *now* is the opportunity, *now* is the time — "the moving finger writes and having writ moves on." Indeed you may well say that now is the time that need and events converge in *duty*. The President has explained the situation to me with compelling logic. I donot — and I think he fully understands this — minimize the solemn implications in any retreat or indecision by the U.S. — Presidential or Congressional. Disintegration of the grand alliance, among other possible consequences, is an appalling reflection for me as it is for so many.

Our talk in Washington Friday night perplexed me a little because I was under the distinct impression from my last talk with the President that he was quite reconciled to running again. If I misunderstood him or if that is no longer the case and the question is whether I would accept the nomination at Chicago and do my level best to win the election, I should like to know it.

If that *is* the case and my decision *is* affirmative, I suppose in sincerity and good conscience I should say publicly and *before* he announces his decision not to run (if such *is* his decision) that all I want is to carry on my work in Illinois, that I have no other ambition, desire or purpose; that I will not seek the nomination; that if my party should nominate me anyway I would accept proudly and prayerfully, of course, confident that the people of Illinois would release me for a larger assignment that I didnot seek.

Thereafter I would continue to run for Governor and do my job with a single minded purpose, and I would have to regret most of the many speaking engagements outside Illinois. What I would do or should do about questions from the press on national matters I hardly know and I would need much advice.

If in these strange circumstances I should still be nominated I would work as hard as if I really wanted to be elected — and I probably would *want* to win *very much indeed* after I recovered from the shock!

Now if you have waded this deep and the President should feel that this offers a plausible solution, I should of course like to know so that I can reach a final decision and inform him at whatever time he prescribes. His confidence and interest in me is a compliment few Americans have ever received and I pray that he — and you — understand my torment, even if you may not wholly sympathize with it.

I am leaving here Wed. noon for Chicago and Springfield. I apologize for this disorderly letter written in the sun and the haphazard way I have marshalled my thoughts. It has helped *me* to try to get them on paper — but I pity you!!

Sincerely yours,

P.S. Reading this over, I trust it is clear that:

1. I think the President could best carry the Democratic banner himself.

2. I would personally prefer to stay out of the national arena this year.

3. If the President does not feel that he can or should run and is not content with [Senator Estes] Kefauver, [Senator Robert] Kerr or [Senator Richard] Russell, I will reach a prompt decision if he wants me, but à la [General Dwight D.] Eisenhower, I can't sincerely and consistently go out and campaign for the *nomination*. And I don't overlook the fact that in these circumstances it may not even be possible to get the nomination.

A.E.S.[63]

[63] Mr. Murphy replied from Key West on March 18, 1952, by handwritten letter:
Dear Governor —
I received your letter this morning and have talked with the President about it. He was much impressed by what you had to say — impressed in the sense that it confirmed and strengthened the high regard he already had for you. I do think it helped a great deal to clarify your situation in his mind. He said that he would like to think the matter over for a few days, and would then talk to me about it again. Until he does, there is little I can add about his views.
I would, however, like to add something on my own behalf. First, let me say I am honored that you should have written me such a letter. I have read it and reread it with great care. I have read it with my heart as well as my head.
The reasons you give for not wishing to seek the nomination are very compelling. I honestly wish I could say that you ought to be left alone. But the more I think about it, the more I am driven to the conclusion that if the President "propositions" you, on the basis indicated in your letter, you should accept. The reasons for this are more than compelling, they are overwhelming. I am not going to try to set them out here — you know most of them better than I do.
I will say this. If the President's final decision is not to run, it will be because he thinks such a decision is in the best interest of the country. I don't think that any of us can lightly challenge the basis of such a decision by him.
And in such a case, you are just "it." Circumstances converge on you. I would be glad for your sake to see the call put off for four years. But this will be one that can't wait. It will be a matter of duty, as I see it.
One word about a practical aspect of this matter. We get considerable information here — not as well collated as it should be, but impressive nevertheless — that you stand well enough in the eyes of your countrymen so that you would be the strongest candidate the Democrats could have, except perhaps the President himself. You can't ignore that either.
Thank you again for the letter.
I shall communicate with you again in the near future.
With all go[od] wishes, no matter how this turns out.

Sincerely,
CHARLES S. MURPHY

Stevenson, en route home from his holiday, wrote a postcard to the
Edison Dicks, who were vacationing with their children at Boca Grande,
Florida.

To Mr. and Mrs. Edison Dick [64]

March 19, 1952

My dear Dicks —

John Fell and I are in the air en route between Atlanta and Jacksonville headed for the frozen north after 3½ lovely days of sunshine and
sunburn! — and a little too much wind for good swimming.[65] I wish we
could have come to you and so does he but this is best. As for me, there
was a call from Key West this morning and the noose seems to be tight-
ning with a kind of inexorable certainty. — Love to the beloved children . . .

THE GUV.

Mr. and Mrs. Robert E. Hatcher, with their young son "Buzzy," lived
across the street from the mansion. On March 11, 1952, Mr. Hatcher sent
the Governor a snapshot of the lad with Artie, the Governor's Dalmatian,
showing them to be fast friends.

To Robert E. Hatcher

March 24, 1952

My dear Mr. Hatcher:

I was enchanted with your letter and the pictures of Buzzy and Artie.
I can't believe that somebody loves my wretched, wandering dog besides
me. I sometimes suspect that he has been a dreadful nuisance in the
neighborhood, which makes your regard for him the more gratifying.

Sincerely yours,

P.S. Tell Buzzy and his mother to come over to the Mansion any time
and they can have as much of King Arthur's time as they wish. Buzzy
might even get a cookie!

A.E.S.

---

[64] This handwritten postcard is in the possession of Mrs. Dick.

[65] The front of the card pictured a man snoozing on a small fishing craft in a calm
sea. Below the picture, the Governor wrote: "This doesn't resemble anything I've
been doing — except the posture — which is exact! ADLAI."

To Mrs. Ernest L. Ives [66]

March 24, 1952

Dear Buffie:

Thanks for your note and the elevating words. I wish I could get elevated and stay there!

The Dutch Smiths daughter, Wendy, gets married on April 12th and I will have my usual wedding present trouble unless you can rescue me in time. If you are not back here and have any suggestions, I am sure Mrs. Munn [67] would execute them. I should send her something quite nice I suppose.

My future is still uncertain but I am making a valiant struggle to stay in Illinois and thus far the noose has not choked me. But there are alarming symptoms of strangulation!

Love,

AD

Signals changed! Bill Blair has found something appropriate & you can forget it.

P.S. I had a splendid, quiet, healthy time in Florida with the Ayres and a lovely day yesterday with John Fell in Lake Forest.

To Lady Mary Spears

March 24, 1952

Dear Mary:

While in New York the other day I saw Betty [68] and she told me that your new book "You the Jury" was a Book-of-the-Month Club selection both in the United States and England. What with Rupert's [69] triumph, it looks as if you had won the sweepstakes. I am delighted and bubbling with pride and congratulations.

Affectionately

Reinhold Niebuhr wrote Stevenson early in 1952, urging him to enter the race for President. He was eager to come to Springfield for a talk, but, having fallen ill, could not make the trip. Later, having left the

---

[66] The original of this letter is in E.S.I., I.S.H.L. It is typewritten with the exception of the two paragraphs following the signature, which were added by hand.

[67] Margaret Munn, one of the mansion secretaries.

[68] Mrs. Ralph Hines, Lady Spears's niece.

[69] Rupert Hart-Davis, the English publisher and Lady Spears's son-in-law. The editors do not know what "triumph" Stevenson refers to.

hospital, he wrote that he was still unable to travel, and added: "It would be presumptuous on my part to press my views upon you, so I will merely express the hope that you will not resist the pressures upon you unduly, and allow your name to become a rallying point for the liberal opinion of America."

To Reinhold Niebuhr

March 27, 1952

Dear Dr. Niebuhr:

A letter from you is flattering to anyone, and especially to me. What you say is even more so, but somehow I cannot feel that I can in good conscience desert a job which I have sought. Moreover, I am a candidate for re-election here and I do not see how I can seek the Democratic presidential nomination even if I wanted it. Certainly a man should not run for two jobs at the same time.

Were I drafted, or threatened with a draft, I should have a most difficult decision to make. I pray that I can measure up to that horror if it should ever come, and I shall not forget what you have said to me.

My secretary reminds me that I have not thanked you for the copy of "The Irony of American History," [70] which arrived lately, together with a very thoughtful letter from Mrs. Niebuhr. I am most grateful, and what's more I shall actually read it!

Let me add that your rapid improvement is an enormous relief to me along with the vast army of your admirers.

Sincerely yours,

To Mrs. Edison Dick [71]

March 28, 1952

. . . The Post Dispatch started it all up again. Chaos hereabouts — and I'm stuck with the big "Meet the Press" television show on Sunday in Wash[ington]. Quelle vie! Guess I've got to say the awful words — No I won't accept the nomination and be damned by the Party forever — maybe. . . .

To Mrs. Edison Dick [72]

March 28, 1952

. . . I've pondered — between 1–2 A.M.! — the last analysis of the Dick

[70] Reinhold Niebuhr, *The Irony of American History* (New York: Scribner, 1952).
[71] This handwritten letter is in the possession of Mrs. Dick.
[72] This handwritten letter is in the possession of Mrs. Dick.

family. As evidence of a very positive state of mind on the general subject of nooses I enclose clippings re the big banquet here last week and my disclaimers of any ulterior ambitions. But somehow the talk goes on and on and I may be driven to answering the final question — would I accept a nomination I didn't want or seek? I'm still hopeful that it can be avoided and the ensuing charges of cowardice, playing safe, etc. But keep the analyses coming. I devour 'em!!

I hope all is well — warm sea — good surf, no wind, hot sun, etc etc. And tell little Eddie to bring me back a trophy something like the enclosed! . . .[73]

P.S. Horrors — [A mutual friend] and daughter & friend have just walked in and me with 2 weeks accumulation of mail & headaches & a speech set for tonight!!

Read the De Voto article in April Harpers.[74] Also my piece in Foreign Affairs.[75] Criticism welcome and the opportunities plentiful!!

When does my political manager & confessor return to Ill? . . .

On March 29, 1952, at the annual Jefferson-Jackson Day dinner in Washington, D.C., attended by Stevenson, President Truman announced that he would not be a candidate for reelection. "The stunned audience was silent for a moment. Then there arose loud groans of 'No, no!' from all over the hall. . . . If the crowd, bewildered by what it had just heard, stood uncertainly in the Armory, the reporters present knew what they wanted. With a deep sense of the needs of the time, they made a beeline for a man who stood talking to a little knot of people at the head table . . . Adlai Stevenson, Governor of Illinois."

Did he want the nomination, he was asked. His answer was no. "I am still a candidate for Governor of Illinois and nothing else."

Would he try to get the nomination? His answer was no.

Would he accept if nominated?

"I'll cross that bridge when I come to it," he replied.[76]

On returning to Illinois two days later, Stevenson made this statement on landing at Midway airport.[77]

[73] Not known what the enclosure was.
[74] Bernard De Voto, "Stevenson and the Independent Voter," *Harper's,* April, 1952.
[75] "Korea in Perspective," *Foreign Affairs,* April, 1952. This article is reprinted below.
[76] Walter Johnson, *How We Drafted Adlai Stevenson* (New York: Knopf, 1955), pp. 5–6.
[77] The statement is in Stevenson's handwriting. He gave it to John Madigan, political reporter for the Chicago *Herald-American,* at Midway airport in Chicago when he got off the plane on his return from Washington. The original is in the possession of Mr. Madigan.

March 31, 1952

My status is quo — or my quo is status.

Illinois looks even better to me after that battle royal in Washington.

I'm running for Governor of Illinois and Illinois is important — at least it is mighty important to me.

Of course the news from Arizona is very significant — *"Stevenson"* hopped to decisive victory over Taft, Truman and Eisenhower in a toad derby at Arizona state college.

But *I'm* hopping down to Manteno State Hospital and then to Springfield — right now. I hope the doctors don't suggest that I prolong my visit to Manteno.

To Harry S. Truman

March 31, 1952

Dear Mr. President:

I was stunned by your announcement Saturday night after that superb speech. I can only accept *your* judgment that the decision was right, although I had hoped long and prayerfully that it might be otherwise. As for myself, I shall make no effort to express the depth of my gratitude for your confidence. I hope you don't feel that I am insensitive to either that confidence or the honor you have done me. Perhaps the reasoning underlying my hesitance is unsound, but my heart is not.[78]

With the utmost respect and gratitude, I am

Faithfully yours,

Late in 1951, Stevenson was asked to contribute an article to Foreign Affairs, *setting forth his views on foreign relations. This article, entitled "Korea in Perspective," was published in the April, 1952, issue as the lead article.*

The strength of America is rooted in a great principle — individuals are an end, not a means. That is the American idea. Schools, colleges, labor unions, political parties and the Government of the United States exist for American men and women; never the other way round. The

---

[78] President Truman in his reply on April 4, 1952, stated that the Democratic party needed a person who would carry on the domestic and foreign policies started by Franklin D. Roosevelt and continued by Truman himself. He added that he hoped Stevenson would not remove himself completely from presidential consideration since the Democratic National Convention should have the right to choose the nominee.

corollary of the idea is that every individual must take responsibility for the whole. He must himself take responsibility for the safety and the wise development of his country, and for the selection of policies which determine its safety and progress. The basic requirement for the success of a democratic system of this sort is, of course, that individuals see their country's problems whole. In a word, they must have perspective.

This is especially true, and especially difficult to achieve, in problems of foreign relations. "Foreign policy," in the year 1952, covers the globe. In no other area is it so easy to have a picture of many single trees and no idea what the forest looks like. But the neatest description of a tree is not a dependable map for making one's way through a forest.

Gaining perspective on American foreign policy begins with gaining a view of America's position in the world — her position as a World Power. This can be indicated in half a dozen words: American interests, power and responsibilities are world-wide. Alongside this must be set two other basic facts which are revealed in any full view of the field of foreign policy. One is that a world-wide imperialist war is now being carried on by the Soviet Union and its Communist satellites. The other is the existence of a world-wide organization of states "united in strength to maintain international peace and security" — the United Nations. The relationship of these three great world forces — the United States, the Soviet Union and the United Nations — are the primary elements in the American problem of foreign policy today.

There is no possibility of doubting (and no reason for ignoring!) the fact that the Soviet objective is one world — one Communist world. Thanks to the interconnections of Soviet imperialism and international revolutionary Communism the Soviet Government is able always to pursue a dual strategy. The strategy is implicit in Bolshevik theory. From the day Lenin seized power in Russia — and indeed even earlier — his strategy was one of "double diplomacy:" a long-range policy, a short-range policy; a set of slogans for home consumption, a set of slogans for foreign confusion; warfare against the Russian people, warfare against all foreigners; political warfare and military warfare, simultaneous or interchangeable. No American foreign policy which does not allow for the over-all view of this Soviet duplicity, and which does not have both political and military weapons to counter it, can provide for our safety or enable us to carry out our responsibilities. The effort to achieve the over-all view is the basic task of Americans.

This is a campaign year in America, and we must expect over-simplification of issues and contradictory advice regarding them. Men, even responsible men, will wander far afield in search of votes. They will capitalize [on] every discontent, every prejudice, every credulity, even in the deadly serious business of foreign policy. Will we emerge from the ordeal of the campaign more aware of the true causes of our difficulties and the magnitude of the stakes involved? Or less aware? Will we emerge better prepared to turn with fortitude to the work in hand? Or worse prepared? These are the central questions which should be answered decisively by the elections.

II

The election campaign has not begun too well in this respect. What, for example, are we to make of the repeated charge that the Korean war is "Truman's war," that the President thrust the United States into it lightly, inadvisedly and against the best interest of the Republic, that it is a "useless" war, and that "we stand exactly where we stood three years ago"? What is the purpose of the petulant animosity shown in some quarters toward the United Nations, and of the despairing conclusion in others that the United Nations has "let us down" and has become more a danger to us than a source of strength? This kind of talk is deplorable because it belittles the heroic sacrifices of American and Allied soldiers and depreciates the value of an international effort that cost us an even greater war to achieve. But it seems to me more than deplorable. It seems to me dangerously misleading. What are we to think of statesmen who don't lead, but who mislead?

The purpose of such utterances apparently is to seek to make a single individual responsible for developments resulting from past actions taken by all the American people. Our present troubles do not stem from the bad judgment or weakness of particular individuals, any more than it would be true to say that any one man's insight has been responsible for our successes — which have been notable. Our setbacks and our victories are alike the products of the full sweep of recent history; and for that we are all of us responsible. Twice within twenty-five years this country felt compelled to intervene in wars to redress the balance of power in the world. At the close of World War II, with Britain exhausted and France demoralized, with German and Japanese power crushed, the United States and the Soviet Union stood virtually face to face, with other nations polarized around them. Imperial Russia, historically a great expanding Power, now heavily armed and equipped with the seductive weapon of revolutionary Communism, soon showed that she was on the move again, seizing weaker nations here, probing there, pressing relentlessly with propaganda and infiltration against the free world. During the Second World War, and with the experience of the prewar period fresh in their minds, our people concluded that isolation was no solution to the problem of security in a shrunken world. Their decision was reinforced by this rising spectre of another ruthless imperial power on the march. They concluded that the time to stop aggression, like a plague, was before it started; and that the way to do it was by organized community action.

It is now some time since we engaged in the formidable task of developing the community of free peoples — first through the United Nations, since the problem is inexorably world-wide; then through the North Atlantic Treaty Organization, designed to strengthen a particularly exposed salient — the Western European "peninsula" of the vast central "Heartland," as the great geographer [Sir Halford John] Mackinder called it; simultaneously by strengthening the important Organization of American States in our own hemisphere; and by numerous other treaties and agencies. The American response to the North Korean aggression, which was supplied and equipped by the Soviet Union and could not have occurred without its instigation or approval, was therefore neither erratic nor impetuous. It was part and parcel of a strategy of collective security which had been in the making for a long time and which had been urged, welcomed and agreed upon long since with virtual unanimity by the American people.

When North Korean forces invaded the Republic of Korea on June 25, 1950, with the full support of Peking and Moscow, most of us knew what was at stake. One of the men who took part in the long, anxious meeting at Blair House gave the simplest explanation of the decision: "This attack on South Korea is like Hitler's reoccupation of the Rhineland." Historians have for years commented on the tragic mistake of France in not ordering the instant mobilization of the French Army when Hitler's troops started marching — and on the shortsightedness of the British and others who failed to urge and support such action.

An American columnist pointed out in June 1950 that President Truman's decision, taken with the virtually unanimous support of the American people and their representatives in Congress, recalled the words of former Secretary of State Henry L. Stimson following what he termed "the tragedy of timidity" in the Far Eastern crisis of the early thirties: "I broke out and said," wrote Mr. Stimson, "that I was living in a world where all my troubles came from the same thing . . . where we are constantly shut in by the timidity of governments . . . and I said that the time had come when somebody has got to show some guts."

Senator [William] Knowland, Republican, of California, a frequent critic of Administration Far Eastern policy, was the first to take the floor of the Senate in support of the President's announcement: "I believe that, in this very important step the President of the United States has taken to uphold the hands of the United Nations and the free peoples of the world, he should have the overwhelming support of all Americans, regardless of their partisan affiliations." In similar vein the approving chorus swept the Congress and the country. One Member of Congress only opposed armed aid to the victims of Communist aggression — Representative [Vito] Marcantonio of New York, subsequently defeated for re-election.

To call Korea "Truman's war" distorts the entire historical significance of our prompt response through the United Nations to the cynical Communist challenge to the whole concept of collective peace and security — the concept which we are pledged to defend and which only the Soviet Union has an interest in destroying. Mr. Truman happened to be the President of the United States when the challenge came. Did the American people wish it to go unanswered, did they wish all hope for the new community of nations banded together in strength to limit war to collapse? *Time* magazine, with a backward glance at the equivocation of the League of Nations, summed up the matter simply: "This time, when the challenge came, the United States accepted it." So did the United Nations. To call this "Truman's war" is to deny the manifest common approval of our prompt action.

Inevitably there are differences of opinion now about the course of events in Korea. The decision to defeat the challenge of aggression by force brought grievous losses in blood and treasure. The first feeling of relief which welcomed the stern, swift action of two years ago has given way to criticism and impatience. In taking stock of where we now stand, however, we should not talk about our problems out of context.

There is nothing to be gained by what General Marshall used to call "fighting the problem." The problem is that the Soviet rulers and their Communist satellites consider themselves at war with us, but that we are not in fact at war with them. It is complicated by the further fact that war in their sense is waged interchangeably by military and political instruments. In view of this it is proper for us to ask ourselves what would have happened if we had "fought the problem" — that is, evaded it — in June 1950. What would have happened if the United States and the United Nations had ignored the Korean aggression?

I can venture a guess. Our friends throughout Asia and in the Pacific would with perfect reason have doubted our intention to resist Soviet design elsewhere in that area, and they would of necessity have taken the path of appeasement. Disillusionment would also have swept Western Europe at this impressive demonstration of Soviet-satellite power and of American indecision in the face of a direct challenge. Then would not the Soviet Union, having challenged us successfully in Korea, have followed that challenge with another? And still another? Munich would follow Munich. Our vacillation would have paralyzed our will and worked havoc in the community of like-minded nations. Then when we did succeed in pulling ourselves together we would have found it too late to organize a common front with our friends. I think there is good reason to believe that the resolute action by the United Nations forces in Korea not only gained time in the East but saved NATO in the West. The alternative was to surrender all positions of strength, to enfeeble if not destroy the grand alliance of the free — and then, perhaps, to resort in desperation to a general war when our moral, political and strategic position had been weakened disastrously.

There is, of course, no tidy solution to the Korean problem, precisely because it is only a part of the whole Soviet imperialist drive — an episode, really, in the sweep of history which relentlessly confronts freedom with thralldom. In a world where the objective of the Soviet Union is to eliminate every rival center of power we must measure our gains and our losses not in absolute terms but in relation to the over-all situation. The Soviet rulers themselves describe their struggle with the non-Soviet world as war. In Korea we have made plain to the Kremlin that we are not fooled by its use of catspaws, and that we recognize war fought at second hand when we see it. Our object is to convince them that other aggressions, disguised or direct, will meet the same response, and thus deter them from a perhaps fatal gamble. At the same time, by limiting the war in Korea, we hope to avoid a third general holocaust. We are trying to use force not only to frustrate our immediate antagonists in the hills of Korea but to preserve world peace. For that reason the full settlement of the Korean problem is likely to take a long time and to wait upon the settlement of many other issues. Once again, perspective.

It is possible, of course, that we may fail in our effort to keep the Korean fighting limited: for just as it takes only one to start a war, so it takes only one to prolong it. The aggressor is the one who decides whether or not the war he has started can be limited. But we have diligently and painfully sought to keep it from spreading. Given the terms of the problem, there is no guarantee of success. It simply seems wiser to pay large insurance premiums than to look forward to rebuilding after the fire.

Meanwhile, some of the positive gains of our policy thus far may properly be noted. Talk of the "uselessness" of the Korean war gained currency only when negotiations for an armistice dragged out, and after we had in fact accomplished the primary objective of stopping the aggression and driving the aggressors back from whence they came — across the 38th parallel. Assured of satisfactory armistice terms, we would have little purpose in continuing hostilities. But what sort of logic is it to say that because the continuation of the war does not serve our interests, the entire enterprise was futile from the start?

And while it is too early to make any final estimate of the Korean experience, it is also foolish and misleading to say we "stand exactly where we stood three years ago." The first reason is that the Korean engagement put the American rearmament effort into high gear. Having virtually obliterated our armed strength after World War II, we were slow to reconcile ourselves to the economic dislocation and sacrifices needed to recreate it. Proof that the Soviet Union would speed the advance of troops across a national frontier dissolved our reluctance. Now our increasing strength not only puts us in a better position to answer further military aggression. We also are in a position to conduct a bolder diplomacy — in other words, to take the initiative politically.

Second, our leadership in fighting aggression in Korea not only saved the moral and psychological defenses of Western Europe from possible disintegration but sparked the rapid build-up there of physical defenses. The demonstration that there could be successful resistance to the Soviet Union and imperial Communism gave the leaders of Europe hope and persuaded their peoples to accept more readily the burdens and risks of rearmament. It is routine politics for even the timid and faint of heart among us to talk about the necessity for American "leadership." Had America not in fact led, but shrunk from the challenge of Korea, would Europe have tackled the vast, costly and painful program of organizing Western defenses?

Third, the Soviet Union now knows that the path of conquest is mortally dangerous. The Korean aggression very likely was planned as merely the first of a series of military actions — initially by satellites, finally to be undertaken by the Soviet Union itself. If so, the lesson of Korea may be of historic importance. Speculation about possible adjustments in the thinking of the men in the Kremlin must be cautious. Perhaps for a time the Soviet Union will now content itself with manoeuvres in the cold war; or perhaps Western strength of will is to be further tested by some other military challenge; or perhaps Stalin and his partners will reason that a full-scale war (which Communist theory foreshadows) had best be waged in the immediate future rather than when the armament programs of the West become more fully effective. It can be argued that Stalin, in his old age, will never risk the loss of the empire he has built up; but it can also be said that he may believe what his sycophants tirelessly chant — that he is "the greatest commander of all times and peoples" * — and that if the "terrible colli-

* *Pravda,* November 6, 1951.

sions" prophesied in Communist dogma are indeed to come, then they had best come while he is still alive. We dare not tie our policies to any one assumption regarding Soviet intentions. Whatever those intentions are, however, the Soviet miscalculation in Korea will make them harder of fulfillment.

Fourth, our support of the first great collective military effort of the United Nations to resist aggression demonstrated that the organization is adaptable to the role of enforcement as well as that of conciliation. In the crisis there emerged proof of the viability of the concept of collective security, a fact of inestimable importance for the security of every free country — including our own. Sixteen countries contributed fighting forces. The policies of the free nations have been concerted consistently in the votes relating to Korea. While troops of the Republic of Korea and the United States have been obliged to carry the main burden of the fighting and we may properly regret the absence of more help from others, we should not overlook the fact that the responsibility for resistance to Communist military aggression in certain other areas is borne more by others than by ourselves. If another showdown is provoked elsewhere, the system of collective security is in better shape now to meet it than it was before June 1950. In short, while Korea has not proved definitively that collective security *will* work, it has prevented the Soviet Union from proving that it *won't* work. And the Korean experience, moreover, has hastened the development of the General Assembly of the United Nations as an agency of enforcement, free from the Soviet veto.[79]

Fifthly, we may record that the successful resistance in Korea has contributed greatly to the successful negotiation of a Treaty of Peace with Japan [1951], as well as of arrangements satisfactory to us regarding the future security of that country. A failure on our part to give evidence of a willingness to act in a time of crisis would not have encouraged the Philippines, Australia, New Zealand and Japan to enter into the recently negotiated [1951] network of the Pacific security treaties.

One further national advantage from this "useless" war deserves at least to be mentioned. We have learned vital military lessons in Korea. I am not competent to discuss improvements in tactics and weapons, nor would it be appropriate here to do so. But a more effec-

[79] The Soviet Union was boycotting the Security Council on June 25, 1950, when the Security Council denounced the North Korean attack on South Korea as aggression and on June 27, 1950, when the Security Council called on all UN members to support the Republic of Korea. After the Soviet Union returned to the Security Council, the UN General Assembly adopted the "Uniting for Peace Resolution" which empowered the Assembly to act in similar situations in case the Security Council was blocked by the veto of a permanent member.

tive use of forces and armaments as a result of long testing under actual combat conditions is to be counted as an important residual return on our investment in this savage conflict.

III

So much for this historic frustration of Communist military conquest. Soviet policy, however, is dual. Indispensable as was the United Nations for the repulse of the aggression in Korea, it is needed even more in the political struggle in which we are engaged.

Obviously the United Nations has not fulfilled all the high hopes that some people entertained when it was founded. The idea that it would automatically usher in an era of sweetness and light was exaggerated at the start, as was soon demonstrated when Soviet imperialism made plain that it was determined to prevent the organization of the world on any but its own terms. But again look at the woods, not the trees. Although the United Nations has worked haltingly, at times badly — it has worked. Since the present *world-wide* coalition of free peoples is inconceivable without a central forum and instrument for discussion and adjustment, it remains an indispensable part of our foreign policy. The problem is to make the organization function more perfectly. Granted that it has done little to adjust the differences between the Soviets and the free world: so long as the Soviet rulers prosecute their dual war — against their own people and against all outsiders — there is no reason to expect that it will. Even so, it maintains at least formal contact between the two worlds. Our willingness to keep the door open for talk and negotiation is essential evidence for our friends (who stand more deeply in the shadow of the Russian fist than we do) that we will accept any reasonable opportunity to better relations and avoid all-out war.

Again, the United Nations is indispensable as an agency for concerting policies among the free states, including (as we found in the case of Korea) enforcement action. The bulk of the members of the General Assembly are free nations. In spite of the discouraging and frustrating debate with the Russians — or perhaps thanks in part to their recalcitrant and dogmatic postures — policies have been developed in the General Assembly to cope better with many of the perils to economic stability and international justice. Obviously not all international questions need or should be put before the United Nations; and certainly we should use our influence to preserve a safe boundary line between those domestic affairs which are our own concern and the external affairs which are of concern to all. These are matters for careful study and progress by stages. But surely to prevent a trespass it is not sensible to shoot the watchman; nor to burn down the barn to roast a pig.

The audible yearning to escape from it all, the murmurs and cries of disdain for the "meddlers," the "globalists" and the "foreigners" now sometimes heard in our midst, are strangely familiar. Are they groans from the ghost of America First, still looking for an unassailable Gibraltar, safe from assault by men — or ideas? I doubt if many Americans will be drawn into a renewal of that wishful search. I think the eagle, not the ostrich, will continue to be the American emblem.

The reality of the matter is that American power is going to be preponderant on our side of the Iron Curtain for many years to come, and that without this concentration of power there would be no possibility of pulling the free world together or providing for an effective common defense. Our friends abroad know this. And the reality is likewise that a successful military defense, and a successful political advance, depend on the cooperation of a large number of governments — in the Far East and the Middle East, in Europe and in this hemisphere. More, our ability to take the initiative depends not simply on the cooperation of governments, but on the good will of peoples who support these governments. We live in a new world — a world where the stronger need the help of the weaker!

We should not be too surprised that the same nations that formerly were alarmed at our isolationism are now concerned about how we will use our power. Just because of our strength we are a target for much unjust resentment. Surely we can call upon a sufficiently long historical perspective, and a sufficiently intelligent understanding of human nature, not to be too much surprised by that. Men in lands which have recently freed themselves from old tyrannies know all too well the temptations of power. Their fear that we may fall into old errors is not unnatural. And indeed, who among us would dare say that we do not have much to learn? No single nation, viewing the world from a particular perspective, can have a monopoly of insight. We must take the criticisms as they come — sometimes as fair warning — and redouble our efforts to develop mutual policies based on adequate understanding between sovereign but interdependent partners.

Sovereign international authorities over a wide area, or fully unified political councils in the whole of the free world, are not in prospect. We must concert our policies with those of our friends by the instruments available. Our aim should be to improve the machinery for mutual give and take, both in the United Nations and in regional agencies. Fortunately, the menace of the Soviet Union tends to promote a common view among those marked out as prey; and it can further be said that despite differences in approach and emphasis, much of the free world now shares a wide range of political and economic interests which move it in the direction of unity. The United Nations is an invaluable instrument for harmonizing differences in those interests. It and other agencies such as the North Atlantic Treaty Organization have given us — and our friends — considerable experience in this unceasing task of mutual accommodation. The United States will find support among peoples in the free states to the degree that they believe that we do not simply consult our own interests but give consideration to their interests as well — that we in truth have a "decent respect for the opinions of mankind." Other nations have a reciprocal obligation to give weight to our interests too. There is no doubt that our power gives us an advantage in this process. But neither is there room to doubt that if we wish allies who will go forward with us with courage and fortitude into the risks of the future, they must be willing and confident allies.

Let us also remember that the alternative to the United Nations is not a vacuum. There would at once be formed another "world organization." The Soviet Union, true to its policy of duplicity, has this alternative organization already in hand — presumably to be based on the "World Peace Council," formed on November 22, 1950, at the "Second World Peace Conference" in Warsaw. Professor Frederic Joliot (known better as Joliot-Curie through his appropriation of a revered name on which he has no claim of blood) [80] presided, as "President of the Bureau," at the most recent meeting, in Vienna last November. Various trained seals were brought from all corners of the world. For the gist of the program one can take almost any of the old Marxist fighting slogans and substitute the word "peace" for the word "revolution." In Soviet double-talk they mean the same.

IV

The burden of my argument, then, based on the meaning of our experience in Korea as I see it, is that we have made historic progress toward the establishment of a viable system of collective security. To deprecate our large and decisive share in that undertaking as "useless" is both mischievous and regressive. It will stiffen no backs, lift no hearts and encourage no one except our enemies.

The particulars of the forward political movement which our successful acceptance of the Soviet challenge in Korea has made possible for us would form the beginnings of a new analysis, not a conclusion for this one. What is incontrovertible, I think, is that America needs

[80] He had married Irène Curie, daughter of the discoverers of radium, and added her name to his own.

and wants allies. I think most Americans know this. I think we believe that the redress in the balance of power in the world must be completed, and quickly. I think we believe that the great experiment in collective security on which we embarked in 1945 is still in the long run our best chance for peace. I think we believe that international cooperation is more than elocution. In short, I think most of us have convictions about the position of the United States in the world today and accept the risks and responsibilities inherent in that position. The nature of the American decision was shown — is shown — in Korea. Shall we retreat from that decision? Shall we go it alone? Or shall we go forward with allies? When our experience in Korea has been placed in perspective, this remains the issue behind the dust and turmoil of this election year.

To Mrs. Edison Dick [81]

April 14, 1952

. . . But do you really think I am not thankful? And do you really think I magnify my misfortunes when there are none — or very few? I want so much to be worthy, to earn, to keep, all the things I have to be thankful for. I feel so *inadequate*, so unworthy. I really want so hard to do the right thing, the wise thing, God's work, if you please. . . .

After the Illinois primary on April 8, 1952, in which he won the Democratic nomination for a second term as governor, Stevenson took a determined step to remove himself from the presidential race. He issued the following statement on April 16. [82]

I have been urged to announce my candidacy for the Democratic nomination for President, but I am a candidate for Governor of Illinois and I cannot run for two offices at the same time. Moreover, my duties as Governor do not presently afford the time to campaign for the nomination even if I wanted it.

Others have asked me merely to say that I would accept a nomination which I did not seek. To state my position now on a prospect so remote in time and probability seems to me a little presumptuous. But I would rather presume than embarrass or mislead.

[81] This handwritten letter is in the possession of Mrs. Dick.
[82] The text is based on a mimeograph copy prepared by the Governor's office for release to the press.

In these somber years the hopes of mankind dwell with the President of the United States. From such dread responsibility one does not shrink in fear, self-interest or humility. But great political parties, like great nations, have no indispensable man, and last January, before I was ever considered for the Presidency, I announced that I would seek re-election as Governor of Illinois. Last week I was nominated in the Democratic primary. It is the highest office within the gift of the citizens of Illinois, and its power for good or ill over their lives is correspondingly great. No one should lightly aspire to it or lightly abandon the quest once begun.

Hence, I have repeatedly said that I was a candidate for Governor of Illinois and had no other ambition. To this I must now add that in view of my prior commitment to run for Governor and my desire and the desire of many who have given me their help and confidence in our unfinished work in Illinois, I could not accept the nomination for any other office this summer.

Better state government is the only sound foundation for our Federal system, and I am proud and content to stand on my commitment to ask the people of Illinois to allow me to continue for another four years in my present post.

I cannot hope that my situation will be universally understood or my conclusions unanimously approved.

I can hope that friends with larger ambitions for me will not think ill of me. They have paid me the greatest compliment within their gift, and they have my utmost gratitude.[83]

To Harry S. Truman

April 16, 1952

Dear Mr. President:

I attach a copy of the statement I have felt obliged to issue in response to the insistent demands. I had hoped to speak to you about it at Omaha this afternoon but there was no convenient opportunity.

This is the hardest thing I have ever had to do, but, as I told you at

---

[83] Stevenson struggled with this statement. There exists a rough draft in his handwriting, undated, with deletions and interlineations (now in A.E.S., P.U.L.). It begins with the flat statement: "I would not accept the nomination if offered me," and continues: "The burdens of this office, the demands of leadership and the solemnity (dread) of the decisions confronting the next President dwarf the imagination. I feel (do not feel) no confidence that I have the strength, the wisdom or the humility (reverence) (grace) (courage) (self confidence) (resources of the spirit) (serenity) (goodness) (virtue) (divine guidance) to (lead the way) (guide us) to coexistence with an inscrutable, hostile and *equal* power in the world. (I marvel that anyone does) (has such self confidence) This is a new and fearsome postion for Am[erica]. Its Pres[ident]. will be sorely tried. May God show him the way. . . ."

Blair House, I could see no best way out of my dilemma, and this seemed to me the right way in all the circumstances. Further agonizing debate since your announcement has only fortified this conclusion.

I know you will be disappointed with me.[84] That you are is my greatest distress — and also my greatest honor. I pray that some time I can serve your confidence better.

Faithfully yours,

The New York Times *observed that Stevenson seemed "effectively to have closed the door to his nomination." Arthur Krock the same day pointed out in the* Times *that President Truman's announcement that he would not run again and Stevenson's statement meant that the Democrats would have their first open convention in twenty years.*

On April 17, Stevenson attended a New York Democratic State Committee dinner in New York City honoring Averell Harriman, feeling that in view of the statement he had just made, his presence would not be misunderstood.[85] But his brief remarks rekindled interest in him, and the next day the New York Post *said: "The man who said he could not accept the presidential nomination . . . was the one speaker whose oratory, wit and liberal commentary evoked a spontaneous and prolonged response. . . . The dinner for Harriman may come to be remembered as the starting point for a real draft-Stevenson movement."*

Stevenson's remarks to the New York Democratic State Committee dinner follow.[86]

I am told that I am here at the head table by misrepresentation and fraud; that you invited a candidate for President but got a candidate for Governor instead. I feel like the weary old Confederate soldier, un-armed, ragged and asleep, whom some zealous young Union soldiers captured. "Git up, Reb, we got you now," they shouted. "Yeah," the old fellow said, "and it's a heck of a git you got."

[84] The President in his reply of April 22, 1952, remarked that he regretted that Stevenson had made the statement. He added that had Stevenson not closed the door, he would have received the nomination.

[85] Prior to issuing his statement of April 16, Stevenson felt he should not attend the dinner because of the continuing attention he was receiving as a potential candidate. On the insistence of Mr. Paul Fitzpatrick, New York State Democratic chairman, who pointed out that he would be more conspicuous by his absence than by attending as originally planned, Stevenson agreed to appear. Letter from Stevenson to Frank E. Karelsen, Jr., April 10, 1952.

[86] The text is based on a mimeograph copy prepared by the Governor's office for release to the press.

But the Democratic Governor of Illinois is profoundly honored to be here tonight, deceitfully or otherwise, among the Democrats of New York and their distinguished guests while you pay tribute to Averell Harriman. It is not often that a midwesterner has a chance to shed a little light on New York — even four minutes worth!

This year we must select a new President of the United States — as well as the old Governor of Illinois, I hope! The burdens of the Presidency dwarf the imagination. And the next President will have something more to face than most any of his predecessors — guidance toward coexistence in this world with a ruthless, inscrutable and equal power in the world. This is a new and fearsome position for the United States, and its President will be sorely tried.

Perhaps it isn't exactly the thing to say to a partisan meeting, but who wins this fall is less important than what wins — what ideas, what concept of the world of tomorrow, what quality of perception, leadership and courage.

For a Democratic victory the omens are good. The Republican party is bereft of common purpose, policy, principles or program — as usual. I don't know what the Republican party is for, and the only thing I am sure the leaders are against is Democrats! Torn with irreconcilable conflicts between men and issues, between a vaporous yearning to retreat to a dear, dead past and the urge to restate and reassert the liberal traditions of its birth — rudderless between forthright conservatism, hopeless reaction and flattering "me-tooism," the Republican party reminds me of the mule who starved to death standing between two stacks of hay trying to make up its mind which to eat.

It was a mule, not a donkey, because the Democratic party knows what it wants for America and how to get it, and the people know where we stand. There have been mistakes, failures and disappointments, and there may be more. But the objectives, the goals, at home and abroad, have been consistent and clear — and, to the everlasting credit of Franklin D. Roosevelt and Harry S. Truman, they have been right!

The twenty years of Democratic direction of the United States have been a period of change as rapid and violent as any in history. Forces have been at work that shattered many societies. But we contained them within the American system of democratic government, popular control and civil liberty. There has been no break in the continuity of our institutions. We have steered by the same course we have been following for 150 years. The party that achieved this triumph of stability in a time of world revolution did so not by pretending that there were short cuts to safety, to prosperity, freedom or social justice, or that they could be bought at a discount. It must not minimize the difficulties or the dangers now.

And during these two decades the United States has risen triumphantly from depression and misery to the pinnacle of prosperity and power. No nation ever reached such a position of world leadership and responsibility with so little premeditation — or so reluctantly. Like bits of a chrysalis, bits of our reluctance still cling to us — a recurrent inability to realize our strength, to ignore its implications, to avoid its responsibilities. But our purpose has been steady and our direction firm. Our goal is peace and every time — from Greece and Turkey to this day — by its deeds a great nation has accepted the full responsibility of its power and its peril; has accepted the leadership from which there is no escape.

We can be proud of our 20 years of faith and service in the American way. But we must look forward, not back. Rather we lose this election than mislead the people by representing as simple what is infinitely complex, or by representing as safe what is infinitely precarious. For there are no painless solutions to war, inflation, communism, imperialism, hunger, fear, intolerance, and all the hard, stubborn problems that beset us.

And no living American knows more about them, or has given more wisdom, patience and relentless effort to their solution, at home and abroad, during the whole span of these two great decades than a great Democrat, your guest of honor, Averell Harriman.

Prior to the dinner honoring Harriman, Stevenson stopped in Chicago on April 15 to open the White Sox baseball season. He returned to Springfield from Chicago that evening, and the following day flew to Omaha, Nebraska.[87] He then went on to New York to the Harriman dinner and returned to Springfield on April 18, when this letter was written.

To Alicia Patterson [88]

. April 18, 1952

. . . En route back to Illinois after an almost frightening 24 hrs in N.Y. for the big Democratic clam bake at the Waldorf — complete with politicians, big & small, radio, TV & whiskey. I like Ill more & more & my once maddening problems there are positively inviting after these forays into the outside world. Its been another awful week — agonizing last minute conferences & pressures from everywhere to "announce"; the zero hour of decision, writing the statement, opening the baseball season in Chicago, then Spfd., then Omaha, then N.Y. & now back I hope to 48 hrs of peace & serious work over the week-end — then to Dallas on

[87] Stevenson's schedule does not show what engagement he had in Omaha on April 16.

[88] This handwritten letter is in the possession of Adlai E. Stevenson III.

Monday for a full dress foreign affairs speech (not yet written); [89] back just in time for the State Convention where they have threatened to adopt a resolution repudiating my "statement"; declaring me still the "favorite son" & starting up the whole wretched business all over again. I think I did allright in N.Y. at the banquet for Averill [Averell Harriman] — too well for my own peace & security from renewed pressure which broke out after the meeting, but I stood fast, privately as well as publicly. [Estes] Kefauver didn't distinguish himself & got a little tight afterward to boot, I'm told. Harriman did well I thought, but not well enough for the politicians' taste. I "sold him" as vigorously as I could — and as a President I really believe he would be the best Democratic possibility, indeed a very good President, but as a candidate I suppose they're right and he would be tough to elect against Taft, let alone Ike.

Dorothy Shiff [90] invited me to a party at her house afterward but I couldn't go & didn't see her in the mob scene. Lloyd Garrison & sundry other friends were there, all full of admiration for my statement and rebukes for my decision. I hope you, at least, agree that it made some sense and that having decided to run for Governor before the Presidential boom started I was in good conscience bound to run for Governor, to lie in the bed I had made. . . .

A

While Stevenson was in New York he called on Trygve Lie, Secretary-General of the United Nations.

To Trygve Lie

April 19, 1952

Dear Trygve:

I was obliged to leave in such haste that I had no proper opportunity to say goodbye. It was a wonderfully interesting experience and I am everlastingly grateful to you for your courtesy — not to mention the opportunity to see you again. My admiration for your balance, good judgment and dedication to your difficult task is boundless.

With affectionate personal regards and warmest thanks, I am

Cordially yours,

[89] Stevenson spoke to the Dallas Council on World Affairs on April 22, 1952. The speech is not included in this volume, since its central theme is the same as that of the *Foreign Affairs* article.

[90] Dorothy Schiff, publisher of the New York *Post.*

On April 19, after Stevenson had returned to Springfield, he discovered
a call from Averell Harriman that he had failed to return while in New
York.

To Averell Harriman

April 19, 1952

Dear Averell:

I was obliged to leave earlier than I expected, and accordingly I had no
opportunity to get in touch with you on Friday. Indeed, I only found
your telephone call among the papers that my secretary brought back to
Springfield.

I am not much of a politician nor can I presume to foretell probable
developments. At all events, I am delighted the New York delegation
has taken an emphatic position and I shall see what can be done to at
least keep the situation here fluid.

Cordially yours,

To Edward D. McDougal, Jr.[91]

April 21, 1952

Dear Ed:

In my recent agony I lost track of you and your illness. I am glad to
hear by your letter from Arizona that all is well.

I enclose a copy of the [April 16] statement I finally felt obliged to
issue and I hope you don't disapprove too emphatically.

Next week-end is a little complicated by virtue of the Democratic State
Convention and the arrival of Governor and Mrs. Schricker [92] who will
be staying with me. The following week I must go to Oregon and California, so I am afraid our reunion must be deferred.

Love to Kate [93] and my heartfelt thanks for your thought of me in my
journey through the wilderness.

Yours,
ADLAI

*Playwright Robert E. Sherwood wrote Stevenson on April 14, 1952,
that Herbert Agar and Barry Bingham had put the question to him
whether, if he were an adviser to Stevenson, he would urge him to be-*

[91] The original of this letter is in the possession of Mr. McDougal.
[92] Henry F. Schricker, governor of Indiana, 1941–1945 and 1949–1953.
[93] Mrs. McDougal.

come a candidate for the Democratic nomination for President in 1952. He wrote that he would urge Stevenson to announce his acceptance of the nomination if tendered by the convention. He had complete confidence that Stevenson would win the election against any Republican other than General Eisenhower. It was his opinion that it was obligatory, in any case, for the Democratic party to name their strongest possible candidate — Stevenson.

To Robert E. Sherwood

April 21, 1952

Dear Bob:

I have read and re-read your letter to me which came just as I was completing the attached statement.

It has been a frightful struggle, with conflicting advice and pressure. Somehow, I have a feeling that seems to be a little novel in such circumstances, that one should keep one's commitments — even politicians! — and my prior commitment was to run for re-election as Governor of Illinois.

I hope you can understand, if not approve, of what I felt obliged to do — and by obliged I don't mean just what I wanted to do either.

You have flattered me profoundly by writing to me and I shall value your letter always.

Sincerely yours,

P.S. I am still hoping and praying that the Sherwoods may find their way to Illinois.

To Mrs. Edison Dick [94]

April 21, 1952

. . . And just now — Sunday night 12:15 — I'm feeling so low & futile & dissatisfied with myself, my work, my campaign, my speech for Dallas, my life, I miss the boys so, the outdoors, that even you would have trouble bucking me up. All of which has nothing to do with humility — no — and not self pity either! Just exhaustion I suppose. Do you ever yearn for the outdoors, for the wild flowers, for the spring, for the green grass and the sky — so you could cry. Thats the way I was today — locked in my cell struggling to write something, without ideas, without knowledge, solutions — even words! Kay Field called this morning about something and told me how beautiful it was at the place, the grass, the

[94] This handwritten letter is in the possession of Mrs. Dick.

flowers popping out — and I found myself splashing tears on the desk! [95]

Tomorrow Dallas — back Wed. Why don't you come down Wed. and talk to Forsyth & Funk [96] about a Women's Division [97] . . . and why didn't you tell me you took a taxi to Peoria? Howard Long, the chauffeur, could have taken you. Really, what you won't do for the welfare dept — and the Governor. . . .

Alan Cranston [98] has been around most of the day — I don't know why & haven't been able to give him much time.

To Frank E. Karelsen, Jr.[99]

April 22, 1952

My dear Mr. Karelsen:

I do appreciate your letter of April 19, and the kind things you have to say about my talk at the New York State Democratic dinner. As always, the trip to New York was great fun and I did enjoy the opportunity to take part in an important function of the Democratic Party in your State. You have an extremely vigorous and intelligent group of people leading the Democratic Party in New York, and I am proud to have been associated with one of their activities.

I appreciate also the friendly spirit which prompts you to suggest that I reconsider my statement of last week. I am certain there will be no occasion to do so, and, in any event, I am convinced, too, that the Democratic Party will win this fall no matter who its nominee may be. I think my contribution to that result can best be made by trying to put Illinois in the Democratic column.

Sincerely yours,

To Doris Fleeson [100]

April 24, 1952

Dear Doris:

I think this is my first letter to a "columnist." Perhaps I have *appeared* "indecisive" because I had hoped that the situation would blow over,

[95] Mr. and Mrs. Marshall Field IV were living on Stevenson's farm at Libertyville.
[96] Donald Forsyth and Donald Funk of the Stevenson for Governor Committee in Springfield.
[97] Mrs. Dick was cochairman with Hermon D. Smith for the Stevenson for Governor Committee, Chicago.
[98] A California businessman, active in Democratic politics in that state and later elected to the U.S. Senate.
[99] Partner in the New York law firm of Karelsen & Karelsen. The original is in the possession of Mr. Karelsen.
[100] The original is in the possession of Miss Fleeson.

but there are many who could testify that there has been no indecision from the start. Moreover, although I hope I am a "friend" of General Eisenhower I have met him only twice, once at the Navy Headquarters in Naples in 1943, of which meeting I am sure he would have no recollection, and again as one of the large audience when he spoke at the Commercial Club in Chicago in 1947 or 1948.

Perhaps it is naive, but I have a very strong feeling that commitments should be kept — even among politicians! — and my prior commitment was to run for Governor. Finally, I think the Democrats have an almost better than even chance of winning with a good candidate, regardless of the Republican nominee. I meant what I said at the New York dinner.

Warm regards, and my apologies for contradicting such a good friend and accurate reporter!

Sincerely yours,

ADLAI

A distant cousin of Stevenson's, Adlai E. Harbeck, on April 23, 1952, sent the Governor his thanks for "a personal service which you have rendered to me. . . . my first name has always been a source of minor irritation. My mail regularly comes addressed 'Dear Madam' and General Batista of Cuba once asked me if my people came from the Middle East. As a result of your activities this situation has changed and my first name, instead of being a source of vague annoyance, is a matter of considerable pride."

To Adlai E. Harbeck

April 25, 1952

Dear Adlai:

That is the most subtle compliment I have yet received! I too have been harassed with "Dear Madam" and sundry insults, conscious and unconscious, all my life.[101] If fortuitous circumstances of late have re-

[101] In later years, when he was at the United Nations, Stevenson recounted this story to his friend Mrs. John Currie: One day when he was alone in the Executive Mansion the doorbell rang. He answered it himself and there on the doorstep was Jack Benny holding a box containing an orchid corsage. When he saw the Governor he clapped his hand to his forehead dramatically and said, "Don't tell me Adlai is a male!" Then he very solemnly and deliberately opened the corsage box and began eating the orchid.

Mrs. Currie had many conversations with Stevenson, of which she kept full notes, copies of which she made accessible to the editors.

When Mr. Benny was asked by Carol Evans to confirm the story he wrote: "This of course is a gag that the late Adlai Stevenson pulled — while I was in the audience."

lieved our situation I am enchanted. It is about the only major comfort in the whole harrowing business.

Cordially yours,

P.S. Did you ever see the verse that Mark Twain wrote once upon a time about the pronunciation? It goes like this:

> *Philologists pray and lexicographers bray,*
>   *But the best they can do is to call him Adlay;*
> *Yet at political clambakes when accents are high,*
>   *Fair Harvard's not present and they call him Adlie!*

Mrs. William Grigsby, who worked in Stevenson's 1948 campaign office, was asked by him to serve in a position with the Illinois Industrial Commission. She was subsequently promoted to be its secretary and security officer. Friction between her and Mr. B. Jay Knight, commission chairman, moved her to write the Governor offering to submit her resignation.

To Mrs. William A. Grigsby

April 25, 1952

Dear Marjorie:

I have your note, and again I am afraid there has been some misunderstanding — or rather a great deal. In all of my conversations with Mr. Knight he always speaks about you with the utmost admiration, confidence, and indeed dependence.

I think it best just to drop it all and recognize that we all have our difficulties and that he may have a little feeling that you are running the show for him. You know how we males are!

For my part, and his too I am sure, there is nothing but gratitude for the splendid work you have done and your devotion to a better quality of public administration. Just take it easy!

With warm personal regards to you and Bill,[102] and I hope that we can see something of each other again if this dreadful turmoil ever subsides a bit.

Sincerely yours,

P.S. I think they have worked out a satisfactory holding arrangement on the matter we discussed the other day until the legislature can clarify the Act.[103]

A.E.S.

[102] Mr. Grigsby.
[103] Not known what Stevenson refers to.

Poet Carl Sandburg wrote Stevenson on April 25, 1952, that he had been "carrying around the speeches made at the Harriman dinner. Your speech has paragraphs and sentences that I have read several times — profound thinking, subtle feeling, exactitude of phrasing — great utterance for this hour and for many tomorrows. . . . It is a hell of a commentary on something or other that you are the only one of the string of candidates being mentioned who seems aware that the next president, if he is in some degree sensitive, will live in a Golgotha."

To Carl Sandburg

April 29, 1952

Dear Carl:

Many, many thanks for your letter. When Sandburg carries around Stevenson's speeches, it's news! — or perhaps it is sinister evidence of a pitiful deterioration in Sandburg's literary tastes.

Anyway, I am bursting with pride.

I am so glad that you share my bewilderment that anyone should *want* to be President. I have not chosen to think that I have any more humility than the next man, but the conceit and arrogance and self-confidence of some of these people fill me with amazement — yes, and a touch of envy too. I have thought of Sing Sing and Alcatraz, but your Golgotha is a better description of the next President's abode.

My affectionate thanks.

Yours,

During the Korean War the Illinois National Guard was activated as the 44th Division and underwent intensive training during the spring of 1952 at Camp Cooke in Southern California. Stevenson, expecting to follow his usual custom of an annual inspection of the Guard, decided to accept speaking engagements in Oregon and California before proceeding to Camp Cooke. On May 1 he spoke in Portland, Oregon, on May 5 in San Francisco, and finally reached Camp Cooke on May 6, where he remained through May 8. En route he stopped in Santa Barbara, California, on the invitation of Thomas M. Storke, owner and publisher of the Santa Barbara News-Press. He returned to Springfield on May 12.

To Thomas M. Storke [104]

May 13, 1952

My dear Mr. Storke:

My West Coast odyssey ended with a couple of bright days in Pasadena, with a little painless politics [105] and a lot of old friends, and now I am back in my torture chamber in Springfield. The natural process of undirected assortment of my memories and impressions of that fabulous land from Portland to Pasadena somehow leaves Santa Barbara and the Storkes on top.

I am still marveling over those nine generations in California and saying less and less of my children's six in Illinois.

I shall long remember my visit with you and the luncheon with Charles [106] and his charming wife, not to mention your extraordinary newspaper and your many courtesies. Even if that enchanted drive through the mustard yellow mountains to the endless madness of Los Angeles had not been beautiful and exciting, the chauffeur and his wisdom and endearing ways would have made it most memorable — and I will be back!

Cordially yours,

P.S. *I* could show *you* New Salem, the restoration of the Lincoln Village near Springfield!

A.E.S.

Marnie Dick, daughter of the Edison Dicks, was attending Bennett Junior College, in South Millbrook, New York, when this letter was written.

---

[104] The original is in the possession of Mr. Storke.

[105] On this trip reporters regularly asked him whether he would accept a draft at the Democratic Convention. In Portland he said: "I cannot speculate about hypothetical situations. But I don't believe there ever has been a genuine draft of an unwilling man for the presidential nomination by either party. I doubt if such a thing is possible. That is all I can say on this story — I regret that I cannot give you a good story." When a reporter persisted, Stevenson replied: "Why don't you put that question in German? It has been put in every other language, it seems."

Two days later when a reporter asked what he would say if the convention attempted a draft, he said: "I had better wait until the improbable arrival of that situation before I comment." Chicago *Sun-Times,* May 2, 4, 10, 1952.

[106] Mr. Storke's son.

To Marnie Dick

May 13, 1952

Marnie dear:

You were an angel to send me that postcard even from the "Shaler *Bar!*" I will say nothing about your non-academic travels!

Your mother and father have given me an account of your performance at the dance recital and I am not the least surprised that you were exquisite. But I am disappointed that the Governor has been deprived of a critic seat so long. Shall we make it the feature of the next Mansion Ball — because I will do my best to stay in the Mansion as you know — to please you of course!!

Best love.

To Alicia Patterson [107]

May 15, 1952

. . . You sound like a happy school girl on her first trip abroad [108] & it all makes me very envious — because thats the way you should feel to enjoy it most & how seldom we do as we get old & more concerned with aching feet than ancient glories.

I too felt that way on my Odessy from Portland to Pasadena — except when the newsmen and photographers closed in 3 or 4 times a day with the inevitable — "Will you accept a draft?" But it was a memorable journey and there was fun and old friends along the way too. I'm being pounded to death by mail, wire, telephone & visit[ors] on the damn nomination. I thought I had it all settled and for keeps but it seems to be hotter than ever now and I wonder if I have to issue a Gen. Sherman. Its a cocky, contemptuous distasteful thing to do and I hate to earn a place in the history books by saying I *won't* do something honorable that has come to few people. Please advise me promptly — shall I say "No" again and more sharply & decisively; shall I keep still; shall I indicate privately that I would accept a genuine draft — i.e. not let them down if it comes? Help, Help . . .

I'm eager to hear all your post Siena news. Ike has plenty of trouble still ahead for all I can see or hear, but I think he's ahead of Taft in spite of the figures.

Of course the poor wretched Italians want peace — and how. Its what

[107] This handwritten letter is in the possession of Adlai E. Stevenson III.
[108] Miss Patterson was traveling in Europe.

people here can't seem to understand who groan about those damn Europeans who won't doing [do] anything for themselves etc. . . .

AES

On May 17, 1952, Stevenson appeared at the celebration of the Norwegian Independence Day, in Chicago, where he spoke briefly.[109]

I feel quite at home here today and not at all like an outsider. For while Norwegian Independence Day is naturally closer to your hearts than it can possibly be to a Scots-Irishman, it is too good a thing for you to keep entirely to yourselves. The really important thing in life are those you can share freely with others without decreasing your own portion, and I am glad that you have given me the opportunity to have some small part of this occasion.

This day belongs not only to Norway and to those of Norwegian ancestry, but to free men and women everywhere and to all throughout the world who hunger for freedom. In 1814, when the revolutionary fires which had swept over Europe were all but extinguished and most of the peoples of the continent were shivering in the cold, relentless grip of reaction, the Norwegian patriots who met at Eidsvoll kept alive the flame of hope in the hearts of freedom loving people everywhere. Even so today may this commemoration of Norwegian independence stir our hearts and lead us all to an increased devotion to the ideals of liberty and democracy to which Norway and America alike are dedicated. . . .

We see on every hand the rich contributions which the various national groups have made to American life. Illinois has one of the largest populations of foreign-born citizens of any of the states. But I confess I didn't realize we had so many Norwegians until I saw this crowd here today. I am told that this is the largest event held by Norwegians in the United States. You can be proud that so many Americans of Norwegian descent remember the significance of this day in the long history of freedom's struggle; you can well be proud of the contribution made by Norwegians to the richness and fullness of American life: to the advancement of our arts, sciences, professions and public life. You have helped fight our wars; you have grown with your adopted country; you have become a part of America and its traditions.

So have we all. That is the essence of the American story. We have learned to live together here, the men and women of all nationalities. We

[109] These excerpts are taken from a mimeograph copy prepared by the Governor's office for release to the press.

have become the world's great sanctuary for those fleeing from oppression and tyranny, and we have gained new vitality from this flow of immigration from overseas. . . .

I know there are those who say that sentiment has no place in the ugly realities of this tormented world. There were those who said we should bar our doors in our own "self-interest." I disagree. I believe that America will gain new vigor, greater understanding, greater tolerance, a keener awareness of the blessings we enjoy in this free, rich land because mercifully we opened our golden doors to worthy refugees from the cruelty, oppression and tyranny we despise.

These are anxious, clouded days and the future is obscure. But I believe our course is clear: we must hold fast to our faith in freedom and the individual. . . .

Twenty years ago this month I was in Norway. And before twenty more years are spent I hope to be there again — in May. Perhaps when the voters have had enough of me I'll go back and lie in spring wild flowers high above the bottomless blue waters of the Sagnefjord, with the mountains behind me and the blue sky overhead and mutter again some words of a Norwegian poet who died in the last war fighting for Norway's freedom:

> In us is born the conviction
> That freedom is life's first law,
> And our faith is as deep and simple
> As the very breath we draw.

To Letitia Dick [110]

May 21, 1952

My dear Miss Dick:

I am in receipt of your invitation to the Commencement exercises at Garrison Forest School. That the Governor is so preoccupied with public affairs that he cannot come and will not be able to see you pass from one important stage of your life to another is deeply distressing. That you will do so with grace, charm — and agility! — the Governor does not doubt, even without his beneficent and tender eyes upon you.

With gratitude for your thoughtfulness, satisfaction in your achievements, and confident expectations for your future, I am obediently and respectfully your most fervent, affectionate — but hopelessly detained — admirer.

[110] The text is taken from a carbon copy. There is no formal closing. It is likely that Stevenson after dictating the letter asked to have it returned to his desk so that he could add a handwritten note.

Mrs. Lloyd Lewis had just visited her husband's grave in Pendleton, Indiana, where she found the lilacs in bloom. She commended Stevenson for his April 17 speech in New York.

To Mrs. Lloyd Lewis [111]

May 21, 1952

Dear Kathryn:

Thanks for your note and for your kind words about the speech. The lilacs will always bloom on Lloyd's birthday, in Pendleton and in myriad hearts.

Affectionately,
ADLAI

To Mrs. Martin D. Hardin [112]

May 26, 1952

My dear Aunt Julia:

I was so glad to have that wonderful quote about grandfather.

I have been in sore travail, as you can imagine, and am still bewildered about what I should do. Illinois is what I want and feel that I should do, but the "draft" is inevitable I am afraid, unless I can extricate myself somehow. But should I? I just don't know, and any advice, intuitive or otherwise, from you would be most welcome and helpful.

Love,
ADLAI

To Mrs. Edison Dick [113]

May 26, 1952

. . . the only major problems on June 3 & 4 aside from corres.[,] appt [appointments][,] schedule[,] etc is preparing speech for June 5 at Harvard [Illinois] Milk Day! (Gov. campaign), and major speech before Executives Club [114] for Fri June 6 (Gov. campaign!) and Commencement speech for Hampden-Sydney [115] for June 9, 2 speeches for June 11 at Freeport and Rockford.

[111] The original of this typewritten letter is in the Lewis collection, Newberry Library, Chicago.
[112] The original is in the possession of Adlai S. Hardin.
[113] This handwritten letter is in the possession of Mrs. Dick.
[114] In Chicago.
[115] Hampden-Sydney College, in Hampden-Sydney, Virginia.

Hope this is on time. What with the Indian Ambassador,[116] Gunther,[117] photographers etc — I couldn't do it before. . . .

Later — Alicia [Patterson] just hung up after telling me that after seeing Ike, I should run & could beat him — *must* accept draft etc. Evidently she came back a little disillusioned.

I'm going to need a labotomy [lobotomy] very soon — bring your instruments, aenesthetics [anesthetics], pump, 26th psalm, and lets have the operation on a fronded island! . . .

To Sherlock Swann, Jr. [118]

May 26, 1952

Dear Sherly:

I was glad to have your note. I wish I could get back for the reunion [119] but it looks as though I would be busy defending right and virtue and the Democratic administration in Springfield around Northern Illinois that week-end.

A politician pays a frightful price for everything he does. Besides, if I were to go to the reunion the Chicago Tribune would have at least two editorials charging me with frivolous neglect of duty!

Why don't you come to see me some time?

Sincerely yours,

On May 28, 1952, Governor Stevenson introduced Averell Harriman at a Roosevelt College Founders' Dinner in Chicago.[120]

The world is very sick. I think of it sometimes as a body which has survived two wars, two very major surgical operations, in rapid succession. They were successful, but a long convalescence with rest, tonic, transfusions, was "indicated," as the doctors say. Instead, the enfeebled patient was promptly attacked by the savage infection of predatory communism. We have joined in doing the only thing possible: administering heroic doses of antibiotics to arrest the infection and the consuming fever.

[116] The Indian consul, G. L. Mehta.

[117] Author John Gunther.

[118] Professor of chemical engineering at the University of Illinois and a Princeton classmate of Stevenson's.

[119] The thirtieth reunion of the Princeton Class of 1922, scheduled to be held in June, 1952.

[120] The text is based on a mimeograph copy prepared by the Governor's office for release to the press.

If the unhappy patient survives the disease he can live and flourish in robust good health, and so can we. But the cure, the stern counter measures, can kill the patient too. We seem to be near the crisis. Perhaps it has already passed, perhaps it is still to come, perhaps this is the crisis. We don't know exactly.

Everyone is prescribing for the patient. Some say more of this, some say less of that, some say let nature take its course. And some just talk, but don't say anything, like the man who asked the judge for a divorce because his wife talked so much. When the judge asked what she said, the poor man thought a moment and replied: "Well, judge, she don't say."

There are many doctors. One of the wisest, most experienced and respected you have invited here to Roosevelt College tonight to receive the 1952 Founders and Friends award for distinguished service to the principles of American democracy.

I am honored that you have seen fit to ask me to introduce to this Illinois audience the Honorable W. Averell Harriman — a man who has given of his time, his comfort, his exceptional talents to his country with selfless, almost reckless, abandon and devotion for twenty years. At thirty his friends thought he would work himself into an early grave. Banking, business, railroading and myriad responsibilities, both inherited and undertaken, all he attacked with a feverish zeal, a civic consciousness, a noblesse oblige that made of him a useful citizen and a leader of his generation.

And now at sixty his friends are still worrying that he will work himself to death. But meanwhile he has been administrative officer of NRA [National Recovery Administration], Lend-Lease administrator in London, Ambassador to Russia, Ambassador to Great Britain, Secretary of Commerce, Marshall Plan Ambassador, Special Assistant to the President, Director of Mutual Security, and for more than a decade international trouble shooter extraordinary under two Presidents, in war and peace. Any of those jobs, and more that I've omitted, would make a proud obituary for any man. But he even feels strong enough, or should I say brave enough, to be President of the United States and chief of the medical staff at the bedside of the world in the hour of its crisis.

He is strong enough and brave enough, wise enough and, most of all, humble enough, to assume burdens that dwarf the imagination and that few understand or appreciate; to undertake a task freighted with the hopes and fears of millions here and more beyond the seas, some heard and seen, some unheard and unseen.

Military power is not an end in itself. The purpose of rearmament is to deter aggression; not to provoke aggression. For many people who have suffered the ravages of war, fear of war itself is far more real than fear of communism. For many hunger, disease, poverty are the real fears. Freedom, justice, democracy have very different meanings in different lands, and no meaning at all to large portions of the globe. For those of us who carry the heaviest burdens the alternatives of military safety at the price of economic disaster, or economic safety at the price of military disaster are not solutions but spectres.

So we do not all diagnose or prescribe for the sickness of the world alike. But there is a common ground, a common prayer — peace. And the purpose of rearmament and the redress of the balance of power in the world is not just to deter aggression, but to enable us to build the peace. It is the means to an end, and the end is negotiation from strength rather than weakness. And the time is coming shortly when we must be prepared to negotiate and initiate negotiations whenever and wherever we can — negotiations not by ultimatum but by give and take. Because we must end the armament race before it ends the gasping patient.

The problems are infinite, infinitely difficult, and imperfectly perceived even in our country. But the realization of the universal dream of freedom; better living conditions for awakening, restless, miserable millions; allaying the ancient fear of the scourge of recurring wars; lifting the crushing burden of armaments, are common goals of all who pray for peace and universal aspirations. It will be for us to help, patiently, persistently, in the face of countless frustrations and failures, to harness the energy in these ideas. And our success or failure will depend much on executive leadership.

But my role tonight is not to talk of these things — or even about the State of Illinois! My assignment is to present to you a man who has earned your esteem because few living men, and none I daresay in the United States, know more about the care and feeding of a sick world or have been in attendance at the bedside longer. Besides, he has profound convictions about America, and the meaning of social justice, equal opportunity and the good life.

If Presidents are chosen for their vision, their courage and conviction, for their depth of understanding of the meaning of this revolutionary era and the mission of America, you will find them all in our honored guest, Averell Harriman.

To Alicia Patterson [121]

June 11, 1952

. . . Ho Hum, quelle vie! I'm back in my eyrie on top of the State Bldg in Chi. after a hectic day in Wash[ington] trying to do my work pursued by newspaper men, preceded by a day of perspiration in broiling Virginia doing a Commencement address at a little college [122] where great grandfather [Lewis Warner] Green was President 100 years ago. Tomorrow to Freeport for a full length noon speech (unprepared!) before the combined service clubs, politics all afternoon and then a speech at the Rockford Centennial in the evening — then two days to do a weeks work in Springfield & then back on the road again with 4 murderous assignments all over the state on Sat. — and so on and on to the end of time.

Meanwhile no summer plans for the boys, . . . no decision on the damn President business, my Governor campaign bogged down — and and and — well what the hell! . . .

In short 'I take my pen in hand' in a bad mood. . . . I really don't want to do it now any more than I did 4 months ago. But I hate to say some further words that may look or sound as tho I deprecate the office or the duty or whatever it is, and, you're right too, that I might well want to try it four years hence. Meanwhile I've hoped, prayed and expected that the draft idea would blow over and that [Averell] Harriman or [Estes] Kefauver would emerge the winner & I could sit aloof and run like hell for Governor and try to find a little time for the children. But it doesn't seem to work that way and everyone (except the big politicians whom [who] seem to be genuinely scared that I'll wash out on them) evidently expects me to run against Taft in any event and probably Eisenhower. I don't know what to do — still! — except to sit tight and hope to get out at the last minute, quietly if possible.

Somehow I got the impression in my 24 hrs in the east that it looks like Taft still thanks to the monkey business in Texas & the south.[123] Per-

[121] This handwritten letter is in the possession of Adlai E. Stevenson III.

[122] Hampden-Sydney College.

[123] On May 27, the forces of Senator Robert A. Taft controlled the Texas state convention. But Eisenhower supporters, who had outnumbered and outvoted Taft supporters at a number of county conventions, and who had been denied seats at the state convention, held their own convention and nominated a rival slate of delegates. There were also disputed delegations from Georgia and Louisiana. The Eisenhower campaign managers denounced Taft and demanded fair play. At the Republican National Convention the Eisenhower forces were able to seat their slate of delegates. Walter Johnson, *1600 Pennsylvania Avenue: Presidents and the People, 1929–1959* (Boston: Little, Brown, 1960), pp. 249–251.

sonally I think Ike has done darn well and [in?] his press conferences with impressive sincerity and warmth and good humor. But somehow the Dems. grow more confident as the Rep[ublican]. division hardens aided and abetted by those fine papers you live off of! Nasty!! . . .

Stevenson was troubled with kidney stones, a painful affliction that recurred from time to time until major surgery in 1954 cleared up the difficulty.

To Dr. Parker Hardin [124]

June 13, 1952

Dear Parker:

Thanks to your shot in the arm I got home without too much discomfort and promptly went out to the hospital for the night. The next day, yesterday, they gave me a cystoscope, etc., and found a small stone in the tube between the kidney and the bladder which seems to have caused my trouble. They say it is too small for surgery and will work its way out in time. Meanwhile, I am armed with pills for the pain if I have recurrences.

God bless you and Catherine.[125] It was a lovely party at your house, and your ministrations were a godsend.

Love to you both.

Yours,
ADLAI

To Mrs. Edison Dick [126]

[no date] [127]

. . . It is all very difficult — what is duty, what is vanity, what is crafty calculation, what is self interest, what is fear, what is bravado, what is irritation? I used to say to myself over and over from childhood — "Wisdom is destiny." Well, what is wisdom?

My love to the dear Titia. . . .

124 The original is in the possession of Dr. Hardin.
125 Mrs. Hardin.
126 This handwritten letter is in the possession of Mrs. Dick.
127 Mrs. Dick thinks this letter was probably written in mid-June, since Stevenson refers in a deleted passage to her daughter Letitia's graduation.

The Reverend Richard Paul Graebel wrote to Stevenson on June 16, 1952: "In a dream . . . I saw the dead elms lining an avenue in Springfield. And on the naked limbs thereof, clustered row on row, the vultures of 'state jobs' past and . . . to come sat sharpening their beaks . . . watching a man walk down the middle of the road. The man carried a gun. . . . At the end of the road, he turned, raised his gun and fired . . . and all of the winged beasts fell into the dust, pulverized. And there came an echo above the noise . . . 'Save the state and you save all.' I continue to urge you — choose not to run for president, we need you here! — P.S. Knowing full well you will be guided aright!! And praying for you!"

To the Reverend Richard Paul Graebel

June 17, 1952

Dear Dick:

I have had the same dream, or something like it. But unhappily when the old blunderbuss goes off *all* the birds don't fall. And indeed a new crop seems to be lining the naked branches even now.

Thanks for thinking of me, and your prayers will help mightily. *This* is what I want, vultures, blunderbuss and all — save dead elms!

Many thanks.

Yours,

On June 21, 1952, Stevenson entered Passavant Hospital in Chicago for a minor operation to remove kidney stones. He was able to return to his desk in Springfield on June 25. During his hospitalization his aide Bill Blair was also ill with a minor ailment. Blair's grandmother, Mrs. Joseph T. Bowen, wrote Stevenson on June 24 to express her concern.

To Mrs. Joseph T. Bowen

June 26, 1952

Dear Mrs. Bowen:

The halt and the blind are taking care of each other as best they can. As for me, I am fully restored to health — thanks in part to your encouraging note. As for Bill, he seems much better today and I think you can record him on the "cures" too. If he should get really sick I think I would have to resign my job. So his health is as important to me as my own!

Affectionately,

To Carroll Binder [128]

June 27, 1952

Dear Carroll:

I was so glad to have your letter and also the reprint of your piece on freedom of information. I had hoped that you and Tommy [129] might be in Springfield for a night with me long before this — and I shall continue to hope both that I shall continue in Springfield and that you will come to see me.

Meanwhile, I shall look forward to a glimpse of you in Chicago during the Democratic convention. I shall probably not dare come to town while the Republicans are there!

Yours,
ADLAI

Kenneth W. Thompson, a political scientist at the University of Chicago, wrote an article on foreign affairs that he expected to have published. In it he set forth what he believed were Stevenson's views on this subject. He sent the Governor a draft of the article for review and asked him to make any substantive corrections necessary.

To Dorothy Fosdick [130]

June 27, 1952

Dear Dorothy:

I am in a pickle. I have had the enclosed manuscript on my desk for a month and have not even been able to read the correspondence, what with the pressure of more pressing things — and you know what! In view of the fact that you know "Stevenson's foreign policy" better than Stevenson does I thought I might be bold enough to ask you to look at this stuff and tell me what it is all about and what I should say to Kenneth Thompson, with whom I am not acquainted. It is curious how self-conscious I am becoming. Is it Presidentitis or rumors of romance with distinguished foreign policy planners and plotters? We must talk about that.

Affectionately,

[128] Editorial editor of the Minneapolis *Tribune*. The original is in the Carroll Binder collection, Newberry Library, Chicago.
[129] Mrs. Binder.
[130] A copy is in A.E.S., P.U.L.

P.S. If this is too much of a chore please return it and I will write Mr. Thompson that I just can't get at it for the present.[131]

To Alicia Patterson [132]

June 27, 1952

. . . Writing is getting harder & harder if thats possible. Saturday night — after a Commencement speech! — I went into the hospital & on Sunday had a kidney stone removed which had caused me two acute agonies. Wednesday I staggered back to Spfd. on the hottest day in history. I'm rapidly getting back to normal & Saturday must go to Houston for the Governors conference. I'm going to take all 3 boys with me & try to have a little fun out of it altho I see small chance hounded by the press & the photographers who haunt me day and night. Certainly we contrive to make life as difficult as we possibly can for our public servants who have little enough peace as it is.

As for my future I'm desperately worried — I want so much to stay here and do this job that I asked for better than its ever been done before — The Chi Trib[une] to the contrary notwithstanding — but at the same time if the country really needs me, if theres a touch of destiny about the draft business, then I don't want to thwart it and make a tragic mistake. I've held off the political leaders who just want a whisper that I would accept the nomination about as long as I can — or can I refuse to give them any encouragement whatsoever until the last minute? What to say when they all assault me in Houston? And why the devil did I ever get in all this mess anyway? I can't or don't want to tell them if its Taft yes, Ike no. That's a deadly thing to do politically. . . .

A

Stevenson had just returned to Springfield after surgery for the removal of a kidney stone when this letter was written. In it he enclosed a clipping from the Chicago Daily News, *beginning: "Governor Stevenson, chipper as he left Passavant hospital Wednesday after his operation, recited a poem he had composed. It was: 'What could be neater/ Than to cheat Saint Peter/ With a nice, clean ureter?' Stevenson said he 'couldn't feel finer.' . . . A red rose danced on his lapel."*

[131] Miss Fosdick replied on July 8, 1952, that the article about Stevenson's foreign policy was an extraordinarily understanding and sympathetic piece and she would have no hesitation in letting it go forward for publication. She added that she greatly enjoyed doing such chores — the more the merrier.

[132] This handwritten letter is in the possession of Adlai E. Stevenson III.

To Mrs. Edison Dick [133]

June 29, 1952

. . . I thought this would amuse Eddie & you. I've had 3 or 4 verses . . . elicited by my casual plag[i]arism from Harriet Welling.

I didn't get anything cleared up in the hospital — except my ureter! I'm trying my best to do just what you say about saying nothing more about my availability so that I can get out if its Ike and go if its Taft and there is a genuine demand for me and I feel I must etc. Its all dreadfully difficult and never more so than since I returned from the hospital. I've been sorely tempted to chuck it all and say I couldn't accept under any circumstances. Perhaps I should and end the agony of doubt. But would I have failed my country, my generation, my convictions, would I have interfered with my destiny and duty etc etc etc. I'm praying it will be Ike even tho he's been an awful disappointment so far and I'm afraid is rapidly alienating the independent progressives & leaving little choice with Taft. But as Pres. I'm sure he would not junk the foreign policy. . . .

I'm in a terrible mess just now — weak & worried and surrounded. 20 people outside waiting for a press conf., Geo. Ball & John [Paulding] Brown upstairs, the boys [134] arriving in an hour; off to Houston tomorrow unprepared; the long distance phone buzzing constantly. Forgive me.

When Stevenson arrived at the annual Conference of State Governors, in Houston, Texas, on June 30, 1952, he made this statement at a press conference.[135]

I think I can anticipate some of the questions which will be asked, and I think we can save both your time and mine. I will now say what I have to say and all I have to say on the Presidential situation — and then we can go on to other subjects, if there are any.

Let me first make it clear that I both intend and consider what I say as a summary of what I have already repeatedly said, and not as an alteration.

Some time ago I said that for many reasons, including my prior candidacy for re-election as Governor, I could not be a candidate for any other office. I have not been nor am I now. I hope to stay in Illinois as Governor. My work there is not finished and it is very important to me.

[133] This handwritten letter is in the possession of Mrs. Dick.
[134] His sons.
[135] New York *Times*, July 1, 1952.

I am not being coy or trying to select my opponent. I have not participated, nor will I participate, overtly or covertly, in any movement to draft me. Without such participation on my part, I do not believe that any such draft can or will develop. In the unlikely event that it does, I will decide what to do at that time in the light of the conditions then existing.

Mrs. Lewis Cuyler wrote Stevenson on July 4, 1952, to say how much she approved of all he had done, said, and not said, as quoted in the public press.

To Mrs. Lewis B. Cuyler

July 7, 1952

My dear Margery:

You were sweet to write me. Tom [Matthews] delivered your letter when we met in Chicago yesterday, and I was deeply touched by your thoughtfulness and good wishes. It has been a hideous ordeal, and I hope and pray that I can emerge as Governor of Illinois, which seems to be the full measure of my meager talents — and then some! I wish so much that I could come back again to see that gay, happy, wholesome household of yours and its enchanting mistress. Perhaps the voters of Illinois will see to that even sooner than I might like.

Tom, whose judgment, sagacity and friendship have been precious to me for many years, has been an invaluable resource and comfort. Perhaps some time when he travels this way you and Buzz [136] could come along and see the Lincoln country under the direction of the Governor — and bring the children.

Sincerely yours,

Alistair Forbes, columnist for the Sunday Dispatch *of London, delivered a letter of introduction in person to Governor Stevenson, written by Herbert Agar. Agar also wrote: "I still feel . . . that they will put the bite on you at the end in a fashion which you cannot refuse. If this should happen, let me know if there is any small thing I can do to help."*

[136] Mr. Cuyler.

To Herbert Agar [137]

July 7, 1952

Dear Herbert:

Alistair Forbes delivered your letter to me in a candle lit garden at a festivity in Lake Forest last night. Only today have I had an opportunity to read it. Nor did I have an opportunity to talk with Mr. Forbes, as I was leaving just as he arrived. You were good to pass him along to me and I shall hope to see him before he leaves.

I am still beseeching the Deity to leave me in Illinois, but the shadows are gathering. However, I am by no means beyond redemption and I may be able to wriggle out and stick to what I both feel I can do and should do.

Should disaster befall me I may holler for your help. Meanwhile, my thanks for your offer, and affectionate regards to the beloved and wonderful Barbie.[138]

As ever,

To Kenneth W. Thompson [139]

July 11, 1952

Dear Mr. Thompson:

I appreciated very much your letter of May 27 with the enclosed manuscript and only regret that with the pressure of other things I have been held up so long in a reply. You have done a very understanding interpretation of my position and I hesitate to make any suggestions at all. On three points, however, you may want to carry your analysis a little further, and I am enclosing two speeches [140] delivered this year which may be of some assistance. In addition, you might wish to refer to my article entitled "Korea in Perspective" in the April 1952 issue of *Foreign Affairs.*

1. One point I had in mind was a further interpretation of the relation of national interest to the interests of other nations in the formulation of foreign policy. You might use, for example, the quotation from the *Foreign Affairs* article:

---

[137] Editor of the Louisville *Courier-Journal,* 1940–1942, director of the English publishing firm of Rupert Hart-Davis, Ltd., author of numerous books including *Abraham Lincoln* (1952).

[138] Mrs. Agar.

[139] A copy is in A.E.S., P.U.L.

[140] Two speeches on foreign policy, one on May 5, 1952, before the Commonwealth Club, San Francisco, California; the other before the Council on World Affairs, Dallas, Texas, on April 22, 1952. These speeches are not included in this volume, since their central theme is contained in the *Foreign Affairs* article, above. Copies are in A.E.S., P.U.L.

The United States will find support among peoples in the free states to the degree that they believe that we do not simply consult our own interests but give consideration to their interests as well — that we in truth have a "decent respect for the opinions of mankind." Other nations have a reciprocal obligation to give weight to our interests too. There is no doubt that our power gives us an advantage in this process. But neither is there room to doubt that if we wish allies who will go forward with us with courage and fortitude into the risks of the future, they must be willing and confident allies.

2. I do not believe your comment on page 28 with reference to "one last supreme effort to achieve a settlement with the Soviet Union" adequately represents my view on this matter. I think we have to approach the problem on a more patient and continuous basis and that, as I have suggested in one of the enclosed speeches, our problem is to conduct a wise diplomacy that takes advantage of any openings but remains undiscouraged. Perhaps the phrase "diplomacy from strength" might be useful in characterizing my position.

3. I suggest you may want to omit the sentence on page 23 referring to the United Nations as the best and only hope for collective security and peace in the world, and draw on material in the *Foreign Affairs* article relating to the United Nations as a world-wide agency to other parts of the collective security system.

I shall not bother you with any further specific comments. I feel I am in excellent hands and that you are more generous than you really should be in evaluating my qualities of statesmanship!

With kindest good wishes to you and good luck with the article. Let me know where it appears! [141]

Sincerely yours,

P.S. I presume it would be appropriate for you to indicate somehow that this would not be an "authorized" discussion of my views. I have, frankly, read it so hastily that I think you understand my attitude.

To Richard Bentley [142]

July 11, 1952

Dear Dick:

The Stevenson for Governor Committee in Chicago tells me you have

---

[141] Mr. Thompson's article appeared under the title "The Study of International Politics: A Survey of Trends and Developments," *Review of Politics,* Vol. 14, No. 4 (October, 1952), pp. 433–467.

[142] The original is in the possession of Mr. Bentley.

sent them a contribution and I want you to know how grateful I am — for this and for countless other kindnesses for countless years.

My affectionate regards.

Yours,

ADLAI

On June 20, 1952, Vincent Sheean sent Stevenson a long letter about his possible candidacy for President. "You probably think I am inordinately presumptuous on slight acquaintance, and yet those days in Springfield when I saw all of Abe Lincoln's things under your protection have made an indelible impression upon me, and I cannot refrain from saying to you what I truly think. It is my belief that you have a supreme duty, as the only Democrat who can possibly win this election, to step forward and state your views and take the consequences."

On July 12, 1952, the day the Republican National Convention adjourned after having nominated General Dwight D. Eisenhower for President and Senator Richard M. Nixon for Vice President, Stevenson's press secretary issued the following statement:

"He [Stevenson] is a candidate for re-election as Governor of Illinois, and as he has often said, wants no other office. He will ask the Illinois delegation to continue to respect his wishes and he hopes all of the delegates will do likewise."

To Vincent Sheean

July 14, 1952

Dear Jimmy:

You asked me "what's the matter?" Actually, I find it very difficult to answer you. It is not cowardice about running against Eisenhower. I have, as you know, felt the same way from the start and been trying to avoid any involvement in this national campaign since last January. Nor is it personal matters other than what weight I have attached to the children's immaturity. It is rather precisely what I have been saying: that I feel my job here is my first obligation, prior in time, importance, and the full measure of my abilities. There are a host of incidental problems; a successor candidate for Governor; prospects for loss of the state; a loyalty to people I have brought into the state government from outside the political arena; keeping faith with the other members of my state ticket and countless local candidates whose fortunes depend on my leadership; etc. etc.

Now, I appreciate fully that all of these things add up to but little when we are talking about the Presidency of the United States. But somehow I seem to be very simple minded about all this and can only do one thing at a time with enthusiasm and any self-confidence and serenity. I made known my position to certain people well before the Republican Convention and I only hope I can emerge from this shattering experience with any public regard and understanding.

What you have written touches me deeply. Perhaps I am confused and my duty — the brave thing — is obscured by lesser considerations. If you pass this way by all means come to Springfield, although our destiny will soon be determined.

Sincerely yours,

P.S. I find now that I have not thanked you for the copy of "A Rage of The Soul" [143] and your inscription. I am most grateful for your thought of me and you may be sure that I will find time to read *this* novel!

To Justin G. Turner [144]

July 17, 1952

Dear Mr. Turner —

It has just come to my attention that you have presented the Illinois Historical Library a fine letter of Elizabeth Edwards to her sister, Mary Todd Lincoln.

I am most grateful to you, and also for the part you played in the formal presentation several weeks [ago] of the Oliver Barrett material to the Library.[145] With this acquisition our Library will house the greatest collection of Lincoln manuscript material in existence, enriched by your fine and thoughtful gift.

With gratitude and good wishes,

Cordially yours,

---

[143] Vincent Sheean, *A Rage of the Soul* (New York: Random House, 1952).

[144] This handwritten letter is in the possession of Mr. Turner, and is reproduced in the illustrations to this volume.

[145] Oliver Barrett had owned one of the largest collections of Lincolniana in the country. His collection was offered at public auction in New York in 1952, and Mr. Turner, a Los Angeles businessman, was the largest purchaser except for the State of Illinois and the Library of Congress. Turner gave many of his items to the Illinois State Historical Library, including the Edwards letter.

Part Five

"And Now, with a Full Heart, I Bid You All Good-by"—Winding up the Governorship

T*he Democratic National Convention of 1952 was held in the International Amphitheater in Chicago, beginning on July 21. Adlai E. Stevenson attended the convention as a delegate, as well as in his official
capacity as governor of the host state. On July 25, he was drafted as his
party's candidate for President of the United States.*[1] *Stevenson's papers
bearing on the convention draft are contained in Volume IV of* The Papers of Adlai E. Stevenson, *as are those relating to his presidential campaign. The papers in this part of Volume III are those which reflect the
closing months of his term as governor of Illinois.*

*On returning to Springfield after his nomination, Stevenson had to plan
the speeches he would deliver and establish a campaign organization
with headquarters in the capital of the state of which he was still the
governor. As he selected a new chairman of the Democratic National
Committee, Stephen A. Mitchell, appointed Wilson W. Wyatt as his personal campaign manager, and assembled a research and writing staff to
assist him, he was also occupied with the affairs of the State of Illinois.*

*Stevenson exerted his influence with the Democratic State Central
Committee to ensure that Lieutenant Governor Sherwood Dixon would
replace him as the gubernatorial nominee. The Governor also called the
directors of all code departments together to map out a plan for conducting the state's business while he was on the national campaign trail.
After this meeting, he wrote each director.*

[1] For a discussion of this genuine draft, see Paul T. David, Malcolm Moos, Ralph
M. Goldman, *Presidential Nominating Politics in 1952: The National Story* (Baltimore: Johns Hopkins Press, 1954); Walter Johnson, *How We Drafted Adlai Stevenson* (New York: Knopf, 1955); Jacob M. Arvey, "The Reluctant Candidate — An Inside Story," *Reporter*, November 24, 1953.

To Leonard Schwartz [2]

August 1, 1952

Dear Director:

At our meeting on Wednesday evening, in which I explained how things will be handled during the period of the presidential campaign, I had intended to stress the importance of continuing the inter-departmental meetings which have been held from time to time under the chairmanship of the Director of Finance.[3] These meetings have all along been very helpful to me. They will obviously be of still more value now. They will not only continue to afford an opportunity for discussion of matters of general interest to all departments, boards and commissions, but will also provide the basis for preparing a summary for my information of current problems and developments.

Because of the increased importance of these interdepartmental meetings, I have asked Director Pois to schedule them on a bi-weekly basis rather than holding them only from time to time as has been done in the past. He will communicate with you as to the date for the next meeting.

I am deeply grateful for the assurances given me by all of you that you will exert every effort to keep the government of our State operating at a high level of efficiency.

Sincerely yours,

During the campaign, Stevenson usually returned to Springfield on weekends. Before starting out on each trip, amidst further planning of the campaign, he found time to consult with some of his aides on state government business.

On November 4, Stevenson went down to defeat, as did gubernatorial candidate Sherwood Dixon. After Stevenson's defeat, he was overwhelmed by a mass of correspondence that poured into his office from disappointed admirers. He insisted that every letter be acknowledged, and, with the help of a corps of volunteers, it was done. Some of his letters in response are included in Volume IV of The Papers of Adlai E. Stevenson. *He also went about the task of winding up the affairs of his administration, due to end in January, 1953, when the newly elected Republican governor, William G. Stratton, was to be sworn into office.*

2 The original is in the possession of Mr. Schwartz.
3 Joseph W. Pois.

On December 7, 1952, Stevenson received a telegram from John A. Corry, the chairman of the Princeton undergraduate newspaper, the Daily Princetonian:

> In light of report in Nov. 24 "Quick" that you will be considered for next president of Princeton by university trustees as well as rumors from other sources would you reply to following questions by wire collect?
> Have you been offered presidency of Princeton?
> To your knowledge, are you under consideration for this post?
> Would you accept Princeton presidency if offered you?

On the bottom of this telegram, Stevenson drafted his reply by hand.

To John A. Corry

Re your telegram I know nothing whatever of the matter you mention and I do not accept or decline proposals I have not received. Regards.

To Edward D. McDougal, Jr.[4]

December 9, 1952

Dear Ed:

Riding to New York on the airplane last week I read your piece in the Alumni Weekly entitled "Governor Stevenson of Illinois." [5] May I say that Governor Stevenson of Illinois has never read anything that pleased him more, and had E. D. McDougal been making the speeches during the campaign I have no doubt the result would have been much different. The accuracy with which you traced the Illinois story confounds me. I don't know how you could have had it so straight and orderly.

Some day I will thank you myself, and I hope soon.

Yours,

ADLAI

At the request of Jacob Arvey, of the Cook County Democratic organization, Stevenson checked with the Illinois Liquor Commission to learn the fate of three applications filed with that agency.

---

[4] The original is in the possession of Mr. McDougal.
[5] *Princeton Alumni Weekly*, November 28, 1952.

To Jacob M. Arvey

December 27, 1952

Dear Jack:

I have looked into the matter you mentioned. He is an applicant for a brewery license as sole stockholder of Bohemian Brewery of Joliet. He is also an applicant for a liquor license in a corporate name and a beer distributor's license in a corporate name. Hearings have been held on all three applications and the only issue is if he is a man of good character and reputation and therefore eligible under the Act. The hearings have just been concluded and he is represented by Stanley Clinton. Many citizens were called on his behalf on the reputation issue. Virgil Peterson,[6] the State's Attorney,[7] the Police Commissioner [8] and one or two others evidently testified that his reputation was bad and that he was known as a Capone hoodlum. Cardinal Stritch [9] recently appointed him to some position in connection with the Catholic Youth Organization.

As to whether these reputation statutes refer to present or past reputation, the law is not clear and there are no satisfactory cases. The arguments pro and con are obvious: But a man who has gone straight should not be everlastingly tarred with his previous conduct. And on the other hand, that a law violator should not be allowed to escape acts of conduct by his subsequent proper behavior. Otherwise, the act is no deterrent.

Hastily,

Mrs. John B. Allen, a Chicagoan appointed by Stevenson to the advisory board of the State Reformatory for Women, wrote the Governor that she had submitted her resignation to Governor-elect William G. Stratton. She wanted Stevenson to know how much she had enjoyed being on the board and said she hoped she had learned something.

To Mrs. John B. Allen

December 30, 1952

Dear Bips:

I have your letter and, while I would have urged you to continue on

---

6 Director of the Chicago Crime Commission.
7 John S. Boyle.
8 Chicago Police Commissioner Timothy J. O'Connor.
9 Samuel Cardinal Stritch, Roman Catholic archbishop of Chicago.

the Board, I suppose you have done the right thing, although, of course, he [Stratton] cannot act upon your resignation until after he becomes Governor.

Perhaps now we will see something more of each other. Bless you!

Yours,

On January 7, 1953, Governor Stevenson made his final report to the people of Illinois by radio broadcast.[10]

I wish I could review here everything that has been done or attempted since 1949 to improve our state government. I should like to review these crowded years department by department — from hunting and fishing and wildlife conservation to insurance regulation — our successes and our failures, our triumphs and defeats, what I've learned that's so and what I've learned that isn't so. I would like to talk to you about politics and patronage, about law enforcement, gambling, corruption, about human beings, the good and the evil, and all the things that have made these four relentless years here in Springfield the best in my life.

You would understand better then why I am so grateful for the opportunity you, the people, gave me and why I wanted so desperately to continue here in Springfield. But my party asked me to run for President, and, after preaching the gospel of public service so long, I didn't see how I could consistently decline. The consequences are familiar to you, and acutely familiar to me now, on the eve of my return to private life!

But all that is past, and it is with the future that I shall deal. I have listed some ten major future goals for the state. They contain no sensations. In the past four years we have instituted extensive legislative and administrative changes. I am happy to say that most of the ambitious original objectives I had four years ago have now been accomplished in whole or in part. What follows are the principal things that remain to be done as I see it:

1. *Foremost is the highway program.* It must be completed as soon as possible. The tempo of that program has been set. Last year $86 million in new contracts were awarded, not counting $23 million of work carried over from 1951 and $11 million contributed by the state to the Cook County super-highway development. This was more than twice as large a program as in any prior year in Illinois history.

---

[10] The text is taken from Adlai E. Stevenson, *What I Think* (New York: Harper, 1956), pp. 117–123.

Moreover, a sound pattern for completing this program in the next ten years has been established. Under laws enacted in 1951 the contribution to the cost of that program will be shared on a more equal basis by highway users — the private vehicle owners and the truckers. I strongly urge the legislature to resist efforts that may be made to radically disturb this fair apportionment. To jeopardize the highway program itself, or to grant special advantages or concessions to particular classes of vehicle operators, at the expense of other classes, would be a grave injustice and disservice.

2. *The urgent needs of the public schools must continue to be recognized.* The schools represent our greatest asset. Important forward strides have been taken in recent years to strengthen the schools of Illinois. To do this the legislature in 1951 appropriated in round figures $150 million to the common schools for the current biennium. State aid has been almost doubled in my four years.

What have been the results? They cannot be measured alone in higher appropriations, but they can be measured in better facilities, better curricula, better trained teachers. The Illinois School Problems Commission surveyed 1,396 schools for the year of 1948–49 and reported that nearly one-half of the elementary schools and almost one-fourth of the high schools had to be rated "inferior." The same schools, surveyed for the year 1951–52, showed that the number of elementary schools now falling short of the foundation program is barely one-fourth instead of one-half. The "inferior" high schools are now fewer than one-fifth. This means that thousands more Illinois children are now receiving a satisfactory instead of an inferior education.

I think the legislature might well consider the creation of a School Building Authority which could finance construction of desperately needed school buildings on a long-term revenue bond basis when local resources are insufficient.

3. *We must extend the gains in welfare services and administration.* As in the case of schools, accomplishment here cannot be measured alone in terms of dollars spent. Real progress has been made in reducing overcrowding and understaffing in the mental hospitals and correctional institutions, but they have by no means been overcome. Our threefold approach has been: Increased efforts to reduce mental disease and public dependency through research and community efforts; extension of the career service idea in the recruitment of more and better hospital personnel; and continuing enlargement of our physical facilities.

On the whole, I think nothing has pleased me more than the improved care and treatment of our unfortunate wards in these past few years and the nationwide recognition of our progress in Illinois.

4. *The state penal system must be re-examined.* Some of our prison facilities are outstandingly good, but others are not. The Menard Penitentiary presents special problems of administration due to obsolete physical plant and the illogical location there of the psychiatric division where mentally deranged criminals are kept. These problems were brought forcefully to public attention by the recent riots that endangered the lives of a number of guards.[11]

It seems to me obvious that the psychiatric division should be moved to another location where psychiatrists and adequate facilities for the treatment of mentally ill prisoners would be more accessible. If the old prison is to be retained some of the buildings will have to be modernized and more shops and facilities provided to keep the prisoners occupied with useful work while they learn trades and skills that will help in their rehabilitation.

In that connection, consideration might well be given in Illinois to the use of the safest prisoners to do necessary work in the state parks and forests. Uncle Sam and one or two other states do it. Some such plan might eventually be extended to solve the old problem of reclaiming, through reforestation or otherwise, the thousands of acres of stripmined land that now are unsightly and largely useless.

More important to me, however, is that our penitentiary system from the wardens on down should be taken out of politics and put on a professional career basis to make it attractive to the most competent people. I have already taken steps in that direction and I hope more will follow.

5. *Law enforcement must be tightened.* Through increased emphasis and activity on the part of the Attorney General and the State Police, we have made conspicuous progress in law enforcement. The overweight truck laws are now being well enforced, but our gambling laws are inadequate and I again urged the General Assembly to give increased powers to the Liquor Control Commission to suspend or revoke tavern licenses where commercial gambling is permitted. Also, since we out-

---

[11] Convicts at Menard State Prison, including prisoners in the psychiatric division, seized prison officials as hostages, in an outbreak of rioting on October 28, 1952. The prison was then under investigation by a state legislative committee as a result of a riot there five weeks earlier. State officials, including Lieutenant Governor Sherwood Dixon, negotiating with the prison rebels, were able to get three of the hostages released. Stevenson was in Pennsylvania on a whistle-stop tour at the time, and after conferring by telephone with Dixon and others at the prison, abruptly suspended his campaign and returned to Illinois. He said that the trip was essential because Illinois's affairs were still his responsibility. On November 1, the Governor personally led a show of force that put down the five-day riot. The New York *Times*, October 28–31, 1952, carried stories of the riot. On November 2, that newspaper commented editorially on the large number of prison riots in the United States during the year and recommended that long-overdue reforms be undertaken.

law gambling, I think it would be consistent to prohibit the manufacture of slot machines and other gambling devices within the state.

Removing the State Police from politics and placing them under a merit system, which I recommended in 1949 and the legislature approved, has already paid important dividends in terms of performance and morale, and I pray that this great reform will be encouraged in letter and spirit in the future.

6. *Efforts to modernize the state Constitution and the state government should continue.* We must have a better judiciary and quicker justice in our courts. Our procedures for the administration of justice are over a century old and clearly outmoded. The Chicago and Illinois Bar Associations have made careful studies of this problem and their plan for modernization of the judicial structure will be presented to the General Assembly at this session.

The proposal to amend the revenue article of the Constitution, which narrowly failed of adoption in the last election, should be restudied and again submitted to the people at the earliest opportunity. The inequities and abuses of our present tax system can never be corrected until the revenue article is brought up to date.

A constitutional amendment giving a greater degree of legislative representation to Cook County's preponderance of population is long overdue. Gross inequalities in population as between the districts within the metropolitan area also must be corrected.

Many recommendations of the Commission I sponsored for reorganization of our state government have already been put into effect, but the General Assembly can accomplish more toward further efficiency and economy by favorable consideration of the remaining recommendations of this Commission.

7. *Better mine safety and labor laws are needed.* The new federal legislation will not, it now appears, relieve the states of their obligation to enact and enforce adequate safety regulations in the mines. Consequently the need continues for a new, up-to-date, effective code of mine safety laws. Illinois also needs a workable state minimum wage law, and a system of temporary disability insurance protecting wage earners from the loss of wages through illness.

8. *The civil rights of all citizens must be steadfastly protected.* Discrimination in any form on account of race, religion, or national origin is repugnant to our ideals of liberty and justice. The proper and most effective initiative in attacking discrimination, wherever it exists, rests with the states. I again express the hope that Illinois will join the other progressive states which have adopted fair employment practices laws.

9. *A single board for higher education should be created.* Little has

been done, except in the teachers' colleges, toward the integration of our system of higher education. There is no orderly, co-ordinated state-wide program; there is much expensive and unnecessary competition and duplication. Two years ago I was convinced that the creation of a single board for higher education, that would take the place of the three virtually autonomous boards we now have, would facilitate that process. I still think so.

10. *The merit idea in personnel policies and recruitment should be extended.* The efficient functioning and integrity of government depend upon attracting to public life honest, competent, loyal men and women. Of all the things I have tried to do nothing is more important than the progress we have made in bringing to and retaining in the state service capable men and women without regard to politics.

The State Civil Service has been expanded and revitalized; the State Police merit system has been established; training programs have been started in the welfare, revenue, public safety, and other departments which need trained career personnel. These are examples of what is needed to improve personnel practices and performances.

When I took office, only 53 per cent of the eligible state employees had civil service status. Today 70.3 per cent are certified. This is a major accomplishment, and it came about not through any magic formula or last-minute manipulation. It has been a slow, steady gain.

If better personnel practices are to have lasting value, this work must go on. I hope very much it will go on here in Illinois because I believe the ultimate results in terms of better service, less cost and waste, and restored public confidence will be tremendous.

Indeed, if I had my way, I would wish history to judge the total worth of my administration by what has been done in this and three other major areas of responsibility.

One of these is the highway program, which I consider the most urgent and vital of the immediate tasks confronting the state. Another has been the dawn of a new day of recognition and state support for our public schools. The third is the positive progress which has been made in meeting the state's welfare responsibilities vigorously and intelligently.

There are many, many accomplishments of other departments and agencies. I have in mind the divorcing of the Commerce Commission, which regulates utility rates, etc., from partisan control and restoring public respect for it; closer screening of public assistance rolls to eliminate many ineligibles; better salaries for state employees; reorganization of the Purchasing Division to place state buying on a strictly business basis; tightening up on abuses in the use of state cars and expense accounts.

And I could go on and on — how the revenue collection services have been improved with reduced personnel, how the Highway Division has been able to carry out its heavier work load without increase in technical staffs, how the Department of Public Health has helped build 17 community non-profit hospitals in areas where the need was greatest, with 21 more under construction.

I'm particularly proud of economies along the way — the weeding out of non-working political payrollers, the reduction in personnel in many departments, the saving of a million dollars a year through new highway resurfacing techniques, the saving of another half-million a year on the State Fair, and the like. Had it not been for many savings, plus various cuts in operating appropriations, we would not now enjoy our substantial treasury balance. The finance department has computed total savings and reductions in appropriations during the last four years at $60 million, almost the exact equivalent of the general revenue fund balance.

This then is my report on the condition of the state:

Our financial position is strong, significant changes have been initiated in state government organization, the people are getting the kind of public service at the state level which they are entitled to expect. Our regulatory agencies have acquired a reputation for objectivity, competence, and freedom from influence. Public employees expect to do, and do, a full day's work for a day's pay.

There has, in short, been a brightening of the tradition of state government in Illinois. With the type of public responsibility we have sought to achieve, with a fearless facing of the people's needs and demands, we can make effective state government a reality, and thus avoid those failures of performance which so often cause public functions to move up the ladder to Washington.

Government — local, state and federal — is not something separate and apart; if it is to be good it must share the attitudes and the competence of the best in our society as a whole. Both business and government are gainers when the best among us from private life will make the sacrifice, if need be, to fill vital public positions.

Illinois, where my family have lived and prospered for a century and a quarter, means a great deal to me, and I am humbly thankful for the opportunity that has been mine to serve it. I leave my high office content in one respect — that I have given to it the best that was in me. It has been a richly rewarding experience, and the satisfactions have far outweighed the disappointments.

To the people of Illinois who have honored me so generously, and to the associates in this great undertaking whose friendship and loyalty have meant so much to me, I shall be eternally grateful.

And now, with a full heart, I bid you all good-by.

Among Stevenson's other tasks in winding up his administration were those of helping his personal staff who were seeking new positions.

To John D. MacArthur [12]

January 8, 1953

Dear Mr. MacArthur:

One of my assistants, Mr. Michael H. Farrin, has told me he is interested in a position in the Legal Department of your company, the Bankers' Life and Casualty Company, and that the emphasis in this position would be on investigations and the collecting of evidence. His training and experience should qualify him excellently for such work.

Mike Farrin came with me as an Administrative Assistant in June 1952 from the Federal Bureau of Investigation in which he had served as a special agent at various points for more than twelve years. Prior to his service with the F.B.I. he engaged in the practice of law at Cairo, Illinois for three years. He was born in Illinois December 27, 1913, graduated from the University of Illinois College of Law in 1936, and since that year has been a member of the Illinois Bar.

Mr. Farrin's legal and investigative experience has been extremely valuable in his work here which, to a large extent, has consisted of "trouble shooting," investigating and collecting evidence in connection with administrative problems involving state employees. I think you might find it worth while to talk with him, and I feel confident from my experience with him that I can underwrite his character as well as his competence.

Sincerely yours,

To Ivan A. Elliott [13]

January 10, 1953

My dear General Elliott:

I have your letter of January 9, with which is transmitted, as con-

[12] President and chairman of the board of Bankers Life and Casualty Company, Chicago.

[13] The original is in the possession of Mr. Elliott.

templated by the Constitution, the Biennial Report of your office for the period ending November 30, 1952. Also as required by the Constitution, I have this day transmitted such report to the General Assembly.

This report is only confirmatory of an impression which is widespread in Illinois, namely, that your tenure in the Office of Attorney General has been marked by conspicuously honorable and distinguished public service. Certainly it has been a great privilege for me to have had my term as Governor coincide with your term of office, and I am satisfied that the splendid spirit of cooperation which has existed between our offices has been greatly in the public interest. You and your associates have unfailingly responded to every request for help which has come from my staff and myself, and our gratitude is correspondingly great.

Sincerely yours,

James Grimmond, of Holyoke, Massachusetts, wrote Stevenson a five-page handwritten letter after his defeat: "I voted for you, supported you, loved you for the truly great man I know you are. . . . I still believe in you as the only American fit to stand with Lincoln. . . . The touchstone of greatness is its awful loneliness." Mr. Grimmond observed that Stevenson's "reluctance to lead" was not "lack of courage, so much as an awareness that you stand virtually alone with the man-breaking and mind-beating task of telling the people, whom you love and who are neither aware of the issue nor prepared to face it, the appalling truth, when they do not want to hear it. You would have to re-direct and re-educate a whole culture. Do the American people know truly that this is the source of your humility?" He added: "The issue is not political corruption, it is social corruption; it is not national morality, it is individual immorality. . . . We in America need to hear you. . . . We need you. We need your kindness, your awareness, your high sense of honour, your humaneness, your humour, your vast understanding. Do not desert us now."

A little later in the letter, Mr. Grimmond stated: "I believe in America in the same way I presume you do, not the America of materialistic greed, of heartless business, of hypocritical posturings, of political chicanery, of spiritual sordidness, of cheap sentimentality, of worship of expediency, of indefinable fears. This is not America — it is the illness of America, as it is the illness of Western culture."

On his last night in the mansion, Stevenson answered this letter by hand. It was typed and mailed on January 12, 1953, the day Governor Stevenson left Springfield.

[596]

To James W. Grimmond

January 12, 1953

Dear Mr. Grimmond:

You need have no doubt that your remarkable letter of Nov. 6 was read. I have read it very carefully and it has enriched me. "Telling the people" *is* a "mind-beating and man-breaking" task. But somehow I think they know, not always at the same time, but *in* time — usually.

You evidently *do* know Lincoln and far better than I do. Indeed I suspect there is much you know that I don't, or at best imperfectly perceive. But I do know — and I knew long before the Convention — that, as you say, no man is really fit for the task of the Presidency in these days, not just the administrative task, or even the policy task, but the monstrous *educational* task. I didn't feel equal to it; had I felt equal to it I should have proved, to my satisfaction at least, that I was not equal to it. Call it humility if you please; I hope it is, but I think true humility is reserved for the saints.

You coined a phrase, "not political corruption, but social corruption" that I shall long remember and shamelessly use. And you said much more that I shall ponder — and said with an eloquence and passion that I wish were mine.

Thank you, sir, and even if you have assigned me roles that I cannot fill, I am flattered and proud that you bothered to write me — so beautifully.

Cordially yours,

P.S. I am writing this at midnight on my last night in the Executive Mansion where I have labored long and fruitfully I think, and where I had wanted to stay within dimensions I had begun to feel I could encompass, or almost. That is why this is not a better letter I have written.

A.E.S.

On January 12, 1953, his aide Lawrence E. Irvin wrote the Governor "to express my everlasting gratitude and appreciation to you for having made possible the most pleasant and enjoyable four years of my life. This association with you has been the source of immeasurable pride and satisfaction and I shall always cherish the memory of it."

To Lawrence E. Irvin

January 16, 1953

Dear Larry:

It was a lovely letter and I shall keep it always — and with it memories of a loyalty and a devotion to a common purpose that meant more to me than perhaps you realize.

I am gone now for a few weeks,[14] but when I get back I hope all will be in order and somewhat to your liking in Springfield.

My love to Marguerite [15] and everlasting gratitude to you.

Yours,

On his last day as governor, Stevenson invited Don Forsyth, of Springfield, to the mansion for breakfast. Forsyth, during Stevenson's administration, served as a member of the Illinois Veterans' Commission. He was downstate Illinois chairman of the Stevenson for Governor Committee and Stevenson's personal campaign manager in his bid for reelection as governor in 1952. After the nomination he assisted in the presidential campaign. Stevenson asked Forsyth to evaluate his four years as governor, to which Forsyth replied: "You are my most expensive friend. For four years as an insurance man I made only $30 on commissions for state business. This is the greatest compliment I can pay you. You brought integrity to government." [16]

The Reverend Richard Paul Graebel was among the throng of friends and well-wishers who bade Stevenson farewell at the Alton Railroad Station in Springfield on January 12, 1953. The following day he wrote Stevenson: "I miss you like the very dickens already and there is a flatness about things, even the beer! . . . If you want me for anything from a wing-ding on New Year's Eve to a literary allusion or to be pastor of a wayside chapel so you can come to church on Sunday, HOLLER, or BLOW THE WHISTLE, or the classic phrase, LEAVE ME KNOW!"

To the Reverend Richard Paul Graebel

January 16, 1953

Dear Dick:

Everything you write is better than anything anyone else writes. I shall remember what you say because I have a feeling — a happy, warm, comforting feeling — that our times together are not over.

Gratefully and affectionately,

14 Stevenson left shortly afterwards for an extended vacation in Barbados.
15 Mrs. Irvin.
16 Don Forsyth, interview with Walter Johnson, April 22, 1966.

Acknowledgments

William S. Dix, Alexander P. Clark and Mrs. Nancy Bressler, of the Princeton University Library, and Paul Spence, of the Illinois State Historical Library, have been most cooperative, as have also Paul E. Edlund, David C. Mearns and John C. Broderick, of the Library of Congress. We also wish to thank Eugenia D. LeJeune and Mrs. Dorothy E. Dean, of the George C. Marshall Research Foundation, and Mrs. Ethel Sinclair and Mrs. Louise Bosworth, of the *Daily Pantagraph,* for their assistance. William L. Day, director of research, and Dorothy Nadasdy, research associate, Illinois Legislative Council, were extremely helpful in checking legislative matters.

We are especially grateful to the following for providing us with special information and material: Mrs. Edison Dick, Archibald MacLeish, Willam I. Flanagan, Juanda Higgins, Eric Sears, Lawrence E. Irvin, Leonard Schwartz, J. Edward Day, William McCormick Blair, Jr., Stephen A. Mitchell, John J. Parish, Walter V. Schaefer, Mrs. Robert Risse, Mrs. Margaret Munn, Mrs. John Paul Welling, Miss Phyllis Gustafson, and Mrs. John Whitaker. We express our gratitude also to Russell Babcock, Mrs. Walter Baumgarten, Jr., Richard Bentley, Barry Bingham, Sherwood Dixon, Mr. and Mrs. Ivan A. Elliott, Don Forsyth, Miss Dorothy Fosdick, the Reverend Richard Paul Graebel, Dr. Parker S. Hardin, the Reverend Martin D. Hardin, Barnet Hodes, Jacob M. Arvey, Miss Anne Alexander, Mrs. Gloria Richter, Frank E. Karelsen, Arthur Krock, Mrs. Lloyd Lewis, Mrs. Carl C. Vrooman, John Madigan, T. S. Matthews, Mrs. Helen Kaste, Miss Maude Myers, Steven Rautenberg, Robert Notti, James F. Oates, Jr., and Thomas M. Storke, for material provided and services rendered.

We are immensely indebted to Adlai E. Stevenson's sister, Mrs. Ernest L. Ives, for her infinite patience and her considerate help in the preparation of this volume. In addition to Mrs. Ives, Professor Stuart Gerry Brown, Carl McGowan, Walter V. Schaefer, William McC. Blair, Jr.,

Lawrence E. Irvin, Edward D. McDougal, Jr., and Mrs. Edison Dick read the entire manuscript. The entire manuscript was submitted to the members of the Advisory Committee to *The Papers of Adlai E. Stevenson,* and their suggestions have been most helpful.

Little, Brown and Company, Mrs. Eugene Meyer, Mrs. Marshall Field and the Field Foundation, Mr. and Mrs. Harold Hochschild, Arnold M. Picker, Robert Benjamin, Newton N. Minow, James F. Oates, Jr., Francis T. P. Plimpton, Benjamin Swig, Philip M. Klutznick, Mrs. John Paul Welling, William McC. Blair, R. Keith Kane, Simon H. Rifkind, Wilson W. Wyatt, the late William Benton, C. Daggett Harvey, Mr. and Mrs. Edison Dick, William McC. Blair, Jr., Lloyd K. Garrison, J. M. Kaplan, Jerrold Loebl, Hermon D. Smith, Edward D. McDougal, Jr., Glen A. Lloyd, Mr. and Mrs. Gilbert Harrison, Irving B. Harris, Edwin C. Austin, Archibald Alexander, Jacob M. Arvey, Paul Ziffren, Frank E. Karelsen, George W. Ball, C. K. McClatchy, Maurice Tempelsman, Barnet Hodes and Scott Hodes generously provided funds to defray the editorial expense of this volume. The University of Hawaii assisted in defraying the cost of typing the manuscript.

We are grateful to Roger Shugg, of the University of New Mexico Press, and Ned Bradford, of Little, Brown and Company, for their encouragement and support.

WALTER JOHNSON
CAROL EVANS

Index